HOLOCAUST MEMORY AND RACISM IN THE POSTWAR WORLD

HOLOCAUST MEMORY AND RACISM IN THE POSTWAR WORLD

EDITED BY SHIRLI GILBERT AND AVRIL ALBA

WAYNE STATE UNIVERSITY PRESS
DETROIT

© 2019 by Wayne State University Press, Detroit, Michigan 48201. All rights reserved. No part of this book may be reproduced without formal permission.

Library of Congress Control Number: 2019938099

ISBN 978-0-8143-4269-5 (paperback)
ISBN 978-0-8143-4596-2 (hardcover)
ISBN 978-0-8143-4270-1 (ebook)

Wayne State University Press

Leonard N. Simons Building
4809 Woodward Avenue
Detroit, Michigan 48201–1309

Visit us online at wsupress.wayne.edu

Contents

Acknowledgments   vii

Introduction   1
    Shirli Gilbert and Avril Alba

Part I. Responses to Racism after World War II

1. Race, the Holocaust, and Colonial/Postcolonial Britain   17
   Tony Kushner

2. "The Jim Crow of All the Ages": The Impact of Hitler, World War II, and the Holocaust on Black Civil Rights in Alabama   41
   Dan J. Puckett

3. From Undesirable to Unassimilable: The Racialization of the "Jew" in South Africa   72
   Milton Shain

4. A Study of Conflicting Images in the Australian Media: Holocaust Suffering and Persistent Anti-Jewish Racism   91
   Suzanne D. Rutland

Part II. Jews and Racism

5. Black and White: Yiddish Writers Encounter Indigenous Australia   121
   David Slucki

6. Who Are the Jews Now? Memories of the Holocaust in Georgia Brown's East End, 1968   146
   James Jordan

7. "A Straight and Not Very Long Road": American Jews, Apartheid, and the Holocaust   168
   Marjorie N. Feld

8. Race, Holocaust Memory, and American Jewish Politics   196
   Michael E. Staub

Part III. Literary Connections across Time

9. In the Nazi Cinema: Race, Visuality, and Identification in Fanon and Klüger   221
   Michael Rothberg

10. Caribbean Literature and Global Holocaust Memory   240
    Sarah Phillips Casteel

11. A Failure of Memory? Revisiting the Demidenko/Darville Debate   272
    Avril Alba

Part IV. Claiming the Holocaust

12. Deliberating the Holocaust and the Nakba: Disruptive Empathy and Binationalism in Israel/Palestine   295
    Bashir Bashir and Amos Goldberg

13. Shifting Responses to Antisemitism and Racism: Temporary Exhibitions at the Jewish Holocaust Centre   327
    Steven Cooke and Donna-Lee Frieze

14. Nazism and Racism in South African Textbooks   350
    Shirli Gilbert

15. "Never Forget": Intersecting Memories of the Holocaust and the Settler Colonial Genocide in Canada   386
    Dorota Glowacka

Conclusion   419
    Shirli Gilbert and Avril Alba

Contributors   421

Index   427

Acknowledgments

This volume originated in "The Holocaust and Legacies of Race in the Postcolonial World, 1945 to the Present," a conference held in April 2012 in Sydney, cohosted by the Department of Hebrew, Biblical and Jewish Studies at the University of Sydney, the Parkes Institute for Jewish/ non-Jewish Relations at the University of Southampton, and the Kaplan Centre for Jewish Studies and Research at the University of Cape Town. The long-standing partnership among our three institutions, expanded recently with the addition of Tulane University, has been a rich and stimulating forum for intellectual exchange on this subject and many others besides. For that, we would like to thank in particular our colleagues Tony Kushner, James Jordan, Suzanne Rutland, Milton Shain, Adam Mendelsohn, and Michael Cohen. The conversation that began in Sydney in 2012 was continued in a panel session at the Association for Jewish Studies in Chicago (December 2012), at the "Jews, Colonialism, and Postcolonialism" international conference at the University of Cape Town (April 2013), and during the course of several smaller meetings. Roughly half the chapters in this volume emerged from those meetings; the rest were invited contributions. We are grateful to the conference participants and to the volume's authors for contributing their thought-provoking ideas and research to this project. We are also grateful to Tom Lawson, A. Dirk Moses, and three anonymous reviewers for constructive feedback on draft versions of the manuscript. Finally, we extend our appreciation to Ceylan Akturk, Jude Grant, Kristin Harpster, Jamie Jones, Emily Nowak, Rachel Ross, Kristina Stonehill, and Kathy Wildfong at Wayne State University Press for their dependably efficient, creative, and professional work in bringing the book to publication.

Introduction

Shirli Gilbert and Avril Alba

IN JANUARY 2015, THE British Prime Minister's Holocaust Commission delivered its report on Holocaust education and commemoration in Britain. "It is vital that people from all walks of life learn about and understand the Holocaust," it declared, "to learn the contemporary lessons from this, the darkest hour of human history.... In educating young people about the Holocaust, Britain reaffirms its commitment to stand up against prejudice and hatred in all its forms. The prize is empathetic citizens with tolerance for the beliefs and cultures of others."[1]

Such universalistic discourse is commonplace today. The Holocaust is frequently invoked as a benchmark for talking about human rights abuses from slavery and apartheid to colonialism, ethnic cleansing, and genocide. Western educators and politicians draw seemingly obvious lessons of tolerance and anti-racism from the Nazi past, and their work rests on the implicit assumption that Holocaust education and commemoration will expose the dangers of prejudice and promote peaceful coexistence.

This volume challenges the notion that there is an unproblematic connection between Holocaust memory and the discourse of anti-racism. Through diverse case studies, it historicizes how the Holocaust has informed engagement with racism from the 1940s until the present, demonstrating that contemporary assumptions are neither obvious nor inevitable and revealing the complicated and unpredictable ways in which the Holocaust has been encountered in racialized societies across more than seven decades. In an attempt to open up such encounters to closer scrutiny, we began this project with a series of interrelated questions. What tensions emerged when countries with an imperial and sometimes genocidal history of racial exploitation confronted the enormity of Nazi crimes? How was memory of the Final Solution reconciled with the formalization of apartheid in South Africa in 1948, for example, or the continuation of the "White Australia" policy and Australia's later transformation to a "multicultural" nation, or the struggle for civil rights in the United States? To what extent was the Holocaust present in postwar public discourse about decolonization, and how did it inflect the articulation of racist and anti-racist politics? How can we explain the connections that were made between the Holocaust and racism in distinct historical and political contexts, and, conversely, how can we explain the not infrequent failure to connect? Does the latter imply an absence of empathy with non-white victims, or was the analogy simply more politically useful at certain times than at others or not considered relevant at all? To what extent did the Holocaust change perceptions of Jews, and how have other "racialized" groups responded to the legacy of Nazism in light of their own histories of suffering and exclusion? The answers to these questions are far from straightforward, and the chapters in this volume only begin to untangle them.

Our concern in the volume is less with empirical connections between the Holocaust and racism than with *imagined* or *metaphorical* connections: the question of why particular actors have chosen to invoke the memory of the Holocaust at certain times and places and not at others. Such metaphorical thinking is far from the sole preserve of literature or the arts but is an integral part of political discourse, intellectual life, and memorial culture. The empirical connections, where they exist, may feed into the imaginative connections that are made, but they are not the same thing and they do not necessarily correspond to or shape one another in predictable ways.

The volume purposefully extends beyond the literary focus of much existing scholarship, presenting carefully researched historical examples of such imaginative connections between the Holocaust and racism in order to account for their specific historical situatedness and development. Why have they arisen in certain contexts and not others? Why do they take particular forms? How have they shifted across time? While such connections are often invoked in highly politicized contexts, we are also less interested in the particular politics that individuals advocate than in how they use the metaphor of the Holocaust to do so. As this is an emerging area of interest, it is not always easy to identify overarching trends, but the work of historicization—establishing the historical contingency of diverse examples—is a necessary starting point for discerning patterns and drawing links.

The historicization of Holocaust-racism intersections is related, unsurprisingly, to the historicization of racism itself. It is by now a scholarly platitude that "race" is a socially constructed category, one whose expressions have shifted radically over time. Racism, similarly, is a phenomenon with markedly different characteristics in specific contexts: as Thomas C. Holt puts it, "There are historically specific 'racisms' and not a singular ahistorical racism."[2] Related terms such as *racialism, race prejudice, discrimination, xenophobia*, and others, often used interchangeably and uncritically, take on radically different meanings in different historical contexts. When links are drawn with the Holocaust, the particularity of discrete historical phenomena is often obscured or ignored.

In particular, while an equivalence is often assumed between racism and antisemitism, the relationship between them has been complex and changeable. Several of the volume's chapters take up this issue, exploring how the Holocaust shaped perceptions about Jews, as well as the perceptions of Jews about racism directed against others. There has already been some fruitful examination of the relationship between Jews, blacks, and wider issues of "race," primarily in the American context, and also in a nascent literature on Jews and colonialism.[3] The volume expands and deepens this focus. To what extent did Jews engage with other oppressed groups in racialized societies, particularly in the global South? What motivated their participation in anti-racist activism? Was there a sense of identification, of empathy, of concern, of indifference?

The presumed anti-racist lessons of the Holocaust have been written back to the postwar years themselves. The historian George M. Fredrickson echoes a common view when he argues that "the Holocaust made blatant racism of all kinds morally disreputable."[4] As Michelle Brattain has shown, however, scientists in the late 1940s and early 1950s struggled to achieve a consensus on racism beyond the rudimentary acknowledgment that Nazism was wrong. Using the example of a 1949 UNESCO project aimed at providing a "final authoritative rebuttal to Nazi-style scientific racism," Brattain shows that most scholars at the time were unwilling to question the essential validity of "race" as a natural category. As a result, while anti-racist activists could argue for equal treatment of races on moral grounds, they were unable to prove equality on the basis of scientific evidence; they thus "played an important, if unintentional, role in facilitating a highly resistant form of popular racism." The Cold War and anticommunism also substantially weakened what might have become large-scale, transnational anti-racist initiatives in the postwar years.[5]

Part of our interest in this volume, then, is to chart the persistence or emergence of new forms of racism in the postwar era, after Nazism had ostensibly discredited the concept, and to examine their relationship, implicit and explicit, with Nazi racial discourse and memory of the Holocaust. In analyzing these encounters, we are not especially interested in the accuracy of the analogies made. Indeed, memory of the past is an inevitably constructed and sometimes inaccurate narrative, shaped at least in part by present-day concerns. As the historian Alon Confino argues, "The greatest danger in attempting to understand post Second World War memory is a cultural anachronism: the attempt to impose present-day moral expectations of what should have been remembered on what actually had been remembered."[6] Our analytical focus is thus more on how the Holocaust was used as an interpretive framework. At what times was that metaphor a productive, provocative, troubling, or even expedient one? At what times was it avoided? Why was this particular metaphor chosen above others at certain places and times?

By foregrounding and historicizing the relationship between the Holocaust and racism, the volume seeks to make a key intervention in the developing historiography on Holocaust memory. The literature on the latter topic has grown steadily over the last two decades, part of a larger boom in memory studies first documented by Jay Winter.[7] The earliest studies of Holocaust memory examined nation-states directly affected by Nazism and its legacy. The impact of the Holocaust in Israel has been the focus of work by Tom Segev, Idith Zertal, Dalia Ofer, and others, with chief emphasis often placed on the Jewish state's role in molding memorial culture.[8] Germany was also unsurprisingly an early area of research, as was the United States, the country of the liberators and a place of refuge for large numbers of Jewish survivors.[9] While some scholars have emphasized the top-down, politically driven nature of memorial cultures in these places, others have sought to excavate the more nuanced ways in which individuals and groups have chosen to remember.[10]

The range of national case studies quickly widened beyond these initial foci. Scholars have traced patterns of Holocaust memory in various European countries, such as Poland and France, and have also increasingly ranged further afield, exploring developments in South Africa, Argentina, Ethiopia, Australia, and elsewhere.[11]

Such studies do more than simply expand the geographical scope of research. The choice of scholarly topics reflects the increasingly widespread dissemination of Holocaust memory itself in the late twentieth and early twenty-first centuries—evidence of what some would call the "globalization" of Holocaust memory since the fall of communism. The Stockholm International Forum on the Holocaust (2000) and the UN-designated International Holocaust Remembrance Day (2005) are frequently invoked as milestones in the Holocaust's transformation from a specific, contextualized event into a universal symbol of racism and injustice.

The global and transnational dimensions of Holocaust memory have accordingly become key concerns in the scholarship. In *The Holocaust and Memory in the Global Age*, Daniel Levy and Natan Sznaider propose the notion of "cosmopolitan memory" to describe Holocaust memory cultures that can be simultaneously universal and particular, taking on distinct meanings in different contexts while still functioning in fruitful ways as a global symbol of evil.[12] In his seminal essay "On the Social Construction of Moral Universals," the sociologist Jeffrey Alexander similarly traces how the Holocaust has assumed a "mythical status," becoming separated from its historical context to be accepted as the dominant symbolic representation of "evil . . . inside all of us and in every society."[13] The cultural historian Amos Goldberg, along with Peter Novick and others, questions the characterization of such memory cultures as "global," arguing that the boom in Holocaust memory is more accurately described as Western or even American.[14]

While most of the case studies in this volume are not focused on the transnational dimensions of Holocaust memory as such, they are centrally concerned with how that memory has been encountered and engaged in racialized societies beyond the countries directly affected by Nazism itself. In probing this question, many have engaged with Michael Rothberg's influential *Multidirectional Memory*, a work of literary and cultural criticism that examines Holocaust memory in the context of decolonization in the 1950s and '60s. Arguing against a "zero-sum game" logic, according to which the Holocaust crowds other histories of victimization out of the public sphere, Rothberg maintains that there are many examples of their productive and dialogical coexistence and that Holocaust memory has enabled and even galvanized the articulation of other histories of victimization, just as those histories have enabled the articulation of the Holocaust. In his work, he seeks to uncover a "not-yet-recognized, six-decade-old tradition" in which writers and intellectuals have made productive metaphorical connections between the Holocaust and the postcolonial experience.[15] The postcolonial condition is, of course, intimately linked with issues of racism, and Rothberg's work has provided a fruitful framework for scholars to explore the diverse and changeable ways in which the Holocaust has shaped postwar racist and anti-racist cultures.

The postcolonial encounter with the Holocaust, or more specifically with Jewish victimhood, is another of the volume's key concerns. Jewish studies and postcolonial studies have historically had very little interaction as disciplines, a disconnect that the literary scholar Bryan Cheyette attributes to political rather than intellectual origins. Central to the disconnect is Israel. As Cheyette explains, once Jews "entered history as nationalists," their historical victimhood could not legitimately be used to illuminate understandings of postcolonial experience. His work, by contrast, explores the ways in which their histories have been intertwined and mutually illuminating. Postwar French intellectuals such as Franz Fanon and Aimé Césaire, for example, made explicit connections with the Nazi death camps in order to formulate their understanding of the effects of colonial racism, while Auschwitz survivor Jean Améry drew on Fanon in order to understand his experiences as a post-Holocaust Jew.[16] As with Rothberg, such literary scholarship has opened up fertile avenues for thinking about historical appropriations of victimhoods of many different kinds.

While the *empirical* links between victimhoods are not themselves the volume's concern, they nonetheless have a bearing on the kinds of imaginative connections that are later drawn. The history of colonial racism in particular underlies several of the volume's chapters, and this too is the subject of a number of studies exploring connections with Nazism. Hannah Arendt's *Origins of Totalitarianism* was one of the first to broach links with anti-black racism in colonial Africa. Arendt's ideas have been developed and challenged in a growing body of scholarship, including work by the historians Jürgen Zimmerer and Shelley Baranowski, who investigate the relationship between

Nazism and the German colonial past, and others who caution against making direct linkages but nonetheless acknowledge the colonial roots of certain kinds of racial thinking.[17]

The scholarly literature on Holocaust memory is large and evolving, and its areas of focus are diverse. In addition to the case studies and topics already mentioned, the literature ranges over a multitude of transnational and transcultural themes, from the relationship between the Holocaust and global human rights issues to histories of mass violence and the experiences of ethnic minorities. There are often important links between these themes, but they also raise distinctive questions and thus deserve focused, discrete investigation. This volume's focus on the Holocaust and postwar racism, with an emphasis on robust historical grounding, is intended to encourage more of the kinds of precise and fine-grained analyses that the broader field sometimes lacks.

In our call for historicization, we also include the scholarship itself. Cheyette, for example, perceives a moral necessity in connecting Jewish and postcolonial histories, while scholars such as Stef Craps and Michael Rothberg similarly make claims not only for the intellectual but also the moral imperative underlying their work: for the "ethical significance of remembering traumatic histories across cultural boundaries." They hope that the kind of noncompetitive remembrance they research will both engender "empathy for the historical experience of others" and actively foster "social solidarity" and "alliances between various marginalized groups."[18] To suggest that such scholarship is unavoidably a product of the present multicultural moment is not to diminish its importance but rather to encourage once again a recognition of the historical contingency of the connections that are identified (or avoided) at certain places and times.

Contemporary educational and memorialization initiatives, while well intentioned, often undermine the effectiveness of their work by assuming the "lessons" of the Holocaust to be self-evident. The contributions to this volume make clear, by contrast, that simplistic connections between the memory of the Holocaust and anti-racist imperatives cannot be assumed. Indeed, the encounter with the Nazi past in racialized societies and political systems has been fluid and unpredictable. Awareness of the Holocaust does not automatically create "empathetic citizens," nor are the connections between Nazism and postwar racisms of very different forms necessarily obvious. Presenting the Holocaust as the ultimate lesson in anti-racism also reduces a complex historical phenomenon to a single root cause, thus obscuring patterns of causation that are critical to gaining a fuller understanding of how the genocide actually happened.[19]

The project of historicization recognizes that the intersections between the Holocaust and racism have a seventy-year history and that they have unfolded in varied ways across disparate geographical spaces. One justification for this project is thus a simple one of historical accuracy. But the relationship between the Holocaust and racism reaches far beyond the academic sphere. Only by understanding its complex history can we understand how we have reached the contemporary consensus, recognize its historical contingency, and begin to evaluate its moral legitimacy and political and social effectiveness.

Notes

1. *Britain's Promise to Remember: The Prime Minister's Holocaust Commission Report*, January 2015, 9, assets.publishing.service.gov.uk/government/uploads/system/uploads/attachment_data/file/398645/Holocaust_Commission_Report_Britains_promise_to_remember.pdf.
2. Thomas C. Holt, *The Problem of Race in the Twenty-First Century* (Cambridge, MA: Harvard University Press, 2000), 21. See also George M. Fredrickson, *Racism: A Short History* (Princeton, NJ: Princeton University Press, 2002), 99.
3. There is a substantial literature on Jews and "race." See, among many others, Eric L. Goldstein, *The Price of Whiteness: Jews, Race, and American Identity* (Princeton, NJ: Princeton University Press, 2006); Mitchell B. Hart, ed., *Jews and Race: Writings on Identity and Difference, 1880–1940*, Brandeis Library of Modern Jewish Thought Series (Waltham, MA: Brandeis University Press, 2011); Iris Idelson-Shein, *Difference of a Different Kind: Jewish Constructions of Race during the Long Eighteenth Century* (Philadelphia: University of Pennsylvania Press, 2014); Eric J. Sundquist, *Strangers in the Land: Blacks, Jews, Post-Holocaust America* (Cambridge, MA: Belknap Press, 2005); Michael Lerner, *Jews & Blacks: A Dialogue on Race, Religion, and Culture in America* (New York: Plume, 1996). On Jews and colonialism, see Ethan B. Katz, Lisa Moses Leff, and Maud S. Mandel, eds., *Colonialism and the Jews* (Bloomington: Indiana University Press, 2017).
4. Fredrickson, *Racism*, 132.

5. Michelle Brattain, "Race, Racism, and Antiracism: UNESCO and the Politics of Presenting Science to the Postwar Public," *American Historical Review* 112, no. 5 (2007): 1387–88, 1397.
6. Alon Confino, "Remembering the Second World War, 1945–1965: Narratives of Victimhood and Genocide," *Cultural Analysis* 4 (2005): 47.
7. Jay Winter, "The Generation of Memory: Reflections on the 'Memory Boom' in Contemporary Historical Studies," *German Historical Institute Bulletin* 27 (Fall 2000): 69–92.
8. Tom Segev, *The Seventh Million: The Israelis and the Holocaust* (New York: Hill & Wang, 1993); Idith Zertal, *Israel's Holocaust and the Politics of Nationhood* (Cambridge: Cambridge University Press, 2005); Dalia Ofer, "The Past That Does Not Pass: Israelis and Holocaust Memory," *Israeli Studies* 14, no. 1 (2009): 1–35; Dalia Ofer, "The Strength of Remembrance: Commemorating the Holocaust during the First Decade of Israel," *Jewish Social Studies* 6, no. 2 (2000): 24–55; and Roni Stauber, *The Holocaust in Israeli Public Debate in the 1950s: Ideology and Memory* (Edgware, UK: Vallentine Mitchell, 2007).
9. See, among many others, Norbert Frei, *Adenauer's Germany and the Nazi Past: The Politics of Amnesty and Integration* (New York: Columbia University Press, 2002); William Niven, *Germans as Victims: Remembering the Past in Contemporary Germany* (Basingstoke, UK: Palgrave Macmillan, 2006); Robert G. Moeller, *War Stories: The Search for a Usable Past in the Federal Republic of Germany* (Berkeley: University of California Press, 2001); Lawrence Baron, "The Holocaust and American Public Memory, 1945–1960," *Holocaust and Genocide Studies* 17, no. 1 (2003): 62–88; Hasia R. Diner, *We Remember with Reverence and Love: American Jews and the Myth of Silence After the Holocaust, 1945–1962* (New York: New York University Press, 2009); Alan L. Mintz, *Popular Culture and the Shaping of Holocaust Memory in America* (Seattle: University of Washington Press, 2001); Peter Novick, *The Holocaust in American Life* (New York: Houghton Mifflin, 1999); and Jeffrey Shandler, *While America Watches: Televising the Holocaust* (New York: Oxford University Press, 1999).
10. Andreas Huyssen, *Present Pasts: Urban Palimpsests and the Politics of Memory* (Stanford, CA: Stanford University Press, 2003); Dominick LaCapra, *History and Memory after Auschwitz* (Ithaca, NY: Cornell University Press, 1998); and James E. Young, *The Texture of Memory: Holocaust Memorials and Meaning* (New Haven, CT: Yale University Press, 1993).
11. See, for example Joan B. Wolf, *Harnessing the Holocaust: The Politics of Memory in France* (Stanford, CA: Stanford University Press, 2004); Jonathan Huener,

Auschwitz, Poland, and the Politics of Commemoration, 1945–1979 (Athens: Ohio University Press, 2003); Geneviève Zubrzycki, *The Crosses of Auschwitz: Nationalism and Religion in Post-Communist Poland* (Chicago: University of Chicago Press, 2006); Estelle Tarica, "The Holocaust Again? Dispatches from the Jewish 'Internal Front' in Dictatorship Argentina," *Journal of Jewish Identities* 5, no. 1 (2012): 89–110; Edward Kissi, "The Uses and Abuses of the Holocaust Paradigm in Ethiopia: 1980–1991," *BRIDGES: An Interdisciplinary Journal of Theology, Philosophy, History, and Science* 10, no. 3 (2003): 235–51; Tom Lawson and James Jordan, eds., *The Memory of the Holocaust in Australia* (Edgware, UK: Vallentine Mitchell, 2008); Ilan Stavans, "The Impact of the Holocaust in Latin America," *Chronicle of Higher Education Review* 47, no. 37 (2001), www.chronicle.com/article/The-Impact-of-the-Holocaust-in/13638; Edna Aizenberg, *On the Edge of the Holocaust: The Shoah in Latin American Literature and Culture* (Waltham, MA: Brandeis University Press, 2015); Judith E. Berman, *Holocaust Remembrance in Australian Jewish Communities, 1945–2000* (Crawley, WA: University of Western Australia Press, 2001); Shirli Gilbert, "Anne Frank in South Africa: Remembering the Holocaust during and after Apartheid," *Holocaust and Genocide Studies* 26, no. 3 (2012): 366–93; and Shirli Gilbert, "Jews and the Racial State: Legacies of the Holocaust in Apartheid South Africa, 1945–60," *Jewish Social Studies* 16, no. 3 (2010): 32–64.

12. Daniel Levy and Natan Sznaider, *The Holocaust and Memory in the Global Age*, trans. Assenka Oksiloff (Philadelphia: Temple University Press, 2006), 3, 20, 5–6. See also Daniel Levy and Natan Sznaider, "The Institutionalization of Cosmopolitan Morality: The Holocaust and Human Rights," *Journal of Human Rights* 3, no. 2 (2004): 143.

13. Jeffrey C. Alexander, *Remembering the Holocaust: A Debate* (Oxford: Oxford University Press, 2009), 35.

14. Amos Goldberg, "Ethics, Identity, and Antifundamental Fundamentalism: Holocaust Memory in the Global Age (a Cultural-Political Introduction)," in *Marking Evil: Holocaust Memory in the Global Age*, ed. Amos Goldberg and Haim Hazan (New York: Bergahn Books, 2015), 3–29; and Peter Novick, "The Holocaust Is Not—and Is Not Likely to Become—a Global Memory," in Goldberg and Hazan, *Marking Evil*, 47–55. See also Aleida Assmann and Sebastian Conrad, eds. *Memory in a Global Age* (London: Palgrave Macmillan, 2010); and Jan Eckel and Claudia Moisel, *Universalisierung Des Holocaust?: Erinnerungskultur Und Geschichtspolitik in Internationaler Perspektive* (Göttingen, Germany: Wallstein Verlag, 2008).

15. Michael Rothberg, *Multidirectional Memory: Remembering the Holocaust in the Age of Decolonization* (Stanford, CA: Stanford University Press, 2009), 27. In

addition to the works already mentioned, aspects of the field have been explored in, among others, Bryan Cheyette, ed., "Jews and Postcolonial Literature/Histories," special issue, *Wasafiri* 24, no. 1 (2009); Stef Craps and Michael Rothberg, "Introduction," in "Transcultural Negotiations of Holocaust Memory," ed. Stef Craps and Michael Rothberg, special issue, *Criticism* 53, no. 4 (2011): 517–21; William Miles, "Third World Views of the Holocaust," *Journal of Genocide Research* 3, no. 3 (2001): 511–13; Falk Pingel, "Teaching about the Holocaust: From European to Global Event" (paper presented at the UNESCO conference Holocaust Education in a Global Context, April 27, 2012); Falk Pingel, "Antisemitism and Racism: Theory, Holocaust Studies and Post-Colonialism" (seminar at the Association for Jewish Studies Annual Conference, Baltimore, December 2014); Willi Goetschel and Ato Quayson, eds., "Jewish Studies and Postcolonialism," special issue, *Cambridge Journal of Postcolonial Literary Inquiry* 3, no. 1 (2016); and Alan E. Steinweis, Philipp Gassert, and Jacob S. Eder, eds., *Holocaust Memory in a Globalizing World* (Göttingen, Germany: Wallstein, 2016).

16. Bryan Cheyette, *Diasporas of the Mind: Jewish and Postcolonial Writing and the Nightmare of History* (New Haven, CT: Yale University Press, 2013). The literary scholar Aamir R. Mufti similarly emphasizes the "metaphorical possibilities of Jewishness" in order to explore the Muslim experience in postcolonial India in *Enlightenment in the Colony: The Jewish Question and the Crisis of Postcolonial Culture* (Princeton, NJ: Princeton University Press, 2007). See also Debarati Sanyal, *Memory and Complicity: Migrations of Holocaust Remembrance* (New York: Fordham University Press, 2015).

17. Hannah Arendt, *The Origins of Totalitarianism* (London: Deutsch, 1986). For subsequent scholarship, see among others Volker Max Langbehn and Mohammad Salama, eds., *German Colonialism: Race, the Holocaust, and Postwar Germany* (New York: Columbia University Press, 2011); Benjamin Madley, "From Africa to Auschwitz: How German South West Africa Incubated Ideas and Methods Adopted and Developed by the Nazis in Eastern Europe," *European History Quarterly* 35, no. 3 (2005): 429–64; Shelley Baranowski, *Nazi Empire: German Colonialism from Bismarck to Hitler* (New York: Cambridge University Press, 2011); Carroll P. Kakel, *The Holocaust as Colonial Genocide: Hitler's "Indian Wars" in the "Wild East"* (Basingstoke, UK: Palgrave Pivot, 2013); A. Dirk Moses, "The Holocaust and Colonialism," in *The Oxford Handbook of Holocaust Studies*, ed. Peter Hayes and John K Roth (Oxford: Oxford University Press, 2010), 68–80; Jürgen Zimmerer, "The Birth of the 'Ostland' out of the Spirit of Colonialism: A Postcolonial Perspective on Nazi Policy of Conquest and Extermination," *Patterns*

of Prejudice 39, no. 2 (2005): 197–219; Jürgen Zimmerer, *Von Windhuk Nach Auschwitz? Beiträge Zum Verhältnis von Kolonialismus Und Holocaust* (Berlin: Lit Verlag, 2011).

18. Craps and Rothberg, "Introduction," 518.
19. Holocaust historiography since the 1970s has identified a wide range of potential factors that account for the genocide, with racist ideology often playing a relatively minor role. For a helpful overview of a huge and complex historiography, see Dan Stone, *Histories of the Holocaust* (Oxford: Oxford University Press, 2010).

Part I

Responses to Racism after World War II

PART 1 FOCUSES ON the encounters between Nazism and racisms of different kinds during and immediately after World War II. Drawing on careful archival research, the four chapters show not only that racist discourse and politics persisted in the postwar period but also, perhaps more important, that links between these racisms and Nazism were identified unpredictably and inconsistently. While some of the chapters attribute this to underlying political agendas, they all bring to the fore a historical contingency that has been obscured by the Holocaust's contemporary status as anti-racist symbol par excellence. The belief that racism was entirely discredited by the Nazis, they suggest, was not borne out in the immediate postwar period. Rather, both antisemitism and anti-black racism continued to be propagated, although often in disguised or socially acceptable forms.

From South Africa and Australia to Britain and the American South, defenders of openly racialized political systems recognized few connections with Nazism despite their broadly shared origins in nineteenth century "scientific" racism. By contrast, their anti-racist opponents often exaggerated the connections, with little recognition of the profound divergences between political systems that might broadly be defined as racialized. In drawing attention to the connections made by contemporaries, the authors of these chapters do not seek to equate the events described or to ignore significant differences between them. Rather, they aim to understand what motivated the making of such linkages, and how these linkages informed contemporary intellectual and political discourse and practice.

Focusing on wartime and postwar Britain, Tony Kushner presents a series of case studies exploring how the histories of slavery, imperialism, and the Holocaust were connected by contemporaries. Challenging scholarship's refusal to compare or connect British imperial racism and antisemitism in the aftermath of the Holocaust, he argues that these histories cannot be properly understood unless considered together. He shows that while blatant discrimination was unacceptable after 1945, racism remained intact—prospective Jewish and black immigrants to Britain continued to face restrictions, for example, and discrimination in the armed forces continued until the 1960s—"as long as it was practiced discreetly."

In his interrogation of the impact of Nazism in Alabama, Dan J. Puckett shows that civil rights activists often compared Jim Crow to Nazism, while southern whites consistently ignored any similarities between them. African American Alabamians regularly referred to Nazism when describing the violent system under which they lived, when mobilizing against racist laws and practices, and when advocating for participation in the war effort. For them, writes Puckett, "the incongruity of a war for the Four Freedoms being waged by a nation that condoned Jim Crow was obvious." White southerners, by contrast, might have criticized Nazi Germany's repressive and antidemocratic nature, but avoided or rejected explicit comparisons, associating the Nazis with extremist organizations like the Ku Klux Klan rather than the white mainstream.

In postwar societies organized along racial lines, the relationship between Jews and "race" was particularly complex. As Milton Shain demonstrates, Jews in South Africa, long perceived as alien outsiders, were subject in the 1930s and '40s to virulent Nazi-inspired racism emanating in particular from the Afrikaner nationalist right. With the implementation of apartheid in 1948, however, Jews were "divested of their racial essence" in order to be incorporated into the white ruling order. The "Jewish question" by and large disappeared, and the new prime minister, D. F. Malan, lauded South African Jews as a model community for managing to maintain their distinctive "racial" identity. In Australia, Suzanne D. Rutland reveals the persistence of antisemitic stereotypes and policies after 1945, particularly surrounding the immigration of Jewish Holocaust survivors, despite the widespread broadcasting of liberation footage and awareness of Nazi crimes. Memory of the Holocaust, she argues, failed to penetrate ingrained prejudices, and few contemporary observers recognized any connection with continuing racist policies.

What these studies demonstrate most powerfully is that victory over Nazism did not entail the erasure of racial thinking. In fact, apart from the efforts of a minority of anti-racist activists, memory of the Holocaust was seldom explicitly linked with contemporary racism. Working against present-day assumptions, the chapters help nuance our understanding by bringing tenacious and multilayered patterns of prejudice to light.

1

Race, the Holocaust, and Colonial/Postcolonial Britain

Tony Kushner

THIS VOLUME MAKES CONNECTIONS that few have previously attempted between "race thinking" in general and the Holocaust and the colonial/postcolonial worlds in particular. Considering how different academic disciplines have approached both Jewish and black studies, however, it seems that connecting attitudes toward these groups would often be viewed as redundant, irrelevant, or even dangerously misleading. For many, it would simply be connecting issues that have nothing in common and indeed had emerged in fundamentally separate spheres with utterly different trajectories and implications. For example, works on Britain and the Holocaust have tended to deal in a narrow way with the state's specific treatment of refugees from Nazism or on postwar cultural responses to the Shoah. They are dealt with as *Jewish*, or *antisemitic*, discourses without reference to other migrant groups or catastrophic histories such as slavery, imperialism, and genocide.[1] Equally, those dealing with so-called race relations have separated out migration from the colonies after 1945 from previous arrivals. Providing a clear example of the latter tendency, the prominent sociologist Harry Goulbourne insists that the inward movement of migrants such as the Jews and the Irish cannot be compared to the "catalytic role black and brown people played in the process of Britain redefining her identity and place as a post-imperial nation-state." Goulbourne presents what is still the mainstream orthodoxy: "Whilst relations between different European groups or between different groups of white people gave rise to patterns of discrimination, the emergence of the notion of racial differentiation and the subsequent race relations ... arose out of the dramatic contact and integration of Africans and Asians." Jews and other "white" Europeans might be part of Britain's "island story," but there is something bigger at stake which they do not relate to—the "colonial/imperial past."[2]

Such compartmentalization is not only present in the sphere of published academic work but has also affected core funding. For example, a major application to Britain's largest and state-funded humanities research council in 2012 was rejected because, according to one reviewer, "One needs to be very careful not to homogenize the diasporic experience of Jews with the post-slavery and Empire experiences of Black British citizens."[3] What is present here is not just a lack of awareness of Jews/discourse about Jews but also a refusal to compare: one that comes out of an approach that is inflexible and based on a crude understanding of colonialism and colonial power relations. Sadly, those who have managed to move beyond these binaries and form a dialogue between Jewish studies and colonial/postcolonial studies, such as Paul Gilroy and Bryan Cheyette, are still in a distinct if talented minority working against the dominant trend.[4] As Cheyette states in *Diasporas of the Mind*, which "argues for a new comparative approach across Jewish and postcolonial histories and literatures," there should be "no need for this book in an ideal world, but there seems to be an increased necessity to indicate the ways in which histories and cultures can be imagined across national and communal boundaries."[5]

Similarly, in studying the memory of the Holocaust and that of colonialism/slavery, Michael Rothberg has provided a "genealogy of works ... without collapsing one history into the other or establishing a hierarchy of suffering." His *Multidirectional Memory* thinks "through a comparative space beyond competition" and one not limited "by a zero-sum logic."[6]

Rothberg argues for an openness that is "necessary in order for the imaginative links between different histories and social groups to come into view."[7] Here it will be highlighted how it is not so much imagination that is required but detailed archival research that reveals the connections that were made by contemporaries between racisms and antisemitisms in the mid-twentieth century. It should be emphasized clearly at this stage that in making such connections, contemporaries did not necessarily ignore differences. Nevertheless, either intellectually or politically they believed there was a purpose in doing so. In continuing this new work of showing how racisms and antisemitisms were often linked, but bringing it beyond the literary and cultural spheres of Rothberg and Cheyette to the historical realm and detailed archival research, it will be illustrated how colonial discourse and what the latter has termed *Semitic* discourse interweave and shed mutual light on each other—as well as informing everyday procedures such as petty discrimination and political interventions at a state and popular level, incorporating, for example, immigration control and recruitment.[8] This is not "special pleading" or a sentimental notion of connecting minorities' experiences. Instead, this chapter argues that to understand how racisms worked during and after World War II in the liberal democracies, a multilayered, historically aware approach is needed that allows for change *and* continuity in race thinking. In the British case, as elsewhere, the Holocaust, colonialism, and postcolonialism were not, I will argue, hermetically sealed in contemporary understanding and praxis, but frequently connected.

The period chosen is a crucial one: the Second World War and the years immediately following. It thus encapsulates not only the Holocaust/Nazi era but also a crucial moment in global history: the withdrawal from empire and the move toward colonial independence. In the British world, while this was slow in relation to Africa, it was abrupt and with violent consequences in India and then Palestine. In terms of comparisons and interconnectivity, there are many questions that will be raised, if only briefly in what is an exhortation for further work.

The first question is whether the war against Nazism changed race thinking in the liberal democratic world. For Britain, John Flint has argued that "the war saw an important change. Whereas in 1939 it had been quite respectable to argue theories of racial inferiority, by 1940 it was not, and by 1945 racial equality was the establishment orthodoxy. Racism had been relegated to the sphere of washroom obscenity and was not considered tolerable in polite society."[9] Flint provides no evidence for this statement, and it is reproduced here because its analysis is widely accepted. The reason for this is simply common sense—surely the horrors of Nazi atrocities would discredit racism and racialism? As will emerge, the logic behind such assumptions can be shown to have some validity in practice, but the story is far more complicated in reality. Thus, in contrast to Flint, David Reynolds, studying the treatment of black American troops during World War II and the continuation of segregation on British soil, was struck by the "lack of reference to any fundamental moral issues" at a governmental level. In fact, although the blatantness of discrimination was regarded as unfortunate, most British officials, especially the home secretary, Herbert Morrison, shared the American army's fear of race mixing, especially at a sexual level and the potential danger of "miscegenation."[10] It will be argued here that varieties of racial discourse at many different levels in Britain and elsewhere in the world of the former Western Allies were too firmly ingrained in culture (and science) to be so easily eradicated by reference to the crimes of the Hitler regime.

More generally, Elazar Barkan has argued for the "retreat of scientific racism" in Britain and the United States in the interwar period. This was partly because of the violence associated with such thinking in Nazi Germany, South Africa, and the American South and its overtly *political* use of racism and also (and more convincingly) because of changes in scientific thinking.[11] Flint's and Barkan's analyses will be at least partly queried in what follows. But it will still be necessary to explore whether the persecution of the Jews and wider Nazi racialism made hostility to other groups, especially those of color, less pronounced and acceptable, or indeed, whether antisemitism in British state or society was curtailed and placed beyond the pale of respectability.

The second question to be raised is the extent to which the Holocaust and/or Nazi racialism impacted on British state responses to its colonial territories, including Palestine. The brief case studies that will inform this overview relate to immigration policy at home and abroad and also to cases of discrimination through the "color bar," that is, the (largely) informal mechanism through which black people in Britain (and elsewhere) were rejected from employment and housing and denied access to social and cultural venues. The emphasis will be on the impact of this discrimination and also an exploration of the rhetoric inside and outside the state that was crucial for underpinning and justifying it. And while the corridors of Whitehall will provide the main focal point, the geographies of this chapter will extend globally to include Africa, the Mediterranean, the Caribbean, Palestine, the United States, and the metropole itself. It includes case studies of immigration control procedures as well as examples of racial discrimination in both Britain and its colonies. The aim is to show how the meanings of the Holocaust, World War II, colonialism, and slavery were brought together—sometimes in conflict, sometimes not—in both official and popular discourse and in a variety of specific case studies covering sometimes small public incidents that ended up having major international ramifications and others that remained secret in government discussions but also had a major impact. Together, they will reveal that the catastrophic histories of slavery, imperialism, and the Holocaust were connected by contemporaries. The migrations they caused, and the exclusions to entry that were then attempted, alongside related racisms, were not the separate worlds put forward by Goulbourne and others.

Recruitment of Colonial Soldiers and the Dilemmas of Race

In the first twelve months of World War II, and under pressure from the Colonial Office especially, all the British armed forces temporarily relaxed their restriction on those deemed not to be of "pure European descent."[12] They did so partly out of pragmatic necessity—the desperate need to increase the size of the British armed forces and labor force in a total war. It was also necessitated in the minds of many (if not all) politicians and senior civil servants that to not do so was to risk a huge propaganda disaster in the fight against Nazism if the racism of the enemy could be connected to that of the British war effort. In turn, this could be exploited by the enemy (and the Soviet Union) as an example of British hypocrisy and also by those in the colonies fighting against imperial rule.

To those who had fought against this color bar, the opening up of recruitment was welcome, but campaigners such as Harold Moody, the leading force of the League of Coloured Peoples, warned that "if the principle is accepted now, surely it must be acceptable all the time."[13] Significantly, Moody, who was a moderate accommodationist in "race" and imperial matters in terms of black leaders in Britain,[14] was explicit in linking the removal of the color bar in the forces with a wider struggle, hoping that "one of the major aims of His Majesty's Government in this conflict was to fight against racial discrimination, prejudice, and persecution in the continent of Europe."[15] Arguing in early

1940 for the banishment of the "Colour Bar from the British Empire," Moody was even more explicit in linking this goal with what he saw as the broader ideological underpinnings of the British war effort: "Nothing has earned for the Nazi Government more world-wide horror, hatred and contempt than its persecution of the Jews and the new races it has conquered. Decent people in every country know that where one race sets out to exploit another there can be no peace in society; freedom and equality for all, whatever their race, colour or creed, is an essential pillar of civilisation."[16] Although Moody's rhetoric and analysis was overstated, he was not totally isolated in his idealistic outlook. Indeed, the support of those in the government for his perspective gives some credence to Flint's analysis that the respectability of racism was being undermined by the reality of total war against Nazism. The Ministry of Information was the British government body formed to monitor morale and design propaganda for consumption at home and abroad. When presented with evidence that the forces were continuing their prewar policy of racial discrimination, it feared that high-profile cases would "constitute a serious handicap to British war-time propaganda which in colonial territories must be based in no small measure on the contrast between Nazi racial theories and our own, and on the fellow-citizenship of all His Majesty's subjects in a single threatened Empire."[17] Yet the lasting impact of liberalizing forces from sympathetic politicians and civil servants, especially linked to the Colonial Office, can be queried. In 1944, all three forces were told to consider their postwar recruitment policies. They were united in their determination to resist such pressure to remove their discriminatory clauses, which they saw as coming only from the Colonial Office. While some official modifications were made, their collective goal, as the chief of the Army Council put it, was to make sure that those not of European descent were still in effect excluded "without intending any of the most undesirable features of a color bar."[18] In short, discrimination was perfectly legitimate, but its implementation should be discreet and away from the public eye. The same attitude was expressed by the Royal Air Force (RAF). Responding to the Chief of Air Staff's demand that the postwar RAF "should maintain the requirement of pure European descent," the secretary of state of the Air Ministry, argued, following a logic that comes straight out of *Alice in Wonderland*, as "coloured candidates would not be accepted," no practical issues would emerge: "There would . . . be no colour bar against them."[19]

That, after five years of conflict against Nazi Germany, racist language had not changed was illustrated by a policy statement made by a senior member of the Admiralty with regard to the Royal Navy. Having outlined all the groups that would continue to be rejected, and describing the hopes of a racially egalitarian world as promoted by the colonial secretary as "more suited to Utopia," he explained how borderline "half-breeds" would be judged for suitability: "The Admiralty view has been that it should be interpreted as excluding persons whom the Lower Deck would be likely to class as 'niggers.'"[20] Furthermore, who was of "pure European descent" continued to exercise the forces after 1945 as much as it had done in the interwar period. The Admiralty in January 1945 believed that the existing regulations "obviously exclud[ed] Asiatics and Negroes." But those to be kept out also included "Turks, Syrians, Armenians, Maltese, and any other near-white races if the blood is wholly of the races concerned."[21]

With regard to "half-breeds," for the Admiralty "the decision depends mainly on the 'Britishness' of the man's appearance and habits."[22] Armenians proved especially slippery and hard to place in the British forces' racial imagination. The Air Ministry before the war spent many months debating the entry of a keen young man who was brought up in Manchester but of Armenian origin who was desperate (and highly qualified) to join the RAF. His supporters within the ministry argued "positively" that "we do not reject Jews on the grounds that they are of Asiatic origin and it is difficult to see why an Armenian should be treated any differently."[23] The problem was that in this case the racial markers produced contradictory "evidence." His "eyes are oriental and perhaps his mouth and head." His skin color was, however, ambiguous and "the colour of his nails is not oriental."[24]

It is thus hard from this evidence from the 1930s and 1940s to detect any change in policy resulting from revulsion against Nazi racialism or a decisive move away from race science that had underpinned exclusion before World War II. The only detectable difference was a desire *not* to be publicly linked (either in the colonies or by liberal forces at home) to the Third Reich by the continued racial classification and discrimination against "non-Europeans" who applied to join the army, navy, or air force. Not surprisingly, because it came from a deeply ingrained state praxis informed and confirmed by "expert" opinion, discrimination in the British armed forces informed by scientific racism continued until the 1960s at least.[25] The major change was that unlike the period immediately following World War I, such racial discrimination had to be disguised—not because it was deemed morally wrong but because it might be misunderstood by "liberal" Britain, hence the contorted efforts to deny the operation of an explicit color bar.

Today those of color are still underrepresented by a factor of 400 percent in the British armed forces.[26] While the world of heritage celebrates the removal of the color bar during World War II, this was far from the case in reality.[27] Cy Grant came from British Guiana to volunteer for the RAF, finding out many years later that his ambition to become a fighter pilot had been thwarted by prejudice. He reflected on the "supreme irony of the . . . racist recruitment policies of the British Armed Forces even whilst waging a war against a racist Nazi regime."[28] It was an irony, however, lost on those in the Air Ministry, War Office, and Admiralty, who were determined to continue discrimination based on race science but did not want to confront their own biological racism in so doing.

The Color Bar in a Context of Nazi Racialism

The Colonial Office, although behind the impetus to change that so irritated the armed forces, had made very slow progress itself in removing the color bar in its appointments—including within the colonies themselves. A key example of this in action will provide the second case study of this chapter. It will reveal the connections made between ongoing discrimination in the British Empire and the still-recent example of Nazi racialism.

In early 1947, Ivor Cummings, principal in the Colonial Office Welfare Department and his superior, J. L. Keith, visited West Africa to aid the process of integrating students from countries such as the Gold Coast and Nigeria to British universities. It was part of a wider mission to promote indirect rule and African participation in the management of Britain's colonies. Nigeria, under its less sympathetic governor since 1943, Sir Arthur Richards, formerly of Jamaica, was deemed problematic in achieving this aim. More generally, his governorship has been described as "disastrous for the relationship between the British and the politically conscious groups and their leaders in Nigeria."[29]

Cummings was of mixed heritage—his father was a doctor from Sierra Leone who had settled in England and married a white nurse. They met when they were working in a hospital in Newcastle upon Tyne before World War I.[30] Ivor was, like Cy Grant, a victim of racial discrimination practiced by the Air Ministry. This was in spite of Cummings's elite education, academic achievements, and integration into the cultural elite of London. He was, in the words of Mike and Trevor Phillips in their popular history of post-1945 black life in Britain, "a fastidious, elegant man, with a manner reminiscent of Noel Coward—he chain smoked with a long cigarette holder, and addressed visitors as 'dear boy.'"[31]

Ivor Cummings applied to the RAF at the start of the war—that is, before policy had been temporarily and partially modified to at least allow Grant and others entry, if at the lowest levels of the RAF. At this point, as Cummings recalled, "[it] excluded all of us. I couldn't join the Royal Air Force because I was not of pure European descent."[32] Cummings then pursued a career in the Colonial Office and was promoted to principal in its Welfare Department in 1941, building on work he had carried out with colonial students in London during the 1930s. Cummings's progress in the civil service was itself remarkable: according to the *Daily Express*, he was "the first coloured man to receive a Colonial Office appointment."[33] Even then, his position in London "society" was not assured.

In October 1942, Sir Alexander Cadogan, undersecretary of state at the Foreign Office, reported in his diary that the cabinet had discussed the "question of [American] coloured troops." At this point there were between 11,000 and 12,000 of them in Britain, a total rising to over 130,000 by the end of the war. There was what Cadogan referred to as a "wild discussion." The cabinet minutes record the clear division between the War Office and the Colonial Office on this subject. The former was happy to provide the American army with full facilities to carry out segregation and regarded it as "most undesirable that there should be any unnecessary association between American coloured troops and British women." It was concerned that the naive British public would dismiss the distinction between "white and coloured troops" as "undemocratic." In fact, it represented a biological reality: "While there are many coloured men of high mentality and cultural distinction, the generality are of a simple mental outlook." In contrast, the Colonial Office was concerned about the impact of such discrimination on "our own coloured people" and its aim was "to secure both in the Colonies and in this country equality of treatment for all races." The cabinet minutes, however, did not record what Cadogan called the "low level" of the discussion.³⁴

In particular, Viscount Cranborne, the colonial secretary, raised the issue of how American discrimination was affecting black Britons. Given the unique position occupied by Ivor Cummings, he was almost undoubtedly the point of reference: "Bobbety [Cranborne's nickname] tried to impress Cabinet with *his* [colonial] difficulties. Said black official at C.O. had always lunched at a certain restaurant which now, because it was patronized by U.S. Officers, kept him out. P.M. [Churchill] said 'That's all right: if he takes a banjo with him they'll think he's one of the band!'"³⁵ Colin Holmes, in his 1988 magisterial history of immigration in modern Britain, *John Bull's Island*, rightly notes that David Reynolds, "somewhat surprisingly, passes this off as an example of Churchill's 'flippancy.'"³⁶ It is significant that in the 1950s Holmes also highlights how Churchill developed "an obsessive interest in West Indian immigration."³⁷ In 1955, he even toyed with the idea of fighting the general election with an explicit "Keep Britain White" campaign.³⁸ The attitude expressed by Churchill thus had an afterlife long after the end of World War II.

Cummings, working closely with his superior Keith, went around the black communities of Britain helping ease their integration, especially those who had come to join the war effort. While the black GIs were officially beyond their Colonial Office remit, in practice the clubs and societies they helped support were happy to allow the isolated black Americans entrance.³⁹ Apart from a genuine care for the welfare of these people, Cummings and Keith were deeply worried about how the color bar at home, whether practiced by white Britons or white Americans, would be received in the colonies.

Beyond this concern, there were some who also linked such discrimination to other (antisemitic) forms of prejudice. A month before the cabinet debate, and at the same time Ivor Cummings was excluded from his favorite restaurant, the left-wing *New Statesman* magazine printed what was undoubtedly an apocryphal anecdote, the folkloric nature of which increased its power. In summer 1942, it was reported that a well-to-do English lady wanted to show willingness in terms of contributing to the war effort and offered to the local American commander Sunday lunch for a half dozen of his men. She added, however, "No Jews please." "Six huge black GIs" appeared at her door at the allotted time. "Horrified, she exclaimed that there must be some mistake. 'Oh no, ma'am', one of them replied. 'Colonel Cohen no make any mistakes.'"[40]

The story did the rounds on the home front and was picked up six months later by a Nazi-controlled radio station in Luxembourg broadcasting to Britain. Rather than recognizing the original article's gentle rebuff to all forms of racism, the broadcast attempted to appeal to the prejudices of its listeners by suggesting that "it ought to be possible for competent military authorities to select [soldiers] without including in their number either negroes, catburglars or Jews."[41] In fact, the British public was largely hostile to the violent antisemitism of the Nazis practiced abroad and to the blatant color bar of the Americans at home.[42] It remained, however, that locally based prejudices against Jews, blacks, and others were largely resistant to change during and immediately after World War II. Even so, Cummings and Keith were not prepared for the shock of experiencing blatant discrimination in the colonies themselves.

As part of their continuing role after the war in integrating black colonial migrants to Britain, they visited Nigeria in 1947. The particular purpose of their visit was the welfare of African students, many of whom were Nigerian, who were coming to British universities in increasing numbers from 1946 onward. The integration of these students was regarded as critical by the Colonial Office—the hope was that they would be informal ambassadors ensuring future good relations between the colonies and the metropole.[43]

The Colonial Office was especially anxious that these West African students should avoid the informal color bar that existed in private accommodation in Britain. There was thus more than a degree of irony that in Lagos Cummings was refused a room at the elite Bristol Hotel because of his skin color.[44] The incident caused a scandal both in Nigeria and Britain. The local African newspapers, especially those of a radical, nationalist and anti-imperialist nature, were not slow to draw a parallel between the rejection of Cummings and the nature of the recent global conflict. The issue was further complicated as the manager of the race-exclusive hotel was Greek, which itself prompted its own form of local xenophobia. The Nigerian *Daily Comet* commented that when a foreigner employs the advantages of the hospitality extended to him to propagate a philosophy which borders dangerously on Adolf Hitler's race theories; when an alien who has been offered every opportunity to pursue an objective in direct contradiction to the declared policy not only of the Government of Nigeria but also of His Majesty's Britannic Government; when such an individual discriminates against an African for no reason than that he is a colored man; Government must . . . consider his expulsion from this country.[45]

The *West African Pilot* made even more of what it thought was the hypocrisy of the proprietor. Here was a refugee from a "Nazi trampled countr[y]" who "resorted to racialism against which the Allied nations, including Greece herself, fought in the last war."[46] Both newspapers were at the forefront of the struggle for independence from British colonial rule and had been briefly banned in 1945 by the authorities for their reporting of the general strike in Nigeria.[47]

Cummings was clearly shaken by this discrimination and he received support from his Colonial Office colleagues but little understanding from the governor of Nigeria. In Whitehall, there were those such as Sidney Abrahams who merely referred to the matter as a "breach of good manners."[48] Others, to compensate for the lack of empathy from Richards, went much further, including the colonial secretary who wrote to Cummings stating that "my Department as a whole sympathizes with you over the disgraceful treatment which you received."[49] Cummings was appreciative of this gesture, writing back that he "found it most encouraging that you should find time personally to have considered what is known as 'The Bristol Hotel Incident.'" It was, he added, "a great pity that I above all people, should have been the innocent victim of stirring up so much discussion and feeling in Nigeria."[50]

And while Abrahams's response was impeccably English, Andrew Cohen was more forceful and aware of the distress and hurt caused to Cummings—it was he who was responsible for the intervention of the colonial secretary.[51] From an elite British Jewish and Unitarian background (in contrast to Abrahams who was second-generation Eastern European),[52] it has been suggested that Cohen was "traumatized by the Holocaust" and as a result became a convinced "anti-racialist and an advocate of African rights."[53] While this reflects a later analysis, it does seem clear that Cohen's anger was markedly different from that of Abrahams's cool response (I will return to Cohen's status at the heart of the late imperial project in the conclusion to this chapter). At a public level, there could, of course, be no comparison made between British rule and Nazism at a time when the hope was to move to a peaceful form of self-government within the British Commonwealth. Nevertheless, among more sympathetic Colonial Office figures, all forms of racialism had been discredited by Nazism and, however patronizingly, the aim was to move to future African self-rule under the paternal British eye.

Postwar British Immigration Policy and the Politics of Race

Cummings, awarded an OBE (Officer of the Most Excellent Order of the British Empire) in the same year as the Bristol Hotel affair,[54] was a great asset to the Colonial Office: he was, as noted, the only Whitehall senior civil servant of black background. As the main liaison officer for African students, it is not surprising that he was brought in to officially welcome the *Empire Windrush* in June 1948 at Tilbury docks. The imminent arrival of this ship carrying five hundred West Indians had created much interest and concern in Britain. There were those such as a group of members of Parliament who wrote to the prime minister fearing that the example of the ship "may encourage other British subjects to imitate their example" and an "influx of colored people domiciled here is likely to impair the harmony and cohesion of our public and social life." They therefore called for control of colored immigration into Britain.[55]

The colonial secretary objected to such demands, warning that such racialism "would give rise to a fierce reaction in the Colonies themselves."[56] The Home Office was more reassuring, not because it was relaxed about the prospect of a large black influx but as it rightly believed that the *Windrush* "episode" was a "comparatively isolated one."[57] In contrast to earlier and later arrivals, great effort was made to welcome and accommodate those on the *Windrush*. Cummings went on board the ship to "express the hope that you will all achieve the objects which have brought you here." He then offered practical advice about the challenges, including discrimination, that might await them. Indeed, he later remembered that he was "desperately anxious about the migrants' prospects." Cummings's final comment, "All that remains for me to say is that I wish you the very best of luck," reflects his genuine concern for these newcomers and confirms the heartfelt and moving sentiment of his speech to those on the *Windrush*.[58]

It was not until 1962 that Britain legislated against the free entry of New Commonwealth migrants. Nevertheless, it would be wrong to assume that there was a laissez-faire attitude before then. As early as a year after the arrival of the *Windrush*, informal procedures were implemented to curtail what was seen as a dangerous influx of colored migrants. Those on the *Windrush*, some returning after having served in the forces or as war workers, were untypical of postwar black arrivals: it was migrants from West Africa, many coming as stowaways, who were the chief concern of civil servants. Measures were thus taken to stop at the source these "illegal" immigrants—in fact, they were still British subjects and could not be deported even though they were immediately criminalized the moment they arrived. The "problem" had been identified before the *Windrush*, and civil servants were convinced that "sooner or later more action must be taken to keep out the undesirable elements of [their] colonial population."[59] But when in 1950 the cabinet discussed the issue, it was recognized that "any solution depending on an apparent or concealed colour test would be so invidious as to make it impossible of adoption." It was decided to continue and intensify unofficial controls that would be "confined to colored persons . . . whose continued presence here is obviously objectionable."[60]

A similar process of informal discrimination was employed against the entry of Jewish immigrants into Britain after 1945. In 1947, the Foreign Office considered a policy toward recruiting displaced persons for labor purposes due to a major shortage of workers in key areas of the economy. Such recruitment, however, it emphasized, "must . . . be highly discriminatory." Antisemitism in Britain "clearly prevent[ed] the recruitment of Jews," even though they represented one quarter of displaced persons. Nevertheless, such discrimination in selection must not be on the grounds of "race, nationality, or residence."[61]

In short, with regard to both Jewish and black groups in postwar Britain, entry had to be restricted. The overall reason was made clear in the report of the Royal Commission on Population in 1949. For the sake of the national interest, large-scale immigration could "only be welcomed without reserve if the immigrants were of good human stock and were not prevented by their religion or race from intermarrying with the host population and becoming merged in it."[62] This was a document in the public domain. What could not be made explicit or even self-acknowledged by referring *directly* to Jews and blacks or other "undesirable" groups was the antisemitism and racism behind such discrimination in the light of horror over Nazi racialism *and* colonial sensitivities. Privately, civil servants and politicians in correspondence and memoranda would explicitly refer to the need to keep out Jews and blacks. But for diplomatic reasons, at home and abroad, and as with discrimination in the British armed forces, it could not be admitted as such because it would be misunderstood as racism. In the convoluted logic of officialdom, it was justified as the desire to *avoid* racism through case-by-case differentiation—a form of selection that would ensure that the dangerous "other" would not enter the metropole.

The emphasis was thus on "discrimination between individuals."[63] Immigration policy was selective and based on racial criteria but could be differentiated from forms that were "anomalous, unjust and most difficult" (i.e., in its Nazi form) by being melded to one of the core elements of liberalism—individualism.[64] And if a colonial discourse was in operation against potential black migrants, it was also present after 1945 in the hostility toward the arrival of *Ostjuden* who were seen as diseased, dangerous, unassimilable, and ultimately oriental. Both groups were seen to be fundamentally un-British and could not be envisaged as being part of the island story.

Returning to Ivor Cummings, the civil servant wrote plaintively (and somewhat optimistically, given the treatment he had received in Britain and its colonies) to the colonial secretary after the Bristol Hotel affair that he saw his mission as "bringing peoples of different races and colours nearer to the English people."[65] Cummings, it should be added, was not simply trying to flatter his civil servant superiors with the prospect of a racially harmonious British Commonwealth. There were those in the Nazi era and the immediate postwar years who could not only imagine but also practice this post-racist world. Indeed, it would be wrong to imply homogeneity or status in race thinking and in the treatment of those of color. One intriguing example is in the artistic world, as exemplified by the Sussex-born artist Edward Burra. He was part of the same cultural milieu in London as Cummings, where race and sexual orientation were partly overcome. For Burra and his circle, otherness could be integrated into the local metropolitan landscape, and his art reflected a new vision of London and a cosmopolitan world that incorporated the vibrancy of New York's Harlem and the new Caribbean arrivals in the West End.[66]

THE LAST YEARS OF THE PALESTINE MANDATE AND "RACE"

The final case study brings together Jewish migrants in a colonial setting—the question of so-called illegal Jewish immigration to Palestine in the last years of the British Mandate. Here, analysis will be confined to the rhetoric associated with this movement and the battles over memory involving two epic themes of slavery/colonialism and World War II/the Holocaust. These were at the heart of a propaganda war between the Zionist world (including non-Jewish supporters) and British officialdom, which accompanied the military struggles over the ships attempting to reach Palestine after 1945.

The propagandists on what was to become *Exodus 1947* (up to the point of summer 1947 the largest and the most notorious of these ships) either accused the British of betraying their noble record during the war or charged them with turning a blind eye when they refused to bomb the death camps. Some on the ship went further and called the outside world to witness the British "act according to all the Nazi methods" or to "come and see with your own eyes how Great Britain is reproducing the evil [that is racism] which the United Nations is striving to exterminate."[67] When the refugees on *Exodus 1947* were returned to Europe and sent to a camp in Germany, an even more juvenile response was generated in the form of a crude ditty:

> Bevin [the British Foreign Secretary] and Hitler are the same
> Fie upon English concentration camp
> Fie upon you hooey English
> Hooey English Hitler's policies.[68]

In response, the Colonial and Foreign Offices emphasized British restraint under provocation and presented themselves as the keepers of peace in a postcolonial world and as the rescuers of Jews during the war. Throughout, the "Final Passage" of the slave trade became the focal point of this polemical divide.

On the British side of the propaganda war, the Royal Navy was presented as revisiting its role *not* of supporting the slave trade, as it did in the eighteenth century, but in *suppressing* it as was the case after 1807—the date of its formal abolition in the British Empire. The naval correspondent of *The Times* saw the movement of illegal immigrants as the success of "sea-gangsters who run this modern slave traffic—the conditions in most of the ships can be compared only to those of the slavers of the last century."[69] Duff Cooper, British ambassador in France, while expressing his sympathy with the ordinary Jews on the ships, felt they were pawns of an international "money-making racket."[70]

The Admiralty even explored the possibility of using the legal precedent of intercepting ships suspected of carrying slaves during the nineteenth century in international waters as an excuse to do the same with those carrying "illegal" Jewish immigrants outside its three-mile area of jurisdiction beyond the coast of Palestine.[71] In response, those on *Exodus 1947* argued that it was the British who were "the damned slave merchants. You traded with Jewish blood during the war and you are continuing to do so now. You are paying with red Jewish blood for black oil."[72] It was a polemic that emphasized both the past and present role of British economic imperialism.

With the return in summer 1947 of the *Exodus 1947* Jews to France and on to Germany, on the one hand, and Jewish terrorism, on the other, no one won this war of rhetoric. It seemed briefly with *Exodus 1947* that the return of Holocaust survivors to the country that had instigated their persecution was a propaganda disaster for the British authorities, especially in the United States. But the brutal murder of two British sergeants as the ships were returning to Europe blunted the moral force of Zionist arguments. What is significant here, however, is that both sides conflated Nazism, racialism, and the alleged abuse of power from a decaying empire to make their moral case. With regard to the last mentioned, in the words of American Jewish journalist Ruth Gruber, who reported its journey to the outside world: "The *Exodus* showed how weakened Great Britain had become. This was not a single misguided act by unfortunate and unhappy civil servants in the field. This was part of a tragic pattern of corrosion and decline."[73] Were Jews or the British the evil modern colonizers? In much present-day progressive thought, Israel is presented as a neocolonial power oppressing the Palestinian population. There is thus a certain irony that in the last days of the Mandate, those on the Revisionist right of the Zionist movement presented themselves as anticolonialist freedom fighters from British rule. In a 1947 document from the Irgun, British "perfidy" was "exposed." The "British had actively helped in the extermination of our people." Against this, the "only way to liberation was . . . armed struggle . . . against British rule in this country." The colonizer's objective, the Irgun claimed, was to confine the Jews of Palestine to "permanent ghettodom, while Britain built up the country as one great military base and oil transit centre."[74]

Nor was this a perspective confined to Palestine itself. Returning to postwar Nigeria, the Colonial Office, deeply concerned about the politics of the pro-independence press, reported in 1947 that the *West African Pilot* supported the "contention of speakers at [a] Communist meeting in Tel Aviv that Britain could bring about agreement between Jews and Arabs but refuses to do so because she knows that such an agreement would end British power in Palestine."[75] Before the State of Israel was created, some anticolonial campaigners could regard Jewish attacks on British rule as part of their own struggles, even if they tended to be linked to Communist Party rhetoric articulated in a variety of national settings. In Britain, for example, the Jewish Committee of the Communist Party declared in July 1946: "Now is the time for Jews to shed their illusions, their reliance on Imperialism, be it British or American. Now is the time to stretch out a hand to the Arab progressives and fight for an independent democratic Palestine."[76]

At the heart of so much of this propaganda war was the question of who were the victims or the heirs of the Nazis. This was an exercise in performativity as much as it was a military struggle—bloodshed was (relatively) minimal. It remains that in late Mandate Palestine the conflicts were refracted through the prisms of war, racialism, colonialism, and postcolonialism.

Conclusion

Bryan Cheyette has argued that for the fin de siècle "a colonial discourse could . . . both locate a minority of Jews within the Imperial ruling 'racial aristocracy' as [the imperial writer John Buchan] put it, as well as representing them as fundamentally 'other' to the Anglo-Saxon 'race.'"[77] By the 1940s, the world was a very different place, but the ambivalence and complexity identified by Cheyette were even more pronounced. British Jews could be and *were* part of a postcolonial elite—Sir Andrew Cohen, for example, became governor of

Uganda, and Sir Sidney Abrahams was in charge of justice in Nigeria.[78] How far integrated the latter was in that role was highlighted in the memoirs of English actor Donald Sinden. Filming on location on the Kagera River, Sir Andrew visited the set. At a formal dinner, Sir Andrew proposed a toast to "Her Majesty the Queen" and then asked the gentlemen present whether they would "care to look at Africa by night?" Unaware that this was a euphemism, Sinden accompanied the others to the garden where "the Union Jack hung limply from the flag post; the whole effect was dreamlike. I just stood there drinking it all in." The trance was cruelly and crudely interrupted, however: "Suddenly I was aware of a splashing sound. I looked around and there was the entire hierarchy of Government House peeing on the lawn!"[79] Through such language and the assumptions behind it, Cohen had taken ownership of Africa. Yet migrant Jews were also seen as undesirable "colonial" settlers, whether in Britain itself or in Palestine or countries such as Uganda where the British authorities had kept Jewish refugee movement to a trickle during the 1930s. Even so, in this (partly) post-imperial world, the winds of change had, if only indirectly, been influenced by what would become known as the Holocaust: the color bar was being morally challenged by abhorrence of Nazi racialism and, to a lesser extent, by politicized racism elsewhere, whether practiced in segregationist America or apartheid South Africa. Furthermore, there was grudging acceptance that black people might have the (future) right to rule themselves. It was still the case, however, that racial discrimination, as long as it was informal and implemented case by case, could be defended as being in *everyone's* best interests.

After 1945, the British world was becoming postcolonial. It was, however, far from being post-racist or post-antisemitic, including even the continuation of biological determinism and the fear of "race mixing." It meant that it was still possible to discriminate against those of color and Jews in immigration procedures and in recruitment of the armed forces with the latter. While blatant discrimination that could be reported in the public realm was, post-1945, regarded as unacceptable in both metropole and empire, as long as it was practiced discreetly that was not only acceptable but also desirable with the goal of keeping people of different "races" apart, especially in the sexual sphere. Change was there, but it was slow and inconsistent. And in such discussions over policy, discourse connected to slavery, imperialism, and Nazi persecution of the Jews was linked both aggressively and defensively. Indeed, the global entanglements at an everyday and ideological level outlined in this chapter reveal how such ambiguities emerged and continued to evolve. It thus insists that only by connecting different racialized histories can the full complexity of this multilayered and still-developing story be fully understood.

Notes

1. See, for example, A. J. Sherman, *Island Refuge: Britain and Refugees from the Third Reich 1933–1939* (Berkeley: University of California Press, 1973); Bernard Wasserstein, *Britain and the Jews of Europe 1939–1945* (Oxford: Oxford University Press, 1979); and, in the cultural sphere, the special issue of *Prism: An Interdisciplinary Journal for Holocaust Educators* 5 (Spring 2013) devoted to the *Kindertransport*. For the move toward a more pluralistic approach, see the chapters in Caroline Sharples and Olaf Jensen, eds., *Britain and the Holocaust: Remembering and Representing War and Genocide* (Basingstoke, UK: Palgrave Macmillan, 2013); and Andy Pearce, *Holocaust Consciousness in Contemporary Britain* (New York: Routledge, 2014).
2. Harry Goulbourne, *Race Relations in Britain since 1945* (London: Macmillan, 1998), x, 26–29.
3. Arts and Humanities Research Council reader response to the author, 2013.
4. Paul Gilroy, *Between Camps: Nations, Cultures and the Allure of Race* (London: Penguin, 2000); Bryan Cheyette, *Diasporas of the Mind: Jewish and Postcolonial Writing and the Nightmare of History* (New Haven, CT: Yale University Press, 2013).
5. Cheyette, *Diasporas of the Mind*, xii.
6. Michael Rothberg, "In the Nazi Cinema: Race, Visuality and Identification in Fanon and Klüger," in "Jews and Postcolonial Literature/Histories," ed. Bryan Cheyette, special issue, *Wasafiri* 24, no. 1 (2009): 13–20, 19, and note 2 (and as chapter 9, this volume); and Michael Rothberg, *Multidirectional Memory: Remembering the Holocaust in the Age of Decolonization* (Stanford, CA: Stanford University Press, 2009).
7. Rothberg, *Multidirectional Memory*, 18.
8. Bryan Cheyette, *Constructions of "the Jew" in English Literature and Society: Racial Representations, 1875–1945* (Cambridge: Cambridge University Press, 1993).
9. John Flint, "Scandal at the Bristol Hotel: Some Thoughts on Racial Discrimination in Britain and West Africa and Its Relationship to the Planning of Decolonisation, 1939–47," *Journal of Imperial and Commonwealth History* 12, no. 1 (1983):

78–79. Much work on the so-called new antisemitism starts from the premise that the restraining factor of the Holocaust has, in the late twentieth and early twenty-first century, worn off. See, for example, Paul Iganski and Barry Kosmin, eds., *A New Antisemitism? Debating Judeophobia in 21st-Century Britain* (London: Profile Books, 2003); and Bernard Harrison, *The Resurgence of Antisemitism: Jews, Israel, and Liberal Opinion* (Lanham: Rowman & Littlefield, 2006).

10. David Reynolds, "The Churchill Government and the Black American Troops in Britain during World War II," *Transactions of the Royal Historical Society* 53 (December 1985): 113–33. For the major cabinet discussion of this issue, see National Archives of the UK, CAB 66/29 (WP [42] 441 and 442, October 3, 1942.

11. Elazar Barkan, *The Retreat of Scientific Racism: Changing Concepts of Race in Britain and the United States between the World Wars* (Cambridge: Cambridge University Press, 1992). For an alternative perspective, see Gavin Schaffer, *Racial Science and British Society, 1930–62* (Basingstoke, UK: Palgrave Macmillan, 2008).

12. Tony Kushner, "Without Intending Any of the Most Undesirable Features of a Colour Bar": Race Science, Europeanness and the British Armed Forces during the Twentieth Century," *Patterns of Prejudice* 46, nos. 3–4 (2012): 339–74; and Roger Lambo, "Achtung! The Black Prince: West Africans in the Royal Air Force, 1939–46," *Immigrants & Minorities* 12, no. 3 (1993): 145–63.

13. David Vaughan, *Negro Victory: The Life Story of Dr Harold Moody* (London: Independent Press, 1950), 96; and for the drafting of the statement, see National Archives of the UK, CO 323/673/5.

14. Anne Spry Rush, "Imperial Identity in Colonial Minds: Harold Moody and the League of Coloured Peoples, 1931–50," *Twentieth Century British History* 13, no. 4 (2002): 356–83.

15. Harold Moody, in *League of Coloured People's Newsletter* no. 3 (December 1939).

16. Moody, in *League of Coloured People's Newsletter* no. 6 (March 1940).

17. Ministry of Information, letter, September 29, 1939, National Archives of the UK, CO 323/673/5.

18. Chairman of the Executive Committee of the Army Council to the secretary of state for war, April 2, 1945, National Archives of the UK, WO 32/14692.

19. Minutes and responses, October 3, 1944, National Archives of the UK, AIR 6/75.

20. O. G. Marrack, Head of Admiralty section CW1, November 1944, National Archives of the UK, ADM 116/6208.

21. W. A. Medrow, head of Admiralty section CW11, January 18, 1945, National Archives of the UK, ADM 116/6208.

22. "Nationality and Descent of Candidates," memorandum, April 16, 1945, National Archives of the UK, ADM 116/6208.
23. J. E. B., minute, February 27, 1936, National Archives of the UK, AIR 2/2248.
24. National Archives of the UK, AIR 2/2248.
25. See, for example, National Archives of the UK, WO 32/12913 and ADM 1/27822, for the 1950s and 1960s.
26. Asifa Hussain, "Careers in the British Armed Forces: A Black African Caribbean Viewpoint," *Journal of Black Studies* 33, no. 3 (2003), 312–34; and Vron Ware, *Military Migrants: Fighting for YOUR Country* (Basingstoke, UK: Palgrave Macmillan, 2012).
27. See, for example, Ministry of Defence, *We Were There: For Two Hundred Years Ethnic Minorities Have Fought for Britain All Over the World* (London: Ministry of Defence Schools Presentation Team, 2004), 13.
28. Cy Grant, "The War Experiences of Flight Lieutenant C.E.L. (Cy) Grant," Imperial War Museum, Department of Documents, 05/68/1.
29. Flint, "Scandal at the Bristol Hotel," 85–86, 89.
30. Val Wilmer, obituary of Ivor Cummings, *Independent*, December 4, 1992.
31. Mike Phillips and Trevor Phillips, *Windrush: The Irresistible Rise of Multi-Racial Britain* (London: HarperCollins, 1999 [1998]), 405.
32. Ivor Cummings, interview in *The Black Man in Britain, 1550–1950*, pt. 4, "Soldiers of the Crown," BBC 2 television documentary, December 6, 1974; quoted in Stephen Bourne, *The Motherland Calls: Britain's Black Servicemen & Women 1939–45* (Stroud: History Press, 2012), 16.
33. *Daily Express* (London), February 25, 1947.
34. David Dilks, ed., *The Diaries of Sir Alexander Cadogan: 1938–1945* (London: Cassell, 1971), 483, entry for October 13, 1942; and National Archives of the UK, CAB 66/29.
35. Dilks, *The Diaries of Sir Alexander Cadogan*, 483.
36. Colin Holmes, *John Bull's Island: Immigration & British Society, 1871–1971* (Basingstoke, UK: Macmillan, 1988), 373n300.
37. Holmes, *John Bull's Island*, 258.
38. Paul Rich, *Prospero's Return? Historical Essays on Race, Culture and British Society* (London: Hansib, 1994), 155.
39. See, for example, National Archives of the UK, CO 876/28, August 12, 1942, which focuses on Cumming's work in South Wales.
40. *New Statesman* (London), September 26, 1942.
41. Graham Smith, *When Jim Crow Met John Bull: Black American Soldiers in World War II Britain* (London: I. B. Tauris, 1987), 219–20.

42. As measured and recorded by the UK government's Home Intelligence unit and the social anthropological organization Mass Observation. See, for example, Mass Observation Archive, File Report 2021, Spring 1943, on Americans and the color bar.
43. See National Archives of the UK, CO 357/1222 and 1914, 1946–. For narratives of some of these students, see Henri Tajfel and John Dawson, eds., *Disappointed Guests* (London: Institute of Race Relations, 1965).
44. See National Archives of the UK, CO 537/1917, March–April 1947.
45. "Bristol Hotel Incident," editorial, *Daily Comet* (Kano, Nigeria), February 27, 1947.
46. "The Negro and the Greek," editorial, *West African Pilot* (Lagos, Nigeria), February 25, 1947.
47. Toyin Falola, *Colonialism and Violence in Nigeria* (Bloomington: Indiana University Press, 2009), 161.
48. Sidney Abrahams, minute, March 15, 1947, National Archives of the UK, CO 537/1917.
49. Arthur Creech Jones to Ivor Cummings, April 8, 1947, National Archives of the UK, CO 537/1917.
50. Ivor Cummings to Arthur Creech-Jones, April 10, 1947, National Archives of the UK, CO 537/1917.
51. Andrew Cohen to T. Lloyd, March 19, 1947, National Archives of the UK, CO 537/1917.
52. W. D. Rubinstein, *The Palgrave Dictionary of Anglo-Jewish History* (Basingstoke, UK: Palgrave Macmillan, 2011), 11. His father was a moneylender born in Eastern Europe.
53. See R. E. Robinson, "Cohen, Sir Andrew Benjamin (1909–1968)," Oxford Dictionary of National Biography, January 2011, doi.org/10.1093/ref:odnb/32478; "Andrew Cohen (Colonial Governor)," Wikipedia, last modified November 7, 2016, en.wikipedia.org/wiki/Andrew_Cohen_(colonial_governor).
54. Wilmer, obituary of Ivor Cummings.
55. Letter of MPs to the prime minister, June 22, 1948, National Archives of the UK, HO 213/244.
56. Draft letter, June 1948, National Archives of the UK, HO 213/244.
57. Draft letter, HO 213/244.
58. For his address, see National Archives of the UK, LAB 8/1516 and HO 213/244, and later testimony reproduced in Phillips and Phillips, *Windrush*, 84.
59. Notes of interdepartmental meeting, February 1948, National Archives of the UK, HO 213/714.

60. "Immigration of British Subjects into the United Kingdom," draft memorandum, 1950, National Archives of the UK, MT 9/5463; cabinet discussion, July 24, 1950, National Archives of the UK, FO 369/4365.
61. "Recruitment of Displaced Persons for GB," March 24, 1947, National Archives of the UK, FO 945/500.
62. Royal Commission on Population, *Report* (London: HMSO, 1949), 124.
63. "Recruitment of Displaced Person for GB."
64. "Recruitment of Displaced Person for GB."
65. Cummings to Creech Jones, April 10, 1947, National Archives of the UK, CO 537/1917.
66. Simon Martin, ed., *Edward Burra* (Farnham, UK: Lund Humphries/Pallant House Gallery, 2011). Gemma Romain is working on the cultural geographies of queer black London in this era, within which Cummings was just one individual.
67. Appeal to the United Nations from those on board *Exodus1947/President Warfield*, summer 1947, National Archives of the UK, CO 537/2400.
68. Reproduced in National Archives of the UK, FO 1032/871, September 12, 1947.
69. *Times* (London), April 9, 1947.
70. Duff Cooper to the Foreign Office, July 23, 1947, National Archives of the UK, FO 371/61818 E6643.
71. National Archives of the UK, ADM 1/235261, September 27, 1947.
72. "Listen to the Voice of the Refugees' Ship 'Exodus 1947,'" July 21, 1947, National Archives of the UK, FO 371/61822 E7699.
73. Ruth Gruber, *Destination Palestine: The Story of the Haganah Ship Exodus 1947* (New York: Current Books, 1948), 121.
74. "Background of the Struggle for the Liberation of Eretz Israel," MI5 report, August 2, 1947, National Archives of the UK, KV 3/438.
75. Review of Nigerian press, 1947, National Archives of the UK, CO 537/1917.
76. C. Chimen, "Palestine: Reality and Illusion," *Jewish Clarion* 8 (July 1946): 1.
77. Cheyette, *Constructions of "the Jew,"* 61.
78. Rubinstein, *The Palgrave Dictionary*, 11; and "Cohen, Sir Andrew Benjamin (1909–1968)." On general issues of colonial recruitment, see A. Kirk-Greene, *On Crown Service: A History of HM Colonial and Overseas Civil Services 1837–1997* (London: I. B. Tauris, 1999). More specifically for Africa, see Christopher Prior, *Exporting Empire: Africa, Colonial Officials and the Construction of the British Imperial State, c.1900–39* (Manchester, UK: Manchester University Press, 2013).
79. Donald Sinden, *A Touch of the Memoirs* (London: Hodder & Stoughton, 1982), 184.

2

"The Jim Crow of All the Ages"

The Impact of Hitler, World War II, and the Holocaust on Black Civil Rights in Alabama

Dan J. Puckett

DURING WORLD WAR II, TWO prominent white Alabamians, journalist John Temple Graves and Governor Frank Dixon, observed how Adolf Hitler and Nazi racial ideas had affected race relations in the United States. In mid-1942, Graves described Hitler as "the Jim Crow of all the ages" and warned that unless agitation for greater black civil rights ceased, it would lead to racial unrest, harm the war effort, and perhaps contribute to a Nazi victory.[1] Graves called Hitler "the greatest race-hater in history" and argued that a Nazi victory would be far worse for African Americans than the existing Jim Crow system. His characterization of Hitler unavoidably linked Nazi racism with southern racism, a connection that southern whites adamantly denied existed and strenuously tried to ignore. In late 1944, the mass murder of the Jews in the Holocaust prompted former governor Frank Dixon to admit that "the Huns have wrecked the theories of the master race with which we were so contented so long."[2]

One cannot reasonably compare the experience of African Americans under Jim Crow with the Final Solution, but the treatment of Jews in prewar Germany and blacks in the American South can and should be examined owing to the striking similarities between the two regarding racial thought—what some scholars have called "a natural racial connection"—despite the repeated denials of such a connection by southern whites. The Nazis recognized the similarities in their racial laws to the Jim Crow laws in the South but chose to try to win the support of German Americans rather than to appeal to southern sympathy by stressing their similar racial views, particularly their anti-black views.[3] American civil rights organizations such as the National Association for the Advancement of Colored People (NAACP) and the black press often directly compared Nazi Aryan supremacy with southern white supremacy and warned that ideas of racial superiority posed a danger to American society. In late 1936, shortly after the Berlin Olympics, an African American student at Talladega College wrote that Hitler

> saw his pet theory crumble before the prowess of American Negroes who defied the dictator himself. This happened in Germany 3000 miles across the Atlantic. Need we go so far from home to see such examples of envy, prejudice, and dislike? Can America point a condemning finger at Germany? It would be well to think thrice before making such a gesture. For in this democratic America, have people always been treated with the courtesy and consideration due them? . . . As long as America sits undisturbed and allows lynchings, and silently permits injustice to exist in the courts of the land, America too, is grossly guilty of intolerance, prejudice, and group discrimination.[4]

Indeed, African Americans clearly recognized the persecution and later the mass murders of the Jews as the bitter fruits of racial supremacy, using terms such as *Nazism* or *Hitlerism* to describe the Jim Crow system under which they lived. These comparisons resonated throughout the black population.[5]

White southerners' views, on the other hand, were more nuanced and complicated. They generally criticized Nazi Germany, but they based their criticism initially on the Nazi government's repressive nature and persecutory tendencies and then, by the mid-1930s, its aggressive foreign policy. Newspaper journalists stressed the incompatibility of Nazism with American democracy. The unpopularity of Nazism in the United States, these writers suggested in mid-1934, had more to do with the antidemocratic nature of the

Hitler regime than with its persecutions of the Jews. They called these persecutions "abhorrent to every instinct of decency and justice," and the many condemnations of Nazi Germany were "the product not only of sympathy for a hounded minority in Germany, but of a profound resentment directed against the whole savage course pursued by the 'New Germany' in rooting out every evidence of democracy, in suppressing freedom of opinion, and in emphasizing preparation for war as the only panacea for German ills."[6] This antisemitic persecution, in their view, was but an aspect of the repression, brutality, and aggression that constituted the vicious modus operandi of the Nazis. It produced an intensely negative view of the Nazis, magnified by the increasingly harsh antisemitic persecution in the 1930s and later the murderous atrocities of the Holocaust, which colored both journalists' and the public's reaction to Germany and which endured even in the postwar period.

Unlike African Americans, most white southerners ignored the similarities between Nazi and southern racism, avoided any such comparison, and frequently attempted to justify white society's treatment of African Americans. An example of this attitude could be found in the *Aliceville Times* in late November 1938, not long after Kristallnacht:

> There are [those] who could readily draw a comparison between the manner in which the Nazis were treating the Jews and the manner in which Southerners are treating Negroes. Heated Hitlerites butcher helpless Jews while heady Southerners lynch helpless Blacks. But they failed to follow through with their logic and see that Negroes had never atained [sic] a proportionate social status of the Jews in Germany, [sic] and furthermore, they failed to see the most important fact that Southern Negroes are satisfied with their status, and that their living conditions are more or less what they themselves make them.[7]

As African Americans pointed out the similarities between Nazi and southern racism, and white southerners largely rejected such notions, World War II and the atrocities of the Nazi regime accelerated the awareness of racial discrimination in the United States, particularly in the South, and brought race, racial discrimination, and civil rights into the national spotlight. Nazi claims of Aryan racial supremacy and the subsequent persecution of racial "inferiors" in Germany called into question white supremacy in the United States. World War II, a war widely proclaimed for the Four Freedoms (freedom of speech, freedom of worship, freedom from want, and freedom from fear) and the preservation of democracy, made white supremacy and Jim Crow segregation hard to justify, a situation that became more acutely perceptible since the United States—including white southerners—condemned Germany for its racial ideology and its persecution of the Jews.

This chapter will examine how Alabamians, both white and black, grappled with civil rights and racial discord in the shadow of war and the Holocaust and how these events fundamentally changed southerners' attitudes toward race. Alabama, in many ways, was a microcosm of the South at the time: part of Appalachia, the center of the industrial New South, dependent on the cotton economy of the Black Belt, and with a thriving port city on the Gulf. Known as the "Heart of Dixie," Alabama was the first capital of the old Confederacy and the center of what would later become the modern civil rights movement. While each subregion of the American South has its own peculiarities, whether the Deep South, Upper South, southern Appalachia, or Atlantic states, the differences are in degrees, not in kind. As such, one can reasonably infer that the responses and views of Alabamians reflect much of the American South, including how Alabamians wrestled with ideas of race, democracy, and equality raised by Nazi racial policy and war.

The media, largely newspaper journalists and editors, those who served as the "public intellectuals" of the day, shaped how the public came to understand these contentious issues. These journalists too are representative of how the larger white population in the South grappled with the complex and often uncomfortable racial dilemmas that arose while the Nazi regime held power. Many of the most influential white southern journalists, such as John Temple Graves, Harry M. Ayers, and Grover C. Hall of Alabama, Virginius Dabney of Virginia, Mark Ethridge of Kentucky, George Fort Milton of Tennessee, and Ralph McGill of Georgia, to name a few, wrote as southern liberals; that is, those who argued for greater political and economic opportunities for African Americans, but opportunities still within the confines of white supremacy and Jim Crow segregation.[8] For example, Grover Hall of the *Montgomery Advertiser* won a Pulitzer Prize in 1928 for his editorial crusade against the Ku

Klux Klan in Alabama, but he adamantly believed in the maintenance of white supremacy and segregation as the foundation of a stable southern society.

Moreover, white southerners bristled at criticism from nonsoutherners, especially when focused on racial issues. In particular, they detested "outside agitators," the nonsoutherners who promoted equal rights for African Americans without consideration for established southern traditions. For white southerners, including southern liberals, good race relations remained in a delicate balance, to be preserved only through the Jim Crow system that demanded that blacks know their place. Such attitudes could be found widely dispersed in many of the white newspapers throughout the region. For example, an editorial in a Black Belt newspaper argued:

> The idea seems to have been placed in many negroes that they are being oppressed, that they should demand equal rights, that they should be given justice in the courts. The people that are spreading this propaganda are not interested in the welfare of the negroes of the South or anyone else. These people have been paid to stir up trouble with the most ignorant negroes. We warn the negroes of Bibb County to turn a deaf ear to these people, and work and live as they should. The white people do not wish to oppress the negroes, as long as they stay in their places, live as they should and work as they should.[9]

As African Americans began to demand greater civil rights during the 1930s and '40s, white southerners worried that it would mean the end of segregation, resulting in social equality and miscegenation. By the beginning of World War II, race had become the measuring stick for liberalism. Liberalism now demanded that the color line be demolished, along with its requisite white supremacy and segregation. This sea change altered the position of white southern liberals, who had been paternalistic in their racial outlook, and they slowly abandoned their liberal positions and withdrew their support from many interracial endeavors. In some cases, they finally abandoned their liberalism altogether, like John Temple Graves who by 1948 had embraced the reactionary and segregationist States' Rights Democratic Party, the Dixiecrats.

As the United States entered World War II, black leaders and journalists questioned whether African Americans actually experienced freedom and democracy in the South. Several issues compelled acknowledgment of this question and demonstrate the difficulty that southern society had in confronting it: lynching, black suffrage, and the role of African Americans in the war effort. African Americans, with some exceptions, saw these issues as obstacles to equality and opportunity in a supposed democratic society. White southerners halfheartedly addressed these issues and complained that black demands for equality were ill timed because of the war. Only after the war ended, they argued, could these issues be rationally examined. By the end of the war, however, the horrors of the Holocaust had been exposed and served to illustrate, most clearly for African Americans, what the idea of racial superiority had to offer to persecuted minorities. For southern whites, it was this changing attitude toward race that led John Temple Graves to argue that Hitler was worse than Jim Crow, and former governor Frank Dixon to lament the inevitable destruction of the South's long-held racial beliefs.

Perspectives on Lynching through the Prism of the Holocaust

No other issue more closely corresponded with Nazism, from both black and white perspectives, than lynching. While the number of lynchings in the American South significantly decreased throughout the 1930s, it remained a viable form of extralegal control over African Americans, and conviction for the crime was rare. Lynchings produced intense emotions from all sides, and the South remained susceptible to charges of fascism by northern critics, the black press, and Nazi propaganda. White southerners consistently condemned lynchings as lawless but opposed, with few exceptions, any legislation put forth by what it considered outside agitators. Federal anti-lynching legislation, championed by the NAACP and other civil rights groups, and sponsored by northern legislators, drew almost unanimous opposition from white southerners while southern senators annually staged filibusters to defeat such measures.[10] This opposition to federal anti-lynching bills, grounded primarily in states' rights principles, gave the impression that white southerners condoned the act and wanted to protect such racial violence. Inaction on the part of the South toward lynching only reinforced this view.

The chasm between black and white perspectives over lynching can be seen in the white-owned *Birmingham Age-Herald*, and the paper's editors could be considered generally progressive for the time. In early 1934, the *Age-Herald* had described a "reign of terror" in Georgia that included three lynchings, two beatings, and a witness run out of town, all of which had "reduced the Negroes ... to a state of utter panic." The editors criticized Georgia authorities who "have done nothing by way of meeting the challenge of anarchy" and called on "every sober and enlightened southerner" to embrace their "civic responsibility" to combat the lawlessness that is "confined to no particular locality." Only the previous day, the *Age-Herald* had urged all Americans "to join in a moral repudiation of Hitlerism" because of the Nazis' "brutal treatment" of the Jews. The similarities between the treatment of Jews in Germany and blacks in the South led the *Age-Herald* to argue that the "inexcusable manifestations in America" did not reflect the governmental policy of the United States, but in Germany it was "the official and avowed policy of the government to deny a whole class of its people their equal rights as citizens on account of their Jewish descent."[11]

On closer examination, however, the complicity of the white power structure in the South to allow a "reign of terror" to go unanswered differed little from the bestial "official" persecution of the Jews in Germany by the Nazis. Moreover, it was "official" policy of southern state governments to deny blacks as "a whole class" their equal rights as citizens on account of their descent, and this unwillingness by the *Age-Herald* and, indeed, by the southern whites in general, to equate the morally repugnant treatment of the Jews in Germany with the equally repugnant treatment of blacks in the South did not go unnoticed. A white Birmingham resident, Drayton Graham, pointed out this inconsistent attitude regarding lynching: "We must bow our heads in shame, but we must do more than this to make Germany and Italy feel that we are able to criticize them in their action toward the Jews."[12]

Politicians, journalists, and civic leaders were quick to condemn lynchings, but they were equally quick to justify the emotions that prompted such violence. They blamed the ignorant, the intolerant, or the outside agitator for the crime but did not see it as indicative of white society at large. While they correctly pointed out that lynchings occurred outside the South, they failed to address the racism that created and perpetuated the inequities and injustice of Jim Crow society, conditions that made such extralegal violence a reality that blacks faced on an everyday basis. The most reactionary often warned that "ignorant negroes" would use northern agitation for an anti-lynching bill as a federal license "to disregard the code of the South . . . to attack white women" and that the product of such events would consequently cause more lynchings unless the South was left alone.[13] Because of the precarious nature of white supremacy in counties with large African American populations, white southerners throughout the Black Belt took a similar stance. Many stories and editorials in the white press pointed to Tuskegee Institute's annual report of lynchings in the United States to show that the number had decreased to a point where it was no longer an unmanageable problem and then laid the blame on ignorant extremists. In fact, Tuskegee's annual report notoriously underreported lynchings in the United States.

Black Americans vigorously condemned lynching, frequently comparing it to Nazism. Most often, lynchings were used to illustrate the second-class status of African Americans in the United States. In July 1942, the black newspaper the *Weekly Review* examined two brutal lynchings in Missouri and Texas, where in one case "10,000 persons witnessed his burning on the Sabbath day on the schoolhouse yard," while the other had been "taken from a hospital, tied behind an automobile speeding through the streets of the city, and hanged by the neck in a gin yard." The paper observed that the latter lynching, which occurred in Texas in mid-June 1942,

> took place at the very time when our government was giving seven saboteurs and German spies who had come to our shore, a fair trial under our laws despite their admitted intention of destroying our property and killing probably tens of thousands of our citizens, while this Negro, who was just a suspect of a crime, never had a chance to deny his guilt or to prove his innocence. This mob did not realize the fact that they were lynching democracy; they were lynching the very cause for which millions of our soldiers are dying. . . . This mob was helping Hitler, who is murdering the Jews. . . . Just look now how they lynch and burn Negroes in America, the arsenal of democracy.[14]

Birmingham World, September 14, 1943.

Another black newspaper, the *Birmingham World* also argued that lynchings were "doing Hitler's work in this country" and by 1943 asked, "Is this what I am fighting for?"[15]

Once again, an account of the Texas lynching in 1942 in the white-owned *Birmingham Age-Herald* demonstrates the dissonance of white southerners regarding Nazi and southern racism. Calling the lynching a blot on "our own record for legal justice," the *Age-Herald* viewed it as an isolated, extreme response to a "deeply deplorable, horrible" provocation of a black man assaulting a white woman. The following day, however, the editors lauded the trial of the Nazi saboteurs as "a very striking example of our American devotion to the methods of orderly, civilized justice," without any mention of lynchings, and simply contrasted the "orderly" trial of the saboteurs with the brutality the Nazis dispensed to their opponents.[16]

White southerners, even the liberal editors of the *Age-Herald*, voiced no reservations toward the differing forms of "justice" meted out to blacks and whites in the American South. By and large, they believed that only the extreme elements of white society supported lynching, but African Americans believed acceptance of lynching to be far more prevalent throughout the white population. Lillian Duncan, a student at Talladega College, a black college located just east of Birmingham, pointed out, "There is a great deal of apathy on the part of influential whites" toward African Americans, and this "better class of whites do not let their good judgement interfere with the actions of their racial brothers when such a small thing as a Negro's life is the difference between interference and noninterference."[17]

Explaining Segregation

The exclusion of Jews and other "undesirables" from German society resembled segregation and the disfranchisement of African Americans in southern politics under Jim Crow. Just as lynching had provided opportunity to compare the racial attitudes of the white South and Nazi Germany, so too did the issue of black suffrage. Through mechanisms such as the poll tax and discriminatory registration procedures, thousands of black Alabamians had been disenfranchised and denied their rights guaranteed by the Fourteenth and Fifteenth Amendments.

Where opinion on lynching and a federal anti-lynching law divided Alabama roughly along racial lines, the controversial issues of suffrage and the poll tax made no such distinctions, despite attempts by conservatives to inject race into the debate. The poll tax, for instance, affected far more than just African Americans. Thousands of poor white Alabamians found themselves barred from the polls because they could not afford to pay the tax. In most cases, the white groups urging repeal of the poll tax, liberals included, were not advocating political equality for African Americans. Southern liberals had long championed allowing greater participation of "qualified" blacks in the southern political process, and the leading liberal newspapers in the state pushed for repeal of the poll tax as an undemocratic mechanism designed to keep certain groups disenfranchised. More moderate positions advocated adjusting the tax rather than eliminating it. All opposed any attempt by the federal government to interfere with a state's right in regard to suffrage.

Although the poll tax affected far more than just African Americans, conservatives injected into the debate the powerful suggestion of "Negro rule," a tactic that southern politicians had used since the end of Reconstruction. By keeping the poll tax, conservatives argued, the state could maintain white supremacy. Federal anti–poll tax legislation pushed by civil rights organizations such as the NAACP and the black press further convinced conservatives of the potential peril to the southern way of life. As such, the debate centered primarily on race and the maintenance of white supremacy, as civil rights organizations and the black press urged passage of federal anti–poll tax legislation. As if on cue, Hamner Cobbs, one of the most outspoken white supremacists in Alabama, declared that "the poll tax fight [was] a negro fight, and that if the negroes withdrew from the fight, and the negro ceased to be an issue, the whole thing would collapse."[18] As another stated, "The civilization of the South can endure only so long as the ballot box is sheltered as it is today."[19]

The question of extending access to the ballot box brought myriad responses from white Alabamians, producing no real consensus on the issue. Meanwhile, African Americans, with a few exceptions, sought to extend the franchise for all African Americans. One of the foremost advocates for extending the ballot was Emory O. Jackson, the editor of the African American *Birmingham World* and a driving force of the Birmingham NAACP. Jackson worked tirelessly during the war years for greater black voter registration. Through numerous *World* editorials and commentary, he crusaded for African American equality in Birmingham, instructing Negro civic groups on registration procedures and voting.[20] Jackson was not alone. Members of the Southern Negro Youth Congress and the Alabama Communist Party marched in Birmingham and organized voter registration drives. John L. LeFlore, the executive secretary of the Mobile NAACP and a staff correspondent for the *Chicago Defender*, also attempted to increase voter registration in the Gulf Coast city.[21] In Montgomery, E. D. Nixon Sr., president of the NAACP chapter, organized the Montgomery Voter League, recruited Alabama-born black New York lawyer Arthur Madison to help with voter registration, and led 750 blacks in a march on the Montgomery courthouse to demand their right to vote.[22]

In early 1942, black Birmingham attorney Arthur D. Shores and K. J. Sullivan, editor of the African American *Gadsden Call-Post*, attempted to run for office as candidates in the Democratic primary but had their applications rejected by officials of the Alabama Democratic Party because both the party and the primary were "white only." The Democratic Party had dominated the American South since the end of Reconstruction. The Alabama Democratic Party's emblem was a rooster that stood under a "White Supremacy" banner and appeared on every ballot cast in the Democratic primary, *the* election in the state. Republicans had not won a statewide election since 1901, so the votes of those blacks who had been allowed to register meant little in determining elections. Jackson of the *Birmingham World* called the reasons for the rejections "in as much contradiction to genuine American law and ways as are the edicts of the Nazi Party."[23]

The April 1944 Supreme Court decision in *Smith v. Allwright*, which outlawed the white-only primary in Texas, gave some hope to blacks that suffrage restrictions might be eased. The *Allwright* decision not only raised African American hopes, but it also coalesced conservative desire to preserve white supremacy, despite the emasculation of black political power via the registration process. In response to *Allwright*, the chairman of the State Democratic Executive Committee, Gessner McCorvey, initiated an amendment to the Alabama constitution that changed voter requirements for the state in order to "constitutionally" bar African Americans from registering. Introduced by state senator E. C. Boswell, the subsequent Boswell Amendment required that "a prospective voter, in addition to displaying an adequate 'understanding' of the U.S. Constitution, would also have to satisfy the local board of registrars that he was of 'good character' and had a proper understanding of 'the duties and obligations of good citizenship under a republican form of government.'"[24] Such restrictions would give registrars the authority to discriminate against any undesirable applicant, either white or black. Nevertheless, the debate over the Boswell Amendment remained racial in nature, just as conservatives like McCorvey wanted.[25]

African Americans, however, saw the Boswell Amendment as another manifestation of southern "native fascism." In June 1945, when the Alabama House of Representatives unanimously approved the amendment, Emory Jackson concluded, "That is a pretty act to climax the end of the war against a similar doctrine in Germany."[26]

In general, African Americans resented the discrimination that disfranchised them, and black leaders spoke out forcibly against it. During the war years, when the United States claimed to be fighting a war to preserve democracy, the lack of access to democracy for African Americans especially burned. Robert Durr condemned the unfair and unconstitutional process of black voter registration, characterizing it as an insidious form of Hitlerism, while Emory Jackson echoed this sentiment when he wrote, "The irony of all this is that a Southern Negro can die for democracy but can't always vote for it."[27]

Mobilizing for Equality and Civil Rights

As war approached, the United States increased national defense, and African Americans clamored for inclusion, primarily for employment in the expanding defense industries. This coming war against a racist enemy, as well as the outlined principles of the war, the Four Freedoms, brought the racial issues concerning democracy, inclusion, and civil rights to the fore. It was common practice that blacks be the last hired for a job and the first fired from a job. They were also excluded from well-paying positions and left with few employment options, if any at all. As a result, A. Philip Randolph's March on Washington movement pressured President Roosevelt to issue Executive Order 8802 that created a Fair Employment Practices Committee (FEPC) to combat discrimination in federal defense jobs.[28] But the FEPC, created prior to the war, and the *Pittsburgh Courier*'s Double V campaign (an initiative to achieve victory abroad against fascism and victory at home against racism), begun in 1942, did not eradicate black apathy toward the war or dissuade African American leaders and organizations from agitating for greater opportunity and rights.

As black civil rights organizations zealously argued for greater inclusion in the war effort and full participation in American democracy, they often compared Nazism to Jim Crow. In 1941, the NAACP's *Crisis* asked "whether there [was] a difference between the code for Negroes under Hitler and the code for Negroes under the United States."[29] By using such rhetoric, the *Crisis* articulated the themes that had emerged in the 1930s. This rhetoric also forced southern liberals not only to address the burgeoning demands by African Americans for greater civil and economic rights but also their own liberalism in regard to race.

John Temple Graves, the *Birmingham Age-Herald* columnist and the most widely read syndicated southern liberal journalist of the period, responded to the *Crisis*'s question by pointing to the harsh treatment of blacks by the Nazis in occupied France. Graves wrote that "less enlightened" black leaders, such as those at the NAACP, should understand "that even though the Negro may not have received all he thinks he should under the Stars and Stripes he [was] infinitely better off under that banner than under the dreadful sign of the Swastika."[30] Graves consistently advocated maintaining the status quo in regard to social reform during the war and had little patience for those arguing for social change, especially in regard to the "delicate" racial question in the South. Only after the war, Graves counseled, could the South gradually move toward racial justice.

By mid-1942, Graves described Hitler as "the Jim Crow of all the ages." His characterization of Hitler as the "greatest race-hater in history" was directed toward black apathy for the war effort, and in it Graves implied that a Nazi victory in the war would be more disastrous for African Americans than would the status quo.[31] African Americans in Alabama certainly feared what a Nazi victory could bring for minorities. The *Birmingham World* argued for "all sane Negroes" to support defense efforts because "in a Hitlerized U.S.A. we would have no rights for anybody else to violate."[32] Yet the status quo meant discrimination, exclusion, and abuse of African Americans under an unjust Jim Crow system, and the *World*'s editor, Emory Jackson, took offense at Graves's assertion that black demands for greater rights imperiled the war effort: "America, and the South in particular, cannot be excused for not treating the Negro better because the Nazi treats him worse.... For [the Negro] to surrender his fight for the best that democracy has for the sake of the approval of his friends would be no more sane [than] for America to cease her fight for democracy for the smiles of Hitler." The *World* editorial also pointedly criticized Graves's position in regard to social reform by stating that "the status quo doctrine play[ed] into the hands of Hitler."[33]

Emory Jackson never fit into the mold of what Graves considered a good or responsible black leader. Conversely, Jackson never considered Graves a true liberal, referring to him on numerous occasions as a "white supremacy" southern liberal. Jackson facetiously accepted Graves as a "southern friend" of the Negro "on faith rather than . . . by deeds and favorable action," but it is clear that Jackson never considered Graves a true friend of African Americans.³⁴ The racial unrest during World War II subsequently caused Graves to abandon his self-proclaimed liberal position and embrace white supremacy as the foundation of southern society. Graves was not alone in doing this. Many so-called southern liberals grappled with this same dilemma. For Emory Jackson, though, "America, Birmingham and the South particularly, [would] be measured either by the American yardstick of 'without race, creed, color, or national origin,' or by the Hitlerite yardstick of 'only Germans and Aryans.'" Some tentative and conservative black leaders, however, warned against agitation because the racial issue had become "dynamite." "If the race question is 'dynamite,'" Jackson wrote, "it should be used to blast Hitlerism from all walks of our American life."³⁵

Federal attempts to eradicate discrimination in defense work, through agencies such as the FEPC, caused tremendous controversy throughout the South, and nowhere more so than in Alabama. Southern white liberals remained wary of the influence of the NAACP and other northern civil rights organizations but lauded the administration's attempt to end racial injustice in the defense program. Liberal editors of the *Birmingham News* argued that "if we would protect this country against the dark prejudices of Nazism, then we should strive to eliminate prejudice from the defense program. . . . The president must have realized that it would do little good to protect the country against Nazism if we were guilty of some of the worst phases of Nazism."³⁶ Conservatives, however, saw such federal attempts as a challenge to states' rights and a threat to white supremacy, despite the statement by the head of the FEPC, Mark Ethridge, who said to an audience in Birmingham that there was "no power in the world—not even in all the mechanized armies of the earth, Allied and Axis—which could now force the Southern white people to abandonment of the principle of social segregation."³⁷

The FEPC clearly raised awareness of racial discrimination in defense industries among both black and white. Those who supported the FEPC's efforts often characterized discrimination as either hurting the war effort or equated it with Hitlerism. One Birmingham labor activist wrote that discrimination in defense jobs limited "the forces which will aid us in our great war against Hitlerism" and called on "patriotic Americans" to give "full help and sympathy to the FEPC." He added, "No one but a fool or a Hitler stooge would

Black newspapers often used cartoons to illustrate injustice. In this case, the *World* cartoon characterized the exclusion of African Americans from defense jobs, including black veterans, as un-American and sabotaging the war effort. *Birmingham World*, May 5, 1942.

want to keep 13,000,000 Negro citizens out of our national war effort." Other working-class whites warned that "all job or training discrimination against Negroes should be ended or we and our children will be Hitler slaves" and that "if we are not to be stooges for 'Adolph Shikklegroober' we must forget our old race prejudices."³⁸

When Alabama governor Frank M. Dixon rejected a federal defense contract in July 1942, opposition to the FEPC in Alabama come to a head. Dixon rejected the contract because it included an antidiscrimination clause that he considered a threat to segregation. The conservative Dixon staunchly supported states' rights and opposed anything that remotely infringed on racial segregation. In his refusal of the defense contract, he condemned the FEPC as an organization designed to place "on trial the entire system of race segregation in the South" by those fostering "their own pet social reforms," independent of the war effort.³⁹ By characterizing the situation in stark language and predicting dire consequences, Dixon fanned the flames of racial discord and caused many to fear an actual breakdown of segregation. For most conservatives that meant miscegenation and the end of Anglo-Saxon racial purity in the South. It meant, for conservatives such as Dixon, the end of the southern way of life.

This fear could be found in the hundreds of letters and telegrams sent to Dixon. As one expressed to the governor, southerners would "rather be dead" than to have FDR "and Eleanor put negroes in our parlors and in our beds." A judge from Birmingham fearfully expressed, "We are about to have a second reconstruction in the South." Others rejected the idea that freedom and democracy included equality for blacks. "Apparently our politicians had forgotten that Democracy in Alabama stood for white supremacy," one complained to Dixon, while another declared, "If it is Democracy to amalgamate and ultimately destroy my Race then to HELL with Democracy."⁴⁰

These were not the ramblings of the uneducated or even the unsophisticated; rather, they were the fears of businessmen, doctors, lawyers, and other educated middle-class whites inflamed by Dixon's reactionary rhetoric. The cognitive dissonance in regard to race and racial equality, especially when placed next to Nazi racism, affected far more than just the conservatives. It was widespread throughout white society.

African Americans and labor leaders lashed Dixon for his stand. Noel Beddow, the southern regional director of the Congress of Industrial Organizations (CIO), told a Bessemer, Alabama, crowd that men such as Dixon "[were] trying to drive a wedge between the white man and Black man in the South and they [were] working for the forces of Adolf Hitler." Black critics saw the contradictions between Dixon's actions and the stated purpose of fighting the war. As one African American wrote to Dixon, "Herr Goebbels and his gang are ever ready to seize on actions such as your rejection of that Defense Supplies contract as proof that the various peoples within the United States are hopelessly divided by racial, nationality, and class barriers." Another suggested that Dixon "had rather have us loose [sic] the war than to see Negroes get the same opportunity in the defense of this country as white people."[41]

But not all black Alabamians rejected Dixon's stand on national defense participation, something that caused tremendous controversy in the black community. Twelve "leading Negro citizens" of Gadsden wired the governor their support for his decision to reject the defense contract, "approved his charging the federal government with seeking to abolish race segregation," and claimed race relations were "satisfactory." "We do not want any strife to mar our pleasant relationship," they said.[42] There is evidence, however, to suggest that the so-called leading Negro citizens had been coerced into supporting Dixon's stand. The telegram caused black resentment and anger toward those men to boil over.

Robert Robinson of the *Weekly Review* lashed out at the twelve who sent the telegram. He believed that Dixon's rejection of the contract hurt black morale in the state, but not so much as the telegram sent by the Gadsden twelve. Robinson argued that it misrepresented the real opinions of black citizens in Alabama, and such misrepresentation had caused significant racial misunderstanding in the South. Nor did Robinson hesitate to invoke Hitler to combat injustice and racism. Of the twelve "leaders," he continued: "We would not want them in the army—they might become leaders there too, and we just couldn't feel strong with them defending Democracy in a war. Suppose they were sent abroad and Hitler should tell them that Democracy was a myth, and that they were apes and had no rights in the world. We are afraid that instead of defending Democracy and themselves they would grab Hitler and kiss him."[43]

To ensure discrimination was minimized in industries that had federal contracts, the FEPC held hearings throughout the South. They met in

Birmingham in July 1942, where the discrimination of Mobile's shipbuilding companies had been exposed and Alabama Dry Dock and Shipbuilding Company (ADDSCO) "admitted discrimination and promised to upgrade Black workers."[44] By November 1942, the FEPC ordered ADDSCO to halt their discriminatory practices.

World War II had transformed Mobile from a midsized port city to a bustling industrial center. Defense work in the city attracted 89,000 people between 1940 and 1943 looking for work. By early 1944, Mobile County had reached a population of 233,000, "having risen 64 percent in four years."[45] The African American community burgeoned as "the city's black population rose from 29,046 in 1940 to 45,814 in 1950, nearly all of the increase occurring in the war years." The tremendous increase in population caused a severe shortage in housing, as well as deficiencies in other vital social services, which affected both blacks and whites. The sharp demographic change challenged long-established traditions. As Melton McLaurin explains, "Nowhere in the country did the war more disrupt established patterns of race relations."[46]

Tensions had increased as more blacks hired under pressure from the FEPC began to fill jobs previously held by whites only. This increase in the number of African Americans in the workplace throughout the South provoked significant protest in both the press and correspondence to congressional representatives, and this was no different in Mobile. The draft and military service had caused acute labor shortages, and the FEPC, along with the Maritime Commission, urged ADDSCO to begin employing more skilled black workers. The FEPC did not, however, urge desegregation. In May 1943, however, a race riot broke out in Mobile when ADDSCO, of its own volition, crossed racial lines and put twelve black welders to work alongside whites. In the resulting riot, federal troops had to be called in to restore order after several black workers had been injured.[47] As a result of this, ADDSCO created four segregated ways, one of only four shipyards to have segregated yards in the Deep South. In his study of southern shipyards, Merl Reed argues that total responsibility lay with ADDSCO, whose "decision to integrate the welding force was drastic and irresponsible."[48]

Conservatives lost no time in affixing the blame for the riot on the FEPC and the government's attempt to break down the racial barriers. Hamner Cobbs charged the FEPC with "handicapping the war effort" and explained that "when the federal meddlers . . . attempt[ed] to use the war effort for the

This is one of the few cartoons that use the graphic images of the Holocaust to illustrate its point. In this image, southern politicians such as Mississippian John Rankin are portrayed as Nazis, and the murdered victims of Dachau represent the FEPC. With the horrors of the camps well known by this point, cartoonist Jay Jenkins used this disquieting representation to show how southern Democrats in Congress voted to end the FEPC. *Birmingham World*, August 7, 1945.

promulgation of racial equality in the South, they [were] helping Hitler."⁴⁹ By this time, however, even white liberals had begun to question the administration's attitude toward segregation, worried that Roosevelt cared more about integration and less about established southern traditions. By early 1944, Birmingham mayor Cooper Green, a New Deal supporter and racial moderate, wrote that the FEPC "[had] done more to stir up racial hate than anything that [had] happened since the Civil War."⁵⁰

As the FEPC came under increased attack in the later years of the war, those in the black press rallied to its defense and consistently alluded to "American fascism" as a threat to American democracy as great as that posed by Hitler's army. Frank Marshall Davis, whose column ran intermittently in the *Birmingham World*, described this "homefront fascism" in the fight against the FEPC. In spite of the many American deaths incurred by fighting for freedom abroad, "our own herrenvolk, in congress and elsewhere, makes strong war against the same ideals here at home." The need for the FEPC, Davis continued, occurred "because of fascist race theories in our country: it is being fought because of American fascism. The power of the blows against [the FEPC] indicates the rising and concentrating power of domestic Hitlerism."[51] Another syndicated column, published in the *Weekly Review* shortly after the European war ended, denounced southern senators in their fight against the FEPC. In doing so, it linked the survival of the FEPC to the plight of blacks and Jews who, without the federal agency, would both "continue to face this rankest kind of discrimination," further commenting, "These [senators] protest slavery in Europe but actually defend it at home."[52]

Identifying Connections

The war against Nazi Germany clearly illustrated the issues of democracy and racial superiority being contested in the South. The incongruity of a war for the Four Freedoms being waged by a nation that condoned Jim Crow was obvious to African Americans. As black writer George Edmund Haynes observed, "Equality of rights and obligations of democracy . . . is just opposite to the Nazi idea that there is a super-race with rights superior to those of other races. Not only must we fight this Nazism abroad, but we must also root out of the American life the idea that there is any superior racial group which has rights over members of other groups." By the end of the war, even conservative and accommodating black leaders, such as Birmingham's Robert Durr, came to see that "it [was] difficult to distinguish between fascism and white supremacy," remarking, "It is dreadful to recognize that the liberty, justice, fairplay for which our boys gave their lives, eyesight and limbs does not exist."[53]

Nothing illustrated the danger of racism and racial superiority more clearly than the Holocaust. The black press, when it published articles or stories concerning the mass killings of Jews, focused primarily on the impact such atrocities had on racial perceptions in America, and the danger in perpetuating ideas of racial supremacy. When the *Birmingham World* ran a story in

January 1945 proclaiming the murder of seven hundred thousand Jews in Eastern Europe, it described the mass murders in language such as "lynched" and "segregated Jewish concentration camp," which obviously resonated with its readers. The article also suggested that changing "the color of these victims to black or brown and you will have and [*sic*] idea of what Africa or the American black belt would resemble under fascist rule." In May 1945, columnist William A. Fowlkes described the mass murders as "horrible" but wrote that "not anti-racially speaking, but for truth, the crimes of the Germans, who under Hitler, were declaring themselves the master Nordic superior race and who hooted down all men of foreign color and strain everywhere, should serve to take some of the wind out of the sails of the Christianity-teaching white man everywhere." American leadership, he proclaimed, should be "ashamed of its inhumanity and of its application of superficial justice under weighty codes of law. It should serve to warn that the Whiteman's civilization is threatening self-destruction because of failure within his heart to be fair and just."[54] Fowlkes used the German atrocities as an example of the arrogance of racial supremacy and later made the connection between Nazism and white supremacy when he suggested that the pictures of the executed Nazi leaders at Nuremberg "should serve as a psychological blow . . . to those perpetrators against human equality, opportunity and freedom—those rank espousers of racial supremacy." "Somehow," he wrote, "I hope the warning is thorough and sufficient to strike for peace around the globe. All Nazis are not dead."[55]

The racial issues influenced by Nazi ideology, policy, and actions altered both attitudes and behavior in Alabama. For white Alabamians, the impact was less obvious than for African Americans. Many white Alabamians and, indeed, many white southerners vehemently rejected any comparison of Nazi and southern racism. Those who did often pointed to the mass murders of the Jews as evidence that no similarities existed. As one asked, "Where are the gas chambers in which we have destroyed millions of Negroes? . . . Where are the concentration camps in which we have starved thousands of Negroes to death?"[56] Such a comparison, however, ignored the fact that Nazi policy toward the Jews had developed from oppression, persecution, and exclusion into systematic murder. Conservatives also used such false comparisons to illustrate the benign treatment of blacks in the South, further contributing to and reinforcing the cognitive dissonance white southerners experienced when confronted by the similarities between Nazi and southern racial thought. Most simply avoided comparing the two.

The contradiction of a war for democracy and the maintenance of southern white supremacy affected white southern liberals more than any other group. The influence of Nazi ideology on public discussions of race and civil rights prior to the war, and certainly the issues of democracy and participation raised by the war, imposed a racial litmus test that most southern liberals, such as Birmingham's John Temple Graves, refused to meet. Graves had previously championed extending certain rights and opportunities to African Americans and had done so since the 1920s. Even in 1942, he wrote of "the difference between the democratic battle-cries with which this nation [had] gone to war and the want-of-democracy in many of our practices, especially toward the Negro."[57] But Graves, who had characterized Hitler as "the Jim Crow of all the ages," could not imagine living in a society without it. By the end of the war, Graves had openly embraced white supremacy and Jim Crow as the cornerstone of southern society, rejecting the increased agitation and activism of African Americans as a dangerous path forward for the South. Throughout his journalistic career, Graves wrote about the march of time and how the liberalism of the day was increasingly making old conservative and reactionary attitudes obsolete, how the modern world was passing them by. It is ironic, then, that as Graves clung tightly to his southern liberalism, the world changed around him. His views remained very much the same—ossified, in a sense. Liberalism had simply passed him by.

Not all white Alabamians avoided comparing the fundamental similarities of white supremacy in the South and Nazi racial ideology, but they were in a distinct minority. No one of any prominence spoke out in this fashion, but numerous letters to newspapers from white readers demonstrate that despite the editors' reluctance to address the topic, some did recognize the hypocrisy. One letter writer asked the editors of the *Birmingham News*, "Are we not fighting the war today in order to kill forever the belief of so-called Aryan superiority? We are nothing but hypocrites when we attack one belief of racial superiority and foster another." Similarly, another letter writer commented, "It is awful for Hitler to speak of the Germans as a superior race . . . but how democratic it is for Alabama's legislators to keep a man from voting just because he is black!"[58] Unlike the black press, of which the majority of the white population in Alabama was relatively unaware, any white editor who made this comparison would have opened himself, and his newspaper, to substantial criticism from the larger white community.

Ultimately, blatant, unjust racism explains why so many white Alabamians embraced and defended white supremacy at a time when the United States warred against a nation condemned for its belief in racial supremacy. They used the loud and aggressive Nazi persecutions as a benchmark "to demonstrate the progressive improvement of race relations in the United States."[59] Yet when white Alabamians refused to break with or even reexamine southern racial practices, in spite of the gross similarities between Nazi and southern racism, they revealed an incredible cognitive dissonance regarding Nazi racial thought and their own attitude toward race. Some recognized these glaring similarities but remained steadfast in their support of southern white supremacy, such as Frank Dixon, who wrote in late 1944, "The Huns have wrecked the theories of the master race with which we were so contented so long." Unlike many of his former constituents, Dixon understood the connection between Nazi and southern racism, that the Nazi ideas of Aryan supremacy and racial purity rested on the same assumptions as southern society: segregation; the political, economic, and social superiority of whites; and an unyielding belief in the inherent inferiority of blacks and other non-whites. Nevertheless, Dixon remained openly "unreconstructed," hidebound to tradition. "As a cosmopolitan and church man," Dixon explained, "I can justify, in theory, racial amalgamation. As a southern man with the normal human dislike of foreigners, both in space and in blood, I doubt my ability to put Christian charity into practice. And knowing my fellow Alabamians as I do, I know that they will not either."[60]

The vehement condemnation of Nazism and Nazi racial beliefs by white southerners led them to compare the Nazis to extremist organizations like the Ku Klux Klan, and the Nazis' brutality certainly support the comparison. While the Nazis' ruthlessness mirrored the violence of the Klan, the Nazis' racial beliefs resembled something more fundamental to the Jim Crow South, as both had a deep and abiding faith in the superiority of the white race. Such semblance produced a cognitive dissonance that many white southerners never resolved or, in Dixon's case, believed could never be resolved. The idea of a "war for democracy" only added to the white southerner's dilemma. Indeed, as Dixon warned, the "intensified democracy" fostered by the

Roosevelt administration would "bring many warnings of storms to come" for the South. Dixon later played a central role in the Dixiecrat revolt in 1948, a revolt spurred by President Harry S. Truman's desegregation of the military.

There was a pointed lack of courage on the part of many whites to speak out against prevailing and ingrained opinion. There were no Dietrich Bonhoeffers or Martin Niemöllers among them. In Alabama, the closest to this, perhaps, was the liberal Baptist minister Charles Bell, who was forced from his pulpit in Anniston, as well as from the state, for maintaining a pacifistic stance during wartime and consistently condemning prejudice and injustice. Bell received vicious letters condemning his pacifism and stance on the racial issue: "The people are tired of a negro loving traitor to our flag. The place for you is in a negro church in Harlem or Springfield, Mo. Go to them and be one of them. The congregation is sorry for your mother and father, but they have no sympathy for you and your yellow to the core brothers. A white person who believes in social equality is lower then [sic] the lowest negro alive. A very potential danger to our South will be removed when you shake the dust of Ala. from your feet."[61] This was a far cry from John Temple Graves, who lamented "that people would get up and leave the table where I sat sometimes at the country club."[62] Journalist Thomas Sancton astutely observed that southerners like Graves or Dixon "grew up in a Southern white society in which it was considered a high crime to employ objective intelligence in studies of race relations. [They] accepted the old prejudices. And even this war, with all its impelling meanings of race and freedom, has failed to make them turn back courageously and gaze upon their fathers' ideas. Instead, they walk backward with cloaks to cover the nakedness of these ideas, as Shem and Japheth covered the nakedness of Noah."[63]

The perception of Nazi ideology, and particularly white hypocrisy in regard to Nazi and southern racism, noticeably encouraged African Americans to demand greater economic and political opportunities as well as civil rights. Prior to the war, African Americans actively campaigned for greater opportunity and forcefully condemned the "Nazi-like" oppression of Jim Crow. Indeed, Alabama's black press argued forcefully for greater equality and did not hesitate to describe southern white supremacy as Hitlerism. Toward the end of the war, and after the revelations of the Nazi mass murders, black leaders and the state's black press became increasingly forceful when agitating for racial justice and civil rights. Such agitation, however, was tempered when compared to northern rhetoric and action. Unlike the northern black leaders or the national black press, African Americans in Alabama refused to call openly for an end to segregation, although they believed that segregation bred injustice. Leaders like Tuskegee president Frederick Patterson argued that the ultimate end to segregation rested only with the "time and technique of its elimination."[64]

The element of race and racism that the war with Nazi Germany brought, the impassioned racial rhetoric surrounding the war, the liberal federal programs designed to aid minorities and help defense efforts, and the war aims set out in the Atlantic Charter provided African Americans a platform on which to seek greater civil rights and inclusion in American democracy. Coupled with pressure from national civil rights organizations, this led to black participation in areas that had been previously "white only." Although the armed forces remained segregated during the war, African American veterans believed strongly that they had fought for "true American democracy," and their experience in the war convinced many of them work for change.[65] Tuskegee's Daniel Beasley and Otis Pinkard, like hundreds of black veterans, joined in voter registration drives after they had been discharged from the army. As Pinkard affirmed, "After having been overseas fighting for democracy, I thought that when we got back here we should enjoy a little of it."[66] But despite the seemingly little progress made toward civil rights in Alabama during the war, small but significant strides had been taken toward greater African American participation in American democracy. With the participation of African American veterans who returned home after the war, the efforts of these early civil rights leaders laid the foundation for the modern civil rights movement.

Notes

1. John Temple Graves, "The Southern Negro and the War Crisis," *Virginia Quarterly Review* 18 (Autumn 1942), 501. Graves wrote a syndicated column published throughout the South, and he was perhaps the most widely read southern liberal journalist of the period.
2. Frank Dixon to Grover C. Hall Jr., November 11, 1944, box 1, folder 1, Grover C. Hall Jr. Papers, Alabama Department of Archives and History (ADAH).

3. Johnpeter H. Grill and Robert L. Jenkins, "The Nazis and the American South in the 1930s: A Mirror Image?" *Journal of Southern History* 58 (November 1992): 685, 688.
4. *Talladega (AL) Student*, November 1936, 7.
5. In many cases, there was a connection between the NAACP and the black press. Black editors such as Emory O. Jackson of the *Birmingham World* and K. J. Sullivan of the *Gadsden (AL) Call-Post* also served as leaders in their community's chapter of the NAACP. Mobile's NAACP leader, John L. LeFlore, was a correspondent for the *Chicago Defender*.
6. *Birmingham Age-Herald*, May 21, 1934, 4.
7. *Aliceville (AL) Times*, December 1, 1938.
8. The best study on this subject is John T. Kneebone's *Southern Liberal Journalists and the Issue of Race, 1920–1944* (Chapel Hill: University of North Carolina Press, 1985).
9. *Centreville (AL) Press*, August 23, 1933.
10. See Robert Zangrando, "The NAACP and a Federal Antilynching Bill, 1934–1940," *Journal of Negro History* 50 (1965): 106–117.
11. *Birmingham Age-Herald*, February 1, 1934, 4.
12. Drayton Graham to editor, *Birmingham Age-Herald*, July 13, 1938, 6.
13. *Tuscaloosa News*, January 12, 1938, 4.
14. *Negro Labor*, quoted in *Weekly Review*, July 25, 1942.
15. *Birmingham World*, October 20, 1942; and February 19, 1943.
16. The African American lynched in Texas had been accused of assaulting a white woman when he was dragged from a hospital and hanged. *Birmingham Age-Herald*, July 15, 1942, 4; and July 15, 1942, 6.
17. Lillian Duncan, "Why I Want the Federal Anti-Lynching Law Passed," *Talladega (AL) Student*, May 1937, 14–15.
18. Cobbs was editor of the *Greensboro (AL) Watchman* and the white supremacist newspaper, the *Southern Watchman* (Mobile, AL). *Southern Watchman* (Mobile, AL), May 19, 1945, 4.
19. *Talladega (AL) Daily Home*, quoted in *Birmingham News*, April 15, 1941, 8.
20. *Birmingham World*, September 15, 1944; June 30, 1944; and February 20, 1945.
21. A useful article that examines Mobile during the war years is Mary Martha Thomas, "The Mobile Homefront during the Second World War," *Gulf Coast Historical Review* 1 (Fall 1985): 55–75. Another article that examines John L. LeFlore and Mobile during the civil rights movement after the war is Nahfiza Ahmed, "A

City Too Respectable to Hate: Mobile during the Era of Desegregation, 1961–1965," *Gulf South Historical Review* 15 (Fall 1999): 49–67.

22. Donald Jones to Miss [Ella] Baker, September 14, 1945, NAACP, Alabama Files, Montgomery Chapter (microfilm), Archives, Birmingham Public Library (BPL); and Dolores Nicholson, "E.D. Nixon Sr.," in *Notable Black American Men*, ed. Jessie Carney Smith (Detroit: Gale, 1999), 879–80.

23. *Birmingham World*, March 6, 1942; and March 20, 1942.

24. William D. Barnard, *Dixiecrats and Democrats: Alabama Politics, 1942–1950* (Tuscaloosa: University of Alabama Press, 1974), 170n18, 62–63. The Boswell Amendment passed in November 1946 by 53.7 percent to 46.3 percent but was declared unconstitutional in 1949, 171n52.

25. Barnard, *Dixiecrats and Democrats*, 62; for a conservative argument for the Boswell Amendment, see Horace C. Wilkinson, "Argument for Adoption of Boswell Amendment," *Alabama Lawyer* 7 (October 1946): 375–82.

26. *Birmingham World*, November 3, 1944; and June 15, 1945.

27. *Weekly Review*, January 15, 1944; and December 11, 1943, 1. Durr could be considered a "race leader" in Birmingham's black community, but he also stayed in contact with white political leaders and journalists such as John Temple Graves. Other black leaders thought Durr too accommodating to the white power structure. See *Birmingham World*, September 20, 1940; and November 3, 1944.

28. Led by A. Philip Randolph, head of the Brotherhood of Sleeping Car Porters, the March on Washington movement encompassed numerous civil rights organizations and threatened a hundred-thousand-strong demonstration at the Lincoln Memorial in June 1941. To prevent a further split in the Democratic Party and avoid the embarrassment of a racial protest in Washington, Roosevelt issued Executive Order 8802, which ended racial discrimination in defense work. To administer this, he established FEPC. Randolph and other civil rights leaders called off the march. See Harvard Sitkoff, *A New Deal for Blacks: The Emergence of Civil Rights as a National Issue: The Depression Decade* (Oxford: Oxford University Press, 1978), 314–22.

29. Quoted in John Temple Graves, "This Morning," *Birmingham Age-Herald*, May 31, 1941, 1.

30. Graves, "This Morning," 1.

31. Graves, "The Southern Negro and the War Crisis," 501.

32. Allen Woodrow Jones, "Alabama," in *The Black Press in the South, 1865–1979*, ed. Henry Lewis Suggs (Westport, CT: Greenwood Press, 1983), 44.

33. *Birmingham World*, June 3, 1941.

34. *Birmingham World*, May 12, 1942.
35. *Birmingham World*, June 16, 1942.
36. *Birmingham News*, June 30, 1941, 6.
37. Graves, "The Southern Negro and the War Crisis," 504–5. Ethridge made the comment at an FEPC meeting in Birmingham in July 1942.
38. W. H. Mooney to editor, *Birmingham Age-Herald*, June 8, 1942, 6. Mooney was the president of Spaulding Red Ore Miners Local No. 556; and Mrs. G. J. Carden, Mrs. Ethel Butler, and Mrs. Paul M'Cool to editor, *Birmingham Age-Herald*, June 20, 1942, 6.
39. Frank Dixon to Ralph D. Williams, July 22, 1942, Dixon Administration Papers, box SG12277, folder 30, ADAH. The nondiscrimination clause read as follows: "The Seller, in performing the work required by this contract, shall not discriminate against any worker because of race, creed, color or national origin." Dixon's letter to Williams was reprinted in the *Birmingham News*, July 26, 1942, 14a; Frank Dixon to Frank Bane, August 24, 1942, Dixon Administrative Papers, box SG12277, folder 30; and Frank Dixon to Mark Ethridge, July 23, 1942, Dixon Administration Papers, box SG12276, folder 12. See also Mark Ethridge to Frank Dixon, July 27, 1942, Dixon Administration Papers, box SG12276, folder12, ADAH.
40. D. E. Henderson to Frank Dixon, July 25, 1942, Dixon Administration Papers, box SG12276, folder 14. Henderson was the district manager of Reliance Life Insurance Company of Pittsburgh, in Huntsville, AL; H. B. Abernathy to Frank Dixon, July 24, 1942, Dixon Administration Papers, box SG12276, folder12. Abernathy was a judge on Jefferson County's Court of Felonies and Misdemeanors; Robert L. Shirley to Frank Dixon, July 25, 1942, Dixon Administration Papers, box SG12276, folder 14. Shirley was a dentist from Fairfield; and J. J. Cockrell to Frank Dixon, July 27, 1942, Dixon Administration Papers, box SG12276, folder14. Cockrell was an attorney in Talladega, AL. Even the head of the Republican Party in Alabama, Oliver D. Street, commented that it was "not the first time that outsiders (high officials of the United States) have attempted to set the Negro astride the necks of the white people of the South." See Street to Frank Dixon, August 15, 1942, Dixon Administration Papers, box SG12276, folder10, ADAH.
41. *Alabama News Digest* is quoted in the *Greensboro (AL) Watchman*, August 20, 1942, 2; Rollins Leonard Winslow to Frank Dixon, 8 August 1942, Dixon Administration Papers, box SG12276, folder 11; and G. F. Porter to Frank Dixon, July 28, 1942, Dixon Administration Papers, box SG12276, folder 11, ADAH.
42. *Gadsden (AL) Times*, July 26, 1942, 1; a press release from the communist *Daily Worker* found in Dixon's files suggests that the Gadsden Chamber of Commerce,

with Rev. E. M. Wilson's assistance, pressured Gadsden's black leaders to sign the telegram supporting Dixon's stance by threatening them with "plenty of trouble." *Daily Worker* (New York) press release, August 7, 1942, box SG12277, folder 31, Dixon Administration Papers, ADAH.

43. *Weekly Review*, August 1, 1942, 4.
44. Another Alabama company, the Gulf Shipbuilding Company of Mobile, "hired Negroes only as porters and janitors although blacks had worked in skilled jobs at the same yard in 1917." Merl Reed, "The FEPC, the Black Worker, and the Southern Shipyards," *South Atlantic Quarterly* 74 (Autumn 1975): 452.
45. Allen Cronenberg, "Mobile and World War II, 1940–1945," in *Mobile: The New History of Alabama's First City*, ed. Michael V.R. Thomason (Tuscaloosa: University of Alabama Press, 2001), 215.
46. Melton A. McLaurin, "Mobile Blacks and World War II: The Development of a Political Consciousness," in *Gulf Coast Politics in the Twentieth Century*, ed. Ted Carageorge (Pensacola, FL: Historic Pensacola Preservation Board, 1973), 47–48; and Thomas, "The Mobile Homefront during the Second World War," 69–70.
47. Thomas, "The Mobile Homefront during the Second World War," 70–71; Reed, "The FEPC, the Black Worker, and Southern Shipyards," 454–55.
48. Reed, "The FEPC, the Black Worker, and Southern Shipyards," 455–59.
49. *Southern Watchman* (Mobile, AL), May 29, 1943, 6.
50. Cooper Green to Lister Hill, March 23, 1944, box 376, folder 2, Lister Hill Papers, Hoole Special Collections, University of Alabama.
51. Frank Marshall Davis, "Passing Parade," *Birmingham World*, January 14, 1944.
52. *Weekly Review*, July 14, 1945, 4.
53. *Service* (Tuskegee, AL), May 1945, 10; and *Weekly Review*, July 7, 1945, 1.
54. "Uncover Bones of 700,000 Victims of German Murder," *Birmingham World*, January 5, 1945, 1, 4; and William A. Fowlkes, Seeing and Saying, *Birmingham World*, May 1, 1945.
55. William A. Fowlkes, Seeing and Saying, *Birmingham World*, October 29, 1946.
56. W. L. Acuff to editor, *Birmingham News*, September 14, 1944.
57. Graves, "The Southern Negro and the War Crisis," 506.
58. *Birmingham News*, August 27, 1944, 2d; and May 24, 1945, 8.
59. John T. Kneebone, *Southern Liberal Journalists and the Issue of Race, 1920–1944* (Chapel Hill: University of North Carolina Press, 1985), 181.
60. Frank Dixon to Grover C. Hall Jr., November 11, 1944, box 1, folder 1, Grover C. Hall Jr. Papers, ADAH.

61. A member to Charles Bell, June 13, 1944, box SC1005, folder 3, Charles Bell Papers, Samford University Archives; and Harry M. Ayers to Charles R. Bell, November 30,1944, box 143, folder 11, Harry Ayers Collection, Hoole Special Collections, University of Alabama (HSC).
62. John Temple Graves to Thomas Sancton, July 7, 1943, John Temple Graves Papers, BPL.
63. *New Republic*, March 8, 1943, 320.
64. Frederick D. Patterson, "The Negro Wants Full Participation in the American Democracy," *What the Negro Wants*, ed. Rayford Logan (Chapel Hill: University of North Carolina Press, 1944), 265.
65. Robert E. Jones to editor, *Birmingham World*, February 14, 1946, *Birmingham World* Papers 1102.29.2, BPL.
66. Robert J. Norrell, *Reaping the Whirlwind: The Civil Rights Movement in Tuskegee* (New York: Knopf, 1985), 60–61.

3

From Undesirable to Unassimilable

The Racialization of the "Jew" in South Africa

Milton Shain

Nativism and the Quota Act of 1930

The Holocaust, an unprecedented event in the long history of Jew-hatred and arguably a unique event in the history of mass murder or genocide,[1] was deeply rooted in what Jacob Talmon refers to as the seedbed of European history.[2] Within that "seedbed," the *Adversus Judaeos* legacy of Christian theology cannot be ignored. But the slaughter of Jews by the state was not part of the medieval Christian world order. For mass death, or the Final Solution, scholars have focused rather on secular ideologies, most notably on race thinking that had its genesis in the eighteenth century. Notions of race, and with these the exclusion of Jews—defined as immutably alien—gradually replaced ideas of brotherhood. Biological politics, writes Christopher Browning, was fundamental to Nazism.[3]

Ideas of race were not restricted to Germany or Europe, and white South Africans—a product of large population migrations (in particular between Britain and South Africa) were certainly among the heirs to those ideas. In an age of increasing literacy and improved communications, this was inevitable. Moreover, a vaguely racial definition of Jewishness ensured that traits traditionally associated with Jews would be ascribed to their coreligionists in South Africa as well. Yet, as argued in this chapter, the characterization of the

Jew—as well as the ebb and flow of anti-Jewish hostility—was a function of specific contingencies rooted in South Africa's historical realities, intellectual traditions, domestic concerns, and political priorities. The "Jewish question," as will be seen, served a political purpose, particularly in the 1930s and early 1940s, but essentialist and racist ideas have persisted, despite Jews being white and color being the cardinal divide in South Africa society.

Characterized in the late nineteenth and early twentieth centuries as "undesirables" and—after the Russian Revolution—as "subversives," the newcomers were now described as "unassimilable."[4] Of course, older stereotypes associated with the alien and undesirable Jew persisted and would continue to be employed for political purposes, but a new racial discourse—informed by a regnant nativism—increasingly defined the Jew. Whereas vaguely racial notions underpinned the alien Jew at the turn of the century, the new nativism of the 1920s was distinctive and ever present. It was led by the English-language *Cape Times* whose editor, the Oxford-educated B. K. Long, persistently advocated curbs on immigration from countries where it was claimed democratic ideals were unknown and "western concepts of morality" quite foreign and unappreciated.[5] "Russians" and "Jews" were now identified with "Orientals," "Africans," "Europeans," "Anglo-Saxons," "English," "Nordics," and "Mediterraneans" as racial groups—a harbinger of trouble at a time when issues of "moral degeneracy" preoccupied South African eugenicists, and "miscegenation" or "cross-breeding"—primarily associated with South African blacks—was widely feared.[6]

These fears were encapsulated in the response of the *Star* (a Johannesburg daily) to a 1925 report on immigration by the census director, John Holloway, who had identified the influx of impoverished Lithuanian Jews as a major cause of concern. The newspaper referred to the "fecundity" of the newcomers and the impact this would have on the country's intellectual and physical development. These immigrants, contended the *Star*, would profoundly modify the racial composition of and affect the whole character of the country, and it would be far better to follow the American example of encouraging "Nordic immigrants."[7] Only a few years later the National Party that was in coalition with the South African Party (forming the so-called "Pact" government under Prime Minister J. B. M. Hertzog) formally called for curbs on the influx of Eastern Europeans by fixing a quota on immigration similar to that of the United States.[8]

Action soon followed. In January 1930, Minister of the Interior Daniel François Malan introduced the Quota Act. Modeled in part on the Johnson–Reed Act of 1924 in the United States, the new legislation planned effectively to halt Eastern European Jewish immigration by imposing an initial limit of fifty migrants per annum from each of a list of "quota countries," which included Lithuania, Latvia, and Poland, the seedbed of South African Jewry. Schooled in a European romanticism that conflated language, state, and nation, Malan knew that he had support across party and language lines: English-speaking merchants appreciated the prospect of less competition and the Afrikaner *volk* wished to limit what it considered a powerful and exploitative alien element that added to the country's "racial" problems.[9] As Malan told an approving House of Assembly, the bill was rooted in the wish of every nation to maintain its own particular identity based on the composition of its original inhabitants. The Eastern European newcomers undermined the character and homogeneity of the nation which, he contended, could not cope with an "undigested and unabsorbed and unabsorbable minority."[10]

Speakers on both government and opposition benches shared Malan's concerns. Some warned that if the characteristics of the "white stock" were undermined, disharmony would result and, moreover, that it was in the interests of future civilization in South Africa that the country's heritage should remain unimpaired. Fears were also expressed that a large influx of Eastern European Jews would pose a very real threat if not diluted with other more acceptable European immigrant stock: "We do not want to keep people out because they are Jews or Lithuanians, but we do want to restrict their numbers so that they shall conform to the present ethnological conditions," argued another proponent. Even the liberal and philosemitic Jan Hofmeyr, a rising star in the South African Party, maintained that the entry of Jews into the country would be advisable only if they were part of a wider immigration stream of the "stock of people from whom we have sprung."[11]

An Additional Racial Problem

These essentialist and racial notions of the Jews became even more pronounced in debates surrounding the growing (albeit small in absolute terms) influx of German Jews in the 1930s. At a time of political instability and an escalating (predominantly Afrikaner) "poor white" problem, the growth of vulgar radical right movements ensured that the Jewish question shifted from the periphery to the center of South African politics. Both Malan (who had broken away from the newly formed United Party to form the Purified National Party in 1934) and Hertzog shared a sense that the racially distinct and unassimilable Jew was a problematic addition to South Africa's already complicated racial mix. In a government memorandum dealing with immigration, the secretary for external affairs, Helgard Bodenstein, accused Jewish immigrants of rigidly retaining their identity as a separate community and being prepared to subordinate the interests of South Africa to those of their own group.[12]

Bowing to substantial pressure—driven largely by *Die Burger*, a Nationalist daily—Hertzog announced stiffer educational and financial immigration requirements during the 1936 parliamentary session to take effect on November 1. But this failed to quell the anti-immigrant clamor, which reached a climax when Jewish organizations abroad hurriedly chartered the *Stuttgart*, a German liner that sailed from Bremerhaven with 537 German Jewish refugees on board to beat the November 1 deadline.[13] Importantly, Afrikaner intellectuals led the charge, making good use of the alleged racial threat posed by the unassimilable Jews that could seriously endanger the delicate social fabric. Stellenbosch professor Johannes Basson made this clear during a lively meeting in the university town, while his colleague, Professor Ebenhaezer "Eben" Donges, warned of "national indigestion" if too many Jews entered the country. The essence of the problem, explained Professor Christian "Krissie" Schumann, was that "the Jew always remained a stranger—even in Jerusalem"—with no real patriotism or love for the country that was his new home.[14] Another academic, Frans Labuschagne of Potchefstroom University College, also voiced concern and secured a resolution at a mass meeting in Potchefstroom protesting the influx of Jews on the grounds that they were "undesirable" on account of their religion and declaring the impossibility of "blood mingling" and "cultural co-operation" with them.[15]

Shortly after the arrival of the *Stuttgart*, the National Party's Orange Free State Congress in Bloemfontein resolved that no Jew, Asiatic, or Coloured (those of mixed descent) could be a member of the party.[16] These sentiments reflected a widely shared segregationist ethos—informed by the conflation of race and culture—that had reached partial fruition in 1936 when Africans were removed from the common voters' roll in the Cape Province, the last bastion (albeit watered-down) of nonracialism. There remained a sense—in certain circles, at least—that Jews were "not white like us," explains the historian Sally Peberdy. South Africa, she writes, understood itself as "a white nation constructed on the basis of only two kinds of founding immigrant and "racial stock": the British and the Afrikaner, the "two great European races" of the Union."[17]

Resolutions approved at the Transvaal National Party Congress in 1936 also reflected obsessions with "racial stock" and fears of racial pollution[18] and would in due course translate into theories of separate development, invested over time with scholarly rationales. As far as Jews were concerned, however, the immediate task was to stop further immigration and limit occupational options. This was spelled out at the National Party's Orange Free State Congress in Bloemfontein where Malan warned that unless the government took the necessary restrictive steps in regard to legislation, he would introduce a bill into Parliament that would be built on the notion of unassimilability.[19] "We already have the natives, the Indians, the coloured people and the Europeans, four great national classes, all of whom stand apart from each other, and live almost as a separate unit," explained J. G. Strijdom, Transvaal leader of the National Party. "We feel that if we allow this streaming in to continue, just as certain as the Indians came here and led to a new national group, we shall be creating a fifth national group by such admission. We with our small numbers are not able to assimilate the great flood of the past years."[20]

Significantly, both the English and Afrikaans press shared these concerns. "The Jewish community in this country," explained the *Cape Times*, "realizes, we are sure, that in a relatively small white community of 2 million people, it is not unnatural that the character of immigration from overseas should be examined with very special attention. A relatively small immigration of a particular type, if continued persistently for several years, might easily change fundamentally the characteristics of the South African people of the future."[21] Other commentators, while not necessarily identifying with nativist views, recognized and feared the tensions surrounding the Jewish question.[22]

In late December 1936 Malan, true to his word, introduced his own immigration and naturalization bill, which was based on the principles he had outlined earlier at the National Party Congress in Bloemfontein[23] in which assimilability as a criterion for entry was uppermost. But Malan's bill was forestalled by the government which introduced its own immigration bill. Although it did not explicitly mention Jews—and would thus not draw the ire of the South African Jewish Board of Deputies and Jewish parliamentarians—it proposed that all aliens would be subjected to an Immigrant Selection Board.[24]

Notably, parliamentary debate demonstrated that Jews were now widely seen as a race apart. At the heart of the Jewish question today, explained the National Party Free State leader, Nico van der Merwe, was "Jewish nationalism" which accounted for "unassimilability" and "the economic power which Jewry has acquired in our country"; and these issues, he pointed out, were not unique to South Africa. The essence of the Nationalist argument was that South Africa should not absorb more than "a certain percentage of Jews" if it was to avoid adding to the already fragmented groups—defined by Strijdom as the natives, the Indians, the Coloured people and the Europeans.[25] Hertzog shared these concerns and, in defense of the bill, argued that South Africa simply could not absorb too many Jews.[26] While Malan's initial request that the word *alien* in the legislation include "a person of the Jewish race" was turned down, the legislation ensured that it would be very difficult for Jews to enter South Africa. Among the new requirements (all subject to an Immigration Selection Board) was a specification of "race" with the form reading "European," "Hebrew," "Asiatic," or "African."[27]

In the final vote on January 27, 1937, the Aliens Act received eighty-seven votes for and twenty-six against. Yet the Nationalists were not assuaged. A month after the legislation was approved, Malan rather ominously called for a "Nordic front" to win back for the English and Afrikaans speakers the ground they had lost.[28] Here, he illustrated the interconnectedness of regnant European currents of thought and South African intellectual traditions—echoing South African nativist thinking of the 1920s with its eugenic obsessions and fears of racial mixing.[29] Quite obviously the alien Jew challenged an emerging sense of "South Africanness" among white English and Afrikaans speakers who were considered to be the founding immigrants.

While the United Party believed that a limited number of Jewish immigrants could be absorbed, Malan's Nationalists—informed by a corporatist *völkisch* mind-set and a powerful neo-Kuyperianism—saw the newcomers as an unassimilable race. It was a weltanschauung that viewed individuals primarily as members of organic communities.³⁰ On the whole, however, white South Africans (both English and Afrikaans speaking) were *ad idem* when it came to concern about Jews, sharing apprehensions that yet another racial group was being added to the already problematic Asian, Coloured, and African mix. Because Jews were immutably alien and unassimilable, they posed a threat to "the delicate balance between the black and white populations of the Union as a result of their perceived difference" and, in fact, could contaminate "the body of the nation itself."³¹ In this essentialist cast of mind, we have hints of a paradigm that would subsequently inform Nationalist thought about culture and ethnicity in general.³² It was a cast of mind that underpinned the apartheid project in its aim to safeguard the values and standards of "white civilization."³³ In this sense, the Jewish question and ways of dealing with it paralleled—and even to some extent presaged—apartheid ideology as it evolved from the mid-1930s.³⁴

Eric Louw, a former high commissioner in London and the United States and (after 1938) member of Parliament for Beaufort West, led the charge against the Jew when he introduced the Aliens Amendment and Immigration Bill in early 1939 whose objectives were wide ranging and built on notions of Jewish lineage. To be sure, "no applicant for permission to enter the Union who is of Jewish parentage shall be deemed to be readily 'assimilable,'" noted a clause in the bill.³⁵ It was this notion of Jewish unassimilability that lay at the heart of Louw's concern: "He has maintained his racial identity and his Jewish customs, he has remained true to the faith of his forefathers, he has maintained the purity of his Jewish blood, and above all he has remained a separate nation," explained Louw. "Now sir, in spite of my being accused of being an anti-Semite, let me say in all sincerity that I think that it is very wonderful that the Jews over a period of two thousand years, often living under unfavourable conditions, have retained the integrity of their race. But that very fact proves that they are, and will remain, a separate nation; in other words, that they are, and will remain unassimilable." Louw was fully supported by Malan who reiterated that Jews from Germany were not welcome as they were not racially appropriate.³⁶ The argument that the country already faced a problem with "kaffirs, Indians, and Coloureds" and did not need an additional Jewish problem was raised once again some months later by a prominent Nationalist Paul Sauer.³⁷

Nazi Echoes

This racial essentialism gained impetus following the South African government's controversial decision to support the Commonwealth war effort to resist Germany. A powerful antiwar movement was orchestrated by the Ossewa Brandwag, or OB (a paramilitary radical right Afrikaner movement founded in 1938), which vigorously promoted fascism and the racial casting of the Jew. The movement excluded Jews from membership on the grounds that they were unable to identify with the main principles of the OB, notably the preservation of Boer traditions and their language.[38] But, in fact, their antipathy to Jews was such that it was envisaged that Jews would eventually be stripped of their civil rights.[39] There was, moreover, a warning that marriage to a Jew should not be condoned because Jews were a product of the mixing of pre-Asiatic races with Semites and their outlook could not be considered European nor their patriotism taken for granted.[40] OB leader Hans van Rensburg's speeches were redolent with anti-Jewish accusations and his rhetoric utilized Nazi-like ideas, among them *bloedsuiwerheid* (blood purity), *die bonde van die bloed* (the bonds of the blood) and *bloed en boden* (blood and soil).[41] In 1942, Van Rensburg issued a manifesto in which he declared that the state must be a "Christian National Republican Authoritarian State" with a government strengthened by "the elimination of nationally harmful and liberal attitudes and so-called democracy." Unassimilable immigrants—meaning primarily Jews—would be banned.[42] As Christoph Marx, a historian of the OB, writes, not only were the Jews unassimilable, but they "represented a fundamentally destructive element that was then given biological significance."[43]

Oswald Pirow's Nuwe Orde—effectively a breakaway group of seventeen members originally elected on a United Party ticket in 1938—also proudly advocated a variant of National Socialism and lauded fascism in Europe.[44] Republicanism remained at the center of its policy, alongside hostility toward "un-Christian" and "unassimilable" elements. The entry of Jews or other unassimilable persons into the country would be forbidden.[45] In a series of "lecture" documents for the movement's incoming cadres, the essentialist or racial notion of the Jew was palpable. These documents dealt in substantial detail with issues of state, governance, law, propaganda, family life, education, health, and the economy. "Jews, non-Europeans and definitely un-Christian elements" would be excluded from citizenship, which would be confined "to bona fide South African National Socialists." Governance was built around "guilds" under an all-powerful president who would rule over an organic state. A homogeneous "Afrikaner National Socialist Fraternity" would be dominant and all "anti-national, un-national and un-assimilable elements" would be excluded. A special lecture, "The Problem of the Jew," considered the matter from three angles: citizenship, right of residence and the right to trade or exercise a profession. Regarding citizenship, a Nuwe Orde handbook laid out the requirements that identified Jews who had come to South Africa after World War I and their children (whether born in South Africa or not) as prohibited immigrants with no citizenship rights. "Right of Residence" was to be granted to Jews who complied with residential or birth requirements, but they were nevertheless to remain aliens subject to good behavior. As far as the right to trade or exercise a profession was concerned, a "special court" could grant Jews who had no residential or citizenship rights the right to follow an occupation or trade subject to a quota but only if the court believed that their special qualifications were in the interests of South Africa. Another recommendation focused on name changes that would have to be reversed and further changes forbidden.[46]

Nuwe orde vir Suid-Afrika (New order for South Africa), a pamphlet issued in December 1940 and reprinted seven times, built on Otto du Plessis's *Die nuwe Suid-Afrika—die rewolusie van die twintigste eeu* (The new South Africa—the revolution of the twentieth century), which unashamedly extolled the corporate state and supported totalitarianism while attacking liberal individualism and "unnational" elements.[47] The state should be founded on a Christian basis, which meant that "anti-Christian" and even "un-Christian elements" would play no part. It had to be national in the sense of unconditional commitment to the Fatherland, and those who did not ascribe to that principle would be regarded as foreigners. Actual power would rest with the "established section" of the population, with the exception of everything "anti-nation, unnational and unassimilable." The intent was to exclude Jews in particular from full participation in the envisaged body-politic.[48]

These racial views of the Jew were now widely shared among the antiwar radical right as spelled out in the Union Omsendbrief 1/41 (a draft constitution for the future South Africa as drawn up by the Afrikanereenheidskomitee, or Afrikaner Unity Committee). This document detailed a proposed republican constitution and demonstrated very clearly the influence of the OB and its racist and anti-Jewish cast of mind. Once again, five racial groups in South Africa were identified: whites (both English and Afrikaans speakers), Jews, Africans, Coloureds, and Indians. Citizenship would be restricted to the white group who would act as state builders. As far as Jews were concerned, the document described them as unassimilable "non-Europeans" or "Semites" who constituted an alien minority race that would fall under the control of the white group. This policy was based on notions of blood, with Jews characterized as a pre-Asiatic race not sharing the blood of the English or Afrikaner.[49]

These ideas were reinforced in Malan's *Draft for a Republic*, which envisaged independence from the British Empire or any other foreign power and endorsed, among other things, a political system that protected the people against "hostile and unnational elements."[50] Significantly, this turn to exclusivism was supported by young Afrikaners: the youth wing of the National Party, the Nasionale Jeugbond (National Youth Union), established in 1940, raised the Jewish question together with other racial issues that demanded urgent attention.[51] A Federation of Calvinist Student Unions also expressed an exclusivist Christian-Nationalist ethnic mood when it included Jews with imperialists, Coloureds, natives, and Indians as constituting threats to the Afrikaner.[52]

As the war drew to a close debates around immigration revealed yet again that Jews were perceived as unassimilable and a race apart. Immigration should be permitted only to persons "who are not members of the Jewish race," Louw bluntly told Parliament in response to a motion advocating the adoption of a policy of large-scale European immigration submitted in early 1944 by Frank Acutt, the Dominion Party's Member for Durban Musgrave. The Jewish population, Louw asserted, was already too large, and when numbers exceeded a certain proportion of the total population, a Jewish question ensued.[53] More than that, Louw accused Jews of being loyal to the nation only when things went well. When there were difficulties, he maintained, "they [shook] the country's dust off their feet . . . then [made] a fresh start in some other country and there they [were] again just as loyal until things [went] wrong there."[54]

Although those supporting increased immigration made no specific mention of Jews during the parliamentary debate, it was apparent—through subtle and not-so-subtle innuendo—that Jews would not be welcome. For example, in supporting Acutt's call for white immigration, Charles Neate, the

Dominion Party's member of Parliament for Natal South Coast, made it clear that the new immigrants would have to be of "the right type" and not people with "ideas foreign to our conditions" and certainly not "traders."[55] This coded language echoed calls made in the 1920s when the English-language press—flushed with nativist impulses—had led a crusade against the influx of Eastern European Jewish immigrants.

Similar ideas were spelled out in the "Draft Programme of Principles" of Malan's National Party, which clearly stated that Jewish immigration would be halted, naturalization strictly controlled, occupational permits introduced for unnaturalized aliens, and steps taken "to equip the original elements of its own European population with the means for making a livelihood and to protect them against unreasonable competition."[56] The racialization of the Jew was now firmly entrenched, and even in the wake of the war when the horrors of the Holocaust were revealed, there remained voices that continued to speak out against Jews. Indeed, Louw, as a member of the Cape Head Committee of the National Party and the party's Federal Council, categorically maintained—despite knowledge that millions of Jews had been murdered by the Nazis—that the "Jewish problem" remained a serious matter, with "unassimilable Jews" taking control of trade, industries, and the professions and extending that control on a daily basis.[57] He was supported by the *New Era*, a Nationalist English-language mouthpiece that propagated notions of Jews as a "separate nation of unassimilable people."[58] Even Jan Hofmeyr—a champion of the Jews who had remained an outspoken critic of antisemitism—had a few months earlier referred to the "distinctiveness" and "otherness" of the Jew when delivering the Hoernlé Memorial Lecture. "The Jew," he said, "is different from the rest of us—we are conscious of that fact—and for all too many people the consciousness of difference acts as a seed-bed of intolerance."[59] Here, Hofmeyr was reiterating the essentialist sentiments he had expressed fifteen years earlier during the debate on the Quota Act.

Postwar Reverberations

Hofmeyr's cultural essentialism was de rigueur in mid-twentieth century South Africa. With their neo-Calvinist and neo-Kuyperian orientation, Afrikaners especially tied culture to a sense of biological descent in which groups had immutable essences. Infused with a strong desire for separation that was manifest in republicanism and a belief in religious mission, they had a sense of "chosenness." Underpinned by deeply Christian beliefs, this inevitably sharpened perceptions of Jews as alien, outsiders, or a people apart. For all that, no one in postwar South Africa seriously conceived of marginalizing or excluding Jews from the wider white population. Antisemitism had, in fact, waned as Hitler's military successes were reversed in the later stages of the war. Indeed, as early as 1942 there had been indications of a changing mood when official days of mourning, coordinated by the South African Jewish Board of Deputies, were addressed by prominent Christian clerics. Many had come to an awareness of the catastrophe overtaking European Jewry. Prime Minister Jan Smuts had, in fact, sent a message in which he condemned wartime atrocities against Jews, describing them as unparalleled "since the emergence of Europe from the darkest ages of its past."[60] Many had come to an awareness of the catastrophe overtaking European Jewry. Malan would certainly have known about these developments and the mounting outrage, which probably accounts for the fact that he made only a couple of references to the Jewish question in the general election campaign of 1943. Even the National Party electoral manifesto said little on the Jewish question. Despite a few hostile voices, anti-Jewish outbursts at the hustings were few and far between.[61] A year later, a Volkskongres (People's Congress)—organized by the Federasie van Afrikaanse Kultuurvereniginge (Federation of Afrikaans Cultural Organizations) and attended by two hundred church and cultural organizations—also ignored the Jewish question and addressed only issues concerning Africans, Coloureds, and Indians.[62] Now, in the closing months of the war, Karl Bremer, a prominent National Party member of Parliament, appealed passionately for white unity and a "new beginning"; although Jews were not mentioned in the speech, many interpreted his words as an indication that wartime divisions would be laid to rest and that hostility toward Jews would be relegated to the dustbin of history.[63]

Now soft-pedaling on the Jewish question, the National Party believed it was time to ensure white survival through formal or legislative separation. Apartheid as an ideology—built on long-established notions of paternalism and trusteeship—was formalized as official racial policy in 1945. Two years later, Malan appointed Paul Sauer to lead a National Party commission to elaborate on the policy.[64] Color—the struggle between black and white—was the cardinal issue. Jews were not a target. No longer as alien and culturally removed as their forebears, most enjoyed the comforts, benefits, and opportunities accorded to whites in apartheid South Africa. Blacks, on the other hand, could never escape the color of their skin in a society defined by pigmentation. Together with Coloureds and Indians they were deliberately excluded from white society. Pigmentation became the arbiter of opportunity and privilege.

There were, however, some voices on the extreme right that persisted with anti-Jewish calumny, but the mood had changed substantially. To be sure, the Jewish question hardly featured in the lead up to the general election of 1948. Jews were now regarded as white South Africans and, as such, beneficiaries of the unfolding apartheid project. Dealing with the broader color question was now paramount for the National Party. There had been a massive move of blacks to the cities, and Nationalists played on fears that (white) Western civilization was under assault with a restive and growing black proletariat threatening white (including Jewish) privilege.

Shortly after the 1948 election, the Jewish Board of Deputies enjoyed a positive meeting with Malan, the new prime minister, who assured them that the Jewish question was now behind them: his government, he maintained, stood "for a policy of non-discrimination against any section of the European population in South Africa," and he "looked forward to a time when there would be no further talk regarding the so-called Jewish question in the life and politics of the country."[65]

In fact, the National Party had little to fear. The prospect of continuing Jewish immigration was negligible and with the political kingdom at hand, Afrikaner economic advancement—a key factor underpinning hostility toward the Jew during the 1930s and war years—was just a matter of time. Most important, there were greater issues with which the National Party had to engage: primarily it had to fashion a new race policy, and it was not long before a range of legislative decisions were presented and acted on. Although the Transvaal National Party continued to exclude Jews from membership until 1951, the Jewish question as such had disappeared. Indeed, in 1953 Malan became the first sitting head of government to visit Israel. Two years later he wrote a preface to Chief Rabbi Israel Abrahams's *Birth of a Community*. Here, in a remarkable and ironic about-turn, he praised the Jews of South Africa for managing to maintain a distinctive "racial" identity while contributing significantly to the society at large. Jews could, he argued, serve as a model for a complex "multi-racial country" like South Africa.⁶⁶ Jewish survival through the centuries now served as a prolegomenon for the Afrikaner—existentially threatened in a decolonizing world. Grand apartheid would be an Afrikaner substitute for the Jewish spiritual fortress. Herein lay the seeds of an important relationship with the Jewish state, which (despite a hiccup in the early 1960s when Israel unequivocally condemned apartheid and supported the liberation movements) evolved into a close alliance between apartheid South Africa and Israel from the early 1970s until the late 1980s.⁶⁷

Malan's praise for the ability of South African Jews to maintain a distinctive administrative racial identity is not surprising. The National Party, after all, favored a multiracial rather than a multicultural society, and it alone would set the tone and define its ethnic template in which it was anticipated that Jews would support—or at least not be hostile to—Afrikaner interests. Acceptance of Jews, in other words, was conditional—a sort of bargain or contract akin to the emancipation of French Jewry in 1791. In South Africa, however, assimilation was not anticipated. Ethnic barriers—even between English and Afrikaans speakers—were subtly structured and endogamy encouraged. It was only with the fall of apartheid in 1990 that the country moved toward inclusivity. Chief Rabbi Cyril Harris was one of four spiritual leaders to deliver a prayer at Nelson Mandela's inauguration as president on May 10, 1994. His presence reflected the "new" South Africa's commitment to multiculturalism and the respect accorded to religious diversity in the self-styled "rainbow nation." For all that, Jews were still perceived by many as distinctive, with innate racial characteristics.

Notes

1. See Steven T. Katz, *The Holocaust in Historical Context*, vol. 1, *The Holocaust and Mass Death before the Modern Age* (New York: Oxford University Press, 1994).
2. J. L. Talmon, "European History—Seedbed of the Holocaust," *Midstream* 19 (May 1973): 3.
3. Christopher R. Browning, *The Path to Genocide* (Cambridge: Cambridge University Press, 1992), 85.

4. For early characterizations of the Jew, see Milton Shain, *The Roots of Antisemitism in South Africa* (Charlottesville: University of Virginia Press, 1994).
5. *Cape Times* (Cape Town), August 16, 1921.
6. Saul Dubow, "Race, Civilisation and Culture: The Elaboration of Segregationist Discourse in the Inter-War Years," in *The Politics of Class, Race and Nationalism in Twentieth Century South Africa*, ed. Shula Marks and Stanley Trapido (London: Longman Group, 1987), 76. See also Saul Dubow, *Illicit Union: Scientific Racism in Modern South Africa* (Johannesburg: Witwatersrand University Press, 1995); Saul Dubow, "Race, Civilisation and Culture: The Elaboration of Segregationist Discourse in the Inter-War Years," in *The Politics of Class, Race and Nationalism in Twentieth Century South Africa*, ed. Shula Marks and Stanley Trapido (London: Longman Group, 1987), 76; and Sally Peberdy, *Selecting Immigrants: National Identity and South Africa's Immigration Policies, 1910–2008* (Johannesburg: Witwatersrand University Press, 2009), 57–63.
7. *Star* (Gauteng, South Africa), September 17, 1925. A short while earlier, the South African Jewish Board of Deputies feared that the Class Areas Bill of 1924—which set out "to make provisions for the reservation of residential and trading areas in urban areas for persons other than natives having racial characteristics in common"—would be applied toward Jews; see Shain, *Roots of Antisemitism in South Africa*, 109.
8. Shain, *Roots of Antisemitism in South Africa*, 136.
9. See Shain, *Roots of Antisemitism in South Africa*, chap. 6.
10. *Hansard*, vol. 14, February 10, 1930, 568.
11. *Hansard*, 14:591.
12. Dr H. D. J. Bodenstein to private secretary, minister of finance, July 7, 1936 (memorandum, June 8, 1936). Jan Smuts Collection, A1, vol. 123, file 46, National Archives and Record Service of South Africa, Pretoria.
13. For details, see Lotta Stone, "Seeking Asylum: German Jewish Refugees in South Africa, 1933–1948" (PhD diss., Clark University, Worcester, MA, 2010), chap. 3 passim.
14. *Star* (Gauteng, South Africa), October 28, 1936.
15. See *Die Vaderland* (Johannesburg), October 30, 1936.
16. *Die Volksblad* (Bloemfontein, South Africa), November 12, 1936. Effectively they said only a Christian republican could join the party.
17. Peberdy, *Selecting Immigrants*, 82.
18. Dubow, *Illicit Union*, 180–89.
19. See *Die Volksblad* (Bloemfontein, South Africa), November 12, 1936.

20. *Hansard*, vol. 28, January 18, 1937, 267.
21. *Cape Times* (Cape Town), December 17, 1936.
22. See, for example, comments made by Sir Carruthers Beattie at December graduation at the University of Cape Town (*Cape Argus* [Cape Town], December 10, 1936) and Jan Smuts's speech at Roodebank, reported in *S.A. Jewish Chronicle* (Johannesburg) December 4, 1936.
23. South African Parliament, House of Assembly, Aliens Bill, *Government Gazette* 106, no. 2400 (December 28, 1936).
24. See Stone, "Seeking Asylum," 97–98.
25. *Hansard* 28:267.
26. *Hansard* 28:263–64.
27. See Government Notice 665 of 1937, Form D (1) (10), Clause 5 (b); and South African Jewish Board of Deputies, Executive Committee Minutes, February 28, 1937.
28. *Die Burger* (Cape Town), February 24, 1937. See also the *South African Jewish Times* (Johannesburg) February 26, 1937; and *Rand Daily Mail* (Johannesburg), February 24, 1937.
29. The idealization of the Nordic race, or "Nordicism," had a long pedigree with strong ties to racial anthropology, Romantic "folk" nationalism, and, from the late nineteenth century, European racism. With race underpinning its categorization, Nordicism was connected in complicated ways with Aryanism and European fascism, especially Nazism. Within this weltanschauung, Jews were a people apart from the Nordic peoples and an ever-present threat. See Christopher M. Hutton, *Race and the Third Reich: Linguistics, Racial Anthropology and Genetics in the Dialectic of* Volk (Cambridge: Polity Press, 2005), chap. 7 passim.
30. For Abraham Kuyper and "Kuyperianism," see Richard Elphick, *The Equality of Believers: Protestant Missionaries and the Racial Politics of South Africa* (Scottsville, South Africa: University of KwaZulu-Natal Press 2012), chap. 15 passim; Charles Bloomberg, *Christian Nationalism and the Rise of the Afrikaner Broederbond in South Africa 1918–48* (London: Macmillan, 1990), 10–12; and Dubow, *Illicit Union*, 259–62.
31. Peberdy, *Selecting Immigrants*, 82.
32. The essentializing of culture was reflected in *Volkekunde*, a branch of social anthropology developed at major Afrikaans universities from the 1930s. Here culture was a special object of study, neatly connected to Christian-National ideology. See John Sharp, "The Roots and Development of *Volkekunde* in South Africa," *Journal of Southern African Studies* 8, no. 1 (1981): 16–36.

33. See Saul Dubow, *Apartheid 1948–1994* (Oxford: Oxford University Press, 2014), 9–16. See also Saul Dubow, "Afrikaner Nationalism, Apartheid and the Conceptualization of Race," *Journal of African History* 33 (1992): 209–37.
34. See Saul Dubow, "A Definitive Study of the Ossewabrandwag," *Historia* 1 (Mei/May 2010): 158, for a review of Christoph Marx, *Oxwagon Sentinel: Radical Afrikaner Nationalism and the History of the Ossewabrandwag* (Pretoria: University of South Africa Press, 2008).
35. South Africa, Aliens (Amendment) Immigration Bill, *Government Gazette*, Bill No. 2596, January 6, 1939, Government Printing Works, Pretoria, 1939.
36. *Hansard*, vol. 33, February 24, 1939, 835.
37. *Die Transvaler* (Johannesburg), August 7, 1939.
38. See comments by C. J. Laas, the first leader of the OB in *Die Transvaler* (Johannesburg), February 26, 1940.
39. See Marx, *Oxwagon Sentinel*, 320.
40. See P. de Klerk, "Die ideologie van die Ossewa-Brandwag," in *Die Ossewa-Brandwag: Vuurtjie in droë gras*, ed. P. F. van der Schyff (Potchefstroom, South Africa: Geskiedenis Department van die Potchefstroomse Universiteit vir Christelike Hoër Onderwys, 1991), 292–331.
41. See Gideon Shimoni, *Jews and Zionism: The South African Experience 1910–1967* (Cape Town: Oxford University Press, 1980), 128. For concerns with race mixing see also *Die OB*, February 24, 1943.
42. See 1942 South African Jewish Board of Deputies Report to Congress, Rochlin Archives ARCH804, South African Jewish Board of Deputies, Johannesburg. For broader policies, see F. J. van Heerden, "Nasionaal-Sosialisme as Factor in die Suid-Afriaanse Politiek, 1933–1948" (PhD diss., University of the Orange Free State, Bloemfontein, South Africa, 1972), 138.
43. Marx, *Oxwagon Sentinel*, 488.
44. See Newell M. Stultz, *Afrikaner Politics in South Africa, 1934–1948* (Berkeley: University of California Press, 1974), 77. See also van Heerden, "Nasionaal-Sosialisme," chap. 4 passim.
45. See Shimoni, *Jews and Zionism*, 131; and *Die Oosterlig*, March 20, 1942.
46. "The Problem of the Jew," Nuwe Orde Correspondence Course, Lecture No. 14, Rochlin Archives 313.2, South African Jewish Board of Deputies, Johannesburg. See also Shimoni, *Jews and Zionism*, 130–32.
47. Oswald Pirow, *Nuwe Orde vir Suid-Afrika*, Christelike Republikeinse Suid-Afrikaanse Nasionaal-Sosialistiese Studiekring, Pretoria, 1940. See also van Heerden, 157–61; and Michael Roberts and A. E. G. Trollip, *The South African*

Opposition 1939–1945: An Essay in Contemporary History (London: Longman, Green, 1947), 79–80.

48. See Shimoni, *Jews and Zionism*, 132–33.
49. See André van Deventer, "Afrikaner Nationalist Politics and Anti-Communism, 1937 to 1945" (master's thesis, University of Stellenbosch, Stellenbosch, South Africa, 1991), 277.
50. *Star* (Gauteng, South Africa), January 12, 1942; and *Die Transvaler* (Johannesburg), January 13, 1942.
51. At one youth congress in Potchefstroom, Professor "Wikus" du Plessis told students that full citizenship should be based on "Afrikanership" and that commerce and "harmful influences" would be purged. *Die Volksblad*, December 23, 1941.
52. H. G. Stoker, "Calvinistiese dinamieka," *Koers* 19, no. 3 (1942): 87–99.
53. *Hansard* vol. 48, February 29, 1944, 2173.
54. *Hansard* 48:2175.
55. *Hansard* 48:2165; and *Zionist Record*, April 21, 1944.
56. National Party Federal, PV 54, section 2, subsection 2, Archives for Contemporary Affairs, University of the Orange Free State, Bloemfontein, South Africa. See also The Social and Economic Policy of the National Party, Kaapstad: Federale Raad van die Nasionale Party, 1944, quoted in William Henry Vatcher, *White Laager: The Rise of Afrikaner Nationalism* (New York: Praeger, 1965), 74.
57. *New Era*, April 12, 1945.
58. For this reason, explained the *New Era*, the National Party supported a National Home for the Jews in Palestine and insisted that all Jewish immigration into South Africa cease. See *New Era*, April 19, 1945.
59. See Jan Hofmeyr, *Christian Principles and Race Problems*, Hoernlé Memorial Lecture (Johannesburg: South African Institute of Race Relations, 1945).
60. See Michael Anthony Green, "South African Jewish Responses to the Holocaust" (master's thesis, University of South Africa, Pretoria, 1987), 59.
61. Milton Shain, *A Perfect Storm. Antisemitism in South Africa 1930–1948* (Cape Town: Jonathan Ball, 2015), 259–60.
62. See Saul Dubow, "Afrikaner Nationalism, Apartheid and the Conceptualization of Race," *Journal of African History* 33 (1992): 216–17; and *Inspan* (Johannesburg), October 1944.
63. *Hansard*, vol. 51, February 22, 1945, 2061.
64. See Hermann Giliomee, *The Afrikaners. Biography of a People* (Cape Town: Tafelberg Publishers, 2003) 475–79.
65. See *Jewish Affairs*, July 1948, 2, and Shimoni, *Jews and Zionism*, 207.

66. Israel Abrahams, *The Birth of a Community: A History of Western Province Jewry from Earliest Times to the End of the South African War, 1902* (Cape Town: Cape Town Hebrew Congregation, 1955) xii–xiii. With great irony, Abrahams expressed his appreciation for "the deeply significant words of this great Elder Statesman of our country" that would he was sure "long be remembered as a notable contribution to better race relations, among all sections of the population," xvi.
67. See Sasha Polakow-Suransky, *The Unspoken Alliance. Israel's Secret Relationship with Apartheid South Africa* (Cape Town: Jacana Media), 2010.

4

A Study of Conflicting Images in the Australian Media

Holocaust Suffering and Persistent Anti-Jewish Racism

Suzanne D. Rutland

IN JANUARY 1948, NOEL Lamidey, at the time in charge of Australia House, London, defined a Jew for the purposes of Jewish immigration to Australia as follows:

1. Any person who is of Hebrew *race* will be considered a Jew regardless of any later baptismal change.
2. Any person who is of the Hebrew *faith* will be considered of the Jewish nationality regardless of his nationality.
3. Any person whose passages are sponsored by HIAS [Hebrew Immigrant Aid Society] or any other Jewish organization will be considered as of the Jewish race.[1]

Lamidey stressed that such a "rigid interpretation" was necessary to prevent Australia from receiving a large influx of Jewish refugees, resulting in "serious official and political embarrassment."[2] The Australian government accepted this definition for Jewish survivors of the Holocaust.[3] Lamidey's definition resonated with Nazi definitions in the sense that the Australian government perceived European Jews as a race as well as a religion. This definition was used to discriminate against European Jewish migrants who from the 1920s had consistently been portrayed in government correspondent files as "undesirable." As elsewhere they were considered to be undesirable because they were depicted as "clannish, aggressive and cosmopolitan," a group that did not assimilate easily and whose loyalty would always be suspect.[4] It is particularly important to note that this policy was formulated in January 1948, a few short years after the end of the Holocaust. It demonstrates that despite knowledge of the Jewish tragedy during the Holocaust, racist notions about Jews persisted so that Jewish survivors who wished to migrate to Australia were discriminated against. This policy was implemented by administrative measures rather than legislation, illustrating the role played by the bureaucrats in the execution of racist immigration policies. This raises the associated question as to why knowledge of the Holocaust failed to impact positively on Australian immigration policy toward Jewish displaced persons (DPs) who had survived the European catastrophe.

This chapter will briefly outline the development of racism in Australia and discuss the information and images that members of the Australian public were exposed to about the Holocaust in the media. It will then examine the ongoing antisemitic narrative in the yellow press, with the use of cartoons that highlighted traditional anti-Jewish stereotypes reviving the anti-Jewish refugee hysteria of the prewar period. In response, the Labor Party government introduced administratively discriminatory policies toward Holocaust survivors, which were continued by the Liberal government from December 1949. This chapter will further argue that there was a connection between the broad backdrop of Australian racism and the specific anti-Jewish policies. This was in spite of the fact that the memory of the suffering created by the Holocaust was portrayed on the movie screens and in newspaper accounts of the destruction of European Jewry, beginning in 1942, but becoming much more explicit by 1944 as more of the details of the Holocaust emerged.

The chapter will also analyze why the prewar anti-Jewish racism toward European Jews persisted after the war. The dichotomy between the sympathy aroused by Jewish suffering in ghettos and concentration camps during the war and the strong opposition to survivors migrating to Australia after the war contributed to a situation of a cognitive dissonance, a concept developed by Leon Festinger in 1956. On the one hand, there was a sense of dismay at the Nazi atrocities, but on the other hand, Jews, who were the Nazis' primary victims, were still depicted in a very negative way, due to the persistence of antisemitic stereotypes in postwar Australia. In contrast, non-Jewish Germans, some of whom were perpetrators, were portrayed as desirable migrants for Australia.[5] Festinger argued that there were three ways of reacting to cognitive dissonance: (1) admitting to a mistake, (2) changing the meaning of conflicting information through interpretation, and (3) denying and repressing.[6] In this case, there was both the changing of the information through the media's portraying potential Jewish immigrants as undesirable and a threat to the Australian way of life[7] as well as a denial of the specificity of Jewish suffering.

THE DEVELOPMENT OF AUSTRALIAN RACISM

Australian racism has had a long history and has related both to Indigenous Australians and to non-British immigration to Australia, especially regarding Asian immigration.[8] The latter was enshrined at federation with the Commonwealth Restrictive Immigration Law (1901), which became known as the White Australia policy. David Hollingsworth has argued that attitudes toward Aborigines and the White Australia policy were "inseparable."[9] He noted that the institution of racial differences was created through legislation relating to immigration, citizenship, and Aboriginal administration, leading to the acceptability of "narrowly exclusivist, cultural and social practices [that] came to be taken for granted well into the twentieth century."[10]

Hostility toward Asian immigration emerged during the early colonial period and intensified after the 1880s owing to the fear of an Asian influx, described as the "yellow peril." The second half of the nineteenth century "witnessed the construction and naturalization of hegemonic ideas of racial exclusivity and reciprocity amongst British settlers."[11] With the Commonwealth Immigration Restrictive legislation of 1901 after federation, the dictation test was introduced as a way of concealing Australian racist intentions. Under this system, the customs officers were required to select a European language with which the immigrant would not be familiar. As Gwenda Tavan argues, the government did not want to draw too much attention to this discrimination because of British government concerns about its relations with India, China, and Japan, so it practiced "quiet diplomacy."[12] Various restrictive laws were also introduced against Islanders and Indigenous voting rights were prohibited.

The central motivations for these restrictive laws were the desire to create a homogenous, cohesive society, emerging from Australian nationalism from the 1880s, and the influence of social Darwinism, including the concepts of survival of the fittest, emerging from the theories of Charles Darwin and Herbert Spencer.[13] The growth of the labor movement, which led to the formation of the Australian Labor Party (ALP) in 1890, also played a key role in the development of anti-Asian immigration feelings, owing to workers' fears of economic competition. By the end of the nineteenth century, "economic fears and racial prejudice were inextricable, with each feeding the flames of the other's fire."[14] Social Darwinism provided a coherent theory and a pseudo-scientific justification, as well as an objective rationale, for the racial policies of maintaining a 98 percent Anglo-Celtic population in Australia.[15]

This rationale applied to both the Aborigines and Asians, but economic fears also applied to European Jewish immigrants. In the 1890s, when there was a fear that Australia would be flooded with Russian Jews, the Sydney nationalist paper *The Bulletin* commented: "Even the Chinaman is cheaper in the end than the Hebrew. . . . The one with the tail is preferable to the one with the Talmud every time. We owe much to the Jew—in more sense than one—but until he works, until a fair percentage of him produces, he must always be against democracy."[16] This perception of Jews as an economic threat continued in the interwar years and was emphasized by opponents to Jewish refugee immigration in the 1930s. For example, Sir Frank Clarke, president of the Victorian Legislative Council, described Jewish refugees as "slinking, rat-faced men" who provided sweated labor for "backyard factories." The economic motif persisted into the postwar years, with ongoing accusations of Jewish wealth and profiteering, as will be discussed. The claim that Jews did not do productive work was part of the modern anti-Jewish stereotype and was highlighted in Nazi racist ideology of Jews as parasites. By the beginning in the 1890s, both the Jews and Chinese were "racialized and in this way othered equally, with the intention that both should be excluded from a white Australia homogenous both racially and culturally."[17]

A key element in the administration of the White Australia policy was the role of the public service, ensuring maximum bureaucratic control of immigration. This was based on the British system of government, so that many decisions in terms of immigration were made at the administrative rather than the legislative level.[18] Social Darwinism also played a major role with this process because "any qualms bureaucrats might have had about the humanitarian implications of white Australia were appeased by referring to the dominant racial ideologies and legal bureaucratic conventions."[19] Often, the true intentions of administrative policies were hidden in the use of technocratic language.

This was also true for the postwar period when the Department of Immigration was established, headed by Tasman Heyes. He reminded the Australian selection team that "*all* instructions received by them as to selection standards, quotas etc., [were] *strictly confidential*. This [was] particularly so where racial considerations [were] involved."[20] Heyes did not specify that he was speaking about Jewish DPs, but by June 1949, when this instruction was issued, the officers in the field would have understood that he was referring to restrictions on Jewish DPs only, since by then they were the only ethnic group where specific restrictions applied.[21]

In terms of immigration, the racist policies developed from 1901 were continued in the interwar period because of the continuing influence of racial theories; economic problems, especially after the onset of the depression in 1929; and the ongoing fear of the Japanese threat. The dictation test remained the major instrument for implementing these policies, with language substituting for race.[22] In this period, the test was also used against Jews and political radicals. The best-known case of this was with Egon Kisch, a Jewish German refugee and communist who had an extensive knowledge of European languages but was excluded when he failed the test in Gaelic.[23] However, there were other instances in which the dictation test was used against Jewish immigrants of Polish background in the 1920s.[24]

While the racial policies mainly targeted Aborigines and colored immigrants, the immigration laws could also be applied to Europeans, including the Irish, Germans, Spanish, Italians, and Greeks, who were also seen as separate races due to linguistic, religious, and/or cultural differences. For example, southern Italians were considered racially inferior and were viewed to have racial characteristics that were in some ways similar to Australian Aborigines.[25]

In the general literature on race and racism in Australia, however, there has been less focus on similar attitudes applying to the Jews as a race. Jon Stratton argues that "the absence of a Jewish voice is most importantly a consequence of a fundamentally ambivalent construction of the Jewish situation in modernity."[26] On the one hand, Jews were perceived as "white," but on the other hand, they were perceived as the "other," making it more difficult for Jews to speak out on racism. Thus, while racist attitudes toward Jews were endemic in both the newspapers and literature following the emergence of Australian nationalism in the 1880s until after World War II, especially in the yellow press such as *Truth*, *The Bulletin*, and *Smith's Weekly*, there has been less focus on this issue in the literature.[27]

The major departure from the attitudes that had dominated the concepts of British superiority and the need to limit immigration to Australia from the European continent occurred in the postwar period, but the attitudes toward the threat posed by Jewish immigration did not change immediately, despite the emerging knowledge of the Holocaust from graphic newspaper accounts, particularly from 1944 onward, as well as some of the newsreels and movies shown in cinemas in Australia from 1944.

Information and Images regarding the Holocaust

During the early years of the war, there was very little reported in the mainstream Australian press about the specific persecution of the Jews. Paul Bartrop has argued that "nothing was seen to be unique about the sufferings of the Jews; everyone caught in the Nazi net was suffering."[28] From the start of Operation Barbarossa in June 1941, more reports began to emerge, and from the beginning of 1942 the Jewish catastrophe unfolding in Eastern Europe began to be better known. There was information about the formation of ghettos, the deportation of Jews to "unknown destinations," and the spread of typhus and other diseases owing to the overcrowded condition in the ghettos, as well as emerging reports of mass shootings and the effects of starvation.[29] The plight of the Jews of Europe was directly acknowledged in the Allied Declaration of December 17, 1942. The major Australian papers reported briefly on this declaration, referring to the statement of Dr. Herbert Vere Evatt, the Australian minister for external affairs, that "the Commonwealth

Government has associated itself with . . . the joint statement . . . regarding German atrocities against the Jews in Europe."[30]

The first reference to gassing appeared in the Jewish press in February 1943 and, according to Bartrop, to Oświęcim (Auschwitz) in the general press only on March 9, 1943, in *The Argus*.[31] Fay Anderson argues that altogether there were a total of twenty-nine articles in which either Oświęcim/Auschwitz were referred to between 1942 and liberation in January 1945, but there was minimal editorial comment. Each article was treated as a separate episode, without any attempt to construct the wider picture.[32] In Eastern Europe, Godfrey Blunden, Australian journalist for the *Daily Telegraph*, began to send accurate eyewitness accounts, such as the killings in Kharkov.[33] As the Soviets gradually began to push the retreating German army back after the battle of Stalingrad in February 1943, more accurate reports began to appear. On November 12, 1943, the *Telegraph* published a particularly graphic account of the Jewish catastrophe, presenting a bar graph listing every country with the number of Jews who had been murdered, adding up to a total of five million. It was believed that these Jews had died as a result of starvation, mass shootings, and with some use of gassing in vans. Yet in this article there is no specific reference to the major death camps.[34]

As more information emerged about Auschwitz in mid-1944, it took time for this news to be reported in Australia. The first detailed article in the Jewish press on Auschwitz appeared under the title of "Mass Murder of Jews in Death Camps" in September 1944, based on the report prepared by Rev. Paul Vogt, head of the Zurich Flüchtlingshilfe.[35] As Anderson argues, in the general Australian press, "despite the horrifying details, there was widespread editorial apathy and indifference,"[36] which mirrored other parts of the English-speaking world,[37] while the Jewish press was also limited by minimal resources. In March 1944, an article published in the *Sydney Jewish News* commented perceptively in relation to Poland's geographical isolation: "Germany can carry out their frightfulness in fairly secure knowledge that little will leak to the outside world. So Poland has become the killing ground for Jews deported from all parts of the world."[38]

On the whole, the Australian press was much more concerned with issues closer to home. There were ongoing reports of the progress of the war effort, particularly in North Africa and the Middle East, where the Australian troops were fighting. For example, newspapers publicized the actions of the "Rats of Tobruk," the Australian soldiers who defended Tobruk from April to August 1941.[39] The tide of the war there only changed with the victory at El Alamein in mid-November 1942. After the Japanese attack on Pearl Harbor, the conflict came much closer to home. In February 1942, the Japanese carried out two raids on Darwin, killing at least 243 people and wounding between 300 and 400.[40] On May 30, 1942, three Japanese midget submarines managed to penetrate into Sydney Harbor. While two were destroyed, the third managed to blow up the depot ship HMAS *Kuttabul*, killing twenty-one sailors.[41] The Japanese navy suffered a major defeat during the Battle of the Coral Sea on May 4–8, 1942, and they did not succeed in invading Australia.[42] However, the episode in Darwin in Australia's north, combined with the Sydney Harbor incident, created great concern. Subsequently, until the end of the Pacific War in September 1945, the Australian press continued to report extensively on the Pacific campaign, led by General Douglas MacArthur. Thus, while the Australian reading public were exposed to some extent to the horrors of the Holocaust, particularly by 1944, the press accounts they read were often not very detailed, did not explicitly refer to Jewish suffering, and were not connected to editorial comment.

There were newsreel accounts of the liberation of the death camps and cinematic representations of the Holocaust. However, with the newsreels, explicit Jewish suffering was often not referred to. When the liberation of Bergen-Belsen was portrayed, the BBC gave the producers instructions not to refer to Jews, even though the majority of the victims of the camp were Jewish.[43] Thus, the horrific and graphic images of the liberation of Bergen-Belsen were presented without the context of the Jewish genocide. Although Australians did not produce these newsreels, the exclusion of Jewish specificity would have influenced the Australian public. A clear awareness of the specificity of the Jewish experience within the overall context of Nazi crimes against humanity emerged only later. However, it took until 1978, when the television program *Holocaust* beamed into people's living rooms, that a full understanding began to emerge of the Jewish Holocaust.

At the end of the war and immediately after, there were also very few films produced that dealt explicitly with either the Jewish Holocaust or antisemitism and were shown in Australian cinemas. Those that did included *None*

Shall Escape in 1944, *The Last Chance* in 1946, and *Crossfire* and *Gentleman's Agreement* in 1947.

None Shall Escape was possibly the most powerful film dealing with the Holocaust shown in Australian theaters. It was produced by Sam Bischoff and directed by André de Toth, who had personal experience of the fighting in Europe, filming there in 1939–40. It was released on October 26, 1944, and played at the Lyceum Theatre in Sydney in November 1944, as well as across Australia in both capital cities and regional theaters. An advertisement in the Jewish press for the movie had the headline "FOR THEIR CRIMES . . . We shall judge them!"⁴⁴ Alfred Neumann and Joseph Than were nominated for the Academy Awards for the "Best Story" category. While the story is completely fictional, it captures much of the violence of the period, presages the Nuremberg trials, and was the first feature film to highlight the Nazi atrocities against the Jews.

However, as with other parts of the world, most of the Australian press reviews made no specific reference to Jewish suffering, just referring in general to the "inhuman and terrible results of Nazi sadism."⁴⁵ This denial of Jewish specificity reflected the response of the free world to the cognitive dissonance between acknowledging the extent of Jewish suffering, on the one hand, and the opposition to Jewish survivor immigration, on the other. One exception was a letter from the Council of Christians and Jews, published in *The Methodist*, which stated: "This picture is a vivid presentation of the sufferings of the people of Poland under the Nazi regime. It shows Christians and Jews suffering alike, though more severely in the case of the latter."⁴⁶ The failure to make specific reference to Jewish suffering occurred again after the full horror of the Holocaust was revealed.

The Last Chance (*Die letzte Chance*) produced in 1946 was an escape story, featuring a British and an American soldier whose prison train was bombed. After their escape, they assisted a group of Italian refugees to escape the Nazis. As such, it was more a war drama than a depiction of the Jewish catastrophe. It played at the Liberty Theatre in Sydney in June 1946.

A different approach focusing on the theme of antisemitism was taken by the 1947 movie *Crossfire*, which played at the Empire Theatre in Sydney in October 1947. Based on the 1945 novel *The Brick Foxhole*, where homophobia was the motive of a murder, the theme was changed to racism and antisemitism in the film. The advertisement for the film in the Jewish press stated: "Some people carry blind HATE within them . . . like a loaded gun. And when they carry it around too long, it goes off and KILLS the way it killed a stranger last night."[47] Thus, there was some exposure to the public of the horrors of the Holocaust and the evils of antisemitism, but this did not change the racial prejudices, including toward Jews, of many Australians. The failure of the Allied countries to highlight Jewish suffering, which included the Australian press, meant that there was little understanding of what has been termed the "Nazis' war against the Jews," that is, the Nazi aim to murder every last Jew.

The Fostering of the Negative Jewish Stereotype

This lack of sympathy to the Jewish plight was also fostered by the portrayal of the negative Jewish stereotype that continued after 1945 of Jews being rich and greedy, out to take over control of the country, and lacking loyalty to Australia. Negative, racist attitudes toward Jews in Australia, as well as to the Indigenous Australians and Asians, which were expressed in popular culture and the media, were fostered over a long period of time. They were closely associated with the emergence of Australian nationalism in the 1880s and were strongly espoused in the pages of *The Bulletin*, founded in 1880 to embrace Australian nationalism. The paper reflected the anti-Aborigine and antiforeign jingoism before Australian federation in 1901—evidenced by the slogan on its masthead from 1880 to 1960, "Australia for the White Man"— and these attitudes persisted after World War II.

Even though Jews did not number more than 0.5 percent of the population in any period from 1788 onward, antisemitic prejudice already existed in nineteenth-century Australia. At no point did it take the form of an "institutionalized" antisemitism in terms of official legislation. From their arrival in 1788, Jews were never subjected to anti-Jewish laws or regulations, persecution, or expulsion, let alone pogroms or murder. However, anti-Jewish sentiments and campaigns erupted in the late nineteenth century as a response to the threat of large-scale immigration from Eastern Europe, and these sentiments reemerged for the same reason both before and after the Holocaust, resulting in administrative measures aimed at limiting the number of Jews permitted to migrate to Australia.

There were several key elements relating to the Jewish stereotype, and even though historical conditions changed over the period from 1880 to the postwar period, these components tended to remain consistent. The first element was the stress on the foreignness of the Jew, represented by the Jewish physiognomy. From its foundation in 1880, *The Bulletin* featured cartoons that depicted stereotypical images of Jews, consistently highlighting Jewish greed and the desire of Jews to control the world.[48] Above all, Jews were cast as physically undesirable—fat and ugly with hooked noses and foreign accents. A cartoon captioned "The Pied Harper," published in *The Bulletin* in 1946, depicted the newly appointed minister for immigration, Arthur Calwell, playing the Jew's harp, attracting Jews as the "imports" while at the same time white British Australians, the "exports," were pushed out.[49] American Jewish leaders commented that this cartoon "was as bad as anything Goebbels ever thought up."[50] While the word *Jew* did not always appear in the captions accompanying the cartoons, the use of these stereotypes made it clear that Jews were the targets of the critique. This is evident in "The Pied Harper" cartoon, which depicts a Jew's harp and the caricatured physiognomy of the "imports."

Other papers, such as the sensational newspaper *Truth*, also consistently portrayed the same negative stereotypes. From its establishment in 1890, *Truth* highlighted pejorative attitudes, with its publisher, John Norton, praising the Tsarist pogroms and opposing Jewish immigration from Eastern Europe.[51] Papers commonly featured antisemitic cartoons and views, including *Punch* (Melbourne) and, later, the independent tabloid newspaper *Smith's Weekly* (Sydney), founded in 1919, which mixed sensationalism, satire, and controversial opinions with sporting and finance news.

Jews were also consistently portrayed as being involved in dubious economic activities and out to fleece members of the non-Jewish public. For example, in the 1890s *The Bulletin* invented a character called John Bull-Cohen, who represented British imperialism acting at the will of Jewish financiers. In the 1890s, fears of a flood of Eastern European Jewish immigrants undermining and destroying the "Australian way of life" became the prevailing pattern of the wider Australian society. A radical journalist and socialist, Harald I. Jensen, authored *The Rising Tide: An Exposition of Australian Socialism*, first published serially in *The Worker* in 1908–9, in which he expounded protectionism as a good balance between capital and labor.[52] He claimed that

Minister of Immigration Arthur Calwell is depicted as the Pied Piper bringing in the rats (i.e., the Jewish "imports") and pushing out the white Anglo-Celt "exports." *Bulletin* (Sydney), December 4, 1946, 15.

Australia and New Zealand were allowing themselves to be fleeced wholesale by "hook-nosed moneylenders" in the guise of British capitalism. A similar cry was taken up in the Labor press and endorsed by W. A. Holman, one of the leaders of the Australian Labor Party in New South Wales and subsequently premier between 1913 and 1920.[53] Some images focused on Jewish economic life and accused Jews, who worked long hours in sweatshops for low wages, of undermining Australian living standards. Conversely, they were charged with being moneylenders who controlled the banks and the media. In addition, Jews were often depicted as a godless people, lacking moral principles when it came to their financial dealings and intent on destroying Christianity.

Another key element in the anti-Jewish hysteria was the belief that Jews were clannish and cared only about themselves. Among the major vehicles for anti-Jewish stereotypes were cartoons published in newspapers, again beginning in the 1880s, which characterized Jews as members of a separate race who were incapable of assimilating.

Anti-Jewish feelings could be found on both sides of the political spectrum. On the left was Australian Labor Party personality Fred Anstey, who wrote a series of articles during World War I attacking Jewish "money power." These were issued in 1917 as a pamphlet titled *The Kingdom of Shylock*, complete with a frontispiece cartoon of a hook-nosed moneylender. On the conservative right, John Norton, demagogue and parliamentarian, in addition to being publisher of *Truth*, promoted similar negative images of the Jew, and in 1938 one article in the paper asserted: "As a racial unit, they are a menace to our nationhood and standards. As an inflow of migrants, they are a menace to employment.... It is a problem of self-preservation."[54]

The same racialized attitudes applied after the Holocaust. Liberal parliamentarian Henry "Jo" Gullett stated: "We are not compelled to accept the unwanted of the world at the dictate of the United Nations or anyone else. Neither should Australia be a dumping ground for people whom Europe itself, in the course of 2,000 years, has not been able to absorb."[55] Labor politician Jack Lang attacked Jewish immigration in parliamentary debates, claiming, for example, that Jewish refugees stranded in the Middle East had boarded the *Strathmore* at Port Said and the berths so taken were withheld from prospective British migrants.[56]

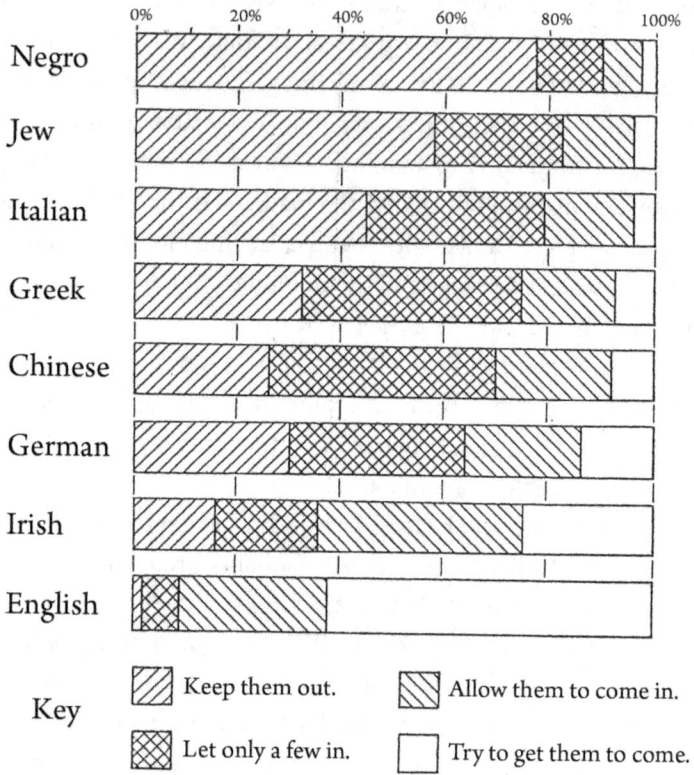

The desirability of eight racial groups based on a survey of attitudes to immigration in Melbourne in 1948. O. A. Oeser and S. B. Hammond, *Social Structure and Personality in a City* (London: Routledge & Kegan Paul, 1954), 55.

Thus, despite the fate of European Jews during World War II, these anti-Jewish sentiments continued to manifest themselves in the Australian media after the war.[57] The ongoing promotion of the anti-Jewish stereotype, particularly in the yellow press, reflected general racist attitudes toward Jews. A 1948 study carried out by Oscar A. Oeser and Samuel B. Hammond showed that the general Australian public perceived a clear hierarchy regarding postwar immigration. Within this hierarchy of race, Germans ranked third in desirability after English and Irish immigrants, while Jews were ranked seventh just above blacks, who were excluded along with other non-whites from immigration to Australia under the White Australia policy.[58]

Oeser and Hammond argued that Australians in 1948 widely believed that "the groups which [had] resisted assimilation and [had] become minority groups [were] mostly Southern Europeans (Italians, Greeks, Yugoslavs) and also Jews."[59] However, adherence to this perception of "hierarchy of race-nation groups"[60] posed a dilemma for Australians whose need to populate the country was in conflict with their fear of foreigners whom they thought unlikely to assimilate. They favored racial groups from northern European countries whose cultures most closely resembled Australia's, with its British origins, and whose people would be more easily absorbed.[61]

In seeking to understand these attitudes, Oeser and Hammond undertook a detailed analysis of attitudes of non-Jewish Australians toward Jews. The questions that revealed the strongest prejudice across all groups related to perceived Jewish clannishness, with 72 percent of respondents replying in the affirmative, and Jewish competitiveness (i.e., always seeking the best jobs), with 76 percent agreeing. In the survey, the authors used two different terms: "Jews" to indicate race and "Hebrews" to indicate religion. There was a much higher level of prejudice in response to the term "Jew," with 22 percent more of the sample wanting restrictive policies being implemented against Jews.[62] Thus, they demonstrated that there was a strong correlation between attitudes to immigration, which obviously affected voting patterns and "immigration policy position of the government."[63]

While the researchers argued that many of the negative attitudes were passive rather than active, they also suggested that "the present situation [lent] itself to political manipulation of the sort used by German Nazis." They concluded: "All that is necessary is to change the place of Jews from being *an* explanation of social evils to being *the* explanation."[64] Two years later, an opinion poll showed 61 percent in favor of the immigration of carefully picked Germans, with only 35 percent against.[65] These attitudes did not change during the 1950s. The 1959 study of Newtown, the small satellite town near Perth in Western Australia, showed that respondents not only ranked the desirability of Jewish immigrants far below that of Germans but also below that of much less favored arrivals from southern Europe.[66] Reflecting the negative images and attitudes toward foreign Jews, Australian government policy throughout the 1950s and early 1960s treated German immigrants as "desirable" while tending to approach Jewish immigrants as "undesirable."⁶⁷ According to Jon Stratton, "From the 1930s the racialization of the Jews as Semites [as compared with the Aryans] was becoming an influential ideology."⁶⁸ He argues that even though there were changes over time, the difficulty of categorizing the Jews as a religion, ethnic group, or race created an ambivalence that "blurs the boundaries of the modern nation-state and upsets the neat modern binary distinction between friends and enemies, or more relevantly, 'our nation' or 'their nation.'"⁶⁹ Within this binary, European Jewish survivors of the Holocaust were viewed as the racialized other and a threat to Australian homogeneity. Given these attitudes in the general Australian population, the Australian governments, first under the United Australia Party before the war, then under the Labor Party, and later the Liberal Party after 1949, introduced restrictive immigration policies toward European Jewish survivors.

Postwar Discriminatory Policies toward Jewish Survivors

In Australia, the ideology of racial hierarchy was intertwined with immigration policy in ways that had mixed results for Jews. On the one hand, the country's core division between whites and non-whites made the government open to accepting, in the words of a 1944 report of a subcommittee on immigration, "any white aliens who [could] be assimilated and contribute satisfactorily to economic development and against whom there [were] no objections on the grounds of health, character or (while the ban is still in force) enemy alien nationality."⁷⁰ On the other hand, all white immigrants were not seen as alike. The same subcommittee, for example, detailed a hierarchy of desirable nationalities, which apart from the British—who were understood as clearly the most desirable—were, in order of preference: Americans, Scandinavians (Norwegians, Swedes, Danes), Dutch, Belgians, Swiss, Yugoslavs, Greeks, and Albanians.

Jews were ranked at the very bottom of the 1944 committee's European hierarchy. In describing the seven thousand to eight thousand refugees—mostly German and Austrian Jews—who had been admitted to Australia in the 1930s before the outbreak of war, the 1944 report underscored what it considered their negative social traits. "Most of them, probably 80 per cent," the report estimated, "settled in Sydney and Melbourne and soon became conspicuous by their tendency to acquire property and settle in particular districts."[71] The committee also pointed out that the professional and university-educated class of Jewish refugees had greater difficulty in settling in Australia than the artisan class. In addition, it concluded that Polish Jews, many of who had arrived prior to 1938 and settled as textile workers in Melbourne, "could not be regarded as desirable types of migrants."[72] Thus, while Australian immigration policy gave some preference to Jews as whites, Jewish immigrants were depicted as less desirable than any other European immigrants.

Before the war, Australia did not have a separate department to deal with immigration. Jewish refugees who arrived before 1939 were processed through the Department of the Interior in accordance with the policy that stated that 98 percent of all immigration to Australia should be Anglo-Celtic. With the impending refugee crisis following the *Anschluss* of Austria, President Franklin D. Roosevelt called a meeting of all relevant countries to discuss the matter at Evian in France in July 1938. Thirty-two nations attended, but no nation was prepared to extend its quota. The Australian representative, Colonel T. E. White, summed up attitudes of the attendees: "Australia does not have a racial problem and is not desirous of importing one."[73]

The majority of Jewish refugees arrived before the war, in 1939, and they became known as the "thirty-niners." During the war years, these numbers were bolstered by the arrival of Jewish internees, including those who were sent out by the British government on the notorious *Dunera*, built to accommodate 1,600 passengers but dispatched with 2,542 men on board, including 451 non-Jewish Italians and Germans, with resultant overcrowding and mistreatment of the internees. The ship arrived in Australia in September 1940 and the Jewish internees were eventually released, with around 1,000 deciding to remain in Australia.

After the war, owing to the Japanese threat of invasion, the Australian Labor government realized that it needed to increase Australia's population, and a new Department of Immigration was created, with Arthur Calwell appointed as the first minister of immigration. In August 1945, Calwell announced that two thousand Holocaust survivors would be permitted to immigrate immediately to Australia through family sponsorship on a humanitarian basis. Immediately after the announcement, there was an outcry in the media and by parliamentarians from both sides of politics against the policy, as discussed above. The negative stereotype of Jews as the racialized other led the Department of Immigration to introduce various administrative measures that discriminated against Jewish survivor migration. Quotas limiting refugee resettlement were introduced through administrative procedures rather than through legislation. For example, from 1946 onward, immigration officials prevented the chartering of ships to bring Jewish refugees to Australia—a practice that had been initiated at the beginning of the Jewish refugee effort—by limiting the number of Jews on each incoming vessel to 25 percent of the total passengers. This rule was later extended to airplanes as well. In 1948, when government officials believed that still too many Jews were arriving, they negotiated a "gentleman's agreement" with the Jewish community that increased the ship quota to 50 percent but allowed a total of no more than three thousand European Jews to be admitted per annum. In 1949, when the limit was exceeded with the arrival of thirty-eight hundred Jewish DPs, the government introduced its "Iron Curtain Embargo," which excluded arrivals from countries under communist rule. While the measure was introduced ostensibly for security reasons, it was intended to reduce the flow of European Jews to Australia, since most Jews were coming from Poland, Hungary, and Czechoslovakia, by then all under communism. The intention underlying the embargo became clear from the way in which the flow of Jews was monitored by a question on the sponsorship forms (both Form 40 for family sponsorship and Form 47 for economic sponsorship) specifically asking if the sponsored person was Jewish (Form 40) or "of the Jewish race" (Form 47) and by medical examinations intended to detect if males were circumcised.[74]

In addition, Jews were excluded from the government-sponsored DP program through the International Refugee Organization (IRO).[75] Gwenda Tavan has argued that the IRO program was "a drastic departure from Australia's traditional emphasis on British immigrants to provide for its population needs. It was also a highly sensitive one, which required careful handling by the government in order to minimise a political backlash."[76]

As a result, the IRO scheme was based on a policy of two-year work contracts, so the newcomers could be sent to where they were most needed. This was to maintain the support of the trade union movement, the voter base of the ruling Australian Labor Party, by controlling the flow of the workforce and sending the DPs to work in remote areas, such as the Snowy Mountains Hydroelectric Scheme in New South Wales, rather than in the cities. This ensured that the Australian jobs and living standards would not be threatened.[77] However, an additional element was also introduced in terms of Jewish survivors, which was clearly based on racial criteria. Secret instructions were sent to recruitment officers: "There appears to be some doubt as to the meaning of the term Jew in relation to the Displaced Persons Scheme. . . . The term refers to race and not to religion and the fact that some D.P.s who are Jewish by race have become Christian by religion is not relevant."[78]

There was a clear nexus between the perceived desirability of an immigrant group and the level of assistance provided by the Australian government. In 1966, Australian demographer and migration expert Charles Price pointed out the differences in government funding for immigrant groups. For example, northern European postwar immigrants, who were seen as desirable, received more government funding than immigrants from Greece and Italy, who were perceived as less desirable. Thus, the Australian government assisted about three-quarters of German and two-thirds of Dutch postwar immigrants. In comparison, the government assisted only 16 percent of Italians and 33 percent of Greeks.[79] Since Jews were considered the least desirable of all European groups, they received almost no government assistance. Rather, obstacles were put in their way. Jewish survivor arrival in Australia was only made possible with the financial assistance of the American Jewish welfare organizations.[80]

Conclusion

As more detailed press reports began to emerge in the Australian media in 1944, the dichotomy between the sympathy aroused for those in the camps and the strong opposition to survivors immigrating to Australia contributed to a nationwide state of cognitive dissonance. As discussed, some Australian political leaders, such as Liberal Party member Gullett and Labor Party member Lang, took the destruction of European Jewry as proof that Jews were unassimilable and that they therefore should not be "dumped" on Australia. In some instances, information about Jewish suffering was repressed when discussions turned to accepting Jewish Holocaust survivors into Australia. This complexity of reactions of the Australian politicians and civil servants resulted in Australia's Jewish community remaining at only 0.5 percent of the total population.

The Australian experience of postwar Jewish immigration mirrored attitudes and responses elsewhere. As scholars such as Leo Dinnerstein for the United States and Irving Abella and Harold Troper for Canada have demonstrated, other English-speaking countries introduced even stricter barriers against Jewish survivor migration, based on similar beliefs of European Jews as the racialized other.[81] As a result, on a pro rata population basis, Australia accepted the second-highest proportion of Jewish survivors after Israel, with 60 percent of these survivors settling in Melbourne. This influx more than doubled the size of Australian Jewry from 23,553 in 1933 to 48,436 in 1954, and the population rose to 59,343 in 1961, but many more could have benefited from the chance of a new life in a new country were it not for the racist perceptions of European Jews. These events highlighted a contemporary explanation that "justice is never complete monarch in the present immoral world."[82] This was true of Australia where, in the past, other groups, such as Asians, were also considered as undesirable and excluded on racist grounds.

In the period between 1945 and 1954, Australia did accept some Jewish Holocaust survivors, but the inbred nature of racism and antisemitism fostered by the negative Jewish stereotype in the yellow press as the racialized other, the development of this concept as an influential ideology, and Calwell's fear of a political backlash if he allowed too many Jews to immigrate to Australia meant that this intake was only a token gesture. There was a clear dichotomy between the sympathy raised in the face of Jewish persecution during the Holocaust, on the one hand, and the support of Australian immigration policies, on the other. Because Holocaust suffering was often not framed as specifically Jewish and because negative racialized stereotypes of Jewish immigrants were deeply entrenched, there existed a cognitive dissonance among Australians in which Holocaust victims were perceived as undesirable immigrants while their German perpetrators were favored. As such, in the immediate postwar period, the Holocaust did not change the perceptions of Jews in Australia as an other who should not be welcomed into Australia.

Notes

1. Cable from Noel Lamidey to Tasman Heyes, "Policy with Regard to DPs from Various Zones in Germany," January 27, 1948, National Archive of Australia (NAA) A1068, item 1C 47/31/14.
2. Cable from Lamidey to Heyes, "Policy with regard to DPs."
3. Reply from Tasman Heyes to Noel Lamidey, January 30, 1948, NAA A1068, item IC 47/31/14.
4. Irving Abella and Harold Troper, *None Is Too Many: Canada and the Jews of Europe, 1933–1948* (Toronto: Random House, 1983), 281.
5. See Suzanne D. Rutland, "Nazis Unwelcome! The Jewish Community and the 1950s German Migration Scheme," in *National Socialism in Oceania: A Critical Evaluation of its Effect and Aftermath*, ed. Emily Turner-Graham and Christine Winter (Frankfurt: Peter Lang, 2010), 219–34.
6. Leon Festinger, Henry Riecken, and Stanley Schachter, *When Prophecy Fails: A Social and Psychological Study of a Modern Group That Predicted the Destruction of the World* (Minneapolis: University of Minnesota Press, 1956).
7. O. A. Oeser and S. B. Hammond, *Social Structure and Personality in a City* (London: Routledge & Kegan Paul, 1954), 95.
8. See, for example, Gwenda Tavan, *The Long Slow Death of White Australia* (Melbourne: Scribe, 2005); David Hollingsworth, *Race and Racism in Australia*, 2nd ed. (Katoomba, NSW, Australia: Social Science Press, 1998); and Andrew Markus, *Australian Race Relations 1788–1993* (St. Leonards, NSW, Australia: Allen & Unwin, 1994).
9. Hollingsworth, *Race and Racism*, 75.
10. Hollingsworth, *Race and Racism*, 75.
11. Hollingsworth, *Race and Racism*, 87.
12. Tavan, *Long Slow Death*, 43.
13. Tavan, *Long Slow Death*, 11.
14. Humphrey McQueen, quoted in Hollingsworth, *Race and Racism*, 99.
15. For a detailed discussion of social Darwinism and Australian racism, see Hollingsworth, *Race and Racism*, 89–94.

16. Quoted in Frank Fletcher, "The Victorian Jewish Community, 1891–1920: Its Interrelationship with the Majority Gentile Community," *Australian Jewish Historical Society Journal* 8, no. 5 (1978): 250.
17. Jon Stratton, "The Colour of Jews: Jews, Race and the White Australia Policy," *Journal of Australian Studies* 20, nos. 50–51 (1996): 55. doi.org/10.1080/14443059609387278.
18. Tavan, *Long Slow Death*, 22–23.
19. Tavan, *Long Slow Death*, 23.
20. Instructions to members of the Australian Mission, Berlin, No. 46, June 30,1949, published in Suzanne D. Rutland, *Edge of the Diaspora: Two Centuries of Jewish Settlement in Australia* (New York: Holmes & Meier, 2001), appendix 2, 407 (emphasis in original). These instructions were provided by Dr. Len Green, one of the doctors in the team.
21. Suzanne D. Rutland, "Subtle Exclusions: Postwar Jewish Emigration to Australia and the Impact of the IRO Scheme," *Journal of Holocaust Education* 10, no. 1 (2001): 50–66.
22. Stratton, "Colour of Jews," 56.
23. Tavan, *Long Slow Death*, 27–28.
24. "Admission of Jews into Australia, 1921–1938," October 3, 1925, NAA CRS A434, item 49/3/3196, CA 31, Department of the Interior (II), 1939–72, correspondence files, class 3 (non-British European migrants), 1939–50.
25. See Joseph Pugliese, "Race as Category Crisis: Whiteness and the Topical Assignation of Race," *Social Semiotics* 12, no. 2 (2002): 157.
26. Jon Stratton, "Speaking as a Jew: On the Absence of a Jewish Position in British Cultural Studies," *European Journal of Cultural Studies* 1, no. 3 (1998): 308.
27. Hollingsworth, in *Race and Racism*, does not refer to Jews and racial policies at all, even though he lists the various European nationalities that suffered from Australian racism. Tavan's *Long Slow Death* does briefly include the Jewish story.
28. Paul Bartrop, *Australia and the Holocaust, 1933–45* (Melbourne: Australian Scholarly Publishing, 1994), 198.
29. See, for example, the headline "Massacre of 700,000 Polish Jews," referring to the "gas vans" in Chelmno, *Argus* (Melbourne), June 26, 1942, 3, with a similar report published in the *Daily Telegraph* (Sydney); reports of the roundup of Jews in Paris in all the major newspapers on August 7; and "Exterminated in Thousands: Treatment of Jews," *Mercury* (Hobart, TAS, Australia), October 31, 1942.
30. "Massacre of the Jews," *Sydney Morning Herald*, December 18, 1942, 4. See also *Argus* (Melbourne), December 18, 1942, 12.

31. Bartrop, *Australia and the Holocaust*, 205.
32. See Fay Anderson, "'They Are Killing All of Us Jews': Australian Press Memory of the Holocaust," in *Aftermath: Genocide, Memory and History*, ed. Karen Auerbach (Melbourne: Monash University Press, 2015), 65–85, esp. 72.
33. Anderson, "'They Are Killing All of Us Jews,'" 74. Blunden was one of the few Australians with some access to the theater of war.
34. *Daily Telegraph* (Sydney), November 12, 1943.
35. *Sydney Jewish News*, September 15, 1944. This article was in a Jewish newspaper cutting file covering the period 1943–54. The file covers the story of the Holocaust country by country, NSW Jewish Board of Deputies Correspondence Files, Archive of Australian Judaica (AAJ), B36, Fisher Library, University of Sydney. While the Vogt report is referred to, there was no reference to the Lichtheim telegram of June 26, 1944. Richard Lichtheim was a representative of the Jewish Agency in Geneva and worked closely with Gerhardt Riegner. In his cable to London he wrote of the murder of Hungarian Jewry. This cable was intercepted by the Horty government, leading to the cessation of the deportations to the death camps until the Arrow Cross seized power on October 15, 1944, when the deportations recommenced. As early as May 1942 Lichtheim began warning of the murder of Jews.
36. Anderson, "'They Are Killing All of Us Jews,'" 65–66.
37. Deborah Lipstadt, *Beyond Belief: The American Press and the Coming of the Holocaust, 1933–1945* (New York: Free Press, 1986).
38. *Sydney Jewish News*, March 10, 1944, AAJ, B36, Fisher Library University of Sydney.
39. This included the role of Jewish doctor Captain Stanley Goulston, "Tobruk Rat" Medal, *Sydney Morning Herald*, December 30, 1941, 9.
40. NAA, "The Bombing of Darwin—Fact Sheet 195: Japanese Air Raids on Darwin and Northern Australia, 1942–43," NAA, www.naa.gov.au/collection/fact-sheets/fs195.aspx, accessed December 28, 2014.
41. "Japanese Midget Submarine Attacks on Sydney, 1942—Fact Sheet 192," NAA. www.naa.gov.au/collection/fact-sheets/fs192.aspx, accessed December 28, 2014.
42. "Battle of the Coral Sea, 4–8 May 1942: Japanese Intentions," Encyclopedia of the Australian War Museum, www.awm.gov.au/encyclopedia/coral_sea/doc.asp, accessed December 28, 2014.
43. Nadia Wheatley Belsen: Mapping the Memories, https://griffithreview.atavist.com/belsen accessed June 22, 2015.
44. *Sydney Jewish News*, October 20, 1944.

45. See, for example, *The Manning River Times and Advocate for the Northern Coast Districts of New South Wales* (Taree, NSW, Australia), November 11, 1944, 5, TROVE.

46. Thomas C. Hammond, Hon. Secretary, Council for Christians and Jews, "An Important and Tragic Picture," correspondence, *Methodist* (Sydney), October 28, 1944, 10, TROVE.

47. *Sydney Jewish News*, October 3, 1947, 7.

48. Bernard Hyams, "What Did They Think of the Jews? The Early Years of the Sydney *Bulletin*," *Australian Jewish Historical Society Journal* 15, pt. 4 (June 2001): 547–63.

49. *Bulletin* (Sydney), December 4, 1946, 15.

50. Letter from Philip Skorneck to Moritz Gottlieb, April 15, 1947, American Jewish Joint Distribution Committee (JDC) Archives, New York, 45/54, #90.

51. Rutland, *Edge of the Diaspora*, 95–96.

52. B. J. McFarlane, "Jensen, Harald Ingemann (1879–1966)," Australian Dictionary of Biography, National Centre of Biography, Australian National University, adb.anu.edu.au/biography/jensen-harald-ingemann-6839/text11843, accessed September 8, 2017.

53. Michael Blakeney, *Australia and the Jewish Refugees, 1933–1948* (Sydney: Croom Helm Australia), 1985, 19. See also Bartrop, *Australia and the Holocaust*.

54. *Truth* (Melbourne), October 16, 1938.

55. Commonwealth Parliamentary Debates (CPD), *Hansard*, vol. 189, November 27, 1946, 661.

56. For a detailed discussion, see Blakeney, *Australia and the Jewish Refugees*, 294–96; and CPD, *Hansard* 189:744–55.

57. Suzanne Rutland, "Postwar Anti-Jewish Refugee Hysteria: A Case of Racial or Religious Bigotry?" *Journal of Australian Studies* 27, no. 77 (2003): 69–79.

58. O. A. Oeser and S. B. Hammond, *Social Structure and Personality in a City* (London: Routledge & Kegan Paul, 1954), 55. See also Gisela Kaplan, "From 'Enemy Alien' to Assisted Immigrant: Australian Public Opinion of Germans and Germany in the Australian Print Media, 1945–1956," in *German-Australian Cultural Relations Since 1945*, ed. Mandfred Jurgensen (Berne, Germany: Peter Lang, 1995), 89.

59. Oeser and Hammond, *Social Structure and Personality*, 53.

60. Oeser and Hammond, *Social Structure and Personality*, 64.

61. Oeser and Hammond, *Social Structure and Personality*, 64–65.

62. Oeser and Hammond, *Social Structure and Personality*, 98.
63. Oeser and Hammond, *Social Structure and Personality*, 74.
64. Oeser and Hammond, *Social Structure and Personality*, 99. The italics were used in the original text.
65. Address by Harold Holt, minister of immigration, January 22, 1951, Citizenship Convention, box E13, Executive Council of Australian Jewry Correspondence Files, 1951–52, AAJ, Fisher Library, University of Sydney.
66. Dan L. Adler and Ronald Taft, "Some Psychological Aspects of Immigrant Assimilation," in *New Faces: Immigration and Family Life in Australia*, ed. Alan Stoller (Melbourne: Cheshire, 1966), 77; and Jan Schmortte, "Attitudes Towards German Immigration in South Australia in the Post-Second World War Period," *Australian Journal of Politics and History* 51 (December 2005): 542.
67. Kaplan, "From 'Enemy Alien' to Assisted Migrant," 88.
68. Stratton, "Colour of Jews," 58.
69. Stratton, "Colour of Jews," 63.
70. This subcommittee consisted of J. Horgan and A. R. Peters of the Department of Interior and W. D. Forsyth of the Department of External Affairs. Memo, "Post-war Migration," September 21, 1944, 10, 16, NAA CRS A373, item 7786/89.
71. Memo, "Post-war Migration," 9.
72. Memo, "Post-war Migration," 7.
73. Speech by Lt. Col. the Honorable T. W. White (Australia), Department of External Affairs (II), Correspondence File, Alphabetical Series, "Intergovernmental Committee (including the Evian Conference), 1938–1940," NAA CRS A981, item Refugees 4.
74. Suzanne D. Rutland, "Are You Jewish?: Postwar Jewish Immigration to Australia, 1945–1954," *Australian Journal of Jewish Studies* (1991): 35–58.
75. Suzanne D. Rutland, "Subtle Exclusions: Postwar Jewish Emigration to Australia and the Impact of the IRO Scheme," *Journal of Holocaust Education* 10 (Summer 2001): 50–66.
76. Tavan, *Long Slow Death*, 43.
77. Tavan, *Long Slow Death*, 43.
78. Berlin Instruction No. 42, "Recruitment of Jews," June 2, 1949, quoted in Rutland, *Edge of the Diaspora*, 407.
79. Charles Price, "Postwar Migration: Demographic Background," in Stoller, *New Faces*, 20–21. The notion that these discrepancies in funding reflected a racialist ideology is supported by Kaplan, "From 'Enemy Alien' to Assisted Migrant," 93.

80. Suzanne D. Rutland and Sol Encel, "Three 'Rich Uncles in America': The Australian Immigration Project and American Jewry," *American Jewish History* (March 2009): 451–87.
81. See Leo Dinnerstein, *America and the Survivors of the Holocaust* (New York: Columbia University Press, 1982); and Abella and Troper, *None Is Too Many*.
82. David Lewis, national secretary of the Co-operative Commonwealth Federation, quoted in Abella and Troper, *None Is Too Many*, 275.

Part II

Jews and Racism

MUCH SCHOLARLY AND PUBLIC debate has explored Jews' motivations for participating in anti-racist activism. Have they been motivated by their history of persecution, by a religious imperative, by secular notions of social justice, or by concerns about antisemitism? While some Jewish groups and individuals have identified obvious connections between struggles against antisemitism and racisms of other kinds, others have responded to antisemitism with calls for increased Jewish self-defense. At the heart of their responses often stands the Holocaust, its memory implicitly or explicitly informing their attitudes toward the racism directed against them and/or other groups.

In the first of four chapters in part 2, David Slucki explores the extent to which the Holocaust changed Jewish perceptions of racism in Australia. Tracing attitudes in Yiddish writing before, during, and after the Holocaust, Slucki argues that writers across the period continued to echo dominant European and Australian tropes of Aboriginal people as backward, uncivilized, and racially inferior. In promulgating such ideas, the writers revealed their own sense of precariousness as "new Australians" and their desire to assimilate into the white mainstream. "The Holocaust did not create universalists out of Jews," Slucki concludes, "and, in fact, may have had the opposite effect." Only in later decades did Australian Jewish perspectives begin to shift, particularly among those on the political left more willing to show solidarity with Indigenous struggles.

James Jordan's focus is the East End of London in 1968 and singer and actress Georgia Brown's analysis of contemporary racism against Pakistani immigrants through the lens of the Holocaust. By the summer of 1968, when Brown's television documentary "Who Are the Cockneys Now?" was broadcast, the Holocaust had become a regular feature of British public discourse around race and immigration, against the background of Enoch Powell's notorious "Rivers of Blood" speech and parliamentary debates around the Race Relations Act. In the documentary, Brown—the granddaughter of Jewish immigrants from Russia—embedded her warning that "Britain was no longer safe for the wrong kind of immigrant" in a narrative of historical Jewish victimhood. Brown's juxtaposition of the Holocaust and British fascism, Jordan argues, sheds light on a key moment for race relations in postcolonial Britain.

Shifting to the United States, Marjorie N. Feld's study traces the tensions between universalism and particularism in American Jewish attitudes toward South African apartheid. While the Holocaust helped shape a liberal postwar agenda among American Jews, the question of how its lessons might apply to global issues like apartheid was less clear. Was the priority the struggle against injustice, or was it the unity and mutual support of Jews around the world? The Jewish commitment to social justice was complicated by the issue of Israel, particularly after the 1967 war; by the 1970s, argues Feld, mainstream American Jewish leaders had shifted decisively away from a universalist perspective. In the final part of her chapter, she explores how invocations of the Holocaust inform contemporary debates around Israel and the BDS (boycott, divest, and sanction) movement. The crucial question that underlay earlier debates around apartheid, she suggests, applies similarly today: Does a commitment to universal anti-racism trump obligations to national survival?

In a similar vein but different context, Michael E. Staub explores how the Holocaust informed Jews' thinking about anti-black racism in the United States. Despite a growing body of scholarship debunking the myth of silence after the Holocaust, Staub argues that little attention has been paid to the crucial role of racism in these discourses. In the immediate postwar decades, it was "*precisely* in the context of debates over Jewish involvement in African American civil rights activism that a series of rich and complicated discussions of the possible interpretations of Holocaust memory for the American context was carried out." Illustrating stark shifts across several decades, Staub shows that while in the immediate postwar period Holocaust memory was linked to an urgent desire to combat racism in all its forms, by the early 1960s such narratives began to be supplanted by a competing, and less liberal, political expression of Holocaust memory, stressing the urgent need for American Jews to focus on communal survival. Throughout the period surveyed, Holocaust memory was inextricably linked with the struggle for

African American equality, though in shifting ways. Why then, asks Staub, does the metaphoric link between racism and Holocaust memory remain so routinely unacknowledged?

In all these chapters, the delicate balance between the particular and the universal is a central concern. Yet neither is a self-evident or stable category, nor are they necessarily mutually exclusive. For some Jews, commitment to global anti-racist struggles has been considered key to ensuring Jewish security and survival. For others, Jewish self-preservation is itself paramount, with a militarily invincible Israel perceived as the ultimate antidote to antisemitism. In the latter view, the fight against racism is often seen to conflict with the need for safe diaspora communities and Israeli national security. In changeable and often politically charged contexts, Holocaust memory is inevitably contingent, its "lessons" harnessed variously for the cause of universal equality or national survival. In the chapters that follow, the symbolic and political utility of the Holocaust is clear, but its meaning is constantly in flux.

5

Black and White

Yiddish Writers Encounter Indigenous Australia

David Slucki

In 1958, the Australian Yiddish journalist Gedaliah Shaiak traveled around northern and central Australia, visiting Indigenous communities and reporting on his impressions in thirty weekly columns in the *Jewish Post*, the Yiddish weekly newspaper he edited. He talked with Indigenous people in Queensland, the Northern Territory, and Western Australia, and discussed the question of Indigenous rights and assimilation with white Australian politicians. In his report, part ethnographic, part historical, and part journalistic, he wanted to convey to Australian Yiddish readers a sense of how Indigenous people lived and how state and federal governments viewed Indigenous disadvantage. Australian Jews in the late 1950s most likely had little contact with or knowledge of Indigenous people, so Shaiak's reports might have been the first or at least the most expansive materials they had read on the topic.

What is most striking about his impressions, which appeared between October 1958 and May 1959 and were later abridged in the *Third Australian Jewish Almanac*, is the way in which he mirrored dominant tropes about Aboriginal people as backward and uncivilized. Shaiak had been the editor of one of Australia's two Yiddish newspapers for twelve years after his arrival in 1949. He was a distinguished writer of prose, poetry, and journalism who had published books and articles covering various aspects of the twentieth-century Jewish experience. Most crucially in this context, he was also a Holocaust survivor who had spent months evading the Gestapo in 1939 before escaping to the Soviet Union, where he was sent to a deportee camp in Siberia. He eventually joined the Polish army and traveled through the Middle East before settling in Australia in 1948.[1] As a victim of racialized thought broadly construed, it is surprising the extent to which he mirrored pre-Holocaust ideas about race.

In this chapter, I will show how Australian Yiddish writers like Shaiak imagined the place of Indigenous people in Australian society, echoing dominant European and Australian tropes. By "othering" the non-white populations with whom they came into contact, they could assert their own Europeanness in the face of continuing antisemitism, exclusion, and discrimination. Following from this, their assertion of their own whiteness allowed them to blend in, to be invisible. This was particularly true after the Holocaust, when survivor writers may not have wanted to stand out against mainstream thinking or set themselves apart from the majority. This was a delicate balance: to maintain their cultural specificity while also conforming to ideological norms. Ultimately, I argue that these writings are evidence that the Holocaust did not seriously reshape Jewish thinking on race as much as it deepened the authors' efforts to assimilate intellectually into the white European mainstream. It was, in the end, changes in the broader intellectual currents that shaped Jewish attitudes to race. If the Holocaust did have any impact, it was that it fostered a survival instinct among Yiddish writers such that they would not argue against the prevailing wisdom in what was a highly racialized society.

The Yiddish writers' responses to their encounters with Indigenous peoples and cultures can be best understood through the framework established in Mary Louise Pratt's *Imperial Eyes,* in which she asks how colonial travel writings created a particular image of Europe through which Europeans would differentiate themselves from "the rest of the world."[2] This chapter will apply that framework to immigrant Jewish writers by asking how Jews in these "contact zones"[3] created a particular image of themselves as European. Through these interactions, how did they construct the image of Jews as white or at least as part of white Australia? How did their contact—or lack of contact—with Indigenous people shape these constructions? And in what ways did their own history of racial persecution—particularly as victims of genocide—shape their perceptions of settler-colonial relations? Did their contact with

Aboriginal Australia serve to differentiate them or integrate them into white Australian society?

These were writers on the periphery of the Jewish world and of Australian society, writing about a people even more marginalized. Theirs was not a substantial body of work, and their accounts do not necessarily represent broader Jewish thinking about Indigenous issues, which garnered very little attention in Jewish public life. They do, however, reveal a deep anxiety about the place of Jews in white society, an ambivalence about Jews' racial status, and perhaps even a protectiveness of the uniqueness of Jewish suffering during World War II. Partly this was an effect of the Holocaust. Jews, even when there was an impulse toward justice, hesitated to place themselves at the forefront of social and political change. Although they had suffered under European regimes that placed great emphasis on racial divisions, some leading Yiddish writers maintained that social inequality could be explained by looking at inherent racial differences. The Holocaust does not seem to have been a major shaping factor in their views, except perhaps to consolidate a demand for invisibility.

There was, by the 1970s, a shift in the attitudes of Yiddish writers, when they started to express solidarity with Indigenous communities. It would be a simple explanation to suggest that this came from their identification with Indigenous suffering and exclusion. The reality, as I will show, is that Yiddish writers came to this position over the course of a number of decades, and the central shaping factor was not the Holocaust and Jewish experience per se but rather their own impulse for acceptance and survival.

Jews in Australia

Jews have been a part of the colonial project in Australia from the very first day of British settlement on January 26, 1788, when a handful of Jews arrived on the First Fleet. Since then, their numbers have steadily risen in line with the population at large, numbering around 0.5 percent from the early colonial period until today.[4] Until the mid-twentieth century, most Jews were immigrants from Britain and their descendants, and so Jewish life in Australia was very much built in the image of Jewish life in Great Britain. Jewish identity was rooted in religion and was a private affair. In the colonial period, before the federation of Australia in 1901, Jews were generally seen to be part of mainstream white society. Although they faced social discrimination, they were not racially othered. Jews passed, as historian Paul Bartrop has argued, as "indistinguishable from the general population."[5]

From the beginning of the twentieth century, a small trickle of Eastern European Jews arrived in Australia, and these numbers were augmented by seven thousand to eight thousand German and Austrian refugees in the 1930s. It was in the postwar era, though, that the Jewish community grew substantially, with Jews a part of the large wave of European immigration during that period. In the decade after the war, Australia accepted around 17,600 Jews from Europe, of which 60 percent settled in Melbourne (mainly from Poland) and about 40 percent settled in Sydney (mainly from Germany, Austria, and Hungary). Overall, between 1933 and 1961, Australia's Jewish population nearly tripled in size, from 23,000 to 60,000.[6] Further waves of refugees from Central and Eastern Europe would follow. Eastern European Jews, particularly Holocaust survivors, came to shape Australian Jewish life in profound ways. This postwar wave of immigration saw Jews increasingly racialized in Australian public discourse, with many harboring fears of an influx of European Jews and the deleterious effects that it might have on Australian society.[7] Moreover, since the acceleration of Jewish migration in the 1930s, many more Jews in Australia had directly experienced systematic discrimination and violence, much less a factor for British Jewish migrants in the nineteenth century.

This othering of the newly arrived Jews can be partly explained by the fact that they came from a world very different from that of the majority of Australian Jews at the time. They brought with them customs, politics, worldviews, and communities that were foreign not only for white Australia but also even for many of the Australian Jews who traced their roots back to England and who identified strongly with British Australia. Perhaps most important, these new Jews brought with them a different language, Yiddish, to which many, particularly in the aftermath of the Holocaust, clung firmly.[8] By the postwar period, a Yiddish-speaking community had crystallized in Melbourne.[9] With a growing number of Eastern European Jews settling in the 1930s, a local Yiddish literary scene was already beginning to take shape. The Kadimah, Melbourne's Yiddish cultural center, was founded in 1911 in the heart of Carlton, the inner-Melbourne suburb that was the first port of call for many Jewish refugees. By the 1930s, the Kadimah was growing in importance as a meeting place and was taking on a more active role in fostering the creation of Yiddish culture in Australia. That decade saw the establishment for the first time of a number of Yiddish newspapers, including *Oystralyer lebn* (Australian life, 1931–34), which became the long-running *Di yidishe nayes* (The Australian Jewish news, 1935–95). In 1949, the *Australian Jewish Post* was founded as Yiddish supplement to the *Australian Jewish Herald*, and for the next two decades Australia was home to two weekly Yiddish newspapers, which serviced the burgeoning Yiddish-speaking community.[10] As well as the birth of a local Yiddish press, the 1930s saw the beginning of Yiddish literary publishing, with the appearance of the first almanac in 1937, a landmark in Australian Jewish life, which was followed in 1939 by Pinchas Goldhar's *Dertseylungen fun oystralye* [Stories from Australia].

The concentration of Jews in Melbourne and Sydney has significantly shaped Jewish attitudes toward race relations, as the nature of British colonization in the southeast of Australia had left a legacy such that there is not a large Indigenous presence in the places Jews have settled.[11] As a result, most Yiddish writers view the question of race relations from a distance—either through an engagement with journalists' reporting on the matter or, in a few cases, by traveling through the larger Indigenous communities in the Northern Territory and Western Australia. There is little evidence in their writings of any meaningful contact with Indigenous people, and in general, Indigenous issues, as historian Colin Tatz has argued, remained a peripheral concern for Jews, particularly on an organized or communal level, throughout the twentieth century.[12]

Antecedents

The first Yiddish writing that touched on questions of race in Australia consisted of interwar travelogues from sojourners exploring the world outside Europe and reporting back to their countrymen and women in Poland. These writers were part of a small wave of Yiddish writers in the twentieth century who visited far-flung locations such as Australia, South Africa, and Latin America and reflected on the local peoples and their cultures. As Jack Kugelmass has argued, this "Yiddish anthropology is always at some level about Jews, or better put . . . Jews and Jewish issues lurk either beneath the surface and are made manifest through the ruminations of the narrator." Jewish matters, according to Kugelmass, appear also in the writers' preoccupation with finding Jews and Jewish communities in even the most remote locations around the world. The writers who came to Australia did so for a variety of reasons—to raise money for Jewish communities around the world, to seek resettlement options for European Jews, or simply to travel—but all practiced what Kugelmass calls "pseudoethnography," in which they tended to "emulate either proto or folkethnography but whose narrative is hopelessly blurred among various conflicting tropes some of which belong to the realm of fiction."[13] Ultimately, reading these narratives reveals more about Jewish imaginings of home and belonging than it does about Australian society and history. In the writers' reproduction of colonial tropes of Indigenous people, we can read the Yiddish writers' own discomfort with their racial positioning in European society. Occasionally these writers saw a direct parallel with Indigenous suffering and the persecution of Jews. Other times, we can read their angst into their depiction of rural Indigenous life.

Two travelers in particular are noteworthy: the distinguished playwright Peretz Hirschbein, who visited Melbourne and Sydney in 1921, and the poet Melech Ravitch, who traveled from Adelaide to Darwin in 1933. Both of these writers published their travel diaries in Yiddish newspapers and journals in Europe and the United States, and versions appeared later in the first almanac. For these two writers, and others who made the journey, Australia was usually not their only destination. They were seasoned travelers, cosmopolitans, and their visit was part of a broader global tour incorporating Pacific Islands, New Zealand, South Africa, and the Americas. Their understandings of race relations, then, particularly in regard to settler-colonial relations, were informed by their global travels.[14]

The first of these visitors was the acclaimed Yiddish dramatist Peretz Hirschbein, best known for his landmark play, *Griner felder* (Green fields). Hirschbein visited Australia in the early 1920s as part of a larger tour of the South Pacific, including New Zealand and Tahiti, and also South Africa. In addition to this tour, Hirschbein traveled to Palestine, India, China, Japan, Burma, and Singapore, as well as a host of Latin American countries. The legacy from these journeys is an impressive body of travel diaries and impressions, both published and unpublished. Hirschbein's impressions of his tour of Australia, the South Pacific, and South Africa were collected and published in a single volume, *Felker un lender* (Peoples and countries) in 1929.[15] His chapter on Australia was reproduced in the 1937 *Australian Jewish Almanac* and reveals his ambivalence toward the country: impressed by its natural beauty and the pioneering spirit of its inhabitants, on the one hand, but, on the other, melancholic at the absence of the continent's original owners.

Hirschbein traveled only between Sydney and Melbourne. When he arrived in the early 1920s, Indigenous people were scarcely to be found in Australia's largest cities. This was the result of a number of factors: the spread of European disease, frontier violence, concentration, and ultimately expulsion to missions and reserves in the farther reaches of the colonies. Cities were built on sacred meeting places, and Aboriginal populations were reduced to a tiny number. Many were sent to live on reserves far from their own ancestral lands. Still, having come from New Zealand, which had its own distinct history of settler-colonial conflict, he was keenly interested in encountering and understanding the plight of Australia's Indigenous population. Given, though, that there were no major urban Aboriginal populations in Australia's major cities at the time, Hirschbein's search for traces of Aboriginal life proved disappointing: "The eyes seek out the local native-born inhabitant, the Aborigine, who once lived in the area. I look for these black, dark-haired, curly-bearded men—but they are nowhere to be seen. The people here are white. The true child of the country is a vestige somewhere along the equator. In the Europeans' midst there is no trace of them." Hirschbein's melancholic musings on the absence of Aboriginal life reflects his ethnographic interest and also a degree of pathos at the outcome of European colonization. Although impressed with the efforts of those who cultivated the land, Hirschbein could not make peace with the brutalization of Australia's Indigenous population: "The country would have far greater appeal for me were its sixty thousand native dark-skinned children to enjoy at least the modest place they deserve. . . . In no young country has the native been so brutally treated by the white settler as the Aborigines of Australia." By then a seasoned world traveler, Hirschbein had seen firsthand the impact of colonization throughout Latin America and the Pacific, which no doubt influenced his view of Australia. "How noble, then, how tall does New Zealand stand in my estimation where the Maoris have been treated, in part at least, like human beings!" Ultimately, Hirschbein dismissed racial categorizations altogether: "It is preferable by far that all primitive notions of colour and skin should die out, rather than these primitive tribes."[16] Although he described the "primitiveness" of Indigenous peoples, his opposition to conceptions of race as a distinguishing characteristic was in marked contrast to many of his contemporaries.

His attitude was at odds with that of Melech Ravitch, whose writing about Australia's Indigenous peoples reflected more clearly his era. Ravitch traveled to Australia in 1933 to explore the opportunity for large-scale European Jewish resettlement in the country's barren deserts. Although he would later live in Australia between 1936 and 1938, it is this 1933 journey from Adelaide to Darwin that is of greatest interest. His diaries were published in various journals and newspapers in Europe at the time, but most significant were two items that appeared in 1937: a chapter in the first almanac describing his impressions of the journey and a poem published in a collection of his poetry titled *Kontinentn un okeanen* [Continents and oceans]. The two pieces illustrate Ravitch's view—widely accepted in that period—that Indigenous Australians were doomed to extinction. This idea is most distinctly expressed in his poem "Aborigines—Extinction Ballad" in which he wrote:

> *Zeyer nekhtn*
> *Hundert toyznt yor,*
> *Zeyer nekhtn*
> *Urvelt tunkle nakht,*
> *Oyf zeyer morgn veln zey*
> *Nisht mer vartn lang—*
> *Oyf zamdikn midbor-untergang*

> [Their yesterday
> One hundred thousand years,
> Their yesterday
> Dark primeval night,
> For their tomorrow
> They won't wait long—
> For a sandy, desert extinction.][17]

If Indigenous extinction was a foregone conclusion, Ravitch argued, then the land was empty and ready for wide-scale Jewish settlement, with only small numbers of Aboriginal people remaining. "We can boldly say," Ravitch wrote, "that in Australia, the Northern Territory is empty and vacant" and might provide Jews shelter from the oncoming storm in Europe.[18] The land, though, was not empty, and Ravitch's assumptions about land ownership did not factor in Indigenous people's own attachment to the land. It reflected the dismissive colonial attitudes toward Indigenous cultures, deeming their spiritual traditions and practices not worthy of preservation and not equal to those of Europeans. The notion that Australia was empty and vacant was the foundation on which the British settled the continent in the eighteenth and nineteenth centuries.[19] It was a premise that ignored Indigenous people's intimate connection to the land and its centrality in Aboriginal cultures.

Ravitch absorbed and promulgated this commonly accepted wisdom as he traveled through Aboriginal Australia in search of a solution to what he saw as the dire prospects of European Jewry. In the most revealing passage of his abridged travel diary published in the first almanac in 1937, he wrote: "We cannot think of the blacks in Australia as the owners of the land. They find themselves on the very lowest rung of human civilization."[20] There is an implication here that Jews are further up this so-called ladder of civilization, perhaps alongside other Europeans at the top. What is of interest here is that a parallel discussion within Europe placed Jews at a lower "rung of human civilization." It may not be surprising that in a period in which racial thinking prevailed, many Jews accepted the notion that humanity was divided on the basis of blood and that some groups were naturally more advanced than others, so Ravitch's observation may simply reflect a broader trend among European Jewish thinkers.[21] And if there were groups, like Indigenous Australians, who occupied those lower rungs, then Jewish writers like Ravitch could imagine themselves as much more like the Europeans in that hierarchy. His dismissal of Aboriginal Australia may tell us more about his own racial anxieties, then, than it does about his subjects'.

Each writer's anxiety manifested itself differently: For Hirschbein, his assertion that categories of race be abandoned altogether can be read as a projection of what he hoped for in Europe. If Jews were not defined as biologically and irreconcilably different from their European neighbors, then they would enjoy equal rights without fear of persecution. Ravitch, by contrast, in reproducing colonial tropes about the primitiveness of Indigenous people, seeks to assert his own whiteness. His solution to his anxiety about European Jewry's precarious situation in Europe is contradictory: he implicitly stresses Jews' whiteness yet argues that only a large-scale resettlement plan would rescue the Jews from European antisemitism.

Yiddish Australia Encounters Indigenous Australia

The 1930s saw the emergence of an Australian Yiddish literary canon, fueled by the arrival of a growing number of Yiddish speakers. This created a larger pool of local Yiddish writers and a bigger audience for local Yiddish content.[22] Yiddish writers were becoming more embedded in Australian society, bringing an Australian Jewish sensibility to their work. These writers and editors better understood Australian cultural mores than did the Yiddish writers who had traveled through Australia previously. Their writings on race, then, were influenced by factors other than their experiences in Europe, based as they were on a closer engagement with Australian political life and a keener understanding of the country's social composition.[23]

Just as the sojourners before them had reflected their anxiety at their place in European society, so too did the reflections of these newly settled writers reveal how they negotiated their position as recent migrants and as outsiders. Their motivations were fundamentally different: they were not simply observing Australian life from the outside but were also contributing to local Jewish understandings of Australia. In these writings, we see the formation of an Australian Jewish consciousness, an analogous process to that by which travel writers to Australia had asserted their Europeanness through their reflections. This consciousness is distinct from the European Jewish writers: these writers absorbed local perceptions about race relations and history, they tapped into literary and cultural traditions that lamented the loss of Aboriginal life and culture but accepted it as part of the march of progress, and they were much more aware of their contemporary political developments.

We first get a sense of how local Yiddish writers perceived Australian race relations from the scientist and linguist Hirsch Munz, who had been active in Australian Jewish life since his arrival in Australia from Poland in 1927.[24]

Munz's contribution to the first almanac, the opening chapter in the volume, provided a brief history and snapshot of Australia. This introductory chapter sought to give readers an understanding of the context in which Jews live, detailing Australia's history and its social, economic, and demographic profile. Munz's account, however, was extraordinarily limited in scope. Much like the English-language histories of the period, it was a story of exploration, discovery, and triumphant colonization.[25] It was a celebratory history whose founding assumption was that Australia was a country that had developed remarkably quickly against the odds. In his historical overview, Munz did not even allude to the Aboriginal people who had lived continuously on the Australian continent for tens of thousands of years. It was not until the fourteenth page (out of twenty-one pages) of his overview that he first mentioned Australia's Indigenous population, and even then, he offered only a single paragraph to give a statistical overview. He passingly referred to the brutal nature of colonization and accepted the inevitability of the Aboriginal people's disappearance before moving onto what he clearly considered the more important matter of the demographics of white settlers.[26]

Munz's chapter was revealing as a relatively early example of the attitudes that Eastern European Jewish immigrants absorbed on arriving in Australia. His approach was unremarkable in its era, reflecting mainstream Australian views of the settlement of the continent. In this retelling, Indigenous people were present in the narrative but only in their absence from contemporary Australian society. "Settler Australians," according to historian Chris Healy, "have, since the beginning, too often thought of Indigenous people . . . as either absent or present—imagining that they were once in place but are now gone." They were seen as "finished and done for."[27] Just like the sojourner Ravitch, this was precisely the view reflected in Munz's history of his adopted country.

In a similar vein, writing on Australia's literary tradition, the most celebrated of Australia's Yiddish authors, Pinchas Goldhar, lauded the social democratic and egalitarian nature of Australian writers, pointing to their representations of Aboriginal people and their plight as an example. He described the "deeply humane sentiments" and "understanding" with which Australian writers represented this aspect of Australian life. They did not "simply appear as defenders of the blacks, but endeavor[ed] to penetrate their unique primitive psychology and to present the problem of black-white as a problem of human equality and brotherhood."²⁸ His tone, more magnanimous than Munz's, reflected his social-democratic outlook. Still, despite his recognition of the destruction that white settlers had wrought on Aboriginal society, he nonetheless accepted the fiction of the primitive essence of Indigenous life. The "primitive culture of the wild Australians," he wrote, was "too lowly" to have any influence on the development of an Australian national literature.²⁹ And like Munz's view of Australian history, Goldhar had a rosy view of Australian literature, in which he emphasized Australian writers' progressive, democratic nature. These two writers did no more than mirror the views that prevailed in Australia in that period. Indigenous issues were seen as peripheral in a young nation that celebrated its unlikely achievements but that closed its eyes to its sinister frontier past.

By far the most in-depth examination of race relations from a local Yiddish writer came from the journalist and poet Gedaliah Shaiak, whose chapter in the third almanac of 1967, "Black and White in Australia," described his 1958 tour around the remote parts of northern and central Australia and Western Australia. The tour was an effort to go deeply into one of the major social and political questions of the late 1950s, the status of Indigenous Australia.³⁰ In the middle of 1958, he spent ten weeks touring remote areas of Australia, having been given government permission to visit a number of Aboriginal reserves. Trans-Australia Airlines, one of Australia's major domestic airlines at the time, was a major sponsor of his "12,000 mile walk through the Australian continent," although it is not clear why the airline supported a Yiddish journalist.³¹ Like others before him, Shaiak was sympathetic to the plight of Indigenous Australians, arguing that they were brutally torn from their way of life and that they had been segregated and discriminated against. He was in favor of granting Indigenous people civil and political rights, and he expressed his concern at their alienation from Australian society and the health and education crises that continued to cripple Indigenous communities. His observations are partly anthropological and partly focused on efforts at alleviating the deep-seated poverty and legal discrimination that Indigenous people faced daily.

Still, Shaiak's answer to the problems Indigenous communities faced reflected the zeitgeist that had changed since Melech Ravitch had visited the Northern Territory in 1933. By the late 1950s, the government was pursuing a policy of assimilation, in which it believed Indigenous people needed to be given the tools to integrate into white society and abandon what was seen as a primitive and nomadic way of life. This shift in policy took place in the context of an emerging international discourse on human rights and racial equality. This was in the aftermath of the United Nations ratifying its Declaration of Human Rights; it was set against the backdrop of decolonization efforts across Africa and Asia and a growing Third World consciousness, which crystallized at the Bandung Conference in 1955. In postwar Australia, this global discourse put pressure on the government to adhere to the new expectations of nationhood. As Anna Haebich has written, "Assimilation promised equal citizenship rights to Aboriginal people through the abolition of discriminatory laws and practices and improved living conditions. . . . In return they were required to abandon their distinctive cultural values, lifestyles, customs, languages and beliefs and conform to the national way of life."[32] Historian Bain Attwood has demonstrated that assimilation was built on the assumption that "history was a story of progress that would inevitably culminate in the triumph of European modernity and the disappearance of Aboriginal tradition or culture."[33] This differed from the earlier ideas that influenced Ravitch only insofar as it was predicated on the vanishing of Aboriginal culture, rather than of Aboriginal people. This marked a minor shift away from a strictly racial discourse, to one that allowed space in mainstream Australian discourse for the possibility of Indigenous survival and renewal.

Shaiak was a proponent of the idea that Aboriginal people could be absorbed into white Australian society, if only given the tools. He wrote positively of the government's policy of assimilation, which, according to then Minister for Territories Paul Hasluck, would see Aboriginal people assimilated into white society within one generation. "After years of research," Shaiak wrote, "pedagogues and psychologists are convinced that the colored child is absolutely not behind the White child in terms of intelligence. In many cases, they are more capable and have better memories."[34] Given the right circumstances, it was possible to assimilate Indigenous people into Australian society, argued Shaiak. The history of dispossession has made that difficult, but their "degradation," he recognized, was a result of "white policies" that confined them to their own Pales of Settlement.[35]

For Shaiak, Jews provided a kind of model for Indigenous people: they had become part of the dominant society, and Aboriginal Australians needed to do as the Jews had done and conform to white civilization. Jews too had "for generations survived so much persecution and prejudice, suffered from the leprosy of mistrust, when [they] were displaced, mocked for [their] beliefs, [their] customs, [their] way of life and traditions" but were now respected in white society.[36] He relayed a number of conversations in which white politicians lament that a proposal for a Jewish settlement in the Kimberley region of Western Australia was never realized. If Jews had settled, they claimed, they would have helped bring "civilization" to the remotest parts of Australia. This suggests that Jews were seen as easily assimilable into white Australian society, whereas Indigenous people were less likely to adapt. Traveling through the remote parts of Australia, Shaiak clearly saw himself as part of white Australia, a position Aboriginal people had yet to attain. It was coming into closer contact with Indigenous people that emphasized his whiteness, although most of his reportage focuses on discussions with white Australians. And although he endorsed the government policy of assimilation, Shaiak still maintained that racial characteristics separated peoples around the world. Citing early twentieth-century ethnographers, in particular James Leyburn, Shaiak presented a number of different theories of race, settling ultimately on one that proposed four main racial types: "Caucasian, or white; Mongol, or yellow; Negroid, or black; and Australoid—proto-Caucasian."[37] Although he did not state it explicitly, by this calculation Jews fit into the white category.

These were categories that one might have expected a Holocaust survivor to hold with some suspicion. Having escaped Nazi-occupied Poland in December 1939, and having written extensively about the destruction of European Jewry, it seems contradictory that Shaiak would rehash racial theories that, particularly by the late 1960s, were more and more out of vogue. His piece, intended to give local and international Yiddish audiences a sense of the place that the vexed question of race relations occupied in Australian life, reflects perhaps a specifically post-Holocaust anxiety about Jews' place in society, although he does not refer specifically to the Holocaust. Desperate to be part of the majority white population, his commentary on race relations in Australia was a perfect way to assert his, and Jews', place within the mainstream of Australia, without having to address it directly. Whereas previously they had themselves been in the lowest social categories, to the point where they were murdered in their millions, in the settler-colonial context, Jews now found themselves with the opportunity to secure their own place as white Australians. This view also serves to eschew the pre-Holocaust view that Jews themselves were a distinct race, an important feature of eighteenth- and nineteenth-century racial discourse.

Shaiak's reporting—along with Ravitch's from decades earlier—may be explained by drawing on Mary Louise Pratt's ideas of "contact zones," spaces of "colonial encounter . . . in which peoples geographically and historically separated come into contact with each other and establish ongoing relations." These relations are often typified by "coercion, radical inequality, and intractable conflict." The encounters are not unidirectional; instead, "subjects are constituted in and by their relations to each other," even though they are characterized by "asymmetrical relations of power."[38] For Shaiak, this encounter with the colonial other was characterized by ongoing inequality. His conception of himself as Australian, his sense of subjectivity, was shaped in part by his firsthand encounter with the subjugated other, strengthening his own sense of power and belonging. This feeling represents a major break from the sense of helplessness that Jews endured under Nazi rule and in the face of European antisemitism.

It is clear, then, that in the wake of Nazi racial persecution and a persistent strain of European antisemitism, Australian Yiddish writers like Munz, Goldhar, and Shaiak clung to the increasingly outdated belief in the racial inferiority and primitiveness of Indigenous Australians. Although recognizing the violence that accompanied the expansion on the frontier, and lamenting the decimation of Aboriginal life, these writers nonetheless promulgated outmoded racial ideas that reveal more about their own feelings of precariousness as "new Australians" than providing an accurate picture to their readers of Indigenous people and their place in Australian society. They absorbed colonial views of the colonized in order to shed the racial stigmatization that had been so central to their experiences of suffering through the first half of the twentieth century.

Changing Winds

In contrast to Munz's and Shaiak's ever more outmoded views on Indigenous hardships, some on the Jewish left were more sympathetic, drawing the links between European colonization and Indigenous poverty and dispossession.

Partly this was a result of politics; the writers who opined most strongly on the topic tended to come from the left. Mostly, though, it was a matter of time. The more prominent the Indigenous question became and the more settled Jews were, the more Yiddish writers there were to address it. Philip Mendes has demonstrated that for the most part the Jewish left, at least on an institutional level, was only marginally involved with the issue of Indigenous rights. Even though many white activists within the Aboriginal civil rights movement were Jewish, Jewish organizations did not tend to focus on those issues.[39] When they did, though, their tone was very different from that represented in the Australian Jewish almanacs. Writers from the Jewish Labor Bund, the inheritors of the Eastern European socialist party, showed their solidarity with Indigenous people and their struggles. Although the movement as a whole did not participate in that struggle, there are some clues that by the 1960s Jews on the left were willing to take a stronger stance to correct historical injustices.[40] They tended to look at the suffering of Indigenous people as the result of centuries of European settlement and government policy rather than as an inevitable outcome of European supremacy over the native population. Their writings also described Indigenous cultures with a greater deal of respect than their forerunners did.

For example, writing in the Bund's journal, *Unzer gedank* [Our belief], Hershl Bachrach protested that in one of the most "highly developed democratic countries" in the world, democracy extended only to "people with white skin." He lamented the "small minded snobs and reactionaries, with their senseless ideas that Aborigines—these truly 'pure' Australians—[were] not grown up enough receive full civil rights in their own country." Unlike earlier writers, Bachrach was clear that Indigenous poverty was linked to the "tragic destiny of the Australian Aborigines under the domination of the first white settlers, how they were slaughtered in the thousands and were decimated to a population of 70,000–80,000 (from around 300,000 in 1770)."[41] In 1970, on the bicentennial of Captain James Cook's first arrival in Australia, Heniek Borensztajn wrote in *Unzer gedank* that for Indigenous Australians, the anniversary could only be a "day of mourning."[42] He recognized the explicit link between British dispossession and Indigenous poverty and disadvantage and argued for the return of land to Aboriginal communities, a growing demand among activists for Indigenous rights.[43]

The work of literary critic Yitzhak Kahn in the 1970s shows most clearly the shift in Jewish attitudes toward race relations in Australia. Kahn, also a Bundist, took a view of Australian history, of Australia's treatment of its Indigenous peoples, and of Aboriginal cultures and traditions very much at odds with the likes of Ravitch and Shaiak. In spite of their sympathies, those earlier writers retained the colonial outlooks of their eras. In analyzing the work of Australian writers dealing with the question of race relations, Kahn demonstrated his sophisticated understanding of Australian history and Aboriginal civilization and also showed how Jewish views of race had shifted since the 1920s and '30s—or at least were beginning to shift. His *Chats with Australian Writers* gave Yiddish readers a deep insight into the history and development of Australian literature, examining the works of over twenty writers from the colonial era to the 1970s. Two chapters in particular were concerned with writers whose work focuses on settler-Indigenous relations. Looking at work of Eleanor Dark and Xavier Herbert, Kahn's analysis demonstrates a close engagement with the political, intellectual, cultural, and social developments that informed government policies and attitudes toward Indigenous people throughout Australian history.

For one, Kahn challenged the ethnographic assumptions that underpinned the writings of earlier observers. He condemned the "racist" assumptions that Aboriginal peoples were racially inferior and culturally primitive compared to Europeans. On the contrary, the former possessed its own "sophisticated" culture, which was disrupted by white settlement. For Kahn, it was more productive to talk of cultural difference than cultural superiority. He acknowledged that Aboriginal people were "a proud people with their own rich culture and civilization" that was "tied up with the land." Theirs was an "entire complicated web of social groups, tribes, gender, kinship, and connection to the land, that together comprise the entire complex organization of ancient Aboriginal life, before and after it came into contact with white civilization."[44] In fact, European settlers even mimicked some Aboriginal spiritual practices, such as meditation and seclusion in the bush. Kahn's was a much more nuanced view than that held by even recent writers such as Shaiak. Indigenous people were not, for Kahn, simply an ethnographic curiosity doomed to extinction but rather the inheritors of a rich, ancient civilization that sought to adapt and survive in the face of substantial existential challenges.

Kahn did not subscribe to notions of racial superiority and inferiority. "Often," he wrote, "we hear the opinion that Aborigines are an inferior race, owing not to the guilt of Whites, but because they are 'lower in the evolutionary scale.' The message: the primitive will always remain lower as a civilization. Such racists want us to forget that Aborigines possess their own sophisticated culture, which provided them with a happy, independent life, until the white man disturbed it." Kahn used a traffic analogy: in some countries, people drive on the left; in other countries, on the right. Neither is more advanced; these are simply different ways of making sense of the world.[45]

Clearly, Kahn had shifted away from the racial prism through which Jewish writers had historically viewed Indigenous people in Australia. The challenges that Aboriginal people faced were not about physical extinction but about the disappearance of historical and cultural practices tied to land that had been usurped by white colonists. As Kahn wrote, when Europeans arrived to "steal that land from them, they began to lose not only the earth under their feet, but even the fabric of Aboriginal society was destroyed. They were lost people and were dying also, when they survived physical destruction."[46] The biggest threat to Aboriginal continuity now, in the eyes of Kahn, was to maintain their culture, having survived the initial colonial onslaught.

This situation, in Kahn's view, was "analogous to Jewish life, in that Aborigines also face this problem: when the older generation dies, will Aboriginal culture die with it?"[47] Indigenous people faced the same challenges to maintain their spiritual and cultural life as Jews did. Aside from the arrival of the British in the late eighteenth century and the widespread physical violence that saw the decimation of the Indigenous population, it was the government's push for assimilation that was a threat to Aboriginal life. Kahn rallied against assimilation policies, which had been proven "bankrupt" for decades. He likened the situation of Aborigines to that of Jews. In this case, though, there was not only a resemblance between the suffering and oppression of the two peoples but also between the assimilation push in both cultures. The assimilation policies of the 1930s to the 1960s, Kahn argued, were unsuccessful because Indigenous people did not want to "give up their language, poetry, music, dance, religion, for the price of full citizenship." This demand was all too familiar to Kahn: "Do we not remember this 'price' that, in the nineteenth century, was demanded for the emancipation of the Jews in Germany?" The issue of assimilation, then, "torments various peoples and races and right now Aboriginal intellectuals are fighting sharply against the assimilation solution."[48] He does not discuss the Holocaust specifically, but the analogy is clear: How do a people, wrought by violence and dispossession, maintain their identity while carrying the burden of the past?

The comparison between Jewish and Aboriginal struggles against assimilation highlights the ambivalent status that Jews continued to hold in Australian society. Indeed, Kahn's book itself testifies to the position Jews still held in the margins. Although writing in a foreign language, Kahn was writing as an insider with a deep knowledge of Australian literature. The title itself implies a deep level of familiarity not only with the work but also with Australian literary circles more broadly. However, in order to access the key works on which Australian national identity had been built, many Jews in this period required an intermediary like Kahn. As with many immigrants, absorbing English was a slow process, and a work like his was a pathway into the tradition of Australian literature that might not have been accessible for those with an inadequate grasp of English. The avenues to full acceptance in Australian society were still limited.

Kahn's observations demarcate the archaic attitudes of earlier Yiddish writers and a more progressive epoch in Australian Yiddish writers' thinking on race. Although by no means a linear progression, Yiddish writers in Australia—both local and visiting—certainly did proceed from a view that reflected the racialized, colonial thinking of the first half of the twentieth century to a more nuanced and sympathetic understanding of Indigenous people and their place in Australian history and society. By the time Kahn's book was published in 1976, however, Yiddish writing was on a steep downward trajectory, paralyzed by the triple blow of the Holocaust, the refusal of Israel's founders to recognize the cultural worth of Yiddish, and the rapid acculturation of Jews in Western countries, which led to the abandonment of Yiddish as a mainstream Jewish vernacular.

As they acculturated into their surrounding societies, Jews in many Western countries no longer carried the stigma of racial difference. Eric Goldstein has argued, for example, that in the case of American Jewry the "events of World War II helped to diminish concern about the far-reaching racial characteristics of Jews and offered them a significant level of incorporation into white America."[49] And although this entry into white society was not without its challenges, Jews throughout the postwar period embraced their newly found acceptance as an "ethnic" rather than "racial" group.⁵⁰ So too in Australia did they now enter the white mainstream, as immigration began to open up to those from East Asia, the Indian subcontinent, and the Middle East. It was precisely in this period, as Philip Mendes and Colin Tatz have argued, that Australian Jews, now secure in their status as Australian citizens (and many now second- and third-generation Australians) also began to participate in the struggle for Indigenous rights more widely.⁵¹ By then, though, Yiddish writers were becoming more and more marginalized in Australian Jewish life.

Conclusion

In their efforts to pass as European, Yiddish writers reproduced early twentieth-century racial tropes in describing their encounters with Indigenous Australians. They occasionally drew some analogies between the Indigenous and Jewish experiences, although they did not directly compare the suffering of Aboriginal Australia to that of European Jews during the Holocaust. Still, the way that the discourse on the issue shifted between the 1920s and the 1970s suggests that the Holocaust may have helped modify and ultimately overhaul the more traditional views of race held by earlier writers.

For the most part, Indigenous issues were, at best, a peripheral matter for Australian Jewry. Partly this was due to a lack of meaningful contact: for the most part, Jewish and Indigenous communities rarely occupied the same geographic space, and even when they lived in adjacent neighborhoods in inner Melbourne, there is scant evidence of sustained engagement. Still, the few insights these Yiddish writers offer into Jewish views on Indigenous matters are revealing and demonstrate a persistent insistence on the Jews' identification as European and white, even by those who suffered the worst of Europe's rejection. Insofar as the Holocaust did come to shape Jewish thinking about race, it did so in implicit ways. It fostered an attitude of self-preservation, discernible in the Yiddish writings on Indigenous Australia, which allowed some writers to ignore the parallels between their own suffering and that of others.

For the most part, though, Jewish attitudes toward the ideas of race in Australia were clearly shaped by the broader national conversations around the question. By the end of the century, Jews would come to be more actively involved in advocating for Indigenous rights, and a narrative emerged that Jews were at the forefront of reconciliation activism.[52] But during the period from the 1930s through the 1970s, with the rise of Indigenous political movements advocating for their rights, the Jewish world, save a small number of individual Jews, seemed to take a much less prominent role. Reading the works of writers such as Ravitch and Shaiak might help explain why, when their counterparts in the United States were more vocal and active in the struggle for civil rights, Australian Jews did not organize for the most beleaguered population in Australia. Their writers and leaders often maintained outmoded views about race and racial hierarchies, which were beginning to wane in the postwar years. Even the experience of Nazi persecution did not change or shape these views substantially. The Holocaust did not create universalists out of Jews and, in fact, may have had the opposite effect. Jewish conceptions of race have never been, as Mitchell Hart has demonstrated, simple or monolithic. They were never uniformly opposed to the ideas of racial science and had routinely "employed the language and images of race to think about the Jewish past and present."[53] This fact becomes starkly evident in colonial spaces like the Australian outback, where Jews' encounters revealed a desperation to blend in and to pass as white Europeans, an objective they achieved in Australia—and elsewhere—by the late twentieth century.

NOTES

I thank Andrew Markus for his comments on an earlier version of this chapter and Shirli Gilbert for organizing a panel on the topic at the Association for Jewish Studies annual conference where I first presented this material.

1. Reuben Havin, "Gedaliah Shaiak—a Tribute," *Melbourne Chronicle*, February/March 1984, 11–12.
2. Mary Louise Pratt, *Imperial Eyes: Travel Writing and Transculturation* (London: Routledge, 1992), 5.
3. "Contact zones" is a phrase Pratt uses throughout her *Imperial Eyes*.
4. W. D. Rubinstein, *The Jews in Australia* (Melbourne: AE Press, 1986), 23.
5. Paul Bartrop, "Living within the Frontier: Early Colonial Australia, Jews, and Aborigines," in *Jewries at the Frontier: Accommodation, Identity, Conflict*, ed. Sander Gilman and Milton Shain (Urbana: University of Illinois Press, 1999), 93.

6. On the population shift, see Suzanne Rutland, *Edge of the Diaspora: Two Centuries of Jewish Settlement in Australia* (New York: Holmes & Meier, 1997), 225–56.
7. Jon Stratton, "The Color of Jews: Jews, Race, and the White Australia Policy," in Gilman and Shain, *Jewries at the Frontier*, 309–34.
8. Jan Schwarz, *Survivors and Exiles: Yiddish Culture after the Holocaust* (Detroit: Wayne State University Press, 2015), has argued that in Europe, Israel, and the Americas, the postwar period was, despite the murder of millions of Yiddish-speaking Jews, a time of Yiddish cultural renaissance and that the Holocaust gave Yiddish writers not only the impetus to cling to their language and culture but also subject matter to sustain a generation of writers. The Polish-Jewish Holocaust survivors in Australia certainly shared these sentiments.
9. Sydney, on the other hand, was the destination for a larger number of Jewish refugees from Germany, Austria, and Hungary, and it also housed a substantial number of British Jews and their descendants. On the resettlement of survivors, see Michele Langfield, "'Don't forget you are Jewish': Holocaust Survivors, Identity Formation and Sense of Belonging in Australia," in *Cultures in Refuge: Seeking Sanctuary in Modern Australia*, ed. Robert Mason and Anna Hayes (Burlington, VT: Ashgate, 2012), 67–78.
10. Alan Crown, "The Jewish Press in Australia," *Arts* 15 (1990): 87–107.
11. One main exception is the inner-city Melbourne neighborhood of Fitzroy, where a substantial urban Aboriginal population grew from the mid-twentieth century. Fitzroy was adjacent to Carlton, the first port of call for many Jewish migrants.
12. Colin Tatz, "An Essay in Disappointment: The Aboriginal-Jewish Relationship," *Aboriginal History* 28 (2004): 100–121.
13. Jack Kugelmass, "A Yiddish Traveller in Peru" (paper presented at Jews, Indians, and the Western World conference, Columbia University, New York, April 25, 2010).
14. These writers followed in the footsteps of the Jerusalem rabbi Jacob Saphir, who in 1861 had traveled to Australia to raise money among the British Jewish migrants. He documented his impressions as part of two Hebrew-language volumes on his travels through the Middle East, Asia, and the Pacific. Saphir's impressions of Australia were translated in the late 1940s by Australia's most important Yiddish writer, Pinchas Goldhar. See Hirsch Munz, ed., *Yaakov Safir un zayne nesiyes: A bazukh in oystralye in 1861* (Melbourne: YIVO-komitet in Melburn, 1950). These impressions include Saphir's amateur anthropological observations about the Aboriginal people still living at the time around Melbourne.

15. Peretz Hirschbein, *Felker un lender: Rayze-ayndrukn fun nayzeland, oystralye, doyrem-afrike* (Vilnius: Vilner farlag fun B. Kletskin, 1929). Hirschbein's other travel writings include collections on journeys to South America, India, and Palestine. See *Fun vayte lender: Argentine, brazil* (New York, 1916); *Indye: Fun mayne rayze in indye* (Vilnius: Vilner farlag fun B. Kletskin, 1929); and *Erets-yisroel* (Los Angeles: Peretz Hirshbein Bukh Komitet, 1951).
16. Peretz Hirschbein, "Australia," trans. Serge Lieberman, *Melbourne Chronicle* no. 60 (1990): 53–57.
17. Melekh Ravitch, *Kontinentn un okeanen: Lider, baladn, un poems* (Warsaw: Literarishe bleter, 1937), 175; author's translation.
18. Melekh Ravitch, "Nordern teritorye rayze—1933," *Oystralyer yidish almanakh* (Melbourne, 1937), 217.
19. This notion was refuted in the High Court of Australia in 1992, when the Court's *Mabo v. Queensland* decision recognized the Native Title of the Merriam people in Australia's north. The key scholarly work tracing the history of *terra nullius* in the Australian context is Henry Reynolds, *The Law of the Land* (Ringwood, VIC, Australia: Penguin, 1987). For a summary of scholarly critiques of Reynolds and the High Court and on the genealogy of the concept of *terra nullius*, see Andrew Fitzmaurice, "The Genealogy of Terra Nullius," *Australian Historical Studies* 38, no.129 (2007): 1–15.
20. Ravitch, "Nordern teritorye rayze," 217.
21. Mitchell B. Hart, ed., *Jews and Race: Writings on Identity and Difference, 1880–1940* (Waltham, MA: Brandeis University Press, 2011), highlights this in an excellent anthology of Jewish writings on race, which shows how Jewish thinkers and scientists were among those that conceived of Jews as a racial group.
22. On the development of Yiddish literature in Australia, see Elise Morera de la Vall, "Jewish Literature in Australia," in *Anglophone Jewish Literature*, ed. Axel Stähler (London: Routledge, 2007), 177–78.
23. Although Ravitch straddled this divide, having lived for a number of years in Australia and worked in local Jewish institutions, he was, as the Australian novelist Arnold Zable noted, "at heart, in the grand tradition, a wandering Jew," whose journey to the antipodes was spurred by an "uncontrollable urge to explore yet another corner of the globe." Arnold Zable, *The Fig Tree* (Melbourne: Text, 2004), 195–96.
24. On Munz, see Malcolm J. Turnbull, "Munz, Hirsch (1905–1979)," Australian Dictionary of Biography, National Centre of Biography, Australian National

University, adb.anu.edu.au/biography/munz-hirsch-11200/text19965, accessed November 28, 2012.

25. For a summary of the development of Australian historiography, see Stuart Macintyre and Anna Clark, *The History Wars* (Carlton, VIC, Australia: Melbourne University Press), 31–49.

26. Hirsch Munz, "Oystralye: An iberblik iber geshikhte un kegnvart," *Third Australian Jewish Almanac* (Melbourne, 1937), 17–37.

27. Chris Healy, *Forgetting Aborigines* (Sydney: University of New South Wales Press, 2008), 9–10.

28. Pinchas Goldhar, "Di oystralishe literatur," in *Gezamlte shriftn* (Melbourne: Farlag Fraynt fun der Yidisher Literatur, 1949), 325; author's translation.

29. Goldhar, "Di oystralishe literature," 325; author's translation.

30. There aren't substantive differences between the original accounts and the abridged version. I focus on the abridged chapter as it appears in the almanac, a compendium of Australian Yiddish culture and thought.

31. Gedaliah Shaiak, "Shvarts un vays in oystralye: An araynfir," *Jewish Post*, October 31, 1958, 4.

32. Anna Haebich, *Spinning the Dream: Assimilation in Australia 1950–1970* (Fremantle, WA, Australia: Fremantle Press, 2008), 12.

33. Bain Attwood, "Rights, Racism, and Aboriginality: Critics of Assimilation in the 1950s and 1960s," in *Contesting Assimilation*, ed. Tim Rowse (Perth, WA, Australia: API Network, 2005), 271.

34. Gedaliah Shaiak (Tschernazon), "Shvarts un vays in oystralye," in Driter oystralish-yidisher almanakh (Melbourne: Jewish Cultural Centre and National Library "KADIMAH," 1967), 368; author's translation.

35. Shaiak, "Shvarts un vays in oystralye," 364; author's translation.

36. Shaiak, "Shvarts un vays in oystralye," 370; author's translation.

37. Shaiak, "Shvarts un vays in oystralye," 360; author's translation.

38. Pratt, *Imperial Eyes*, 6–7.

39. Philip Mendes, "The Australian Jewish Left and Indigenous Rights," *Journal of the Australian Jewish Historical Society* 20, no. 3 (2011): 430–43.

40. On the history of the Bund after World War II, including in Australia, see David Slucki, *The International Jewish Labor Bund after 1945: Toward a Global History* (New Brunswick, NJ: Rutgers University Press, 2012).

41. Hershl Bachrach, "Der shand-flek fun oystralye," *Unzer gedank* (May 1959); author's translation.

42. Heniek Borensztajn, "Di oystralisher aborigines," *Unzer gedank* (November 1970): 9–10; author's translation. The Day of Mourning was an allusion to a protest held by Indigenous activists in 1938 against the celebrations of Australia Day and against the government's exclusion of Indigenous people from Australian life. On the Day of Mourning, see Bain Attwood and Andrew Markus, *Thinking Black: William Cooper and the Australian Aborigines League* (Canberra, NSW, Australia: Aboriginal Studies Press, 2004), 82–88.
43. On the struggle for Aboriginal rights in Australia, see, for example, Attwood and Markus, *Thinking Black*; Bain Attwood and Andrew Markus, *The Struggle for Aboriginal Rights: A Documentary History* (Sydney: Allen & Unwin, 1999); Bain Attwood, *Rights for Aborigines* (Sydney: Allen & Unwin, 2003); Frank Brennan, *No Small Change: The Road to Reconciliation for Indigenous Australia* (Brisbane, QLD, Australia: University of Queensland Press, 2015).
44. Yitzhak Kahn, *Shmuesn mit oystralisher shrayber* (Melbourne: York Press, 1976), 217; author's translation.
45. Kahn, *Shmuesn mit oystralisher shrayber*, 225; author's translation.
46. Kahn, *Shmuesn mit oystralisher shrayber*, 216; author's translation.
47. Kahn, *Shmuesn mit oystralisher shrayber*, 226; author's translation.
48. Kahn, *Shmuesn mit oystralisher shrayber*, 224; author's translation.
49. Eric L. Goldstein, *The Price of Whiteness: Jews, Race, and American Identity* (Princeton, NJ: Princeton University Press, 2006), 194.
50. Goldstein, *Price of Whiteness*, 189–239. On Jews and whiteness in the United States, see also Karen Brodkin, *How Jews Became White Folks and What That Says about Race in America* (New Brunswick, NJ: Rutgers University Press, 1998).
51. See, for example, Philip Mendes, "Australian Jewish Left and Indigenous Rights," 433–39; and Colin Tatz, "Essay in Disappointment," 100–121.
52. Colin Tatz dismantles this idea in "Essay in Disappointment," 109.
53. Mitchell B. Hart, "Jews and Race: An Introductory Essay," in Hart, ed. *Jews and Race*, xiii.

6

Who Are the Jews Now?

Memories of the Holocaust in Georgia Brown's East End, 1968

James Jordan

IN 2008, TOM LAWSON and I coedited a volume titled *The Memory of the Holocaust in Australia*.[1] To celebrate its publication we attended a book launch at the Sydney Jewish Museum where we spent time with Avril Alba discussing the absence from the collection of an article that discussed in depth how the Holocaust had been remembered in Australia alongside the memory of colonial violence and genocide, the White Australia policy, and racial prejudice. It struck us as a significant absence, particularly in the year that Prime Minister Kevin Rudd had apologized to Australia's Indigenous peoples for the "pain, suffering and hurt" of the Stolen Generations.[2] While there had already been some important work undertaken in this area, it was clear that more was needed, and not only in respect of Australia. In the United Kingdom, for example, more needed to be done in terms of recognizing connections and similarities between the origins and implementation of the Holocaust and imperial violence of the nineteenth century, understanding how knowledge of the Holocaust influenced race relations in the postwar and postcolonial context, and assessing the impact this has had on national memory and culture against the seemingly overlooked backdrop of empire, slavery, racism, and genocide.

In the decade since those discussions, as the introduction to this collection makes clear, there has been sustained engagement with these questions, and yet some areas, such as the cultural intersection, remain relatively underexplored. The following makes an original contribution to that area by considering the influence of the memory of the Holocaust on race relations in postwar Britain. In particular, it looks at television and "Who Are the Cockneys Now?," a forty-two-minute documentary that followed the singer Georgia Brown as she returned to the Jewish East End streets of her youth to see what had changed across the thirty years.[3] As the *Radio Times* explained, while the area had once been "largely Jewish, as fortunes improved over the years, there [was now] a dispersal. Now, new immigrant groups [were] moving into the area: Indians, Pakistanis and West Indians. Georgia Brown want[ed] to know what [was] in store for the new Cockneys."[4] Although that synopsis implied that the focus was to be on the new immigrants, only occasionally did Brown look at what the future held for the new Cockney. More often the program looked backward to tell the story of Jewish immigration, offering the Jewish experience as an archetype for the immigrant experience more generally. In what could at times be an uncritical, nostalgic, and celebratory narrative, Brown, local residents, and three famous friends—songwriter Lionel Bart, hairdresser Vidal Sassoon, and playwright/writer Wolf Mankowitz—offered their own views on the East End of the 1930s, the influence it had on their careers, and what had changed in recent years. Brown also used this as an opportunity to reflect on her own family history, in the process arguing that the Jewish immigrant population of the 1890s–1910s, impoverished and alien, had been able to survive and then flourish in Britain thanks in part to the support network provided by the established Anglo-Jewish community.

The following explores the program's structure in terms of narrative and editing, placing it within the broader context of race relations in the United Kingdom and beyond in 1968, and examining how on-screen connections were made between the experiences of the old and new immigrant. In particular, it considers how Brown represented her own Jewishness and what it meant to be a Jew in the East End in 1968. It also highlights the parallels the program made between the persecution of the Jews in Germany in the 1930s and the position of the non-white Commonwealth immigrant in Britain in the 1960s, including the implicit suggestion that there was the potential for another genocide, this time enacted by the British on British soil against British subjects.

ONE PAIR OF EYES

"Who Are the Cockneys Now?" was an episode of the critically acclaimed television documentary series *One Pair of Eyes*, which initially ran on the BBC from 1967 to 1974. Each episode saw a famous guest presenter offer her or his personal perspective on a subject of their choice, with freedom to approach the subject in her or his own way. The series produced a fascinating array of programs and subjects from a variety of speakers, with highlights including "The Road to Kingdom Come," in which journalist James Cameron visited Italy, Israel, Egypt, and India to look at notions of God, and "No, but Seriously" with comedian and writer Marty Feldman asking what makes us laugh. These could be contentious and political subjects. In 1971 in "A Region of Shadow," for example, the writer Laurens van der Post explored the impact of apartheid on his native South Africa.[5] In a *Radio Times* preview to accompany that episode, journalist George Rosie made connections between the treatment of the non-white population in South Africa under apartheid and the prejudice that van der Post had witnessed against Jews in Russia and Nazi Germany. Van der Post continued by offering his explanation as to why such prejudices existed: "You see, we all have a dark man inside us. He is the side of our personality that is suppressed by our culture. The irrational, instinctual, perhaps feminine side of us. So, when we confront the other people who seem to embody those suppressed qualities—be they Negroes, gypsies, Jews, whoever—then we dislike them. We hate in others what we hate in ourselves."[6]

These issues and connections had been very much at the front of people's minds three years earlier when in the spring of 1968, two days before Georgia Brown started the location filming for her own *One Pair of Eyes*, the Conservative member of Parliament (MP) Enoch Powell made his notorious, highly inflammatory "Rivers of Blood" speech to a Conservative association in Birmingham. Delivered in the wake of the 1968 Commonwealth Immigrants Act and concurrent to parliamentary debates surrounding the 1968 Race Relations Act, Powell's speech offered both his own personal vision of the current state of the United Kingdom and a warning for its future, predicting dire consequences if immigration from the Commonwealth were to remain unchecked. Powell did not hold back, outraging many with his description of "charming, wide-grinning piccaninnies" and sharing a prediction that "in 15 or 20 years' time the black man will have the whip hand over the white man" in the United Kingdom. He famously concluded with an allusion to Virgil, which has since given the speech its popular name in public memory:

> As I look ahead, I am filled with foreboding. Like the Roman, I seem to see "the River Tiber foaming with much blood." That tragic and intractable phenomenon which we watch with horror on the other side of the Atlantic but which there is interwoven with the history and existence of the States itself, is coming upon us here by our own volition and our own neglect. Indeed, it has all but come. In numerical terms, it will be of American proportions long before the end of the 20th century. Only resolute and urgent action will avert it even now.[7]

One person deeply affected by the words of Powell and their consequences was the Oxford-educated, Indian-born poet and journalist Dom Moraes. The son of the editor of the *Times of India*, Moraes had first come to England in 1954 as a sixteen-year-old after a childhood spent in India, Sri Lanka, and Australasia. The youngest winner of the Hawthornden Prize for poetry and married into what he called "an English County family," Moraes described Powell's speech as the moment his self-perception changed. "It suddenly seemed," he wrote, "that he [Powell] was expressing the feeling of the man in the street in England. It seemed to me that the whole of my life here must be based on a false premise, and I suddenly started to think—what about the other poor sods, the million and a half immigrants in this country. I suddenly felt for the first time that I should identify with them."[8] These issues were addressed by Moraes in his own *One Pair of Eyes* called "One Black Englishman," which was first broadcast in December 1968.[9] Moraes wanted to know "to what extent he [could] identify with ordinary immigrants" and then in turn explored "his situation as a colored Englishman who suddenly [felt] he [was] an immigrant."[10] Moraes initially set out his thoughts on how to do this in some "basic ideas" for the production team. He wanted the program to depict "immigrant life as contrasted with [his] own" and include a visit to the English northern city of Bradford, particularly the Lumb Lane area "where hardly a Pakistani ever [saw] a white skin." This would show not simply the area but demonstrate that Moraes in some respects had little in common with the new Commonwealth immigrants: "I do not speak their language, eat their food, or share their interests. I am much more a foreigner amongst them than amongst English people. Yet (and I think this is the key point of the programme), I differ from my white liberal friends in that I can truthfully identify with immigrants. . . . I am a consequence of Powell. I identify with immigrants only when I see them oppressed or verbally attacked. The rest of the time I identify with English friends and family."[11] To highlight this, Moraes wanted the program to begin by establishing his "past milieu."

> This would include stills of my father's house, numerous servants, etc: live films of myself talking to Oxford dons, friends such as James Cameron, etc: if obtainable, film of the Eichmann trial, where I spent 8 months, and of Negro riots in the USA where I was last year. This would establish the following points: I was brought up in a wealthy family which though in India had English habits. I was brought up as a more or less English undergraduate, and later as an English writer and poet. My friends, mainly English, mainly hold, in common with myself, certain views about poetry and are mainly of the liberal left. Thus the persecution of Jews obsessed me for years, the Eichmann trial forming an important point in my life. Similarly I felt as most white liberals do about Negroes in America, the color problem in South Africa, etc.[12]

The importance of the Holocaust to Moraes and his associated sense of identification with the oppressed were both articulated more fully in the commentary for the program itself:

> I suppose I am what's called a liberal intellectual. I tend to identify with the oppressed. I wrote about the Eichmann trial. Day

after day in the hot courtroom in Jerusalem I listened to the details of six million Jewish deaths. I identified with the Jews as I did last year with the rioting negroes in America. I wasn't a Jew or a negro so it was easy and safe to identify with them. My own problem is that I'm an immigrant, a coloured man in England, but I wasn't even aware I had a problem.[13]

Moraes's response was simply one example of how the Holocaust was being referenced more regularly in the years following Eichmann's trial, and often with reference to broader issues of racism and prejudice. For example, a July 1961 edition of *Meeting Point*, the long-running BBC religious program about people and God, prompted the question "What light does [the Eichmann trial] throw on human nature?" The answer took the form of an interview with Dr. Heinrich Grüber, provost of Berlin, who had recently given evidence at Eichmann's trial, followed by discussions on the defense of "only obeying orders," whether Israel had a moral right to try Eichmann, and the underlying causes of the Nazi genocide. Opening the program, Grüber spoke of the help he had received from the Nazis and Eichmann himself, in smuggling Jews out of prewar Germany: "I went to Eichmann thirty or forty times to plead for my Jewish friends—he was always cold, lacking in feeling, and convinced of his own importance. Only once did he show a spark of humanity when I came one evening into his office very tired, he said to me 'Why do you do this for the Jews? They won't thank you for it.' So I told him the story of the Good Samaritan."[14]

Grüber also suggested that the underlying root of the Holocaust was antisemitism, an idea that was taken up by the consultant psychiatrist in the program's final section, although rather than dwell on this, he made connections that suggested other perpetrators for other crimes that extended beyond Nazi Germany: "[Antisemitism is] not in essence a different problem from anti-Negro feeling and we have both to some extent in this country. This whole problem of condemning in other people what we can't stand in ourselves, is really the basic psychological mechanism at the back of this. . . . But of course it's really a worldwide problem, and it's a problem which is just as much in us here as it was in Nazi Germany."[15]

The employment of the Holocaust in this comparative way was not new, not even for the still relatively new medium of television. As early as November

1956, *A Man from the Sun*, John Elliot's groundbreaking drama about "the first wave of West Indian immigrants" in postwar Britain, contained this warning: "If we [the white majority] start treating them [the Caribbean immigrants] like the natives in South Africa, they may end up like the Jews in Hitler's Germany,"[16] a reference that made superficial connections between prejudices old and new at home and abroad. Such comparisons took on a new meaning in the wake of Powell's speech, with television once more capturing those concerns across drama, news, and talk programs. For example, on the evening of May 29, 1968, in an edition of the current affairs magazine show, *Europa*, a program that tried to break down national boundaries by showing television films from every country across Europe, translated into English for the British audience, that week's program considered how Swiss, West German, French, and Dutch television were covering Powell's speech and Britain's "immigration problems," featuring extended extracts from the programs of those other European broadcasters. The sequence from Dutch television included a chaired discussion between Joseph Hunte, Ian Mikardo, and John Pardoe. Mikardo, a Labour MP whose parents were Jewish refugees from tsarist Russia, ascribed those tensions to an economic cause, suggesting that the non-white population of the United Kingdom was being used as a scapegoat. In doing this, he made direct comparisons with Nazi Germany, arguing that it was in this way that "Hitler brought millions of Germans into the Nazi Party" and in turn instilled "militant anti-Semitism" into many "who had never set eyes on a Jew in their lives." In response, Hunte, a member of the West Indian Standing Conference and author of the 1966 *Nigger-Hunting in England?*, a book that exposed the racial bias of police practice, argued that the current prejudice went beyond economic scapegoating, seeing it as more deeply rooted in anti- and pro-white prejudice; else, he asked, why were the "Irish, Dutch, French, Jews and all others" not also considered by the language of the Powellites? In concluding the discussion, the Liberal MP Pardoe called for the immediate end to all forms of discrimination as practiced by landlords, schools and councils. To do so, he said, would come at a considerable financial cost, but, it was one that had to be paid. In fact, he continued, "[C]an we afford not to pay it? What is the alternative? Thirty years ago in another supposedly civilised European country, ordinary decent men and women lay down and buried their heads in the sand and they allowed the waves of irrational fear and prejudice to roll over them. And by so doing they destroyed their country and condemned six-million people to the Final Solution. It couldn't happen here? Couldn't it?"[17]

The East End through Other Eyes

In the summer of 1968, therefore, the persecution and murder of European Jewry was for some people at least an important feature of public debates about race and immigration in the United Kingdom. They were certainly pertinent for Georgia Brown who argued in "Who Are the Cockneys Now?" that those "first generation British" like herself, born to immigrant parents, needed to acknowledge the common ground they shared with the new immigrants, advocating solidarity regardless of place of birth, color, religion, culture or race, and celebrating an increasingly multicultural Britain. It was a central theme of her program, which opened with Brown celebrating the East End as a "great big melting pot" of "all races and colours," which for her meant "chicken soup and warmth and acceptance and enormous ability to change very rapidly."

A similar observation about the area had been made on British television during the days of Brown's childhood when, on the evening of Wednesday July 12, 1939, the BBC had broadcast a forty-five-minute documentary, *East End*. A precursor to Brown's program in some ways, this saw anthropologist and Mass Observation founder Tom Harrisson exploring London's East End, introducing the television audience to "Cockney and Jew, Lascar and Chinaman, and others of its inhabitants." In this program Harrisson too had attempted to capture the great vibrancy of the "huge mixed population [that] has silted up to make the most varied, colourful, confusing hubub in the world."[18] It was a depiction of the East End as a cosmopolitan world that had also been found in A. B. Levy's *East End Story*, a description of the area and particularly the Jewish East End that had first been published in serial form in the *Jewish Chronicle* in 1948. Levy's book contained a chapter, "Our Dark-Skinned Neighbours," which, like Brown's program, focused in part on Hessel Street and Petticoat Lane. Preempting Brown, Levy described how "in recent years" there had been an "increasing number of dark-skinned customers" in the area. These newcomers brought with them "social problems... varying in seriousness according to whether they [were] Indians, West Africans, British West Indians or Maltese." Levy, in language more widespread in the 1940s but unacceptable by the 1960s and irrevocably tainted by association with Powell, wrote of how "down Christian Street . . . some piccaninnies and Jewish tots... busily play[ed] together."[19] More recently, BBC radio had made similar points in *Our East End*, a celebration of the area written and presented by Jo Joseph that featured actors and performers including Lionel Bart, Alfie Bass, Lee Montague, and Georgia Brown herself. This again explored the Jewishness of the area as simply one aspect of the "rich mixture of races and faces, languages, mannerisms, philosophies which co-exist[ed] in every building, in every side street." Indeed, for comedian Bud Flanagan, the East End was always diverse, and that meant that in his lifetime the area didn't change, even if the people did: "I don't think there is any difference, even now. . . . I think the . . . Jewish people in my day, down there, they just strove to get out of the neighbourhood and they did. . . . And then their places were taken by the Maltese, and the Pakistanis. And I was down there recently and it is just the same to me–but with different people."[20]

It was a point also made by Rose Henriques in *50 Years in Stepney*, the serialization of her memoirs broadcast on the Home Service in 1966, in which she considered parts of the East End that would be discussed by Brown two years later: "Our Hessel Street market was formerly almost an enclave of Eastern Europe, with its stalls and shops owned by venerable old Jewish men and women. Today it's more like Marseilles or Port Said. Very few Jewish shopkeepers remain, but every kind of Asian, African, Indian and West Indian spices, vegetables and pulses are on sale by their Commonwealth owners. Add a great proportion of Maltese and Cypriots, and our cosmopolitan population is complete."[21]

Perhaps most similar to Brown's documentary was Robert Vas's 1962 film *The Vanishing Street*. Only nineteen minutes in length, this also captured the Jewish East End around Hessel Street as the area's architecture and demographic started to change, containing many of the same themes, camera angles, and subjects as Brown's film but with a striking difference: whereas Vas created a montage of sound and image without commentary, Brown was the narrator of her journey, guiding the viewer as she moved through the East End inviting others to tell their stories.

WHO WAS GEORGIA BROWN, AND WHO IS LILLIAN KLOT NOW?

Georgia Brown was born Lillian Klot in the largely poor Jewish area of Whitechapel in October 1933. Her grandfather had fled Russia in 1910 to escape pogroms, taking the first ship he could: "It might just as well have been going to New York, but, in fact, arrived at London Docks. It was a shipload of disposed Jews, willing to settle in any country that would take them. Without money they had to move into the poorest and cheapest part of London, into houses that nobody else wanted. The Jewish community of the East End of London grew."[22]

Her professional career started in the early 1950s; she performed standards such as "These Foolish Things," "Begin the Beguine," and "Night and Day" on the stage across Europe. On television she made her debut as a singer on the BBC's *Top Hat* in January 1951, performing "Lover Man," "Saint Louis Blues," and "Georgia on My Mind." Appearances followed in light entertainment and cabaret shows and even in a 1956 episode of *Panorama*, the BBC's flagship current affairs program, that reported on the success of Sam Wanamaker's revival of Brecht/Weill's *Threepenny Opera*, the show that brought Brown to prominence. As an actress she starred as Yvette Pottier in Rudolph Cartier's 1959 version of *Mother Courage and Her Children*, but it was playing Nancy in Lionel Bart's *Oliver!*, a role written for her by her childhood friend, that confirmed her place as a superstar.

To show how much she had changed across that period, "Who Are the Cockneys Now?" opened to the sound of Brown singing "Ta-ra-ra Boom-de-ay," the music hall standard that had once been associated with Lottie Collins, another celebrated Jewish performer, but was now firmly established as part of Brown's repertoire and one of her signature songs. This was played over a medium shot of Brown sitting with her old friend Lionel Bart in the back of an open-top Bentley being driven through Hyde Park and along Park Lane. The car and the location were both indicators of their personal journeys from poverty to international success, a journey that both found hard to explain. As Bart asked with a deliberate double meaning in that opening scene, "What are we doing here, folks? I mean, what is it all about?" Brown's reply was less playful:

> I'm talking about having a look at what's happening down there in the East End, because it seems to me that of late with the whole sort of immigrant situation coming up so strongly in the papers—about what they're going to let in, what they're not going to let in—I suddenly realised that I'm first generation British . . . and that I'm from an immigrant family, and you too, and lots of people we know . . . and it would seem to be that to go back and have a look at what we came from, what we were allowed to do when we were there, what we weren't allowed to do, what opportunities we had, what we did with those opportunities, how many of us had those opportunities and what kind of opportunity is there now.

Brown, that is, was already signaling that her interests were in both present and past, to look back at where she had come from and to see what opportunities there were now and in the future for the new immigrant. To emphasize this visually, the on-screen image cut from the opulent surroundings of Park Lane to the run-down East End streets of Brown's childhood, with the sound bridge of "Ta-ra-ra Boom-de-ay" providing both continuity and contrast between the scenes. Brown was now seen wandering almost wistfully through Black Lion Yard, the "Hatton Garden of the East End," then pictured outside Bullen House in Whitechapel, where, looking directly into the lens, she declared for the camera: "My name's Georgia Brown. I was born here in the East End within the sound of Bow Bells and that makes me a Cockney." For this affirmation of identity, Brown was framed in close-up, the camera showing her gazing confidently out of the screen, looking the audience in the eye. Two very similar shots followed, each time the camera pulling back from close-up to medium shot to reveal Brown in her surroundings as she described the experiences that helped nurture her sense of self. First, while standing outside Deal Street school she spoke of her school years and air-raid shelters before finally, this time framed by the doorway of the Great Garden Street Synagogue on Greatorex Street, she again looked directly into the camera, smiling as she stated clearly, confidently, and with pride: "I'm a Jew. And this was the family synagogue. I haven't been here for seventeen years."

In that opening triptych, therefore, Brown established herself as an East End native, both Cockney and Jew.[23] It also demonstrated the way in which memory, space, place, and identity were linked and the impact that the past had on understanding the present, and vice versa. Throughout the remainder of the program, she would continue to make similar connections, moving from Park Lane to Hessel Street and Petticoat Lane, allowing the camera to share her journey and memories as she interviewed well-known local Jewish figures such as Tubby Isaacs and Jo and Jack Joseph. In the process, she cataloged the area's specifically Jewish past, including the influx of new immigrants from Eastern Europe at the turn of the century, which was told through the lens of her own family as she went from Old Montague St. and St. Katherine's dock to her grandparents' home on Spelman St., a house that was now occupied by immigrant Cypriots.

In this autobiographical and often uncritical account, Brown structured the narrative around the key events of her childhood, including the destruction of Hughes Mansions, the block of flats in Stepney that was struck by a V2 rocket in 1945. It was that tragic loss of life, in conjunction with the inequality between men and women she saw in Great Garden Synagogue as a twelve-year-old, that triggered her movement away from Judaism.[24] After that moment of revelation, Brown found security and safety in theater and performance, particularly performing at Brady Club, the local Jewish youth club group. Brown celebrated this influence by returning to the club with the camera in order to watch her participate in two different events: a prize-giving ceremony and a Holocaust commemoration. Although it is a point not made explicitly in the narrative, the inclusion of these scenes foregrounded the importance of the Holocaust for Brown's conceptualization of what it meant to be a Jew while also providing her with a platform to ask why Brady remained almost exclusively Jewish in spite of the fact that the surrounding area had undergone such a transition.

In covering such a range of subjects, *One Pair of Eyes* is a combination of viewpoints in spite of its title, and yet this array of perspectives seldom includes that of the new Cockney and indeed fails almost entirely to give a voice to the new immigrant, who is largely passive, a piece of scenery rather than active in formulating an opinion of the area or Britain more generally. While it is true that there are many faces seen of the new immigrant, and shop fronts advertising halal food, there is only one interview, with a shopkeeper who is asked first to identify the unusual vegetables he sells. When subsequently asked if he likes it "here," the awkward answer given is simply "It's not bad. . . . I wouldn't say anything else. . . . It's alright."

Brown's focus for the film was really the Jewish past and present. When she returned to Hessel Street and Black Lion Yard to show the new shop fronts and the faces of the new immigrants, she was nostalgic for that past, but it was of course, to a degree, an imagined past. In the wake of Powell, for example, Brown spoke of the East End as containing "a tension which wasn't there before," a point she illustrated with an impromptu conversation with a young housewife. The woman in question told Brown that the only thing to have changed in the area in recent years was "the colour," adding, "I think *we're* in the wrong country, aren't we?" It is another uncomfortable moment in a program full of such encounters.

Writing about that moment in the *Daily Telegraph*, Sean Day-Lewis noted that "something very sinister seemed on the point of happening when a native housewife—with a complexion both political and facial similar to that of Mr Enoch Powell—confronted a group of Pakistanis. But nervous cutting muddled the effect."[25] The cutting may have been nervous, but the effect it created, when understood alongside Brown's commentary, was to expose her fears for the future while simultaneously revealing that this vision of the past was being seen through nostalgic eyes: "All the tension [in the area] erupted yet again when the Dockers marched in support of Enoch Powell's speech. It was terrifying that this could become the East End of the thirties, of the black shirts, the Ridley Road riots. Obviously the Docker has a right to protect his livelihood and has a right to protect his home. But surely we're not going to allow the Pakistanis and the Indians to go through the same thing the Jews did? We must have learnt something from the past."

In that question and observation, Brown connected directly two migrant experiences that were separated by forty years, foregrounding, contrary to her narrative elsewhere, that the Jewish experience of the East End had not always been free from tension. It also seemed to warn that the attitudes of the 1930s were being resurrected, a warning that was made more explicit and more direct in the moments that followed as the screen cut from footage of the Dockers' protests to Brown in conversation with Wolf Mankowitz outside the Royal Albert Hall.

> Mankowitz: If they want to throw the blacks out of the country then that's what they'll do because their constitution gives them a right to do that.... Whether ethics gives them a right to do that is another question, but it's not a political question. What can liberals, humanistic people who feel that this is ethically wrong, do about it? They should be rallying to create a unified force for whatever it is they represent as opposed to the Powell point of view, within the left wing groups and parties that exist, but there's no sign of them doing that at all. In fact, every liberal intellectual you meet is destroyed and distressed by this whole situation and is in a state of shock. Now that state of shock is exactly what happened in Weimar just before Hitler.
>
> Brown: Do you think it's possible that that sort of thing could happen again?
>
> Mankowitz: I think it is happening again, isn't it?
>
> Brown: In what way?
>
> Mankowitz: I mean it's quite clearly the same kind of elements. The same sort of enterprise, political enterprise, is present in the—in this immediate situation vis-à-vis the recent black immigrants.

To underline the point, the interview with Mankowitz was followed by black-and-white archive footage of the East End demonstrations of the 1930s and then images of Oswald Mosley speaking at Belle Vue, Manchester, in 1939. Brown explained what was being seen and its significance: "Oswald Mosley came to the East End in 1936 and he gave kids—poor kids—shirts and shoes to wear. Unfortunately the shirts were black and the shoes marched them against my mother and father. It seems to me that those who have been persecuted must stand up for those who are being persecuted now."

From this narrative and the black-and-white footage of Mosley in full flow, the screen returned to colour, and with it returned to Brady Club, although that was not immediately obvious. Earlier the club had been the site for an awards ceremony, happy memories and celebrations, but now the tone was markedly different. "Who were the victims? Where did they come from?" asked an unidentified voice as the camera panned across a packed room and an audience composed predominantly of young people wearing yellow stars. Once again Brown's commentary supplied the meaning to what was being seen: "Every year at Brady Club there's a ritual memorial service, complete with horror films." Filmed on April 25, 1968, this was Brady's annual Yom HaShoah, Holocaust Remembrance Day. Films showing scenes of liberation were accompanied by readings of witness testimony and victims' accounts, concluding with an extract from Richard Dimbleby's iconic account of the liberation of Belsen in April 1945. This closed the circle, completing the transitioning of the Jewish experience to that of the new immigrant, seemingly Judaizing the new immigrant, in the process suggesting in word and image that there was a potential Holocaust coming, one that would see the persecution and potentially genocide of the non-white immigrant by the British. But whereas one might anticipate that Brown would make explicit the connections and warnings being made by the editing, the program in fact took an unexpected turn to focus not on the prospects of the new Cockney but on the Jewish community and Brown's fears of Jewish insularity:

> Brown: How do you show a teenage Jew the horrors of the past without making him feel inferior, defensive, and ready to isolate himself the way his father did, for the fear that this could happen to him?
>
> Dryer: Basically I think it's something that, as a Jewish organization, as a Jewish club, we feel it's our duty to remind the members today, who had no bearing before the war years, what it was all about.
>
> Brown: What kind of reactions do you seem to have? I mean, does anything happen because of it? Is there any response to it?

> Dryer: It's hard to tell, you know. Immediately afterwards everybody saw the films and they all said how terrible it is. I think you can hear them, you know, the shudder and the intensity of the actual film. A lot of the members feel that it's a terribly important thing, and this is what the club stands for, and this is some of the things that we should be doing.

The program ended with a discussion between some of the Brady Club members about multiculturalism, intermarriage, and whether the club should embrace more non-Jews. Brown's conclusion: "It's the Pakistanis now who are Jews of the East End, isn't it? . . . The Jews have gone through all the same kinds of problems the Pakistanis are going through now. Why should it be so difficult for them to communicate? Why shouldn't it draw them closer together?"

The next week David Attenborough, the controller of BBC2, wrote to Brown to congratulate her on a "marvellous" program, saying that he had returned to work on Monday "full of pride and pleasure" at what was "quite the most moving thing I saw on television over the weekend." The BBC's own internal audience research review recorded that viewers found it "thought-provoking," "revealing and informative." It "was evidently of great interest to three out of every five of the small sample audience," with Brown's "view that the Jews'" place was now being taken by Pakistanis and Indians regarded as "interesting—and to some surprising." The remainder of the responses in the review were, however, less enamored, with complaints pointing out that it looked to the past and the prospects of the Jewish community: in view of the title, it was felt that the program should have enlarged on the present Cockneys ("it seemed to me to be more concerned with 'Judaism' in the East End than with the 'Cockneys'"), and some felt it "lacked continuity" and needed "more interviews with ordinary local people."[26]

As has been seen above, Brown's program was indeed focused more on the Jews of the East End, but the other reviews tended to overlook that point. Philip Purser, for example, writing in the *Sunday Telegraph*, started his review of the weekend's shows with the appearance of Esther Ofarim in her show *Just Esther*, in which she sang in English, Irish, French, German, and Hebrew. Purser linked Ofarim to Brown, noting, "Both are Jewesses, both children of the pogroms and the dispersals of the 20th century." Brown's program, Purser argued, attempted to demonstrate that "the East End has always been a melting pot" and asked not only "what was to prevent the latest wave of immigrants, the Pakistanis, from becoming the next generation of Cockneys?" but also "where was the confidence and the togetherness they needed to accomplish this?" "If her arguments were sometimes . . . simple," he continued, "I warmed to this cheerful, funny, unsentimental girl who instead of trying to make everyone feel guilty about racial prejudice, accepted it and looked at it and hinted how it might be usefully converted."[27] To make his point clearer, he compared Brown's approach to that of the CBS documentary *Of Black America*, which also aired that week, a program that did not advocate assimilation: "So often the programme professing to expose racial prejudice ends up by seeking to inflame it. Ah sweet Georgia Brown, who preached only coolness and wit and assimilation. Thirty years ago it would have mattered hugely that she was Jewish. Hands up all those of you today who even knew she was. And did either of you care?"[28]

Other sections of the mainstream British press focused on Brown's advocacy of integration and assimilation. Michael Billington in *The Times* noted that the program demonstrated "the same urgent need for racial assimilation as before,"[29] while Peter Black in the *Daily Mail* felt that Brown made it clear "that [Brown] distrust[ed] all segregation, even the well-intentioned exclusivity of the Brady community settlements in the East End, where a non-Jew [was] still as uncommon a sight as raspberries at Christmas." He concluded: "Georgia has a decent conviction that those who had been persecuted in the past should stand up for those who are being persecuted now."[30] However it was not all positive. Sean Day-Lewis in the *Daily Telegraph* was critical of "an over-simplified but valid contribution towards the better understanding of racial problems," particularly Brown's use of "the melting pot" which was "a generalisation that exactly contradicted the rest of the programme . . . [which in fact] realistically showed that the East End Jews, far from being dipped into a melting pot, felt obliged to remain apart from the not always friendly natives, and even today still pursue the doctrine of separate development in youth clubs and elsewhere."[31] Brown was also criticized by Hyam Corney in the *Jewish Chronicle*: "While she is rightly concerned for the area's new immigrants . . . it is arguable whether the answer is turning clubs like Brady into multi-racial centres. . . . Her heart is in the right place, only her reasoning is at fault."[32] The subsequent correspondence in the *Jewish Chronicle* sided with Brown. "This presumably is," said the correspondent, "because she showed a real interest in the area's new immigrants and developed the tight exclusiveness of the Jewish clubs and the narrow attitude of the Jewish population. Some of the young people she talked to at the Brady Club agreed with her, but obviously those in charge did not. What is wrong with her attitude of the 'brotherhood of man'?"

The episode was also the subject of a discussion at the BBC weekly program review board. Norman Swallow, one of the foremost TV documentary producers of the period, expressed his reservations about Brown's view of the East End, finding it difficult to decide what was genuine and what was "the result of manipulation by the director." Christopher Ralling, who had joined the BBC in 1955 and would later be the BBC head of documentaries, denied this, arguing that there had been no manipulation and that Brown's commentary was "quite spontaneous," although he too noted that considerable effort had been devoted to the editing.[33] The production folder held at the BBC's Written Archives sheds some light on this, revealing a different filmed but unused sequence in the transcripts of the rushes. One of these shows how Brown and Bart devoted a longer segment in that opening scene to a discussion of what the East End and being Jewish meant to them, along with a discussion of the old and the new. Bart was far more critical of Brown's approach in this unseen section:

> Bart: You're comparing the Jewish bit I presume with the Pakistani and West Indian and . . .
>
> Brown: I'm comparing the immigrant Jew, yes. . . .
>
> Bart: It's entirely different. For openers, at the time our families came over just after the turn of the century more or less the British Empire was at the height of its time . . . And there were great opportunities for everybody. Also you've got to remember, as far as the Jewish bit is concerned . . . the rest of our families have been here . . . [for two hundred or three hundred years].

It is then Bart who argues that what made success possible for the immigrant Jew was "an establishment . . . that had power, and anybody that wanted to make good, could make good." However, he does not mean the Jewish establishment but "the British Empire." The difference for immigrants now is that they can only take menial jobs, and that means not unlocking their full potential. Bart is, however, overwhelmingly positive about Britain, calling it "the most civilised firm in the world."[34]

The production folders also show that Brown's memories of growing up included a visit to a kosher slaughterhouse—a scene that would have further strengthened the similarities to Vas's *Vanishing Street*. According to the surviving documents, Brown was horrified to see chickens being killed, and it was that scene that was to lead to the shots of the interior of the Great Garden Synagogue, where the camera picked out the Klot family plaques. It also included an interview with Rabbi Shaposnik, during which Brown questioned the relevance of the synagogue in modern Jewish life. In this version, it was that discussion rather than the footage of contemporary tensions that was to precede the Yom HaShoah memorial service, a markedly different juxtaposition. That remembrance service was to be followed by Brown's conversation with Brady manager, David Dryer. Again the longer transcripts reveal the extent to which Brown was questioning the club's continued preference for Jewish members: "Don't you think you've encouraged it [antisemitism]? I mean being separate, making yourself separate, making yourself unattainable, or making yourself a group. Don't you think this encourages antisemitism because we can soon reach or perpetrate the feeling that we're 'other than.'"[35]

It was only at that point that Brown was to return to her memories of the war, of her evacuation to Wales, the bombing of Hughes Mansion and filmed shots of the local Jewish cemetery where many of the dead were buried. The programme would then return to Brady for the prize-giving and questioning of the current members of intermarriage and Jewish segregation, ending with the shots of Petticoat Lane, Hessel Street and the Jewish dispersal.

Who Are the Jews Now?

While there are clearly flaws in the logic and the editing, Anthony Searle's film in combination with Brown's narrative is thoughtful, evocative, and provocative. It did occasionally slip into the sentimental and the nostalgic. Moreover, it failed to give any depth or substance to the Asian immigrant, most noticeably to the extent that there was neither any extended interview with the new immigrant nor any direct engagement with Islam and what it meant to be a Muslim, even though Brown was interested in religion and culture as unifying forces. But there is a clear political message that captures the contemporary concerns and delivers the uncomfortable message that Britain was no longer safe for the wrong kind of immigrant. This was more explicit in sections not included in the final cut. As Brown lamented in one of those extracts, while it's "all very well for the Jewish teenagers to be shown" the images of liberation "year after year," she would like these to be shown to the striking dockers "every year, every month, every week if necessary." Powell's viewpoint and the support of the dockers was "so against everything that England means to me, so against every human feeling that I felt this could be Hitler's manifesto all over again. It could be Germany of the thirties."

The program asked, "Who are the Cockneys now?," highlighting the changing nature of the area's demographic in light of postwar movements and migrations, but in fact it actually addressed the question "Who are the Jews now?" The answer was twofold: the Jews were now integrated and prosperous, British, and responsible for policies of inclusion and support, but the Jews were now also the non-white Commonwealth immigrants, recently arrived in the United Kingdom and facing levels of intolerance that were, the program implied, the first steps on the path to genocide.

NOTES

1. James Jordan and Tom Lawson, eds., *The Memory of the Holocaust in Australia* (London: Vallentine Mitchell, 2008).
2. Prime Minister Kevin Rudd to the Parliament of Australia, Apology to Australia's Indigenous peoples, February 13, 2008, www.australia.gov.au/about-australia/our-country/our-people/apology-to-australias-indigenous-peoples.
3. "Who Are the Cockneys Now?," *One Pair of Eyes*, with Georgia Brown, directed by Anthony Searle, BBC2, tx. August 17, 1968. Unless otherwise stated, all quotes are taken directly from the program itself. In the United Kingdom, this can be viewed at www.bbc.co.uk/iplayer/episode/p00t3mkz/one-pair-of-eyes-georgia-brown-who-are-the-cockneys-now.

4. "Georgia Brown on 'Who Are the Cockneys Now?,'" *Radio Times*, August 15, 1968, 7.
5. "The Road to Kingdom Come," *One Pair of Eyes*, with James Cameron, directed by Richard Marquand, BBC, tx. September 23, 1967; "No, but Seriously," *One Pair of Eyes*, with Marty Feldman, directed by Francis Megahy, BBC, tx. June 7, 1969; and "A Region of Shadow," *One Pair of Eyes*, with Laurens van der Post, directed by Stephen Cross, BBC, tx. July 10, 1971.
6. George Rosie, "Anthony Grey: 'I learned what really matters'; Van der Post: 'We all have a dark man inside us,'" *Radio Times*, June 24, 1971, 6.
7. Enoch Powell, MP, "Rivers of Blood" speech, April 20, 1968, www.telegraph.co.uk/comment/3643823/Enoch-Powells-Rivers-of-Blood-speech.html.
8. Dom Moraes, "One Pair of Eyes," *Radio Times*, August 14, 1969, 21.
9. "One Black Englishman," *One Pair of Eyes*, with Dom Moraes, directed by Francis Megahy, BBC2, tx. December 21, 1968. See also Sarita Malik, *Representing Black Britain: A History of Black and Asian Images on British Television* (London: Sage, 2002); and Graziano Krätli, "Crossing Points and Connecting Lines: Nissim Ezekiel and Dom Moraes in Bombay and Beyond," *Journal of Postcolonial Writing* 53, nos. 1–2, 176–89, doi.org/10.1080/17449855.2017.1283746.
10. Dom Moraes, "One Black Englishman," *Radio Times*, December 19, 1968, 5.
11. BBC WAC T56/202, *One Pair of Eyes: One Black Englishman*, "Basic Ideas," 1. BBC Written Archives Centre, Caversham, England.
12. BBC WAC T56/202, "Basic Ideas," 1.
13. BBC WAC T56/202, *One Pair of Eyes: One Black Englishman*, "Commentary," 10. BBC Written Archives Centre, Caversham, England.
14. *Meeting Point: The Eichmann Trial*, produced by Oliver Hunkin, BBCtv, tx. July 30, 1961, genome.ch.bbc.co.uk/72ac2bdfa9f54bb2a3715e0c7bece9b0.
15. *Meeting Point*.
16. *A Man from the Sun*, directed by John Elliot (uncredited), BBCtv, tx. November 8, 1956.
17. *Europa*, May 29, 1968, BBC WAC TV Talks Scripts 1965–70, Film 7/8. BBC Written Archives Centre, Caversham, England.
18. For more on Harrisson's program, see James Jordan, "'The Most Varied, Colourful, Confusing Hubub in the World': The East End, Television and the Documentary Imagination, July 1939," in *Migrant Britain: Histories from the 17th to the 21st Centuries*, ed. Jennifer Craig-Norton, Christhard Hoffmann, and Tony Kushner (London: Routledge, 2018).
19. A. B. Levy, *East End Story* (London: Vallentine Mitchell, 1951).

20. *Our East End*, BBC Home Service, tx. January 16, 1962.
21. *50 Years in Stepney*, BBC Home Service, episode 5, tx. January 21, 1966.
22. "Georgia Brown on 'Who Are the Cockneys Now?'"
23. This was in marked contrast to *East End* thirty years before in which Tom Harrisson clearly considered Cockney and Jew as two separate categories of "race," which did not overlap.
24. Brown did not consider herself to be "a religious Jew" and indeed viewed Jewishness "more as a race than a religion," something that was evident throughout "Who Are the Cockneys Now?" See Pamela Melnikoff, "What Yom Kippur Means to Me," *Jewish Chronicle* (London), September 27, 1968, 24; and Pamela Melnikoff, "Sweet Georgia Brown: From Brady to Stardom," *Jewish Chronicle* (London), December 22, 1961, 29.
25. Sean Day-Lewis, "Singer Recalls Her Childhood in Stepney,"*Daily Telegraph* (London), August 19, 1968.
26. BBC WAC R9/7/94, Audience Research Reports Television, VR/68/500, "One Pair of Eyes." BBC Written Archives Centre, Caversham, England.
27. Philip Purser, "In White and Black," *Sunday Telegraph* (London), August 18, 1968.
28. Purser, "In White and Black."
29. Michael Billington, "What Makes Actors Tick?" *Times* (London), August 19, 1968.
30. Peter Black, "The Only Silly Thing about Lillian Klot Is Georgia Brown," *Daily Mail* (London), August 19, 1968.
31. Day-Lewis, "Singer Recalls Her Childhood in Stepney."
32. Hyam Corney, "Georgia Goes Back East," *Jewish Chronicle* (London), August 23, 1968, 23.
33. BBC Programme Review board minutes, August 21, 1968, 4, minute 236.
34. BBC WAC T56/197, Television Documentaries, "One Pair of Eyes, Who Are the Cockneys Now?," 3, 4, 5. BBC Writing Archives Centre, Cavensham, England.
35. BBC WAC T56/197.

7

"A Straight and Not Very Long Road"

American Jews, Apartheid, and the Holocaust

Marjorie N. Feld

FIVE YEARS AFTER THE end of World War II, the left-leaning editors of the English-language *Labor Israel* expressed their disappointment that some South African Jews supported Prime Minister Daniel F. Malan, leader of South Africa's National Party, a principal architect of apartheid and a supporter of Hitler during World War II. The editors for the monthly periodical of the socialist Zionist organization Hashomer Hatzair (Youth Guard) had long condemned colonialist oppression in Africa, including the rise of South African apartheid.[1] They offered a stinging critique of Malan: "The South African Nationalists are persecuting the African people on the false grounds of racial superiority. But 'White v. Black' is merely the thin end of the wedge, as American Jewry know to their cost." The editors drew lessons from the Holocaust in attacking apartheid: "There is a straight and not very long road between sneering at "n-----s" and gassing Jews," they wrote, lamenting that "many leading South African Jews, judging from their nauseating praise of Malan, seem[ed] as yet unaware of this elementary truth."[2]

These and other Western Jews on the left drew from Holocaust consciousness in their anticolonialist activism. They did not shy away from attacking other members of Jewish communities—including leaders of Jewish South Africa and of Israel—for allying with imperialism and racism.[3] Indeed, liberal and left Jews in South Africa rejected Malan as well as Jewish communal leaders who supported his National Party, and they opposed apartheid in part by citing the universalist lessons of the Holocaust.[4] In Israel's first decades, its leaders also drew from these same ideas as they built commercial ties to independent black African nations and repeatedly supported anti-apartheid resolutions in the United Nations. Foreign Minister Golda Meir consistently drew parallels "between the "common history" of Jews who have been subject to persecution and various forms of prejudice and the sufferings and prejudice encountered by the colored people of Africa."[5] Into the 1960s, lessons of the Holocaust still served as the foundation of the alliance between Israeli and other Western Jews and black Africa, in support of black independent nations and in opposition to all forms of prejudice: "For us, the Jews," said Joel Barromi, Israeli representative at the United Nations, in 1961, "the question of apartheid is first and foremost a matter of principle and of conscience. It is a facet of our impassioned condemnation of each and every form of racial discrimination." The editors of *Israel Horizons* (the second incarnation of *Labor Israel*) agreed that Israel could not "do otherwise." "Apartheid is wrong," they wrote. "To fight it is an imperative."[6] They praised Israel for being "on the side of the angels" on this issue and noted that "a Jewish State, the haven of so many refugees from the worst Holocaust a people has ever known, cannot condone racial discrimination anywhere."[7]

American Jewish leaders' stands on civil rights, apartheid, and colonialism were inextricably tied to their positions on Zionism and Israel, and, to borrow a phrase from Hasia Diner, the Holocaust served as the "background, context, and justification" for all these issues. However, this assessment of the Holocaust's prominence in shaping a "liberal agenda" for American Jews in the postwar period rests almost exclusively on historians' analyses of domestic issues.[8] On the world stage, and especially beyond Jewish areas of interest and influence such as Israel and Soviet Jewry, American Jews never reached a consensus on how the lessons of the Holocaust would apply to global issues such as South African apartheid. Should American Jews follow the lead of Hashomer Hatzair members, calling out injustice even when it threatened Jewish unity by potentially placing South African Jews in harm's way? Or should Jews around the world come together at all costs, fortifying Jewish existence, difference, and futures through unity, even if that meant silencing intracommunal criticism for the sake of those urgent priorities?

Immediately after World War II, Western Jews debated whether protesting apartheid—and implicitly criticizing South African Jews who supported white supremacy—would be an act of betrayal of Western Jewish unity or whether the failure to speak up would be a betrayal of core Jewish commitments to social justice; whether such protests were necessary in light of the Nazi Holocaust or whether they imprudently threatened the relationship between American and South African Jews and, later, American Jews and Israel. After 1967, as Israel faced increasing international isolation and built an alliance with apartheid South Africa, these questions grew more pressing. Israeli and other Jewish leaders flipped Golda Meir's analogy, arguing that the Holocaust's destruction lent the greatest urgency to Jewish survival and that Israel must pursue "security" with all nations and national groups at any cost. Activists in the United States and South Africa who linked their Jewishness to universalistic causes such as anti-apartheid were put on the defensive and often marginalized by mainstream Jewish leaders in the late 1960s and 1970; railing against leaders who said they had "true" Jewish communal interests in mind, these activists were sometimes even likened to Nazis.[9]

The powerful global anti-apartheid movement forced a reckoning with this complex legacy in the 1980s. It was then that mainstream American Jewish leaders once again tapped into Holocaust memory to support their return to anti-apartheid activism. Indeed, this shift back to a more universalist stance mirrored what was occurring among South African and other Western Jewish communities as well.[10]

Along with other developments in the United States and abroad, these events set the stage for a series of contests over apartheid and the legacies of the Holocaust, contests that continue in contemporary, high-stakes debates over the use of the word *apartheid* in Israel/Palestine.[11] These contests demonstrate the shifting role that Holocaust memory still plays in shaping contemporary Jewish identity and Jewish commitments to liberation movements in the United States and in the wider world.

American Jews, South African Apartheid, and Civil Rights

As evidenced by the editorials in *Labor Israel* and *Israel Horizons*, contests over apartheid and Holocaust memory for Western Jews began in the early 1950s, just as South African leaders began to build the apartheid state. In 1954, India and other nations newly freed from colonialism flexed their power in the United Nations, proposing a strong anti-apartheid resolution that came across the desk of all nongovernmental organizations (NGOs), including the World Jewish Congress (WJC), which had been founded in Europe in August 1936. A stormy debate ensued among WJC leaders about whether or not to support the anti-apartheid resolution, with those on both sides of the issue referencing the lessons of the Holocaust. British rabbi Maurice Perlzweig felt strongly that these lessons lay in Jewish unity, and, importantly, the WJC was at that moment courting the membership of the South African Jewish community. Though his regret was "deep and genuine," he felt that not supporting the anti-apartheid measure was "inevitable in view of our relationship with" the South African Jewish community.[12] "It would manifestly be a very foolish thing for us to send a highly critical document on South Africa to the U.N., and it would certainly wreck the hope of doing anything in regard to affiliation," he wrote. Using language indicative of his powerful feelings of allegiance to world Jewry, Perlzweig asserted that South African Jewish leaders "would rightly regard it as a betrayal" if American Jews were to speak out against apartheid.[13]

American Jewish leader David Petegorsky responded to Perlzweig with "vigorous protest." "The refusal of the WJC ... on one of the worst cases of racial segregation in the world cannot be regarded simply as a matter of expediency," Petegorsky wrote. "It seems to me to go to the very heart of the principles for which we stand." He inserted a reference to the American civil rights movement and to Jewish organizational involvement in a pivotal event within US borders in 1954, the case of *Brown v. the Board of Education of Topeka, Kansas*. "You may not be aware of the fact," he wrote to Perlzweig,

> that last year, the AJ [American Jewish] Congress filed a brief amicus in the segregation case before the Supreme Court. A

> delegation of three Jews from the South came to New York ... to demand that we withdraw our brief and threatened that if we did not ... we would be denied allocations from Welfare Funds in the South. [We] promptly told them that while [we] had no idea how we would be financially affected, this was to us a matter of basic principle and we could under no circumstances yield to any such demands.[14]

Petegorsky followed the lead of American Jews who drew from Jewish teachings and Holocaust consciousness in asserting a place for Jews in the civil rights movement, and he put the anti-apartheid struggle in line with that activism, no matter its impact on Jewish unity.[15]

Rabbi Joachim Prinz, a towering figure in the American civil rights movement who had been expelled from Nazi Germany, sounded off to Perlzweig six years later, in 1960, when the debate flared up again. He had recently organized and led a picket line at the Woolworth's on New York's Fifth Avenue, drawing attention to the practices of racial segregation at its southern stores. Just as British and French Jews have the right to "criticize the United States for its failure to implement the Supreme Court decision on segregation in the public schools," Prinz reasoned, American Jews can speak out about apartheid. He called it "a matter of deep Jewish concern" and cited his own experiences in Germany, when American Jews spoke out about Hitler. "We will not be silent in the face of any injustice that we feel is being committed."[16]

With few exceptions, Jewish communal leaders spoke of protecting South African Jews from any reprisals from their own government. The desire to court South African membership in the WJC along with the urgent sense of a need for Jewish unity kept most American Jews from taking strong, public stands against South African apartheid. Though many radical South African Jews were active in the anti-apartheid movement, members of that nation's organized Jewish community remained silent on apartheid, positioning themselves as vulnerable to loyalty tests and perhaps other forms of discrimination should they or other members of the Jewish diaspora actively oppose apartheid.[17] The debates that ensued between Prinz and Petegorsky, on one side, and Perlzweig, on the other, demonstrate the centrality of Holocaust memory to all sides of American Jewish contests over apartheid, universalism, and particularism, even in these early years.

Throughout the 1960s and '70s, mainstream American and other Western Jewish leaders shifted away from the universalist perspective that linked the Holocaust to civil rights and anti-apartheid stands. Instead, they increasingly embraced a more strident particularism, arguing that the paramount importance of Jewish unity left little room for opposition to white supremacy. The new, inward-facing agendas of mainstream American Jewish organizations were a crucial component of this shift. As scholar Stuart Svonkin explains, the intergroup relations project that occupied the energies of these organizations immediately after the war had explicitly linked the struggle against Nazism to struggles against all kinds of prejudice. The civil rights work of Prinz and Petegorsky and their protests against South African Jews for their silence on apartheid drew as much on their sense of Jewish loyalty as from their liberal, universalist commitments. By the 1960s, however, the "paradigm of intergroup relations established during the 1940s and '50s was no longer adequate."[18] Socioeconomic mobility brought many American Jews closer to the privileged majority, so the case for a shared fate with disadvantaged groups weakened. Increased assimilation made Israel central to American Jewish visibility in ways that had a profound impact on the brands of Zionism American Jews embraced in the following decades, and that then affected American Jews' positions on the anti-apartheid movement.

American Jewish positions on apartheid were also affected by changes in black/Jewish relations. Cold War activists across the world linked liberation struggles against colonialism in nations such as Algeria and Vietnam to the global struggles of all oppressed people, and US black nationalists joined this Third World movement in fighting white supremacy. Criticisms of Israel among these activists sometimes veered into blatant antisemitism. The promulgation of such ideas in African American organizations particularly alienated liberal Jews, as did the purging of whites, including Jews, from civil rights coalitions with the rise of the Black Power movement in the mid-1960s. Tensions between African Americans and American Jews also rose in these years owing to their encounters in urban neighborhoods, with Jews amply represented among landlords and business owners when civil rights activists protested high rents and prices as well as consumer fraud.[19] While once invoking the Holocaust as the motivation for their liberal and left activism, many American Jews came to feel uncomfortable, even unsafe, in civil Rights coalitions, and thus they departed organizations active in anti-apartheid campaigns.

Finally, the impact of the 1967 war in Israel on all American Jews cannot be overstated, perhaps especially with the defining, even urgent, postwar quest for Jewish unity among Jewish leaders. "The fateful period before, during, and immediately following the Six Day War in June 1967," writes historian Jonathan Sarna, "jolted the American Jewish community from [its] universalistic agenda" of social justice and militarism, of fighting for Civil Rights and against the war in Vietnam.[20] As Arab troops massed on Israel's borders, Jews around the world experienced tremendous anxiety over that nation's future, invoking the Holocaust as they expressed their fear of another "abandonment of the Jews."[21]

In the wake of the war, many Western Jews reconfigured their theological and political commitments to become a part of this shift away from universalism. Increasingly, Jews in the United States expressed their Jewishness through community building, religious observance, and unquestioning support of Israel while dismissing those who linked Jewish teachings to social justice, antiwar, civil rights, and anticolonial campaigns. Liberal and left American Jews who continued to embrace these campaigns as Jews, at times criticizing Israel's policies, faced accusations: they were traitors to the Jewish community, consumed by self-hatred, and they harbored communist sympathies and were unconcerned with the future of the Jewish people. "By the late 1960s," writes historian Michael Staub, who documents this turn comprehensively, "[i]t was scarcely possible to speak in an uncomplicated way about the direct relationship between Judaism and justice."[22]

Human rights scholar Michael Galchinsky also argues that the 1960s marked the end of the "honeymoon between Jews and international human rights." Suburbanization contributed to this move "away from their traditional liberal stance toward conservatism," as did the increasingly vocal, international criticism of Israel by global human rights bodies, which came to see Israel's policies, especially its occupation, as outgrowths of colonialism. "Since the 1970s," Galchinsky writes, "Jews have found repeatedly that they have had to choose between commitments to human rights and Israel."[23] As human rights groups came to follow the lead of anticolonialist activists, linking Israel and

South Africa in their global critiques, American Jews had to choose sides in their struggles over apartheid.

In short, Israel and Holocaust memory emerged as central to the calculus of American Jewish positions on apartheid and human rights. If "never again" served as the bedrock to twentieth-century human rights discourses, seeking to protect all "Jews"—a universal stand-in for victims—from genocide, then the implications for Israel were twofold and opposing. On the one hand, linking Israel's existence to the Holocaust made Israel's actions exempt from the protections of human rights discourses (i.e., Israel must do what it has to do to prevent another Holocaust, including joining forces with apartheid regimes and abusing the human rights of Palestinians in order to protect a Jewish future). On the other hand, Israel's claim to victimhood also encouraged individuals to hold Israel to a higher standard of conduct (i.e., Jews have learned their lessons firsthand about oppression and oppressors and now must not stand in for Nazi oppressors in abusing any group or people). South African apartheid—and particularly Israel's commercial and military relationship with the apartheid regime—brought this tension into sharp relief and played a crucial role in conversations about Jewishness and Zionism throughout the world.[24]

AMERICAN JEWS, SOUTH AFRICAN APARTHEID, AND ISRAEL

Despite the profound nature of these clashes over apartheid and Jewishness, over the meanings of "never again" for the anti-apartheid movement, these debates took place largely out of view. American Jewish presses dedicated little space to apartheid during the 1960s and '70s. The few public airings of contests among Jews about apartheid and Israel in this period made clear that the usage of Holocaust consciousness had clearly shifted from the postwar perspective of Prinz and Petegorsky. Though once the Holocaust meant that American Jews had no choice but to actively oppose apartheid—"never again" taking on a universal meaning—now the Holocaust was likened to anti-Israel hostility among the Arab world, Palestinians, and their Third World allies. "Never again" served as the justification for mainstream Jewish leaders' taking care of their own: overlooking or defending the growing commercial alliance between Israel and South Africa as key to Israel's (and thus Jewish) survival and stepping outside American coalitions against apartheid in fear of anti-Israel and antisemitic sentiment.

American Jews with diverse positions on Israel and Zionism who wanted to protest apartheid, who felt allied with global and domestic anticolonialist movements *as Jews*, were left with few places to go. Those who continued to link their Jewishness and the idea of "never again" to universalist positions such as anti-apartheid often also leveled criticisms of Israel's occupation and advocated for dialogue with Palestinian groups. The refusal of mainstream Jewish organizations to hear these positions meant that these American Jews had to take their activism to alternative Jewish organizations, often working in local chapters of the progressive, multi-issue, feminist, LGBTQ-inclusive New Jewish Agenda.[25]

American Jews who inextricably linked their Jewishness to their anti-apartheid activism frequently had to leave the world of organized Jewry to join the movement. After being removed from the speakers' list of the American Jewish Congress "because [he] was using the term "Palestinian" prematurely," Peter Weiss, a lawyer and human rights activist, worked against apartheid exclusively as a leader of the American Committee on Africa.[26] Rabbi Sharon Kleinbaum, a lifelong human rights activist and rabbi of the largest LGBT synagogue, felt alienated by the political conservatism and homophobia of campus Jewish organizations when in college, and she led Barnard and Columbia (secular) student protests against apartheid.[27] Former Manhattan borough president and New York City mayoral candidate Ruth Messinger, who recently ended her twenty-year leadership of the American Jewish World Service, "had plenty of differences with the organized Jewish community" in the 1980s, consistently hoping to see "rabbis take more vibrant stands, federations and synagogues get more involved" in world issues, instead of focusing so exclusively on American Jewish assimilation and Israel.[28] She worked for the divestment of New York municipal funds from South Africa as a member of the city council, and she ran for the Harvard Board of Overseers as a candidate representing Harvard and Radcliffe Alumni/ae against Apartheid, a group that worked tirelessly to convince Harvard to divest.[29] These activists' departure from the Jewish world spoke to the emerging realpolitik among American Jews.

These activists had only to tune into formal conversations at the United Nations in New York to understand the contours of this changing realpolitik.

Israeli ambassadors there tapped into the uses of Holocaust memory, first to deny and then to reinforce the necessity of the new arrangement in which Israel buffered its declining reputation and downplayed its shift in Cold War allegiances from independent black African nations to apartheid South Africa. In 1980, with commercial and military cooperation between the two nations in full swing, Ambassador Yehuda Z. Blum, permanent representative of Israel to the United Nations, defended Israel (in bad faith) against those who testified to the emerging Cold War alliance.[30] "Once again I wish to reaffirm from this rostrum Israel's long-standing opposition to the concept and policies of apartheid," he stated.

> Our own national identity was forged in the crucible of persecution. Our people spent hundreds of years in ghettoes, in Europe and elsewhere, subject to humiliating and discriminatory laws, to vicious pogroms and to a succession of expulsions. Within the memory of many in this Assembly hall, the Jewish people were victims of the ultimate expression of racism and racial discrimination, the maniacal and methodical massacre of six million persons whose only crime was to be born of Jewish parents or grandparents.

Thus Blum spoke for Israel with "deep moral conviction and from bitter experience when [he] declare[d] yet again before this Assembly that Israel [would] give to bigotry no sanction, to persecution no assistance."[31]

Blum's successor as Israel's permanent representative to the United Nations was Benjamin Netanyahu. He too had to respond to reports linking Israel to South Africa. Netanyahu labeled the "Israel-baiting" as "so much part of the proceedings" of the United Nations that he assumed many of his listeners could "barely suppress a yawn." To defend Israel from these accusations, Netanyahu noted that "Israel categorically condemns racism in all its forms, including *Apartheid*"; invoking the Holocaust, he asserted that "we are a people who have suffered more from racism, murderous racism, than any other."[32]

The comments that followed marked the turning of the tide away from universalist uses of Holocaust memory, for Netanyahu hoped to win the contest over victimhood in order to open up the opportunity to engage in Cold

War battles. He dismissed Israeli trade with South Africa as "scarcely visible" against the "substantial commerce" between South Africa and "the Soviet bloc, but especially the massive trade with Arab countries." He went still further, urging that "the nations of Black Africa [most of whom had by now cut all ties with Israel] not be sidetracked by the Arab campaign of vilification against Israel," warning that the anti-apartheid movement would suffer for singling out Israel so unfairly.[33] Americans listening in on Netanyahu's speech heard a new, Cold War paradigm utilizing Holocaust memory and "never again" to divert attention from Israel's trade with apartheid South Africa.

The clearest, most profound, and most far-reaching example of the new paradigm exemplified by the words of Israel's ambassadors was South African prime minister John Vorster's April 1976 visit to Yad Vashem, the Holocaust Memorial in Jerusalem, on his official state visit to Israel.[34] People around the world saw this visit as crucial evidence of Israel's growing ties to South Africa's apartheid regime.[35] The visit turned the Holocaust analogy on its head: a former Nazi supporter, architect of South African apartheid, visited Israel's Holocaust memorial to crystallize South Africa's trading partnership with Israel, born in the aftermath of the Holocaust. The symbolism of Vorster's visit, his presence at what many considered a sacred site of historical memory, prompted visceral responses from across the world. For American Jews and others who worked against apartheid, the visit prompted nothing short of disgust.

Though only a small group of powerful Israeli leaders supported the apartheid regime, the complicated relationship between Israel and South Africa grew harder to ignore after Vorster's visit.[36] To Israel's allies *and* critics, Vorster's visit offered evidence, or further confirmation, of Zionism's connection to racism, recorded in UN resolution 3379 of 1975 and vigorously protested by Israel and its allies throughout the world.[37] The *New York Times* recorded the strong criticism of Vorster's visit by global leaders: the Dutch government issued a statement saying "that the visit would complicate the efforts of Israel's friends abroad to persuade the world that there is no connection between Zionism and racism"; the Organization of African States, the Arab League, and the Soviet Party paper *Pravda* also condemned the visit.[38] An editorial in the *Ghanaian Times* read: "Israel's active cooperation with South Africa makes it impossible for any African country which is committed to the African Liberation Movement to extend sympathy to its cause in the

Middle East."³⁹ Eastern bloc and African nations consistently drew attention to Israel's military, commercial, and economic ties to apartheid South Africa, their strongest enemy on the continent.⁴⁰ Vorster's visit to Israel made their criticisms still louder, more urgent, and more powerful.

To individuals and groups around the world who were committed to the independence, integrity, and stability of black Africa, these links—between Palestinians and black South Africans, between Zionism and apartheid/racism—grew harder to ignore. Some African American presses reprinted a *Time* magazine article on the "blossoming relationship between South Africa and Israel" even as others printed the American Jewish organizations' defensive arguments over this relationship: their insistence that other nations' trade with apartheid South Africa was far more noteworthy and that "the singling out of Israel" for wrongdoing was unjust.⁴¹ African American leaders in US anti-apartheid and other anti-colonialist efforts noted how the visit from Vorster would only enhance anti-Israel feelings in the Third World.

American Jewish responses to Vorster's visit to Africa fell along predictable lines. The matter was marginalized by mainstream Jewish leaders who invoked Holocaust memory only in conversations about intracommunal Jewish issues such as assimilation and Jewish invisibility; left political activists, however, offered their impassioned criticisms of the visible linkages among the Holocaust, Israel, and apartheid. The left Zionist journal *New Outlook* editorialized Vorster's visit as "both wrong and stupid," asserting that such an alliance cut against Israel's "long range interest" and its "true interests" in the "development, survival, and well-being of the peoples of Asia and Africa, all opponents of the South African racist regime."⁴² *Jewish Currents*, edited by communist, historian, and educator Morris Schappes, noted the building up of military ties between Israel and South Africa and dismissed the statement made by an Israeli cabinet minister that said "there [was] no ideological significance to our trade relations." Most strongly, he stated succinctly and finally: "Whatever diplomatic reasons Israel may have, U.S. Jews should resist being sucked into South African tourism or weakening opposition to apartheid."⁴³

Jewish students active in the liberation movements of the 1960s and '70s also sounded off about the symbolic weight of Vorster's visit. University of California–Berkeley student David Hammerstein wrote a frank assessment of Israel's relationship with South Africa in the *Jewish Radical*, published by students in Berkeley's left-leaning Radical Jewish Union. He began his piece by evoking Vorster's visit to Yad Vashem in order to document the dramatic and striking parallels between Nazi Germany's racialism and that of the apartheid regime in South Africa, as well as the growing alliance between the two nations in the 1970s. "Israel, a country founded upon the ashes of Jewish victims of racism, has, in the last ten years, dramatically strengthened its diplomatic, commercial, and military ties with the most racist country in the world, South Africa. At a time when much of the world has begun to disengage from ties with South Africa, Israel is basing a major part of its future on an alliance with the apartheid regime."[44]

Students at Brandeis University in Massachusetts also contributed to the anti-apartheid movement in the wake of Vorster's visit. Brandeis's unique origins as a Jewish-sponsored, nonsectarian university, its large undergraduate Jewish population, and its myriad other ties to the American Jewish community made it, in many ways, appear as a microcosm of the larger American Jewish world in its responses to apartheid. Jewish newspapers throughout the United States covered the tensions that flared throughout Brandeis's anti-apartheid movement. Students accused administrators of holding a "wait and see" attitude toward divestment and apartheid, when that attitude was "historically implicated in the murder of six million Jews in World War II."[45] The student senate in particular noted that Brandeis, "with its heritage built on the legacy of the Holocaust, should be especially sensitive to the urgency of [apartheid]."[46]

Rabbi Albert Axelrad, Brandeis's progressive chaplain and B'nai B'rith Hillel director, made this linkage explicit, calling apartheid "the single most heinous, nefarious outrage to have been perpetrated on members of the human family since the horrors of Nazism. It is both morally and educationally inappropriate," he wrote, "for a university, especially ours, rooted as it is in the history and values of the Jewish people, to accept funding which accrues from such an atrocious system, thereby participating in propping it up and perpetuating it."[47] Active in politically progressive campaigns, Rabbi Axelrad had long advocated for full divestment, submitting a resolution to the Massachusetts Board of Rabbis in April 1978 for all Jewish individuals and institutions to boycott South African products.[48] He too walked a fine line, simultaneously recording his defense of Israel's trade with South Africa with his strong anti-apartheid position.⁴⁹ While asserting that he did "lament and deplore Israeli trade with oppressive regimes"—from South Africa to Nicaragua—he noted that Israel had few options for survival. Citing a statement from the Union of American Hebrew Congregations, the organization of the US Reform movement, Axelrad enumerated South African, Israeli, and American Jewish contributions to fighting apartheid, and warned of those who would "co-opt" the movement, "seeking the delegitimization and diplomatic isolation of Israel." He praised the "integrity and decency" of Brandeis's means of protest for not devolving into "unjustifiable and unnecessarily divisive sidetracking and recrimination." Axelrad concluded by expressing his hope that Brandeis's contributions to the global movement would have a "salutary influence" and that all could be "collaborators in creative and dogged struggle" in seeking to "rid the world of the unspeakable evil" of apartheid.⁵⁰

American Jews against Apartheid

Though Israel retained ties to leaders of the apartheid regime in South Africa into the early 1990s, even after the end of apartheid, the growing momentum and strength of the global anti-apartheid movement by the mid-1980s meant that mainstream Jewish groups began to line up their support for the cause.⁵¹ The paradigm of Holocaust consciousness among Western mainstream Jewish communal leaders shifted back again, in line with the rhetoric of activists once marginalized: now the historical Jewish lessons in suffering and loss translated to an alliance with anti-apartheid activists. Indeed, Jewish organizational leaders' statements opposing apartheid nearly all reference the Holocaust in these years. The National Jewish Community Relations Advisory Council, the umbrella group for major Jewish organizations, adopted a position paper on apartheid in 1989 that read: "Our own experiences through the millennia of suffering egregious discrimination, deliberate exclusion, and physical violence by some in the communities in which we lived, has sharpened our commitment to ensuring that neither Jews nor any other people should be subjected to such treatment."⁵²

Acknowledging the long gap in mainstream American Jewish organizational leaders' contributions to anti-apartheid, journalists labeled the new activism of the mid-1980s an attempt to "revive the accord" between blacks and Jews.⁵³

Rabbi David Saperstein of the Reform Movement's Religious Action Center stood at the Free South Africa movement protest in front of the South African embassy in Washington, DC, in December 1984. "This protest and demonstration today," he asserted, "is the start of what we see as increased Jewish involvement against apartheid in South Africa."[54] This language began to take an accounting of the cost of mainstream Jewish groups' abandonment of the anti-apartheid movement, the damage done to black/Jewish relations and to Jewish representation in progressive, anticolonialist coalitions.

Yet the reclaiming of Holocaust consciousness for anti-apartheid and for American mainstream Jewish groups' involvement in the movement did not signal a global Jewish consensus on the issue. For even when the Holocaust was not directly mentioned in US anti-apartheid campaigns, intracommunal, cross-continental debates erupted over what side might lay claim to its legacies. In 1986, for example, the American Jewish Congress tapped into the widespread support for the global anti-apartheid movement by integrating the cause into a massive membership drive. Founded in 1918, the Congress passed resolutions against apartheid until the late 1960s and then followed the trajectory of much of the American Jewish mainstream community in picking it up again two decades later. For this 1986 membership drive, Theodore Bikel, an actor, folk singer, composer, and American Jewish Congress vice president, penned a letter with the tagline "Apartheid Is a Jewish Issue." Though Bikel made no direct reference to the Holocaust, he made the case for apartheid as a Jewish issue with these words: "As Jews, we are well-acquainted with racial and religious persecution. Our people have been—and are today, in the Soviet Union, Syria, Ethiopia and other countries—singled out for brutal repression."[55] In light of that repression, Bikel urged the letter's reader to sign an enclosed petition that signaled support for divestment from South Africa.[56]

The reception of Bikel's letter among South African Jews spoke to the long-standing contest over the role of the Holocaust in American Jewish opposition to apartheid. Liberal Jews and non-Jews in South Africa stood strongly against the strategy of divestment from South Africa, and in part Rabbi Bernard Moses Casper, chief rabbi of South Africa, wrote to Bikel to give voice to that position. "Of course Jews are concerned at every evidence of injustice and oppression," he wrote, based on "our entire history and on the basic teachings of Judaism." But from the wider world, he argued, South

Africa needed greater investment, not an economic boycott. Most offensive to the rabbi was that Bikel's letter used Jewish teachings and history to try to persuade American Jews to support divestment. In Bikel's lines, the rabbi read a direct comparison between apartheid and the Holocaust, and on his rejection of that analogy Rabbi Casper built his argument against apartheid as a "Jewish issue":

> There is a world of difference between the circumstances facing the Black population in South Africa on the one hand and the horrors of the Holocaust as it affected Jews on the other. It is almost offensive and obscene to begin to make the comparison. On the one hand one sees a policy of hurtful discrimination and an absence of opportunity for human advancement. On the other there was a deliberate policy of brutal murder with a view to the physical extermination of an entire people.

Rabbi Casper elided Bikel's justification and context for anti-apartheid activism with his attack on the institution of apartheid itself. But comparing and measuring oppression in this way allowed Rabbi Casper to sound a cautionary note. To see apartheid as "a specifically Jewish issue," he observed, meant to link arms with some who may not care about "the problems that face us specifically as the Jewish people. Indeed," he wrote, some of them "may well be linked with groups hostile to our own cause."[57] To take a stand on apartheid, he warned, might mean to befriend an enemy of Israel and thus all Jews. His argument reached back across the decades to the first encounters of American and other Western Jews with South African apartheid, suggesting that Jewish unity (in this case, unity around unqualified support for Israel) should weigh more heavily on American Jews than anti-apartheid commitments.

Even after the anti-apartheid movement succeeded in peacefully dismantling the apartheid state, American Jewish leaders continued to wrestle with balancing what they saw as their "own cause" with a celebration of the end of apartheid. The controversy surrounding Nelson Mandela's 1990 visit to the United States demonstrated this very point. As Mandela was heralded as a hero throughout the world, many Jews expressed shock and dismay over his embrace of Yasser Arafat, chairman of the Palestinian Liberation Organization

(PLO), his analogizing the liberation movements of black South Africans and Palestinians. Mainstream Jewish leaders labeled Arafat a terrorist and an enemy of the Jewish people and rejected his leadership of the Palestinian liberation movement. Following the lead of South African Jewish leaders,[58] American Jewish leaders hesitated in welcoming Mandela as a hero in New York and met with him in Europe beforehand to obtain his assurances that he was a friend of Jews and of Israel.[59]

Other Jews in the United States, however, expressed their frustration and anger with mainstream Jewish leaders for not welcoming Mandela unconditionally, and they utilized the moment to reclaim Jewish history for progressive causes. These individuals saw in the PLO the possibility for negotiation and diplomacy and had long linked the colonialism of Israel's occupation to that of white supremacist apartheid.[60] Active in campaigns for justice in Latin America and South Africa, Donna Nevel, Marilyn Kleinberg Neimark, Alisa Solomon, and other progressive Jews in New York City decided to form a Jewish organization dedicated to local struggles for justice—where they felt mainstream Jewish organizations were far too underrepresented. "When just at that moment the 'official' Jewish organizations announced that they would not participate in the city's welcome of Mandela,"[61] Solomon recalled, "that seemed to crystallize all too well the direction the "official" community was going—and it was also a sign of the way Israel politics was skewing the local agenda. In discussing some kind of inaugural event at the meeting . . . someone suggested that we welcome Mandela and there was unanimous enthusiasm for the idea."[62]

A small committee organized the evening on June 15, 1990. The Welcome Service for Nelson Mandela was the first-ever event of the organization named Jews for Racial and Economic Justice (JFREJ), which works for local causes of social justice.[63]

The service that night aimed at "rededicating ourselves to the struggle for racial and economic justice." There were greetings from Mayor David Dinkins, from performer and activist Harry Belafonte (who was co-chair of the Nelson Mandela New York Welcome Committee), and Manhattan borough president Ruth Messinger. On the list of supporters were Messinger, Morris Schappes, Peter Weiss, and New Jewish Agenda's Manhattan chapter. A civil rights and civil liberties activist and fellow JFREJ founder, Henry Schwarzchild, offered the evening's concluding remarks. Schwarzchild had fled Nazi Germany after

Kristallnacht in 1938 and that evening he pledged that "whatever the cost, I would not live in a period of major social, moral events and be a bystander." Taking a clear position on debates over the legacy and meaning of the Holocaust for American Jews, Schwarzchild introduced JFREJ members as "a group of disparate people," who had come together "around the intuition that the Jewish task of justice [was] being neglected in our own society."

> We here no longer suffer much from the handicaps of ethnicity or poverty, but we thrive in the presence of, even partly as a consequence of, the social sins of the racial distress and economic pain of others. Jews for Racial and Economic Justice came together to find a way not to stand silently by at the blood (literal and metaphoric) of our brothers and sisters, or at their joy. We expect that the African American community of this city and this country will receive Nelson Mandela much the way East European Jewry is said to have received Theodor Herzl, as an emblem and harbinger of liberation. We rejoice with them at this visit.[64]

Reaching back into Jewish history, Schwarzchild found his analogy for black liberation in the earliest moments of the modern political Zionist movement. That analogy, had long sustained a kinship among African Americans, Africans, Israelis, and American and other nations' Jews. With it, Schwarzchild signaled unqualified allegiance to anticolonialist causes such as anti-apartheid in a moment when mainstream American Jewish organizations distanced themselves from that cause with qualifications about Mandela's "loyalty" to Israel, Zionism, and Jews.[65]

Joining a long history of Jews on the left, JFREJ sought to push back against those who claimed Jewish history and Holocaust memory for narrower interests that precluded alliances with groups working for progressive causes—and also to push back against leaders who prioritized a certain brand of Zionism as central to Jewish identity and community.[66] Certainly Schwarzchild's speech, and the founding of JFREJ in 1990 broadly, drew attention to the years when American Jewish leaders had been absent from the anti-apartheid movement; it also encouraged a critical look at community leaders who refused to engage in dialogue with those who were critical of communal priorities, especially the place of Israel in those priorities.

In the twenty-first century, a new movement—this time aimed at Israel's policies toward Palestinians—put these dynamics into sharp relief, and the same stark choices emerged. This is the world in the age of the boycott, divest, and sanctions (BDS) movement, founded in 2005 by 170 Palestinian organizations and modeled on the anti-apartheid movement. BDS seeks to isolate Israel as punishment for its treatment of Palestinians and its occupation.[67] It also builds on the use of the word *apartheid* to describe those policies, a practice that began in the 1960s and '70s and now culminates in Israel Apartheid Week, a weeklong series of events and rallies held across the world and linked to the BDS movement since its founding.

From the vantage point of Holocaust consciousness, debates over criticisms of Israeli policies and the BDS movement offer compelling parallels to the historical contests over American Jews and anti-apartheid. As discussed above, in the late 1960s through the 1980s, mainstream American Jewish organizational leaders alienated or purged those who openly criticized Israeli policies, who drew attention to Israel's alliance with South Africa, and who joined coalitions against apartheid that included members critical of Israel and Zionism. In this century, still citing Jewish unity as the top priority, mainstream American Jewish communal leaders alienate Jews who criticize Israel and who wish to link their Jewishness to the BDS movement or to broad anticolonialist activism in Israel/Palestine.

References to the Holocaust are employed in (slightly) new directions in this debate. In addition to avoiding those who criticize Israel, these leaders also urge the abandonment of global conversations about colonialism and racism, especially when such conversations occur in any proximity to those who downplay or deny the Holocaust.[68] Indeed, critics use the term *Nazis* to describe Jews who directly engage in these conversations, discrediting all such activism as ultimately contributing to the destruction of Jewish communities.[69] Jewish leaders once again see an anti-Israel and, by extension, anti-Jewish conspiracy in the human rights community; they reject activists who draw from Holocaust consciousness as motivation for fighting contemporary racism. Gerald M. Steinberg, a political scientist and president of NGO Monitor, accused "some of the most publicly-identified anti-Israel activists involved in BDS and IAW" of the "cynical abuse of human rights for the purposes of political warfare. These abuses include anti-democratic and decidedly anti-Israel strains, exploiting the Holocaust to advance the idea that Zionism denies justice to Palestinians."[70]

Once again, American Jews can draw from the language of Israeli authorities in attempts to marginalize or dismantle the BDS movement. In April 2015, for example, the Israel High Court upheld the so-called boycott law in Israel, which gives "ground for individuals to sue anyone who calls for a boycott of Israel, or areas under its control." In their decision, according to one journalist, the justices utilized the world *terror* eleven times and *Holocaust* three times in order to demonstrate the seriousness of threats from the BDS movement.[71]

Today, as the BDS movement gains momentum, Jewish leaders in the United States might find lessons in the history of American Jews' encounters with apartheid; they might utilize these lessons to take an accounting of the costs of defending Israel's current policies and fighting BDS. As late as the early 1980s, Jewish leaders failed to listen to the voices of activists in their own community, who drew attention to the urgent injustices of apartheid and the growing momentum of the anti-apartheid movement. These activists never stopped linking Holocaust memory to anti-colonialism, even when Jewish leaders looked the other way while Israel collaborated with South Africa.

A prominent voice of the contemporary American Jewish left is Henry Siegman, past president of the American Jewish Congress, who led that organization to speak out against apartheid beginning only in the mid-1980s. Many consider him then to have been a "consummate insider." After leaving that world in 1994, Siegman became an increasingly vocal critic of Israeli policies, analogizing Israel's policies toward Palestinians to South African apartheid in 2010.[72] As Israel invaded Gaza in 2014, Siegman said in an interview that his own experience with the Nazis—"I lived two years under Nazi occupation, most of it running from place to place and in hiding"—had a profound effect on his current view of the Israeli government:

> [T]he important lesson of the Holocaust is not that there is evil. . . . The great lesson of the Holocaust is that decent, cultured people, people we would otherwise consider good people, can allow such evil to prevail. . . . Now I draw no comparisons

between the Nazi machine and Israeli policy. And what I resent most deeply is when people say, "How dare you invoke the Nazi experience?" The point isn't, you know, what exactly they did, but the point is the evidence that they gave that decent people can watch evil and do nothing about it. That is the most important lesson of the Holocaust, not the Hitlers and not the SS, but the public that allowed this to happen.[73]

Siegman indicted Israeli voters with that pronouncement and also, importantly, American Jews, saying, "There's much more to Judaism and to the meaning that you give to your Jewish identity than support for the likes of Netanyahu."[74] In the past few years, Siegman has become a defender of the BDS movement.

The history of the debate over South African apartheid offers insights into contemporary contests over the Holocaust, Israel, the BDS movement, and contemporary Zionism, perhaps especially with histories of individuals such as Henry Siegman, whose life intersected with so many of those currents. Contemporary leaders might look to this past for lessons in balancing particularist priorities—such as creating vibrant and stable Jewish communities—with universalist commitments to social justice that work toward an end of oppression. To study American Jewish invocations of the Holocaust is to examine a record of a community wrestling with its fraught and conflicted relationship to the legacy—and future prospects—of liberation for itself and for other groups and nations.

Notes

I thank the Babson Faculty Research Board for their support in the research of this chapter.

1. A history of Hashomer Hatzair in the United States and its "effort to synthesize Zionism and revolutionary socialism" can be found in Ariel Hurwitz, ed., *Against the Stream: Seven Decades of Hashomer Hatzair in North America* (Tel Aviv: Association of North American Shomrim, 1994), quote on 71.
2. "The Black Man's Burden," editorial, *Labor Israel* 38 (March 24, 1950): 2. *Labor Israel* became *Israel Horizons* in 1952.

3. See, especially, C. C. Aronsfeld, "The New Challenge to the Jew in South Africa and Argentina," *Labor Israel* 43–44 (June 1950): 4. A scholar of the Holocaust, Aronsfeld wrote about the oppressive regimes of South Africa's D. F. Malan and Argentina's Juan Perón, warning that Jews in both nations "must fear not for the security of their bodies, but for the integrity of their souls," 4.
4. See Shirli Gilbert, "Jews and the Racial State: Legacies of the Holocaust in Apartheid South Africa, 1945–60," *Jewish Social Studies: History, Culture, Society* 16, no. 3 (2010): 32–64.
5. Golda Meir, quoted in Jack Raymond, "15 African Nations Laud Israeli Aid," *New York Times*, October 9, 1960.
6. "The Vote against Apartheid," editorial, *Israel Horizons* 15, nos. 9–10 (1967): 5.
7. "Apartheid Isolates South Africa," editorial, *Israel Horizons* 9, no. 5 (1961): 6; and "Israel Is Counted on South Africa Issue," editorial, *Israel Horizons* 11, no. 7 (1963): 8.
8. Hasia Diner, *We Remember with Reverence and Love: American Jews and the Myth of Silence After the Holocaust, 1945–1962* (New York: New York University Press, 2009), 295, 293.
9. Michael Staub writes about these analogies, in which leaders compared Jewish civil rights activists and Jewish critics of Israeli policies to Nazis, in *Torn at the Roots: The Crisis of Jewish Liberalism in Postwar America* (New York: Columbia University Press, 2004) 16, 17. I write about the invocation of these analogies for critics of apartheid and Israel's occupation in *Nations Divided: American Jews and the Struggle over Apartheid* (New York: Palgrave Macmillan, 2014), 148.
10. See Shirli Gilbert, "Jews and the Racial State: Legacies of the Holocaust in Apartheid South Africa, 1945–60," *Jewish Social Studies: History, Culture, Society* 16, no. 3 (2010): 32–64.
11. See Feld, *Nations Divided*.
12. Maurice Perlzweig, memorandum, March 17, 1954, World Jewish Congress Papers, American Jewish Archives, Cincinnati, OH.
13. Rabbi Maurice Perlzweig to Dr. [Nahum] Goldmann, March 19, 1954, World Jewish Congress Papers, American Jewish Archives, Cincinnati, OH.
14. David Petegorsky to Maurice Perlzweig, March 17, 1954, World Jewish Congress Papers, American Jewish Archives, Cincinnati, OH. Petegorsky was born in Ottawa and educated in London before settling in the United States.
15. Stuart Svonkin, in *Jews against Prejudice: American Jews and the Fight for Civil Liberties* (New York: Columbia University Press, 1997), writes that leaders of the American Jewish Congress such as Petegorsky hoped that Civil Rights activism

"would provide American Jews with a strong sense of group identity," counteracting the "communal disintegration" that some feared would lead to "assimilation and ultimately... annihilation," 81.

16. Joachim Prinz to Maurice Perlzweig, May 20, 1960, World Jewish Congress Papers, American Jewish Archives, Cincinnati, OH. See Michael Meyer, ed., *Joachim Prinz, Rebellious Rabbi: An Autobiography—the German and Early American Years* (Bloomington: Indiana University Press, 2007).
17. On this point, see Gideon Shimoni, *Community and Conscience: The Jews of Apartheid South Africa* (Waltham, MA: Brandeis University Press, 2003).
18. Svonkin, *Jews against Prejudice*, 191.
19. Cheryl Lynn Greenberg documents the tensions of this era comprehensively in *Troubling the Waters: Black-Jewish Relations in the American Century* (Princeton: Princeton University Press, 2006), chap. 6.
20. Jonathan Sarna, *American Judaism: A History* (New Haven, CT: Yale University Press, 2004), 315.
21. Sarna, *American Judaism*, 315.
22. Staub, *Torn at the Roots*, 149.
23. Michael Galchinsky, *Jews and Human Rights: Dancing at Three Weddings* (Lanham, MD: Rowan & Littlefield, 2008), 49.
24. My thinking here has been influenced by Peter Beinart, *The Crisis of Zionism* (New York: Picador Press, 2013); and Robert Meister, *After Evil: A Politics of Human Rights* (New York: Columbia University Press, 2012).
25. On New Jewish Agenda, see Ezra Berkley Nepon, *Justice, Justice, Shall You Pursue: A History of New Jewish Agenda* (Oakland, CA: Thread Makes Blanket Press, 2012).
26. Peter Weiss, email to the author, July 27, 2009.
27. Rabbi Sharon Kleinbaum, interview with the author, January 26, 2011. This sit-in led to Columbia's divestment from stocks and bonds directly associated with South Africa; Columbia did not fully divest until 1991. See "Student Sit-In at Columbia," *New York Post*, May 2, 1978; "Demonstration at Columbia," *New York Daily News*, May 2, 1978; Rabbi Sharon Kleinbaum, email to the author, May 18, 2011; and "275 Occupy Business School; 700 Rally for CU Divestiture; McGill to meet sit-in Leaders," *Columbia Daily Spectator* (Columbia University, New York), May 2, 1978. That issue of the *Spectator* was devoted almost entirely to the protest and its aftermath. Kleinbaum also led a meeting the following January at which about a hundred students discussed several pressing issues, including divestment. Ann Koshel, "Campus, Community Issues Aired at Informal Gripe

Session in BHR," *Columbia Daily Spectator* (Columbia University, New York), January 31, 1979.
28. Ruth Messinger, interview with the author, January 6, 2011.
29. The Board of Overseers is a thirty-member governing body for Harvard second only to the seven-member Harvard Corporation in decision-making powers for the university. Sara Frankel, "Alumni Urge Harvard to Divest," *Mother Jones*, May 1987, 12; Messinger, interview with the author.
30. On the Cold War alliance between Israel and South Africa, see Sasha Polakow-Suransky, *The Unspoken Alliance: Israel's Secret Relationship with Apartheid South Africa* (New York: Pantheon, 2010).
31. "Statement of H.E. Ambassador Yehuda Z. Blum, of Israel to the United Nations in the Plenary on Policies of Apartheid of the Government of South Africa," November 12, 1980, 1–2.
32. "Statement in the General Assembly by H.E. Ambassador Benjamin Netanyahu, Permanent Representative of Israel to the United Nations, *Policies of Apartheid of the Government of South Africa*, Wednesday 21 November 21, 1984," papers of the American Jewish Congress, Center for Jewish History, New York, 2 (emphasis in the original).
33. "Statement in the General Assembly by H.E. Ambassador Benjamin Netanyahu," 4.
34. Polakow-Suransky begins his book on Israel and South Africa, *Unspoken Alliance*, by capturing the moment and import of Vorster's visit; see 3, 159.
35. Polakow-Suransky interprets Vorster's visit to Israel as a move toward pragmatism. "By the time Vorster set foot in Jerusalem," he writes in *The Unspoken Alliance*, "the idealism of Israel's early years had been replaced by hardened self-interest." Further, the visit "gave South Africa a surge of self-confidence and helped relieve its feelings of growing isolation," 92.
36. On the close ties between South African and Israeli officials, see Polakow-Suransky, *Unspoken Alliance*, esp. chap. 5.
37. On this point, see Polakow-Suransky, *Unspoken Alliance*, 233–34.
38. Terence Smith, "Vorster Visit to Israel Arouses Criticism," *New York Times*, April 18, 1976.
39. *Africa Research Bulletin*, April 1976, 4009, quoted in Joel Peters, *Israel and Africa: The Problematic Friendship* (London: British Academic Press, 1992), 163.
40. See Polakow-Suransky, *Unspoken Alliance*, 164–70.
41. "Friendship between Israel and So. Africa Blossoming," *Oakland Post* (Oakland University, Oakland, CA), May 5, 1976; and "From Where I sit: Women Prisoners in South Africa," *Tri-State Defender* (Memphis, TN), December 4, 1976.

42. "Both Wrong and Stupid," editorial, *New Outlook* (September/October 1976): 3–4.
43. "Junket for U.S. Jewish Editors to South Africa," editorial, *Jewish Currents* 30 (October 1976): 29.
44. David Hammerstein, "Marching to Pretoria," *Jewish Radical* 9, no. 3 (1978), Tamiment Library, New York University.
45. "Brandeis University's Involvement in Corporations Doing Business in South Africa: The Students' Perspective," report by the Brandeis University Student Senate, March 26, 1979, Brandeis University Archive, Waltham, MA.
46. Keith W. Jenkins, Brandeis University Student Senate President, to professors, student leaders, the Brandeis community, March 22, 1979, Gordon Fellman Papers, 1949–2006, Brandeis University Archive, Waltham, MA. Brandeis's radical student magazine, *The Watch*, often invoked Holocaust analogies with apartheid. See Danny Weinstraub, "Will We Never Forget?" *Watch* 7, no. 1 (1986): 3.
47. Rabbi Albert S. Axelrad, "Israel and South African Apartheid: Toward a Proper Perspective," *Watch* 6, no. 9 (1986): 14–15.
48. "Resolution," April 3, 1978, submitted by Rabbi Albert S. Axelrad. In his accompanying letter, Rabbi Axelrad asked the executive director of the Board of Rabbis to consider "the particular appropriateness of the history and ideals of Pesach [Jewish holiday of Passover] as they related to the plight of Blacks in South Africa." Rabbi Albert Axelrad to Rabbi Arnold Fine, April 6, 1978, Gordon Fellman Papers, 1949–2006, Brandeis University Archives, Waltham, MA.
49. Axelrad, "Israel and South African Apartheid," 14–15. While awaiting a decision from the Board of Trustees about full divestment in February 1987, Rabbi Axelrad joined with Brandeis's two other chaplains in fasting as a sign of protest. "Chaplains Speak on Fast," *Justice* (Brandeis University, Waltham, MA), February 17, 1987.
50. Axelrad, "Israel and South African Apartheid, 14–15.
51. "By the mid-1990s," writes Polakow-Suransky in *The Unspoken Alliance*, "the economic interests that gave birth to the alliance [between Israel and South Africa] and the ideological affinities that sustained two decades of lucrative and intimate cooperation had ebbed away," 229.
52. "NJCRAC [National Jewish Community Relations Advisory Council] Position Paper on Apartheid, Adopted by the NJCRAC Plenary Session, meeting in Washington, D.C. 19–22 February 1989," papers of the American Jewish Congress, Center for Jewish History.
53. Sam Roberts, "Blacks, Jews Seeking to Revive Accord," *St. Louis Post-Dispatch*, December 15, 1984, B1, papers of the American Jewish Congress, Center for Jewish History. On black/Jewish relations, see Greenberg, *Troubling the Waters*.

54. Gerald M. Boyd, "Jews Back Blacks in Racism Protest," *New York Times*, December 11, 1984, www.nytimes.com/1984/12/11/us/jews-back-blacks-in-racism-protest.html.
55. Theodore Bikel to "Dear Friend," April 1986, papers of the American Jewish Congress, Center for Jewish History.
56. Bikel's letter was mailed with a form: the top half was for membership fees and/or donations to the American Jewish Congress; the bottom half asked for a signature to a letter to the president pledging "unequivocal support for the withdrawal of American investment in the repressive Republic of South Africa." A letter from New York Representative (and American Jewish Congress leader) Stephen Solarz also accompanied Bikel's letter: on congressional letterhead, Solarz indicated his support for anti-apartheid measures and also noted that the American Jewish Congress agenda was "*not* limited to one issue." Stephen Solarz to "Dear Friend," April 1986, papers of the American Jewish Congress, Center for Jewish History.
57. Letter from Office of the Chief Rabbi (signature unreadable), Federation of Synagogues of South Africa, to Mr. Theodore Bikel, American Jewish Congress, August 8, 1986, papers of the American Jewish Congress, Center for Jewish History.
58. Nelson Mandela met with South African Jewish leaders before he departed for his tour of Europe and the United States. These individuals communicated to American Jewish leaders that Mandela remained committed "to the wellbeing of the South African Jewish community" and pledged "his unswerving opposition to racism and antisemitism" and to Israel's right to exist in "secure borders." Mandela also "expressed appreciation for the role Jews had played in the struggle against apartheid." Herbert Wander, co-chair, Ad Hoc Committee on Apartheid, and Diana Aviv, assistant director, memorandum to NJCRAC and CJF [Center for Jewish Future] Member Agencies, July 31, 1990, Religious Action Committee Papers, American Jewish Archives, Cincinnati, OH.
59. On June 10, 1990, Mandela met with American Jewish organizational leaders in Geneva and spoke about their positions with regard to Israel and the PLO. The leaders felt "the American Jewish community could fully and actively participate in the welcome of Mr. Mandela to the United States." Wander and Aviv, 7.
60. Although vigorously rejecting terrorist responses to Israeli aggression, these activists granted Arafat the political legitimacy and visibility they felt was necessary to begin peacemaking.
61. This was prior to Mandela's meeting Jewish leaders in Geneva.
62. Alisa Solomon, email to the author, March 22, 2011.

63. In her important examination of the racial arrangements and politics of the twenty-first-century United States, *The Color of Jews*, Melanie Kaye/Kantrowitz, the first director of Jews for Racial and Economic Justice, writes of the organization's first meeting. See Kaye/Kantrowitz, *The Colors of Jews: Racial Politics and Radical Diasporism* (Bloomington: University of Indiana Press, 2007), 19.
64. Henry Schwarzchild's remarks at the Welcome Service held by Jews for Racial and Economic Justice and Congregation B'nai Jeshrun, New York, June 15, 1990, in Jews for Racial and Economic Justice, *Mensches in the Trenches*, tenth anniversary booklet, December 10, 2000, emailed to the author by Alisa Solomon.
65. Daniel Rozsa Lang/Levitsky notes the "clear, consistent politics of anti-racism and anti-colonialism of [JFREJ's] founding moment." Lang/Levitsky, "Hidden Agenda: Lessons from NJA, Lost and Learned," in *Justice, Justice, Shall You Pursue: A History of New Jewish Agenda*, ed. Ezra Berkley Nepon (Oakland, CA: Thread Makes Blanket Press, 2012), 103.
66. In the JFREJ tenth anniversary booklet, Marilyn Kleinberg Neimark and Donna Nevel list the reasons that they founded JFREJ, among them the following: "In New York City, a conservative Jewish voice not only defined what were so-called Jewish interests, but also influenced the City's priorities—and still does"; "it was time to reexamine the centrality American Jews gave to the state of Israel and in forming Jewish identity and building political alliances—and still is"; and "to offer a place where Jewish identity and commitment to social justice are not at odds." *Celebrating Ten Years of Jews for Racial and Economic Justice*, December 10, 2000, pamphlet, emailed to the author by Alisa Solomon.
67. Website of the Palestinian BDS National Committee (BNC), www.bdsmovement.net/, accessed June 16, 2013; and Naomi Klein, "Israel: Boycott, Divest, Sanction," *Nation*, January 26, 2009, posted online January 7, 2009, www.thenation.com/article/israel-boycott-divest-sanction#axzz2btLTqiAu.
68. Here I refer to the 2001 United Nations Conferences against Racism in Durban, South Africa, and the 2009 Durban Review Conference in Geneva, Switzerland. See Feld, *Nations Divided*, chap. 8.
69. *Tikkun* editor Rabbi Michael Lerner presented the Tikkun award to Justice Richard Goldstone of South Africa in spring 2011; Goldstone had just chaired a UN Human Rights Council fact-finding mission to Gaza and authored a report in which he found both Israel and Hamas guilty of war crimes. Goldstone endured scathing criticism from Israel's prime minister, Benjamin Netanyahu, and other Jewish leaders. In response to his show of support for Goldstone, vandals attacked Lerner's home three times, leaving behind posters that depicted Lerner and

"Islamic extremists" as "Nazis" intent on destroying Israel. See "Zionist Extremist Hate Crime against Rabbi Lerner: Third Attack on His Home and the Limits of 'Freedom of the Press,'" *Tikkun Daily* (blog), March 16, 2011, www.tikkun.org/tikkundaily/2011/03/16/zionist-extremist-hate-crime-against-rabbi-lerner-3rd-attack-on-his-home-and-the-limits-of-freedom-of-the-press/.

70. Gerald M. Steinberg, "The Goldstone Myth," book review of Adam Horowitz, Lizzy Ratner, Philip Weiss, eds., *The Goldstone Report* (New York: Nation Books, 2011), Scholars for Peace in the Middle East, March 29, 2011, spme.org/spme-research/book-reviews/book-review-by-gerald-m-steinberg-philip-weiss-adam-horowitz-and-lizzy-ratner-eds-the-goldstone-report/9622/.

71. Yael Marom, "High Court on BDS: Somewhere between Terror and Holocaust Denial," *+972*, 972mag.com/high-court-on-bds-somewhere-between-terror-and-holocaust-denial/105656/, accessed July 24, 2015.

72. Henry Siegman, "'Imposing Middle East Peace," *Nation*, January 7, 2010, www.thenation.com/article/imposing-middle-east-peace/.

73. "Henry Siegman, Leading Voice of U.S. Jewry, on Gaza: 'A Slaughter of Innocents,'" *Democracy Now!* July 30, 2014, www.democracynow.org/2014/7/30/henry_siegman_leading_voice_of_us .

74. "U.S. Jewish Leader Henry Siegman to Israel: Stop Killing Palestinians and End the Occupation," *Democracy Now!* July 31, 2014, www.democracynow.org/2014/7/31/us_jewish_leader_henry_siegman_to.

8

Race, Holocaust Memory, and American Jewish Politics

Michael E. Staub

IN DECEMBER 1955, THE very month an African American bus boycott began in Montgomery, Alabama, to protest segregation on public transportation, historian Louis Ruchames—who would later become the first chair of the Academic Council of the American Jewish Historical Society—published an essay on what he saw as the parallels between Jewish and African American history. As he reflected on three hundred years of Jewish life in America, Ruchames wrote that he knew "of no more appropriate and meaningful act than to join our observance with that of the Negro people, whose history touches ours at so many points and whose welfare is so directly related to ours." Ruchames continued:

> We Jews have known within our lives and the lives of our fathers the problems which have confronted the Negro—the meaning of persecution, of segregation, and of the deprivation of elementary human rights. And in our own day, the lesson that men have had to relearn in every generation, that the rights of all men are interrelated, that no minority group is safe while others are the victims of persecution, has been seared into our minds and hearts through the burning flesh of six million of our brethren in Europe.[1]

I open with this quotation from Rabbi Ruchames because it is, first of all, an eloquent summary of what many American Jews felt with respect to the interrelationship between African American civil rights and the mass murder of European Jewry during the early postwar era. Certainly, once the civil rights movement gained force by the early 1960s, we find ample evidence that young Jews got involved in African American civil rights activism in the context of an evolving sense that to do so was to be responsive to one important "lesson" of Holocaust memory in the American context. In fact, civil rights activist Paul Cowan put it exactly like this many years later in his memoir, observing that his participation in African American civil rights had emerged from his "deep commitment to the belief that [Jews] had a lifelong debt to the six million dead."[2]

I also open with this quotation from Louis Ruchames to highlight what has been (and remains) a subject of contestation for many American Jews. For there has persisted "a broad consensus that public awareness of the Holocaust was low in the first decade and a half after the end of World War Two." While scholars have also been careful to observe that this "lack of a widespread consciousness" should not "be confused with silence," they have often nonetheless reinforced an impression that Jews did not reflect very much on the meaning of Holocaust memory for their American lives at least until the early 1960s.[3]

My own contention has been that it was *precisely* in the context of debates over Jewish involvement in African American civil rights activism that a series of rich and complicated discussions of the possible interpretations of Holocaust memory for the American context was carried out—already since the late 1940s. Far from keeping silent about the mass murder of European Jewry—either out of horror or out of sensitivity to survivors—and far from finding it irrelevant to the US context, American Jewish commentators drew extensively on the memory of the Holocaust already in the 1940s when they analogized on its meaning for African American civil rights. This habit of drawing lessons may, in hindsight, seem deeply disrespectful. In more recent decades, we have become more attuned to the Holocaust's grim specificities and the inappropriateness of facile comparisons (even as facile comparisons continue to proliferate widely among both Jews and non-Jews, and for a broad array of political agendas). Many thoughtful commentators may insist that lesson-making of all kinds is a dishonor to the dead, and they may emphasize that the essential meaninglessness of the Holocaust is one of the most important things to grasp about it.⁴ Yet this notion that it might be indecent to engage in lessons or comparisons was not initially considered.⁵

After the horrifying revelations of 1945, the Nazi genocide of European Jews was invoked almost at once in debates concerning American Jewish political engagement with African American civil rights. Indeed, it would be appropriate to say that these debates came centrally to shape the future course and direction of Holocaust memory in the postwar United States. And yet, and while scholarship has increasingly acknowledged that there existed no real silence after the Holocaust, the focus of this research continues largely to sidestep the key role that race and racism played in these developments. Therefore and while we do now have invaluable accounts of how post-Holocaust memory in America came centrally to be represented in film and television and in American Jewish communal life, there still tends to be a hesitancy fully to bring into the frame an analysis of how African American civil rights struggles factored centrally in this history.⁶

This erasure may have something to do with the complexity of the story itself. For one thing, and far from incidentally, already by the mid-1960s assumptions about the lessons of Nazism for political life in the United States had gone through at least three distinct stages. Political commentary (especially—though not exclusively—in the Jewish press) made frequent reference to Nazism and the mass murder of European Jewry, particularly in the context of the African American civil rights movement.

In the first stage of drawing lessons from the genocide of European Jewry for the US context, both left-wing (that is, pro-communist) and liberal (pro-Democratic) American Jews continued—as they had done already during World War II—to elaborate analogies between German Nazism and American anti-black racism. These Jews often identified directly with African Americans. In a racist and antisemitic environment—according to the prevailing logic—in helping blacks, Jews were also helping themselves.

We find, for example, that when renowned journalist Max Lerner reported to the annual convention of the American Jewish Congress in 1949 about his recent trip to Germany, he argued that the example of the Nazi past made it imperative to combat racism also in the United States. Racist and antidemocratic movements, he announced, were "not just jokes": "They are a grim thing that ends in the furnaces of Auschwitz and Dachau. We have come to understand what the meaning of racism is. We know that racism ends in death. We know that racism ends in charred bodies."[7] And we find as well, and along related lines, Leo Pfeffer, a lawyer on the staff of the American Jewish Congress, writing in 1946 in the Labor Zionist journal *Jewish Frontier* that "as Hitler well knew, [a lie] will be believed, no matter how big it is, if only it is repeated often enough." So too, he went on, the "continued repetition of the fairy tale that Negro blood is different from and inferior to Caucasian has caused millions of uneducated or partially educated poor whites to consider Negroes an intermediate species between simian and human." In the same way, ordinary German citizens had "participated or acquiesced in mass murder of Jews because for years they had been exposed to the lie that the Jews were their enemy and that all would be well when Jewish blood would flow."[8]

Although the Cold War undermined that particular analogy as un-American, and a new analogy between Nazism and Stalinism grew in its place, by the late 1950s a second form of Holocaust consciousness had emerged. Inspired by the Reform rabbis' movement for "prophetic Judaism," and led by committed Zionists within the American Jewish Congress, anti-racist activists began to argue that if they did not help blacks, American Jews would be no better than the gentile German and Polish bystanders who had done nothing to prevent the Holocaust. This line of reasoning came to full flowering in the early 1960s, which also saw the beginnings of a third (more particularist and to us now more familiar) strand of argumentation: one that identified the most important lesson of the Holocaust as the need for Jews—within the United States and around the world—to protect themselves and fight for their own survival.

From Holocaust Memory to African American Civil Rights Activism

In the aftermath of World War II, the Nazi genocide of European Jewry quickly emerged as a key topic for discussions within the American Jewish community—and it did so often in the context of debates over African American civil liberties. Leading commentators agreed that the Nazi genocide was a logical reference point from which to draw conclusions about the bitter persistence of anti-black racism in the United States. Leading Jewish liberal periodicals in the immediate postwar era were especially receptive to the analogy between German fascism and American racism.

The new journal *Commentary*, sponsored by the American Jewish Committee, repeatedly invoked a Nazi analogy to dramatize its disapproval of racial discrimination in the United States, especially in housing and employment practices. A 1947 essay in *Commentary* titled "Homes for Aryans Only" put a distinctly American spin on the possible lessons of Nazism. The author argued that a libertarian tradition did not give American property owners a legal right to refuse to sell their homes to "non-Caucasians" (including Jews). Rhetorically linking the emancipation of slaves with the liberation of European Jewry, the author wrote: "Eighty years after Gettysburg, and two years after Hitler, the proposition that all men are created equal is again being whittled down, and in the area perhaps most crucial for a future democratic America—the area of our neighborhood life."[9]

For at least a few years, the Nazi genocide became a relevant reference point for making sense of American racial (and racist) realities. These analogies were not only taken to be inoffensive to most American Jews, but they were also widely understood to reflect common sense. It was a double standard, many felt, for the United States *not* to turn its full attention to the eradication of white racism at home after German fascism had been defeated abroad.

An early and prominent—if also now largely forgotten—venue that repeatedly made the connection between German fascism and white racism was the pro-communist Jewish periodical, *Jewish Life*. Established in 1946 by the Morning Freiheit Association, *Jewish Life* hammered away at the analogy between a resurgence in US white racism and the rise of German Nazism. It noted in its inaugural issue, for instance, how the "recent activity of the [Ku Klux] Klan is reminiscent of the SS terrorism before 1933," adding: "Like the SS, the Klan specializes in beatings, terrifying torch parades, burnings."[10] References specifically to the genocide of European Jewry recurred in the pages of *Jewish Life*. In 1947, the journal observed that "symptoms of the alarming situation" that "led to the rise of Hitlerism in Germany" were disturbingly present in the United States as well. It argued that all Americans—white and black, Jewish and gentile—had a moral responsibility to combat white supremacy. The lessons of Nazism and the Holocaust were clear, perhaps especially for American Jews:

> Skillfully promoted antisemitism in nazi-Germany [*sic*] helped to brutalize certain elements among the German people and to create the conditions under which the annihilation of Jews and the bestial destruction of millions of members of other nations was made possible. In the same way American lynch-breeding jimcrowism [*sic*] leads to the brutalization of significant sections of the American masses and may create the necessary conditions and sentiments for a new Hitlerite destruction of the Jews in America. In the interests of the security of Jewish life, of the future of the Jews in America, we must fight with all our strength all forms of race prejudice and discrimination against the Negro people, as American citizens, as neighbors, as workers, as fellow-members of unions.[11]

Throughout the remainder of the forties, *Jewish Life* continued to document a direct analogical link between racism and antisemitism in America and German fascism. At all points it made abundantly clear that attempts to suppress or deny the civil liberties of American communists were really one crucial early signal that domestic capitalist forces (many of whom, *Jewish Life* claimed, had profited from their investments in German companies successful during the Third Reich) intended to follow through on a plan to institute an American-style fascist state.

With the rise of the Cold War, however, nearly every element of American society—including many American Jewish individuals and organizations—endorsed the anti-communist consensus. In prior years, many Jewish liberals (along with leftists and left-wing sympathizers) had proclaimed American white racism and German Nazism comparable evils. By 1949, this analogy had virtually vanished—ridiculed as the product of "Communist-fabricated hysteria." Only those few sympathetic to communism continued to press the anti-racist linkage, and they were declared anti-American because their rhetoric "furnished new grist for the Kremlin propaganda mill."[12] In 1948, New York University philosopher Sidney Hook had already spelled out a new analogy: it was Soviet communism that most resembled Nazism.[13]

Increasing numbers of Jewish commentators suggested that Jews made the best and most loyal Cold War Americans precisely because their suffering at the hands of Nazism had taught them to abhor the excesses of totalitarianism. Fear that Jews might be tarred with the communist brush was great. Suspected Jewish communists and communist sympathizers were expelled from every major American Jewish organization. Many Jews abandoned their active roles in left-wing causes. Analogies between Nazism and American racism grew far less acceptable among Jewish liberals. The vast majority of Jewish intellectuals and leaders retreated wholesale from making pronouncements that could possibly be interpreted as anti-American or pro-communist. Civil rights continued to be supported but far more cautiously.

References to Nazi crimes in American Jewish discourse began to drop off dramatically. It was only at the end of the 1950s and increasingly in the early 1960s that the Holocaust and its relationship to American politics began to resurface. However, it did so in competing and mutually irreconcilable forms.

Bystander Anxiety

On August 28, 1963, at the March on Washington rally, Rabbi Joachim Prinz, president of the American Jewish Congress, gave a brief address titled "The Issue Is Silence." At Prinz's side stood Martin Luther King Jr., who was to deliver his "I Have a Dream" speech that same afternoon. The crowd that late summer day numbered two hundred thousand. Prinz spoke of his years as a rabbi in prewar Berlin, an intimate witness to the advance of Nazism. Standing before the Lincoln Memorial, his speech revitalized the link between German antisemitism and American racism that had been all but erased during the early Cold War years. Elaborating on why American Jews struggled for racial justice after Auschwitz, Prinz offered a Holocaust lesson distinctly different from the sort of analogy that had motivated a pro-communist journal like *Jewish Life* in the 1940s:

> When I was the rabbi of the Jewish community in Berlin under the Hitler regime, I learned . . . that bigotry and hatred are not the most urgent problem. The most urgent, the most disgraceful, the most shameful and the most tragic problem is silence.
> A great people which had created a great civilization had become a nation of silent onlookers. They remained silent in the

face of hate, in the face of brutality and in the face of murder. America must not become a nation of onlookers. America must not remain silent. Not merely black America, but all of America. It must speak up and act, from the President down to the humblest of us, and not for the sake of the Negro, not for the sake of the black community, but for the sake of the image, the idea and the aspiration of America itself.[14]

A rabbi attending the March on Washington told *Hadassah Magazine* that Prinz's speech mirrored his own feelings: "Had this march taken place in the 1930s in Germany, there might never have been the mass murder of Jews. The conscience of the Christians in Germany might have been awakened as our consciences are being awakened today."[15] Thus, Prinz had formulated a kind of Holocaust analogizing that might best be called "bystander anxiety." While bystander anxiety spoke to all Americans—gentile and Jewish alike—it was to have a particular resonance within the American Jewish community, both laypersons and leadership, as the argument became that if Jews failed to put themselves at risk to work on behalf of African Americans, then they would be behaving no better than German citizens had under Nazism.

Bystander anxiety had already begun to find expression in rabbinic and other Jewish circles. In 1958, Rabbi Jacob M. Rothschild of Atlanta asked, regarding civil rights activism: "How can we condemn the millions who stood by under Hitler, or honor those few who chose to live by their ideals, when we refuse to make a similar choice now that the dilemma is our own?"[16] In 1962, in an indicative turn of phrase, gentiles who had rescued Jews from the Holocaust were honored as "Freedom Riders."[17]

A year later, Rabbi Richard Rubenstein, describing a discussion at the convention of the Conservative movement's Rabbinical Assembly (concerning the proposed establishment of an institute "to document altruistic deeds done by non-Jews to save Jews during the Hitler holocaust"), reported the following exchange: "The proposal touched an understandably sore nerve. In the midst of the debate, one rabbi queried why we were concentrating our energies on what had happened twenty years ago [during the Holocaust]. . . . Then, almost as an afterthought, the rabbi asked whether the Rabbinical Assembly was doing the right thing by meeting together rather than adjourning to

Birmingham, Alabama, to aid Dr. Martin Luther King and his followers in their struggle for human rights."[18] These were far from isolated cases. In 1964, Rabbi Richard Hertz, responding to the question "What has the moral crisis over race to do with Judaism?," answered (in the pages of *Ebony*): "Everything! . . . We lived in the blackest ghettos of misery. We tasted the salt of our own tears. . . . We who have experienced humiliation cannot humiliate others. We who have suffered segregation cannot segregate others." Hertz continued: "The current theme of Jewish leaders is that America must not be a nation of neutral onlookers in the civil rights struggle—that Jews and others must speak up and act, otherwise be as guilty as the non-Nazis in Germany were who looked the other way when Jews were persecuted."[19] Similarly, journalist and activist Nat Hentoff (also in 1964) contended that although "there are no Dachaus here" in the United States, "the ghetto is a form of concentration camp." He also underscored that "although a protestor under Hitler put his life in danger, no American White—except in parts of the South—would run any risk to his personal safety by denouncing and working to change the practices of the real-estate interests, the mortgage-lending banks, the schools, the businesses, the police, and all the other institutions which keep the Negro down."[20] Remarkably, Hentoff here implied that nonresistance on the part of Jews to American racism was arguably more shameful than nonresistance on the part of non-Jewish Germans to the Nazi genocide.

In sum, then, reference to the Holocaust found recurrent and strenuous articulation at least in part in the encounter with and discussions of the African American struggle for civil rights. As an Auschwitz survivor put it succinctly in 1964 at a public Jewish forum, it was in dismay that she could compare American Jews' "bigoted" remarks against African Americans with "the same expressions and opinions that were so familiar to me as a Jew living in Hungary." She continued: "I have worn the yellow Star of David with pride as I shared the slave labor with my fellow camp-mates. But I cannot walk with my head erect among my neighbors who, after only twenty years, have forgotten that six million Jews were the victims of prejudice. It is sad that six million of us died in vain if today similar attitudes are being used toward the Negro in this country."[21] Jews who saw social justice concerns as integral to their faith and ethnic identity found in the Holocaust a crucial reference point that underscored the moral righteousness of their anti-racist activism. The years

1963–64 witnessed the full flourishing of this line of argumentation.[22] It was not, however, to go unchallenged for very long.

Jewish Survival

A competing (and implicitly less liberal) political expression of Holocaust memory came to prominence also in the early 1960s. It stressed the urgent need for American Jews to focus on their own communal survival. Interestingly, this opposite perspective came also to be formulated in the context of African American civil rights activism.

At the start of the 1960s, a number of prominent Jewish communal leaders expressed frustration at the community's ardent involvement in black civil rights. In 1960, Milton Himmelfarb accused the American Jewish Congress of being more concerned with African American struggles than with Jewish religion, education, or culture.[23] That same year, *Midstream* editor Shlomo Katz wondered aloud whether black civil rights wasn't simply a fad wherein students engaged in cathartic, social guilt-releasing bouts of group therapy. Protesting segregation seemed just to be a "fashion" and a "salve for the conscience."[24]

In 1963 and 1964, the attacks on Jews involved in African American civil rights activism became more fervent. In his now-famous essay, "My Negro Problem—and Ours," *Commentary* editor Norman Podhoretz confessed to "twisted feelings about Negroes." But he also expressed annoyance at white liberals who, in his view, "romanticize Negroes and pander to them [or] who lend themselves . . . to cunning and contemptuous exploitation by Negroes they employ or try to befriend." Podhoretz expressed condescension toward African Americans even as he also invoked Auschwitz:

> Did the Jews have to survive so that 6 million innocent people should one day be burned in the ovens at Auschwitz? It is a terrible question and no one, not God himself, could ever answer it to my satisfaction. And when I think about the Negroes in America and about the image of integration as a state in which the Negroes would take their rightful place as another of the protected minorities in a pluralistic society, I wonder whether

> they really believe in their hearts that such a state can actually be attained, and if so *why* they should wish to survive as a distinct group. I think I know why the Jews once wished to survive (though I am less certain as to why we still do): they not only believed that God had given them no choice, but they were tied to a memory of past glory and a dream of imminent redemption. What does the American Negro have that might correspond to this? His past is a stigma, his color is a stigma, and his vision of the future is the hope of erasing the stigma by making color irrelevant, by making it disappear as a fact of consciousness.[25]

If Jews on the left had in the late 1940s argued antisemitism and white racism were the principal dangers to Jewish security, and anti-communist liberal Jews in the early 1950s named Soviet communism the central threat, Podhoretz by the start of the 1960s looked to the psychopathological demons within. Auschwitz had left scars on every Jew, but these were seldom if ever visible to the naked eye. Podhoretz believed that every Jew was in a pitched internal struggle to reclaim emotional well-being after the Holocaust, whether that individual knew it or not. Indeed, a lack of consciousness (or denial) that there even existed a struggle was arguably the surest sign that there was. Jews after Auschwitz had to grasp that the genocidal campaign the Nazis waged against them was not over. The genocide had merely moved to a more ambiguous place, one that involved the health and emotional security of each Jew's own mind.

This line of thinking soon inflected opinions on the unmistakably prominent role played by Jewish activists in the black civil rights struggle. An increasing number of Jewish commentators began to argue that the fact of the Holocaust meant that Jews should withdraw immediately from their involvement in civil rights activism. And not unlike Podhoretz, they began to make an argument that Jews who stayed involved in civil rights activism were self-hating.

In seeking to revise the proper meaning for Holocaust memory, for example, Abraham G. Duker attacked Jewish civil rights activists. Duker was an editor of *Jewish Social Studies* and a professor of history at Yeshiva University. Blacks were turning on Jews, Duker suggested, because of their own "disappointments with the pace of integration." The Jewish community's very survival was at risk, he said, if Jews did not recognize how black "demands on [them] are sometimes veiled with threats [and] are reminiscent of prolegomena to quotas, robberies, confiscations and pogroms." Duker explicitly compared demands for the "Negroization" of Harlem stores to German "Aryanization" propaganda. Warning that "genocidal Negro extremists have been given respectability and recognition," he analogized: "That is what happened to anti-Semites in Germany, and the world is still paying for it." Duker was no less harsh on Jews advocating for the rights of blacks, calling this a "masochistic approach to their own people." Speaking at a conference on black-Jewish relations, and through an extended chain of associations, Duker brought together Holocaust imagery with Jewish involvement in civil rights:

> The gas chambers and crematoria have proved at least to one generation the bankruptcy of assimilation in Europe. Nevertheless, the pressures of acculturation, Jewish deculturation and thereby de-Judaization have been increasing, with hedonism and deracination as their most visible hallmarks. Departure from the community through intermarriage and indifference follows. . . . In the United States escapism from Jewishness has also found expression in the integrationist movement. I know of cases of escapist identification of Jews with the integration struggle to the extent of extreme *jüdischer Selbsthass* [Jewish self-hatred] and active antisemitism.

Duker continued by conceding that the legitimacy "of this intensive interest in the Negro struggle on the part of so many Jews . . . stems from the Jewish tradition of social justice (usually called 'prophetic' tradition)." However, Duker stressed the necessity of taking into account the consequences of such interest—for "in many cases Jewish communal involvement in integration [has come] at the cost of neglecting . . . Jewish survival."[26]

Marie Syrkin, editor of the *Jewish Frontier*, offered another influential example of this new interpretation of Holocaust memory coupled with disdain for African Americans. In "Can Minorities Oppose 'De Facto' Segregation?" Syrkin gave several reasons why a civil rights push for desegregation was "not only self-depreciating but deflect[ed] energy from more meaningful demands." She made overt reference to her post-Holocaust Jewish identity in the essay:

> I am impelled to write not as a white liberal, though I believe the label fits, but as a member of a minority which knows more about systematic discrimination and violent persecution than any group in history. In the immediate as well as historic experience of Jews, a ghetto is not a metaphor; it is a concrete entity with walls, stormtroopers and no exit save the gas chamber. And wherever Jews have lived, varying gradations of bias and social exclusion have been their daily diet. I offer these credentials to indicate Jewish expertise in what it means to be a suffering minority. However brilliant his individual success, Auschwitz is in the consciousness of the modern Jew, reinforcing historic memories of catastrophe.

Syrkin's analogies revealed a wholly negative view of integration efforts. She likened full integration to "discover[ing] that most of my fellow passengers on some bus routes or subway trains happened to be Jews. Would I then be justified in protesting *de facto* segregation on my bus?" No more, she concluded, than she should "be expected to travel to Harlem in the interests of integrated dining." And Syrkin also introduced the theme of self-hate in her essay. History, she claimed, had taught the Jewish people how a minority survives. "Self-respecting" Jews knew survival could—and should—mean a desirable degree of voluntary communal separateness. Only "self-hating Jews" would ever view de facto segregation of the Jewish community "as oppressive.... Except for avowed assimilationists, Jews have never made complete integration a goal."[27]

A subsequent exchange of views about black-Jewish relations printed in *Midstream* in 1966 included more such comments. Akin to Duker's analogy between "Negroization" and "Aryanization," historian and journalist Lucy Dawidowicz, for instance, compared African American militancy to Nazism. It was "hard to distinguish Black Power from Black Shirts," she observed. Furthermore, Jews involved in Students for a Democratic Society, Student Nonviolent Coordinating Committee [SNCC] and the Congress of Racial Equality were "alienated" from their own heritage, "spitting in the wells from which they drank."[28]

These trends did not go uncontested. For instance, in their challenge to Norman Podhoretz's "My Negro Problem—and Ours," civil rights activists Shad Polier and Justine Wise Polier labeled the *Commentary* editor's vision of Jewishness "woefully insensitive" to the broader context of black lives. They proposed that it was Podhoretz who suffered from self-hate and appeared to have "a preference, conscious or unconscious, to be part of the powerful white *goyim* who could oppress, rather than to be part of any minority which might suffer oppression."[29]

But it was Podhoretz's more neoconservative vision that was in ascendance. Tensions grew in the years that followed, when the Six-Day War between Israel and the Arab nations marked a turning point in American Jewish politics. But as the intense debates over American race relations so decisively show, this seeming turning point of 1967 needs to be understood as the culmination of an extended conflict that had been brewing for quite some time. That it was radical, left-liberal, and black-identified Jews who were "not Jewish enough" came to be seen by many as the new communal common sense. A new set of associations and arguments was emerging. Blacks were not like Jews; blacks, especially when militant, were like Nazis. Jews who worked on behalf of blacks were seeking to escape their Jewishness. And memories of the Holocaust meant that Jewish survival should be paramount. Jews who continued to adhere to liberalism, the new theory went, must not be proud of their heritage. This cluster of convictions was in dramatic contrast with earlier interpretations of Holocaust memory, which had either urged Jews to identify directly with other oppressed minorities or to refuse to be bystanders to injustice.

Jewish Power

One broad outcome after the Six-Day War in 1967 was a deepened commitment among American Jews to a very particular form of Jewish pride and Jewish power. A notable example came from the right-wing Zionist Jewish Defense League (JDL), cofounded by Orthodox rabbi Meir Kahane in 1968. Kahane made the Jewish capacity for self-defense central to his message. He urged each Jewish man to stop being a "Nice Irving."[30] He warned Jews to stop being "patsies."[31] In "A Small Voice," Kahane's regular column for the Brooklyn-based Orthodox *Jewish Press*, he wrote:

> Vandals attack a Yeshiva—let that Yeshiva attack the vandals. Should a gang bloody a Jew, let a Jewish group go looking for the gang. This is the way of pride—not evil pride, but the pride of nation, of kinship. . . . There are those who will protest: This is not the Jewish way. And yet since when has it been a *mitzvah* [good deed] to be punished and beaten? Since when is it a *kiddush hashem* [sanctification of God's name] . . . ? It is not a *kiddush hashem*, it is quite the opposite. It is a disgrace to the pride of our people, our G-d.³²

Kahane became a central figure in the reconfiguration of Holocaust memory among American Jews—and here again Holocaust memory and race commingled freely, albeit (and again) in a new way. The JDL's philosophy blamed an inability to confront the legacy of the Holocaust for all the Jewish community's problems. The spiritual sickness of American Jewish identity lay precisely in a reflexive refusal to defend oneself against aggression, according to JDL thinking. Along with the slogan "Never Again," the JDL advocated that all Jews learn martial arts and that all Jewish children join rifle associations.

But it was anti-black racism that really glued the JDL together, a fact signaled by the group's most controversial recruitment tool: a large *New York Times* advertisement that appeared in June 1969. Prompted by SNCC leader James Forman's decision to read aloud a demand for reparations for slavery at New York City's leading white Christian churches and at Temple Emanu-El, the ad showed several JDL toughs, armed with baseball bats and lead pipes, gathering to defend the synagogue. The ad's caption asked: "Is This Any Way for Nice Jewish Boys to Behave?" The answer followed:

> Maybe. Maybe there are times when there is no other way to get across to the extremist that the Jew is not quite the patsy some think he is.
>
> Maybe there is only one way to get across a clear response to people who threaten seizure of synagogues and extortion of money. Maybe nice Jewish boys do not always get through to people who threaten to carry teachers out in pine boxes and to burn down merchants' stores.

> Maybe some people and organizations are too nice. Maybe in times of crisis Jewish boys should not be that nice. Maybe—just maybe—nice people build their road to Auschwitz.[33]

In this way, and in the specific context of African American political activism, the JDL resuscitated the popular and profoundly problematic theory that Jews had been passive under Nazi persecution. Indeed, one of the most striking aspects of Holocaust memory in the late 1960s and early 1970s was the exacerbation, rather than the rejection, of the myth that Jews in Europe's ghettos and death camps had gone "like lambs to the slaughter." This stereotype—strongly endorsed in Bruno Bettelheim's *Informed Heart* (1960) and Hannah Arendt's *Eichmann in Jerusalem* (1963)—was eloquently refuted during the course of the 1960s. Jewish power advocates chose, however, to reinforce the "passive Jew" myth at this moment to advance their cause both in Israel and the United States.

At the same time, and however paradoxically, the JDL articulated an overt anti-black racism even while JDL members often directly *appropriated* black militant styles for their own purposes. As one JDL woman said, explaining why she no longer straightened her naturally curly hair: "I used to straighten it because it seemed animal-like, but now it's a question of Jewish identity not to ... that happened to blacks when they got their movement." Along similar lines, another JDL member, drawing both on the example of black militancy and the memories of Nazism, described his own commitment to the militant Zionist movement this way: "The government, made up of WASPS, is willing to throw Jews to the dogs to save themselves. The Jew must make an intense militant effort just like the black did, or he'll be pushed out like in Europe in the 20s and 30s. Life will become impossible for Jews—politically, socially, and eventually physically."[34] The legacy of the Holocaust and the struggle for African American equality remained intertwined.

Jewish Radicalism

The radical Zionist movement was set officially in motion in February 1970 at Camp Ramah in Palmer, Massachusetts, where Jewish students from seventy-five campuses in the United States, Canada, and Israel gathered for a two-day conference. Voicing "total rejection of the assimilationist position and strong affirmation of the need for a liberation movement for the Jewish people," a caucus of conference members drafted the founding manifesto of the Radical Zionist Alliance. It read in part: "North American Jews are a marginal people in a society of economic, political, and cultural oppression. . . . We call for the liberation of the Jewish people and the restructuring of our people's existence in such a way as to facilitate self-determination and development of our institutions so as to control our destiny as a nation."[35] The radical Zionist movement also came to view Holocaust memory through the lens of American race relations. Left-wing radical Zionism—like the right-wing JDL—was not so much a movement developed in backlash against black power as it was a movement modeled on black power and conceived as parallel to it. Perhaps no one put this linkage in clearer perspective than Aviva Cantor Zuckoff, editor of the radical Zionist *Jewish Liberation Journal*. In 1970, Zuckoff wrote:

> Try to imagine, if you can, a group of Jews demanding reparations from the Church or some other oppressive institution, for 2,000 years of oppression. Of course it's a complete wild fantasy. We wouldn't do it, we would tell ourselves we're above all that. The truth is, Jews are terrified of asserting their power in this manner. One of the main roots of so much Jewish antagonism to the black power movement is Jews' jealousy of blacks for not being afraid to do this. . . . Jewish defenselessness is among the most dehumanizing aspects of the oppression of Jews—and the most dangerous. For it is precisely this defenselessness that provokes and encourages attack. Jews will not riot and the goyim count on this. We do not know what would have happened had German Jews rioted against Hitler before or just when he came to power; but we do know the Nazis counted on the fact that they would not do so.[36]

Whereas Jewish neoconservatives had stressed the incommensurability of the African American and Jewish experiences, radical Zionists made an almost opposite claim. For them, it was Jews (and not only New Left Jews) whose psyches were horribly disfigured—and African Americans who showed the way to self-acceptance and self-renewal in group distinctiveness. Elaborating on this perspective sometimes involved taking a strong stand against black militancy or against those New Left Jews perceived to be subservient to it. But usually radical Zionists engaged in a kind of double move, which reflected some anger at African Americans and more at New Left Jews but also borrowed heavily from black power motifs. Radical Zionists tended often to insist that Jews could—and ideally would—become as militant as African Americans.

In 1969, M. Jay Rosenberg, a student at the State University of New York at Albany, stated that radical Zionism condemned any Jew who remained in the New Left as behaving like "today's Uncle Tom." The New Left Jew, in Rosenberg's view, was someone who "scrapes along . . . ashamed of his identity," an "aspiring WASP." Using the common radical Zionist epithet for the Jewish equivalent of an Uncle Tom—"Uncle Jake"—but referring to members of his own generation rather than older Jewish establishment figures, Rosenberg elaborated on his idea of what it meant to be an Uncle Jake:

> He joins black nationalist groups, not as a Jew but as a white man. . . . He does not understand that his relevance to the black struggle is as a Jew and a fellow victim of endless white exploitation. He can comprehend the black struggle but only in the context of his own. . . . The sad fact is that the Jewish Tom is an inevitable product of American civilization. But it is time that he realizes that he, not today's black, is the invisible man; he, like yesterday's Negro, wanders in a no man's land.

Nor was Holocaust memory absent from Rosenberg's discussion. On the contrary, Rosenberg concluded his own assault against those young Jews "who [were] so trapped in [their] Long Island split level childhood that [they] can't see straight": "In the aftermath of the crematoriums, you are flippant. After Auschwitz, you are embarrassed. Thirty years after the holocaust, you have learned nothing and forgotten everything. *Ghetto Jew*, you'd better do some fast thinking."[37]

Yet another twist on these various motifs came in Tsvi Bisk's essay, "Uncle Jake, Come Home!" published in May 1969 in the *Jewish Liberation Journal*'s founding issue. Bisk was, as the paper noted, "a young Philadelphian-born Jew who [had] settled in Israel." Bisk, like Zuckoff and Rosenberg, saw a lot of psychological sickness in American Jewry and called for "a healthy solution." Bisk emphasized Israel's difference from "the West," stressing especially the "utopian" possibilities of the kibbutz and workers' cooperatives and the contrast between them and the West's "massive urban concentrations [which] have caused an alienation that is almost endemic." Bisk considered "Black-Jewish relations in America" another matter of foremost concern for Jews, and his suggested remedy was for "the total disengagement of the Jewish and Black peoples." Bisk argued that some Jews' roles as slumlords or merchants in black communities were "a socio-political embarrassment to the Jewish people" and a "chronic source of public dishonor." And he called not just for "the ending of Jewish financial interests in the black ghetto"—and especially "the ending of the employment of Black maids by Jewish housewives" (because "one cannot entertain a dignified relationship with another who is on his hands and knees scrubbing one's floor")—but also for "the removal of Jewish teachers and social workers from the Black ghetto" and "the ending of all Jewish contributions to the Black revolution."[38]

Unlike an ex-liberal like Norman Podhoretz, then, Bisk was not only scathing in his indictment of "Jewish participation in civil rights" (which he believed was "caused as much by Jewish anxiety as by any objective loyalty to a greater social ethic") but eager as well "to purify Jewish society and make it a beacon of morality (a 'light to the Gentiles' if you will)." He too invoked Nazism; Bisk argued that if the Jewish community did not self-purify "we will have done to ourselves what all the Hitlers and Hamans couldn't do to us—we will have committed national suicide." But he found "fighting other people's battles" an inexcusable and indeed "degrading" exercise. Bisk saw the emergence of black power both as an inadvertently fortuitous development for Jews, and—in this way like Rosenberg—wished Jewish activists would model themselves on it. Particularly disdainful of the sort of Jew who "rejects vociferous Jewish pride in Jewish history and Jewish accomplishments . . . as manifestations of the Ghetto neurosis while, in the same breath, he defends the similar claims of the black nationalists as a necessary purging of the collective inferiority complex of the black after centuries of persecution (it never occurring to him that the same justification may be used in a Jewish context)," Bisk also suggested that "Black nationalism may have saved Jewish identity in the U.S. by removing the route of escape (participation in black causes) from the radical Jew and by making ethnic identity once again fashionable in the U.S."³⁹ In this way, memories of the Holocaust and the symbolism of black militancy became potent reference points for radical Zionists by the end of the 1960s.

Conclusion

It is no longer newsworthy to declare the genocide of European Jews to have already become an active departure point for public discussion and debate during the immediate postwar era in the United States. That the years between 1945 and 1960 were marked by a relative silence concerning the Holocaust—one that only "began to dissipate in the 1960's, first with the trial of Adolf Eichmann in Israel in 1961, and then with the six-day war in June 1967"—is an assertion that no longer carries with it much historical credibility.⁴⁰ The volume of evidence that has been amassed in recent decades has made such an assertion sound like counterfactual fiction.

And yet questions still remain. Even as a historical consensus now states that Holocaust memory began to be constructed—and reconstructed—in the United States quite soon after the defeat of German Nazism, why does the topic of racism continue to remain outside the frame of many (if not most) of these important revisionist analyses? If anti-black racism and antiracist activism alike were—as this chapter documents—key discourses within which the Holocaust got so routinely invoked during the so-called years of silence from 1945 to 1960 (and then continuing throughout the 1960s, but with ever-changing valences and messages), why does this metaphoric link between race and Holocaust memory remain so routinely unacknowledged? As our capacity to reconstruct Holocaust memory has expanded so immensely, we still see an erasure of race from this narrative—a fact that becomes its own sort of historical development. While we remember more fully on the one hand, we continue to forget on the other. And it is this continued erasure of historical knowledge concerning the complexities of earlier American Jewish conflicts over Holocaust memory and its deep connection to racism that has formed the subject of this chapter.

Thus, when we turn to the question of how the Holocaust was commemorated by American Jews, we need increasingly to ask not if the Holocaust was actively remembered after World War II but rather by what mechanisms, and in the context of what ideological conflicts, certain memories or lessons or communal rituals have gained the aura of legitimacy—while other memories and lessons have slipped into historical limbo. This is *not* to propose that the lessons and memories that were erased from the subsequent retrospective narratives were superior to the memories and lessons that came to dominate later discussions and debates, nor vice versa. Rather it is to suggest that processes of remembrance and forgetting are complexly intertwined with ideological processes and that interrelationships between politics and memories require careful reconstruction and analysis.

Notes

1. Louis Ruchames, "Parallels of Jewish and Negro History," *Negro History Bulletin* 19 (December 1955): 65.
2. Paul Cowan, *An Orphan in History: Retrieving a Jewish Legacy* (New York: Quill, 1996), 6.
3. Neil Levi and Michael Rothberg, *The Holocaust: Theoretical Readings* (New Brunswick, NJ: Rutgers University Press, 2003), 6. Also see Deborah E. Lipstadt, "America and the Memory of the Holocaust, 1950–1965," *Modern Judaism* 16 (October 1996): 195–214; and Peter Novick, *The Holocaust in American Life* (Boston: Houghton Mifflin, 1999).
4. Lawrence L. Langer, "The Dilemma of Choice in the Death Camps," in *Holocaust: Religious and Philosophical Implications*, ed. John K. Roth and Michael Berenbaum (New York: Paragon House, 1989), 222–32; and Alvin H. Rosenfeld, "The Americanization of the Holocaust," in *Thinking about the Holocaust: After Half a Century*, ed. Alvin H. Rosenfeld (Bloomington: Indiana University Press, 1997), 119–50.
5. For fascinating comparable dynamics in other nations, see Gideon Shimoni, *Community and Conscience: The Jews in Apartheid South Africa* (Hanover NH: University Press of New England, 2003); Shirli Gilbert, "Jews and the Racial State: Legacies of the Holocaust in Apartheid South Africa, 1945–60," *Jewish Social Studies* 16, no. 3 (2010): 32–64; and, on Japan and Israel, Ran Zwigenberg, *Hiroshima: The Origins of Global Memory Culture* (Cambridge: Cambridge University Press, 2014).
6. See, for instance, Jeffrey Shandler, *While America Watches: Televising the Holocaust* (New York: Oxford University Press, 1999); Lawrence Baron, "The Holocaust and American Public Memory, 1945–1960," *Holocaust and Genocide Studies*

17 (Spring 2003): 62–88; and Hasia Diner, *We Remember with Reverence and Love: American Jews and the Myth of Silence after the Holocaust, 1945–1962* (New York: New York University Press, 2009).

7. Max Lerner, "Role of the American Jew," *Congress Weekly* 17 (January 16, 1950): 10.
8. Leo Pfeffer, "Defenses against Group Defamation," *Jewish Frontier* 13 (February 1946): 6.
9. Charles Abrams, "Homes for Aryans Only," *Commentary* 3 (May 1947): 421.
10. Arthur D. Kahn, "The American SS," *Jewish Life* 1 (November 1946): 19.
11. Moise Katz, "A Warning against Race Hatred," *Jewish Life* 1 (August 1947): 25.
12. "The Peekskill Riots," editorial, *Crisis* 56 (October 1949): 265.
13. See Sidney Hook, "Why Democracy Is Better," *Commentary* 5 (March 1948): 203–4.
14. Joachim Prinz, "'America Must Not Remain Silent . . . ,'" reprinted in Michael E. Staub, ed., *The Jewish 1960s: An American Sourcebook* (Waltham, MA: Brandeis University Press, 2004), 90–91. Prinz's speech originally appeared in *Congress Bi-Weekly* 30 (October 7, 1963): 3.
15. Ruth Gruber Michaels, "March on Washington: The Enemy Is Silence," *Hadassah Magazine* 44 (September 1963): 40.
16. Jacob M. Rothschild, quoted in Melissa Fay Greene, *The Temple Bombing* (Reading, MA: Addison-Wesley, 1996), 189.
17. "The Embattled Minority," editorial, *Reconstructionist* 28 (June 2, 1962): 4.
18. Richard L. Rubenstein, "The Rabbis Visit Birmingham," *Reconstructionist* 29 (May 31, 1963): 5.
19. Rabbi Richard C. Hertz, "Rising Tide of Negro-Jewish Tensions," *Ebony* 20 (December 1964): 124, 118.
20. Nat Hentoff, *The New Equality* (New York: Viking, 1964): 81.
21. Quoted in "The Evil to Be Eradicated," *Congress Bi-Weekly* 31 (September 24, 1964): 3.
22. For a richer sense of the terms of debate at this historical moment, see Staub, *The Jewish 1960s*, chap. 4.
23. Milton Himmelfarb, "In the Community," *Commentary* 30 (August 1960): 160.
24. Shlomo Katz, "Notes in Midstream: Negroes and We," *Midstream* 6 (Spring 1960): 33.
25. Norman Podhoretz, "My Negro Problem—and Ours," *Commentary* 35 (February 1963): 93–101.
26. Abraham G. Duker, "On Negro-Jewish Relations—a Contribution to a Discussion," *Jewish Social Studies* 27 (January 1965): 20–29.

27. Marie Syrkin, "Can Minorities Oppose 'De Facto' Segregation?" *Jewish Frontier* 31 (September 1964): 9. Syrkin also pointedly asked: "A minority may justly oppose the quality of housing, schooling or job opportunities available to it, but with what grace can it object to a preponderance of its own people?," 10.
28. Lucy S. Dawidowicz, "Negro-Jewish Relations in America: A Symposium," *Midstream* 12 (December 1966): 17.
29. Justine Wise Polier and Shad Polier, "Fear Turned to Hatred," *Congress Bi-Weekly* 30 (February 18, 1963): 5–6.
30. Yossi Klein Halevi, *Memoirs of a Jewish Extremist: An American Story* (Boston: Little, Brown, 1995), 79.
31. *The Jewish Defense League: Principles and Philosophies* (New York: Education Department of the Jewish Defense League, n.d.), 275.
32. Meir Kahane, "A Small Voice," *Jewish Press*, July 26, 1968, 36.
33. "Is This Any Way for Nice Jewish Boys to Behave?," advertisement, *New York Times*, June 24, 1969, 31.
34. JDL members quoted in Janet L. Dolgin, *Jewish Identity and the JDL* (Princeton: Princeton University Press, 1977), 160.
35. "Radical Zionist Manifesto," *Genesis 2* 1 (April 1970): 8; and "Jewish Leftists Form Anti-Establishment Body," *Jewish Post and Opinion*, February 27, 1970, 1.
36. Aviva Cantor Zuckoff, "Oppression of Amerika's Jews," *Jewish Liberation Journal* 8 (November 1970): 1–2.
37. M. Jay Rosenberg, "To Uncle Tom and Other Such Jews," *Flame* 1 (March 26, 1969): 3. Rosenberg's essay originally appeared in the *Village Voice* on February 13, 1969.
38. Tsvi Bisk, "Uncle Jake, Come Home!," *Jewish Liberation Journal* 1 (May 1969): 7–14.
39. Bisk, "Uncle Jake, Come Home!," 13–14.
40. Gabriel Schoenfeld, "Death Camps as Kitsch," *New York Times*, March 18, 1999, A25.

Part III

Literary Connections across Time

PART 3 EXPLORES THROUGH a literary lens the connections made between the Holocaust and other instances of racial persecution. The contributors examine literary efforts to connect the Holocaust and racism in geographically, culturally, and temporally diverse settings, approaching their examples as simultaneously imaginative and historically contingent. They attempt, in other words, to historicize literary productions that may themselves be inherently, or even deliberately, ahistorical.

Thanks to their imaginative nature, literatures connecting Holocaust memory with varied examples of racism have the potential to widen the former's cultural and political reach. Fiction's focus on the symbolic and the emotive might jeopardize historical specificity, but empathetic identification is almost always enlarged. While such connections may be problematic from the historian's perspective, the goals of literature lie elsewhere, expanding the Holocaust's analogical power to shed light on other instances of racial persecution and, conversely, to bring the legacies of a diversity of racial conflicts back to bear on the memory of the Holocaust. The task that faces the scholar interested in these literatures is to pay due attention to the contexts in which they forge their imaginative connections. Only through such historicized analyses can we understand the political and social utility of such memory work.

Given these considerations, it is perhaps no coincidence that literary scholars have been some of the first to explore the intersections between the Holocaust and racism, particularly in a postcolonial context. In the following chapters, some of the field's prominent representatives explore the intellectual possibilities of "thinking together" postcolonial and Jewish victimhoods with specific reference to the Holocaust.

Michael Rothberg juxtaposes the work of the postcolonial theorist Frantz Fanon and the Auschwitz survivor Ruth Klüger to link two disparate instances of "becoming a racialized subject," urging us to probe the intersections between the Holocaust and colonialism. Focusing on the intersection between literature and film, Rothberg's work provides a deep and sustained meditation on the many layers of interpretation that generate the process of racialization at the level of both the individual and the group. In his reading of Klüger through the lens of Fanon, Rothberg pushes us to consider the benefits for both post-Holocaust and postcolonial fields of inquiry in creating new models of comparative critique.

Providing another compelling example of how such comparative work enlarges our understanding of the dynamics of racialized societies, Sarah Phillips Casteel examines how postwar Caribbean writers have drawn on Holocaust imagery in an identificatory rather than competitive manner, to make sense of black histories of trauma. In so doing, she aims to break down the often binary "north-south" paradigm in which Holocaust memory operates, providing a more nuanced understanding of the motivations of Caribbean writers who invoke the analogical power of Holocaust memory. In these cases, Casteel posits, the Holocaust functions less as a site of competitive victimhood than as a site of memory and identification.

Yet literature has also constituted a divisive force, as Avril Alba's revisiting of the Australian-based Demidenko/Darville debate demonstrates. Here, Holocaust memory succeeded in igniting, rather than disavowing, age-old racist stereotypes, threatening to expose the nascent and still somewhat shaky foundations of multicultural Australia. Despite its somewhat perverse inversion of Holocaust memory, Alba argues that this literary hoax can be fruitfully understood (but not excused) as a "refraction of Australia's racial and identity politics at the time." Thus, while acrimony and scandal followed in its wake, Helen Demidenko/Darville's novel also served to reveal important fault lines in Australian political life.

Taken together, these three contributions illustrate literature's ability to cross borders and cultures in unexpected and often counterintuitive ways. Indeed, fiction's capacity to transgress historical boundaries can paradoxically bring histories to bear in radically new contexts, creating new encounters between seemingly disparate memories.

9

In the Nazi Cinema

Race, Visuality, and Identification
in Fanon and Klüger

Michael Rothberg

THE OPENING SECTION OF Ruth Klüger's 1992 memoir *weiter leben*—self-translated and published in a revised English version in 2001 as *Still Alive*—recounts everyday life in Nazi Vienna from the perspective of a young Jewish girl. In describing a youth spent under the shadow of National Socialism and later in several Nazi camps, Klüger grants a central place to cinema as an exemplary site of fantasy, identification, and social control. Besides evoking in general terms the fascination that Nazi propaganda, ideology, and film held for her as a child, Klüger briefly recounts watching several films in particular. In addition to four German films from 1940 to 1941—*Jud Süss*, *Ohm Krüger*, . . . *reitet für Deutschland*, and *Carl Peters*—Klüger mentions seeing Disney's first animated feature, *Snow White and the Seven Dwarves*. While the viewing of *Snow White* plays a significant role in the memoir, to which I will return, the film that left the greatest impression on the young Klüger, she reports, was the one about nineteenth-century German colonialism in East Africa: Hubert Selpin's *Carl Peters*, a politically inflected biopic portraying a legendary imperialist adventurer. In accounting for the film's power to imprint itself on her memory, Klüger draws attention to "a central scene [in which Peters] stood in his lily-white suit, whip in hand, in front of a group of barely clad and cringing black natives. . . . [T]he symbols of brutality . . . vibrated among the audience. . . . They must have inspired the boys who were watching in their short pants and their Hitler Youth daggers . . . just as they appalled the Jew girl with vague premonitions."[1] Klüger's account of watching *Carl Peters* in the forbidden realm of the Nazi cinema establishes both an identification between an Austrian Jewish subject and colonized Africans and an analogy between colonial violence and the violence of the Holocaust. Why does Klüger—both as a young girl in Vienna and as a much older memoirist long since immigrated to the United States—look to the colonial scene to make sense of the experience of living under Nazism? What is at stake in her identifications and analogies, and how can they help shed light on the relationship between Jewish and postcolonial writing?

The analogy Klüger constructs between colonial and Nazi violence does not suggest an equivalence between what are quite distinct histories. Rather, something more interesting emerges. Klüger's cinematic stories occupy what may seem an exceptional space and time: after the 1938 *Anschluss* in which Nazi Germany annexed Austria but before the genocidal killing of the Holocaust had begun. Focusing on this seemingly unrepresentative moment of everyday life under extreme threat and foreboding allows Klüger to reveal something paradoxically central but often minimized in accounts of the Holocaust: the importance of the *process* of racialization in the Nazi genocide. She reveals both how she was turned into a racial "other" and how that process also produced racially "superior" subjects capable of complicity with the genocide of their neighbors. While the moments before and after this transitional period would imply a very different relation between European Jews and the subjects of European colonialism—because they would necessitate confronting periods of relative assimilation and of the most extreme annihilation, respectively—Klüger's focus on racialization and complicity in an exceptional moment suggests that both postcolonial and Holocaust scholars can gain comparative insights by opening up their disciplinary borders.

Klüger's cinematic scenes possess a strong intertextual resonance with important works in the postcolonial canon. Most crucially for the analysis I undertake here, the scene of furtive spectatorship Klüger describes in her memoir strongly recalls the famous discussion of colonialism and cinema in Frantz Fanon's *Black Skin, White Masks*.[2] Juxtaposing Fanon and Klüger reveals the intersection of race, visuality, and identification as a prominent meeting ground for Jewish and black histories marked by trauma and diaspora. The texts of these very different writers thus provide an opportunity to take up some seldom-explored issues, for the writings that have emerged out of and confronted the legacies of the Nazi genocide are rarely considered alongside the writings that have emerged out of and confronted the legacies of European colonialism. Yet, as the texts of Fanon and Klüger illustrate, these two bodies of writing are compelled to confront many of the same ethical and aesthetic questions and problems. Like the literature of the Holocaust, the literature of the colonial and postcolonial conditions testifies to the underside of European modernity. Both literatures bear witness to forms of extreme and everyday violence perpetrated in the name of racial ideologies and imperial political projects, and both literatures grapple necessarily with the burden of history, the destruction of cultures and communities, and the fracturing of time—not simply into the familiar categories of before, during, and after but also into uncanny, if not traumatic, constellations.

In the following pages, I look closely at scenes of cinema, racialization, and identification in Fanon and Klüger to reveal how visual culture becomes a site of articulation between histories often kept isolated from each other. This conjunction also reveals, however, that such reckoning does not take place in a "homogenous empty time"—or a homogenous space. The locations that bring together supposedly autonomous histories also raise problems of translation and reveal gaps between histories. Reading Klüger through Fanon and the insights of postcolonial critique allows us to situate the experience of becoming a racialized subject within the unfolding of the Holocaust—an insufficiently explored line of inquiry. Simultaneously, Klüger's account of the experience of racialization points to ambivalences and blind spots about Jewishness in much postcolonial scholarship, including that of Fanon. Finally, however, Klüger's memory of watching *Carl Peters* contains a cautionary tale about the nature of our access to the past and the modes through which we construct historical analogies. Taken together, the texts of Fanon and Klüger testify to the need for new models of comparative critique between the postcolonial and the post-Holocaust and beyond competitive notions of history and identity.

In the Colonial Cinema: Fanon's Footnotes

In a well-known footnote to the chapter "The Negro and Psychopathology" in *Black Skin, White Masks*, Frantz Fanon anticipates Klüger's cinematic anecdotes and invents a new mode of cultural critique that links affect and psychic disruption to the "cultural situation" of the colonized. The explicit theorization of racialization, visual culture, and identification in *Black Skin, White Masks* can help illuminate Klüger's narrative. Fanon's famous footnote annotates his claim that "every neurosis, every abnormal manifestation, every affective erethism in an Antillean is the product of his cultural situation. In other words, there is a constellation of postulates, a series of propositions that slowly and subtly—with the help of books, newspapers, schools and their texts, advertisements, films, radio—penetrate the individual by constituting the world view of the group to which he belongs" (*pénètrent un individu—en constituant la vision du monde de la collectivité à laquelle il appartient*).³ Demonstrating his characteristic critical prescience in the footnote to that sentence, Fanon suggests that the racializing effect of the media might best be understood through a comparative study of audience reception:

> I recommend the following experiment to those who are unconvinced: Attend showings of a Tarzan film in the Antilles and in Europe. In the Antilles, the young Negro identifies himself de facto with Tarzan against the Negroes. This is much more difficult for him in a European theater, for the rest of the audience, which is white, automatically identifies him with the savages on the screen. It is a conclusive experience. The Negro learns that one is not black without problems. A documentary film on Africa produces similar reactions when it is shown in a French city and in Fort-de-France. I will go farther and say that Bushmen and Zulus arouse even more laughter among the young Antilleans. It would be interesting to show how in this instance the reactional exaggeration betrays a hint of recognition. In France a Negro who sees this documentary is virtually petrified. There he has no more hope of flight: He is at once Antillean, Bushman, and Zulu.⁴

In this passage, Fanon draws attention to two important aspects of the cinematic scenes to which he and Klüger grant prominence. First, he reveals that these scenes are not simply scenes *depicting* racialization but are in fact scenes *of* racialization. That is, cinema as an everyday institutional space supplements film's representational powers. Second, he demonstrates that within that institutional space racialization takes place through the simultaneity of conflicting forms of identification. In other words, cinema plays at least a double role in the process of racialization: as text, film seems to offer a set of naturalized identifications ("In the Antilles, the young Negro identifies himself de facto with Tarzan"), while as institution, the cinema produces what Mary Ann Doane has called "a space of identificatory anxiety" in which text and context exist in tension with each other.[5] The "traumatic break"[6] that occurs in such moments of everyday racialization derives from the conflict between the cinema's two roles: racist culture elicits certain identifications (for example, with white heroes) that a racist society then renders impossible. As Ella Shohat and Robert Stam put it, "The conventional self-denying identification with the White hero's gaze . . . is shortcircuited through the awareness of being looked at in a certain way, as if one were being 'screened' or 'allegorized' by a colonial gaze within the movie theater."[7] Cinema leaves the colonial subject "virtually petrified" because it simultaneously elicits cross-cutting identifications that transgress racial categories *and* reproduces a Manichean colonialist worldview that fixes subjects in racialized slots (a Manicheanism Fanon theorized even more explicitly in *The Wretched of the Earth*).

Yet the act of revealing this petrifying bind also constitutes the critical, resistant edge of Fanon's account. While colonialism, like the cinema of the time, sees the world in black and white terms (as Klüger will also remark), Fanon renders both the gaze and identification *relational*; that is, he makes visible the crisscrossing looks that always constitute the production, distribution, and consumption of visual culture. Here, the operative points from which gazes and identifications emerge are already at least fourfold—the Antilles forms part of a web connecting the site of Hollywood production, the controlling gaze of the French metropole, and another colonial periphery in Africa. *Black Skin, White Masks* as a whole creates a web of what Shohat and Stam call "analogical identifications"[8]—a web that also echoes in Klüger's experience in the Nazi cinema. Fanon's emphasis on relationality does not relativize the moral or political meaning of racism or colonialism; rather, he suggests that questions of moral and political responsibility do not map onto psychic disorder in any clear way. Political context disrupts psychic order across the board. Colonial and race societies intensively police relations among social groups and seek to produce various kinds of segregation, of course. But Fanon's analysis reveals how, nevertheless, the traumas associated with racism create a psychically and socially relational intimacy across groups.

To this relational account of racialization, *Black Skin, White Masks* adds another comparative dimension: it includes extensive discussion of antisemitism and traumas suffered by Jews.[9] When Fanon published his treatise in 1952, World War II (which Fanon fought in) and the discovery of the Nazi camps were still relatively recent events. With frequent reference to Sartre's 1948 *Anti-Semite and Jew* (*Réflexions sur la question juive*), Fanon carefully relates and distinguishes antisemitism and anti-black racism based on what he understands as the different place occupied by the Jew and the "Negro" in the racist imaginary. If, Fanon writes, "to suffer from a phobia of Negroes is to be afraid of the biological" or sexual, to fear Jews is to possess a phobia about the "intellectual danger" that accompanies "civilization."[10] Yet Fanon's text proves ambivalent on the question of how to relate black and Jewish histories. While Fanon sometimes points to what Jews and blacks share, he also often assimilates Jews to the category of whiteness—an assimilation that recent history should have complicated, as analysis of Klüger's text will indicate.

On the one hand, Fanon links blacks and Jews as "brother[s] in misery" because of parallels between European racism and antisemitism, and he famously cites his "philosophy professor, a native of the Antilles, who recalled the fact to me one day: 'Whenever you hear anyone abuse the Jews, pay attention, he is talking about you.'"[11] Once again, such insight sometimes emerges in the liminal space of a footnote. As Bryan Cheyette has observed, "Much of Fanon's response to Sartre takes place in the footnotes to *Peau noire*, which often act as a kind of Möbius strip which enables him to tell the differing stories of colonial racism and antisemitism simultaneously."[12] Not long before Fanon introduces the Tarzan example, he explicitly links the experience of "becoming Black" under the racist gaze to "becoming Jewish" in the face of antisemitism. Having commented that the black man's "first encounter with a white man oppresses him with the whole weight of his blackness,"[13] Fanon appends a note citing Sartre's discussion of Jews only becoming aware of their Jewishness in relation to the non-Jewish world. The example Sartre uses, and that Fanon cites without further comment, obliquely evokes the Holocaust: "During the Occupation there was a Jewish doctor who lived shut up in his home in Fontainebleau and raised his children without saying a word to them of their origin. But however it comes about, some day they must learn the truth: sometimes from the smiles of those around them, sometimes from rumour or insult. The later the discovery, the more violent the shock. Suddenly they perceive that others know something about them that they do not know."[14] The traumatic "shock" that Sartre describes anticipates the shock that takes place in the French cinema when, under the white gaze, the Antillean learns that "one is not black without problems."[15] As Klüger will also note, both blacks and Jews are vulnerable to trauma via encounter and exposure—hence the recurrent use of visuality as an index of violence in both of their texts.

On the other hand, because of the primacy Fanon grants to the "racial epidermal schema"[16] in the constitution of the colonial subject, he ultimately separates the experience of blacks from that of Jews by virtue of Jews' allegedly greater ability to pass as white, even as, once again, he obliquely references the Nazi genocide:

> The Jew can be unknown in his Jewishness. He is not wholly what he is. . . . His actions, his behavior are the final determinant. He is a white man, and, apart from some rather debatable characteristics, he can sometimes go unnoticed. . . . Granted, the Jews are harassed—what am I thinking of? They are hunted down, exterminated, cremated. But these are little family quarrels. The Jew is disliked from the moment he is tracked down. But in my case everything takes on a new guise. I am given no chance. I am overdetermined from without. I am the slave not of the "idea" that others have of me but of my own appearance.[17]

Fanon clearly employs an ironic rhetoric, here laced with litotes, which cannot be read literally. Nevertheless, even leaving aside the deliberate minimization of Nazi genocide as a "family quarrel," Fanon's passage ignores the contradictions and legacies of antisemitism that make it a very peculiar kind of family affair. Seen from the present, Fanon's distinction between the central role that the visual plays in anti-black racism and the centrality of ideas and ideology in antisemitism may seem like common sense. But this commonsense account amounts to a surprisingly unhistorical theory of Jewish visibility; it ignores the relative consistency of the image of the Jew over time, the frequent association of Jews with various "anomalous" physical traits, including blackness (as demonstrated, for example, in the work of Sander Gilman) and—at the time Fanon was writing—the still-recent production and mobilization of a visible, highly biologized, and even sexualized Jewish difference in the context of a genocidal project.[18] In addition, whether employed in the early 1950s by Fanon or today in the works of some postcolonial critics, this simplified binary between blacks and white Jews risks homogenizing Europe and casting blacks definitively outside European "familial" space. Without doubt, Fanon provides critical resources for a post-Holocaust, postcolonial theory of racialization, and in linking colonialism to Nazism and racism to antisemitism anticipates insights only now being reclaimed. Yet his ambivalence about Jewish difference and about its relation to blackness also makes "visible" ambivalences that continue to haunt postcolonial studies.[19]

IN THE NAZI CINEMA: A DOUBLE DEFIANCE

In a discussion of cinema remarkably reminiscent of Fanon's, Klüger's *Still Alive* focuses on a moment when, contra Fanon, Jewishness does become visible. At the same time, Klüger also reveals, as Fanon has taught us to expect, how during such moments the process of racialization itself becomes visible in the institutional spaces of spectatorship and spectacle. In documenting the transitional period of everyday life under Nazism, Klüger stages two cinematic scenes that are linked in the English version of the memoir by the appearance of the ambiguous word "native," a word that turns out to mark a site of transfer between Holocaust and colonial discourse.

The discussion begins with a story in which Klüger, like Fanon, becomes the object of the racial gaze: "In 1940, when I was eight or nine, the local movie theatre showed Walt Disney's *Snow White*. I loved movies. I had been weaned on Mickey Mouse shorts and traded pictures of Shirley Temple with classmates. I badly wanted to see this film, but since I was Jewish, I naturally wasn't permitted to. I groused and bitched about this unfairness, until finally my mother proposed that I should leave her alone and just go and forget about what was permitted and what wasn't."[20] When, spurred on by her mother, Klüger summons the courage to attend, she finds herself seated "next to the nineteen-year-old baker's daughter from next door with her little siblings, enthusiastic Nazis one and all."[21] After "sweat[ing] it out" in the theater for ninety minutes, wondering "whether the baker's daughter was really glaring at me, or if I was only imagining it,"[22] Klüger is finally castigated by her young neighbor and threatened with the police if she transgresses again. Summing up the experience, Klüger writes:

> The story of Snow White can be reduced to one question: who is entitled to live in the king's palace and who is the outsider. The baker's daughter and I followed this formula. She, in her own house, the magic mirror of her racial purity before her eyes, and I, also at home here, a native [*auch an diesem Ort beheimatet*], but without permission and at this moment expelled and exposed. Even though I despised the law that excluded me, I still felt ashamed to have been found out. For shame doesn't arise from the shameful action, but from discovery and exposure.[23]

In this allegory of whiteness, the Jewish girl is simultaneously at home and uncanny, fixed and expelled. The appearance of the ambivalent word "native"—not present in the German version, which deploys instead the discourse of *Heimat*—suggests at once a naturalized claim to belonging and the presence of a colonial discourse in which it is precisely "natives" who are subject to displacement. The ambiguous deictics "here" and "at this moment" reinforce the traumatic destabilization of location and identity that, as Fanon famously theorizes in *Black Skin, White Masks*, results from the everyday racializing gaze.[24] The spatial and temporal division at the heart of this act of racialization suggests both the specific position of "native" German and Austrian Jews under the Nazis and the more general uncertainty about Jewish positioning in the post-Holocaust and postcolonial moment of the text's enunciation. Marking expulsion from the "here and now" of unproblematic belonging, Klüger's post-Holocaust, diasporic narration of the displacement of "natives" by a project of "racial purity" makes an implicit claim to postcolonial positionality. In other words, Klüger both confirms Fanon's links between racialization and the visual and exposes the gaps in his assumption about what constitutes Jewish invisibility; in Nazi Vienna, the Jewish girl does not go "unknown" and "unnoticed." Against the backdrop of a spectacle of whiteness, she becomes visible as a racial other. Perhaps equally important, the passage charts the conversion of neighborliness to enmity, as the "baker's daughter from next door" takes on the role of state agent policing the everyday. While this somewhat haphazard enforcement of racial segregation seems far removed from the systematic genocide to come, the very everydayness of this scene suggests how the preconditions for genocide were established—in part, as Fanon has suggested, through the relations of looking staged in the cinema.

Klüger's further cinematic memories illustrate the possibilities and limits of resistance to the dominant racial gaze that both she and Fanon locate in that cinematic space. Klüger describes her encounter with the baker's daughter as taking place in 1940, that is, after Jews had been banned from the cinema and other public spaces but before the September 1, 1941, "identification of Jews" police ordinance, which required Jews to wear a "clearly visible" yellow star on their clothing.[25] While such a law seems to confirm Fanon's point that under ordinary circumstances Jews can go "unnoticed"—hence the need for supplementary forms of identification—Klüger's memoir reveals that this inconspicuousness is itself of limited value due to the everyday panoptic gaze of a profoundly racialized society like that established by National Socialism and embodied by the baker's daughter. Yet neither the young Klüger's disturbing encounter at *Snow White* nor even the identification ordinance prevents her from attending films. "The cinema," she writes, "was a magnet." That magnetism indicates both the ideological pull of visual culture and the possibilities for countervision it sometimes makes possible:

> The movies I wanted to see were Nazi propaganda films, which gave me the satisfaction of a double defiance: I was thwarting both the discriminatory laws of the state and the rules of my family, who had never permitted me to listen to a speech by Hitler on the radio. . . . These films taught me the dominant

ideology, which concerned me, I reasoned, and which I couldn't just ignore because it wasn't palatable. The attraction lay in the critical distance I had to maintain, the resistance against any temptation to identify or agree.[26]

In this scene, the young Klüger's "double defiance" recalls what cultural theorist José Muñoz has called "disidentification": "a survival strategy that is employed by a minority spectator . . . to resist and confound socially prescriptive patterns of identification." Disidentification is not the opposite of identification, but a particular kind of appropriation of the dominant ideology, "one that neither opts to assimilate within such a structure nor strictly opposes it; rather, disidentification is a strategy that works on and against dominant ideology."[27] Klüger's framing of her discussion of Nazi propaganda as "forbidden" but "irresistible"[28] suggests that what is at stake is indeed not a simple resistance to identification but the necessity of passing through identification's magnetic pull on the way toward a defiant subjectivity.

As Klüger continues her discussion of cinema, the ambiguous disidentificatory relationship between Nazi and Jew becomes further complicated by the entry of a third term: the colonial African subject. Here, at greater length, is the passage in which Klüger describes Hubert Selpin's propagandistic film about colonialism in East Africa:

> The representative of German power was named Carl Peters . . . and in a central scene he stood in his lily-white suit, whip in hand, in front of a group of barely clad and cringing black natives [*Schwarzen*]. You have to remember that it was decades before violence, realistically acted out, became part and parcel of common movie fare. In those days the symbols of brutality had a disturbing effect, which vibrated among the audience. They must have inspired the boys who were watching in their short pants and their Hitler Youth daggers . . . just as they appalled the Jew girl with vague premonitions. That is, I felt personally threatened by the whip, the boots, and the racist black-white confrontation in black-and-white. I call up this remembered image from the flickering screen as meaningful

background to my later experience of a power structure that involved real men with boots and whips, for the film tried to make sense of it—to which I could oppose my contrary sense—whereas the reality was clumsy chaos.[29]

Mobilizing for a second time in the English version of the memoir the concept of the displaced "native," the temporality of this passage is complex: Klüger's post-Holocaust account of her "Holocaust girlhood" (to cite the memoir's subtitle) draws on a "postcolonial" Nazi-produced account of Germany's erstwhile colonial experience in order to map out relations of power and ideology that the subject had not yet fully experienced.[30] Identification serves as a means of cutting across the "clumsy chaos" of reality and establishing lines of affiliation. But what exactly is the relationship between German master, colonized subject, and Jew in this passage? On the one hand, the scene suggests a process of active identification in which the Jewish girl takes the place of the ungendered "natives," just as the Hitler Youth boys take the place of the colonial master. It is precisely the native's visible difference from the master, doubled in the very medium of black-and-white film, that seems to support these parallel identifications. The shared, affective "vibration" Klüger tracks in the cinema points once again to the simultaneous production of the racially "superior" and the racially "subaltern." On the other hand, however, while the passage mobilizes a series of oppositions—black and white, German power and cringing native, Hitler Youth and Jew girl, film and reality, sense and chaos—it concerns equally the transgression of the laws and boundaries that hold such terms apart. Klüger's presence in the theatre is impelled by a desire to move into forbidden space and to see forbidden images, despite the "shame" that her earlier exposure by the baker's daughter entailed. The struggle to disidentify—to maintain critical distance—entails reoccupying the ideological machinery of exclusion.

It is not at first easy to understand why a minority subject would want to move into this deadening and deadly space—to identify not only with the victims of German power but with the whole technical apparatus of Nazi ideology. Again, Muñoz's insights into the subjection and subjectivation of minority subjects are useful: "To disidentify is to read oneself and one's own life narrative in a moment, object, or subject that is not culturally coded to 'connect' with the disidentifying subject. It is not to pick and choose what one takes out of an identification. It is not to willfully evacuate the politically dubious or shameful components within an identificatory locus. Rather, it is the reworking of those energies that do not elide the 'harmful' or contradictory components of any identity."[31] The colonial film is clearly not intended to "connect" with the young Klüger—in fact, she is actively excluded from its address. And yet it clearly offers her something otherwise unavailable: "sense." In this scene, the already racialized subject passes through desire for and identification with that which is shameful because, under extreme circumstances, that toxic force also offers the only available vision of order. The powerful other and his fetishized accoutrements, the boots and whip on which the young spectator focuses, are representative of the will-to-order of that other, his ideological "sense." The young Klüger's willful submission to the ideological machinery of Nazi interpellation reveals a desire for meaningful structure and hints that without disidentification the experience of the subaltern would tend toward chaos and thus subjective dissolution (the phenomenology of which Fanon powerfully captures in *Black Skin*).

The active, productive quality of Klüger's disidentification helps us identify a shortcoming in the dominant discussions of racialization. As Rey Chow argues in *Primitive Passions*, much postcolonial theorization has been invested in a binary framework in which the gaze is always European and the non-European world is mere object or spectacle.[32] As we've seen, Fanon's work both fits that binary model and complicates the one-sidedness of the racializing gaze by revealing the multiplicity of gazes at work in the colonial cinema. Klüger also stages multiple gazes but, in addition, challenges the European/non-European binary that continues to structure Fanon's and Chow's arguments. While postcolonial studies has no doubt developed since Chow originally made her observation about the one-sided gaze, the countermodel she proposes, which takes into account the "dialectics of [the colonized subject's] seeing,"[33] is nonetheless illuminating for the texts under consideration here. In Chow's model—paradoxically but fittingly for Klüger's text—taking account of the nondominant gaze also entails recognizing that gaze as emerging from the subject's previous objectification; she thus could be seen as arguing for a kind of disidentification. Chow's reflections on the possibility of a postcolonial counterethnography supplement Muñoz and may be of use in unpacking the importance of spectatorship in Klüger's text.

Chow's suggestion that the "new ethnography [of] those who were previously ethnographized" must take account of the "memory of past *objecthood*—the experience of being looked at" resonates with Klüger's scenes of Nazi Vienna as much as with Fanon's anticolonial counterethnography. To the self-reflexivity of postmodern anthropology and the well-known theorization of the male gaze by Laura Mulvey, Chow adds the postcolonial insight that "being-looked-at-ness, rather than the act of looking, constitutes the primary event in cross-cultural representation." For Chow, the "memory of past *objecthood*" can be translated into a moment of subjective agency: she writes that "the state of being looked at not only is built into the way non-Western cultures are viewed by Western ones; more significantly it is part of the *active* manner in which such cultures represent—ethnographize—themselves."[34] Read through the lenses of Fanon, Muñoz, and Chow, Klüger's *Still Alive* becomes a form of disidentifactory counterethnography in which she recognizes the violence of the production of "Aryan" whiteness by working through the scene of colonial spectacle and spectatorship. The scene of colonial domination in Klüger's text, as well as the scene of exposure at *Snow White*, is part of an *active* disidentification with Vienna, the terrain of her childhood, "the original slime from which life developed . . . a city that hated children—Jewish children, to be precise."[35] Returning in memory and discourse to the slime of Nazi Vienna allows Klüger to stage a form of resistance to historical erasure and to ethnographize a culture that expelled her after rendering her uncanny in her own home.

Yet Klüger's counterethnography bears one further cautionary lesson—a warning about memory, history, and analogy. What is most fascinating about her description of the scene of colonial domination in *Carl Peters* is that while all the elements Klüger describes from the film are in fact there—a remarkable feat of memory if she has not seen the film for a half century—the scene itself is not. That is, a scene exists that features whips, shackled, half-naked Africans, and Peters in his white suit, but in this scene—the only one to which Klüger might be referring—Peters is in the position not of the sadist but of the liberator. The scene takes place early in the film, when Peters and his crew have set out across East Africa for the first time to claim land for Germany. Coming over a hill, they see a village burning and, on closer inspection, Arab slave traders on horses whipping shackled Africans. Peters challenges the slave traders, who claim in heavily accented English that they have British permission for their trade. But after Peters yells at them, the Arabs ride off, leaving the Germans to rip up the British papers and free the slaves. In subsequent scenes, tribe after tribe begs Peters for protection and, after performing "exotic" dance and drum rituals before the colonizers, sign over their land in return.

Despite Klüger's understandable misremembering, we can profitably read the film as allegorizing the relationship between the Holocaust and German colonialism—only in a more indirect mode. On the one hand, Klüger is correct about the character of the historical Peters as she is about the contemporary significance of the film. Strictly speaking, all of *Carl Peters* constitutes a sort of Freudian screen memory in which innocent scenes of liberation, protection, and intercommunal harmony cover over the brutality of Peters and German colonialism. Additionally, as Sabine Hake argues, "German films about the colonies partook not in 'the battle over Africa' but in the battle over Europe," a battle in which "the terms of racial and national identity [were] in fact worked out."[36] Having lost its non-European colonies after World War I, Nazi Germany's postcolonial representations of Africa were part of its neocolonial projects of *Lebensraum* and genocide.[37] Yet, on the other hand, Africa's place in this battle was not simply that of a site of racial otherness that could be analogized to Jewishness. Rather, as Hake shows, the connection made by the film between colonial relations and relations between Nazis and Jews is more mediated and passes through a "conflation of antisemitic and anti-*British* positions."[38] The film is, on its own terms, "pro-African."

At the same time, the fact that Klüger remembers the film as providing a more immediate image of her own condition is not without significance. Her translation of the scene seems to point to a two-way reshaping of history and experience: while the film clearly made enough of an impression on the young "Jew girl" to mark her experience of the Nazi period, it also may be that her future experiences of the camps re-formed her experience of the film. While assuredly only one person's experience, such a mutual determination of the colonial and the genocidal remains suggestive for thinking about the cultural legacies of two autonomous histories that have continued to intersect in cultural memory and collective consciousness despite the disciplinary divide between "things Jewish" and "things postcolonial" that has come to keep them apart. As scholars continue to seek links between German and European colonialism and the Holocaust, *Carl Peters* and Klüger's misremembering of it stand as a methodological warning: the form of the colonialism/Holocaust relationship should not be considered in the mode of simple historical analogy, a mode that the passage reveals as imaginary in the Lacanian sense. Both the film and Klüger's memory of it work at the level of the imaginary, defined by identification, mirroring, and binary logic. A critical reading of the film and memoir suggests the contours of a different conception of the relationship between German colonialism and Nazi genocide as indirect, mediated, and triangulated between multiple historical and phantasmatic positions.

The particularities of German colonialism, staged in Klüger and in *Carl Peters*, also serve as a reminder of the differentiated legacies of diverse European imperial projects. The same holds for Fanon's reflections on the particular stakes of racial representation in the Antilles. While both situations have implications for general theories of race, empire, and genocide, as I have tried to suggest, we cannot assume generalizability and translation—they must be constructed from the ground up. Such construction demands new forms of interethnic, transnational comparison.

Conclusion: Beyond Competition

The dynamic interplay of colonial and Nazi domination and of racialization and visual culture in the texts of Fanon and Klüger suggests the need for a new way of thinking about twentieth- and twenty-first-century global histories. Too often in recent years the "black-Jewish" question has been rendered according to a logic of competitive victimization and viewed through a lens of mutual accusation. According to this story, we must identify either blacks or Jews as the most suffering subjects of modernity and consider their histories in isolation from each other. Bringing together Fanon and Klüger produces neither a simple solidarity nor the pure symmetry of historical analogy, but it does reveal the inadequacy of the framework of competition with its zero-sum logic of either/or. Situating these writers under the overlapping signs of the postcolonial and the post-Holocaust demonstrates that cultural production, identification, fantasy, and deadly violence do not respect the borders of the nation or of identity. To reoccupy the Nazi and colonial cinemas in order to learn their lessons and resist their logics demands the double task of disidentification: we must recognize the ideological force of their spectacle while transgressing their prescribed subject positions. One way to begin is by thinking though a comparative space beyond competition.

Notes

This chapter originally appeared, in slightly modified form, in "In the Nazi Cinema: Race, Visuality, and Identification in Fanon and Klüger," in "Jews and Postcolonial Literature/Histories, ed. Bryan Cheyette, special issue, *Wasafiri* 24, no. 1 (2009): 13–20.

1. Ruth Klüger, *Still Alive: A Holocaust Girlhood Remembered* (New York: Feminist Press, 2001), 51–52.
2. Frantz Fanon, *Peau noire, masques blancs* (Paris: Seuil, 1952); and Frantz Fanon, *Black Skin, White Masks*, trans. Charles Lam Markmann (New York: Grove Press, 1967).
3. Fanon, *Black Skin*, 152; Fanon, *Peau noire*, 124 (translation modified).
4. Fanon, *Black Skin*, 152–53n.
5. Mary Ann Doane, *Femmes Fatales: Feminism, Film Theory, Psychoanalysis* (New York: Routledge, 1991), 227.
6. E. Ann Kaplan, "Fanon, Trauma and Cinema," in *Frantz Fanon: Critical Perspectives*, ed. Anthony C. Alessandrini (New York: Routledge, 1999), 151.
7. Ella Shohat and Robert Stam. *Unthinking Eurocentrism: Multiculturalism and the Media* (New York: Routledge, 1994), 348.
8. Shohat and Stam, *Unthinking Eurocentrism*, 351.
9. See Cheyette's nuanced account of Fanon's writings on blacks and Jews. Using a method congruent with that employed here, Cheyette explores the "heterogeneous juxtapositions which bring together diasporic Jewry and the history of antisemitism with the colonial struggle and anti-Black racism," 75.
10. Fanon, *Black Skin*, 165.
11. Fanon, *Black Skin*, 122.
12. Bryan Cheyette, "Fantz Fanon and the Black-Jewish Imaginary," in *Frantz Fanon's "Black Skin, White Masks": New Interdisciplinary Essays*, ed. Max Silverman (Manchester, UK: Manchester University Press, 2005), 85.
13. Fanon, *Black Skin*, 150.
14. Jean-Paul Sartre, quoted in Fanon, *Black Skin*, 150n.
15. Fanon, *Black Skin*, 153n.

16. Fanon, *Black Skin*, 112.
17. Fanon, *Black Skin*, 115–16.
18. Sander Gilman, *The Jew's Body* (New York: Routledge, 1991).
19. The ambivalence of postcolonial scholars is, of course, matched and perhaps even exceeded by scholars of the Holocaust faced with questions of colonialism, slavery, and race. In my book *Multidirectional Memory*, I provide a genealogy of works that articulate memory of the Holocaust alongside memory of colonialism and slavery without collapsing one history into the other or establishing a hierarchy of suffering. Making this countertradition visible requires rethinking the dynamics of memory and leaving behind the lens of "competitive memory" through which these problems are generally thought. My concept of "multidirectional memory" describes the dynamic intersection of different historical memories as productive and not as limited by a zero-sum logic. Michael Rothberg, *Multidirectional Memory: Remembering the Holocaust in the Age of Decolonization* (Stanford, CA: Stanford University Press, 2009).
20. Klüger, *Still Alive*, 45–46.
21. Klüger, *Still Alive*, 46.
22. Klüger, *Still Alive*, 46.
23. Klüger, *Still Alive*, 47; and Ruth Klüger, *weiter leben: Eine Jugend* (Munich: DTV, 1994), 47–48.
24. Fanon, *Black Skin*, cf. 109–10.
25. A selection from the September 1, 1941, ordinance is included in the editorial notes to Victor Klemperer, *I Will Bear Witness: A Diary of the Nazi Years, 1933–1941*, trans. Martin Chalmers (New York: Random House, 1998), 495. Upon hearing of the new ordinance, Klemperer writes that the star will mean "upheaval and catastrophe" for him and his "Aryan" wife, 429.
26. Klüger, *Still Alive*, 47.
27. José Muñoz, *Disidentifications: Queers of Color and the Politcs of Performance* (Minneapolis: University of Minnesota Press, 1999), 28, 11.
28. Klüger, *Still Alive*, 50.
29. Klüger, *Still Alive*, 51–52; and Klüger, *weiter leben*, 54–55.
30. For excellent collections of essays on German colonialism and its legacies, see Eric Ames, Marcia Klotz, and Lora Wildenthal, eds., *Germany's Colonial Pasts* (Lincoln: University of Nebraska Press, 2005); and Sara Friedrichsmeyer, Sara Lennox, and Susanne Zantop, eds., *The Imperialist Imagination: German Colonialism and Its Legacy* (Ann Arbor: University of Michigan Press, 1998).
31. Muñoz, *Disidentifications*, 12.

32. Rey Chow, *Primitive Passions: Visuality, Sexuality, Ethnography, and Contemporary Chinese Cinema* (New York: Columbia University Press, 1995), 12–13.
33. Chow, *Primitive Passions*, 13.
34. Chow, *Primitive Passions*, 180.
35. Klüger, *Still Alive*, 59–60.
36. Sabine Hake, "Mapping the Native Body: On Africa and the Colonial Film in the Third Reich," in Friedrichsmeyer, Lennox, and Zantop, *The Imperialist Imagination*, 174–75.
37. Historian Pascal Grosse makes the pertinent argument that it is precisely Germany's peculiar experience of "postcolonialism" that ties its colonial past to its later genocide of the Jews: "While the major colonial powers underwent a process of decolonization much later and as a result of independence movements in the colonies themselves, Germany was stripped of its colonial possessions as a direct consequence of its defeat in World War I, which left a complete vacuum in the sphere of expansionism exactly when expansionist aspirations had reached their height. I therefore suggest that Germany's postcolonial experience—what might be called 'colonialism without colonies'—became the fundamental factor in the interwar radicalization of pre–World War I ideas and practices of expansionist biopolitics." Pascal Grosse, "What Does German Colonialism Have to Do with National Socialism?," in Ames, Klotz, and Wildenthal, *Germany's Colonial Pasts* 118–19.
38. Hake, "Mapping the Native Body," 181 (emphasis added).

10

Caribbean Literature and Global Holocaust Memory

Sarah Phillips Casteel

"Why would a writer from the Caribbean want to write about the Holocaust?" This is the question with which Caryl Phillips opens his 1998 essay "On 'The Nature of Blood' and the Ghost of Anne Frank."[1] In an accompanying photograph, Phillips sits at his desk with a poster of the Jewish diarist hanging prominently behind him. I was reminded of Phillips's essay while visiting the Mikve-Emanuel Synagogue Museum in Willemstad on the Dutch Caribbean island of Curaçao. In the museum, amid a wealth of ritual objects documenting the Curaçao Jewish community's 350-year history, is a small exhibit about the Holocaust. On display are an edition of Anne Frank's *Diary* in the Dutch Antillean patois Papiamentu and an exhibition pamphlet on whose cover is a photograph of an Afro-Caribbean girl cradling a portrait of Frank.

At the Anne Frank House in Amsterdam, visitors are invited to read responses to the museum from around the world. By pressing on a touch screen displaying a map of the globe, museum visitors can access comments such as those of Nisha (age forty-one) from Trinidad and Tobago, who wrote on June 24, 2014: "Anne was such an inspiration for me growing up. I asked for my own diary at 13. I still write and aspire to become a writer like her. In 1992 my country had a coup d'etat. I wrote in that diary every day and thought, I am not experiencing half as much suffering as she did." Another

The author Caryl Phillips at work, with a poster of Anne Frank behind him. Photo John Biggins.

Caribbean visitor to the Anne Frank House, Lauren (age twenty-six) from Jamaica, wrote on January 15, 2015: "This history is so important, as it can be related to so many other histories & adversities in our lives & our own personal roots. I'm not Jewish, but when I read Anne's story as a child, it broke my heart. Not just because of her, but because of how inhumane the situation was. God bless her family for making her story known." Along with these visitor responses, the numerous different language editions of the *Diary* both on display in the Anne Frank House and for sale in the museum bookstore confirm Frank's status as a global Holocaust icon.

The Caribbean literary texts that I will discuss in this chapter further illustrate the global circulation of memories of Anne Frank and the Holocaust. As I have argued elsewhere, postwar Caribbean writing makes repeated reference to two Jewish historical traumas: the Iberian expulsion and the Holocaust.[2] This Caribbean literary tradition of engaging Jewish historical experience has been obscured by the institutional divide between Jewish and postcolonial studies as well as by the almost exclusive focus on the United States in discussions of black-Jewish relations—discussions that tend to be inflected by persistent political tensions between African Americans and Jewish Americans. Indeed, despite both the geographical breadth and historical depth of black and Jewish diasporic encounters in the Americas, the question of black-Jewish relations and their literary representation has rarely been broached outside a twentieth-century US framework. As a result, the broader hemispheric American terrain of black-Jewish relations and the purchase of Jewishness on the Caribbean literary imagination in particular have been neglected. In my view, Caribbean literary invocations of Jewish historical experience cannot be interpreted through the lens of black-Jewish relations in the United States and especially not through a paradigm of ethnic competition. Instead, they need to be contextualized with regard to histories of contact between blacks and Jews in the colonial and postcolonial Caribbean. These complex and multifaceted histories range from the participation of early modern port and plantation Jews in the colonial project, including the practice of slaveholding, to the resettlement of Holocaust refugees in various parts of the Caribbean.

Approached from this vantage point, Caribbean Holocaust literature not only attests to the Holocaust's global reach but also encourages us to consider how Holocaust memory is localized in particular colonial and postcolonial settings. For as Daniel Levy and Natan Sznaider emphasize in *The Holocaust and Memory in the Global Age*, Holocaust memory is produced reciprocally and dialectically. Thus "the Holocaust does not become one totalizing signifier containing the same meanings for everyone. Rather its meanings evolve from the encounter of global interpretations and local sensibilities."[3] How, then, has Holocaust memory been reanimated in the Caribbean in the service of particular needs and political projects such as decolonization? To what extent does the deep historical presence of Sephardic Jews in the Caribbean inflect this creolized form of Holocaust memory? More broadly, how does Caribbean Holocaust literature conform to or complicate current theorizations of the Holocaust as a global icon, and how might it help advance the development of a postcolonial memory studies?

In this chapter, I argue that Caribbean Holocaust literature offers a neglected case study of the transcultural operations of memory and of Holocaust memory in particular. Opening up a space for the exploration of historical and cultural relationships that have been obscured by academic discourse, Caribbean imaginative literature serves as a corrective to what Bryan Cheyette calls "disciplinary thinking"[4] by bringing suppressed knowledge to the surface. For these reasons, it is important to give the subject of Caribbean-Jewish encounter not only the historical and empiricist treatment that it has received by scholars of the Jewish Atlantic but also a literary and aesthetic analysis. Thus far, the Caribbean has figured in discussions of global Holocaust memory largely through an examination of the early postwar francophone theoretical writings of Aimé Césaire and Frantz Fanon. Scant consideration has been given to Caribbean creative expression as a vehicle for transcultural memory with the notable exception of Caryl Phillips, whose 1997 novel *The Nature of Blood* has been treated as a unique instance of Caribbean-Jewish intersectionality. A more in-depth examination of Caribbean and Caribbean diaspora literature reveals that Phillips's much discussed novel participates in a larger generational practice of cross-cultural identification with Jewish historical experience. This chapter seeks to resituate Phillips's Holocaust fiction as part of a generational trend in Caribbean literature while decentering the United States as the locus of black-Jewish relations.

Postcolonial Memory Studies

In the 1980s, memory studies emerged as a major focus of scholarly inquiry. Initially centered on the nation-state, the discussion subsequently has shifted to the transnational transmission of cultural memory, with the Holocaust typically cited as the paradigmatic instance of how "memory claims themselves are increasingly globalized."[5] In "Present Pasts: Media, Politics, Amnesia," Andreas

Huyssen traces the emergence of new forms of memory discourse back to two key historical moments: the era of decolonization in the 1960s and the memorialization of the Holocaust in the 1980s.[6] Yet while the Holocaust is disproportionately present in memory studies, colonialism is notably undertheorized. Indeed, a peculiarity of memory studies, which has largely addressed European national memorial cultures, is its scant reference to colonialism.[7]

In a valuable essay on the relationship between cultural memory studies and postcolonial studies, Michael Rothberg details what he describes as a "missed encounter" between the two fields in the 1980s and '90s.[8] He remarks that with its predominantly metropolitan orientation, focus on canonical archives, and emphasis on cultural coherence and continuity, "cultural memory studies may have inadvertently done as much to reproduce imperial mentalities as to challenge them."[9] If memory studies has tended to neglect the colonial dimensions of European memory cultures, neither for its part did the founding texts of postcolonial studies foreground memory as one of the field's organizing concepts. Yet, as Rothberg demonstrates, while anticolonial and early postcolonial theorists may not have overtly employed this vocabulary, they were deeply engaged with questions of memory and forgetting and especially with the problem of colonial amnesia resulting from imposed (or "prosthetic") metropolitan memories. Nonetheless, it is only by reading foundational texts of postcolonial theory somewhat against the grain that Rothberg is able to draw out the theme of memory in these works, where it largely remains implicit rather than explicit.[10] By contrast, postcolonial studies scholarship published since the turn of the millennium has taken up the question of postcolonial memory cultures more directly, analyzing various forms of postcolonial memory work and tracking the emergence, in the words of Nicola Frith and Kate Hodgson, of "more dynamic and transnational conceptualizations of memory."[11]

One explanation for the traditional cleavage between cultural memory studies and postcolonial studies is suggested by historian Charles S. Maier's discussion of the twentieth century as a period best understood through moral narratives rather than structural ones. In Maier's analysis, two distinct narratives of moral atrocity compete with each other to capture the meaning of the twentieth century: a Western narrative that focuses on the Holocaust and Stalinist killing as emblematic of twentieth-century experience and a non-Western narrative that prioritizes imperialism and its legacy of economic neoimperialism. Recognizing that the two narratives are frequently entwined, Maier nonetheless emphasizes their diverging political implications for the present. His account may help explain why, until the recent "colonial turn" in Holocaust studies, there had been little dialogue between Holocaust and postcolonial studies that could elucidate the connections between these two narratives of moral atrocity.[12]

A second obstacle to understanding the place of memory and the Holocaust in postcolonial studies is cultural memory studies' tendency to present the transnational circulation of memory as a new phenomenon. The transnational turn in memory studies identifies a significant reorganization of the field of memory since the start of the millennium.[13] In this account, a reconfiguration of memory brought about by globalization is exemplified by the emergence of the Holocaust as a decontextualized global icon that travels freely across borders and mediascapes.[14] Thus in shifting its focus to transnational memory cultures, memory studies largely has presented the emergence of these cultures as a direct consequence of globalization, which has led to the creation of a new "grammar of memory in a global age."[15]

This rhetoric of newness obscures the transnational and transcultural operations of memory that—as the Caribbean literary examples discussed below will attest—significantly preceded globalization. Accordingly, several recent alternative theorizations of memory have stressed its historical mobility and relationship to non-Western contexts. Preeminently, in *Multidirectional Memory: Remembering the Holocaust in the Age of Decolonization*, Rothberg recovers an early postwar moment, before arguments about the uniqueness of the Holocaust had taken hold, in which there was a particular openness to comparing colonial and Jewish histories of trauma in a multidirectional rather than competitive fashion. In this period, analysts of fascism such as Hannah Arendt and anticolonial thinkers such as Aimé Césaire and Frantz Fanon drew key parallels between antisemitism and colonialism. In Césaire's *Discourse on Colonialism* (1955) and Fanon's *Black Skin, White Masks* (1952), such analogies animate a powerful critique of European imperial formations and promote a "multidirectional" understanding of memory.[16] Multidirectionality thus offers an alternative to competitive memory and to the "conceptual traps" of uniqueness and universality.[17]

Rothberg's influential theorization of multidirectional memory is further taken up in his coedited special issue with Stef Craps, "Transcultural Negotiations of Holocaust Memory" (2011), and in Rick Crownshaw's edited collection *Transcultural Memory* (2014).[18] In his introduction, Crownshaw emphasizes the "inherently transcultural nature of cultural memory" and points out that concepts central to memory studies such as Marianne Hirsch's "postmemory" and Alison Landsberg's "prosthetic memory" suggest how memory can travel and transcend ethnic boundaries.[19] In her contribution to Crownshaw's collection, Astrid Erll goes still further, maintaining "that *all* cultural memory *must* 'travel,' be kept in motion, to 'stay alive.'"[20] Rejecting the container culture model that traditionally has informed memory studies in favor of anthropologist James Clifford's "travelling cultures," Erll insists that memory is constituted through movement. Thus she writes that in what she deems a "third phase" in the development of the field, "memory studies should develop an interest in mnemonic itineraries."[21]

These "mnemonic itineraries" are powerfully embodied by the Caribbean literary narratives examined below. Caribbean Holocaust literature helps advance the project of a postcolonial memory studies by nuancing current models of global Holocaust memory while simultaneously recasting our understanding of black-Jewish relations. Caribbean literary invocations of the Holocaust challenge memory studies' periodization of the emergence of global memory and understanding of Europe as the only authentic memorial landscape of the Holocaust. Both anticipating and coinciding with globalization, this literature articulates a form of postcolonial countermemory that challenges hegemonic narratives of colonial history.[22] Thus it conjoins the two narratives of moral atrocity that Maier identifies as vying with one other to explain the twentieth century. Moreover in Caribbean Holocaust writing, instead of competing with or diverging from one another, these two narratives of atrocity tend to be mutually animating. Contrary to expectations of a competitive relationship between black/Jewish and colonial/Holocaust memory, the Caribbean literary examples that I cite more closely adhere to Rothberg's model of multidirectional memory while also establishing the historical and cultural specificity of Caribbean discourses about Jewishness and the Holocaust.

Because Holocaust memory has dominated the cultural memory studies discussion, there are certain risks entailed in reproducing this focus here.

Attempts to effect a rapprochement between postcolonial and Holocaust studies must inevitably confront thorny issues surrounding the Holocaust's status as a yardstick for other historical atrocities as well as fears that the global distribution of Holocaust memory will result in the erasure of authentic historical knowledge of the Shoah.[23] Some contributors to the debate have argued that comparisons between the Holocaust and colonial and Indigenous atrocities can be as much harmful as beneficial. Aleida Assmann and Sebastian Conrad emphasize that "claims to the Holocaust's universality . . . are received in many parts of the world as a form of Euro-American imperialism in the field of memory." In their analysis, "it may well be that imperialism/colonialism emerge as competitors of the Holocaust as the fundamental historical experience on which to base claims of morality, recognition and recompensation."[24] Relatedly, Amos Goldberg cautions that rather than fostering cross-cultural alliances, global Holocaust memory "perhaps still functions primarily as a mechanism of exclusion that may indeed dismantle the old iniquitous structures but that builds others that might be no less problematic in their stead."[25] Accordingly, critics such as Goldberg, Jeffrey Alexander, and Peter Novick have expressed skepticism regarding whether Holocaust memory is truly global or whether we are in fact conflating *global* with *Western* or even *American*.[26] In this chapter, I remain mindful of these key concerns. I am neither interested here in imposing a Holocaust focus onto Caribbean writing nor in weighing the merits of the Holocaust/slavery analogy. Instead, I seek to account for Caribbean writers' own persistent introduction of Holocaust motifs into their work and to consider the implications of this pattern of imagery for larger discussions of global Holocaust memory. Because of the Holocaust's centrality to cultural memory studies, it becomes particularly important to nuance our understanding of how Holocaust memory operates in global and postcolonial contexts.

Caribbean Literature and the Holocaust

The "Black-Jewish relations industry" in the United States, as Daniel Itzkovitz has dubbed it, has largely characterized that relationship as one of competition and antagonism.[27] In particular, discussions of Holocaust memory and its connection to African American culture often take for granted a logic of competition and appropriation while assuming the fundamentally discrete character of Jewish and black histories of trauma.[28] Recentering discussions of black-Jewish relations on the Caribbean encourages us to rethink such expectations. Taking some distance from a US setting in which Holocaust memory competes for real estate on the Washington Mall with memories of black and Native American atrocities, Caribbean literary invocations of the Holocaust are predominantly sympathetic rather than competitive. At the same time, they are informed by an awareness of the overlapping nature of Jewish and African diaspora histories and identities—one that calls into question charges of appropriation (who "owns" the Holocaust?) as well as an automatic association of Jewishness with narratives of victimhood.

Jewish and Holocaust motifs are favored by Caribbean and Caribbean diaspora writers who came of age during World War II and in the early postwar decades. Signaling the formative impact of the Holocaust on this generation of Caribbean intellectuals, Caribbean Holocaust narratives often revisit their authors' adolescence and are set either during the war or in the early postwar years. For the most part, the Jewish-themed works that they produced were published in the last two decades of the twentieth century, an important period in the public memorialization of the Holocaust as well as the Middle Passage. Also commemorated during this period were the five hundredth anniversary of Columbus's so-called discovery of the New World and the Iberian expulsion. Finally, the quincentenary celebrations coincided in the early 1990s with the height of black-Jewish tensions in the United States. The convergence of these factors helps account for why, whereas African American sympathy toward Jews peaked in the early and mid-twentieth century, Caribbean writers exhibit a rising interest in Jewish experience that carries through the 1980s, 1990s, and into the 2000s. Indeed, the predominantly noncompetitive orientation of Caribbean narratives about Jewishness reflects their authors' rejection of a divisive American race politics. Rather than offering a close reading of any single literary example of this philosemitic tendency in Caribbean literature, I will delineate the contours of a Caribbean literary discourse about the Holocaust and illustrate how in this discourse, the Caribbean itself emerges as a memorial landscape of the Holocaust. This synthetic approach will highlight some of the implications of the Caribbean example for larger attempts to bridge the gap between postcolonial and Holocaust studies and to theorize global Holocaust memory.

A Generational Phenomenon

For those critics seeking to break down barriers between Holocaust studies and postcolonial studies, Caryl Phillips's novel *The Nature of Blood* has become a kind of touchstone, so much so that it overshadows other examples of cross-cultural identification with Jewishness that are available in the literature of the Caribbean and its diaspora.[29] Phillips's formally experimental and deeply intertextual novel has drawn critical attention for its interweaving of a Holocaust victim's narrative with that of Shakespeare's *Othello*. Phillips's engagement with the Holocaust in *The Nature of Blood* and other writing tends to be presented as exceptional, particularly when read against US literature and its more polarizing approach to black-Jewish relations.[30] Rather than being an isolated case, however, *The Nature of Blood* highlights a broader pattern of adolescent cross-cultural identification with the Holocaust that emerges in the work of Caribbean and Caribbean diaspora writers and intellectuals who came of age during World War II or in the several decades following.

By way of illustration, we can compare two passages, the first from an essay by Caryl Phillips and the second from an essay by Caribbean Canadian writer M. NourbeSe Philip:

> As a child, in what seemed to me a hostile country, the Jews were the only minority group discussed with reference to exploitation and racialism, and for that reason, I naturally identified with them. At that time, I was staunchly indignant about everything from the Holocaust to the Soviet persecution of Jewry. The bloody excesses of colonialism, the pillage and rape of modern Africa, the transportation of 11 million black people to the Americas, and their subsequent bondage were not on the curriculum, and certainly not on the television screen. As a result I vicariously channeled a part of my hurt and frustration through the Jewish experience.[31]

> At twelve, possibly, thirteen, I was outraged and upset at what had happened to the Jews. In the silence surrounding my own history and my own memory, I took to myself the pain of what had happened to Jewish people in Europe. Perhaps—I am sure that at some deeper level I knew what had happened to my own people . . . , and that I was on the journey to my own past albeit through a surrogate issue. It matters not *how* we come to understand oppression, provided we take the lessons to heart and apply them to our lives.[32]

In these strikingly similar autobiographical accounts, the Holocaust enables the adolescent Caribbean or Caribbean diaspora subject to explore the slavery past in societies that made little space for discussions of the Middle Passage. Phillips, born in 1958 in St. Kitts and raised in the north of England, and NourbeSe Philip, born in 1947 in Tobago and raised in Trinidad and Tobago, came of age in a postwar moment in which the Holocaust had become an accepted topic of discussion but slavery had not yet been afforded the same recognition. In the absence of books such as W. E. B. DuBois's *Souls of Black Folk* from her local library, NourbeSe Philip's first introduction to the subject of racial persecution came through Leon Uris's novel *Exodus*.[33] Similarly, for the adolescent Caryl Phillips, viewing a television documentary titled *The World at War* served as his initiation into questions of historical trauma and displacement. Accordingly, NourbeSe Philip and Caryl Phillips turned to the Holocaust as a "surrogate issue" (in NourbeSe Philip's phrase) through which they could gain access to the memory of a suppressed slavery past.

The first passage, from Caryl Phillips's *European Tribe* (1987) is frequently cited, but set alongside this lesser-known extract from NourbeSe Philip, it reveals a pattern of Caribbean cross-cultural identification and of linking together the histories of fascism and racism that extends beyond both Phillips's oeuvre and the early postwar francophone anticolonial context of Césaire and Fanon. Indeed, along with the Anne Frank House visitor comments that I cited at the opening of this chapter, a number of other examples are available. Phillips's contemporary Paul Gilroy, born in 1956 to a Guyanese mother and raised like Phillips in Britain, describes in his introduction to *Between Camps* how he was compelled as a child by the Holocaust like a "painful wobbly tooth" to which he "returned ... compulsively." Gilroy writes of his youthful friendships with the children of Holocaust survivors, recounting how he "struggled with the realization that their suffering was somehow connected with the ideas of 'race' that bounded [his] own world with the threat of violence."[34]

Caribbean scholars and writers of the generation preceding that of Gilroy and Phillips also identify the impact of the Holocaust on their intellectual formation.[35] The adolescence of St. Lucian poet and playwright Derek Walcott (b. 1930) "was marked by World War Two and by the news of the concentration camps"[36] so that for him, the Holocaust is unrivaled as "the deepest question of the 20th century."[37] Relatedly, Surinamese author Cynthia McLeod (b. 1936) has described how her literary career was partly inspired by her childhood contact with a European Jewish family during the war.[38] Among those who left the Caribbean to pursue their studies in Europe, the impact of the war was perhaps even more keenly felt. When asked about his interest in the Jewish political theorist Isaiah Berlin, the Jamaican scholar Rex Nettleford (b. 1933) explained:

> I was so concerned about race discrimination, and I had a particular interest in the Jews with all they had suffered with the Holocaust. Because from early I had this concept that *our* Holocaust was the Middle Passage. And of course you use the word diaspora now liberally. I remember as a student traveling on the train from Paris to Amsterdam ... and I would go talk to people who might have been in the war, to hear their stories about the war. The Second World War interested me a great deal; the suffering of the Jews interested me a lot.[39]

Autobiographical accounts of the Holocaust as a surrogate issue through which Caribbean writers could explore their own postslavery histories illustrate the phenomenon of multidirectional memory theorized by Rothberg in which memories of different traumatic events interact in a reciprocal and productive fashion.

The multidirectional operations of memory also help explain the presence of Holocaust imagery in Caribbean fiction and poetry. A case in point is

NourbeSe Philip's short story "Stop Frame" (1993), in which World War II looms large for the twelve-year-old heroine Miranda, a "young girl on a tiny Caribbean island—far away from events like 'the final solution,' panzer divisions, and the Desert Fox."[40] In the story, Miranda launches her own "war effort"[41] by playing pranks on the émigré Dr. Ratzinger, whom she imagines as an incarnation of the Hollywood image of the evil Nazi dentist. For Miranda, living on a Caribbean island in 1958, the Holocaust is the most readily available means of accessing the memory of a deeper historical trauma that is symbolized by her aching tooth. Anticipating Gilroy's "wobbly tooth" metaphor, the rotten tooth that plagues Miranda symbolizes the pain of slavery. Refusing to allow her tooth to be extracted by Dr. Ratzinger, she resists the excision of painful memories. Yet neither, the story suggests, can these memories be approached directly. Accordingly, slavery and racism are not explicitly addressed in "Stop Frame" but instead are alluded to through analogies with antisemitism. For example, expressing his disbelief that Dr. Ratzinger could be having an affair with his mixed-race nurse, Miranda's father exclaims, "'Me don't care how mix-up she is—as far as those Nazis go she is a member of an *inferior* race. Me read about it—they even killing Jews and they have white skins!'"[42] For Philip's young protagonist, the Holocaust functions as a surrogate issue through which she can explore the deeper, unnamed pain of slavery that remains unspoken in the colonial Caribbean of the late 1950s.

The most vivid treatment in Caribbean literature of the phenomenon of adolescent cross-cultural identification with the Holocaust is Jamaican American writer Michelle Cliff's first novel *Abeng* (1984). Like other Caribbean writing from the 1980s and '90s discussed in this chapter, Cliff's autobiographical fiction draws inspiration from her youthful encounters with cinematic and literary representations of the Holocaust. In interviews, Cliff has pointed to the role of mass media in the global circulation of Holocaust memory. She recalls seeing the 1959 film *The Diary of Anne Frank* as a child in Jamaica: "I cut school to see the movie. I then read her diary and started to keep my own, the one my parents read—which was based on Anne Frank's diary. I would never have thought to keep a diary without having read her. She gave me permission to write, and to use writing as a way of survival."[43] Cliff draws on this autobiographical material in *Abeng*, which is set in preindependence

1950s Jamaica. *Abeng*'s light-skinned, middle-class heroine, Clare, is characterized by her "naivete," for she "was a colonized child, and she lived within certain parameters—which clouded her judgement."⁴⁴ Midway through the novel, however, Clare has a transformative experience that profoundly alters her relationship to narratives of familial and collective history. Just as Cliff herself had done as an adolescent, in *Abeng* Clare cuts class to see the film *The Diary of Anne Frank*. This episode catalyzes a process whereby Clare begins to question the dominant beliefs of her society:

> This twelve-year-old Christian mulatto girl, up to this point walking through her life according to what she had been told—not knowing very much about herself or her past—for example, that her great-great-grandfather had once set fire to a hundred Africans; that her grandmother Miss Mattie was once a cane-cutter with a cloth bag of salt in her skirt pocket—this child became compelled by the life and death of Anne Frank. She was reaching, without knowing it, for an explanation of her own life.⁴⁵

After viewing the Anne Frank film, Clare undertakes an intensive study of the Holocaust against her father's wishes, hiding library books under her mattress, and begins to question her father's and teachers' colorist ideology. Her contact with the *Diary* has a radicalizing impact on her colonized adolescent consciousness much as encounters with Holocaust survivors, Holocaust memoirs, and Nazi persecution have on the protagonists of other Caribbean novels such as Michèle Maillet's *L'étoile noire* (1990) (discussed below) and NourbeSe Philip's *Harriet's Daughter* (1988).

In her discussion of postcolonial memory, Anita Rupprecht identifies a postcolonial practice of historical recollection that "is neither nostalgic nor forgetful of the importance of a conception of historiography that is 'active.'" Instead of seeking to recover a lost, precolonial essence, this postcolonial mode of retelling the past "explore[s] the ways in which historical categories are assigned, the way they position subjects, and the processes by which ascribed identities are either embraced or resisted."⁴⁶ Caribbean Holocaust narratives such as *Abeng* develop just such a postcolonial mode of historical recollection.

Notably, however, they do so by reanimating Holocaust memory. In *Abeng*, Holocaust memory is reactivated in order to decolonize dominant historical narratives and expose the ideological structures that underpin them.

The Diary Genre and "Permission to Write"

A recurring motif in Caribbean Holocaust narratives is the diary. This motif reflects both the particular impact of Anne Frank's *Diary* on a number of the Caribbean authors discussed here and the relationship of testimonial narrative forms associated with the Holocaust to postslavery writing. More profoundly, the prevalence of the diary trope signals a connection between Caribbean authors' encounters with the Holocaust and the act of writing itself.

Martinican writer Michèle Maillet's Holocaust novel *L'étoile noire* tells the story of an Antillean woman living in Bordeaux who is deported along with her two children to Auschwitz in December 1943.[47] Maillet's Martinican protagonist, Sidonie, documents her experience in Ravensbrück and Mauthausen in a moleskin notebook whose entries make up the text of the novel. Maillet frames her novel as a camp diary in keeping with the priority of testimony in Holocaust writing. At the same time, Maillet's deployment of the testimonial voice and the diary form points to a Caribbean collective amnesia about the slavery past that her heroine must challenge through the act of writing. In a fascinating image for the multidirectionality of memory, Sidonie writes her diary in two directions simultaneously, both forward into the present of her camp internment and backward into her Antillean and slavery past. Thus, in Maillet's rendering, the emblematic scene of shaving the camp inmates' hair is defamiliarized when it transitions seamlessly into reflections on the significance of hair texture in the Caribbean. Correspondingly, the dogs used by the camp guards evoke for Sidonie an ancestral slave terror of dogs. In this respect, Sidonie's notebook, which is situated at the intersection of Holocaust and postslavery memory, represents the meeting of two literary genres: the Holocaust diary and the fugitive slave narrative. *L'étoile noire* not only exhibits the palimpsestic operations of memory (to borrow Max Silverman's metaphor), then, but also overlays the genres of the camp diary and the slave narrative through its use of first-person testimony.[48] In so doing, Maillet's novel vividly stages the operations of multidirectional memory by invoking the history of the Middle Passage within the frame of a camp narrative. Thus Maillet participates in a Caribbean practice of historical recollection in which the Holocaust functions as a countermemory that unlocks the slavery past.

Maillet's presentation of her Caribbean heroine as a camp diarist reflects the historical status of "art [as] an important medium of defiance" during the Holocaust.[49] At the same time, it signals the more particular role of the Holocaust and Holocaust narratives in giving Caribbean authors what Cliff describes as "permission to write." As we saw, in interviews Cliff identifies a link between her own early encounter with Frank's *Diary* and the onset of her writing career.[50] Cliff's response to Frank's diary suggests that its value for her lay not only in its subject matter but also in the literary ambition that it embodied on the part of someone who made for an unlikely candidate for literary immortality.

Similarly, Frank's *Diary* emerges in Caryl Phillips's nonfiction essays not simply as a source text but also as a text that licenses the act of writing itself. Phillips has described how he wrote his first work of fiction directly following his viewing of a Holocaust documentary. He remarks that "a tangible legacy of that episode of 'The World at War' and the story that it gave rise to is that for the past ten years or so I have worked with a large poster of Anne Frank above my desk. In some strange way she was partly responsible for my beginning to write, and as long as I continue to write her presence is a comforting one."[51] Thus it is not only (as one critic has argued) that Phillips's relationship to the Holocaust is mediated by narratives such as Frank's *Diary* but also, *conversely*, that his relationship to writing is mediated by the Holocaust.[52] Read from this vantage point, Phillips's novel *The Nature of Blood*, which is itself an intertextual reworking of Frank's *Diary*, expresses a desire to honor and come to terms with the experience of cross-cultural identification that launched his literary career.

It is also from this perspective that we can understand Phillips's statement that in composing his Holocaust novel, "Anne Frank's narrative wasn't the most important narrative. The example of Anne Frank has obviously been important to *"free me."* There were any number of books that had a pretty profound effect on me, but there was no one story or one person about whom I thought let me try to recreate her voice."[53] In other words, although the *Diary* is a key intertext of the novel, the framework of intertextuality in a narrow sense does not capture the full significance of the *Diary*, which, more than providing literary inspiration, "frees" Phillips to write.

Entangled Histories

In his discussion of global Holocaust memory, Huyssen contends that "it is precisely the emergence of the Holocaust as universal trope that allows Holocaust memory to latch on to specific local situations that are historically distant and politically distinct from the original event."[54] Commentaries such as Huyssen's tend to assume that global Holocaust memory links together experiences that are temporally and geographically disparate. Postwar Caribbean literature, by contrast, reveals the *proximity* of the Holocaust, the mutual entanglement of cultural formations and geographies that we tend to perceive as separate. Novels such as Maillet's *L'étoile noire* and Oscar Hijuelos's *Simple Habana Melody* (2002) as well as stories such as Cliff's "A Woman Who Plays the Trumpet Is Deported" (1990) not only introduce the Holocaust as a surrogate for slavery but also concretize Holocaust slavery analogies by drawing attention to the experiences under the Nazis of Caribbean musicians and students as well as other black émigrés and black Europeans. Paralleling the literary archaeologies undertaken by postslavery fiction, this subgenre of Holocaust fiction, which also includes African diaspora texts such as John Edgar Wideman's "Valaida" (1989) and Esi Edugyan's *Half-Blood Blues* (2011), recovers the history of black victims of the Nazis and contributes to recent efforts to expand our understanding of the Holocaust.[55] In so doing, this literature reminds us that the relationship of the Holocaust to African diaspora experience is not simply an abstract one between disparate historical traumas.

Holocaust memory also intersects with the Caribbean landscape in a concrete and historically grounded fashion in a second set of Caribbean literary texts that recall the flight of Jewish refugees from the Nazis to the Caribbean. In the late 1930s, hundreds of European Jewish refugees arrived in Trinidad, where they formed a "Calypso Shtetl" and dubbed themselves the "Calypso Jews." Moreover, not only Trinidad but also Jamaica, Barbados, Cuba, the Dominican Republic, Martinique, and Curaçao served as havens for Jews during World War II.[56] This little known chapter of Holocaust history, which Claude Lévi-Strauss briefly recounts in *Tristes tropiques* (1955), is a recurring motif in postwar Caribbean fiction.[57] Trinidadian author Sam Selvon's *Brighter Sun* (1952), for example, opens with the following lines: "On New Year's Day, 1939, while Trinidadians . . . were attending the races in the

Gravestones of the Calypso Jews in the Bet Olam section of the Mucurapo Cemetery, Port of Spain, Trinidad. Photo Sarah Phillips Casteel.

Queen's Park Savannah, Port of Spain, a number of Jewish refugees fleeing Nazi persecution in Europe landed on the island."[58] Also evoking this historical episode is the figure of the Jewish refugee doctor who briefly appears in V. S. Naipaul's classic novel *A House for Mr. Biswas* (1961). More recently, this figure resurfaces in Antiguan American writer Jamaica Kincaid's novel *Mr. Potter* (2002), which adopts an imagistic and associative strategy in which Jewish refugee experience illuminates the impact of a suppressed slavery past on the twentieth-century Caribbean psyche. A European refugee Jew also features prominently in Jamaican writer John Hearne's *Land of the Living* (1961), which promotes an identificatory model of cross-cultural empathy, eliding some of the tensions and ambivalences that Kincaid's novel embraces.[59]

In contrast, then, to some postcolonial and multicultural writing, the Jew does not simply function in Caribbean literature as a deracinated figure of postmodern displacement. Neither is Jewishness an empty metaphor in these texts, a litmus test for the multicultural condition that relies on an ahistorical and superficial understanding of Jewish experience, as Sander Gilman has charged of some postcolonial and multicultural fiction that incorporates Jewish themes.[60] Instead, as my examples attest, Jewish and Holocaust references appear in Caribbean literature not only for allegorical reasons but also for historical and biographical ones. In these texts, the Caribbean itself becomes a memorial landscape of the Holocaust.

Sephardism

One final aspect of Caribbean literary invocations of the Holocaust that encourages us to reconsider some of the prevailing expectations regarding the relationship of postcolonial fiction to Jewish experience is the tendency of Caribbean Holocaust memory to become entangled with memories of the 1492 expulsion. The Caribbean not only served as a haven for Holocaust refugees in the mid-twentieth century but also, several centuries earlier, for Sephardim who resettled there in the aftermath of the 1490s expulsions from Spain and Portugal. Accordingly, while discussions of Jewishness and postcolonial literature have focused on the cross-cultural resonance of the Holocaust, 1492 emerges in Caribbean literature as an equally significant node of multidirectional memory. Registering the Caribbean's deep and multilayered relationship to histories of Jewish refugee resettlement, contemporary Caribbean literature engages in a complex triangulation of memories of slavery, Sepharad, and the Holocaust. This interpenetration of Holocaust and Sephardic memories in Caribbean literature illustrates how global Holocaust memory may be still more complex and multilayered than current models register.

Signaling their awareness of this deeper history of black-Jewish encounter in the colonial Caribbean, Caribbean writers periodically insert into their Holocaust narratives references to the Iberian expulsions. Cuban American writer Achy Obejas's novel *Days of Awe* (2001), for example, intertwines a Holocaust refugee narrative with a Sephardic Caribbean plotline.[61] In *Days of Awe*, a crypto-Jew of Sephardic ancestry works in the Havana flower shop of an elderly Polish Auschwitz survivor. Layered together in Obejas's consciousness and literary imagination, then, are two stories: that of early modern Sephardic Jews' attempt to make a homeland in the Caribbean in the aftermath of the Iberian expulsion and that of the Ashkenazi Jewish refugees from the Nazis who fled to Cuba and other islands in the late 1930s.

The fiction of Michelle Cliff similarly weaves together Holocaust and Sephardic memory. Notably, while the most prominent Jewish historical references in Cliff's *Abeng* are to Anne Frank and the Holocaust, the novel also invokes the Sephardic presence in the Caribbean, a theme that she would later develop in her novel *Free Enterprise* (1993) by incorporating a Surinamese Jewish protagonist.[62] By contrast, Caryl Phillips's Holocaust fiction and essays make no reference to the Sephardic Caribbean—this despite his own Sephardic ancestry.[63] In his essays on Anne Frank, Phillips remarks on the presence of Surinamese, Arubans, and Curaçaoans in Amsterdam and makes much of the fact that at the time of writing, next to the Anne Frank House was a Caribbean bar, an adjacency that suggests a relationality between black and Jewish histories of trauma. But, in fact, as an emerging body of historical scholarship on the Jewish Atlantic is exploring, the links between the Dutch empire and Jewishness go much deeper than analogies between colonialism and European fascism convey. Ironically, Amsterdam, the site of Frank's victimization, was also the center of a colonial empire that made possible one of the greatest examples of Jewish privilege in early modern history: the self-governing Jewish agricultural settlement of Jodensavanne (Jews' Savannah) in seventeenth- and eighteenth-century Suriname. This conjunction of colonial and Holocaust histories is suggested in Frank's *Diary* by her companion Peter van Pels's colonialist fantasy of living on a plantation in the Dutch East Indies in his version of an attempt to imagine a future beyond the war.[64] The 2011 erection of a statue of Anne Frank in Aruba and the Papiamentu edition of Frank's *Diary* that is displayed in the Curaçao Jewish museum give further testament to these complicating linkages between Anne Frank's Amsterdam and the colonial Netherlands Antilles—between the Holocaust and the Sephardic Caribbean.

Conclusion

Caribbean Holocaust narratives participate in a tradition of cross-cultural engagement that has been obscured by the institutional divide between postcolonial and Jewish studies. Paradoxically, Caribbean Holocaust discourse is also in many ways obscured by current theorizations of global Holocaust memory. Discussions of global Holocaust memory tend to trace a trajectory from national containers of memory to the emergence under globalization of "cosmopolitan memory cultures."[65] Such accounts posit that if in the 1970s and '80s Holocaust memory was *Americanized,* in the late 1990s and 2000s it was *globalized.*[66] Aleida Assmann, for example, asserts that "the year 2000 marks the starting point of a new era. In retrospect, we may say today that with the beginning of the new millennium the Holocaust went global."[67]

The rhetoric of newness that attends such analyses of global memory belies the extent to which colonial and diasporic formations such as the Caribbean were always cosmopolitan and that as a result, memories were "on the move"[68] in the colonial world long before the era of globalization. More specifically, theorizations of global memory that confine their discussions to the turn of the twenty-first century neglect the ways in which, as Rothberg has demonstrated, Holocaust memory was activated by anticolonial intellectuals in the early postwar period. Relatedly, Caribbean literary narratives about the Holocaust that were published in the late twentieth century draw autobiographical inspiration from their authors' adolescent contact with media and textual representations of the Holocaust in the 1950s, '60s, and '70s as well as from historical encounters between Jewish and African diaspora populations in the Caribbean dating as far back as the seventeenth century. Thus, if some of the Caribbean texts I discuss participate in the millennial moment highlighted by theorists of global Holocaust memory, others anticipate it.

Caribbean Holocaust literature also challenges the assumption that Europe is the exclusive memorial landscape of the Holocaust and that therefore the relationship of non-Western populations to Holocaust memory is necessarily an abstract or inauthentic one. In particular, it calls into question sociologist Jeffrey Alexander's claim that "obviously, non-Western nations cannot 'remember' the Holocaust."[69] Alexander concludes his influential essay "On the Social Construction of Moral Universals," in which he traces how the Holocaust came to be constructed as a free-floating event with universal resonance, with a brief section titled "Is the Holocaust Western?" Here, Alexander argues that the process of universalization that he has identified applies primarily to Western societies. Citing the examples of Mexico and Japan, he suggests that non-Western societies are consumed with their own "identity-defining trauma dramas,"[70] although over time they have gained some awareness of the

Holocaust through cultural globalization. Thus, situating the non-West as an appendix to his discussion of social constructions of the Holocaust's meaning, and identifying the non-West as a latecomer to a discourse about the Holocaust shaped by the United States and Western Europe, Alexander positions Western and non-Western histories as essentially separate from each other. By contrast, the Caribbean literary texts that I have examined illustrate the extent to which the Holocaust spills over into non-Western spaces and testify that metropolitan and colonial memorial landscapes are much more deeply imbricated with each other than Alexander's account registers.[71] A reciprocal relationship between metropolitan and colonial geographies and memory cultures is evidenced by stories of Holocaust refugees such as Claude Lévi-Strauss, who in 1941 fled to Martinique on the same ship as the surrealist writer André Breton. While on the Vichy-controlled island, Breton met the anticolonial theorist and founder of Negritude Aimé Césaire and went on to write the preface to Césaire's poetic masterpiece *Cahier d'un retour au pays natal* (1939). The deeply entangled character of metropolitan and colonial memories is further suggested by the wartime experience of the Surinamese portrait artist Josef Nassy, who was arrested in Belgium in 1942 and interned by the Nazis for three years.[72]

While not attuned to such entanglements, what Alexander's analysis importantly reveals is the extent to which the Holocaust's transformation into "an archetype, an event out of time"[73] has generated anxiety surrounding how the Holocaust is narrated and whether it is being deprived of its historically specific meaning. For example, discussing the International Task Force on Holocaust Education, Remembrance and Research that was founded in 1998, Assmann worries that the historical memory of the Holocaust is "in danger of being covered over by a unified and locally disconnected memory."[74] I would suggest that it is useful in this context to consider literary mediations of Holocaust memory alongside institutionalized forms of remembrance. Caribbean novels such as Cliff's *Abeng* and Phillips's *Nature of Blood* illustrate how literature can serve as a counterweight to the standardizing, delocalizing tendencies of public historical narratives.[75] It is in fact precisely these amnesiac tendencies that literary inscriptions of Caribbean Holocaust memory challenge. They do so by offering highly personalized, localized, and historically grounded accounts of how the Holocaust's impact was felt in colonial settings. They illustrate how encounters with globally circulating media and textual representations of the Holocaust helped generate particularized forms of countermemory that challenged the dominant society's suppression of local memories of slavery and colonialism.

Finally, as I have shown, the Caribbean case suggests that discussions of global Holocaust memory need to look beyond the slavery/Holocaust binary to address other salient historical traumas. In particular, in a New World context that was doubly shaped by 1492 as both the moment of Columbus's "discovery" and the Iberian expulsion that led to Sephardic Jewish resettlement in the Americas, Caribbean Holocaust memory often becomes entangled with sephardism. Discussions of black-Jewish and postcolonial-Jewish literary connections have focused overwhelmingly on Holocaust references. This is the case even in analyses of a text such as British Guyanese writer David Dabydeen's slavery novel *A Harlot's Progress* (1999), which although specifically referencing the presence of Sephardic Jews in eighteenth-century London, has been interpreted as a response to the Holocaust.[76] I am interested not only in the compelling question posed by some scholars of the relationship of Holocaust memory to slavery and colonialism but also in how the ground of comparison shifts when the postcolonial-Jewish analogy is not rooted exclusively through the Holocaust. The Caribbean literary examples I have cited suggest that taking some distance from the Holocaust frame of reference opens up still greater possibilities for multidirectional memory.

At the same time, to consider 1492 alongside the Holocaust is also to complicate notions of black-Jewish affiliation by drawing attention to a more ambivalent chapter of Jewish history in which early modern port and plantation Jews were both victims and agents of empire. As the emerging field of Jewish Atlantic history is revealing, the early modern Caribbean was a contradictory space of both renewed oppression and unusual freedom for Jews, who played a key role as cultural and economic brokers of colonialism and participated in the practices of slaveholding and slave concubinage. Moreover, I note a connection between Caribbean authors' cross-cultural references to Jewish experience and the ambivalent critical reception that occasionally has greeted their own work. It is no accident that Jewishness is a recurring trope in the work of writers such as Hearne, Walcott, and Cliff, who have been accused of having an insufficiently Afrocentric perspective. Indeed, Jewishness, which is itself defined by its racial indefinability, proves especially useful to Caribbean writers who have an interest in exploring mixed-race identity and in acknowledging the European—including Jewish—components of their ancestry alongside their New World African heritage.

To end with one last literary example, in Guadeloupean writer Gisèle Pineau's novel *L'exil selon Julia* (1996), the young French Antillean protagonist abruptly abandons the diary that she had begun composing in the style of Anne Frank when she realizes that she is merely *une copieuse*, an imitator, of Frank.[77] Pineau casts doubt on the universalist model of identification and cross-cultural empathy that the protagonist's reading of Frank's *Diary* initially inspires. Ultimately, the practice of diary writing that she learns from Frank appears to be of limited use in negotiating her own anguish. Moreover, the illiteracy of the girl's Guadeloupean grandmother, who takes the place of Frank's Kitty as the diary's addressee, raises questions about the suitability of Frank's diaristic and textual model to the Guadeloupean context.

As I have shown, in the course of launching their literary careers in the 1980s and '90s, a number of Caribbean writers looked back to their early postwar adolescent experiences of cross-cultural identification with the Holocaust and drew inspiration from those experiences. Their invocations of Jewishness were further stimulated by several late twentieth-century societal developments including the intensification of public memorialization of the Holocaust, the quincentenary of the Sephardic expulsion, and heightened black-Jewish tensions in the United States from which these writers sought to distance themselves. A younger generation of Caribbean writers may prove less inclined to address the Holocaust, both because of difficulties surrounding Israel politics and especially because of the significant expansion in recent decades of public discourse about slavery—illustrated most recently by a spate of films and television series as well as the 2016 opening of the National Museum of African American History and Culture in Washington, DC. Indeed, the decision of the Caribbean Standard Examination Committee in the mid-2000s to remove Frank's *Diary* from its list of examinable texts because of waning student interest[78] suggests that the mode of cross-cultural identification with the Holocaust that I have traced in this chapter, while significant as a historical and generational phenomenon, may have run its course.

Notes

1. Caryl Phillips, "On 'The Nature of Blood' and the Ghost of Anne Frank," *CommonQuest: The Magazine of Black-Jewish Relations* 3, no. 2 (1998): 4.
2. This essay draws from and expands on arguments contained in Sarah Phillips Casteel, *Calypso Jews: Jewishness in the Caribbean Literary Imagination* (New York: Columbia University Press, 2016).
3. Daniel Levy and Natan Sznaider, *The Holocaust and Memory in the Global Age*, trans. Assenka Oksiloff (Philadelphia: Temple University Press, 2006), 11.
4. Bryan Cheyette, *Diasporas of the Mind: Jewish and Postcolonial Writing and the Nightmare of History* (New Haven, CT: Yale University Press, 2013), 6.
5. Aleida Assmann and Sebastian Conrad, "Introduction," in *Memory in a Global Age: Discourses, Practices and Trajectories*, ed. Aleida Assmann and Sebastian Conrad (New York: Palgrave, 2010), 8.
6. Andreas Huyssen, "Present Pasts: Media, Politics, Amnesia," *Public Culture* 12, no. 1 (2000): 21–38.
7. One exception is Rossington and Whitehead, who identify postcolonial studies as a "contributing factor to the surge of interest in memory in the 1990s" and point to postcolonial studies' "inherent interest in temporality and the past." Michael Rossington and Anne Whitehead, "Introduction," in *Theories of Memory: A Reader*, ed. Michael Rossington and Anne Whitehead (Baltimore: Johns Hopkins University Press, 2007), 8.
8. Michael Rothberg, "Remembering Back: Cultural Memory, Colonial Legacies and Postcolonial Studies," in *The Oxford Handbook of Postcolonial Studies*, ed. Graham Huggan (Oxford: Oxford University Press, 2013), 361.
9. Rothberg, "Remembering Back," 364.
10. Rossington and Whitehead thus perhaps overstate the case somewhat when they claim that for Spivak and Bhabha "memory is central to postcolonialism and they draw out the ways in which personal and cultural memory can be used to analyse, and potentially to undermine or contest, the structures of empire." Rossington and Whitehead, "Introduction," 9.
11. Nicola Frith and Kate Hodgson, "Slavery and Its Legacies: Remembering Labour Exploitation in the Francophone World," in *At the Limits of Memory: Legacies of Slavery in the Francophone World*, ed. Nicola Frith and Kate Hodgson (Liverpool, UK: Liverpool University Press, 2015), 17. Memory appears increasingly focal in more recent postcolonial studies scholarship. See, for example, Frith and Hodgson, eds., *At the Limits of Memory*; Michael R. Griffiths, ed., *Biopolitics and*

Memory in Postcolonial Literature and Culture (Farnham, Surrey, UK: Ashgate, 2016); D. Venkat Rao, *Cultures of Memory in South Asia: Orality, Literacy and the Problem of Inheritance* (New Delhi: Springer India, 2014); Uta Fenske, Daniel Groth, Klaus-Michael Guse, Bärbel P. Kuhn, eds., *Colonialism and Decolonization in National Historical Cultures and Memory Politics in Europe* (Frankfurt: Peter Lang, 2015); Iain Chambers, Alessandra De Angelis, Celeste Ianniciello, Mariangela Orabona, Michaela Quadraro, eds., *The Postcolonial Museum: The Arts of Memory and the Pressures of History* (Farnham, Surrey, UK: Ashgate, 2014); and Abigail Ward, ed., *Postcolonial Traumas: Memory, Narrative, Resistance* (New York: Palgrave, 2015).

12. Charles S. Maier, "Consigning the Twentieth Century to History: Alternative Narratives for the Modern Era," *American Historical Review* 105, no. 3 (2000): 807–31. For recent attempts to overcome the divide between the two fields, see Cheyette, *Diasporas of the Mind*; Michael Rothberg, *Multidirectional Memory: Remembering the Holocaust in the Age of Decolonization* (Stanford, CA: Stanford University Press, 2009); Max Silverman, *Palimpsestic Memory: The Holocaust and Colonialism in French and Francophone Fiction and Film* (New York: Berghahn, 2013); and Casteel, *Calypso Jews*.

13. See, for example, Assmann and Conrad, "Introduction," 1.

14. For an overview of this discussion and critical responses to it, see Amos Goldberg "Ethics, Identity, and Antifundamental Fundamentalism: Holocaust Memory in the Global Age (a Cultural-Political Introduction)," in *Marking Evil: Holocaust Memory in the Global Age*, ed. Amos Goldberg and Haim Hazan (New York: Berghahn, 2015), 3.

15. Assmann and Conrad, "Introduction," 6.

16. Aimé Césaire, *Discourse on Colonialism*, trans. Joan Pinkham (New York: Monthly Review Press, 1972 [1955]); Frantz Fanon, *Black Skin, White Masks*, trans. Charles Lamm Markmann (New York: Grove, 2008 [1967]).

17. Rothberg, *Multidirectional Memory*, 37.

18. Rothberg and Craps's introduction to their special issue argues that to ignore the multidirectional operations of memory is to impoverish our "understanding of the dark underside of modernity" as well to deny the potentialities of transcultural empathy. Stef Craps and Michael Rothberg, "Introduction," in "Transcultural Negotiations of Holocaust Memory," ed. Step Craps and Michael Rothberg, special issue, *Criticism* 53, no. 4 (2011): 518.

19. Rick Crownshaw, "Introduction," in *Transcultural Memory*, ed. Rick Crownshaw (London: Routledge, 2014), 3.

20. Astrid Erll, "Travelling Memory," in Crownshaw, *Transcultural Memory*, 17 (emphasis in original).
21. Erll, "Travelling Memory," 19.
22. On postcolonial countermemory, see Rothberg, who argues that "postcolonial and minoritized cultural production acts . . . as a form of counter-memory—a resignification of the past in the present—that unsettles canonical cultural memory." Rothberg, "Remembering Back," 368; cf. 366 n11. See also Anita Rupprecht, "Making the Difference: Postcolonial Theory and the Politics of Memory' in *Temporalities, Autobiography and Everyday Life*, ed. Jan Campbell and Janet Harbord (Manchester: Manchester University Press, 2002), 35–51. Rupprecht makes a related argument about the function of postcolonial recollection.
23. On the debate surrounding whether using the Holocaust as "a sort of global yardstick for understanding the past and the duties it casts in the present" is a positive or negative phenomenon, see Goldberg, "Ethics, Identity," 12.
24. Assmann and Conrad, "Introduction," 9.
25. Goldberg, "Ethics, Identity," 15. Further, Craps and Rothberg suggest that "because they are generally better remembered, the atrocities of Europe are perceived as morally more significant than atrocities elsewhere." Craps and Rothberg, "Introduction," 518. Relatedly, in his discussion of the globalization of Holocaust memory, Huyssen cautions that "one must always ask whether and how the [Holocaust as universal trope of traumatic history] enhances or hinders local memory practices and struggles, or whether and how it may perform both functions simultaneously." Huyssen, "Present Pasts," 26.
26. See Jeffrey Alexander, "On the Social Construction of Moral Universals," in *Remembering the Holocaust: A Debate* (Oxford University Press, 2009), 68; Peter Novick, "The Holocaust Is Not—and Is Not Likely to Become—a Global Memory," in Goldberg and Hazan, *Marking Evil*, 47–55; and Goldberg and Hazan, "Preface," in Goldberg and Hazan, *Marking Evil*, xi.
27. Daniel Itzkovitz, "Notes from the Black-Jewish Monologue: Civil Rights, Nostalgia, Israel and Twenty-First Century Jewish Identity," *Transition* 105 (2011): 4.
28. Naomi Mandel's *Against the Unspeakable: Complicity, the Holocaust, and Slavery in America* (Charlottesville: University of Virginia Press, 2006), for example, focuses on the slavery fiction of writers such as William Styron and Toni Morrison who have been charged with appropriation and blackface.
29. Caryl Phillips, *The Nature of Blood* (New York: Vintage, 1997), has been cited by numerous critics as exemplifying a multidirectional rather than competitive mode of memorializing the past. Such critics have sensitively analyzed the formal

techniques that enable Phillips to draw black and Jewish histories into relation without sacrificing the specificity of these experiences. They have argued persuasively that these techniques mitigate the accusations of appropriation that have been leveled against Phillips, most notoriously by Hilary Mantel in a 1997 review in which she asserted that "it is indecent to lay claim to other people's suffering: it's a colonial impulse, dressed up as altruism." Hilary Mantel, "Black Is Not Jewish," review of *The Nature of Blood*, *Literary Review*, February 1, 1997, 39.

30. See, for example, Wendy Zierler, "'My Holocaust Is Not Your Holocaust': 'Facing' Black and Jewish Experience in *The Pawnbroker*, *Higher Ground*, and *The Nature of Blood*," *Holocaust and Genocide Studies* 18, no. 1 (2004): 46–67. See also Eric J. Sundquist's description of Phillips's Holocaust writing as "unparalleled in recent literature and commentary." Sundquist, *Strangers in the Land: Blacks, Jews, Post-Holocaust America* (Cambridge, MA: Harvard University Press, 2005), 145n*.

31. Caryl Phillips, "In the Ghetto," *The European Tribe* (Boston: Faber & Faber, 1987), 54.

32. M. NourbeSe Philip, *Showing Grit: Showboating North of the 44th Parallel* (Toronto: Poui, 1993), 84.

33. Philip comments: "I find it interesting that my introduction to racial persecution came through the events of Jewish history—in particular reading Leon Uris' *Exodus* and I was so outraged. Interesting, given that I am a descendant of formerly enslaved Africans and lived in a post-colonial, post-slavery society. Very little was taught about our history when I went to school" (personal correspondence, October 4, 2014).

34. Paul Gilroy, *Between Camps: Nations, Cultures and the Allure of Race* (London: Routledge, 2004 [2000]), 4.

35. There is also some evidence that this pattern of identification was one that could be passed on from one generation to another. The British journalist Gary Younge, born in 1969 to Barbadian parents, "was ten years old when his mother told him and his brothers to stay up to watch the television series *The Holocaust*. His mother explained to him that this was part of his history." Gemma Romain reports that watching the series had a "huge impact" on Younge. Romain, *Connecting Histories: A Comparative Exploration of African-Caribbean and Jewish History and Memory in Modern Britain* (London: Kegan Paul, 2006), 227.

36. Paula Burnett, *Derek Walcott: Politics and Poetics* (Gainesville: University Press of Florida, 2000), 69.

37. Derek Walcott, "An Interview with Derek Walcott," interview with J. P. White, *Green Mountain Review* 4, no. 1 (1990): 14–37. Rpt. *Conversations with Derek*

Walcott, 151–74, ed. William Baer (Jackson: University Press of Mississippi, 1996), 154. Accordingly, Walcott, much like Césaire and Fanon, uses Nazism in his poetry "to access related European oppression, and its universally deplored racism is held up as an image of the deeply entrenched racism still widely sanctioned in white culture." Burnett, *Derek Walcott*, 189–90. For a fuller discussion of Jewish imagery in Walcott's poetry and drama, see Casteel, *Calypso Jews*, chaps. 1 and 3.

38. Cynthia McLeod, personal interview with Ken Victor, Paramaribo, July 20, 2013.
39. Rex Nettleford, "'To Be Liberated from the Obscurity of Themselves': An Interview with Rex Nettleford," interview with David Scott, *Small Axe* 10, no. 2 (2006): 149.
40. NourbeSe Philip, "Stop Frame," *Prairie Schooner* 67, no. 4 (1993): 63.
41. Philip, "Stop Frame," 64.
42. Philip, "Stop Frame," 68.
43. Michelle Cliff, "The Art of History: An Interview with Michelle Cliff," interview with Judith Raiskin, *Kenyon Review* 15, no. 1 (1993), 68.
44. Michelle Cliff, *Abeng* (New York: Plume, 1995 [1984]), 121, 77.
45. Cliff, *Abeng*, 71.
46. Rupprecht, "Making the Difference," 39.
47. Michèle Maillet, *L'étoile noire* (Paris: Oh!, 2006 [1990]).
48. Silverman, *Palimpsestic Memory*.
49. Sidra DeKoven Ezrahi, *By Words Alone: The Holocaust in Literature* (Chicago: University of Chicago Press, 1980), 16.
50. Cliff's account is echoed by the comments of Anne Frank House visitor Nisha who was quoted at the opening of this chapter.
51. Phillips, "On 'The Nature of Blood,'" 7.
52. See Anne Whitehead, *Trauma Fiction* (Edinburgh: Edinburgh University Press, 2004), 106.
53. "Disturbing the Master Narrative: An Interview with Caryl Phillips," interview with Renée Schatteman, *Commonwealth Essays and Studies* 23, no. 2 (2001): 93–106. Rpt. *Conversations with Caryl Phillips*, 53–66, ed. Renée Schatteman (Jackson: University Press of Mississippi, 2009), 61 (emphasis added).
54. Huyssen, "Present Pasts," 24.
55. Oscar Hijuelos, *A Simple Habana Melody* (New York: Perennial, 2003 [2002]); Michelle Cliff, "A Woman Who Plays the Trumpet Is Deported," *Everything Is Now: New and Collected Stories* (Minneapolis: University of Minnesota Press,

2009), 124–28; John Edgar Wideman, "Valaida," *Fever: Twelve Stories* (New York: Henry Holt, 1989), 27–40; and Esi Edugyan, *Half-Blood Blues* (Toronto: Thomas Allen, 2011).

56. The history of Jewish refugee immigration into the British Caribbean has been the subject of two unpublished doctoral dissertations: Joanna Newman, "Nearly the New World: Refugees and the British West Indies, 1933–1945" (PhD diss., University of Southampton, 1998); Alisa Siegel, "An Unintended Haven: The Jews of Trinidad, 1937–2003" (PhD diss., University of Toronto, 2003). For further discussion on the Dominican Republic, see Marion A. Kaplan, *Dominican Haven: The Jewish Refugee Settlement in Sosúa, 1940–1945* (New York: Museum of Jewish Heritage, 2008); and Simone Gigliotti, "'Acapulco in the Atlantic': Revisiting Sosúa, a Jewish Refugee Colony in the Caribbean," *Immigrants and Minorities* 24, no. 1 (2006): 22–50. On the Dutch West Indies, see Oscar E. Lansen, "Victims of Circumstance: Jewish Enemy Nationals in the Dutch West Indies 1938–1947," *Holocaust and Genocide Studies* 13, no. 3 (1999): 437–58. On Trinidad, see Tony Martin, "Jews to Trinidad," *Journal of Caribbean History* 28, no. 2 (1994): 244–57. See also Eric T. Jennings, *Vichy in the Tropics: Pétain's National Revolution in Madagascar, Guadeloupe, and Indochina, 1940–1944* (Stanford, CA: Stanford University Press, 2001), 96, which uncovers archival evidence that in late 1940, a scheme was proposed to relocate French Jews to the Antilles.

57. Claude Lévi-Strauss, *Tristes tropiques*, trans. John and Doreen Weightman (New York: Penguin, 1992 [1955]).

58. Sam Selvon, *A Brighter Sun* (New York: Viking, 1952), 3.

59. V. S. Naipaul, *A House for Mr. Biswas* (London: Penguin, 1992 [1961]); Jamaica Kincaid, *Mr. Potter* (New York: Farrar, Straus & Giroux, 2002); and John Hearne, *Land of the Living* (London: Faber & Faber, 1961).

60. Sander Gilman, *Multiculturalism and the Jews* (New York: Routledge, 2006), chap. 9.

61. Achy Obejas, *Days of Awe* (New York: Ballantine, 2001).

62. Michelle Cliff, *Free Enterprise* (New York: Plume, 1993).

63. In a striking moment in his nonfiction work *A New World Order*, Caryl Phillips relates how a few years after leaving university, he came to discover that his grandfather was "Emmanuel de Fraites, a Jewish trader with Portuguese roots that reached back to the island of Madeira." Phillips, *A New World Order* (New York: Vintage, 2001), 130.

64. Anne Frank, *The Diary of a Young Girl* (New York: Pocket, 1958 [1953]), 139.

65. Levy and Sznaider, *Holocaust and Memory in the Global Age*, 2.

66. Huyssen observes that while the founding of the United States Holocaust Memorial Museum in 1993 inspired debates about the "Americanization" of the Holocaust, "the resonance of Holocaust memory did not stop there." Instead, "by the end of the 1990s, one must indeed raise the question of to what extent we can now speak of a globalization of Holocaust discourse." Huyssen, "Present Pasts," 23.
67. Aleida Assmann, "The Holocaust—a Global Memory? Extensions and Limits of a New Memory Community," in Assman and Conrad, *Memory in a Global Age*, 98.
68. Assmann and Conrad, "Introduction," 2.
69. Alexander, "Social Construction of Moral Universals," 69.
70. Alexander, "Social Construction of Moral Universals," 69.
71. Levy and Sznaider appear more open to the dialectical dimensions of Holocaust memory and its potential to cross ethnic and geographical borders when they ask, "Can an event defined by many people as a watershed in European history (Bartov 1996; Diner 1999) be remembered outside the ethnic and national boundaries of the Jewish victims and the German perpetrators? Can this event be memorialized by people who do not have a direct connection to it?" Levy and Sznaider, *Holocaust and Memory in the Global Age*, 4. Nonetheless, their claim that it is only in the late twentieth century that the Holocaust becomes "a concept that has been dislocated from space and time, resulting in its inscription into other acts of injustice and other traumatic national memories across the globe," including memories of slavery and colonialism, appears premised on an understanding of metropole and periphery as fundamentally separate formations. Levy and Sznaider, *Holocaust and Memory in the Global Age*, 5.
72. Nassy, who was of African and Jewish descent, was born in Paramaribo in 1904 and later moved to Belgium, where he married a Belgian woman in 1939. Arrested in 1942 as an enemy national, Nassy was imprisoned in the Beverloo transit camp in Belgium and then in the Laufen internment camp and in its subcamp Tittmoning in Germany. During his internment, Nassy created a visual record of his experience that is now in the collection of the United States Holocaust Memorial Museum.
73. Alexander, "Social Construction of Moral Universals," 32.
74. Assmann, "Holocaust—a Global Memory?," 103.
75. *The Nature of Blood*, for example, powerfully juxtaposes a Holocaust victim's testimony with more impersonal forms of historical discourse.
76. David Dabydeen, *A Harlot's Progress* (London: Vintage, 2000). On connections between Dabydeen's novel and the Holocaust, see Jutta Schamp, "Transfiguring Black and Jewish Relations: From Ignatius Sancho's *Letters* and Olaudah Equiano's

Interesting Narrative to David Dabydeen's *a Harlot's Progress*," *Ariel* 10, no. 4 (2009): 19–46. For an alternative reading of Dabydeen's novel that emphasizes the Sephardic context, see Sarah Phillips Casteel, "David Dabydeen's Hogarth: Blacks, Jews, and Postcolonial Ekphrasis," *Cambridge Journal of Postcolonial Literary Inquiry* 3, no. 1 (2016): 117–33.

77. Gisèle Pineau, *L'exil selon Julia* (Paris: Éditions Stock, 1996), 156.
78. I thank Aliesha Hosein for sharing this information with me.

11

A Failure of Memory?

Revisiting the Demidenko/Darville Debate

Avril Alba

APPEALS TO HOLOCAUST MEMORY in literature are frequently made with the goal of harnessing its analogical power to illuminate other instances of racial or antisemitic persecution and to highlight the injustice at hand.[1] Against this backdrop, the curious Australian case of Helen Demidenko/Darville, the author of the novel *The Hand That Signed the Paper*, stands in startling opposition. Beyond the bizarre nature of the literary hoax enacted by Demidenko, the supposed descendant of Ukrainian peasants who was subsequently unmasked as Helen Darville, the daughter of middle-class English migrants, perhaps the most perplexing aspect of the episode was its use of antisemitic and racist tropes to provide the scaffolding for a book that claimed to explore and explain the history and memory of the Holocaust.

Had the work been judged "a shallow, immature and ultimately anti-Semitic novel," as political scientist Peter Christoff described it,[2] it would barely have rated a mention in its time, and even less so would it be worthy of retrospective analysis. Yet the fact that Demidenko/Darville's *Hand That Signed the Paper* was awarded three of Australia's top literary awards means that the Australian literary establishment received it very seriously indeed, and, as such, it remains of interest with regard to its significance in and for Australian cultural and political history. In what follows, I revisit the "Demidenko/Darville debate" with the aim of delineating and unpacking its import as a refraction of Australia's racial and identity politics at the time, revealing the somewhat shaky foundations on which the nascent Australian multiculturalism of the 1990s rested.

In recovering the controversy surrounding *The Hand*, we find that the memory of the Holocaust in the Australia of the early 1990s was not necessarily an edifying or unifying one. Rather, this memory holds within it as much potential to provoke anger and division as it does to facilitate justice and reconciliation. While the controversies over the book's literary worth and its author's identity are now largely forgotten, what remain intriguing about the episode are the unresolved racial and cultural animosities it brought to light. Ironically, through its facile and arguably antisemitic treatment of the Holocaust, *The Hand* and the controversy surrounding it forced deep reflection on the nature and composition of Australian multiculturalism, a point that does not redeem the novel's content but does speak to its utility for understanding the complex intersection between Holocaust memory and race in the Australian public sphere.

The Demidenko/Darville affair revealed a fundamental confusion with regard to the relationship between justice and diversity in Australian cultural and political discourse. For those who would defend or even endorse Demidenko/Darville's version of history, "forgetting" past injustices would "heal old wounds" and enable Australia to move into a harmonious multicultural future. Those shocked, offended, and incensed by the novel's treatment of Holocaust history saw a threat of equal magnitude—one in which forgetting threatened the very foundations of a just society that would allow Australia's racial, cultural, and religious diversity to flourish. As Demidenko/Darville herself was unmasked, so too were assumptions about the nature of Australian "tolerance" and "commitment to diversity" revealed and found wanting. This chapter charts the contours of these disagreements and in so doing lay bare the surprisingly fractious connection between the memory of the Holocaust and the battle for racial and cultural tolerance in Australia.

What becomes evident is that Demidenko/Darville's (mis)use of Holocaust history and memory exposed the nature and limits of what political commentator Robert Manne characterized as a "sentimental multiculturalism."[3] For in the curious case of Helen Demidenko/Darville's *Hand That Signed the Paper*, it would be those who demanded that history be held to account who would ultimately be accused of threatening the fabric of Australia's now multicultural society. Indeed, in forcing Australians to confront the less-than-salutatory aspects of their migration history as well as its potentially divisive contemporary resonance, the Demidenko/Darville debate would expose a historic and ongoing proclivity to "forget" those elements of the past that might threaten a supposedly harmonious multicultural present. Rather than providing an occasion for a "working through" of the past in which justice and accountability were vital components, the memory of the Holocaust ignited by *The Hand* exposed an Australia not yet ready to confront the less salubrious aspects of its history; an Australia convinced that a peaceful present hinged on what a future prime minister would eventually refer to as a "relaxed and comfortable"[4] vision of the past.

Given the sheer amount of media coverage and debate *The Hand* generated, what follows does not pretend to offer a detailed narration of all aspects of the Demidenko/Darville affair.[5] Rather, it focuses on popular and scholarly responses to the novel's use of Holocaust history and memory. These responses provide insight into what maintaining racial and cultural diversity in 1990s Australia was deemed to require. First, the historical ignorance evinced both in the novel and its reception as to the antecedents and events of the Holocaust are outlined and addressed. Second, the moral confusion that resulted from this historical ignorance and the related championing by some of a form of moral relativism as a more constructive (and supposedly "Australian") method of confronting the past is also examined. Finally, these responses to the novel and the controversy it created are contemplated with regard to one of *The Hand's* dominant narrative frameworks—the events and consequences of the Australian War Crimes trial that took place in South Australia in the early 1990s. Taken together, the reception of Demidenko/Darville's novel and the controversy that surrounded the trials reveal that the memory of the Holocaust and its relationship to racial and cultural diversity in late twentieth-century Australia was far from obvious, with its ultimate utility the topic of often-fierce public debate.

THE HAND AND HISTORY

The Hand That Signed the Paper is a short novel that narrates the wartime history of the Kovalenko brothers, Ukrainian peasants who with the German invasion of the Soviet Union in 1941 volunteer to serve in the SS death squads, aiding the Nazis in the murder of Eastern European Jewry both in shooting campaigns and in the death camps of occupied Poland. What makes the novel "Australian" is that its narrator, first-generation Australian Fiona Kovalenko, tells her uncle and father's stories from the vantage point of Queensland in the late 1980s/early 1990s. The narrative recounts in often gratuitously horrific detail the wartime deeds of these men, interspersed with Fiona's reflections on their migration to Australia, her own childhood as the daughter of migrants and her path to understanding her family's history. The text connects the Kovalenko brothers' brutal past to the Australian present from the outset, beginning at the moment that Fiona Kovalenko is driving to visit her uncle Vitaly on hearing that he had recently been charged with war crimes.

The initial success of the novel was arguably driven by Demidenko/Darville's authenticity as a supposed first-generation Australian of mixed Ukrainian/Irish background and her connected claims that some of the materials for her novel were based on oral history acquired from relatives. In her own words, "it would be ridiculous to pretend that this book is unhistorical; I have used historical events and people where necessary throughout the book."[6] When interviewed by Rosemary Soreson on 3RN on September 4, 1994, Demidenko referenced her family's influence in a refrain that she would consistently reiterate until her true identity was exposed a year later, stating unequivocally: "This is from my own experience."[7] Indeed, Demidenko not only capitalized on her supposed ethnic origins but reveled in them, turning up to prestigious literary events dressed in Ukrainian peasant blouses and regaling the media with accounts of her colorful, if at times embarrassing, ethnic upbringing. Commentators both disposed toward and disgusted by the book noted that Demidenko's claim to authenticity was undeniably a factor that strengthened its reception both in literary and popular circles.[8] When "outed" by the *Courier Mail*'s David Bentley on August 19, 1995, as the daughter of British migrants Harry and Grace Darville, the book and its author's infamy were assured as the greatest literary hoax in Australian history since the "Ern Malley affair" began to unfold.[9]

Beyond the identity fraud perpetrated by Demidenko/Darville, what makes the novel controversial is that from these materials supposedly based on the oral testimonies of her Ukrainian relatives, Demidenko/Darville connected the experience of Stalin's engineered famine in Ukraine in the 1930s (the Holodomor) with the Holocaust in an explicitly *causal* paradigm. As Fiona

Kovalenko states in the opening pages of the novel, what is clear in the mind of this protagonist is "how the Ukrainian famine bled into the Holocaust and one fed the other."[10] Thus begins a tale in which the genocide of European Jewry is characterized as an unfortunate but inevitable episode in a vicious cycle of revenge, one in which "Jewish communists" inflicted a brutal famine on Ukrainians who then retaliated through active participation in the Final Solution. The Judeo-Bolshevik myth was thus resurrected in sunny, suburban Queensland.

Now living out their twilight years in the multicultural landscape of 1990s Australia, Fiona's uncle Vitaly and father Evheny find themselves yet again victims of "the Jews," those determined to set the "cycle" of vicious revenge in play again through their insistence that even in distant Australia, war crimes trials must be undertaken. Of course, similar to their role in the former USSR, the said "Jews" are too clever to undertake such ventures themselves but rather do so through their influence and control of key politicians, most notably the "silver budgie Zionist, bloody Hawkie, Bob Hawke."[11] In 1990s Australia, these now "Zionist" Jews are portrayed in the novel as bringing hatred and revenge on themselves yet again, this time through manipulating the Australian political and legal establishment into initiating war crimes trials. In a stunning reversal of victims and perpetrators, the novel thus set the events and memory of the Holocaust firmly into an Australian setting, with the war crimes trials undertaken in South Australia in the early 1990s, providing a new canvas on which these accusations and prejudices were redrawn.

Even prior to publication, *The Hand* had sparked controversy. Demidenko/Darville had entered her work in the 1993 Vogel Award, an Australian literary prize for unpublished, first manuscripts by authors under thirty-five. On first reading, author Roger McDonald, who together with crime and children's fiction writer Jennifer Rowe and radio broadcaster and literary journalist Jill Kitson, made up the judging panel for 1993, gave this warning: "There will have to be a lot more work on the roots of Ukrainian antisemitism otherwise this manuscript will be seen with justification as antisemitic."[12] McDonald's warning was not to be heeded by the other judges, and the book was awarded the prestigious Vogel on September 22, 1993.

Publisher Allen and Unwin, as a condition of the award, publish all its winning novels. During the publishing process, three editors—Brian Castro, Lynne Segal, and Stephanie Dowrick—refused to edit the book on the grounds that they thought it antisemitic.¹³ Expert historical advice was sought from Dr. Geoffrey Jukes, a recently retired military historian from the Australian National University and a specialist on the eastern front during World War II. Focusing more on matters of detail, Jukes argued that Demidenko could only really be faulted for attributing too much of Ukrainian antisemitism to the Bolshevik rather than pre-Bolshevik era. Jukes did not question either the antisemitic reasoning given for Ukrainian participation in Nazi death squads, nor did he note its placement within the broad framework of antisemitic ideology: what Robert Manne described as "the irrational force of antisemitism—the hatred of Jews not for what they had done but for what they were."[14] With this academic imprimatur, an editor was finally found in Neil Thomas, who despite misgivings as to the quality and depth of the novel overall, and noting in his report to Allen and Unwin that the novel "teeters on the edge of apologetics,"[15] agreed to edit the manuscript.

Following publication, *The Hand* continued its triumphant march through Australia's literary circles, first being awarded the most prestigious prize in Australian fiction, the Miles Franklin Award, in June 1995 and the Australian Literature Society Gold Medal in July of the same year.[16] Demidenko had taken the hat trick of Australian literary honors, yet the controversy surrounding her book was only just beginning. When Demidenko was exposed in August 1995 as Darville, debate over the novel and its author again raged in the op-ed and letters pages of Australia's major newspapers. The most acrimonious of these debates were those concerned with the book's ostensibly "historical" aspects. Was Demidenko/Darville simply rehashing some of the vilest antisemitic myths employed by the Nazis to justify their genocide or probing deep into the minds of those who committed genocide to try and understand the most inhuman of human actions? This question animated debates in literary, political, and historical circles and created fierce tension within and between the two groups at the heart of the debate—Australia's Jewish and Ukrainian communities.[17]

In retrospect, what was startling about *The Hand*'s entry into the Australian literary scene is that with the exception of McDonald's report, the three sets of literary judges displayed a complete lack of awareness that the history of the Holocaust, as recounted in *The Hand*, could prove contentious. So shallow was their grasp of the historical facts of the Nazi campaign in Eastern Europe that the judges who bestowed the 1995 Miles Franklin on *The*

Hand—Professor Dame Leonie Kramer, Professor Harry Heseltine, Associate Professor Adrian Mitchell, and Ms. Jill Kitson—credited the novel in their report as containing "a powerful literary imagination coupled with a strong sense of history."[18] Demidenko's thesis and indeed the underlying logic of the book, that Ukrainian participation in the Holocaust was driven by revenge, was thus accepted without question both by the judges and subsequently by a fair chunk of Australia's literary and news establishment.

Even the Jewish press was at first less than critical about the book. In an interview that appeared in the Sydney edition of the *Australian Jewish News* on August 26, 1994, striking historical inaccuracies were reported without critique. These included Demidenko's assertion that "the extent of the Ukrainian collaboration depended on how many Jews were in the Communist party in the area, how close to the frontline people were and how severe the famine had been in a particular area."[19] Demidenko herself consistently stood by the version of history propagated in the book, insisting her work was more than simply "art for art's sake" and remarking, "I cannot stand a bar of the art for art's sake school of writing. It makes me ill. . . . My view of good art is that without browbeating people I still think art is a political act and that is something that should be acknowledged and not denied."[20]

As the debate progressed, many political and literary figures such as Robert Manne, Gerard Henderson, and Peter Christoff [21] attacked and deconstructed the novel's historical framing while others, most notably literary critic Andrew Reimer, would defend the version of history mainly on ground of artistic license.[22] As the news of the Franklin Award broke, however, it was Holocaust survivor and historian Jacques Adler who provided one of the first historical correctives and a clear statement on why, in his view, the novel was both historically and morally bankrupt: "Contemporary Australian fiction has taken many directions. But no one has so far tried to find historical justification for genocide. . . . The crime that this 'novel' commits is not that it is bad fiction masquerading as honesty. The travesty of history at this work's core is that it is an apologia for genocide. One can only hope that history serves its victims more honorably in next year's round of prizes."[23] Adler continued, "Ukrainians volunteered for genocide duty—they chose their path, their friends and their enemies." Adler's piece was subsequently perceived by some members of the Ukrainian community to be engendering "hate." For example, George Jaworsky, the then director of public affairs for the Association of Ukrainians in Victoria wrote in *The Age*: "We are all victims of history. All our hands are stained with blood. Let us resolve to but these hatreds behind us, and not seek to imply that the horrors of the times are the responsibility of one side only. All that will succeed in doing is establishing the conditions for a repetition of the past. There is no place for this in Australia."[24] Jaworsky thus not only reinforced the ideas of "equal responsibility" that Adler sought to refute by recourse to the historical record but also reproduced this version of history with the express aim of warning that such "history" could repeat itself even on Australian shores.

Similarly Stefan Romaniw, the then president of the Australian Federation of Ukrainian Organisations, wrote in *The Age* that Adler's article falsely propagated a charge of "collective responsibility" and that such a perspective was "equally rooted in racism." Romaniw also stated that "Ukrainian Australians believe in dialogue that seeks to unite rather than divide communities," noting that "Ukrainian Australians support processes for dealing with war criminals resident in Australia." Romaniw concluded: "Thus we welcome Ms Helen Demidenko's *Hand That Signed the Paper* as a significant contribution to that vital dialogue. As Ms Demidenko's efforts have been recognized by the Australian literary community it is bizarre for Dr Adler to accuse her of being an apologist for genocide. Indeed, Dr Adler's main intent seems to be perpetuating hate-filled stereotypes about Ukrainians." He then proceeded to offer to introduce Alder to Ukrainians who assisted Jews to escape the Holocaust, ending his letter with the following statement: "Hate has no place in our tolerant, multicultural Australian society."[25]

Members of the Ukrainian community strongly (and rightly) opposed Demidenko's caricaturing of all Ukrainians as murderous antisemites.[26] Indeed, Romaniw and Jaworsky were clearly legitimately concerned with all Ukrainians being tarred by the same brush. Yet what was troubling about their responses was the accusation that it was Adler's exposure of the historical and moral inversion of Holocaust history and memory as articulated in *The Hand* that would threaten Australia's multicultural status quo. In Romaniw and Jaworsky's logic, telling the truth about the past could only serve to fuel hatred in the present. This disagreement as to the accuracy of the history contained in Demidenko/Darville's novel provided a preview of the historical and moral confusion yet to come.

The Hand and Morality

The echo of these early debates continued to animate deliberations concerning the literary and historical worth of the novel as well as its resonance for contemporary Australian life. Vogel and Miles Franklin judge Jill Kitson remained throughout the various debates accompanying the novel one of *The Hand's* greatest advocates. Her reasoning is evidenced in the many interviews she gave following the Franklin award. Speaking to the *Sydney Morning Herald's* Angela Bennie, she enthusiastically explained that Demidenko's book fit the award criterion admirably, referring to a key phrase in Miles Franklin's will that required that the award go to a work portraying "any phase of Australian life." For Kitson, one of Demidenko's greatest achievements had been her ability to synthesize her family's European history with her own Australian identity: "Helen had to exercise an extraordinary literary imagination in order to create some aspects of this book. . . . She creates a protagonist who needs to understand this difference between who she is as an Australian and what makes her very different from her migrant parents. She becomes the family's recording angel."[27]

Further, not only did Demidenko illuminate the past for Kitson, but she also showed us what we might do with that past in the present, in order to "integrate" it into our own experience. Describing what she saw as an obvious strength of the novel, Kitson opined that "this book is about the migrant experience, which we as Australians all share. This country has always taken in migrants, whether they were as convicts or refugees. We Australians, so many of us, all seem to carry some dead heart of shame or guilt about the past generation or generation's actions. Helen shows us how to integrate this."[28] Kitson's comments not only revealed a rather rose-colored view of Australia's past migration policies but also demonstrated a belief that somehow the version of history outlined in *The Hand* provided a model par excellence for coming to terms with the past. As prefigured in the exchange between Adler and Romaniw, others were not so easily convinced. In June and July 1995, the battle raged as to whether the history of the Holocaust as told in *The Hand* would prove divisive or instructive in contemporary Australian life.

One of the first journalists to interrogate both the history contained in *The Hand* and question its contribution to "cultural harmony" was *The Age's* Pamela Bone. In a scathing attack, she described what she saw as the moral failings of the novel's historical framing: "The central thesis of the book, as Demidenko explained in an interview on ABC radio, is that the Jewish Holocaust was 'probably a fairly inevitable facet of European history.' Yes, Uncle Vitaly is guilty. But guilty only because of the wrongs done to him and his people. . . . This is the other side of the Holocaust. Except, as John Pilger has said, there is no other side to the Holocaust."[29] Focusing on the issue of individual choice, Bone refuted the "inevitability" that Demidenko and her novel advocated, in particular its position that there was no possibility for moral choice in the Holocaust: "I am speaking from a position of safety. Even so, I refuse to excuse mass murder by saying that we are all capable of it. Because most people are not capable of it. Some Ukrainians, some Germans, some Poles committed acts of terrible cruelty during that terrible time. Some chose to die rather than take part in it. Many were able to pretend they didn't know it was happening."[30] Judith Armstrong directly responded to Bone's article, taking issue with her assessment of Demidenko's work as a "justification of murder." Rather, she opined, in Demidenko's view,

> the "identical horseshit" of Soviet and German propaganda had turned the Ukrainian peasants into savages, conditioned to kill without argument. Pamela Bone proclaims this to be a justification of murder. Another reader might see that the atrocities at Treblinka, or Babi-Yar, are totally condemned in this novel, as are the demands the Nazis put on their minions. Tolstoy would have understood that. Famously pacifist though he was, he blamed the leaders, not the foot-soldiers, for the carnage of war.[31]

Bone and Armstrong's exchange provides a microcosm of the moral confusion wrought by historical ignorance. Armstrong clearly did not either know or fully grasp the circumstances of Ukrainian involvement in the genocide, its voluntary nature, and the historical antecedents of antisemitism in Ukraine.[32] As such, while she sought to enlighten her Australian readers, whom she believed could not possibly understand the circumstances under which such acts were carried out, in actuality she muddied the historical and moral waters, turning voluntary killers into martyrs, death camp guards into "Tolstoy's foot soldiers" rather than war criminals. Indeed, for Armstrong, Demidenko enlarges our understanding

A Failure of Memory? • 281

of the limited options available to Uncle Vitaly as she "challenges her cushioned Australian readers to imagine the terrifying boundary between heroism and survival, martyrdom and brutalisation."[33]

For Armstrong, the relative safety of Australian life made judgment of the murderers impossible and the attribution of volition to them unthinkable. Armstrong's lack of knowledge as to the historic experience of antisemitic violence in Ukraine, the context of Ukrainian participation in the Holocaust and her complete lack of ability to assess the Judeo-Bolshevik myth as permeating all aspects of the book's "reasoning" given for Ukrainian collaboration, fed into her assessment that Australian readers of the book could neither judge its author nor the characters it described.

Other commentators, such as Susan Geason, also missed the historical inaccuracies in the novel but nonetheless picked up on the moral and ethical slippage that commentators such as Armstrong overlooked. Considering the ethical implications of "excusing" rather than explaining history through recourse to cycles of revenge, Geason remarked: "It seems to me that a writer trying to understand criminal behavior can attribute it to "history" (to the social, cultural, religious environment if you like) or to the psychological make-up of the individuals who perpetrate the deeds. . . . If one decides history is to blame, then individuals, by extension, are not. This defence is popular, often trotted out in courts as mitigation for criminal behaviour, but it does rest on the dangerous assumption that humans do not possess a free will."[34] But for many others, including the *Sydney Morning Herald*'s Miriam Cosic, the version of history propagated by the novel—that Ukrainians killed Jews because "Bolshevik Jews" starved Ukrainians—was accepted and *then* became the baseline for contemplating the "problem of evil." The faulty reasoning that emerges from such a reading of history was clear. Cosic wrote, "It is the scapegoating behaviour of the authoritarian personality par excellence and it sets the scene for the horror that follows, because if they really did believe that communists and Jews were responsible for the bestial conditions in which they lived, the murderous orgy of retribution which eventuated, if nauseating in its excess, is also explicable."[35] But not only is the murder explicable, according to Cosic; it is also *applicable* with regard to racism and racist acts in contemporary Australian life. "And there, but for the Grace of God," she continued, "go us all: every Australian who doesn't want Aborigines living next door, who believes Asian migration should be lowered, who is irritated by the person who can't spit out his English fast enough."[36] Cosic was clearly attempting to argue for increased racial tolerance, yet her premise was fundamentally flawed as she based her argument for acceptance on the belief in an erroneous, and ultimately murderous, racist myth.

And so the battle raged over the novel's reading of history and its ethical and moral implications. Gerard Henderson led the charge from Sydney against *The Hand* while Peter Christoff, Robert Manne, Jacques Adler, and others composed the core of the Melbourne critics.[37] Those arguing for Demidenko, even after her unmasking as Helen Darville, either accepted the version of history contained in the novel or at least were prepared to overlook the inaccuracies in light of what they considered the book's literary and moral achievements. For example, Padraic P. McGuiness, writing in *The Age*, proclaimed with reference to the historical inaccuracies in the book that "this does not mean that we should not try to understand the horrors of the total situation, which was as much Stalin's fault as Hitler's."[38] What exactly McGuiness meant by this statement is hard to pinpoint, yet what is strange about his pronouncement is that none of the commentators objecting to *The Hand* denied Stalin's implementation of an engineered famine against Ukraine in the 1930s. What was being objected to was the use of this horrific event as an "apologia" for the genocide to follow.

Again, this lack of historical accuracy would then lead McGuiness and others to all sorts of unfounded conclusions, according to which those who had pointed out Demidenko/Darville's faulty history and the book's resultant antisemitism stood accused of censorship. In actuality, no such censorship had occurred. No critic of *The Hand* had argued that the book be banned or its author censored.[39] At what was possibly the lowest ebb of the debate, those Jewish community leaders who had condemned the novel were even chastised for pointing out its antisemitism. Frank Devine's description of Jewish community leader Isi Liebler's reaction when news of Demidenko's identity fraud broke provides a case in point: "Liebler acted before the TV cameras as if he were celebrating the downfall of an enemy. To me, at that moment, he represented the unacceptable bullyboy face of anti-anti-semitism."[40] This nexus between flawed history and moral confusion reached perhaps its fullest articulation in Andrew Riemer's *Demidenko Debate*. In a concerted effort to understand the book's literary worth and impact, Riemer referenced the point, made by many commentators, that the book would not have been taken seriously "even for five minutes" in Europe. He considered whether the willingness to do so in Australia reflected negatively on its literary establishment but then opined, "Or were we perhaps, as I had begun to suspect, a more resilient society, more liberal and tolerant in fundamental ways than Germany, despite the sophistication and intellectual vigour that literary life there seemed to display?"[41] Where critics of *The Hand* had seen Australian ignorance, Riemer saw "tolerance"; where they had seen an indictment of evil, he saw a postmodern suspicion of all standards of certainty. For Riemer, Helen Demidenko/Darville was simply a product of her time. Objecting to those who saw the book as embodying a "fundamental immorality," he believed that it was rather a "particular morality ... centred on distrust of most systems of belief, suspicious of the claims of ideologies, whether national, political or to do with concepts of ethnicity or race."[42]

While such arguments are reminiscent of familiar and seemingly benign postmodern literary approaches, the moral confusion of Riemer's position becomes apparent not only in his seeming acceptance of the version of history *The Hand* tells but also in his acceptance of the work that *The Hand*'s version of the past does in the present. Riemer pointed out that Demidenko/Darville "insisted that she wished to tell the story of the persecution of Jews by her Ukrainian compatriots not from the perspective of 'us and them' but as a chapter in the continuing history of hatred, prejudice, brutality and revenge—which the forthcoming war crimes trial in Adelaide would only perpetuate."[43] That this history is instructive in the present is a key point for Riemer and other commentators on all sides of the debate. Despite his acknowledgment that "this short and inescapably limited work of fiction was asked to sustain more critical and political scrutiny than any novel—let alone the first work of a young writer—should be required to bear,"[44] Riemer saw the novel as containing legitimate commentary on key social and political issues of the time. Not the least of such issues were the recent Australian war crimes trials. It is to this connection between the Demidenko/Darville affair, the trials and their import for understanding the intersection between the memory of the Holocaust and struggles for racial tolerance in Australia, that this chapter will now turn.

Justice or Revenge: *The Hand* and the Australian War Crimes Trials

The Australian war crimes trials took place in Adelaide, South Australia, from 1990 to 1993. While there were a variety of legal and political attempts to bring attention to the number of suspected war criminals who had entered Australia in the postwar period, these remained largely unsuccessful until journalist Mark Aarons's investigation of Australia's postwar migration policies. The results of these investigations made headlines when first televised on leading ABC radio and television current affairs programs in 1986 and were eventually chronicled by Aarons in *Sanctuary: Nazi Refugees in Australia* and *War Criminals Welcome: Australia, A Sanctuary for Fugitive War Criminals since 1945*.[45] An estimated four thousand to five thousand war criminals were allowed to migrate to Australia in the immediate postwar period, with most hailing from Eastern Europe. Providing false information on documents, in interviews, and screening processes, they most often claimed to have been forced laborers under National Socialism. Many were found to have been collaborators in the extermination process.[46]

Scholars have pointed to the fact that in all likelihood Australian migration officials knew of such activities but turned a blind eye as they sought to recruit Soviet double agents from within these migrant groups. While there was a small spate of protests from within the Jewish community in the 1950s as survivors of Nazi terror found themselves sometimes cheek by jowl with their former persecutors on ships and in migrant hostels, they were not long lived as support at that time for what was viewed as a "Jewish cause" was not forthcoming.[47] Hence, the War Crimes Amendment Act only came into force in 1988 as a result of lobbying by both Jewish and other individuals, although the Special Investigations Unit (SIU),[48] the federal body charged with investigating suspected war criminals, had already been in operation since 1987. While the SIU investigated hundreds of cases over a five-year period, only three perpetrators, two of Ukrainian background (Ivan Polyukhovich and Mikolay Berezowsky) and one an ethnic German serving in the Ukrainian auxiliary police force (Heinrich Wagner), were brought to trial. No convictions were obtained due to insufficient eyewitness testimony. The trials were abandoned in 1992 under the Keating government, and to this day Australia has not recommitted itself to reopening war crimes trials with regard to either Nazi war criminals or criminals from other genocides now residing in Australia.

Helen Demidenko was awarded the Vogel in September of 1993, some four months after Ivan Polyukhovich was acquitted by an Adelaide court of war crimes. Demidenko/Darville's book is premised on her interpretation of these trials as deeply divisive and fundamentally unjust. As outlined, *The Hand* begins with Fiona Kovalenko's distress at hearing the news of war crimes charges being laid against her Uncle Vitaly and is peppered throughout with references to the Australian war crimes trials. At one point, Fiona's best friend tells her, "I want you to understand that . . . I think it's wrong to try them. That trying people for what they did in a war legitimises other wartime activities that are left untried. War is a crime, in itself." The novel's consistent position on the trials is that they are unnecessary at best and destructive at worst. Vindicating this overall perspective, the work ends with Uncle Vitaly escaping his day in court through death, absolved both by the priest who administers his last rites and surrounded by loving family. After his death, Fiona writes "letters to various Australian newspapers and magazines, protesting against the trials"[49] and finds some kind of solace in conversation with the descendent of a Quaker victim of the Nazis at the site of the former death camp of Treblinka.

In interviews and her own articles, Demidenko/Darville would time and again link the impetus for writing of *The Hand* to the Australian war crimes trials.[50]

> I was very upset by the war crimes trials because I thought they were very specifically directed at the Ukrainian community and were very vindictive and sanctimonious. They seemed to be this incredible "holier-than-thou, we-are-right, we-are-going-to-get-you, you-nasty-people, you-shouldn't-have-come-to-Australia-and-polluted-our-holy-shores" and it wasn't motivated by a sense of justice but by a sense of revenge.[51]

And:

> For all that some people don't like the way I've told this story, I prefer my method to war crimes trials. This may seem strange. I've been threatened with rape and death. But I've also spent a

> good part of my life in courtrooms. And I know from experience which hurts more, costs more, sets up adversarial winners and losers. Most lawyers talk to win. This lawyer prefers to talk.[52]

So too, those who would honor *The Hand* with the Miles Franklin would also connect the import of the novel to the trials and the moral challenge they placed on Australian society:

> Novels about the migrant experience seem to us to be seizing the high ground in contemporary Australian fiction, in contrast to fiction about the more vapid aspects of Australian life. In particular they are incorporating into the cultural memory first-hand experience of the major historical events of the century, events from which Australia has been largely insulated, but which are a growing component of contemporary Australian life—even to the extent of requiring of us intricate moral judgements, as the most recent debate over the war crimes legislation highlighted.[53]

Indeed, the trials arguably underpin the novel's Australian framework; in the moral universe of the text, they are the contemporary setting in which the Holocaust as "cycle of revenge" continues to be played out on Australian shores. In short, *The Hand* portrays these exceedingly complex legal undertakings as the work of a vengeful "lobby group," intent on causing distress to those who simply wish to retain the peaceful status quo of multicultural Australia. This point was not lost on Alan Dershowitz, who attacked the moral slippage with regard to the novel's characterization of the trials: "Demidenko's greatest anger is directed against the Jewish survivors who sought to bring their Ukrainian tormentors to justice after the war by having them tried as war criminals. The 'silver budgie Zionists' [sic] are destroying the families of the Ukrainian killers who emigrated to [sic] Australia after the war. It is the Jews who are making them hate. 'My sister is starting to hate . . . my sister who never hated anything.'"[54] In point of fact, while Jewish communal leaders were active in lobbying the then Hawke Labor government to undertake trials, they did not find unequivocal support in the Jewish or survivor community.

Konrad Kwiet, chief historian for the trials, pointed to the fact that many survivors were not publicly supportive of the trials as they feared that they would trigger an increase of antisemitic sentiment in Australia.⁵⁵ He noted:

> Fierce criticism was articulated by the ethnic communities to which the suspected war criminals belonged. Their spokespersons chose to speak of injustice or an act of revenge, of defamation of innocent people. Their disapproval found its most vehement expression in the form of a warning that the war crimes debate would stir up animosities and ethnic tensions, in particular between Jewish and Eastern European communities. It was claimed that this, in turn, could threaten the fabric of Australia's exemplary multicultural society.⁵⁶

In other words, if Jewish migrants spoke about and indeed testified as to their experiences at the hands of the Nazis and their collaborators both during and after the Holocaust, it was they who would threaten the multicultural status quo. Such sentiments could be said to embody a uniquely Australian version of the quotation ascribed to Israeli psychoanalyst Zvi Rex that "the Germans will never forgive the Jews for Auschwitz."⁵⁷ *The Hand* and those who would defend its history and applaud its morality would perform a similar moral inversion. In its framing of the Australian war crimes trials as "show trials," the novel's historical and moral distortions find their logical end: an end in which justice was neither possible nor desirable, where keeping Australia a tolerant and "harmonious" multicultural society could only be achieved through forgetting rather than "working through" the past.

Puzzled as to how such a reversal of victim to victimizer could have eventuated in the multicultural and supposedly tolerant Australia of 1990s, Robert Manne wondered, "Are we not part of that common civilization that absorbed the shock of Auschwitz and which internalized its meaning?" Admitting that it was at this very point that the moral confusion prompted by the novel's version of the Holocaust threatened to overwhelm understanding, he wrote:

> There is one aspect of the Demidenko affair I still find extremely puzzling. *The Hand that Signed the Paper*, a work honoured by

three sets of Australian literary judges, seems to me to be not only an unmistakeably antisemitic novel, but an unmistakably antisemitic novel *about the Holocaust*. And yet it is clear that it would be absurd to regard Australia as an antisemitic country or as a country where antisemitism is on the rise or to fail to notice that, until the Demidenko affair, no segment of Australian society was more reliably hostile to expressions of racism or antisemitism than its literary community.[58]

Whether Manne's description of Australia as a country largely free of antisemitism is accurate is open to debate. But what *The Hand*, in revealing historical ignorance and generating moral confusion, showed was that in Manne's prescient phrase, Australia's "culture of forgetting" proved itself yet again to be unable or unwilling to face up to the less "relaxed and comfortable" aspects of its past, seeing such episodes as impediments rather than opportunities to create a just foundation for a truly tolerant present. It is doubtful that when resurrecting the Judeo-Bolshevik myth in sunny Queensland, Helen Demidenko/Darville aimed to do anything beyond characterize the history of the Holocaust in Europe and its memory in Australia as embodying a simplistic and ongoing story of ethnic revenge. Whatever her intentions, in actuality her novel reignited and laid bare a complex and enduring debate as to what preserving ethnic and racial harmony in Australia truly entailed.

Notes

1. In Australia, such references can be found consistently in the popular media but are also evident in scholarly and political discourses. See Neil Levi, "'No Sensible Comparison?' The Place of the Holocaust in Australia's History Wars," *History and Memory* 19, no. 1 (2007): 124–56.
2. Peter Christoff, "Assassins of Memory," *Arena Magazine*, no. 18 (August/September 1995), 48.
3. Robert Manne, *The Culture of Forgetting: Helen Demidenko and the Holocaust* (Melbourne: Text, 1996), 190.
4. The phrase comes from John Howard, before he became prime minister, in an interview with Liz Jackson on "An Average Australian Bloke—1996," *Four Corners*, February 19, 1996, www.abc.net.au/4corners/an-average-australian-bloke—1996

/2841808. Howard was not commenting on the Demidenko/Darville affair but rather giving his vision for Australian life in the twenty-first century.

5. The most comprehensive single collection of the media coverage surrounding the affair can be found in John Jost, Gianna Totaro, and Christine Tyshing, *The Demidenko File: Who Said What, Where and When in Australia's Most Inflammatory Literary Debate* (Ringwood, VIC: Penguin, 1996).

6. Helen Demidenko, *The Hand That Signed th e Paper* (St. Leonards, NSW, Australia: Allen & Unwin, 1994), vi.

7. Jost, Totaro, and Tyshing, *Demidenko File*, 7.

8. Prior to her unmasking and even after, Demidenko/Darville's ethnicity was noted by key writers in the debate as a factor that deeply influenced the reception of the novel. See Manne, *Culture of Forgetting*; Gerard Henderson, "Playing Loose with the Truth in This Work of 'Faction,'" *Sydney Morning Herald*, June 27, 1995; Andrew Riemer, *The Demidenko Debate* (Sydney: Allen & Unwin, 1996).

9. Michael Heyward, *The Ern Malley Affair* (Sydney: Vintage Australia, 2003).

10. Demidenko, *Hand That Signed the Paper*, 3.

11. Demidenko, *Hand That Signed the Paper*, 81.

12. Roger McDonald, quoted in Manne, *Culture of Forgetting*, 32.

13. Castro in particular also had concerns over the quality of the manuscript. See Jost, Totaro, and Tyshing, *Demidenko File*, viii.

14. Manne, *Culture of Forgetting*, 41.

15. Manne, *Culture of Forgetting*, 45.

16. The medal winner was decided on earlier in 1995 but only announced after the Miles Franklin. See Manne, *Culture of Forgetting*, 62–65.

17. See Philip Mendes, "Jews, Ukrainians, Nazi War Crimes and Literary Hoaxes Down Under," *Patterns of Prejudice* 30, no. 2 (1996): 55–71.

18. "Forum on the Demidenko Controversy," *Australian Book Review* 173 (August 1995): 19.

19. "Analysis of Mindless Hatred," interview with Vic Alhadeff, *Australian Jewish News*, Sydney edition, August 26, 1994, in Jost, Totaro, and Tyshing, eds., *The Demidenko File*, 6.

20. Catherine Taylor, "Helen's Our New Young Literary Lioness," *Daily Telegraph-Mirror* (Sydney), June 2, 1995.

21. Peter Christoff, "Assassins of Memory," *Arena Magazine*, no. 18 (August/September 1995); Henderson, "Playing Loose with the Truth in This Work of 'Faction'"; and Robert Manne, "The Strange Case of Helen Demidenko," *Quadrant* 39, no. 9 (1995): 21–28.

22. Riemer, *Demidenko Debate*; and A. P. Riemer, "After Demidenko. -American Novelist William Gass and Miles Franklin Award Winner for 1997 David Foster-," *Voices: The Quarterly Journal of the National Library of Australia* 7, no. 2 (1997): 104.
23. Jacques Adler, "The Hand That Hides an Ugly History," *Age* (Melbourne), June 22, 1995.
24. George Jaworsky, "Washing Our Hands of Past Hatreds," *Age* (Melbourne), July 3, 1995.
25. Stefan Romaniw, "The Hand That Seeks to Rule Out Hate," *Age* (Melbourne), June 26, 1995.
26. See Bernard Freedman, "Demidenko No Innocent Multiculturalist," *Australian Jewish News* (Melbourne), August 25, 1995.
27. Jill Kitson, quoted in Angela Bennie, "First Novel Wins Helen the Nation's Top Prize at 24," *Sydney Morning Herald*, June 2, 1995.
28. Kitson, quoted in Bennie, "First Novel Wins Helen the Nation's Top Prize at 24."
29. Pamela Bone, "A Harsh Sting in the Tale," *Age*, June 9, 1995.
30. Bone, "A Harsh Sting in the Tale."
31. Judith Armstrong, "'Swords Cross over the Terror of Words," *Age*, June 17, 1995.
32. For an overview of this history, see Mendes, "Jews, Ukrainians, Nazi War Crimes and Literary Hoaxes Down Under."
33. Armstrong, "Swords Cross over the Terror of Words."
34. Susan Geason, "War Criminal Next Door," *Sun Herald* (Sydney) September 4, 1994, 11.
35. Miriam Cosic, "The Evil Within: Blind Revenge of the Victims," *Sydney Morning Herald*, September 20, 1994, 9.
36. Cosic, "Evil Within," 9.
37. Again, for a comprehensive sense of the heat and extent of the debate, see Jost, Totaro, and Tyshing, *Demidenko File*
38. Padraic McGuinness, "'Confusing the Literary Merit with the Message," *Age*, August 24, 1995.
39. For a specific refutation of such charges, see Manne, *Culture of Forgetting*, 164–88.
40. Frank Devine, "Guilty of an Unseemly Rush to Demonise," *Australian* (Surry Hills, NSW), August 24, 1995.
41. Riemer, *Demidenko Debate*, 11.
42. Riemer, 63.

43. Riemer, *Demidenko Debate*, 51–52.
44. Riemer, 52.
45. Mark Aarons, *Sanctuary: Nazi Refugees in Australia* (Melbourne: Heinemann, 1989); and Mark Aarons, *War Criminals Welcome: Australia, A Sanctuary for Fugitive War Criminals since 1945* (Melbourne: Black Inc., 2001).
46. See David Fraser, *Daviborshch's Cart: Narrating the Holocaust in Australian War Crimes Trials* (Lincoln: University of Nebraska Press, 2010); and Konrad Kwiet, "A Historian's View: The War Crimes Debate Down Under," *Dapim: Studies on the Shoah* 24, no. 1 (2010): 319–31.
47. Fraser, *Daviborshch's Cart*; and Kwiet, "A Historian's View."
48. Eight hundred forty-three cases were investigated by the SIU over a five-year period. See Attorney-General's Department, *Report of the Investigations of War Criminals in Australia* (Final SIU Report). Canberra: Australia Government Publishing Service, 1993.
49. Demidenko, *Hand That Signed the Paper*, 157.
50. Examples abound: "'The war crimes tribunals here triggered it,' she said yesterday of her novel. I suddenly thought, what if I found out that my family was in some way involved in that utterly, utterly appalling thing, what if that were me? After all, I am half-Ukrainian. 'I realised I would go off the edge, I would just wipe out, I would die. I love my family, and I am very close to them.'" Bennie, "First Novel Wins Helen the Nation's Top Prize at 24."
51. Interview with Terry Lane, 3RN 11 June 1995, in Jost, Totaro, and Tyshing, eds., *The Demidenko File*, 42
52. Helen Demidenko, "Stories and Stereotypes: Critics Miss the Mark," *Age*, June 27, 1995. Sections of this article are also printed in an article by Demidenko, "All People Are Capable of Atrocities," *Sydney Morning Herald*, June 27, 1995.
53. The Miles Franklin Citation, in Jost, Totaro, and Tyshing, *The Demidenko File*, 26.
54. Alan Dershowitz, "Holocaust 'Abuse Excuse' Fails to Disguise Murder Most Foul," *Australian Financial Review*, June 29, 1995.
55. Interview with Professor Konrad Kwiet, December 2, 2009; and Kwiet, "A Historian's View," 47.
56. Kwiet "A Historian's View," 47.
57. The origins of the quotation and idea remain controversial but is first thought to appear in Henryk M. Broder, "Der Täter als Bewährungshelfer oder Die Deutschen werden den Juden Auschwitz nie verzeihen," *Der ewige Antisemit: Über Sinn und Funktion eines beständigen Gefühls* (Frankfurt: Fischer-Taschenbuch-Verlag, 1986).
58. Manne, *Culture of Forgetting*, 189.

Part IV

Claiming the Holocaust

PART 4 BRINGS THE volume into the present, focusing on contemporary political causes for which the Holocaust provides a benchmark for racial equality and justice. The authors carefully trace historical developments, unpacking how Holocaust memory has been invoked as a framework for redress, recognition, and reconciliation. Its power to do so effectively is assessed and, at times, found wanting.

Beginning with perhaps the most politically contentious of connections, the first chapter by Bashir Bashir and Amos Goldberg draws on their important Hebrew-language study, *The Holocaust and the Nakba*. The authors propose a theoretical framework based on Dominick LaCapra's concept of "empathic unsettlement," which would allow for the recognition of the Holocaust alongside the Nakba and, by extension, the mutual recognition of others in the Israeli-Palestinian context. In their chapter, the memories of these two events are not equated but rather sit in creative tension, challenging readers to engage with the discomfort they evoke as a meaningful pathway to eventual reconciliation.

Turning to the Southern Hemisphere, the next two contributions consider the "lessons" of the Holocaust in Australia and South Africa. Steven Cooke and Donna-Lee Frieze chart the evolution of temporary exhibitions in Melbourne's Jewish Holocaust Centre, a progression that sees survivors move from being presented as victims of racial persecution to agents of change, promoting a strong message of civic awareness and anti-racism. Yet the "great Australian silence" concerning Indigenous genocide remains glaringly absent in these productions, illustrating perhaps a failure of Holocaust memory to engender empathetic identification in an organization committed to promoting racial equality. Shirli Gilbert explores how the Nazi past has been taught in South Africa from the 1950s to the 2010s, problematizing the post-apartheid linkage between Nazism and apartheid and showing that connections considered obvious today were for several decades not seen as such. Many apartheid-era textbooks use the language of "race" and racism to explain Nazi actions in a way that recognizes no relationship to their contemporary reality, while post-apartheid textbooks often associate the Holocaust and apartheid in simplistic and unquestioning ways. Her contribution illustrates that the assumption that Holocaust education provides a panacea for all manner of social ills remains untested.

In the book's final contribution, Dorota Glowacka explores how First Nations activists in Canada have invoked the Holocaust in order to draw attention to their own "very different historical injustice," arguing that this is a powerful means through which their claims are recognized. Significantly, her work also shines a light back onto Holocaust studies itself: she maintains that the discipline has remained largely trapped within Eurocentric epistemologies, limiting not only its power to evoke empathetic engagement across racial divides but also its own possibilities for development. She challenges us to think about how Holocaust studies itself may be transformed through an engagement with postcolonial critiques and ongoing processes of decolonization, creating new possibilities for cross-disciplinary work that may well provide the foundations for renewed political engagement across national and racial divides.

Taken together, these case studies stand as challenge and corrective to contemporary assumptions that appeals to Holocaust memory will result in racially tolerant communities. They also provide an opportunity to reflect on how we might draw on these memories to unsettle, rather than confirm, how we think about and construct contemporary struggles for racial equality. From such a perspective, we posit, the generative power of Holocaust memory may be more fruitfully harnessed.

12

Deliberating the Holocaust and the Nakba

Disruptive Empathy and Binationalism in Israel/Palestine

Bashir Bashir and Amos Goldberg

THIS CHAPTER DEVELOPS A theoretical framework for shared and inclusive Jewish and Palestinian deliberation on the memories of the Holocaust and the Nakba,[1] arguing that a joint Arab-Jewish public deliberation on the traumatic memories of these two events is not only possible, however challenging and disruptive it may be, but also fundamental for producing an egalitarian and inclusive ethics of binationalism in Israel/Palestine. There are several reasons justifying common deliberations on these two foundational events.

First, the Holocaust and the Nakba are defining events in the political consciousness and collective identity of the two increasingly intertwined peoples, and both generate a dominant collective awareness that incorporates elements of victimhood. Thus, in Arab-Jewish debates and conversations, it has become very hard to address one without mentioning the other.

Second, the two events are historically related. It is beyond the scope of this chapter to fully discuss the exact ways in which this is the case, but it is clear that the events of 1947-48 in Palestine/Israel—namely, the establishment of the State of Israel and the Palestinian Nakba—were in various direct and indirect ways strongly influenced by the events in Europe between 1933 and 1945.[2] They have emerged as inseparable in light of the seeming intractability of the conflict.

Third, the "ethics of catastrophe," for which the Holocaust serves as its major trope and symbol, is mainly premised on the rejection of "the metaphysics of comprehension."³ Therefore, while the metaphysics of comprehension demands and emphasizes closure, consensus, and unity, the ethics of catastrophe insists on acknowledging the constitutive yet disruptive role of various forms of "otherness" in the social and political domains. The mainstream and endorsed national narratives of the Holocaust and the Nakba largely operate according to the metaphysics of comprehension rather than the ethics of catastrophe. Stated differently, they produce and reinforce total comprehension and essentialist identities that oppress the disruptive otherness. One way of restoring the critical and ethical force and meaning of these two catastrophic events, we argue, is by discussing them together in a disruptive fashion.

Fourth, and intimately linked to the previous point, these two "foundational pasts"⁴ are deeply exclusionary and conflicting in current dominant Jewish and Palestinian identity politics. They are often used to demonize the other side and establish a complete self-justification. Hence, they further widen the gap between the two peoples and disable the possibilities of conductive Jewish-Arab discussion on the question of Israel/Palestine. The unavoidable inseparability and interdependence of Arab and Jew means that productive engagement between the two memories, histories, and identities has become both inevitable and timely. This productive engagement, we argue, produces a conceptual frame within which these two mutually and radically exclusionary traumatic memories can become politically and ethically transformative in establishing a common, even if minimal, binational "we" and ethics.⁵

Before we proceed to describe the structure of the chapter and its various sections, it is critical to mention at least two important caveats. First, we must stress already at this point that we do not suggest that these two disastrous events are identical or even similar in extent and character. Indeed, as Gilbert Achcar argues in *The Arabs and the Holocaust*, although the Nakba is a catastrophic event that should not be undermined, "the Holocaust was clearly incomparably crueler and bloodier than the Nakba."⁶ Nonetheless, when it comes to the manner in which they are remembered, narrated, historicized, and understood, it may be possible to associate them in a helpful way.

Second, when we invoke public deliberation, we do not refer to thin and confining liberal notions of public deliberation but to thick and robust notions of deliberations. More specifically, unlike the conventional and restrictive liberal notions of democratic deliberation (for example, Jürgen Habermas and John Rawls) that place "public reason" at their center, privilege rational argumentation, and demand bracketing particularities and asymmetries for the sake of achieving legitimate democratic decisions, our notion of public democratic deliberation is more expansive by respecting not only "rational and reasonable arguments" but also other modes of speech, such as testimony, storytelling, and narrative. These latter modes of discourse are exceptionally important both because they allow for contestation (rather than consensus) and deliberation from within particularities/contextualized positions and because they are central to deliberating the memories and histories of the Holocaust and the Nakba.[7] Civil partnership within the public sphere is not necessarily achieved through agreement, but first and foremost through debate and contestation, which in itself situates adversaries in a joint discursive framework.

This chapter is divided into three sections. The first section identifies and explores some of the fundamental difficulties and challenges that face such a joint deliberative enterprise. Unlike the conventional Jewish and Palestinian discussions on the Holocaust and the Nakba, which usually follow and reinforce exclusionary, dichotomous, and self-referential logic that excludes and demonizes the other, the second section presents some examples, most notably Elias Khoury's epic novel, *Gate of the Sun* (*Bab al-Shams*), which bring the memories of the Holocaust and the Nakba together and thus challenge and disrupt this exclusionary and binary logic. We interpret Dominick LaCapra's notion of "empathic unsettlement," which transforms otherness from a problem to be disposed of into a moral and emotional challenge, as a political concept that best captures and explains the disruptive potential of a joint deliberation on the Holocaust and the Nakba. The third section proposes to move from the critical potential of the empathic unsettlement as an ethics of disruption to its more productive potential. We suggest that its productive potential transcends intractable and antagonistic binary politics and gives rise to a binational approach to the question of Israel/Palestine vis-à-vis the memories of the Holocaust and the Nakba. In this section, we focus on the centrality of the figure of the refugee, constitutive of Palestinian and Jewish histories and identities, in contributing to the development of an egalitarian ethics of binationalism. More specifically, we claim that the figure of the refugee, a product and victim of the ethnically homogenizing modern nation-state, who is intimately connected to both the Holocaust and the Nakba, serves as a herald of disruptive politics, a politics that challenges the rigidity and dichotomy of identity politics and favors empathy, partnership, joint dwelling, and integration instead of separation, segregation, ghettoization, and oppressive assimilation in Israel/Palestine.

DIFFICULTIES

To deliberate on these traumatic and foundational pasts under present conditions of animosity and asymmetry is exceptionally challenging.[8] After all, creating such an enterprise is not a technical matter. As we have stated, not every exchange of words turns into a public deliberation, and not every shared discussion generates civil partnership. Regrettably, an inclusive and joint public sphere seldom evolves among Jews and Palestinians, even more so when it comes to the Holocaust and the Nakba.[9] This is first and foremost because the traumas of the Holocaust and the Nakba continue to be experienced firsthand by each of the societies and constitute an open wound, and anything perceived to reframe it in an unorthodox manner generates extreme reactions.[10]

Several additional factors make it yet more difficult to conduct an egalitarian and inclusive deliberation in these contexts. On the one hand, the Holocaust is indeed an event of enormous proportions in modern history. Some go so far as to contend that it is a unique or unprecedented occurrence.[11] To Jews and large sections of the Western world, the Holocaust has become the ultimate symbol of evil and human criminality.[12] The Holocaust, some have argued, is the best candidate to serve as a "global memory" and the measuring reference for crimes against humanity.[13] As such, any comparative discussion of the Holocaust with another event, especially the Nakba, is likely to be perceived by Jews and many others as a reductive, tasteless, or even morally and politically questionable banalization of the topic.[14]

On the other hand, most of the Jews today live under completely different and better historical conditions in comparison to the 1930s and '40s. As Yehuda Bauer stated already in the 1970s, Jews after the Holocaust emerged from a complete state of powerlessness.[15] Holocaust survivors inevitably bear the scars of this terrible trauma on their bodies and souls, as do their successors, albeit in different ways.[16] Yet Jews now live in a strikingly different period: Israel is a reasonably well-established state in possession of nuclear weaponry, the Jews are one of the most successful ethnic groups in the United States, and antisemitism does not exist in the same ways it did prior to World War II, at least in Europe and the United States.[17] The Jews, as individuals and as a group organized in collective institutions (for example, the State of Israel), are far from being powerless historical agents as they were during the 1930s and '40s.

By contrast, since the Nakba, most Palestinians largely live under conditions of statelessness, occupation, and dispersion. The Nakba is an explicitly continuing present, and its consequences are still unfolding and affecting contemporary Palestinian life. Its aftermath of suffering and political weakness affects nearly every Palestinian, Palestinian family, and the Palestinian collective on an almost daily basis.[18]

But beyond all this, a deeper asymmetry in the context of these two events renders joint discussion even more charged. The Palestinians bear no responsibility whatsoever for the Holocaust that occurred in Europe.[19] The Holocaust is a case of genocide that grew out of European racism and World War II. It was German and European antisemitism and the failure of nationalism to include Jews that gave rise to the "Jewish question" in Europe and were among the primary ideological factors that led to the Holocaust. The State of Israel, however, generated and was fully involved in the events of the Nakba. The Haganah, the Palmach, the Etsel, and the Lehi (the prestate Zionist armed forces) and, subsequently, the Israeli army caused the Palestinian national devastation during the confrontation of 1947–48, which, among other phenomena, manifested itself in the expulsion or flight of many Palestinians, making some 750,000 of them refugees.[20] And it is the State of Israel that has prevented and continues to prevent the return of the refugees since the end of the war to this day. Toward that end, it had passed the Absentees' Property Law, which allows the confiscation of all land and property left behind by the refugees and placed its Palestinian citizens under military rule from 1948 until 1966, citizens who continue to experience discrimination to this day. The State of Israel has also controlled the occupied territories of the West Bank and Gaza since 1967 by means of a discriminatory occupation regime that deprives the Palestinians of most of their individual and collective rights. Many Palestinians therefore regard Zionism and the State of Israel as bearing prime responsibility for their catastrophe and suffering. Whether one accepts Israel's justifications of these events as legitimate acts of self-defense or not, it is certainly not an uninvolved party in the Palestinians' ongoing catastrophe and suffering; the same cannot be said for the Palestinians with respect to the Holocaust. The actual events in Palestine/Israel place the Jews and the Palestinians in different political and moral positions, and it is extremely difficult to conduct a joint and egalitarian civil conversation in such an asymmetrical context.[21]

In the context of the Holocaust, these issues are in fact far more complex. The vast majority of Israeli Jews generally perceive the Holocaust as a catastrophe that justifies their Zionist position favoring a Jewish nation-state on the land of Israel/Palestine. There is a prevalent sense among many Jews, including many Holocaust survivors after the war, that they must establish a robust sovereignty of their own in the wake of the Holocaust.[22] Thus, it follows that any denial of the Holocaust or its dimensions, or antisemitic utterances, as enunciated by some Arab and Palestinian leaders, let alone the rejection of Jewish sovereign existence itself, provokes among many Jews considerable anger and existential anxiety that harks back to those horrific events.

The majority of the Palestinians, for their part, perceive Zionism as a European colonial movement that emerged as one of the many responses to the "Jewish problem," itself a European problem exacerbated by the Holocaust.[23] The very attempt to find and then implement a solution to such a European question in Palestine, as well as Zionism's frequent use of colonial discourse and practice manifested in expressions such as "progress," "modernity," and "settlement," aroused resistance among Arabs generally and Palestinians in particular. Confronting Zionism is regarded by many Palestinians as a legitimate, even necessary and justifiable, form of anticolonial resistance. Within this context, the Holocaust is perceived as a catastrophe for which the Arabs were compelled to pay, even though they bore no responsibility for its occurrence. Moreover, several Palestinians believe that Zionism and the State of Israel have made cynical political usage of the Holocaust in order to divest themselves from taking responsibility for their actions toward the Palestinians and to suspend the latter's collective and individual rights.[24] Indeed, this instrumental use of the Holocaust has been identified and critically explored by the research of scholars such as Idith Zertal, Moshe Zuckermann, and others.[25]

In light of the above, it appears that the equality and symmetry that could enable the debate to establish some common public egalitarian sphere are generally absent from this discussion. This brings us back to the question of whether and under what conditions Israeli Jews and Palestinian Arabs are capable of creating a public sphere, however confined and local, within which a common civil and democratic deliberation on the memories of the Holocaust and Nakba can take place. And even if this is a deliberation between adversaries, it still establishes and rests on some sort of partnership.

THE ETHICS OF DISRUPTION

Elias Khoury's novel *Gate of the Sun* (*Bab al-Shams*)[26] narrates the Palestinian catastrophe. Khaleel, the novel's narrator and protagonist, in a monologue addressed to Yunes, a hero of the Palestinian struggle who lies unconsciously on his deathbed in a hospital in one of the refugee camps in Beirut, says:

> But tell me, what did the [Palestinian] national movement posted in the cities do apart from demonstrate against Jewish immigration?
> I'm not saying you weren't right. But in those days, when the Nazi beast was exterminating the Jews of Europe, what did you know about the world?
> ... [D]on't worry, I believe, like you, that this land must belong to its people, and there is no moral, political, humanitarian, or religious justification that would permit the expulsion of an entire people from its country and the transformation of what remained of them into second-class citizens. . . . But tell me, in the faces of the people being driven to slaughter, don't you see something resembling your own?
> Don't tell me you didn't know, and above all, don't say that it wasn't our fault.
> You and I and every human being on the face of the planet should have known and not stood by in silence, should have

prevented that beast from destroying its victims in that barbaric, unprecedented manner . . . because their death meant the death of humanity within us.[27]

This critical passage that the narrator directs at the Palestinian national movement, which failed to recognize the "unprecedented barbarity" that occurred in Europe and the refugee status of the Holocaust survivors, should be read in the context of the divergent positions on the Holocaust among Palestinian and Arab intellectuals. While some of them were skeptical and others flatly denied its occurrence, another influential current of thought, to which Khoury adheres, not only recognized the Holocaust but sought to instill awareness of its importance and the centrality of its memory in shaping modern Jewish and Western identity and history.[28]

Moreover, we claim that this passage may also serve as a key to the issue at hand, since it marks the problematic aspects of simultaneously addressing the Holocaust and the Nakba—and the anxiety that this arouses. This is primarily an anxiety about foregoing absolute justice, which is shared by both Jews and Palestinians. The Nakba underlines Palestinian political justice, while the Holocaust currently underpins many Jews' ultimate claim to justice. Yet the willingness to weave the catastrophe of the other side into each party's national narrative does not imply a dismantling of the core justification of the national narrative. Or, in the words of the narrator in *Bab al-Shams* who here refers to the Palestinian perspective: acknowledging the Holocaust does not undermine the justness of the Palestinians regarding the wrong done to them or to question "that this land must belong to its people."

Taking account of the origin of the Jews who came to Palestine does not, from the narrator's viewpoint, detract from the claim to justice on the part of the Palestinians. Neither does it imply that things would necessarily have turned out differently had the Palestinians taken into account why Jews came to Palestine. In other words, this empathy toward the Jewish victims of the Holocaust does not amount to a complete identification with them and their point of view. It does retain one's otherness in relation to the other. It does not erase difference. But, nonetheless, from this very position the narrator, and seemingly Khoury himself, demands that this be recognized for two reasons: first, because of some sort of identification, as when he asks "in the faces of the people being driven to slaughter, don't you see something resembling your own?" and, second, because of the moral obligation that constitutes entry to history—"their death meant the death of humanity within us"; as he continues referring to the consequences of the Palestinian national movement's failure to acknowledge this "death of humanity," he says: "but we—you were outside of history so you became its second victim."[29] The narrator demands from the Palestinians then a double move: acknowledging themselves as different from the Jewish other while identifying with their suffering.

It is noteworthy that Khoury's narrator assigns, in a Levinasian gesture, a critical significance to the "face" of the other as an indicator of ethical commitment. As Levinas argues, the contact with alterity, responding to and engaging with the claims/demands of those who are not well known to us and with whom we did not choose to dwell, animates the ethical scene. This infinite constitutive alterity makes itself known through the face of the person (i.e., the face) that generates infinite ethical demands and obligations. According to Levinas, the face commands us to preserve life and not to kill.[30]

Khoury's protagonist's views on the memories of the Nakba and the Holocaust could be understood within this Levinasian conceptual framework of radical ethical obligation toward the other. But there is also a fundamental difference. Whereas Levinas places strong emphasis on the otherness of the face, Khoury's narrator combines this notion of otherness with a sense of empathy. For him, it is not only about otherness but also about empathy and resemblance.

Furthermore, in response to the applicability of his ethical frame to the oppression of the Palestinians, Levinas insisted that his proposed ethical frame is not universally applied. It is culturally and geographically restricted. He claimed that he meant to extend ethical obligations to those who are bound together, keeping in mind those with Judeo-Christian and classical Greek origins.[31]

Following Hannan Hever,[32] we further deliberate on Khoury's narrator's notion of otherness and empathy in regard to the Nakba and the Holocaust by means of "empathic unsettlement," coined by Dominick LaCapra in his protracted discussion of trauma and the Holocaust.[33] This concept manages to closely and convincingly link memory, ethics, history, and trauma in a way that we believe suits our and Khoury's notion of empathy. But before further elaboration on the usefulness of empathic unsettlement, we should note that in utilizing LaCapraian psychoanalytical concepts we are not seeking to reduce the narrative of conflict to the realm of psychology. Like LaCapra,[34] who declares that he is not using these concepts in the orthodox way, we try to extract from this conceptual world a theoretical structure that facilitates understanding and analysis of political reality. Otherwise stated, it is through politically conceptualizing "empathic unsettlement" that we hope to offer a path toward that common civil partnership with which we began this chapter.

Dominick LaCapra contrasts empathy and empathic unsettlement with complete identification: "empathy is mistakenly conflated with identification or fusion with the other.... In contradistinction to this entire frame of reference, empathy should rather be understood in terms of an affective relation, rapport, or bond with the other recognized and respected as other."[35] Identification follows the risky fantasy of universal likeness, which seeks homogeneity and eradicates difference.[36] It operates on one of two levels—appropriation or subjugation—since, if it is to occur, the individual must either reduce the other to his own concepts or subjugate himself to the concepts of the other. Thus, identification is always connected to narcissistic impulses and indicates a type of illusion that is potentially aggressive and violent.[37]

As we have argued, Khoury's narrator is aware of this and rejects this form of identification. He refuses to relinquish his point of view for that of the enemy even as the latter has experienced extreme trauma in the form of the Holocaust. Nevertheless, he finds some similarity: "Don't you see something resembling your own in the faces of the people being driven to slaughter?" But what is the significance of this recognition? How does it exert an influence? And what does it mean? The narrator gives us no immediate or unequivocal answer to these questions. This response is suspended for the time being[38]—it only destabilizes an overly stiff narrative.

This, in fact, is how empathic unsettlement undermines meaning. For, by contrast to identification, which seeks to blur the distance between the self and the other, empathic unsettlement requires the subject to make, like Khoury's narrator, two opposite movements simultaneously. On the one hand, it recognizes the fundamental inherent otherness of the individual who experiences the trauma, defined as an excessive experience that transcends the existing array of social symbols and images.[39] On the other hand, and despite the recognition of the radical and ineradicable otherness of those who experience trauma, empathic unsettlement calls for a sense of empathy toward them. Therefore, the ethics of trauma is an ethics of disruption that compels us to react empathetically to others while being fully aware of their otherness and at the same time to recognize the component of trauma that disrupts and prevents any structure, narrative, or relationship from reaching wholeness and closure. As LaCapra indicates:

> At the very least, empathic unsettlement poses a barrier to closure in discourse and places in jeopardy harmonizing or spiritually uplifting accounts of extreme events from which we attempt to derive reassurance or a benefit... but involve affect and may empathetically expose the self to an unsettlement, if not a secondary trauma, which should not be glorified or fixated upon but addressed in a manner that strives to be cognitively and ethically responsible as well as open to the challenge of utopian aspiration.[40]

The forms and consequences of the empathic unsettlement required to address traumatic events cannot be predictable or known. Its role is precisely this—to disrupt. It emanates from a fear of any type of closure, to which all political discourse aspires and which itself is a harbinger of fascist logic.[41]

Disruption is the key word here, since it is located between the two poles that trauma is liable to generate: disruption neither completely dismantles the discourse (as a field of distinctions), nor does it fortify dichotomous opposition. It introduces some rather indigestible otherness to the discursive sphere, which emanates from some ethical commitment to those experiencing the trauma, but that cannot necessarily be formulated immediately. As such, empathic unsettlement disrupts and constantly undermines every "redeeming narrative" of suffering that offers a melancholic pleasure,[42] and this is the source of its considerable political value. One might say that it compels us to take the otherness of the other seriously. It operates in the twilight zone between full identification that appropriates the other or requires her to submit to the concepts of the "self," and outright alienation, which generates a sphere from which communication is absent, in which only power dictates.

Deliberating the Holocaust and the Nakba • 305

The weakened identification experienced as part of empathic unsettlement is therefore sensed not only vis-à-vis the person experiencing the trauma as someone who is suffering but first and foremost as an other in whose core experience there is something that goes beyond the symbolic and political contours that purport to represent him. And this turns him into a symbol and manifestation of intense ethical commitment toward radical otherness.

This is the precise demand that Khoury's narrator makes of his interlocutor when he asks him: "In the faces of the people being driven to slaughter, don't you see something resembling your own?" This type of empathic partnership leads neither to appropriation nor to submission. It likewise does not necessarily or immediately produce practical results. It does, however, create a type of disruption. It prevents a harmonious closure of the narrative, exposing it to new even if yet unforeseen possibilities.

For LaCapra, this is an essential component in working through the trauma as it confronts a tendency to fetishize a national redemptive narrative in cases of massive collective trauma, which violently excludes any otherness in a kind of a scapegoat mechanism. In such cases, as Vamik Volkan warns us and as we stated above regarding our context, "past [traumatic] events may become the fuel to ignite the most horrible human dramas."[43] Introducing a disruption into a tightly foreclosed national traumatized narrative, as in the cases of the dominant Palestinian and Israeli national narratives, is therefore essential.

In fact, Khoury himself critically reflects on such kind of fetishized narratives in many parts of *Bab al-Shams*. Thus, for example, the narrator warns: "We mustn't see ourselves only in their mirror, for they're prisoners of one story, as though the story had abbreviated and ossified them. Please, father [Yunis]—we mustn't become just one story. . . . Believe me, this is the only way, if we're not to become ossified and die."[44] Indeed, it seems that many Jews and Palestinians are trapped in such kind of a fetishized, exclusionary, and deadly closed traumatic narrative of which empathic unsettlement disrupt and undermine.

Khoury is not the only example of this type of empathic unsettlement. It also happens in Jewish Israeli literature. One of the "prophets" of this unsettling binding of the Holocaust and the Nakba in Jewish Israeli literature was the poet Avot Yeshurun. Already in 1952, he published a poem in this spirit, "Passover on Caves," which raised a huge controversy and marginalized him for more than two decades. He was even more explicit and radical in his 1958 poetic prose "Reasoning": "The Holocaust of the Jews of Europe and the Holocaust of the Arabs of Eretz Yisrael [Palestine] are one Holocaust of the Jewish people. The two gaze directly into one another's face."[45]

Another interesting example is the Palestinian author Ghassan Kanafani's 1969 novella *Return to Haifa*, which was staged by the widely famous and celebrated Israeli Cameri theater group in 2008. The plot is about a Palestinian couple who fled Haifa out of horror in April 1948 while leaving behind their baby. After the 1967 war, they return from Ramallah to visit their home, which is now occupied by Holocaust survivors who have adopted the left-behind child and raised him to become an Israeli soldier. The encounter between the two couples and the heartbreaking dilemma of the child is extremely unsettling to all readers/viewers—Jews, Palestinians, and others. The play's actors comprised both Jews and Palestinians, and the process they underwent during the production was extremely empathically unsettling. Peter Marks described this in the *Washington Post*:

> In rehearsals, the passions of the Israeli Jewish and Israeli Arab actors sometimes could not be contained by what was on the page. There were many instances where the actors said, "I have to have a line now, because I have to respond!" And we said: "Say it!" Gaon [the playwright] recalls. Some of these improvisations made their way into the script. "Every side wants all of its story to be told, all of it," the playwright adds. "And that's the whole deal, that's what the play is about: It's very comfortable to be surrounded by your own story, but what do you do when you find someone who is opposite to you?"[46]

Indeed, the play managed to stimulate precisely what we call an empathically unsettling shared public deliberation inside and outside the theater.[47]

It is also worth mentioning in this context the book by historian Yair Auron *The Holocaust, Rebirth, and the Nakba*. Relevant for our discussion here is the book's title. "From Holocaust to rebirth" (*MiShoah Letekumah*) is the most rigid form of the Zionist teleological redemption narrative, with its ultimate closure whose positive ending redeems its catastrophic beginning and lends some meaning to it. Adding the Nakba to the title in the same continuum fundamentally disrupts and unsettles this narrative, although, as is evident in the book's content, does not abolish it altogether.

Such unsettling deliberations are not only textual or theatrical: they also manifest themselves in the activities and the symbolic discourse of small Jewish and Palestinian joint political groups. One can mention, for example, Zochrot. According to its website, Zochrot will act to promote Israeli Jewish society's "acknowledgement of and accountability for the ongoing injustices of the Nakba and the reconceptualization of Return as the imperative redress of the Nakba."[48] However, as such, much of Zochrot's activities and discourse follow Holocaust remembrance habitus and discourse, for instance, special emphasis on victims' and perpetrators' testimony and tours to the ruins of Palestinian villages. Even its very name is an unsettlement of a loaded Holocaust-related signifier. As the cultural scholar Louise Bethlehem has asserted, "The linguistic subversion present as a willed différance is played out in the very name of the organization itself. Zochrot is the feminine plural form of the verb to remember—an imperative which is routinely associated with the Holocaust for Jewish Israelis."[49] As the photo below demonstrates, this unsettling slippage of signifiers seems to have gone beyond Zochrot.

Saleh Diab, depicted in this photo, is one of the leading activists in the joint Palestinian-Jewish struggle against the Judaization of the Palestinian neighborhood of Sheikh Jarrah in East Jerusalem. His family, originally from Jaffa, was expelled during the Nakba events of 1948. Together with twenty-seven other families, they settled in Sheikh Jarrah in 1953. Following long juridical discussions in Israeli courts in which the alleged prior-to-1948 Jewish land owners reclaimed their property in the neighborhood, some of these Palestinian families were recently evicted from their homes while others remain under this threat. The photo was taken in May 2013 during a joint Jewish and Palestinian demonstration against these processes. As Saleh noted, they deliberately chose the "Nakba Survivor" on his shirt since the word *survivor* is automatically associated in Israeli and US cultures with Holocaust survivors. It seems that while the slogan implicitly acknowledges the catastrophic fate of the Jews, it also wishes to provoke a moral reaction to the Nakba.

Another interesting case is the Holocaust exhibition displayed on January 27, 2009, in the village of Ni'lin—a village that has become the symbol for

Photo copyright Amos Goldberg.

the joint battle by Palestinians and Israelis who oppose Israel's construction of a separation wall in the West Bank. To mark the International Holocaust Remembrance Day, the village, whose inhabitants suffer greatly from oppressive measures by the Israeli military against their ongoing struggle against the wall, erected a display of photographs purchased from Yad Vashem Holocaust Museum and invited the public to learn more about the persecution of the Jews.[50] This exhibition was initiated by Khaled Kasab Mahameed, a lawyer from Nazareth, who mounted a small Holocaust exhibition at his home's ground floor. He dedicated many years of his life to promoting historical knowledge of the Holocaust among Palestinians. He believed that without understanding the Holocaust, the Palestinians could not really understand

Photograph copyright Khaled Kasab Mahameed.

the Israeli Jewish society and politics and therefore could never reach an agreement with them.

The exhibition in Ni'lin was indeed profound. As the photo depicts, Palestinian residents, despite hardships imposed on them by the Israeli military, were willing to confront the catastrophic history of their enemy. But also on display was a sign that stated: "Merkel, why should we Palestinians continue to pay the price for the Holocaust?" The message of this exhibition to Israeli Jews was yes, we are willing, however hard and challenging for us, to engage with your history, but we do not wholly accept your narrative—precisely as we saw in Khoury's novel.

All these examples and many others of empathic unsettlement deserve a lengthy ethnographic description and analysis, but that is beyond the scope of this chapter.[51] They all demonstrate different and at times contradicting ways by which small groups of Jews and Palestinians in various social and political arenas and contexts struggle to jointly establish a new empathic and unsettling discourse on the two catastrophes. These examples offer something more than merely bringing the Holocaust and the Nakba together to create a kind of rupture in the foreclosed national narratives.

More specifically, maybe the disruptive "other" in both traumatic narratives can be located in a way that would make empathic unsettlement more meaningful and constructive, that is, by creating a joint and egalitarian Jewish and Palestinian binational "we" and ethics that many of the groups and individuals mentioned above seek to achieve, even if sometimes it is not their officially stated aim. To make this claim, we first elaborate on the figure of the refugee in order to return to what we consider the radical implications of empathic unsettlement in our context. The figure of the refugee takes us from the disruptive potential of empathic unsettlement, important in itself, to its productive potential that gives rise to binationalism.

Empathic Unsettlement and Binationalism

As we have shown, Khoury offers what we named a kind of an empathic unsettling recognition toward the Jewish refugees. Edward Said proposes a similar position with regard to this disruptive power in the Israeli-Palestinian context, at the center of which stands the figure of the refugee (or of a people that seeks refuge). In his reading of Freud's *Moses and Monotheism*, Said recasts Moses, an Egyptian, among the refugees and traces the diasporic origin of Judaism and Jewish identity. Put differently, he emphasizes the constitutive role non-Jewish others played in the formation of what he calls the "irremediably diasporic, unhoused character" of Jewish life.[52] He argues that Palestinian identity and history are also constitutively diasporic and have been constructed in relation to alterity and under conditions of dispersion, exile, plurality, and heterogeneity.[53] Said concludes that these Palestinian and Jewish experiences of refugeeism give rise to disruptive and diasporic politics that invites adversarial partnership and joint dwelling instead of separation and segregation; they challenge the ethnically homogenizing and exclusionary drives of the existing mainstream political order and identity politics discourse in Palestine/Israel.

It is thus no coincidence that the figure of the refugee ("Jews fleeing European antisemitism"),[54] a disruptive presence, plays such a major role in our interpretation of empathic unsettlement. For, as Hannah Arendt and subsequently Giorgio Agamben have pointed out,[55] the refugee is precisely the one who stands outside the political order and is thus, by definition, a figure that disrupts the established order of things. In many cases, the refugee is from the outset created as a result of the aspiration toward homogeneity by modern societies and in particular the ethnically exclusive nation-state. The nation-state, in certain circumstances, is inclined to "cleanse" or to "purify" itself of every "stranger" or "other" that threatens to spoil the picture of its complete, unified, and close-knit identity, which it seeks to create. And when she is uprooted or expelled because she is different, because of her political position or ethnic origin, because she is perceived to be an enemy, or for any other reason, the refugee loses her civil status and is therefore no longer protected by the law and inevitably becomes a permanent victim. An empathic view of the refugee disrupts the validity of the foundations of the political order that created her in the first place and now abandons her to her fate. For the refugee, more than any other figure, also constitutes the most radical threat to this aspiration for some utopian ethnic homogeneity. And as soon as she unwillingly becomes a refugee, her radical "incompatibility," which sparked the crime against her in the first place, is merely exacerbated. The refugee is thus a paradigmatic figure since she symbolizes a prevalent and pervasive modern phenomenon, while at the same time arousing disquiet and presenting an enormous threat to the existing social and national order.

The refugee issue was high on the international agenda in the period preceding World War II partly because of the Nazis' persecution of the Jews, although Armenian refugees were prominent in European and American consciousness in the 1920s.[56] By the late 1930s, though, they became identified above all with the "Jewish problem." Following the war and the Holocaust, Jews remained the most problematic group of refugees on Europe's political agenda. Many countries did not want them back, and many displaced persons refused to return to their former homelands.

As such, the figure of the refugee historically links the Holocaust to the Nakba, both of which are located on a plane on a type of continuum, despite the radical difference between these two events. Written in 1951, the words of Hannah Arendt,[57] who herself underwent the refugee experience and wrote a fair amount about it, are worthy of extensive citation:

Hitler's solution of the Jewish problem first to reduce the German Jews to a nonrecognized minority in Germany, then to drive them as stateless people across the borders, and finally to gather them back from everywhere in order to ship them to extermination camps, was an eloquent demonstration to the world how really to "liquidate" all problems concerning minorities and stateless. After the war it turned out that the Jewish question, which was considered the only insoluble one, was indeed solved—namely by means of a colonized and then conquered territory—but this solved neither the problem of the minorities nor the stateless. On the contrary, like virtually all other events of our century, the solution of the Jewish question merely produced a new category of refugees, the Arabs, thereby increasing the number of stateless and rightless by 700,000 to 800,000 people. And what had happened in Palestine . . . was then repeated in India on a large scale. . . . Since the Peace Treaties of 1919 and 1920, the refugees and stateless have attached themselves like a curse to all the newly established states on earth which were created in the image of the nation state.[58]

According to this political thinking, refugees and stateless persons are not merely unfortunate beings deserving of pity and empathy. They are above all symptomatic of the ethnically exclusive nation-state's modern political structure, which encompasses intrinsic and potentially disastrous dangers, whose severity may vary from case to case, even though they are located on the same general conceptual plane and follow fairly similar logic. The refugee, whose radical difference within a given political order has turned her into what she is, becomes yet more different and threatening once she becomes a refugee who lacks a place and the protection of the political order. As such, she is almost completely exposed to all the ills of this world. This is why empathy toward the refugee is unsettling, since it is directed at the traumatic element within the modern nation-state. For this reason, empathy toward the refugee, especially the one coming to your territory or the one for whose refugeeism you are responsible, is not an easily acquired and nonpolitical pleasurable identification. It forces one to reconsider the political system that produced the refugee in the first place and to translate this empathy into an inevitably unpopular political action. It is an empathy that casts very worldly responsibility toward the refugee.

Perhaps no one experienced firsthand these tendencies of the nation-state with more intensity than European Jews.[59] From the European perspective, always seen to possess a dual (local and Jewish) identity, the "Jew" was perceived as someone who transcended borders, who was often multilingual and multicultural, whose religion was different, and who hailed from a different ethnic origin, constantly challenging and disrupting this desire for homogeneity. The Jews of different societies and nation-states in Eastern and Western Europe suffered from this image in very different ways, not only in Nazi Germany but also in interwar Poland and, more severely in the latter half of the 1930s, in Romania, certainly in Russia, as well as in France and in other places. To be sure, one cannot explain the fate of the Jews in every location only by this context of the national urge toward homogeneity. Nevertheless, once the Jews were marked as others whose belonging to the political structure of the nation-state was questionable, they inevitably became an object of some sort of persecution, discrimination, or exclusion and frequently also of expulsion or murder. The most extreme example of this tendency is Nazi Germany's self-conceptualization as a *Volksgemeinschaft* of which the Jews were its major victims.[60]

The Nakba appears to be a further such example. It too was the outcome of national and colonial confrontation in which the victorious Jewish side's aspiration to ethnic homogeneity within its state was among the factors that created the large number of Palestinian refugees. From the mid-1930s onward, during the course of its struggle against the Palestinians, Zionism (or at least its mainstream variants) largely adopted the Eastern-Central European model of ethnocentric nationalism, which is constantly engaged in defining the ethnic identity of the nation-state and its projects of ethnic exclusivity and homogenization.[61] At the same time, the majority of Palestinian Arabs refused to recognize the legitimacy of the new Jewish settlement and the growing Jewish nationalism in Palestine, and therefore they rejected the 1947 partition plan, opposed Jewish nationalism and settlement in Palestine, and related to them as a colonialist outpost of Western imperialism. In these contexts, the non-Jewish other—namely, the Palestinians—became an alarming threat to the very legitimacy of Jewish sovereignty, on the one hand, and a threatening ethnic presence, on the other. The logic of modern cleansing, particularly during wartime, almost inevitably led them to the outcome of the Nakba.

Thus, even if the Holocaust and the Nakba are incomparable events of different magnitude, in other senses they structurally and albeit partially share the same type of dangerous political rationale, together with many other historical phenomena. We underscore the "partially" since neither the Holocaust nor the Nakba, nor the other events to which we have alluded, can be entirely reduced to this political logic alone. Yet this historical and political context, however unsatisfactory, is certainly important and essential to understanding these events. The refugee is therefore a major political and cultural figure who, despite all the difference, links the Jewish Holocaust to the Palestinian Nakba and stands as a figure of radical critique of the exclusionary ethnic model of the nation-state.

More specifically, the Palestinian and Jewish refugees of the Nakba and Holocaust not only serve as disruptive and alarming reminders against the exclusionary forces of identity politics in Israel/Palestine but also as a challenge to the statist mainstream Palestinian and Israeli politics that view exclusive and separate ethnic nation-states as the ultimate and desired institutional frame within which the political rights of the respective peoples are realized and protected. Consequently, one could view the refugee as a herald of alternative and creative forms of politics, ones that are premised on partnership, cooperation, joint dwelling, and integration rather than on segregation, balkanization, separation, and ghettoization. In what follows, we suggest that these are the disruptive and productive potentials of LaCapra's empathic unsettlement that give further, however partial and initial, meaning, shape, and content to the alternative and integrationist forms of politics heralded by the refugee.

How, then, does LaCapra's empathic unsettlement confront these problems of refugeeism, otherness, collective trauma, and an egalitarian public deliberation that could bear the mark of a shared "we"? As we have seen, empathic unsettlement transforms otherness from a problem to be disposed of into a moral and emotional challenge. It requires a type of paradoxical action—namely, to empathize precisely with that alienating, traumatic, and hard-to-digest element of radical otherness. Empathic unsettlement enables this traumatic otherness, which breaks out of the political, social, and discursive structures, to render, in a controlled manner and through a paradoxical identification, the preordained narratives more flexible and to enhance receptiveness to new structural possibilities that seek to reduce the very likelihood that these traumas will be generated. Moreover, according to LaCapra, in response to this disruptive and excessive otherness that transcends discursive political structures and the existing array of images, empathic unsettlement seeks to avoid two extreme situations. Each of these is a temptation that lurks amid the encounter of the individual or collective subject with the unsettling otherness of trauma.

One such possible extreme reaction is the validation and extreme entrenchment of unbridgeable dichotomies. This exceptional rigidity and lack of flexibility is a prevalent response to trauma. It is demonstrated in the Jewish-Palestinian case by the present mainstream political system with regard to Jewish-Palestinian relations: exacerbation of the dichotomy between Israeli and Jew and between Palestinian and Arab as two national identities that establish themselves above all through the rejection of the other identity. As such, they maintain themselves as political and cultural identities that are unable to generate even the most partial common sphere and sense of "we." Moreover, according to LaCapra, such dichotomies are extremely dangerous as he notes in regard to the Holocaust: "I think the binary opposition is very closely related to the scapegoat mechanism and that part of the process of scapegoating is trying to generate pure binary oppositions between (self-identical) self and (totally different) other, so that the other (let's say in the context of the Holocaust, the Jew) becomes totally different from the Nazi, and everything that causes anxiety in the Nazi is projected onto the other, so you have a pure divide: Aryan/Jew—absolutely nothing in common."[62]

On the other hand, empathic unsettlement seeks to avoid the posttraumatic collapse of all distinctions into a single indistinct jumble. Therefore, we believe that the translation of empathic unsettlement into political concepts produces thinking along binational lines as a moral and political principle (which is not necessarily manifested in a binational state). It does not reject the existence of two separate communitarian collectives, however internally diverse, but refuses to accept that the removal and exclusion of the one by the other provides the only solution to the traumatic experience of each of the collectives and to the encounter with trauma of the other collective. On the contrary, working through the traumas demands that the national dichotomies are made more flexible without dismantling them altogether. Indeed, Khoury himself adopts a position along these lines in an interview he gave to the Israeli cultural critic Yaron Mor: "I hope that a binational state will exist in Palestine-Israel," and he even further expands this idea to multinationalism which would encompass the whole region.[63]

In conclusion, let us be more concrete on our proposed binationalism and briefly utilize its meaning in relation to other notions of binationalism, most notably Judith Butler's. Following Edward Said, Judith Butler argues that the constitutively diasporic Jewish and Palestinian identities and histories considerably contribute to giving rise to binationalism in Israel/Palestine. Butler further argues that the increased political, economic, and demographic entanglements and entwinements in Palestine/Israel have created a de facto binationalism, a "wretched form of binationalism"[64] premised on oppression, discrimination, colonial expansion and occupation, and hatred and mistrust. Her ethical and relational notion of binationalism is grounded on different principles—namely, democratic values of equality, justice and cohabitation. She argues that it is through the conditions of dispersion (geographic and ethical) and cohabitation that we can think about such democratic values. Dispersion (conditions of heterogeneity and plurality) involves a relation to alterity. This relationality, she insists, destabilizes and interrupts ontological claims and goes beyond identity and nation as constitutive frameworks.[65]

While the binationalism that stems from our reading of empathic unsettlement has few similarities with Butler's account of binationalism (including largely agreeing with the diagnosis of the realities on the ground in Israel/Palestine), it nevertheless remains considerably different. Unlike Said, Butler, and other scholars who equate binationalism with a binational state as the ultimate institutional governing frame, our proposed binationalism can be achieved within the frame of several institutional arrangements. Put differently, various forms of governing polities such as federation, confederation, parallel state structure, condominium, binational state, and/or an expansively cooperative, overlapping, and interlinked two-state solution can realize and respect the egalitarian individual and collective national rights of Arabs and Jews in Palestine/Israel. Moreover, Butler's binationalism seems to run the risk of collapsing into a radical individualistic liberalism. For when she argues that her notion of binationalism leads to a "postnational polity" that "would eradicate all forms of discrimination on the basis of ethnicity, race, and religion,"[66] this postnational state seems closer to classical liberalism of benign neglect/difference blind or excessive individualism and destabilizing differentiation and pluralization than to agonistic relational binationalism. Our proposed binationalism, denoted by "empathic unsettlement," allows for more ontological stability than Butler's excessive individualistic hybridity and radical alterity. Otherwise stated, our binationalism endorses a thin form of communitarianism that acknowledges the role ethnicity and nationalism play in Israel/Palestine. More precisely, our account recognizes the right to national self-determination of both national groups while insisting that this right ought not be realized in the form of an exclusive ethnic state.

Our emphasis on some degree of ontological stability resonates with LaCapra's claim that "deconstruction does not blur or undermine all distinctions; it leaves you with a problem of distinctions that are, if anything, more difficult and more necessary to elaborate, given the fact that you cannot rely on simple binaries. . . . It is *not* a pure binary opposition but rather involves a notion of difference, but a difference that's not a pure or total difference."[67] LaCapra's ethics, like our notion of binationalism, seeks a middle ground between complete separation, on the one hand, and blurring all (ethnic and communal) distinctions, on the other. As LaCapra notes: "Deconstructing a binary opposition does not automatically cause it to go away or to lose its often constraining role in social and political reality."[68] This is particularly valid in intractable conflicts such as the case of the Jews and the Palestinians in Palestine/Israel. Similarly, our attempt in this chapter has been to suggest a way to jointly think and deliberate on the two traumatic memories of the Holocaust and the Nakba without conflating them but also without completely separating them as if they had nothing to do with each other. A joint discussion on the Holocaust and the Nakba informed by the requirements and effects of empathic unsettlement does not only require expansive public deliberation that nourishes civic virtues of tolerance, reciprocity, mutual legitimacy and active engagement in public affairs; it also gives rise to an adversarial democratic politics that necessitates achieving compromises, forming alliances likely to cut across ethnic and national lines, and paving the way for creative thinking and challenging existing paradigms. Finally, it is precisely in the context of the policing dominance and hegemony of paradigmatic and foreclosed narratives and epistemologies that we view this joint chapter as a modest contribution to identifying possible venues for alternative thinking and democratic joint dwelling.

Notes

This chapter was first published as an article with the same title in *Journal of Genocide Research* 16, no. 1 (2014): 77–99. For comments on earlier versions, our thanks go to the journal editors Rachel Busbridge, Alon Confino, Azar Dakwar, Avner de-Shalit, Yasmine Haj, Ammon Raz-Krakotzkin, Adel Manna, Sidra Ezrahi, and four anonymous referees. We also thank the Van Leer Jerusalem Institute for hosting the project from which this chapter emerged.

1. *Nakba* is an Arabic word that means "catastrophe," and it has been used to refer to the dispossession, expulsion, and national ruin of Palestinians before and after 1948.
2. For a related and careful historical analysis, see, for example, Yehuda Bauer, *Rethinking the Holocaust* (New Haven, CT: Yale University Press, 2001), 241–60; Arieh J. Kochavi, *Post-Holocaust Politics: Britain, the United States, and Jewish Refugees, 1945–1948* (Chapel Hill: University of North Carolina Press, 2001); Gilbert Achcar, *The Arabs and the Holocaust* (New York: Metropolitan Books, 2010); and Yair Auron, *The Holocaust, the Rebirth, and the Nakba: Memory and Contemporary Israeli-Arab Relations* (Lanham, MD: Lexington, 2017).
3. Robert Eaglestone, *The Holocaust and the Postmodern* (Oxford: Oxford University Press, 2004), 3.
4. Alon Confino, *Foundational Pasts: The Holocaust as Historical Understanding* (New York: Cambridge University Press, 2012).
5. There have been several attempts to write a joint (or parallel) Palestinian/Israeli narrative. See, for example, Adel Manna and Motti Golani, *Two Sides of the Coin: Independence and Nakba 1948; Two Narratives of the 1948 War and Its Outcome* (Dordrecht, Netherlands: Republic of Letters, 2011). Nevertheless, our aim in this chapter is different. We aspire to identify the enabling conditions and the guiding principles of such a joint discussion.
6. Achcar, *The Arabs and the Holocaust*, 18.
7. For a relevant critique of the Habermasian notion of public deliberation, see Bashir Bashir, "Reconciling Historical Injustices: Deliberative Democracy and

the Politics of Reconciliation," *Res Publica* 18, no. 2 (2012): 127–43; and Lynn Sanders, "Against Deliberation," *Political Theory* 25, no. 3 (1997): 347–76.

8. See also Michael Rothberg, *Multidirectional Memory: Remembering the Holocaust in the Age of Colonization* (Stanford, CA: Stanford University Press, 2009), 199–226. Some of the ideas presented here owe him much.

9. See, for example, the debate in Saree Makdisi, "The Architecture of Erasure," *Critical Inquiry* 36, no. 3 (2010): 618.

10. See, for example, in a very different context, the debate over Timothy Snyder's argument for reframing the Holocaust within Eastern Europe's catastrophic history in the 1930s and 1940s in *Bloodlands: Europe between Hitler and Stalin* (New York: Basic Books, 2010). For the debate, see "Review Forum: Timothy Snyder, *Bloodlands: Europe between Hitler and Stalin*," *Journal of Genocide Research* 13, no. 3 (2011): 313–52.

11. See, for example, Steven Katz, *Historicism, the Holocaust, and Zionism: Critical Studies in Modern Jewish Thought and History* (New York: New York University Press, 1992), 162–92; and Bauer, *Rethinking the Holocaust*; Saul Friedländer, *Memory, History, and the Extermination of the Jews of Europe* (Bloomington: Indiana University Press, 1993), 113.

12. Daniel Levy and Natan Sznaider, *The Holocaust and Memory in the Global Age* (Philadelphia: Temple University Press, 2006); Jeffrey C. Alexander, "On the Social Construction of Moral Universalism: The 'Holocaust' from Mass Murder to Trauma Drama," *European Journal of Social Theory* 5, no. 1 (2002): 5–86; and Tony Judt, *Postwar: A History of Europe since 1945* (New York: Penguin, 2005).

13. See, for example, Avishai Margalit, *The Ethics of Memory* (Cambridge, MA: Harvard University Press, 2002); John Torpey, *Making Whole What Has Been Smashed: On Reparation Politics* (Cambridge, MA: Harvard University Press, 2006); and Elazar Barkan, *The Guilt of Nations: Restitution and Negotiating Historical Injustices* (New York: Norton, 2000). It is precisely this exceptionalism positioning the Holocaust as a benchmark for "global memory" that blocks the memory of the Nakba, according to Karin Fierke, "Who Is My Neighbor? Memories of the Holocaust/al Nakba and a Global Ethic of Care," *European Journal of International Relations* 20, no. 3 (2014): 787–809, doi.org/10.1177/1354066113497490.

14. During the mid- and late 1980s, *Historikerstreit* in Germany was on the issue of comparison and banalization of the Holocaust. See, for example, Richard J. Evans, *In Hitler's Shadow: West German Historians and the Attempt to Escape from the Nazi Past* (New York: Pantheon Books, 1989); Martin Broszat and Saul

Friedländer, "A Controversy about the Historicization of National Socialism," *Yad Vashem Studies* 19 (1988): 1–47.

15. Yehuda Bauer, *The Jewish Emergence from Powerlessness* (Toronto: Toronto University Press, 1979).

16. See Marianne Hirsch, *The Generation of Postmemory: Writing and Visual Culture after the Holocaust* (New York: Columbia University Press, 2012).

17. The question of when and in what sense a traumatic event ends is a very complicated and contentious, yet conceptually underexplored, topic, and it is beyond the scope of this chapter to navigate through this complex issue in relation to genocides. For related literature on the them, see Jens Meierhenrich, "How Genocides End: An Analytical Framework" (unpublished paper, Harvard University, Cambridge, MA, May 5, 2008); and Francois Furet, *Interpreting the French Revolution* (Cambridge: Cambridge University Press, 1981), 1–79; and Yehuda Elkana, "The Need to Forget," *Haaretz*, May 2, 1988, ceuweekly.blogspot.com/2014/08/in-memoriam-need-to-forget-by-yehuda.html.

18. On the centrality of the Nakba in Palestinian identity and nationalism, see Rashid Khalidi, *Palestinian Identity: The Construction of Modern National Consciousness* (New York: Columbia University Press, 1997), 177–210; Yezid Sayigh, *Armed Struggle and the Search for State* (Oxford: Oxford University Press, 1999), 25–57; Baruch Kimmerling and Joel S. Migdal, *The Palestinian People: A History* (Cambridge, MA: Harvard University Press, 2003), 214–39; Nur Masalha, "60 years after the Nakba: Historical Truth, Collective Memory and Ethical Obligations," *Kyoto Bulletin of Islamic Area Studies* 3, no. 1 (2009): 37–88; Ahmad H. Sa'di and Lila Abu-Lughod, eds., *Nakba: Palestine, 1948, and the Claims of Memory* (New York: Columbia University Press, 2007); and Mustafa Kabha, ed., *Towards a Historical Narrative of the Nakba: Complexities and Challenges* (Haifa, Israel: Mada—Arab Center for Applied Social Research, 2006).

19. The issue of the Mufti Haj Amin al-Husseini's links to the Nazis inevitably arises in this context. Yet this matter may be regarded as a moral stain and a political error deserving of strong condemnation. See Azmi Bishara, "The Arabs and the Holocaust: An Analysis of the Problematical Nexus," *Zmanim* 13, no. 53 (1995): 54–71 (in Hebrew). It had, however, no effect on Nazi policy toward the Jews or on the murderous implementation of this policy. This may be an important symbolic issue but has no historical importance with regard to the Final Solution. Nevertheless, as Peter Novick has noted, the Mufti was accorded an entry in the *Encyclopedia of the Holocaust* twice as long as those of Goebbels and Goering. See Peter Novick, *The Holocaust in American Life* (Boston: Houghton Mifflin, 1999),

158. A number of works have been written on the attitude of the Arab world and the Palestinian National Movement toward the Holocaust, which reach virtually opposite conclusions. See, for example, Achcar, *The Arabs and the Holocaust*; Meir Litvak and Esther Webman, *From Empathy to Denial: Arab Responses to the Holocaust* (New York: Columbia University Press, 2009); and Jeffrey Herf, *Nazi Propaganda for the Arab World* (New Haven, CT: Yale University Press, 2009).

20. The Nakba has been analyzed as ethnic cleansing by Ilan Pappé, *The Ethnic Cleansing of Palestine* (Oxford: Oneworld Publications, 2006); and Nur Masalha, *Expulsion of the Palestinians* (Washington, DC: Institute for Palestine Studies, 1992). This analysis in turn has drawn sharp criticism, as, for example, by Seth J. Frantzman, who rejects the assertion of ethnic cleansing as well as the academic value of Pappé's book. See his review, "Flunking History: Ilan Pappé's *The Ethnic Cleansing of Palestine*," *Middle East Quarterly* 15, no. 2 (2008): 70–75. Recently, some scholars have attempted to understand the events of 1948 within a global perspective and comparative modern history of ethnic cleansing and forced migration while staying away from polemics and accusations. Richard Bessel and Claudia Haake view 1948 within a history of forced removal in the modern world, arguing that the concept of forced removal "can perform descriptive and explanatory work of a kind that the frameworks offered by 'genocide' or 'ethnic cleansing' seldom attempt or cannot undertake." Bessel and Haake, "Introduction: Forced Removal in the Modern World," in *Removing Peoples: Forced Removal in the Modern World*, ed. Richard Bessel and Claudia Haake (Oxford: Oxford University Press, 2009), 5. Alon Confino placed 1948 within a global history of modern forced migration, arguing for the benefits of this concept over ethnic cleansing both on grounds of method and of public debate because ethnic cleansing is now associated with a tribunal and prosecutorial atmosphere, which blocks discussion and leads to reflexive denials. Confino, "Miracles and Snow in Palestine and Israel: Tantura, a History of 1948," *Israel Studies* 17, no. 2 (2012): 25–61.

21. The disgorgement of Arab Jews after 1948, although the Palestinians were not involved in it and later even denounced it, is often held up as a sort of equal population exchange with the Palestinian refugees. See Irwin Cotler, David Matas, and Stanley A. Urman, "Jewish Refugees from Arab Countries: The Case for Rights and Redress," November 5, 2007, www.justiceforjews.com/jjac.pdf. On Palestinian opposition to this disgorgement, see Nabil Shaath, "The Democratic Solution to the Palestine Issue," *Journal of Palestine Studies* 6, no. 2 (1997): 15.

22. See, for example, Zeev W. Mankowitz, *Life between Memory and Hope: The Survivors of the Holocaust in Occupied Germany* (Cambridge: Cambridge University

Press, 2002); and Hagit Lavsky, *New Beginnings: Holocaust Survivors in Bergen-Belsen and the British Zone in Germany, 1945–1950* (Detroit: Wayne State University Press, 2002). For a different view, see Idith Zertal, *From Catastrophe to Power: Holocaust Survivors and the Emergence of Israel* (Berkeley: University of California Press, 1998).

23. See, for example, article 22 of the Palestine National Charter of 1968, avalon.law.yale.edu/20th_century/plocov.asp, accessed September 27, 2018; and Edward Said, *The Question of Palestine* (New York: Times Books, 1979).

24. Report of a radio address by Mahmoud Darwish on the fiftieth anniversary of the Nakba, which appeared on the Festival Internacional de Poesía de Medellin website, www.festivaldepoesiademedellin.org/pub.php/en/Diario/03.html?print, accessed October 19, 2012, but is no longer available at the time of this book's printing; and Edward Said, "Israel-Palestine: A Third Way," *Le Monde Diplomatique* (Paris), September 1998.

25. Idith Zertal, *Israel's Holocaust and the Politics of Nationhood* (Cambridge: Cambridge University Press, 2005); and Moshe Zuckermann, *Zweierlei Holocaust: der Holocaust in den politischen Kulturen Israels und Deutschlands* (Göttingen: Wallstein, 1988).

26. The epic novel *Bab al-Shams* by Elias Khoury was originally published in Arabic in 1998, fifty years after the Nakba. It soon became acknowledged as one of the masterpieces in Palestinian and Arab literature. See, for example, Adina Hoffman, "'Recollecting the Palestinian Past," *Raritan* 26, no. 2 (2006): 52–61.

27. Elias Khoury, *Gate of the Sun* (*Bab al-Shams*), trans. Humphrey Davies (New York: Archipelago Books, 2006), 295–96.

28. See Achcar, *The Arabs and the Holocaust*. In March 2001, Khoury, along with thirteen other Arab intellectuals (including Mahmoud Darwish, Samir Kassir, and Adonis), signed a statement opposing the holding of a Holocaust denial conference in Beirut.

29. Khoury, *Gate of the Sun*, 296.

30. Emmanuel Levinas, "Peace and Proximity," in *Emmanuel Levinas: Basic Philosophical Writings*, ed. Adriaan T. Peperzak, Simon Critchley, and Robert Bernasconi (Bloomington: Indiana University Press, 1996), 161–70.

31. Emmanuel Levinas, "Ethics and Politics," in *Levinas Reader*, ed. Sean Hand (Oxford: Blackwell, 1989), 289.

32. Hannan Hever, "The Post-Zionist Condition," *Critical Inquiry* 38, no. 3 (2012): 630–48.

33. Dominick LaCapra, *Writing History, Writing Trauma* (Baltimore: Johns Hopkins University Press, 2001).

34. LaCapra, *Writing History, Writing Trauma*, 141.
35. LaCapra, *Writing History, Writing Trauma*, 212.
36. Zygmunt Bauman, *Postmodernity and Its Discontents* (New York: New York University Press, 1997), 5–16.
37. Sigmund Freud, "Totem and Taboo and Other Essays," in *The Standard Edition of the Complete Psychological Works of Sigmund Freud*, ed. and trans. James Strachey (London: Hogarth Press, 1955), 13; Jacques Lacan, "The Mirror Stage as Formative of the Function of the I as Revealed in Psychoanalytic Experience," in *Écrits: A Selection*, trans. Alan Sheridan (New York: Norton, 1977), 1–7.
38. This theme returns again as a dominant one toward the end of the novel. Khoury, *Gate of the Sun*, 397 passim.
39. See, for example, LaCapra, *Writing History, Writing Trauma*, 90–94.
40. LaCapra, *Writing History, Writing Trauma*, 41.
41. As Saul Friedländer sums up the ethics of the French philosopher Lyotard, "The striving for totality and consensus is, in Lyotard's view, the very basis of the fascist enterprise." Friedländer, "Introduction," in *Probing the Limits of Representation*, ed. Saul Friedländer (Cambridge, MA: Harvard University Press, 1992), 5.
42. See Amos Goldberg, "The Victim's Voice in History and Melodramatic Aesthetics," *History and Theory* 48 (2009): 220–37.
43. Vamik D. Volkan, "Transgenerational Transmissions and Chosen Traumas: An Aspect of Large-Group Identity," *Group Analysis* 34, no. 1 (2001): 95.
44. Khoury, *Gate of the Sun*, 275.
45. Avot Yeshurun, *Hashever Hasuri Afrikani* (Tel Aviv: Siman Kri'a, 1974), 130 (in Hebrew). For more on this, see Hannan Hever, "'The Two Gaze Directly into One Another's Face': Avot Yeshurun between the Nakba and the Shoah—An Israeli Perspective," *Jewish Social Studies* 18, no. 3 (2012): 153–63.
46. Peter Marks, "'Return to Haifa' Crosses Borders of War," January 22, 2011, www.washingtonpost.com/wp-dyn/content/article/2011/01/21/AR2011012107180.html.
47. On the extensive debates that the play generated, see David Goldenberg, "'Return to Haifa': Controversy at the Cameri," January 4, 2011, vimeo.com/18436295.
48. Zochrot, zochrot.org/en, accessed November 24, 2013.
49. See Louise Bethlehem, "Apartheid: A Double-Crossing," Zochrot, February 2011, zochrot.org/en/content/apartheid-double-crossing.
50. Roi Mandel, "Ni'lin Holds Holocaust Exhibit," Ynetnews.com, January 27, 2009, www.ynetnews.com/articles/0,7340,L-3662822,00.html.
51. See, for example, the skit by the Israeli performance artist and poet Natalie Cohen Waxberg, "How Would You Manage without the Holocaust?," www.youtube

.com/watch?v=gPLGczT6Hjw, accessed December 2, 2013. Educational deliberations that largely follow our proposed empathically unsettling direction took place at the Van Leer Jerusalem Institute and are regular activities of the Center for Humanistic Education at the Ghetto Fighters' House Museum, www.gfh.org.il/eng/?CategoryID=86, accessed December 2, 2013. It also stands at the basis of the joint Jewish/Palestinian village of Neve Shalon/Wahat al-Salam (Oasis of Peace). wasns.org, accessed December 2, 2013.

52. Edward Said, *Freud and the Non-European* (London: Verso, 2003), 53.
53. Surely Said is not the only Palestinian intellectual who emphasizes the diasporic identity of the Palestinians following the Nakba of 1948. Mahmoud Darwish's poetry extensively refers to the centrality of exile in the formation of Palestinian identity. However, unlike Said, Darwish didn't propose an alternative to the two-state solution or explicitly favor binationalism. For more on Darwish's focus on exile, see Hala Khamis Nassar and Najat Rahman, eds., *Mahmoud Darwish, Exile Poet: Critical Essays* (Northampton, MA: Olive Branch Press, 2008).
54. Said, *Question of Palestine*, 119.
55. Hannah Arendt, *The Jew as Pariah: Jewish Identity and Politics in the Modern Age* (New York: Grove Press, 1978), 59–66; and Giorgio Agamben, "We Refugees," *Symposium* 49, no. 2 (1995): 114–19.
56. Keith David Watenpaugh, "'The League of Nations' Rescue of Armenian Genocide Survivors and the Making of Modern Humanitarianism, 1920–1927," *American Historical Review* 115, no. 5 (2010): 1315–39.
57. Some scholars have challenged the usefulness and guidance of Arendt's intellectual contributions on modern nation-state, violence, statelessness, and refugees to our contemporary times. See, for example, A. Dirk Moses, "'Das römische Gespräch in a New Key: Hannah Arendt, Genocide, and the Defense of Imperial Civilization," *Journal of Modern History* 85, no. 4 (2013): 867–913.
58. Hannah Arendt, *The Origins of Totalitarianism* (New York: Harcourt Brace Jovanovich, 1973), 290. See also Zygmunt Bauman, "The Dream of Purity," in *Postmodernity and Its Discontents* (New York: Blackwell, 1997), 12.
59. Yet it was not only the Jews who suffered from the desire for homogeneity on the part of the nation-state (or ethnically dominated empires). Many European minorities, including Greeks, Armenians, Ukrainians, Belarussians, and Germans, likewise suffered from this inclination, which led to a prolonged series of discrimination, exclusion, expulsion, ethnic cleansing, mass killings, genocide, and even to the Holocaust itself. On the link between genocide and ethnic cleansing and the nation-state, see Eric D. Weitz, *A Century of Genocide: Utopias of*

Race and Nation (Princeton: Princeton University Press, 2005); Donald Bloxham, *The Final Solution: A Genocide* (Oxford: Oxford University Press, 2009); Michael Mann, *The Dark Side of Democracy: Explaining Ethnic Cleansing* (Cambridge: Cambridge University Press, 2005); Mark Levene, *Genocide in the Age of the Nation-State*, vol. 2, *The Rise of the West and Coming Genocide* (London: I. B. Tauris, 2005); and Benjamin Lieberman, "'Ethnic Cleansing" versus Genocide?," in *The Oxford Handbook of Genocide Studies*, ed. Donald Bloxham and H. Dirk Moses (Oxford: Oxford University Press, 2010), 42–60.

60. Michael Wildt, *Hitler's Volksgemeinschaft and the Dynamics of Racial Exclusion* (New York: Berghahn Books, 2011); Peter Longerich, *The Wannsee Conference in the Development of the "Final Solution,"* trans. Ian Gronbach and Donald Bloxham, Holocaust Education Trust Research Papers, vol. 1, no. 2 (London: Holocaust Educational Trust, 1999–2000); LaCapra, *Writing History, Writing Trauma*, 165; and Zygmunt Bauman, *Modernity and the Holocaust* (Cambridge: Polity Press, 1989).

61. Dimitry Shumsky, "Brith Shalom's Uniqueness Reconsidered: Hans Kohn and Autonomist Zionism," *Jewish History* 25, nos. 3–4 (2011): 339–53. For an illuminating comparison between the situation of the Jews in interwar Poland and the Palestinians in Israel, see Yoav Peled, "The Viability of Ethnic Democracy: Jewish Citizens in Inter-war Poland and Palestinian Citizens in Israel," *Ethnic and Racial Studies* 34, no. 1 (2011): 83–102.

62. LaCapra, *Writing History, Writing Trauma*, 149.

63. haemori.wordpress.com/tag/%D7%91%D7%90%D7%91-%D7%90%D7%9C-%D7%A9%D7%9E%D7%A1/ (in Hebrew). For more on the cultural and historical roots of this regional approach, which capitalizes on the cultural diversity of the Levantine, see, for example, Ammiel Alcalay, *After Jews and Arabs: Remaking Levantine Culture* (Minneapolis: Minnesota University Press, 1993).

64. Butler, *Parting Ways: Jewishness and the Critique of Zionism* (New York: Columbia University Press, 2012), 210.

65. Butler, *Parting Ways*, 5–6.

66. Butler, *Parting Ways*, 16 and 208.

67. LaCapra, *Writing History, Writing Trauma*, 150

68. LaCapra, *Writing History, Writing Trauma*, 150.

13

Shifting Responses to Antisemitism and Racism

Temporary Exhibitions at the Jewish Holocaust Centre

Steven Cooke and Donna-Lee Frieze

THIS CHAPTER BRINGS TOGETHER two underresearched areas—temporary exhibitions and community Holocaust museums—by examining the Jewish Holocaust Centre (JHC) in Melbourne, Australia. The JHC opened in March 1984, the result of the work of a small number of Holocaust survivors and the coming together of two Jewish organizations: the Federation of Polish Jews and the Kadimah (a Yiddishist cultural group). Funding for the project was primarily provided by Melbournian Jew Mina Fink (who was not a survivor of the Holocaust), and the original building that housed the exhibition spaces, meeting room, library, and archives was named Leo Fink House in memory of her late husband.[1] The location of the new museum in Elsternwick, an inner eastern suburb of Melbourne, was also important. Located adjacent to the Kadimah, and close to the Sholem Aleichem Jewish day school, the museum is in the center of a vibrant Jewish area.

The JHC had rudimentary origins and began as a "grave" for the survivors to mourn loved ones murdered during the Holocaust. Mina Fink was an early advocate of educating the public and especially school children on the values of tolerance and warnings of antisemitism. While teaching lessons about antisemitism did not change, the concept of "tolerance," as discussed below, shifted dramatically. Over the next thirty years, the JHC grew in both scope and size, although these dual narratives of Holocaust-specific issues (such as antisemitism) and broader social concerns (such as tolerance, which later developed into the broader notion of racism) have remained a prominent theme within the educational remit at the JHC. As well as this symbolic grave, commentary at the opening argued that the JHC would combat antisemitism and create understanding between Jews and non-Jews and eliminate racial prejudice.[2] The JHC would also serve as a place of documentation: an archive and also a personal chronicle of the survivors involved, providing a symbolic link with the Warsaw ghetto Oyneg Shabes archive of Emanuel Ringelblum, where prisoners of the ghetto would gather on the afternoon of the Sabbath to discuss material pertaining to their plight.[3] This combined mission of education, evidence gathering, and a record of personal testimony has been the JHC's mission from its inception, although these interests would, at times, vie for greater importance.

Professional state-run Holocaust museums, with their purpose-built architecture reflecting their function as memorial and pedagogic spaces, have a monumentality that contrasts with the JHC, which is housed in a former dispensary building. This neighbored locality allowed the survivors to feel "at home": the JHC was a permanent refuge where they could share their stories, remember the dead, and feel connected to a unique survivor community.[4] Despite the idea of the JHC as a refuge and a safe place for survivors, expansion was inevitable if the message of tolerance and, later, anti-racism was to reach as many schoolchildren as possible. Increased professionalism on the part of volunteers and calls for paid staff in the years after opening led to major changes in personnel and structure in the early 2000s. From the beginning, there was anxiety about the inevitable: that the survivor generation that built the JHC and sustained it would pass. At the same time, the mission of the organization required the JHC to grow into a relevant community organization that would be a broader community resource for promoting anti-racist behavior. In order to grow philosophically, the JHC had to expand materially and proposals were made for redevelopment. The broadening message was reflected in the iconography of the new architecture: from an ordinary house on an ordinary suburban street[5] to a space immediately identifiable as a Holocaust museum through sculptures by Andrew Rogers, which framed the new entrance.

Considering the tension between desiring a refuge and memorial for the survivors and seeking a center for combating racism, a focus on temporary exhibitions in community Holocaust museums is long overdue, as these types of exhibitions can satisfy the topics and interests overlooked or minimized in the main exhibition. Temporary exhibitions in Holocaust museums may allow the curators to be released from formulaic Holocaust images and both focus on issues or topics that are specific to the Holocaust community attached to the museum and engage in broader debates about other genocides. While we have argued elsewhere the permanent exhibition responded to local geographies and the narratives of the survivors provided specificity to orthodox narratives,[6] our argument in this chapter is that the temporary exhibitions at the JHC are a key indicator of the institution's changing focus since its inception from a community museum to a professional museum. Andrew Markus, writing in 2004, argued: "The Museum today, since the extension and the opening-up of the exhibit space, is very different. To my mind commemoration has receded and its educative role is now pre-eminent."[7] This has resulted in changing concerns: from finding a place of comfort and as recognition as survivors, to being more assertive about the civic role of the JHC and the contemporary relevance of the Holocaust. It has also marked a shift, as we argue below, from an emphasis on antisemitism to a broader notion of racism. Temporary exhibitions at the JHC illustrate this refocusing from antisemitism (self-identity) to anti-racism (the civic role of the museum); a journey from the survivors as embodying victimhood to survivors as powerful civic agents, and from an internal focus to an external one. This change has happened within a number of contexts, including debates over the representations of the Holocaust, the civic role of the museum, and the passing of the survivor generation, as well as changing Australian government policy regarding multiculturalism and the treatment of asylum seekers. While providing a space for a more explicit and assertive stance on racism in contemporary Australian society, mostly absent is an engagement with what W. E. H. Stanner called "the Great Australian silence"[8]: Australian settler colonial genocide. From celebratory exhibitions detailing the positive impact that survivors have had on the Australian community, through a more assertive stance of critiquing contemporary Australian government policy toward refugees and challenging the visitor to use the resources of the past to act in the present, this chapter will examine five temporary exhibitions at the JHC, held between 1985 and 2012, that illustrate this change.

THE CIVIC ROLE OF TEMPORARY EXHIBITIONS

Museums have long been associated with a civic role within society, from forming part of the disciplinary apparatus for the creation and regulation of citizens, to the museum as forum: as an affective space with the potential for humanization of the "other."[9] The selection and arrangement of objects in a museum and the narratives of people, place, and events through which they are understood and given meaning are a tangible location in which to recover the motivations of those involved in their production. Reflecting the worldview of those involved with their conception, design, and installation, they can also serve as a focal point for sometimes-heated debate, where the ideological construction of history is made material and therefore open to contestation.[10] Often these museums embody a connection among their mission statements, philosophy, and broader societal values, and they use temporary exhibitions to creatively connect these ideals.

Temporary exhibitions within permanent museums are a comparatively recent development. Grace McCann Morely, writing in 1951, argued that the view of temporary exhibitions was changing: having once been seen as a distraction from permanent exhibitions, they were increasingly seen as part of the public orientation of the museum, including providing impetus for repeat visits.[11] Another motivation for temporary exhibitions was their social role. For example, during World War II, temporary exhibitions in the United Kingdom, were part of "a valiant struggle to maintain exhibition services to the public when valuable permanent collections had to be put into safer shelters and galleries were left empty."[12] These temporary exhibitions were generally held outside the museum, with the social role having a political aspect in the need to maintain public morale during the time of war. However, since the New Museology from the late 1980s onward, political uses for exhibitions, particularly temporary exhibitions, have become more evident, in particular for institutions that seek to promote values of human rights.[13] As

Richard Sandell argues, temporary exhibitions may be more likely to "provoke debate and public reaction, both positive and negative" owing to their profile and content but, conversely, precisely because to their impermanence, "may be perceived as less authoritative, more open to scrutiny and question than more permanent displays."[14] Tony Bennett draws the distinction between the "solidity and permanence" of museum displays and the flexibility of world fairs and exhibitions, which could more easily "respond to shorter-term ideological requirements."[15] This distinction is directly applicable to the case of temporary exhibitions that are held within museums. Rather than the longer life span of permanent exhibitions, which, because of their resource implications need to be shown for more prolonged periods, temporary exhibitions, because of their comparatively low costs, can be held more often and change depending on the shorter-term needs of the organization, external events, or visitor interest.[16]

Temporary exhibitions in community museums (as opposed to professional museums run by qualified practitioners) reveal the complex set of relationships within groups as well as the relationship between the group and wider society. Community museums are often administered by people with a vested interest in the subject of concern in the museum, whether this applies to local community concerns or issues of genocide. In the latter's instance, the journey from the individual victim of racism to a civic agent, can empower those that operate the museum with tools to help create an ethical community beyond the museum. Elizabeth Crooke argues that there is a "symbiotic relationship" between museums and communities[17] and that there is a particular relationship to professionally run museums: "Rather than being guided, monitored and even restricted by professional museum standards, expectations and the glare of peers, it is more likely that this form of governance will come from within the community itself. Therefore, community initiatives will develop reflecting the community, as defined by its leaders, incorporating its strengths, as well and weaknesses."[18] As Moira G. Simpson states, "In the past, community-based museums established by immigrant communities have had a tendency to be nostalgic memorials to the past"[19] whereby Chen Yunqian states that "the establishment of a museum can provide a means of recalling what has been lost, and exempting to preserve traditional skills and knowledge. Such activities can be important for immigrants as they seek to retain a sense of cultural identity and community in a new environment, and to share and take pride in those things which they feel makes their culture unique."[20] Immigrant community museums have traditionally been formed through a nostalgia for a time and a place often far removed from the present and with a focus on movable and intangible cultural heritage, through which to tell stories about the home country. However, Yunqian also argues, some exhibitions work as commemorative spaces for mobilizing support for new political formations, particularly around anniversaries.[21]

Exhibitions at the JHC

While academic analysis has focused primarily on state-run Holocaust museums and exhibitions such as Yad Vashem and in particular the United States Holocaust Memorial Museum in Washington DC, smaller community Holocaust exhibitions have received less attention.[22] Understandably, studies of state museums consider the (non)equilibrium between national politics and Holocaust remembrance, and the scholarly community is divided on the question of whether state-run institutions should impose national values on Holocaust commemoration and education or whether this proscription is inevitable.[23]

Most museums of atrocity, trauma, and dislocation will have as a key aspect of their exhibition strategies primary documents, objects, and photographs, asserting the empirical nature of these items as necessary to the narrative of evidence: the exhibitions are a witness, proof of the veracity of the events. Indeed, the founders of the JHC began collecting evidence of atrocity during the Holocaust. For example, Bono Wiener and Abram Goldberg (both among the founders of the JHC) were together in the Łódź Ghetto where they hid personal items such as diaries in one box and Nazi announcements of liquidations and other evidence of life in the ghetto in another. After the Holocaust, Goldberg returned to Łódź and retrieved the box of nonpersonal items (the other box could not be found), and he immigrated to Melbourne in the late 1940s with this in hand. Some of the items would be incorporated into the permanent museum, and the items would also later form a unique temporary exhibition on the Łódź Ghetto, providing the survivors' specific perspective within the context of broader Holocaust historiography. At the same time, the institutional rhetoric was on the civic role of the JHC. Remembrance was instrumentalized, with a civic purpose beyond commemoration. As Avril Alba has argued, the injunction to *zachor* is both to remember and to act.²⁴ Remembering antisemitism during the Holocaust has been a mission from the outset: acting against racism became a priority over time. Cyla Sokolowicz would write in the first edition of *Centre News*: "The Centre's group of dedicated volunteer workers have great ambitions for the future and hope to be able to use the lesson of the Holocaust as a starting point in an effort to build bridges of understanding between Jews and non-Jews, so that they may work together *towards a future in which racial prejudice and hatred will forever be eliminated*."²⁵

While remembrance and a civic purpose were clearly delineated and specific to the JHC's function, the concepts of antisemitism and racism (discussed below) were complicated. The term *antisemitism* was used as a vehicle to specify survivors' Holocaust experiences and was articulated in the exhibitions from the beginning, whereas "racism" and, in the words of Sokolowicz, "racial prejudice" were terms used as force to drive civic education.

At first the JHC included a "hand made"—nonprofessional—permanent exhibition²⁶ consisting of photographs of murdered family members of the survivors, items that the survivors had collected and images from newspapers, books, and other museums such as Yad Vashem, which, knowingly or not, were often perpetrators' images of Jews. Thus, while the survivors were creating an educational space for students and other visitors, they were also creating a photographic collage of the perpetrators' antisemitic perspective of dehumanized objects. The narrative constructed through the displays was twofold: to provide evidence, in the face of Holocaust denial, that the Holocaust happened and to remember loved ones, also with evidence.

The focus for the first exhibition was described by the philosopher Harry Redner, writing for the launch of the JHC in March 1984: they were part of what we argue was the JHC's healing function. For Redner, to see the vanished world "materialize . . . might until now have seemed like a shameful act of exhibitionism—and this was what for so long dissuaded many of us. . . . Now it is a necessary act of release both for us and for our dead." This was a place where those who mourn could unburden themselves, and for the dead, he continued, "it is to gain a resting place, a local habitation somewhere close to the surviving nearest, even though far from their former places of life and death." Redner went further: the JHC would be a museum like no other. It would be a site of mourning rather than a museum: "This is not a museum of culture or a museum of knowledge, this is a resting place for these remains of our dead. Let us tend them with love so that we may be at one with them and with each other."[27]

As the museum grew, the space for permanent exhibitions was reworked to include space for changing temporary displays. The permanent exhibition included generic images of the Holocaust that did not directly relate to the Melbourne survivors' personal experience (for example, photographs and items from Yad Vashem and the Ghetto Fighters' House Museum, both in Israel), as well as items that were directly linked to the lived experience of Melbourne's Holocaust survivors. The items and photographs were expected to speak for themselves: there were few labels that would contextualize and explain them. The exhibition slowly became more professional in its design, and six years after its inception in 1990, a new permanent exhibition opened, including new themes such as "Righteous amongst the Nations." The exhibition space was completely revised again in 2010.[28]

As well as the permanent exhibition, the JHC also staged temporary exhibitions, beginning one year after the opening, and it is through these temporary exhibitions that changes to the organization's approach can be most clearly identified. Most were developed in-house by the curatorial team. These included exhibitions devoted to particular places and events, exhibitions that coincided with commemorative events (for example, the 1994 temporary exhibition acknowledging the tenth anniversary of the JHC, the 2001 art exhibition in November on Kristallnacht, and the 2003 *Regeneration* exhibition commemorating the sixtieth anniversary of the Warsaw ghetto uprising), and also exhibitions on diaspora and identity as survivors of the Holocaust within a Melbourne context. More recently, a smaller number of exhibitions hosted at the JHC were developed by other institutions and organizations such as *The Rescuers* exhibition by Proof: Media for Social Justice, a New York City–based organization that uses visual responses to human rights' atrocities.

The JHC's temporary exhibitions were an opportunity to commemorate key events, tell personal survivor stories, and reach new audiences. In particular, this was a chance to recognize other groups such as Hungarian Jews, Roma and Sinti victims, and others who may not have felt as involved in the mainly emigre Polish Jewish survivor community in Melbourne, but would also respond to a broadening focus at the JHC to include other genocides and to fulfill the JHC's mission, which has remained unchanged since its commencement, to "combat antisemitism, racism and prejudice in the community and [foster] understanding between people."[29] As the mission statement reveals, combating antisemitism is of utmost importance. Antisemitism is linked specifically with the Holocaust and its survivors: *zachor* and *yizkor* (remembering/acting and memorializing). Racism and prejudice is aligned with the broader educational function of the JHC that connects with the current Australian "community" and "people." That, for survivors of the Holocaust, antisemitism and racism are different modes of thinking, will be explored below in the discussions of the temporary exhibitions.

Although temporary exhibitions were seen as important to some, such as Saba Feniger, the honorary curator at the JHC between 1985 and 2001, they were not prioritized by the executive committee: apart from the practical considerations such as lack of space, the focus was on the main exhibition.[30] Given this attitude, very few funds were allocated to support them. Feniger adjusted: she overcame the space issue by working from home, using her personal connections to obtain discounts for art supplies and then picking the materials up herself to avoid delivery charges. Eva Marks, in her role as assistant curator, recalled that the team had to work in a "small, back room at the Centre, which no longer exists. We boiled in the summer, froze in the winter and the roof leaked when it rained. We even worked sheltering under an open umbrella. The room had one table and two chairs."[31] The focus for these *early* temporary exhibitions was an internal one: the permanent exhibition was for the schoolchildren and the temporary ones for the survivors. For Feniger, the temporary exhibitions were

> a verification of what really took place and what happened to them because invariably, when I made exhibitions, I knew that they would be of no great interest to the students. But they were of great value to the Jewish community, to the survivors . . . because it verified, it witnessed, it showed what they were talking about. . . . They came to every one of those . . . exhibitions that commemorated certain events or certain places . . . very much because you want to have it confirmed . . . a confirmation of your survival . . . and your experiences.[32]

Over time, however, the permanent and temporary exhibitions increasingly had an explicit civic role: not just nostalgia for a "lost world" but also a commentary on the present. They also were a reflection on certain issues surrounding Holocaust memory and representation. For example, Saba Feniger curated a temporary exhibition titled *Art of the Holocaust* (1985) at a time when issues of representing the Holocaust were being fiercely debated in the broader Jewish community.[33] A year later, a civic approach was taken in which the survivors were at the center of the exhibition *Survivors amongst Us Work for Peace*, not as victims but instead as united activists for peace. The twin philosophies of tolerance and warnings around antisemitism that were promulgated at the opening of the JHC, were reflected in the themes of the future temporary exhibitions.[34] As we have shown elsewhere, rather than breaking the perceived silence of Holocaust museum making, the numerous temporary exhibitions held in Melbourne in the postwar era allow us to see the JHC as a continuation of the plethora of meaning-making rather than a dramatic break with what went before.[35] In addition, as they changed from an internal audience to an external one, the temporary exhibitions reflected a shift from notions of antisemitism to a broader understanding of racism.

Art of the Holocaust (1985)

The first temporary exhibition was mounted in October 1985 by Feniger with the help of Mietek Muchnicki and titled *Art of the Holocaust*.[36] The exhibition was a reaction to normative photographic representations of the Holocaust, which were usually taken during the Holocaust by the Nazis and their collaborators "who, at the time, did not contemplate the possibility of the Third Reich's defeat and the eventuality that the photos might become damning evidence against themselves. They were the work of oppressors."[37] This temporary exhibition was a step toward defiance. Rather than explicitly addressing issues of anti-racism, the exhibition connoted that the authoritative voice of responses to antisemitism belonged to the survivors.

By eschewing photographs and using art, the first exhibition by survivor volunteers was an act of resistance. Rather than themselves being the subjects of Nazi photographs, the drawing and paintings were from prisoners in Theresienstadt, Buchenwald, Auschwitz, Bergen-Belsen, Dachau, Łódź, and

Kovno, among others, and as such demonstrated that creative and spiritual resistance was apparent during the Holocaust. The artists and their work were sourced from around the world and included survivors and those who were killed during the Holocaust. Although all the artists were victims during the Holocaust, not all were Jewish, testifying to the notion that the witness of the Holocaust victim was more relevant to the exhibition than the identity of their religion or ethnicity.

Survivors amongst Us Work for Peace (1986)

The year 1986 was the United Nations International Year of Peace,[38] and the JHC responded with an exhibition about the role of Holocaust survivors living in Melbourne and their journey from birth to experiences during the Holocaust. The exhibition took as its focus the journeys of twenty-eight Holocaust survivors and mainly comprised a collage of materials on maps, some family photographs, photographs from books, and excerpts from official documents. Some also included present-day photographs or postcards from towns and cities across Europe. The journeys of the survivors were indicated by colored arrows, which linked key places and events in their narrative. Many of the survivor journeys intersected at various locations, such as Auschwitz-Birkenau or Stutthof. This approach was part of a growing appreciation of both the individual experiences and stories of survivors (as opposed to the processes of destruction) and a sensitivity to the geographies of the Holocaust.

The movements of the survivors were mainly forced, via transportations on railways or death marches, and only occasionally with agency. Within the surviving images of the exhibition panels, there is no focus on the journey to Australia (usually because this journey through displaced persons camps and sometimes Palestine and/or Israel was complicated) nor their experiences of life in Australia after the Holocaust. The main focus of the aftermath is that there *was* life: each panel included a comparison of family members who were murdered in the Holocaust and provided details of the family who survived and where they had settled.

There were no examples of *how* they worked for peace, although the exhibition also included letters from students (which were not recorded in the temporary exhibition archive). Implicit in the stories is the need for peace and the consequences of genocide—as though the very fact of survival is enough to demonstrate that they are working for peace. The exhibition also demonstrates that genocide is not only complete destruction; the mapped journeys illustrate the consequences of destruction and the intent of genocide—deportation, ethnic cleansing, mental and bodily harm, and the forcible removal of children. While the exhibition did not focus specifically on antisemitism, it did highlight the survivors (as the title suggests) while illuminating a civic and participatory purpose to their new life in Australia.

Although the focus in the exhibition was primarily on the European geographies of Holocaust journeys, with the inclusion of surviving family members in other parts of the world, the exhibition also referenced an expanded geography, not only in terms of physical spaces and places of destruction but also in other (non-European) spaces and places of tolerance and survival. While the material and imaginative distance from Europe was important in this exhibition, later exhibitions would emphasize more explicitly the contribution and civic reception of the survivors in their new country.

From Holocaust to New Life (1988)

The next temporary exhibition at the JHC marked a shift from the past and antisemitism to contemporary issues of race and racism, exploring the contribution of sixteen Holocaust survivors to the Australian community, as part of Australia's bicentennial celebration in 1988. The exhibition focused on the survivors' contributions to Australian society and economy rather than their wartime experiences, highlighting those who achieved prominence in various spheres, including community work, education, music, and science. It concentrated on Jewish survivors, not all of whom were connected to the JHC but who had established themselves as contributing, law-abiding citizens who had enhanced the society that adopted them.[39] Each panel took the form of an overview of these survivors' lives, including their occupations in Australia and the evidence of their contributions, and a quotation from the survivors about what they saw as their role in Australian society. It is important to note that this exhibition coincided with the Australian bicentennial celebrations, demonstrating the need for survivors to insert themselves into the themes of rebirth, multiculturalism, and relevancy, despite the racist implications of a colonial state celebrating the arrival of the First Fleet. The exhibition spoke to the then opposition leader John Howard's One Australia policy, which excluded Aborigines as citizens: a "decisive rebuttal of [the previous prime minister, Malcolm Fraser's] multiculturalism."[40] While not explicitly stated, it is difficult to overlook the connection between survivors' experiences of antisemitism and the then racist ideologies being discussed as potential policy. Thus, while the core sentiment of the JHC's mission statement (antisemitism) was the framework for this exhibition, the subsequent civic notions of community, understanding, and anti-racism revealed the JHC's dual roles. The link connecting the "internalized" theme of antisemitism and the broader notion of "racism" was multiculturalism.

The variety of different experiences illustrated the breadth of the survivor's contribution. For example, the panel relating to JHC survivor guide Moshe Ajzenbud, who identified as a "fitter and turner/storeman," stated his contribution in this way: "To continue Yiddish cultural traditions in the framework of multiculturalism. To link the Australian way of life with the specific Yiddish heritage." Other panels included one on Dr. Frank Vajda and his contribution to medicine. Survivors chosen for the exhibition were obvious achievers in Australia, such as Irene Capek who stood out for her work with migrants; Paul Huppert, a principal experimental scientist with the Commonwealth Scientific and Industrial Research Organisation; and Malvina Malinek, a scientist and community leader. Felix Werder wanted to be "remembered in this country for having played the prophet Ezekiel." He said: "I stirred them. Australia will never be the same in music, music criticism, art and literature." Of note is Werder's language, which illustrates an ambivalent belonging: "*this* country" rather than *my* country; "stirred *them*" rather than stirred *us*. While the exhibition could be viewed as a celebration of Australia's multicultural society, it also contained suggestions of the tensions involved in multiculturalism.

A number of the panels related directly to the JHC. Walter Lippmann (a Jewish community leader who had various roles, including president of the Victorian Jewish Board of Deputies, and was dedicated to multiculturalism, as reflected in his senior involvement with the Ethnic Communities' Council of Victoria) had arrived in Australia in 1938 from Germany. Having not experienced the Holocaust during the war period, Lippmann was to offer a quotation that reflected Australia's colonial history: "The Holocaust Centre's Exhibition on the occasion of Australia's Bicentenary is very valuable. It emphasizes not only our Jewish Association with Australia in the early days of settlement, but also the more recent history, through which many citizens have passed and of which many other Australians are quite ignorant."[41] Unsurprisingly perhaps, the founding copresidents of the JHC, Bono Wiener and Aron Sokolowicz, focused on their contribution to Holocaust commemoration. Unlike Lippman, both Wiener and Sokolowicz experienced the Holocaust in ghettos, concentration camps, and death camps. Wiener focused on his contribution to the JHC (and also to the Australian Labor Party), stating that "it was a sense of history which led [him] to hide two boxes of documents in the ghetto." Sokolowicz's focus was on the museum and commemoration— "We rebuilt our lives emotionally and spiritually which consequently enabled us to contribute . . . [to] the country which adopted us"—and further stated that "every country needs organised ethnic communities." The emphasis here is on the reconstruction of life and nation building through multiculturalism and implicitly points to the health of a nation-state's vigor in combating racism. While contributions such as Sokolowicz's focused on his identities as a Holocaust survivor and an active Australian citizen, the message behind the exhibition was *how* these Holocaust survivors were well situated to comment on the nation's racial barometer. Howard's new blueprint for the left-leaning Wiener in particular, which addressed a wave of Asian immigration as a "clear target,"[42] arguably was distressing for survivors.

Despite this emphasis on multiculturalism, the exhibition concluded with an art installation by Charlotte Neumann, which depicted the journey of survivors moving from Europe to Australia, with "optic fibres light[ing] up in a sequential manner, showing the movement of the masses leaving Europe and eventually *merging* into a brightly lit Australia":[43] an assimilationist message which contrasted with the assertiveness of the displays.

These early temporary exhibitions from the volunteer body of the JHC represent the survivors creating their own narratives and demonstrate the growing confidence of the JHC in making the links among the Holocaust and contemporary race and racism, Australian history, and politics, including contemporary politics. As the JHC employed more paid staff, including the appointment of a new curator in 2002, the temporary exhibitions grew less from survivors' initiatives and more from traveling exhibitions and "retrospectives" on the early days of the JHC and its survivor communities. They also took a more assertive tone in broadening the definitions of victims of the Holocaust, providing a commentary on contemporary as well as historic issues, and acknowledging other genocides. For example, the first temporary exhibition at the JHC, which focused exclusively on non-Jewish victims of the Holocaust, was *Gypsy Reflections: Remembering the Romani Victims of the Holocaust through Art*. Opened by George Lekakis from the Victorian Multicultural Commission and held between November and December 2003, this was a time when the JHC was reaching out to groups and organizations outside the Jewish community. In appreciation of the JHC's efforts, the Romani-Gypsy Association presented the JHC with a Romani memorial sculpture the following year.[44] It now became clear why the JHC mission statement separated the notions of antisemitism and racism: while the former depicted something that had been the ideological underpinning of the Holocaust, the broader notion of racism could occur anywhere and at any time.

Shelter from the Storm: Jewish Refugees to Australia 1933–1945 (2006)

An example of this shifting focus was the temporary exhibition *Shelter from the Storm: Jewish Refugees to Australia 1933–1945*, which ran for four months in 2006[45] and was funded by a $20,000 federal government fund.[46] The JHC's curator worked with academics Eileen Wright, Michele Langfield, Paul Bartrop, and Susanne Wright to produce a highly acclaimed exhibition. The exhibition focused on the experiences of Jews in Nazi-occupied Europe, the choices made by Jews to stay or leave, the response of the Australian government, and the treatment of Jewish refugees during World War II, including internment in Australia and treatment of refugees on the HMT *Dunera*. As with other temporary exhibitions, *Shelter from the Storm* used personal testimony of Holocaust survivors who made their home in Melbourne to illustrate the story. While the testimonies provided an almost overwhelmingly positive narrative about adjusting to life in Australia, continuing the discursive framing of immigration and settlement represented in a section of the exhibit titled "From Holocaust to New Life," elsewhere the curatorial voice hinted at the problems faced by refugees, especially children: "They faced the stigma of being branded 'reffos' [derogatory Australian slang for "refugees"] and the conflict of wanting to fit in with Australia schoolmates, whilst struggling with their European heritage and identity" (exhibition panel "Long Way from Home"). While there was muted criticism of Australian government policy during World War II and no criticism of the response of the Australian Jewish community, the *contemporary* policies of the Australian government toward asylum seekers were critiqued explicitly through the exhibition's text and through a comparison with the historic context of World War II. Twenty years after the exhibition that addressed Howard's One Australia policy (*Survivors amongst Us Work for Peace*) Australia now found itself impacted by over ten years of Howard's anti-refugee and racist policies. Perhaps as a result of this, the JHC was wary of using the word *tolerance* as an educational tool. In the words of one Holocaust survivor, "Tolerance shouldn't be used because the word 'tolerance' means someone is different" and, similarly, in the words of another, "I object to the word 'tolerate' . . . we're not teaching tolerance, we're teaching that everyone is equal, that we're all human, we're all one race, we're human."[47] The politics associated with the word *tolerance*—that Australians should "tolerate" refugees—suggested complacency and inaction. Anti-racist actions fitted better with the philosophical growth of the JHC.

The panel titled "Between Hope and Despair" included a quotation from barrister and longtime refugee advocate Julian Burnside, which typified *zachor*—the need to act: "Asylum seekers are human beings and they deserved to be treated properly. . . . We diminish ourselves by the way we treat them. Once we recognize that these people are human beings, we will see that the problem is in truth a moral problem and they have made a profound mistake in the way we have handled it. *We must not rest until this outrage to humanity is ended*" (emphasis added). The text of the exhibition further condemned current policy:

> Every nation reserves the right to determine its own immigration policies with respect to its resources and social considerations and to assess the legitimacy of claims for asylum. However a measure of an advanced culture must surely be how it treats the vulnerable, how it heeds its international obligations and the moral underpinning of its policy towards refugees. Active deterrence or a punitive response to refugees violates the humanitarian spirit of international laws of asylum.

A quotation from an asylum seeker held in the Maribynong Detention Centre contrasted with the positive testimonies of survivors: "Being detained without any crime is very traumatic, shameful, self-destructive and awful hardship, prisons may sound very hard but knowing an exact duration of a sentence is less stressful. . . . I feel I'm in a grave with four walls." Only five years since the *Tampa* affair,[48] Australia's treatment of asylum seekers was still a matter for fierce debate.[49] As well as being quoted in the exhibition, Burnside spoke at its launch, using the occasion to make the connection between the exhibition and what Robin Rothfield, reporting on the launch, called the "Howard Government's cruel and heartless policy of issuing temporary protection visas."[50]

The Rescuers (2012)

The expanding focus of the JHC is further exemplified by *The Rescuers*, a 2012 exhibition. Created by Leora Kahn from New York, it included photographs of rescuers from many genocides around the world.[51] The sixteen panels of photographs and stories were supported by a monthlong series of public programs. Because of the breadth of case studies, it was attended by many local and foreign diplomats and representatives from varied communities.[52] Kahn's exhibition vividly and effectively communicated "what qualifies people as rescuers, what motivates them and the contexts within which the rescue behaviour takes place."[53] As well as representing a further shifting of the non-universalist narrative that Judith Berman argued had been dominant at the JHC since 1984,[54] through a focus on the rescuers from a number of genocides rather than the Jewish victims of the Holocaust, the exhibition asked the visitors to act in the present, making explicit the civic role of the JHC. This exhibition illustrated the process of an institution that focused inwardly (on Holocaust antisemitism) to an outreach center that had the authority to communicate on community anti-racist policies and actions and global genocides. As retired lieutenant general the Honourable Roméo A. Dallaire, then a senator for Canada, who led the UN forces that attempted to prevent the 1994 genocide in Rwanda, stated in the introductory text of the exhibition:

> Mass violence and genocide do not occur by accident. They are caused by human will, and they can be prevented by human

will. And when we bear witness to those ultimate failures of humanity—failures to prevent the worst in our nature—ordinary heroes and rescuers are needed more than ever to maintain hope that, one day we will do better, that one day we will make "never again" mean to never again accept atrocities against innocent civilians for all of humanity.[55]

We argue that while the sentiments toward combating racism have been present from the outset—in particular in a formal sense through the mission statement—it was the temporary exhibitions that gave this material form. Temporary exhibitions provided a space through which the JHC could increasingly comment on contemporary issues and expand the scope of the organization. They provided a platform for survivors, who have highlighted the impact of antisemitism on them and their communities during the Holocaust, to use that authority in the present: acknowledging other genocides and instances of racism within contemporary Australian society. Given the welcome "outside" communities were receiving at the center (through these exhibitions and other public programs), it is not surprising that the executive director, Warren Fineberg, would now describe the JHC as a "healing centre," for Holocaust survivors and other victims of genocide.[56]

Conclusion

Reflecting on the role of Bono Wiener, a founder of the JHC, Alex Dafner has argued that "the Holocaust Centre was started by his generation of survivors . . . [but] they would not be the ones to finish this important task."[57] For much of the JHC's history, the temporary exhibitions responded to internal motivations—they were for the survivors, to tell their individual and collective stories. Despite the rhetoric of being an institution motivated to effect change within society, the early temporary exhibitions maintained this internal focus. However, as the institution changed over the next thirty years, so too did the temporary exhibitions, reflecting a more outward focus, both in terms of the connections between the Holocaust and Australian history and contemporary issues but also to other genocides.

The early rhetoric of an institution founded to combat antisemitism and racism in Australian society gradually emerged in temporary exhibitions, which showed signs of a journey from race (survivor identity) to contemporary anti-racism (the civic role of the museum and its outreach capacities). What has not emerged through this process is an engagement with the history of racism within an Australian context. While the story of William Cooper (1860–1941), an Australian Aboriginal activist who protested over the treatment of German Jews after Kristallnacht by attempting to deliver a message to German consulate in Melbourne, is now briefly told in the permanent exhibition, any links to the genocide of Australia's Indigenous population are absent. The temporary exhibitions, however, allowed the Holocaust survivors to demonstrate the connection between Australia's racist past and refugee xenophobia and Europe's antisemitic past and the world's responses to current genocides. While the narratives of the permanent exhibition remain focused primarily on the Holocaust and antisemitism, the temporary exhibitions have been a space through which the JHC can increasingly speak out as authority on other examples of racism and make explicit the need to act in the present. Despite seminars in recent years focusing on other genocides, the main exhibition and the focus of school programs have until today concentrated on the Holocaust. While this is appropriate and unsurprising for a Jewish Holocaust center founded by Holocaust survivors, the mission statement of the JHC required a broadening of its content and activities. Further, the geographical specificity of a Holocaust center located in Australia necessitates, we would argue, an engagement with Australia's genocide.

Although the impact of these temporary exhibitions on visitors, as with all museum exhibitions, is difficult to quantify,[58] an examination of the temporary exhibitions illustrates the changing roles, mandates, and philosophies of those involved in their production. As the temporary exhibitions continue to bring a broader range of ethnic groups to the museum, the JHC's emphasis has shifted from a survivor refuge to an organization that is more outwardly focused and increasingly assertive in providing a space through which to critique contemporary government policy and to challenge visitors to act in the present. As such, the temporary exhibitions illustrate the transition of survivors from victims to agents—in particular in the survivor-driven temporary exhibitions—and have increasingly asserted the JHC's civic role and a changing emphasis from personal, internal commemoration to public, external education.

Notes

We thank the Jewish Holocaust Centre, particularly Jayne Josem, for providing access to the temporary exhibition archive. We also thank Philip Maisel, Holocaust survivor and longtime volunteer at the Jewish Holocaust Centre, for the initial funding for research into the history of the Jewish Holocaust Centre on which this chapter is based.

1. Leo and Mina were both from Białystok in Poland. In 1932, they immigrated to Melbourne, where Leo became president of the Kadimah ten years later. Leo and Mina were instrumental in providing refuge and resettlement to Holocaust survivors through the United Jewish Overseas Relief Fund, later to become the Australian Jewish Welfare and Relief Society, of which Leo became president. He died in 1972 at age seventy-two. See Rodney L. Benjamin, "Fink, Leo (1901–1972)," *Australian Dictionary of Biography*, National Centre of Biography, Australian National University, adb.anu.edu.au/biography/fink-leo-10183/text17993, accessed September 1, 2016.
2. Steven Cooke and Donna-Lee Frieze, *The Interior of Our Memories: A History of Melbourne's Jewish Holocaust Centre* (Melbourne: Hybrid, 2015).
3. Moshe Fiszman, interview with Pam Maclean and Andrea Witcomb, December 10, 2010; and Samuel D. Kassow, *Who Will Write Our History? Emanuel Ringelblum, the Warsaw Ghetto, and the Oyneg Shabes Archive* (Bloomington: Indiana University Press, 2007).
4. Cooke and Frieze, *Interior of Our Memories*.
5. Harry Redner, in JHC, commemorative booklet produced to mark the opening of the JHC, Melbourne, 1984.
6. Cooke and Frieze, *Interior of Our Memories*; and Steven Cooke, Avril Alba, and Donna-Lee Frieze, "Community Museums and the Creation of a 'Sense of Place': Holocaust Museums in Australia," *reCollections* 9, no. 1 (2014): recollections.nma.gov.au/issues/volume_9_number_1/papers/community_museums.
7. Andrew Markus, quoted in Cooke and Frieze, *Interior of Our Memories*, 39–40.
8. W. E. H. Stanner, *The Boyer Lectures 1968: After the Dreaming* (Sydney: Australian Broadcasting Commission, 1969).
9. Philip Schorch, "Experiencing Differences and Negotiating Prejudices at the Immigration Museum Melbourne," *International Journal of Heritage Studies* 21,

no. 1 (2015): 46–64; Andrea Witcomb, "Migration, Social Cohesion and Cultural Diversity: Can Museums Move Beyond Pluralism?" *Humanities Research* 15, no. 2 (2009): 49–66; and Tony Bennett, *The Birth of the Museum: History, Theory, Politics* (New York: Routledge, 1995), 80.

10. See, for instance, Reesa Greenberg, "*Mirroring Evil*, Evil Mirrored: Timing, Trauma, and Temporary Exhibitions," in *Museums after Modernism: Strategies of Engagement*, ed. G. Pollack and J. Zemans (Malden: Blackwell, 2007), 104–18. Greenberg highlights the difficulties of exhibiting controversial art about the Holocaust.
11. Grace L. McCann Morley, "Museums and Temporary Exhibitions," *Museum International* 53, no. 4 (2001): 5.
12. Morley, "Museums and Temporary Exhibitions," 5.
13. Richard Sandell, ed., *Museums, Society, Inequality* (London: Routledge, 2003).
14. Richard Sandell, "Museums and the Combating of Social Inequality: Roles, Responsibilities, Resistance," in Sandell, *Museums, Society, Inequality*, 2.
15. Tony Bennett, *Birth of the Museum*, 8.
16. Sue M. Davies, "The Co-production of Temporary Museum Exhibitions," *Museum Management and Curatorship* 25, no. 3 (2010): 305–21.
17. Elizabeth Crooke, *Museums and Community: Ideas, Issues and Challenges* (Hoboken, NJ: Routledge, 2008), 1.
18. Crooke, *Museums and Community*, 9.
19. Moira G. Simpson, *Making Representations: Museums in the Post-Colonial Era* (London: Routledge, 2001), 81.
20. Simpson, *Making Representations*, 81.
21. Chen Yunqian, "Local Exhibitions and the Molding of Revolutionary Memory (1927–1949)," *Chinese Studies in History* 47, no. 1 (2013): 29–52.
22. Yunqian, *Local Exhibitions*. See also, for example, Paul Gediman, "This Museum Is Not a Metaphor: Confronting the Hard Facts of the Holocaust," *Commonweal* 120, no. 11 (1993): 13–15; Philip Gourevitch, "Behold Now Behemoth: The Holocaust Memorial Museum: One More American Theme Park," *Harper's*, July 1993, 55–63; and Barbara Kirshenblatt-Gimblett, "Imagining Europe: The Popular Arts of American Jewish Ethnography," in *Divergent Jewish Cultures: Israel and America*, ed. Deborah Dash Moore and S. Ilan Troen (New Haven, CT: Yale University Press, 2001): 155–91.
23. See Amos Goldberg, "The 'Jewish Narrative' in the Yad Vashem Global Holocaust Museum," *Journal of Genocide Research* 14, no. 2 (2012): 187–213; Jennifer Hansen-Glucklich, "Evoking the Sacred: Visual Holocaust Narratives in National Museums," *Journal of Modern Jewish Studies* 9, no. 2 (2010): 209–32; Tim Cole,

"Nativization and Nationalization: A Comparative Landscape Study of Holocaust Museums in Israel, the US and the UK," *Journal of Israeli History* 23, no. 1 (2004): 130–45; and Michael Bernard-Donals, "Synecdochic Memory at the United States Holocaust Memorial Museum," *College English* 74, no. 5 (2012): 417.

24. Avril Alba, "Integrity and Relevance: Shaping Holocaust Memory at the Sydney Jewish Museum," *Judasim* 54, nos. 31–32 (2005): 108–15.
25. Cyla Sokolowicz, editorial, *Centre News* 1, no. 1 (1984): 2 (emphasis added).
26. Helen Light, quoted in Judith E. Berman, *Holocaust Remembrance in Australian Jewish Communities, 1945–2000* (Perth, WA: University of Western Australia Press, 2010), 107.
27. Redner, in JHC, commemorative booklet, 1984.
28. Cooke and Frieze, *Interior of Our Memories*, 96–121.
29. JHC, Mission, www.jhc.org.au/about-the-centre.html, accessed September 1, 2018.
30. Cooke and Frieze, *Interior of Our Memories*, 98.
31. Eva Marks, "The Privilege of Working with Saba," *Centre News* 20, no. 3 (2001): 17.
32. Saba Feniger, interview with Andrea Witcomb and Linda Young, April 29, 2009.
33. See Cooke and Frieze, *Interior of Our Memories*, 80–95.
34. See Cooke and Frieze, *Interior of Our Memories*.
35. Cooke and Frieze, *Interior of Our Memories*.
36. Saba Feniger, "My Creative Years at the Holocaust Centre," *Centre News* 3, no. 20 (2001): 16–17.
37. JHC, *Art of the Holocaust*, pamphlet, box 15:2220, folder 8, 1985, JHC, Elsternwick, VIC, Australia.
38. United Nations, Forty-Ninth Plenary Meeting, October 24, 1985, A/Res/37/221, www.un.org/en/ga/search/view_doc.asp?symbol=A/RES/40/3, accessed January 29, 2019.
39. Cooke, Alba, and Frieze, "Community Museums and the Creation of a 'Sense of Place.'"
40. Marian Maddox, *God under Howard: The Rise of the Religious Right in Australian Politics* (Crows Nest, NSW, Australia: Allen & Unwin, 2005), 112.
41. JHC, temporary exhibition archive.
42. Maddox, *God under Howard*, 113.
43. Marks, quoted in Cooke, Alba, and Frieze, "Community Museums and the Creation of a 'Sense of Place'" (emphasis added).
44. "Gypsy Sculpture for Holocaust Centre," *Centre News* 26, no.4 (2004): 10.
45. Tali Borowski, "Shelter from the Storm," *Australian Jewish News* (Darlinghurst, NSW), August 11, 2006, 6–7.

46. "Centre's $20,000 Government Grant," *Centre News* 27, no. 2 (2005): 13.
47. Phillip Maisel, interview with Donna-Lee Frieze and Michele Langford, July 8, 2009; and Saba Feniger, interview with Andrea Witcomb and Linda Young, April 28, 2009.
48. The *Tampa* affair involved the Norwegian vessel MV *Tampa*, which was carrying over four hundred Hazara refugees stranded in the Indian Ocean, trying to land in Australia. The Howard government introduced the Border Protection Bill (2001) to prevent refugees and ships from landing in Australian territory. See "Defining Moments in Australian History," National Museum Australia, www.nma.gov.au/online_features/defining_moments/featured/tampa_affair, accessed September 1, 2016.
49. "Exhibition Covers Refugee Experience," *Centre News* 28, no. 2 (2006): 6–7.
50. Robin Rothfield, "Australia's Great Shame on Refugees," *The Age*, August 26, 2006, 9.
51. Pauline Rockman, "From the President," *Centre News* 34, no. 1 (2012): 3.
52. This included Faina Iligoga, a Rwandan genocide survivor; Dr. Hariz Halilovich, born in Srebrenica and studying in Sarajevo during the genocide; and John Searle, chair of the Board of the Victorian Human Rights and Equal Opportunity Commission. See JHC, "The Rescuers: An Overview," *Centre News* 34, no. 2 (2012): 8.
53 "The Rescuers: An Overview," *Centre News* 34, no. 2 (2012): 8–9.
54 Judith E. Berman, *Holocaust Remembrance in Australian Jewish Communities*, 149.
55 Roméo A. Dallaire, quoted in "Picturing Moral Courage: The Rescuers," Proof: Media for Social Justice, proof.org/rescuers-intro-dallaire, accessed October 24, 2017.
56 Warren Fineberg, personal communication with Donna-Lee Frieze, November 2012.
57 Alex Dafner, "Kadimah's Role in Founding a Holocaust Centre," *Centre News* 21, no. 2 (2002): 17.
58. Volker Kirchberg and Martin Tröndle, "Experiencing Exhibitions: A Review of Studies of Visitor Experiences in Museums," *Curator: The Museum Journal* 55, no. 4 (2012): 435–52.

14

Nazism and Racism in South African Textbooks

Shirli Gilbert

IN SOUTH AFRICA, ONE of the world's most reviled racial states after 1945, Nazism has been a complex but surprisingly consistent public presence. Memories of Nazism and the Holocaust were regularly invoked during the apartheid period (1948–94), although different groups drew starkly different conclusions about the implications of the connection. Following apartheid's demise in 1994, the Nazi past was perceived as a potent and seemingly obvious historical benchmark for understanding what had happened in the country, for envisioning reconciliation, and for thinking about how apartheid might be remembered and memorialized. The history of Holocaust memory in South Africa still awaits full exploration, although scholars are beginning to chart this complex terrain.[1]

This chapter takes as its focus the sphere of formal education, surveying the changing ways in which the Nazi past has featured in curricula and textbooks from the 1950s through the 2010s. For a wide range of groups—including apartheid leaders, liberation movements, successive post-1994 governments, and the Jewish community—history was integral to conceptions of national identity, belonging, and resistance. The Nazi past was considered especially significant, though it was taught in markedly different ways and accompanied by divergent explanatory narratives.

In present-day South Africa, the Holocaust occupies a prominent position in the national curriculum for history. It was first officially included in the early 2000s, a time when it also featured increasingly in the public sphere as part of the post-apartheid nation's narratives of reconciliation and democracy. In syllabi and textbooks alike, the Nazi genocide was presented as an exemplary instance of human rights abuse, a medium for encouraging learners to recognize racism and stand up against it.[2]

The chapter places this post-apartheid linkage between Nazism and apartheid in broader historical perspective. The largely unquestioned linking of these histories, rooted in their shared origins in racist ideology, has led to the widespread assumption that the Holocaust could only have been taught after apartheid's demise.[3] The chapter demonstrates, however, that the connections considered obvious today were for several decades not seen as such. Many apartheid-era textbooks use the language of "race" to explain Nazi actions in a way that recognizes no relationship to apartheid's anti-black racism. They also do not shy away from the consequences of Nazism's racist ideology, providing open descriptions of persecution and genocide. Post-apartheid textbooks in turn often associate the Holocaust and apartheid in simplistic and unquestioning ways, effacing the specificity of the two events and the complex factors that explain them historically.[4]

The empirical question of links between Nazism and apartheid requires brief mention. Afrikaner nationalism—the broad political movement from which apartheid emerged—was indisputably influenced by ideas derived from Europe, particularly Nazi Germany, in the 1930s and '40s. In particular, while antisemitism had not been absent from South African life before this period, the 1930s saw it enter the political mainstream, with several openly pro-Nazi movements attracting popular support.[5]

The enduring impact of Nazism in South Africa has nonetheless been a topic of sustained debate, much of it political rather than scholarly. In the decades following the introduction of apartheid in 1948, establishing connections with Nazism was a powerful way for apartheid's opponents to explain the nature of the racist regime and the struggle against it. A number of quasi-scholarly texts, not all of them bound by principles of academic rigor, advanced this thesis during the apartheid era.[6] In the post-apartheid period, commentators across the political spectrum have variously minimized the historical links,[7] gently disparaged the "hyperbole" employed by activists during the apartheid era,[8] and stressed the continuing relevance of the analogy to South Africa's ongoing efforts to confront its past.[9]

Even if the two shared broad nineteenth-century roots, apartheid was a fundamentally distinct ideological and political system to Nazism. To begin with, it was a system of exploitation rather than of genocide. And although race was the key organizing principle for all areas of life, according to the sociologist Deborah Posel apartheid ideologues "eschewed a science of race, explicitly recognising race as a construct with cultural, social and economic dimensions."[10] While the precise meaning of apartheid was disputed from the outset, in Nationalist rhetoric it was justified not on the basis of white racial superiority but rather in terms of "separate development." The narration of history in textbooks largely reflects this ideology, extolling the importance of the "separate development" of South Africa's many "nations,"[11] and glossing rather impassively over issues of "race" and racism.

The current prominence of Holocaust education in South Africa is partly shaped by global trends, as is the interpretive framework of anti-racism, social justice, and human rights that underpins it. Patricia Bromley and Susan Garnett Russell note that the Holocaust began to feature in curricula in the United States, Canada, Germany, and the United Kingdom in the late 1970s and '80s, and they link this development with the general growth of Holocaust consciousness. Since the 1990s, Holocaust education across the globe has increasingly been framed in the language of human rights.[12] Over the past two decades, there has been a worldwide growth in programs using the Holocaust to teach human rights and anti-racism, spurred by initiatives such as the UN-designated International Holocaust Remembrance Day and the Stockholm International Forum on the Holocaust.[13] The relationship between Holocaust and human rights education is widely debated among scholars, however, and even those convinced that "teaching the Shoah effectively can contribute . . . to protecting human rights and strengthening democracy" acknowledge that there is very little empirical research to confirm these assumptions.[14] Notwithstanding this, those who speak of "Holocaust education" often intend it unproblematically as a tool for human rights education.[15] While South Africa's trajectory in part mirrors these international developments, it is a distinct case for examination given its history.

My chapter focuses on syllabi and textbooks, analyzing examples from the 1950s to the present. When I began my research I expected that these sources would be relatively meager for the apartheid period, but this was emphatically not the case. The focus on formal education, as opposed to private or nongovernmental initiatives,[16] offers particular insight into notions of "official knowledge," the key ideas that a society seeks to convey.[17] Many scholars argue that education policy is inevitably "political and ideological," especially in a state such as apartheid South Africa.[18] Although the degree of the South African state's control has varied over time, it has been broadly responsible for creating curricula, approving textbooks, overseeing exams, and granting school-leaving certificates.[19] As such, formal education is a valuable marker of leadership's changing conceptions of the relationship between apartheid and the Nazi past.

Syllabi and textbooks are of course limited in what they can tell us, and we cannot assume that what is written in them is always taught or learned.[20] My focus here is on how the past has been narrated over time in government syllabi and (largely) government-approved textbooks rather than how it has been understood and received by learners. The latter is an important but different question, and since observation is not possible for anything but contemporary classrooms, it is also one that poses methodological challenges. I have nonetheless gained some insight into the relationship between written sources and classroom practice through individual teachers' accounts and examiners' reports.[21]

Scholars have noted the particular importance of textbooks in the South African context.[22] Under apartheid, textbooks were a key vehicle for the transmission of information, considered to be "authoritative bodies of factual knowledge."[23] They were subject to a closely controlled process of approval and adoption that was regulated by local departments of education. Led primarily by profit incentives, publishers usually took a conservative and self-censoring approach in order to ensure that their textbooks made it onto the "approved textbook" lists.[24] Delays in curricular reform after 1994 meant that apartheid-era textbooks continued to be used until at least the late 1990s, although this may also have been part of a deliberate government effort to reduce conflict during the fragile period of transition.[25] Hundreds of new textbooks have been published since 2000 to support the revised post-apartheid curricula, although the Department of Basic Education has recently reinstituted approved textbook lists.[26] Textbooks are still sometimes the only source of information for learners and even teachers, particularly in rural schools, and they are still relied on heavily.

The existing scholarship on history education during the apartheid period has focused largely on textbooks, particularly the ways in which they portrayed South African history in order to justify the political status quo. Much emphasis has understandably also been placed on Bantu education, apartheid's educational system for Africans.[27] Relatively little work has been done on how "general" or world history (as it was designated in some syllabi) was portrayed, beyond the reflection that it was largely Eurocentric. In focusing on this underresearched area, my study is underpinned by several key questions.[28] When did South African schools begin teaching the Nazi past? Which aspects of that past were taught at different times, and which omitted? What was the historical framework within which Nazism was located, and how was it interpreted and explained? How was racism defined, and to what extent was the Nazi persecution of the Jews considered explicitly as an instance of racism? What links, if any, were made between Nazi Germany and the South African context? The answers to these questions, as the chapter demonstrates, are not always straightforward or predictable.

No comprehensive collection exists of apartheid-era syllabi, but I have gathered fragments from a wide range of sources to obtain a clear, if incomplete, picture.[29] Despite the strict segregation of learning under apartheid, Jonathan Jansen argues that curricula were less differentiated during apartheid than they had been before 1948, largely because the context of Bantu education—untrained teachers, overcrowding, poor facilities and equipment—was itself so successful at institutionalizing racial discrimination.[30] The documents and syllabi I studied reinforced this finding. I have also examined over seventy secondary school textbooks published from the 1950s until the present, primarily in the subjects of history and social sciences.

A detailed history of South African education is beyond the chapter's scope, but a brief overview is a necessary background against which to understand what follows. A cornerstone of apartheid legislation was the Bantu Education Act (1953), which brought black education under central government control. The act aimed to prevent the mixing of cultures and to prepare black people for their designated subordinate role in society. It was informed by the ideology of Christian National Education (CNE), which was based on principles of racial supremacy and trusteeship, the God-willed separation of nations, and Calvinist-nationalist ideals. By the time the far-reaching National Education Policy Bill No. 39 was passed in 1967, the segregation and centralization of South African education was largely complete. The bill made CNE uniform policy across the country, standardizing syllabi and exams. The four designated racial groups had their own separate schools, but control over syllabi and budgets was in the hands of the white parliament.[31] In short, apartheid education "was an instrument of division and oppression, . . . a major tool for legitimising the apartheid state."[32]

The 1976 Soweto uprising initiated a protracted period of resistance against apartheid education that saw the widespread "disintegration of learning."[33] The government introduced reforms, but they fell far short of students' demands, exacerbating the crisis and provoking further unrest. Several alternative education initiatives gained ground during the 1980s, including attempts to construct alternative histories of South Africa. Key to this effort was the work of revisionist South African historians, many of them based in the United Kingdom, and the People's History movement, which emerged from the broader People's Education movement. Both were limited in their influence, but they provided content for teachers who wished to teach "against the grain" of apartheid history.[34]

After 1994, it took some time for syllabi to reflect political changes. Interim syllabi drawn up by the Department of Education were intended simply to remove the most egregious aspects of apartheid-era syllabi without the need for new textbooks. Given the explosive political situation, leaders opted for careful and gradual change that would facilitate reconciliation, rather than radical revisions. Jonathan Jansen argues that educational reform in this period "was simply about achieving a symbolic and visible purging of the apartheid curriculum" and that substantial revisions of content and implementation were not on the agenda.[35] The first post-apartheid curriculum, adopted in March 1997 and grounded in ideas of outcomes-based education, subsumed history into the human and social sciences, where the subject ceased to exist in any recognizable form. In 2000, however, the new minister of education, Kader Asmal, initiated a thoroughgoing process of revision that saw history education reframed as a necessity for promoting strong democratic values. The first entirely revised curricula appeared in 2002–3, "informed by a strong values and human rights framework," and a subsequent revision resulted in the National Curriculum Statement Grades R-12 (2012), still current at the time of writing.[36]

The Apartheid Period

During the apartheid period, history was a compulsory subject from the age of nine or ten, and an optional (but unpopular) choice for the final three years of school. A central syllabus was drafted by the director-general of National Education together with the directors of white education in South Africa's four provinces. Content was divided equally each year between "general" history and South African history, the former heavily Eurocentric and the latter overwhelmingly a history enacted by whites.[37]

Nazism began to feature in syllabi as early as 1957. In that year, the "General History" section of the Transvaal Education Department History syllabus for Standards IX and X, the final two years of secondary school, included options on "[t]he origin and development of National-Socialism in Germany" and "[t]he expansionist policy of Germany, Italy and Japan, together with other causes leading to the outbreak of the Second World War."[38] By 1964, German totalitarianism and the lead-up to World War II were compulsory topics in the national curriculum adopted by all the provinces for the Senior Certificate (school-leaving qualification).[39] In 1976 and 1979, provincial as well as Joint Matriculation Board (independent school) syllabi included sections on Nazism focused on the rise of the Nazi party, Hitler's domestic and foreign policy, and the nature of totalitarianism.[40] Another round of syllabus changes took place in the early to mid-1980s, when Nazi Germany again appeared in compulsory sections on totalitarianism and events leading up to World War II, particularly in the final years of secondary school.[41]

It is thus clear that Nazi Germany was a consistent subject on apartheid-era history syllabi, and it was compulsory from at least 1964. It also appeared frequently on exam papers for three decades.[42]

How was the subject of Nazism contextualized in the syllabi? First, it was framed within the rise of totalitarianism in the interwar period, alongside fascist Italy in particular. Second, it was presented as part of a chronology of events leading to the outbreak of World War II, with a focus on Hitler's foreign policy. Finally, it was understood in the context of the growth of world powers in the interwar period, considered alongside the United States, the Soviet Union, and Japan. The focus in all three cases was on the prewar Nazi period (1933–39) rather than the war itself. Syllabi did not usually mention Jews or any other victims, nor, given the prewar emphasis, did they specify study of the genocide. The word *Holocaust* was not used.[43]

Syllabi provided skeletal frameworks of topics to be studied. These frameworks were largely reflected in the textbooks, although the detail of how specific topics were to be covered was left to individual authors. In the vast majority of textbooks, the rise of Nazism was charted as a chronological narrative, beginning with the punitive and humiliating postwar agreement at Versailles, Germany's economic crises during the 1920s, and the failure of Weimar democracy.[44] The rise of the Nazi Party was detailed against this background. Hitler's foreign policy during the 1930s was a significant focus, underscored by the frequent use of maps depicting Hitler's designs on Europe and his expansionist exploits.[45] Examiners noted that questions on these topics were among the most popular among students.[46] World War II was largely explained in the textbooks as the result of the world's failure to stem Hitler's aggressive expansionism. The war itself was generally described briefly, in military terms.[47]

Some of these portrayals revealed clear sympathy for the Nazi cause, describing Hitler as "a talented speaker" and "an extraordinary politician" who "restored order and stability in the country."[48] This ideological bias was emphasized by the author of an early study of apartheid textbooks, who pointed out that "there is no word of anti-Semitism or Jews, not a word on any other perhaps unacceptable aspect of the Hitler regime. There is much complimentary reference to Hitler's achievements and a description of how he set about uniting all Germans in one Reich. The course of the war is presented with care to show German successes as much as Allied ones, if not more."[49]

Examples of such bias are evident in a handful of textbooks. According to one published in 1978, "Germany was in trouble and only a particularly strong and gifted leader would be able once again to create order in this once mighty state. The man whom the German people were seeking, emerged in the person of Adolf Hitler. . . . On the economic front Hitler and his Nazis carried out all their promises. Without using force or alienating important people, they achieved a large measure of success with their reforms." The same textbook defended Germany as "the only real bulwark against Communism," explaining that Nazism had played a key role in combating the "communist menace." Together with "the ingenious Goebbels," Hitler's main objective was simply "to unite all Germans inside Germany in the interest of the state." Such depictions resonated clearly with the apartheid regime's political priorities and anticommunism. While antisemitism was mentioned, its significance was understated, to say the least: according to one textbook, for example, "the persecution of the Jews" created an image of the Führer and his party that was "unfavourable."[50] Other textbooks discussed the Nazi Party's "impressive policy programme," Germany's "remarkable revival" under the Nazis, and the development of the air force "by the ingenuity of Goering into the strongest in the world."[51] In explaining Hitler's wide appeal, some textbooks stressed that he "gave the Germans something they wanted and in return they were prepared to sacrifice their democratic rights and to ignore the persecution of the Jews."[52] *Mein Kampf* was described as "one of the best-read books in Germany," the "textbook" and the "Bible" of the Nazi movement, "of great value as it explains [Hitler's] programme and ideas."[53]

While contemporary audiences might expect such bias during the apartheid period, however, it was not widespread. Most interpretations of Nazism in the textbooks were more balanced. Detailed descriptions were given of the Nazi Party's virtual omnipotence in Germany, the suppression of democracy and personal freedoms, the control of society at all levels, and the widespread use of violence and terror.[54] While some textbooks stressed the legal means by which the National Socialist German Workers' Party gained power,[55] most emphasized the Nazis' "ruthless use of violence and intimidation" and their "policy of terrorizing all opponents into submission"; "indeed, in their violence they did not scruple at murder."[56] Fascist Italy and Nazi Germany were presented as prime examples of the "mighty totalitarian state," and the connection between Hitler and Mussolini was reinforced through the use of cartoons and photographs depicting the two leaders.[57] Totalitarianism as a political system was the subject of unguarded censure.

There were also many critical portrayals of Nazi leaders. Hitler achieved his aims by "the most unscrupulous means," and his foreign policy successes only "encouraged his arrogance."[58] Movements such as Nazism "were led by men who had never fitted into a peaceful, ordered society," and their audiences were "hypnotized into uncritical acceptance of views expressed by hysterical orators."[59] Hitler was repeatedly depicted as the chief protagonist of Nazi Germany. "The history of National Socialism," proclaimed one popular 1965 textbook, "is the history of one man."[60] The vast majority of textbooks reinforced this claim, devoting many pages to the rise of Hitler and the Nazi Party and providing detailed accounts of Hitler's biography.[61] Other individuals were mentioned, including Goebbels, Goering, Himmler, and Hess, but they received at most a line or two of text.[62] Sympathetic portrayals of these figures tended to come from Afrikaans-speaking authors rather than English-speaking ones, but this was not always the case.

The emphasis on totalitarianism was sometimes used to differentiate between Nazi Germany and contemporary South Africa, as in this excerpt from a 1952 publication: "Governments may take different forms. In some cases the supreme power is centered in one man (a dictator). This was the case in Germany during the time of Hitler. In South Africa the constitution is a democratic one. That is to say the persons who govern are chosen by the people of the land, and they only remain in office if their actions meet with the approval of the majority of the people."[63] Such pointed comparisons were not frequently made, but the widespread portrayal of Nazism as the product (at least in part) of the failure of democracy came with the implicit suggestion that South Africa, in line with most of the postwar world, had chosen a different course. Indeed, history syllabi consistently included sections on South African governance, stressing its basis "on the Westminster system."[64]

There are other ways in which apartheid-era textbooks do not conform to contemporary assumptions. Present-day observers often presume that apartheid ideologues, including educators, would have avoided discussion of Nazism because of the obvious links that would have been drawn with South African racism. However, many textbooks from throughout the apartheid period contain extensive discussion of Nazi "racialism" and "racial superiority." References were regularly made, for example, to the *Herrenvolk*, or "master race." Describing the training of youth in Nazi ideology, one 1957 textbook explained that "the Herrenvolk ideal was brought home to them, namely, that the German nation, as an Aryan race, was superior to others, and consequently had to be purified of its non-Aryan elements, especially the Semites."[65] Many textbooks similarly described Nazi theories of the "absolute superiority of the Aryan race."[66] In a section titled "Racial Intolerance," a popular 1959 textbook described the Nazis' "doctrine of racial superiority," citing the influences of Arthur de Gobineau and Houston Stewart Chamberlain on Hitler's thinking.[67] "The Herrenvolk (master race) outlook was assiduously fostered," wrote another 1980 textbook, "the proposition being that the Germans, being of Aryan stock, were a superior people and must therefore be purified of non-Aryan elements, especially the Jews."[68] It was made clear that the "pseudo-scientific theories" on which these ideas were based "are not supported by the conclusions of biology and ethnology."[69]

The textbooks also make little attempt to sidestep the murderous consequences of Nazi ideology, offering open descriptions of the persecution of and genocide against the Jews. In a section titled "The Persecution of the Jews," a popular 1965 textbook noted:

> One of the most reprehensible features of the Nazi ideology was the so-called *race theory*. The Nazis were firmly convinced of the superiority of the so-called Aryan race, to which the Germans also belonged. The Aryan race was destined to rule over the inferior races, such as the Slavs. The purity of the race had to be maintained at all costs, i.e. there was to be no miscegenation with inferior races. And according to them the Jews were the most inferior. That was one of the reasons for the *persecution of the Jews* which was a feature of the Nazi regime in Germany. But there were others too. Hitler himself was obsessed with hatred for the Jews. From the beginning of his career as party leader in Munich until he committed suicide in a bomb shelter in Berlin in 1945, he railed against the Jews. He held them responsible for all the calamities which had befallen Germany, and international Jewry for all the ills in the world. Wars, Communism, democracy, international capitalism—everything that he was opposed to he sooner or later attributed to the Jews, and he felt himself called upon to exterminate the Jewish race.[70]

Today, the phase of Nazism most frequently likened to apartheid is the pre-war period (1933–39), with its antisemitic prohibitions on interracial sexual relations and marriage ("miscegenation with inferior races"), denial of citizenship rights, and segregated facilities. Again, such subjects were openly covered in many textbooks, with no implication that they were particularly sensitive or controversial. Indeed, textbooks included straightforward and sometimes lengthy descriptions of the "terrible persecution of the Jews." In a section titled "Antisemitism and Treatment of the Jews," one 1976 textbook explained:

> It should be noted that the Jews were not persecuted because of their religion but on account of their race. Various discriminatory laws were passed and persecution increased as Goebbels' propaganda machine stirred up feeling against these people. In April 1933 Jews were dismissed from posts in government service and the universities. Under the Nuremberg Laws (1935), Jews were deprived of citizenship rights and they were forbidden to marry non-Jews. After an incident in Paris in 1938 a pogrom was carried out under the direction of the S.S. The greater part of Jewish property was confiscated and these people had to live in restricted areas. The Jews were debarred from most professions and their business concerns were boycotted.[71]

How is it possible that apartheid-era textbooks could address such issues so dispassionately? A key reason is that apartheid conceived of itself in fundamentally different terms: not as a racist regime but instead as one dedicated to the "separate but equal" development of its racial groups. Deborah Posel rejects the idea that this position was merely a strategic one, calculated to give a veneer of respectability to biological racism in the aftermath of Nazism. While there were some in Afrikaner nationalist circles who insisted that "race" was determined by blood, this was not the understanding of race implemented in apartheid legislation. Instead, race was understood as a mix of biology, class, and culture, something that could be determined using "common sense," on the basis of a person's social habits, education, speech, and "demeanour in general."[72] Apartheid's solution to the fundamental "incompatibility between African nationalism and the European personality" was to allow South Africa's racial groups—each with their own distinctive and much-vaunted cultures, heritages, languages, and nationalisms—to develop autonomously.[73] Such formulations help explain why descriptions of Nazism generated hardly a glimmer of recognition.

After 1994, the topic of "bystanders" became a key medium for emphasizing individual responsibility in the "new" South Africa, in implicit contrast with the "old." In the apartheid-era textbooks, however, the widespread involvement of ordinary Germans in discriminatory behavior was openly and quite neutrally discussed:

> The German people took an active part in the persecution of the Jews which the Government launched in 1933. First the Jews were excluded from State offices, the legal and medical professions, education and cultural activities. The Nuremberg Laws of 1935 deprived Jews of German citizenship, and prohibited marriages between Jews and Germans or the employment of Germans by Jews. Jews could leave the country, but could not take their money or possessions with them. Hundreds of thousands preferred to flee; those who remained were subjected to increasing discrimination and persecution. The murder of a German diplomat in Paris by a Jewish youth in 1938 led to an organized reign of terror directed against the Jews in Germany in which their possessions, houses and synagogues and shops were looted and destroyed.[74]

In addition to racial ideology and prewar persecution, both English- and Afrikaans-language textbooks also covered wartime persecution and genocide. There were frequent references to concentration camps and their victims, not only Jews but also clergy and, above all, communists (a reflection of the apartheid government's fierce anticommunism).[75] There were explicit descriptions of the "systematic extermination of the Jewish race" and "six million Jews [who] were shot or gassed during the war."[76] Accompanying images unambiguously depicted the mass murder of the Jews at the hands of the Nazis.[77]

While a handful of textbooks were blatantly biased, as I have suggested, many advocated history study as a tool for critical thinking and informed citizenship. One of the aims of history education, affirmed a 1979 examination handbook, is to "[foster] an appreciation of such fundamental values as justice, liberty, truth and integrity" and to make the pupil "aware of his privileges and duties as a citizen."[78] Rather than simply memorizing information, insisted a 1961 textbook, students should be educated "to take a wider and more intelligent interest in the study of current problems and establish for themselves the reasons for the existence of divergent opinions."[79] "The point of history is not just to learn facts," wrote another 1965 textbook. "The point is to encourage thinking among pupils. By teaching [the pupil] to associate critically with the events of the past he will resist hasty or superficial verdicts. He will cultivate considered opinions—the highest fruit of historical education. This includes tolerant and cautious reflection on the realities of the past. Reflection brings about, of its own accord, a critical attitude."[80] Of course, there is often a gap between statement and reality. Examiners' reports from the 1960s to the 1980s made clear that rote learning for history exams was a long-standing problem, fueled in part by the huge span of the syllabus.[81] At the same time, these ideas cannot simply be dismissed as empty or disingenuous. The textbooks offer few reasons to doubt that those writing at the time were sincere in their views about the value of history for critical thinking; indeed, some educators went to great lengths to demonstrate their commitment to this ideal.[82]

For at least three decades, then, the Nazi past was an integral part of a curriculum aimed at cultivating thoughtful, informed citizens. While a few textbooks expressed sympathy for Nazism, the vast majority provided unguarded descriptions of Nazi racism and its consequences. There were few indications that this history bore any particular relevance for apartheid South Africa.

THE POST-APARTHEID PERIOD

The revised post-apartheid curriculum billed itself as a human rights curriculum, one that "seeks to promote human rights, inclusivity, environmental and social justice,"[83] informed by the "values of our Constitution."[84] Teaching was designed to give voice to the marginalized, to encourage learners to think critically, and to instill in them a sense of agency and informed citizenship.[85] The adoption of human rights education was influenced by alternative anti-apartheid educational initiatives that had been developed in the 1980s, as well as by the growth of international trends. As two key stakeholders note, "There is no doubt that South Africa's re-birth [in 1994] into a world of human rights treaties, conventions and declarations impacted on the trajectory of human rights infusion into the curriculum."[86]

The decision in the 1990s to include the Holocaust in the curriculum was closely linked to the post-apartheid agenda of promoting democracy and non-racialism. The revised curricula first introduced Nazism in Grade 9, the last school year in which history is a compulsory subject, in a unit titled "Human Rights Issues during and after World War II." While the curricula provided only brief topic outlines, with no specifications for timing or measurement of progress, the arrangement of subjects and brief interpretive suggestions made clear the linkage among the Holocaust, apartheid, and other racially based violations of human rights. Guiding questions included "how the Nazis used [Aryan] 'identity' to define and exclude others," "how and why the Holocaust happened," and "what choices people had in Nazi Germany." Subsequent units considered the "struggle for human rights" after World War II, including the American civil rights movement and anti-colonial struggles, and "[a]partheid in South Africa." A section on "dealing with crimes against humanity" explicitly compared the South African Truth and Reconciliation Commission to the Nuremberg Trials.[87]

Learners who chose to continue with history as a subject for matric (the school-leaving certificate) encountered Nazism for a second time in Grade 11. Here, again, the focus on racism explicitly linked the Holocaust with apartheid and other historical examples. Topics in the first part of that year included colonialism in Africa and Asia and its impact on ideas of "race" and racism. Nazism then appeared in the context of the Great Depression and the emergence of fascism and, subsequently, in a unit on "the impact of pseudo-scientific racism and Social Darwinism on the nineteenth and twentieth centuries," including the impact of eugenics on racism in Africa, the United States, Australia, and Europe "and particularly leading to genocide in Nazi Germany." The following Grade 11 unit considered conceptions of race under apartheid and its relationship to other neocolonial movements in the postwar world.[88]

In the most recent revised curricula, the words *race*, *racism*, and *human rights* no longer appear in connection with Nazism, but the arrangement of topics continues to make an implicit linkage between the Holocaust and apartheid based on racism. In Grade 9, the first term of the year is devoted to "World War II (1919–45)," with Nazi Germany and the Holocaust allocated ten of twelve content hours. Topics listed for study include the failure of Weimar democracy and rise of Nazism, the Nazis' aggressive foreign policy, "Nazi Germany as an example of a fascist state (compared with democracy)," the Nuremberg Laws "and loss of basic rights of Jewish people," the fates of other persecuted minorities, and the Nazi genocide. Subsequent sections focus on the "Universal Declaration of Human Rights after World War II," definitions of racism and apartheid South Africa.[89] In Grade 11, Nazism again appears as a case study—"Ideas of Race in the late C19th and C20th"—followed by examination of nationalisms in Africa and apartheid. This syllabus explicitly states that the topics are connected.[90]

The textbooks usually provide historical context for the Holocaust in Grade 9 by describing World War I and the Treaty of Versailles, the rise of the Nazis, the Weimar Republic and the Depression. Nazi foreign policy before 1939 and the military progress of World War II are usually covered quite briefly.[91] Compared with apartheid-era textbooks, there is more extensive focus on the Holocaust. Details about anti-Jewish actions in the prewar period are followed by discussion of the "euthanasia" program, the ghettoization of Eastern European Jewry, mobile killing units in the Soviet Union, and the death camps, sometimes in graphic detail. Extensive sections are also devoted to the topics of resistance and rescue, with emphasis on the Warsaw Ghetto uprising and on victims' responses in the ghettos and camps.[92] There is a focus on the wide range of victim groups targeted by the Nazis, which included Jews as well as political opponents, Roma and Sinti, Jehovah's Witnesses, homosexuals, Slavs, black people, and people with physical or mental disabilities. Very little background is provided about Jewish life before 1933 or after 1945.[93]

Many post-2000 textbooks focus on Nazi Germany as a fascist or totalitarian state that is highly militaristic and exercises complete control over its population, an emphasis that closely mirrors that of apartheid-era texts. "The Nazi totalitarian government had total control over men, women, youth, newspapers, radio, art, books, music, universities, schools, police, army, law courts and religion," writes one publication. "In other words, they controlled every aspect of life in Germany."[94] In the post-apartheid textbooks, however, there is an added emphasis on the individual's obligation to resist such repressive regimes. Obedient and unquestioning German children are a foil for thoughtful, questioning South African ones. "Not all German people supported the Nazis," states one textbook. "But most were too scared to openly criticise or oppose them. Most people just closed their eyes and minds to what was happening. It was easier not to know."[95] Another textbook is more explicit about why learners should study the subject:

> One reason that genocide occurs could be the complicity of bystanders within the nation and around the world. Probably the vast majority of people in a society such as Nazi Germany were bystanders—they stood by and did nothing. At some point, some of them became perpetrators and others became resisters or rescuers. It is important to try to understand what makes a bystander choose to go one way or another. The Nazis carried out their murderous activities with the active help of local collaborators in many countries, and the indifference of millions of bystanders. Bystanders, just by being passive witnesses, affirm the actions of the perpetrators—they allow them to carry on.[96]

As this example makes clear, the post-apartheid textbooks focus not only on content but also on cultivating "an active and critical approach to learning, rather than rote and uncritical learning of given truths," in line with the aims of the curriculum.[97] The emphasis on bystanders highlights questions of individual choice and responsibility and is often accompanied by discussion of the wide range of people involved in the Nazis' crimes.[98] There are also frequently sections on those who courageously resisted the Nazis, including Sophie Scholl and the White Rose movement, and the Confessing Church.[99]

The chief explanatory factor given for the Holocaust is racist ideology, an emphasis that again echoes apartheid-era textbooks. "The Holocaust was a frighteningly clinical and cold-blooded exhibition of racism," declares one 2010 textbook.[100] "Nazis believed that Germans belonged to the Aryan race, a superior or 'master race,'" asserts another. "They thought others, especially Jewish people, were inferior. Hitler blamed the Jews for much of what was wrong in Germany."[101] A third textbook states:

> Hitler believed that great, large, pure "races" were great nations, and had to be preserved for good health, necessary militaristic aggression and superior intelligence to become the master race and nation in the world. The weakest nations would be those "mongrel races" who were mixed, impure, with "poor inferior cultures" and "poor intelligence." The worst group were [sic] believed to be the Jewish people who were "parasitic" and the "impure" gypsies, homosexuals and disabled. Called *untermensch* [sic] or "subhumans," Hitler saw them all as deficient and inferior in some way, and wanted to wipe them out by force.[102]

The key difference from apartheid-era textbooks is that racism is not limited to the Nazis but is presented as a universal malaise, manifest in behaviors ranging from stereotyping all the way through to genocide—and, crucially, linked to apartheid. One textbook places the Holocaust on a continuum of racial ideas stretching from the early classification of humans in the eighteenth century, through German colonialism in South and West Africa in the twentieth century, and the Human Genome Project in the twenty-first.[103] Grade 11 textbooks explore scientific racism and its many consequences, including eugenics, colonialism, and Jim Crow.[104] Some texts emphasize the concept of antisemitism and the Nazis' particular targeting of Jews, but antisemitism is presented as an instance of racism rather than a distinct phenomenon.[105]

Racism is thus an umbrella concept for discussing a range of related examples. One Grade 11 textbook, for example, states:

> As one would expect pseudo-scientific theories shaped the racial policies of many countries across the globe. In some instances the idea of white supremacy was carried to extreme levels which was to have grave consequences as was evident in the following cases: The rise of Nazism in Germany; The racist activities of the Ku Klux Klan in the USA; The destruction of the Aborigines culture in Australia; The detribalization of African societies as a result of colonialism and racism.[106]

Here, Nazism is misleadingly portrayed as an example of "white supremacy." In another 2006 example, it is described as "institutionalized racism" and explicitly linked with apartheid:

> Communities of people who practise racism engage in "institutionalized racism" such as the system of apartheid in South Africa and the anti-Semitic policies in Nazi Germany. The supporters of both these political systems believed that one group of people were inherently superior to another. Therefore, they ruled and oppressed the group of people they perceived to be the "problem." In Nazi Germany the Nazis annihilated the Jewish people. Today international conventions outlaw racist policies and racism. They have declared apartheid and the Holocaust in Nazi Germany crimes against humanity.[107]

Despite the fundamental differences between the two systems, many textbooks present similar comparisons, emphasizing that the difference between the various examples offered is one of degree only: "Were Hitler's ideas any different from ideas expressed in the USA and Australia? No, they weren't different. What was the difference between how Nazi Germany applied eugenics and how other countries applied it? The difference is one of scale. Hitler became a dictator and used the resources and power of the German state to apply these ideas practically to millions of people. Nothing was attempted in the USA and Australia on the same scale."[108] In these and other examples, diverse instances of racism are thus subsumed under a single category of explanation, with little analysis of their distinct historical contexts. The Holocaust simply represents the nadir of racist ideas and practices.

Human rights is a key organizing concept in most textbooks. One 2006 text, for example, anachronistically describes extermination camps and genocide as instances of "the gross violation of Human Rights"[109] and portrays the persecution of German Jews as follows: "Laws were passed by the Nazis called the Nuremburg [sic] Laws. These laws took away all the human rights of Jews. They were not allowed to go to German schools or universities, use sporting facilities, sit on park benches or run businesses."[110]

"The Nazis solved some problems," maintains another textbook, "but they turned Germany into a police state with no respect for human rights."[111]

Human rights and social justice are also the subject of many questions and activities for learners, in line with the curriculum's stated goals. For example, alongside descriptions of Nazi "euthanasia" and genocide in one 2009 textbook is a "Topic for Discussion" box, which states: "In the new South African history curriculum, there is an emphasis on teaching values, such as respect for democracy, equality, human dignity and social justice. Why are these sorts of values particularly important in a country like South Africa? How would you respond to people who said that learning scientific or technical skills is more important?"[112] The placement of the box clearly encourages learners to recognize the relevance of studying the Holocaust in post-apartheid South Africa. Similarly, a unit on Nazi propaganda in another text asserts that "it is an important life skill to learn to think critically, and to make up your own mind about things. In a democratic society we have the opportunity to make up your [sic] own minds!"[113]

The pedagogical emphasis on individual choices and responsibility is a product of the immediate post-apartheid agenda of reconciliation and nation building.[114] Many of the textbooks are explicit in embracing this agenda. "How have white South Africans explained their involvement in apartheid?" asks one. "Are there any similarities to the German explanation about the extent of their involvement in the extermination of the Jews?"[115] Another suggests the following activity: "How can we try to ensure that there will never be another Holocaust? Work in groups. Discuss what you think is needed to ensure that atrocities such as the Holocaust are prevented. Consider what ordinary people, civil society organisations and governments can do."[116] In all these examples, study of the Nazi past is unambiguously linked with post-apartheid South Africa and conceived as an instructive means through which to promote its democratic values and responsibilities.

Conclusion

As the preceding overview has demonstrated, Nazism has been a subject of formal education in South Africa for many decades. There have been marked changes over time as to which aspects of the topic are taught and how they are explained, but these changes do not always correspond with political shifts in the ways that we might assume.

There are some obvious differences in syllabi and textbooks published across the seven decades surveyed in this chapter. Apartheid-era history syllabi tend to focus more straightforwardly on factual content than do more recent ones, which emphasize critical thought and applied skills. In keeping with these aims, textbooks published in the last decade include many more activities and questions than the earlier textbooks. These activities are presented in visually engaging boxes alongside maps, images, and other material intended to sustain learners' attention, and the language used is often simpler. By contrast, the older textbooks are more traditional linear accounts, with dense and sometimes complex passages of text, sparse illustrations, and very little in the way of participatory content. The Holocaust specifically is allocated far more space in post-apartheid textbooks than it was previously, and it is presented within an unambiguous framework of human rights.

However, there are also significant continuities. From as early as the 1950s, Nazi Germany has been presented in South African textbooks as a totalitarian state that exercised absolute control over its population. Post-2000 textbooks are distinct from earlier ones in situating their narratives within the framework of human rights and encouraging learners to respond actively to social injustice, but across the apartheid and post-apartheid periods Nazi Germany is portrayed as an example of a failed democracy, implicitly or explicitly in contrast with South Africa.

Nazism is also consistently described using the language of racism, with a focus on its belief in a superior "master race" and rejection of inferior groups. There are few attempts to gloss over the murderous consequences of its racial ideology, even in the apartheid-era textbooks. The Nazi Party itself is presented as a nationalist, fervently anticommunist party promising to restore German pride after the humiliation of Versailles. Across both periods, textbooks tend to devote between eighteen and thirty pages to the subject, with the focus shifting from Nazi foreign policy in earlier textbooks to the Holocaust in more recent ones.

There are also intriguing resonances in the articulation of pedagogical aims. Although definitions of critical thinking and citizenship have shifted considerably since the 1950s, across both periods students are consistently encouraged to think for themselves, to evaluate sources critically, and to develop informed attitudes and interpretations. The texts themselves do not necessarily do much to facilitate these aims, however, and most have serious limitations in this regard.

In apartheid-era textbooks, there is hardly a hint of a connection between the Holocaust and apartheid. Nazi Germany is openly portrayed as a racist, totalitarian state, and where links are made with the local context, they serve to affirm South Africa's democratic order rather than to recognize possible parallels. The widespread coverage of the subject in apartheid-era textbooks, and particularly the explicit emphasis on racism, suggests that rather than links being denied, they were more likely not made in the first place and that apartheid notions of "separate development" firmly distinguished it from Nazi racism.

In the post-apartheid curricula, by contrast, the connections between Nazism, apartheid and a range of other distinct examples boil down to a single explanatory factor: racial ideology. Such simplistic analogies obscure the fact that race is only one of a number of factors that explain the complex origins and nature of both apartheid and the "Final Solution."[117] In addition, they discourage learners from considering the myriad factors that lead people to act in particular ways in different places and times. To be sure, the various examples of racism covered in the textbooks have some common features. Authors also have the added challenge of conveying complicated ideas in a limited space to often poorly educated audiences. Nonetheless, if critical thinking and active citizenship are the ultimate pedagogical aims, such reductive portrayals not only are inaccurate but also potentially hinder learners' ability to understand the complicated historical contexts within which racism originates and within which individual responses are fashioned.

While shifts in Holocaust education in South Africa have been shaped in part by the local political context, they have also been considerably informed by international trends. For several decades after 1945, the Holocaust was considered an aspect of World War II rather than a subject to be studied and taught in its own right. In early scholarship, the framework within which Nazism was analyzed was primarily that of totalitarianism.[118] It was only in the late 1970s and '80s that both historiography and pedagogy began to develop significantly. The focus in apartheid-era textbooks on totalitarianism, political events, and foreign policy thus reflects the state of the broader historiography, perhaps more than it suggests an attempt by the apartheid government to downplay racism and its consequences.[119] Indeed, the historiography of apartheid placed relatively little focus on "race" and racism until after the collapse of apartheid. Similarly, the increasing shift toward human rights and democratic values in Holocaust education has been evident in many countries since the end of the Cold War, which was also, not coincidentally, a significant factor in apartheid's demise.[120]

In sum, apartheid-era education about the Nazi past cannot simply be characterized as an ideologically driven refusal to recognize "obvious" links, in the same way that post-apartheid education cannot accurately be described as critical engagement with racism as a historical phenomenon.[121] The explanations for both are more complex and ambiguous, as are their implications. What they do demonstrate unequivocally, however, is that the assumption that Holocaust education can help eradicate racism and promote tolerance is a naive one and that a great deal more work is needed to devise educational strategies that are historically informed and, ultimately, effective.

Notes

My thanks to Chana Teeger, Milton Shain, Chaya Herman, and Sarah Phillips Casteel for their helpful comments on earlier drafts of this chapter.

1. See, among others, Annie E. Coombes, *History after Apartheid: Visual Culture and Public Memory in a Democratic South Africa* (Durham, NC: Duke University Press, 2003); Shirli Gilbert, "Anne Frank in South Africa: Remembering the Holocaust during and after Apartheid," *Holocaust and Genocide Studies* 26, no. 3 (2012): 366–93; Shirli Gilbert, "Jews and the Racial State: Legacies of the Holocaust in Apartheid South Africa, 1945–60," *Jewish Social Studies* 16, no. 3 (2010): 32–64; and Roni Mikel-Arieli, "Holocaust Memory in South Africa during Apartheid and in its Aftermath" (PhD diss., Hebrew University, Jerusalem, 2018).
2. Throughout the chapter, I have used contemporary terminology to describe pupils (apartheid era) and learners (post-apartheid).
3. See, for example, "Anne Frank Room Opens at Holocaust Centre," *Berea News*, November 14, 2008; and Zohra Mohamed, "Reality Checkpoint, *Financial Mail*, November 20, 2008.

4. Katalin Morgan, "From Auschwitz to Apartheid: Conceptual Representations in History Textbooks," *Education as Change* 16, no. 1 (2012): 3–20, esp. 7.
5. Shirli Gilbert, "Jews and the Racial State: Legacies of the Holocaust in Apartheid South Africa, 1945–60," *Jewish Social Studies* 16, no. 3 (2010): 32–64.
6. See, for example, Brian Bunting, *The Rise of the South African Reich* (Middlesex, UK: Penguin, 1964); and Sipo E. Mzimela, *Apartheid: South African Naziism*, 1st ed. (Nairobi: Evangel Publishing House, 1983).
7. Hermann Giliomee, "The Making of the Apartheid Plan, 1929–1948," *Journal of Southern African Studies* 29, no. 2 (2003): 373–92; and Heribert Adam, "Antisemitism and Anti-Black Racism: Nazi Germany and Apartheid South Africa," in *The Holocaust's Ghost: Writings on Art, Politics, Law and Education*, ed. F. C. DeCoste and Bernard Schwartz (Edmonton: University of Alberta Press, 2000), 244–59.
8. Lionel Abrahams, *The Democratic Chorus and Individual Choice*, Alfred and Winifred Hoernlé 37th Memorial Lecture (Johannesburg: South African Institute of Race Relations, 1996).
9. Kader Asmal, Louise Asmal, and Ronald Suresh Roberts, eds., *Reconciliation through Truth: A Reckoning of Apartheid's Criminal Governance* (Cape Town: David Philip, 1996). For a more extensive literature review, see the preface to Patrick J. Furlong, *Between Crown and Swastika: The Impact of the Radical Right on the Afrikaner Nationalist Movement in the Fascist Era* (Middletown, CT: Wesleyan University Press, 1991). See also Shirli Gilbert, "Remembering the Racial State: Holocaust Memory in Post-Apartheid South Africa," in *Holocaust Memory in a Globalizing World*, ed. Jacob S. Eder, Philipp Gassert, and Alan E. Steinweis (Göttingen, Germany: Wallstein, 2017), 199–214.
10. Deborah Posel, "What's in a Name? Racial Categorisations under Apartheid and Their Afterlife," *Transformation* 47 (2001): 53.
11. Leonard Thompson, *The Political Mythology of Apartheid* (New Haven, CT: Yale University Press, 1985), 60.
12. Patricia Bromley and Susan Garnett Russell, "The Holocaust as History and Human Rights: A Cross-National Analysis of Holocaust Education in Social Science Textbooks, 1970–2008," in *As the Witnesses Fall Silent: 21st Century Holocaust Education in Curriculum, Policy and Practice*, ed. Zehavit Gross and E. Doyle Stevick (New York: Springer, 2015), 300, 308, 312–13.
13. Avril Alba, "Holocaust History and Ethics Education: Teaching at the Crossroads," in *The Wiley-Blackwell Companion to the Holocaust*, ed. Simone Gigliotti and Hilary Earl (Hoboken, NJ: Wiley Blackwell, 2017). There is a large body of

scholarship on Holocaust education. For a helpful overview of recent international trends, see Peter Carrier, Eckhardt Fuchs, and Torben Messinger, *The International Status of Education about the Holocaust: A Global Mapping of Textbooks and Curricula* (Paris: UNESCO, 2015); Bryan L. Davis and Eliane Rubinstein-Avila, "Holocaust Education: Global Forces Shaping Curricula Integration and Implementation," *Intercultural Education* 24, nos. 1–2 (2013): 149–66.

14. Zehavit Gross and E. Doyle Stevick, "Introduction," in Gross and Stevick, *As the Witnesses Fall Silent*, 3–5. On the Holocaust and human rights education, see, among others, Bromley and Russell, "Holocaust as History and Human Rights"; Bruce Carrington and Geoffrey Short, "Holocaust Education, Anti-racism and Citizenship," *Educational Review* 49, no. 3 (1997): 271–82; P. Cowan, and H. Maitles, "Does Addressing Prejudice and Discrimination through Holocaust Education Produce Better Citizens?" *Educational Review* 59, no. 2 (2007): 115–30; William R. Fernekes, "Developing Reflective Citizens: The Role of Holocaust Education." *Internationale Schulbuchforschung* 22, no. 1 (2000): 73–88; Henry Maitles, Paula Cowan, and Eamonn Butler, "Never Again!: Does Holocaust Education Have an Effect on Pupils' Citizenship Values and Attitudes?" Scottish Executive Education Department, Edinburgh, September 2006; Anja Mihr, "Why Holocaust Education Is Not Always Human Rights Education," *Journal of Human Rights* 14, no. 4 (2015): 525–44; Alice Pettigrew, "Limited Lessons from the Holocaust? Critically Considering the 'Anti-Racist' and Citizenship Potential," *Teaching History*, 141 (2010): 50–55; Paul Salmons, "Universal Meaning or Historical Understanding? The Holocaust in History and History in the Curriculum," *Teaching History*, 141 (2010): 57–63. For the South African context, see Tracey Petersen, "Moving beyond the Toolbox: Teaching Human Rights through Teaching the Holocaust in Post-Apartheid South Africa," *Intercultural Education* 21, suppl. S1 (2010): S27–S33; Tracey Petersen, "Holocaust Education in Post-Apartheid South Africa—Impetus for Social Activism or a Short-Lived Catharsis?" (paper presented at Museums Fighting for Human Rights conference, Liverpool, September 2010); Tracey Petersen, "Teaching Humanity: Placing the Cape Town Holocaust Centre in a Post-Apartheid State" (PhD diss., University of the Western Cape, Cape Town, 2015), etd.uwc.ac.za/xmlui/handle/11394/5033; and Sofie Geschier, "Beyond Experience: The Mediation of Traumatic Memories in South African History Museums," *Transformation: Critical Perspectives on Southern Africa* 59 (2005): 45–65.

15. Monique Eckmann, "Is Teaching and Learning about the Holocaust Relevant for Human Rights Education?" in Gross and Stevick, *As the Witnesses Fall Silent*, 53–65.

16. There are many additional educational initiatives and developments that lie beyond the scope of this chapter. In the Jewish community, for example, education began in the 1950s in connection with commemorative initiatives, although it was only in the 1980s that schools began to institute formal Holocaust education. There were other Jewish initiatives as well, including the work of the Yad Vashem Foundation, the Student Holocaust Interviewing Project begun in 1981 under the auspices of the South African Union of Jewish Students, and many others. The Holocaust also featured in educational work beyond the Jewish community, including in Afrikaans schools. Alternative educational initiatives under apartheid, such as the African Night School Movement and the African Education Movement, did not engage substantially with the Holocaust for various reasons, although the subject is not entirely absent. The decades since the end of apartheid have seen an explosion of educational initiatives beyond state-funded education, including the Foundation for Tolerance Education, Shikaya, various high-profile international exhibitions, and in particular the South African Holocaust and Genocide Foundation. Many of these initiatives have close links with international organizations such as the United Nations, UNESCO, Facing History and Ourselves, and Yad Vashem.
17. Stuart J. Foster and Keith A. Crawford, eds., *What Shall We Tell the Children? International Perspectives on School History Textbooks* (Greenwich, CT: Information Age, 2006).
18. Jonathan D. Jansen, "Curriculum as a Political Phenomenon: Historical Reflections on Black South African Education," *Journal of Negro Education* 59, no. 2 (1990): 196; Ryôta Nishino, "Political Economy of History Textbook Publishing during Apartheid (1948–1994): Towards Further Historical Enquiry into Commercial Imperatives," *Yesterday & Today* 14 (December 2015): 2; and Gail Weldon, "A Comparative Study of the Construction of Memory and Identity in the Curriculum in Societies Emerging from Conflict: Rwanda and South Africa" (PhD diss., University of Pretoria, 2009), 35.
19. R. E. Chernis, "The Past in Service of the Present: A Study of South African School History Syllabuses and Textbooks, 1839–1990" (PhD diss., University of Pretoria, 1990), 29.
20. Linda Chisholm, "Migration, Citizenship and South African History Textbooks," *South African Historical Journal* 60, no. 3 (2008): 354–56; and Lynn Maree, "The Hearts and Minds of the People," in *Apartheid and Education: The Education of Black South Africans*, ed. Peter Kallaway (Johannesburg: Ravan Press, 1984), 148–59.

21. There is a small literature on the experiences of apartheid-era teachers: see, for example, Elizabeth De Villiers, *Walking the Tightrope: Recollections of a Schoolteacher in Soweto* (Johannesburg: Jonathan Ball, 1992); William Finnegan, *Crossing the Line: A Year in the Land of Apartheid*, 1st ed. (New York: Harper & Row, 1986); Alan Wieder, *Voices from Cape Town Classrooms: Oral Histories of Teachers Who Fought Apartheid*, History of Schools and Schooling 39 (New York: Peter Lang, 2003). On the post-apartheid period, see, for example, Chana Teeger, "'Both Sides of the Story' History Education in Post-Apartheid South Africa." *American Sociological Review* 80, no. 6 (2015): 1175–1200; and Chana Teeger, "Teaching Transformations: History Education and Race Relations in Post-Apartheid South Africa" (PhD diss., Harvard University, Cambridge, MA 2013).
22. Elizabeth Dean, Paul Hartmann, and May Katzen, eds., *History in Black and White: An Analysis of South African School History Textbooks* (Paris: UNESCO, 1983), 102; J. M. du Preez, *Africana Afrikaner: Master Symbols in South African School Textbooks* (Alberton, South Africa: Libranius Felicitas, 1983), 19; Rosemary B. Mulholland, "The Evolution of History Teaching in South Africa: Vol I and II" (master's thesis, University of the Witwatersrand, Johannesburg, 1981), 287; and Chernis, "The Past in Service of the Present," 42.
23. Weldon, "Comparative Study," 98.
24. Nishino, "Political Economy of History Textbook Publishing," 2–3. See also Rob Siebörger, "The Dynamics of History Textbook Production during South Africa's Educational Transformation," in Foster and Crawford, *What Shall We Tell the Children?*, 227–43; and Melanie Walker, "History and History Teaching in Apartheid South Africa," in *History from South Africa: Alternative Visions and Practices*, ed. Joshua Brown, Patrick Manning, Karin Shapiro, Jon Wiener, Belinda Bozzoli, and Peter Delius (Philadelphia: Temple University Press, 1991), 268–76.
25. Sasha S. Polakow-Suransky, "Historical Amnesia? The Politics of Textbooks in Post-Apartheid South Africa" (paper presented at the annual meeting of the American Educational Research Association, New Orleans, LA, April 4, 2002), 2–3, files.eric.ed.gov/fulltext/ED466677.pdf, accessed March 2, 2016). See also *Report of the History/Archaeology Panel to the Minister of Education* (Pretoria: Ministry of Education, 2000).
26. On the textbook selection process, see Chisholm, "Migration, Citizenship and South African History Textbooks," 367–9; Rob Siebörger, "The Dilemmas of Textbook Selection: The Department of Education's 2007 Screening of Grade 12 History Textbooks: A Case Study," *Yesterday & Today* 14 (December 2015): 41–57. Current

textbook lists are found on the website of South Africa's Department of Basic Education, www.education.gov.za/Curriculum/LTSM/tabid/703/Default.aspx.

27. In addition to sources cited above, see Franz E. Auerbach, *The Power of Prejudice in South African Education: An Enquiry into History Textbooks and Syllabuses in the Transvaal High Schools of South Africa* (Cape Town: AA Balkema, 1965); Franz E. Auerbach, "Soos Ek Dit Sien—'N Antwoord Aan Prof. van Jaarsveld," *Historia* 7, no. 4 (1962): 228–30; Marianne Cornevin, *Apartheid: Power and Historical Falsification* (Paris: UNESCO, 1980); Thompson, *Political Mythology of Apartheid*, 46–64; Carol Bertram, and Johan Wassermann, "South African History Textbook Research—A Review of the Scholarly Literature," *Yesterday & Today* 14 (December 2015): 151–74; Jonathan Hyslop, *The Classroom Struggle: Policy and Resistance in South Africa, 1940-1990* (Pietermaritzburg, South Africa: University of Natal Press, 1999); Kallaway, *Apartheid and Education*; Peter Kallaway, ed. *The History of Education under Apartheid, 1948-1994: The Doors of Learning and Culture Shall Be Opened* (New York: Peter Lang, 2002); and Cynthia Kros, *The Seeds of Separate Development: Origins of Bantu Education* (Pretoria: Unisa Press, 2010).

28. In devising my research questions, I have drawn on several important studies, including Carrier, Fuchs, and Messinger, *International Status of Education about the Holocaust*; Falk Pingel, *UNESCO Guidebook on Textbook Research and Textbook Revision* (Paris: UNESCO, 2010).

29. I have compiled information about syllabi from the following sources: documents from the National Library of South Africa, the UNISA archives, and the National Archives (Pretoria); appendices in Mulholland, "Evolution of History Teaching in South Africa" and Chernis, "Past in Service of the Present"; and several of the textbooks cited in my study.

30. Jansen, "Curriculum as a Political Phenomenon," 201.

31. Penny Enslin, "The Role of Fundamental Pedagogics in the Formulation of Educational Policy in South Africa," in Kallaway, *Apartheid and Education*, 139–47; Weldon, "Comparative Study," 16; Mulholland, "Evolution of History Teaching in South Africa," 254–59; and Walker, "History and History Teaching in Apartheid South Africa," 270–76.

32. Weldon, "Comparative Study," 16–17. It should be stressed that the history of Bantu education is not a monolithic one. For a nuanced overview, see Elaine Unterhalter, "Changing Aspects of Reformism in Bantu Education 1953–89," in *Education in a Future South Africa: Policy Issues for Transformation*, ed. Elaine Unterhalter, Harold Wolpe, Thozamile Botha, Saleem Badat, Thulisile Dlamini, and Benito Khotseng (London: Zed Books, 1991), 35–72. See also Pam Christie

and Colin Collins, "Bantu Education: Apartheid Ideology and Labour Reproduction" in Kallaway, *Apartheid and Education*, 160–83; and Abraham Leslie Behr, *New Perspectives in South African Education: A Review of Education South Africa 1652–1984*, 2nd ed. (Durban, South Africa: Butterworths, 1984).

33. David Alexander Black, "Changing Perceptions of History Education in Black Secondary Schools, with Special Reference to Mpumalanga, 1948–2008" (master's thesis, University of South Africa, Pretoria, 2009), 68.

34. Black, "Changing Perceptions of History Education," 195–99; Shireen Motala and Salim Vally, "People's Education: From People's Power to Tirisano" in Kallaway, *Apartheid and Education*, 178; Weldon, "Comparative Study," 102–5; Leslie Witz, "A Brief Examination of the Development of People's History in South Africa, 1977–1988," *South Africa International* 19, no. 2 (1988): 90–95; and A. Wieder, "A Mother and Her Daughters: Jewish Teachers and the Fight against Apartheid," *Teachers College Record* 109, no. 5 (2007): 1235–60. On alternative education, see Adrienne Bird, "The Adult Night School Movements for Blacks on the Witwatersrand 1920–1980" in Kallaway, *Apartheid and Education*, 192–221; Luli Callinicos, "Popularising History in a Changing South Africa," *South African Historical Journal* 25, no. 1 (1991): 22–37; Melanie Walker and Ghaleeb Jeppie, *Reconstructing Schooling: A Survey of "Alternative" Curriculum Materials in South Africa* (Johannesburg: University of the Witwatersrand, Education Policy Unit,1991); and Seán Morrow, Brown Maaba, and Loyiso Pulumani, *Education in Exile: SOMAFCO, the ANC School in Tanzania, 1978–1992* (Cape Town: Human Sciences Research Council Press, 2004).

35. Jonathan Jansen, "Political Symbolism as Policy Craft: Explaining Non-Reform in South African Education after Apartheid," *Journal of Education Policy* 17, no. 2 (2002): 199, 203.

36. Rob Siebörger, "Dealing with a Reign of Virtue: The Post-Apartheid South African School History Curriculum," in *History Wars and the Classroom: Global Perspectives*, ed. Tony Taylor and Robert Guyver (Charlotte, NC: Information Age, 2012), 145–47; Weldon, "Comparative Study," 122–3, 134–40, 162–73; Linda Chisholm, "The History Curriculum in the (Revised) National Curriculum Statement: An Introduction," in *Towards "New" Histories for South Africa: On the Place of the Past in Our Present*, ed. Shamil Jeppie (Cape Town: University of Cape Town Press, 2004); Linda Chisholm, "The Making of South Africa's National Curriculum Statement," *Journal of Curriculum Studies* 37, no. 2 (2005): 193–208; Colin Bundy, "New Nation, New History? Constructing the Past in Post-Apartheid South Africa," in *History Making and Present Day Politics: The Meaning of Collective*

Memory in South Africa, ed. E. Stolten (Uppsala, Sweden: Nordisk Afrikainstitut, 2007); and Rob Siebörger and J. Reid, "Textbooks and the School History Curriculum," *South African Historical Journal* 33 (November 1995): 169–77.

37. Walker, "History and History Teaching in Apartheid South Africa," 273–74.
38. Mulholland, "Evolution of History Teaching in South Africa," 356.
39. Republic of South Africa, "Handbook: National Courses, Syllabuses and Examinations (Commercial, Art and General Subjects)," 1964, 199. The Transvaal Education Department removed Nazism from its syllabus in 1967, but the subject remained in the syllabi for all the other provinces; the 1972 TED syllabus again included Nazi Germany.
40. Department of Education, "Seniorsertifikaat: Geskiedenis Sillabus: Std 10 Hoër en Standaard Graad 1976," Pretoria; and Joint Matriculation Board, "Matriculation Examination Handbook for 1979, Part II: Syllabuses and Faculty Requirements," Pretoria, 1979, 300.
41. Joint Matriculation Board, "Core Syllabus for History Higher Grade Stds 8–10," Pretoria, 1983; and Transvaal Education Department, "Syllabus for History Standard Grade, Standards 8–10, Implementation Years 1985–7"; and Joint Matriculation Board, "Standard Ten Examination Requirements for History Higher Grade and Standard Grade," Pretoria, 1987.
42. Joint Matriculation Board, History Matriculation Examination papers, 1962–64, 1967–69, 1971–2, 1974–77, and 1979–92.
43. Leonard Schach notes that Anne Frank's *Diary* was prescribed reading in Afrikaans schools in the 1970s, but he was probably referring to the text's informal use in schools; I have found no evidence that it was included on the syllabus. Schach, *The Flag Is Flying: A Very Personal History of Theatre in the Old South Africa* (Cape Town: Human & Rousseau, 1996), 91–92.
44. Arnold Napier Boyce, *Europe and South Africa: A History of the Period 1815–1939* (Cape Town: Juta, 1959), 313, 328; A. G. Coetsee, J. C. Otto, and A. G. Roodt, *Geskiedenis Vir Die Senior Sertifikaat. Transvaalse Leerplan* (Cape Town: Nasionale Boekhandel Beperk, 1960), 399; Floris Albertus van Jaarsveld, and Theo van Wijk, *Illustrated History for Senior Certificate: Stds. IX and X, etc.*, 3rd ed. (Johannesburg: Voortrekkerpers, 1965), 218; and A. P. J. van Rensburg and F. S. G. Oosthuizen, *Active History, Std 9* (Pretoria: De Jager-Haum, 1986), 166.
45. A. P. J. van Rensburg and F. S. G. Oosthuizen, *Active History, Std 10* (Pretoria: De Jager-Haum, 1980), 34, 58; S. F. Malan, M. S. Appelgryn, and B. M. Theron, *New History to the Point Std 10* (Johannesburg: Educum, 1988), 79. Maps and cartoons were also often used in examination papers; see, for example, Joint Matriculation

Board, "Matriculation Examination History (Higher Grade)," Pretoria, March 1975, November/December 1976, November/December 1977, March 1978, November/December 1980, November/December 1981, March 1983, November/December 1984, November/December 1988, November/December 1991). See also *Educamus*, Government Printer, Pretoria, October 1988, 25.

46. See, for example, Joint Matriculation Board, "Examiners' Report on the Work of Candidates, Matriculation Examination November/December 1982," Pretoria, 1982, 29; Joint Matriculation Board, "Examiners' Report on the Work of Candidates, Matriculation Examination November/December 1988," Pretoria, 1988, 44.

47. C. de K. Fowler, and G. J. J. Smit, *History for the Natal Senior Certificate* (Cape Town: Maskew Miller, 1961), 358, 361; M. C. E. Van Schoor and J. J. Oberholster, *Geskiedenis Vir Die O.V.S.-Skooleindsertifikaat*, 3rd ed. (Cape Town: Nasou Beperk, 1962), 189; M. C. E. Van Schoor, A. G. Coetsee, H. A. Lambrechts, J. J. Oberholster, and K. J. Pienaar, *Senior History for South African Schools Standard 10* (Cape Town: Nasou, 1979), 66; and F. A. Van Jaarsveld, Nic Dreyer, B. J. Van der Merwe, and P. H. Kapp, *New Illustrated History Std. 7* (Johannesburg: Perskor, 1974), 56.

48. A. J. Böeseken, J. J. Oberholster, M. C. E. Van Schoor, and N. J. Olivier, *Geskiedenis Vir Die Senior Sertifikaat*. 2nd ed. (Cape Town: Nasionale Boekhandel Beperk, 1957), 276; Coetsee, Otto, and Roodt, *Geskiedenis Vir Die Senior Sertifikaat*, 407; and G. J. J. Smit, H. G. J. Lintvelt, T. A. Eckstein, and F. P. J. Smit, *History for Standard 10* (Cape Town: Maskew Miller, 1976), 52.

49. Franz Auerbach, "Different Pictures from a Common Past" (paper presented at a National Union of South African Students seminar on education, University of the Witwatersrand, June 5, 1962); Auerbach, *Power of Prejudice in South African Education*.

50. E. H. W. Lategan and A. J. De Kock, *History in Perspective, Standard 10* (Johannesburg: Perskor, 1978), 29–35.

51. S. P. Jordaan, A. Jordaan, and H. A. Mocke, *Exploring History Standard 10* (Pretoria: Via Afrika, 1995), 35; and A. J. Böeseken, J. J. Oberholster, M. C. E. Van Schoor, and N. J. Olivier, *History for the Senior Certificate*, 2nd ed. (Cape Town: Nasionale Boekhandel Beperk, 1957), 260, 262.

52. Van Rensburg and Oosthuizen, *Active History, Std 9*, 186.

53. Jordaan, Jordaan, and Mocke, *Exploring History Standard 10*, 36; H. A. Lambrechts, I. T. Bennison, J. J. Bester, J. Fourie, M. H. Trümpelmann, and J. S. Labuschagne, *History 9: New Syllabus 1986* (Cape Town: Nasou, 1986), 54; Arnold Napier Boyce, *Europe and South Africa, Part 2: A History for Standard 10* (Cape

Town: Juta, 1974), 42; and Boyce, *Europe and South Africa: A History of the Period 1815–1939*, 343.

54. Van Jaarsveld and van Wijk, *Illustrated History for Senior Certificate*, 224; Oberholster, Van Schoor, and Olivier, *History for the Senior Certificate*, 259; Van Schoor, Coetsee, Lambrechts, Oberholster, and Pienaar, *Senior History for South African Schools Standard 10*, 40; and Fowler and Smit, *History for the Natal Senior Certificate*, 356.
55. Coetsee, Otto, and Roodt, *Geskiedenis Vir Die Senior Sertifikaat*, 406; and Lategan and De Kock, *History in Perspective, Standard 10*, 31.
56. Van Rensburg and Oosthuizen, *Active History, Std 9*, 183; and Coetsee, Otto, and Roodt, *Geskiedenis Vir Die Senior Sertifikaat*, 344.
57. Böeseken, Oberholster, Van Schoor, and Olivier, *History for the Senior Certificate*, 233, 273; Smit, Lintvelt, Eckstein, and Smit, *History for Standard 10*, 54; and A. P. J. Van Rensburg and F. S. G. Oosthuizen, *Active History, Std 10* (Pretoria: De Jager-Haum, 1987), 78.
58. Boyce, *Europe and South Africa: A History of the Period 1815–1939*, 345; C. J. Joubert, *History for Standard 10*, 3rd ed. (Johannesburg: Perskor, 1979), 74.
59. Van Rensburg and Oosthuizen, *Active History, Std 10*, 1987, 43; Boyce, *Europe and South Africa: A History of the Period 1815–1939*, 344.
60. Van Jaarsveld and van Wijk, *Illustrated History for Senior Certificate*, 222.
61. See, among many others, F. E. Graves and E. Viglieno, *History for Today 10* (Cape Town: Juta, 1989), 174; Böeseken, Oberholster, Van Schoor, and Olivier, *History for the Senior Certificate*, 257; Van Rensburg and Oosthuizen, *Active History, Std 10*, 1980, 36; and Van Schoor, Coetsee, Lambrechts, Oberholster, and Pienaar, *Senior History for South African Schools Standard 10*, 35.
62. Coetsee, Otto, and Roodt, *Geskiedenis Vir Die Senior Sertifikaat*, 410; Van Rensburg and Oosthuizen, *Active History, Std 10*, 1987, 46; Van Rensburg and Oosthuizen, *Active History, Std 9*, 180; Lategan and De Kock, *History in Perspective, Standard 10*, 30.
63. Anthony Dennis Dodd and Winston Arthur Hutchings Cordingley, *Social Science: History (Standards VI, VII and VIII)* (Cape Town: Juta, 1952), 161.
64. See, for example, Transvaal Education Department, "Syllabus for History Standard 7," 1985.
65. Böeseken, Oberholster, Van Schoor and Olivier. *History for the Senior Certificate*, 260.
66. Malan, Appelgryn, and Theron, *New History to the Point Std 10*, 70; Smit, Lintvelt, Eckstein and Smit. *History for Standard 10*, 51.

67. Boyce, *Europe and South Africa: A History of the Period 1815–1939*, 347.
68. Van Schoor, Coetsee, Lambrechts, Oberholster, and Pienaar, *Senior History for South African Schools Standard 10*, 38.
69. Arnold Napier Boyce, *Europe and South Africa: A History for South African High Schools*, 3rd ed. (Cape Town: Juta, 1972), 563.
70. Van Jaarsveld and van Wijk, *Illustrated History for Senior Certificate*, 229.
71. Smit, Lintvelt, Eckstein, and Smit, *History for Standard 10*, 56.
72. Posel, "What's in a Name?," 52–56.
73. William Beinart, *Twentieth-Century South Africa*, 2nd ed. (Oxford: Oxford University Press, 2001), 146–47. See also Hermann Giliomee, *The Afrikaners: Biography of a People* (London: C. Hurst, 2003), 520–21; Rob Skinner, *Modern South Africa in World History: Beyond Imperialism* (London: Continuum, 2017), 90–91; and Hilgard Muller, "Separate Development in South Africa," *African Affairs* 62, no. 246 (1963): 53–65, here 54, 57–58, 61. See also Milton Shain and Andrew Lamprecht, "A Past That Must Not Go Away: Holocaust Denial in Apartheid and Post Apartheid South Africa," in *Remembering the Future: The Holocaust in the Age of Genocide*, vol. 1, ed. John K. Roth, Elisabeth Maxwell, Margot Levy, and Wendy Whitworth (London: Palgrave Macmillan, 2001), 858–69.
74. Van Jaarsveld and van Wijk, *Illustrated History for Senior Certificate*, 229.
75. See, among many others, Coetsee, Otto, and Roodt, *Geskiedenis Vir Die Senior Sertifikaat*, 411; Fowler and Smit, *History for the Natal Senior Certificate*, 355; Van Jaarsveld and van Wijk, *Illustrated History for Senior Certificate*, 228.
76. Van Jaarsveld and van Wijk, *Illustrated History for Senior Certificate*, 229; Van Rensburg and Oosthuizen, *Active History, Std 9*, 185.
77. Smit, Lintvelt, Eckstein, and Smit, *History for Standard 10*, 82; Malan, Appelgryn, and Theron, *New History to the Point Std 10*, 93.
78. Joint Matriculation Board, "Matriculation Examination Handbook for 1979," 1979, 296; Joint Matriculation Board, "Matriculation Examination Handbook 1973," Pretoria, 1973, 214.
79. Fowler and Smit, *History for the Natal Senior Certificate*, preface.
80. Van Jaarsveld and van Wijk, *Illustrated History for Senior Certificate*, 4.
81. See, for example, Joint Matriculation Board, "Examiners' Report on the Work of Candidates, Matriculation Examination December 1969," Pretoria, 1969, 13.
82. Floris Albertus Van Jaarsveld, "Probleme by die skrywe van skoolgeskiedenisboeke." *Historia* 7, no. 3 (1962): 147–63.
83. *National Curriculum Statement Grades 10–12 (General): History* (Pretoria: Department of Education, 2003), 4.

84. *Revised National Curriculum Statement Grades R-9 (Schools): Social Sciences* (Pretoria: Department of Education, 2002), 6.
85. *Revised National Curriculum Statement Grades R-9 (Schools): Social Sciences*, 6; *Curriculum and Assessment Policy Statement Grades 10–12: History* (Pretoria: Department of Basic Education), 2011, i; *Curriculum and Assessment Policy Statement Grades 7–9: Social Sciences* (Pretoria: Department of Basic Education, 2011), 3.
86. Andre Keet and Nazir Carrim, "Human Rights Education and Curricular Reform in South Africa." *Journal of Social Science Education* 5, no. 1 (2006): 100.
87. *Revised National Curriculum Statement Grades R-9 (Schools): Social Sciences*, 61, 92.
88. *National Curriculum Statement Grades 10–12 (General): History*, 26.
89. *Curriculum and Assessment Policy Statement Grades 7–9: Social Sciences*, 41.
90. *Curriculum and Assessment Policy Statement Grades 10–12: History*, 21, 24.
91. J. Bottaro, S. Cohen, L. Dilley, D. Duffett, and P. Visser, *Oxford Successful Social Sciences: Learner's Book Grade 9*, 2nd ed. (Cape Town: Oxford University Press, 2013), 41; E. Brink, C. Fowler, A. Grundlingh, E. Varga, and J. Verner, *Solutions for All History: Grade 11 Learner's Book* (Northlands, South Africa: Macmillan, 2012), 129; Jean Bottaro and Pippa Visser, *In Search of History: Grade 12 Teacher's Guide* (Oxford: Oxford University Press, 2000), 59; and "World War II (1939–1945)," South African History Online, www.sahistory.org.za/article/caps-grade-4-world-war-ii-1939-1945-term-1, accessed June 24, 2016.
92. Bottaro and Visser, *In Search of History*, 58; Lindiwe Sikhakhane, Carol-Anne Stephenson, Dina Moodley, Niri Dorasamy, Reggie Subramony, Jabu Hlongwane, Fiona Frank, Kumarasen Naidoo, Sham Randhani, Pinglan Naidoo, and Muzi Vuma, *History Grade 11: Learner's Book* (Durban, South Africa: New Generation, 2010), 180; R. Deftereos, C. Dugmore, C. Geldenhuys, D. Ramoroka, M. Snail, M. Stoltz, V. Titus, and V. Van Reenen, *Making History Grade 11 Learners' Book*, Ed. Irene Stotko (Sandton, South Africa: Heinemann, 2006), 167; Sue Grové, Jake Manenzhe, André Proctor, Bridget Tobin, and Gail Weldon, *Via Afrika History: Grade 11 Learner's Book* (Cape Town: Via Afrika, 2012), 141; K. L. Angier, J. Hobbs, P. McMahon, R. L. Mowatt, and G. Nattrass, *Viva History: Learner's Book Grade 11* (Cape Town: Vivlia, 2012), 155; Brink et al., *Solutions for All History*, 153; and P. Ellis, S. Haw, B. Karumbidza, P. Macallister, T. Middlebrook, P. Olivier, and A. Rodgers, *Shuters Top Class History: Grade 11 Learner's Book* (Pietermaritzburg, South Africa: Shuter & Shooter, 2015), 126.
93. *Curriculum and Assessment Policy Statement Grades 7–9: Social Sciences*, 41; Grové et al., *Via Afrika History*, 136; Bottaro and Visser, *In Search of History*, 98;

and Jean Bottaro, Pippa Visser, and Nigel Worden, *Oxford in Search of History: Grade 11 Learner's Book*, 8th ed. (Oxford: Oxford University Press, 2009), 159. See also Carrier, Fuchs and Messinger, *International Status of Education about the Holocaust*, 162–63.

94. "The Use of Propaganda," South African History Online, www.sahistory.org.za/article/human-rights-issues-during-and-after-world-war-ii-focus-nazi-germany-grade-12-0, accessed June 24, 2016. See also Grové et al, *Via Afrika History*, 133; Brink et al., *Solutions for All History*, 127; Bottaro and Visser, *In Search of History*, 58; Ellis et al., *Shuters Top Class History*, 124; and Bottaro, Visser, and Worden, *Oxford in Search of History*, 124–25.

95. Bottaro et al., *Oxford Successful Social Sciences: Learner's Book Grade 9*, 39, 44.

96. Grové et al., *Via Afrika History*, 145.

97. *Curriculum and Assessment Policy Statement Grades 10–12: History*, 4.

98. Grové et al., *Via Afrika History*, 143; and Angier et al., *Viva History: Learner's Book Grade 11*, 161.

99. Bottaro et al., *Oxford Successful Social Sciences*, 45; Brink et al., *Solutions for All History*, 150; and Ellis et al., *Shuters Top Class History*, 125–26.

100. Sikhakhane et al., *History Grade 11: Educator's Guide* (Durban, South Africa: New Generation, 2010), 165.

101. Bottaro et al., *Oxford Successful Social Sciences*, 37.

102. Deftereos et al., *Making History Grade 11 Learners' Book*, 186.

103. Grové et al., *Via Afrika History*, 108–9.

104. Bottaro, Visser, and Worden, *Oxford in Search of History: Grade 11 Learner's Book*, 140–59; Deftereos et al., *Making History Grade 11 Learners' Book*, 169–85; Ellis et al., *Shuters Top Class History*, 116; Angier et al., *Viva History: Learner's Book Grade 11*, 149–51; and Brink et al., *Solutions for All History*, 94.

105. Sikhakhane et al., *History Grade 11: Educator's Guide*, 154; Michelle Friedman, Christopher C. Saunders, Mzamo Jacobs, Yonah Seleti, and Judith Gordon, *Looking into the Past: Source-Based History for Grade 11 Learner's Book* (Cape Town: Maskew Miller Longman, 2006), 180; and Grové et al., *Via Afrika History*, 136.

106. Sikhakhane et al., *History Grade 11: Learner's Book*, 177.

107. Deftereos et al., *Making History Grade 11 Learners' Book*, 183.

108. K. L. Angier, J. Hobbs, P. McMahon, R. L. Mowatt, and G. Nattrass, *Viva History: Teacher's Guide Grade 11* (Cape Town: Vivlia, 2012), 72.

109. "Grade 9—Term 1: World War II (1939–1945)," South African History Online, www.sahistory.org.za/article/grade-9-term-1-world-war-ii-1939-1945-0, accessed June 24, 2016.

110. "How and Why Did the Holocaust Happen?" South African History Online, www.sahistory.org.za/article/human-rights-issues-during-and-after-world-war-ii-focus-nazi-germany-grade-12-2, accessed 24 June 2016.
111. Bottaro et al., *Oxford Successful Social Sciences: Learner's Book Grade 9*, 32.
112. Bottaro, Visser, and Worden, *Oxford in Search of History*, 159.
113. "How did the Nazis Construct an Aryan Identity?," South African History Online, www.sahistory.org.za/article/human-rights-issues-during-and-after-world-war-ii-focus-nazi-germany-grade-12-0, accessed June 24, 2016.
114. Shirli Gilbert, "Remembering the Racial State"; Shirli Gilbert, "Anne Frank in South Africa"; and Sasha S. Polakow-Suransky, "Historical Amnesia?"; see also June Bam, "Negotiating History, Truth and Reconciliation and Globalisation: An Analysis of the Suppression of Historical Consciousness in South African Schools as Case Study," *Mots Pluriels* 13 (April 2000), motspluriels.arts.uwa.edu.au/MP1300jb.html.
115. Friedman et al,. *Looking into the Past*, 186.
116. Grové et al., *Via Afrika History*, 152.
117. For introductions to the large and complex historiographies of apartheid and the Holocaust, see, among many others, Philip Bonner, Peter Delius, and Deborah Posel, eds., *Apartheid's Genesis, 1935–1962* (Braamfontein, South Africa: Ravan Press, 1995); Paul Maylam, *South Africa's Racial Past: The History and Historiography of Racism, Segregation and Apartheid* (Aldershot, UK: Ashgate, 2001); and Dan Stone, *Histories of the Holocaust* (Oxford: Oxford University Press, 2010).
118. Jeremy Noakes, "Hitler and the Third Reich," in *The Historiography of the Holocaust*, ed. Dan Stone (Basingstoke, UK: Palgrave Macmillan, 2004), 24–51, esp. 32.
119. Falk Pingel, "The Holocaust in Textbooks: From a European to a Global Event," in *Holocaust Education in a Global Context*, ed. Karel Fracapane and Matthias Hass (Paris: UNESCO, 2014), 77–87, esp. 78.
120. For a comparison of international trends, see Carrier, Fuchs, and Messinger, *International Status of Education about the Holocaust*, esp. 160–69. On international influences in post-apartheid education, see Jansen, "Political Symbolism as Policy Craft," 204; Weldon, "Comparative Study," 34.
121. On the latter, see, for example, Chana Teeger, "'Both Sides of the Story' History Education in Post-Apartheid South Africa." *American Sociological Review* 80, no. 6 (2015): 1175–1200.

15

"Never Forget"

Intersecting Memories of the Holocaust and the Settler Colonial Genocide in Canada

Dorota Glowacka

> The Indians of our surviving nations, like Jews, should never forget.
> —Osage scholar Carter Revard

INDIGENOUS USES OF THE HOLOCAUST

CHRYSTOS, A PROMINENT AMERICAN poet and LGBTQ activist, identifies solely with her father's Menominee ancestry, despite her mixed Indigenous and European heritage.[1] Chrystos's rejection of her mother's ethnic identity is a symbolic punishment meted out to the entire settler culture: by expunging her European roots, she wants to draw attention to the erasure of her country's genocidal history. In the poem "Winter Count," from the volume *Dream On* (1995), she writes:

> By their own report america has killed
> forty million of us in the last century
> . . . .
> We have died as children, as old men & women without defenses

> We have been raped, mutilated, we have been starved
> experimented on, we have been given gifts that kill
> . . . .
> We have been killed on purpose, by accident, in drunken rage
> As I speak with each breath
> another Indian is dying   Someone part of our Holocaust
> which they have renamed civilization
> . . . .
> Down the long tunnel of death my grandmothers cry
> *Give no solace to our destroyers*
> Into the cold night I send these burning words
> *Never forget*
> *america is our hitler.*²

The phrase "Never forget," accentuated in the poem, evokes the rallying cry of Holocaust remembrance. Chrystos recites a litany of horrors and signposts the number forty million, in juxtaposition to the symbolic six million of murdered European Jews. Thus she mobilizes familiar cultural tropes in order to rescript the atrocities as "our Holocaust" while also presenting them within the framework of an Indigenous calendarium.³ Her denunciation of colonial violence ends with an injunction to remember, which she shouts into the "cold night" of historical amnesia, because, in contrast to the Jewish *Zachor!*, it has not yet found a global addressee.

Chrystos's poetic exhortations are representative of comparisons with the Holocaust that were frequently mobilized by Indigenous scholars and activists in the 1990s in order to draw attention to the violence of North American colonial history. Notably, few references to the Holocaust were made in the late 1960s and early 1970s, at the height of the Red Power movement, which culminated in 1973 in a violent standoff at Wounded Knee between a chapter of AIM (American Indian Movement) and the FBI.⁴ Comparisons between the Holocaust and settler colonial genocide were only occasionally made in the 1980s.⁵ In the 1990s, however, the Holocaust rose to prominence in North American popular memory and culture, especially following the release of *Schindler's List* in 1993 and the opening of the United States Holocaust Memorial Museum in the same year. At the same time, the increasing awareness of historical and social injustice and growing demands for redress were fueled by controversies around the five hundredth anniversary of Columbus's arrival in the Western Hemisphere and, after 1994, by the revolutionary Zapatista movement in Mexico, which emphasized its Lacandon Maya roots.

In Canada, the recognition of the genocidal nature of the country's colonial history also began to emerge in the 1970s, with the Canadian branch of AIM undertaking direct actions to ensure the rights of Indigenous peoples and assert their land claims (such as boycotts of government institutions in Ottawa, highway blockades in British Columbia, and an occupation of a municipal park in Kenora, Ontario). The protests were sparked by Pierre Trudeau's white paper of 1969, which aimed to extinguish the distinct status of First Nations people. In the 1990s, widespread political mobilization of Indigenous communities was galvanized by the July–September 1990 Oka crisis, which started as a protracted land dispute and devolved into a military siege of the Mohawk reserve of Kanehsatake.[6] At the same time, the history of the atrocities against Indigenous peoples began to emerge, following a public disclosure in 1990 by Phil Fontaine, the grand chief of the Assembly of Manitoba Chiefs, about his experiences of abuse and neglect at the Fort Alexander school in Manitoba.[7] With little purchase on political power and denied access to cultural capital, Canadian Indigenous activists and those advocating on their behalf feared that the Holocaust's growing popularity, which coincided in time with the aftermath of the Oka crisis and the first public disclosures about the Indian residential schools, had created a hierarchy of suffering that would become an obstacle in obtaining recognition for colonial atrocities and obliterate their own traumatic history.

The United States and Canada share the history of the annihilation of Indigenous lives and cultures over the centuries of colonial conquest and rule. Patterns of destruction, however, have varied considerably, with Canada priding itself on having chosen a more civilized path of assimilation in contrast to the documented brutality of its southern neighbor. Yet Canada has been equally successful at erasing the memory of genocidal policies toward Indigenous peoples from its foundational narratives of nation building, resulting in widespread ignorance about the violent nature of that history. This willed historical amnesia about the fact that Canada was founded on the elimination of Indigenous groups from the social, political, and geographic landscape has been sustained by the undercurrent of systemic racism. The sentiment that "Canada should remain a white man's country," expressed in the Parliament by Prime Minister Mackenzie King in 1947, has remained largely impervious to change.[8] Hence, the prevailing opinion among Indigenous scholars and activists today is that "while Canada may be described by the settler society as a postcolonial state, it is not postcolonial for Indigenous peoples. . . . The colonial experience has never ended for us."[9] It is only in recent years that Canadians have been forced to question their cherished belief in Canada as a benevolent peacemaker and to recognize that its ideal of an inclusive multicultural mosaic has rested on the nonrecognition of the primacy of sovereign Indigenous presence. At the same time, Indigenous groups have been increasingly forceful in asserting their treaty rights, including their right to self-determination, and in demanding that the history of colonial settlement in Canada be recognized as genocidal.

The debate among genocide scholars as to whether the five-hundred-year history of colonial conquest and the disastrous demographic collapse caused by European-Indigenous contact should be recognized as "genocide" hinges on the interpretation of the UN definition of the term.[10] Article II of the Convention on the Prevention and Punishment of the Crime of Genocide places emphasis on the mental element (mens rea, or guilty mind) of the "intention to destroy a national, ethnical, racial or religious group," and it stipulates a quantitative element: the destruction of a group "in whole or in part." If numbers are taken as the primary criterion, then colonial genocide appears to be unparalleled in the history of humankind: an estimated 95 percent of North American Indigenous populations prior to contact perished as a direct or indirect result of European conquest and settlement. The necessity to prove premeditation, however, complicates that count: none of colonial settler states would admit that they carried out the destruction deliberately, an argument that has been supported by some Holocaust scholars who have used it to defend the thesis about the uniqueness of the Jewish genocide.[11] In Canada, as in the United States, Indigenous communities were decimated by infectious diseases brought by the settlers, but it is impossible to establish with certainty whether viruses such as smallpox and tuberculosis (the number-one killer of children in Canadian Indian residential schools) were deployed as biological weapons. The measure of intentionality is similarly unclear in the case of famines and the despoliation of Indigenous land, which were the result of settler greed for territory and natural resources.[12] In Canada, this was especially poignant in the case of the hunting-gathering Beothuk people of Newfoundland, who became extinct in the first half of the nineteenth century when their access to fishing grounds was cut off by settlers.[13]

When Indigenous grievances about these lethal practices came to the fore in the public debates in the 1990s, the term *genocide* was metonymically equated with the extermination of European Jews, while no comparisons were made with other colonial genocides, such as the extermination of the Herero and Nama peoples in German Southwest Africa.[14] The definition of genocide, as it was adopted in 1948, emerged in response to the barbarities of World War II, and its conceptual framework was shaped by the cultural and political circumstances of postwar Europe, although the fate of European Jews was not singled out in the UN deliberations.[15] The extermination of the Jews, including the murder of almost all his family members, was a catalyst in Raphaël Lemkin's fight for the adoption of the Genocide Convention, and in *Axis Rule in Occupied Europe* (1944), in which he formulates the concept of genocide, he focused mainly on the events of World War II in Europe.[16] In his other works, however, written both before and after the war, it is clear that Lemkin strove for a much more comprehensive historical and geographic perspective, and he regarded colonialism, including Hitler's territorial ambitions, as an integral part of the world history of genocide.[17] In unpublished essays and notes on the history of genocides, Lemkin wrote extensively about the conquest of the Americas and described in detail the destruction of Tasmanian Aborigines by the British in the first half of the nineteenth century. In Lemkin's account, after the final resettlement to a nearby island, the last Tasmanian died in 1876, a poignant example of a forced extinction of the entire tribe, which could serve as a cautionary tale to underscore the paramount importance of implementing the new concept.[18]

In 1948, references to colonial genocides were not included in the convention, largely at the insistence of colonial settler states, and Article III of the original draft, containing provisions about cultural genocide, was struck from the definition, despite Lemkin's efforts to retain it.[19] In the last decade of the twentieth century, however, advocates for the recognition of these terms began to call on Lemkin's original formulation that genocide consists in the "destruction of the national pattern of the oppressed group" and "the imposition of the national pattern of the oppressor," and they referenced his argument that the annihilation of culture is inseparable from physical destruction.[20] Returning to the spirit and letter of Lemkin's formula helped Indigenous scholars in the 1990s reinterpret Indigenous history amid proliferating representations of the Holocaust and a growing number of Holocaust memorial projects. Thus Chrystos's evocations of the Holocaust, quoted at the beginning of this chapter, echoed polemical theses advanced by proponents of the indigenization of the Holocaust, such as David A. Stannard and Ward Churchill. Both of these scholars were sharply critical of the escalation of Holocaust memory in North American culture. They saw the dogma of Holocaust uniqueness as harmful to Indigenous interests, and they questioned it by establishing direct links between the extermination of Indigenous peoples and Hitler's population policies: "The road to Auschwitz led straight through the heart of the Indians of North and South America."[21]

At the same time, both in Canada and in the United States, Indigenous writers and activists began to appropriate Holocaust tropes as a strategy to undermine the tightly scripted narratives of the settler states' national beginnings and to bolster their claim that mass atrocities committed against Indigenous peoples in North America should be recognized under the UN definition of genocide.[22] For instance, Alice M. Azure, a writer of Mi'maw descent, affirmed that "for indigenous peoples, the story of genocide, of holocaust, is present in every cell and fibre of our being, in every step we take as we walk this remembering earth."[23] Tuscarora writer Eric Gansworth argued that although his ancestors "were not living in a death camp, per se . . . , the world around their small sanctuaries had become one giant, all-encompassing death camp."[24] By casting the Holocaust as the paradigmatic genocide, these comparisons have drawn on the immense scope of destruction, killing methods (including the state's bureaucratic machinery and the role of the state as perpetrator), the intensity of racist hatred that allowed targeted populations to be construed as subhuman, and finally the denial of genocide during and after the fact.[25] These competing claims between Holocaust memory and the memory of settler colonial genocide have occasionally descended into expressions of antisemitism and Holocaust denial. In Canada, such was the case with David Ahenakew, the former national chief of the Assembly of First

Nations who in 2002 made unsavory remarks about the purpose of the Final Solution and was subsequently stripped of the Order of Canada.[26]

THE CASE OF CANADA: A POSTCARD FROM NOVA SCOTIA

> Oh, Canada!
> Your home's on Mi'kmaw land
> True genocidal drive
> By all your Queen's command.[27]

In the province of Nova Scotia, the strategy of mobilizing Holocaust tropes to bolster Indigenous claims lies at the heart of Daniel N. Paul's efforts to document the history of the Mi'kmaq and of the colonial expropriation of Mi'kma'ki. Paul, a Mi'kmaw Elder, scholar, and community activist, is also highly regarded for his service as a justice of the peace and as a member of the Nova Scotia Human Rights Commission. In his book on Mi'kmaw history, *We Were Not the Savages: Collision between European and Native American Civilizations*, first published in 1993, Paul finds historical links between the persecution of the Jews and the extermination of North American Indigenous peoples. He points out, for instance, that 1492, the year of Columbus's "discovery" of America, was also the year of the historic expulsion of the entire Jewish community from Spain, and Columbus's voyages were partly funded by property seized from the Jews by the Spanish emperors.

In his detailed chronicle of Nova Scotia's history from an Indigenous perspective, Paul recounts that Halifax, the capital of the province, was established as a settlement on the Mi'kmaw moose-hunting territory known as K'jipuktuk. Since the Mi'kmaq never signed land treaties or otherwise ceded their ancestral land, and they never capitulated to the British in a military defeat, Halifax is located on unsurrendered Mi'kmaw territory. Faced with land theft by British settlers, the Mi'kmaq allied themselves with the French, but at the Treaty of Utrecht (1713), following the British conquest of New France, France ceded large parts of Mi'kma'ki to Britain without including the land's rightful owners in the negotiations. The Mi'kmaq continued to wage war on the British and to defend their territory by capturing British fishing vessels and attacking smaller settlements. Refusing to accept a declaration of war from "the savages," the British resorted to deceptive and brutal tactics. Notoriously, in 1749, Governor Edward Cornwallis, who was sent to the restive territory following his previous success in pacifying the Scottish Highlanders, proclaimed a scalp bounty, setting off a killing rampage by both the military and the settlers.[28] This violent history of British-Mi'kmaq relations was mitigated by periods of relative peace and treaty making.[29] In 1783, following the American War of Independence, an estimated thirty thousand British loyalist settlers migrated to Nova Scotia and took possession of the land, on the assumption of royal dominion of the territory, thus bringing an end to what had been until then a strained yet reciprocal relation based on treaty making.[30] Thousands of Mi'kmaq also perished from diseases brought by the newcomers and from starvation because the settlers' limited their access to fishing and hunting grounds, overhunted game for furs, and cut off their transportation routes. Compounded by the government's reneging on treaties and withholding of provisions, these measures brought the Mi'kmaq to the brink of extinction in the early twentieth century.

These ignominious pages of Nova Scotia's history remain little known, while Governor Cornwallis has been amply memorialized in the topography of the province as "the founder of Halifax," with streets, parks, rivers, schools, and establishments named after him, a dark exemplar of another line from the same poem by Chrystos: "The names of those who murdered us are remembered / in towns, islands, bays, rivers, mountains, prairies, forests."[31] In 2011, the Mi'kmaq and their allies scored a victory when the Nova Scotia School Board voted in favor of the proposal, presented by the board's Mi'maw representative, to change the name of Cornwallis Junior High School, amid a vituperative public debate, which included arguments about whether "it would be nice [for the larger Halifax community] to have that school re-named Hitler Jr. High."[32] An advocacy group led by Paul also started lobbying to tear down the statue of Cornwallis in a popular park and to rename Cornwallis Street, both in downtown Halifax. In August 2017, the Cornwallis debacle was reignited, with rallies, educational and social media initiatives, and, in January 2018, following a vote by the Halifax City Council, the statue was removed and placed in storage. Two months later, Cornwallis Street Baptist Church quietly removed Cornwallis's name from its designation, renaming itself New Horizons Baptist Church.[33] These new developments only seem to confirm

Paul's reflection from more than two decades prior that "the hardship and discrimination [the Mi'kmaq] suffered . . . in the midst of plenty . . . [do] not greatly pale in comparison to that suffered by the Jewish people at the hands of Hitler in the 1930's and 40's. . . . They, like Jews, were treated as 'non-persons' in their own country."[34] Unlike the Jewish people, however, the Mi'kmaq still await the recognition of the historical wrongs against them, and they continue to suffer intergenerational consequences of the genocidal past.

Although Indigenous history is not mandatory in Canadian schools and many Canadians are oblivious to the nation's violent beginnings, gruesome facts about Indian residential schools have become public knowledge as a result of the work of the Truth and Reconciliation Commission, which was established in 2008 and concluded its proceedings in December 2015. Indian residential schools were founded by the federal government based on the Indian Act of 1876, and they were run by churches of various denominations—an aggressive strategy of assimilation that became an effective way of eliminating First Nations and Inuit populations.[35] At the schools, where attendance was mandatory from 1920 to 1948 (the parents were jailed for noncompliance), children were prohibited from speaking their language and practicing their customs and religion. They endured tremendous neglect, physical and sexual abuse, poor sanitation, inadequate nutrition, and lack of medical care, leading to mortality rates between 30 percent and 69 percent, although such summaries callously underestimate the extent of the children's suffering. The inhumane treatment was compounded by eugenic measures, such as compulsory sterilization in Alberta (1923) and British Columbia (1933), and malnutrition experiments in the late 1940s. Duncan Campbell Scott, the head of the Department of Indian Affairs in the 1920s, confirmed that the policies were designed to "kill the Indian in the child," echoing the motto of "kill the Indian, save the man," coined by Richard H. Pratt, a leading American proponent of assimilation through boarding schools. The violent measures were routinely justified by the mantra of the Canadian civilizing mission, about which Paul comments, : "If what they [the British and Canadian governments] did was civilized behavior, may we never be civilized again."[36] The belief in the long-term benefits of assimilation is still widely shared by Canadians, even though intergenerational trauma and the detrimental legacy of the schools continue to impact Indigenous communities.

The disclosures about the Indian residential schools put pressure on the federal government to initiate procedures to address the wrongs, including Prime Minister Stephen Harper's official apology in 2008.[37] Indigenous communities initially welcomed these developments but increasingly have found them inadequate when it comes to addressing the systematic and long-term nature of settler colonial violence. Dene scholar Glenn Sean Coulthard concludes that the state-imposed idiom of national reconciliation is an expression of "neocolonial politics," designed to undermine the Indigenous groups' desire for self-determination and to deny them the recognition of their diverse individual and collective practices in coming to terms with the damaging past.[38]

In oral depositions given to the Truth and Reconciliation Commission and in written accounts, former students of Indian residential schools referred to themselves as "survivors" of historical trauma, echoing the idiom of Holocaust testimonies. The schools were frequently compared to Nazi concentration camps, and Hitler and other Nazi figures appeared as an emblem of evil, used to convey the memory of the inhumane treatment by the staff. Doug Knockwood, for instance, a Mi'kmaw Elder from Indian Brook, Nova Scotia, described his experiences at Shubenacadie Residential School as "torture and the harsh concentration-camp behavior."[39] Augie Merasty, a retired Cree trapper, who spent eleven years at St. Therese Residential School in Saskatchewan, commented on the physical and sexual abuse at the hands of one of the priests as follows: "I remember him, he was and still is one of the worst human beings I have ever known about, except maybe Hitler."[40]

In their 1997 searing exposé, *The Circle Game: Shadows and Substance in the Indian Residential School Experience in Canada*, Roland Chrisjohn and Sherri Young contended that "Canada's treatment of Aboriginal Peoples in general, and its creation and operation of Residential Schools in particular, was and continues to be nothing short of genocide."[41] Chrisjohn, an Oneida scholar, a former member of the Canadian branch of AIM and, later, chair in Native Studies at St. Thomas University in New Brunswick, has been an outspoken proponent of the recognition of settler colonial atrocities under the definition of genocide, and he has relied on Holocaust testimony and scholarship to build his indictment against the Canadian government. In *The Circle Game*, he refers to Zygmunt Bauman's critique of modernity as "a system in which

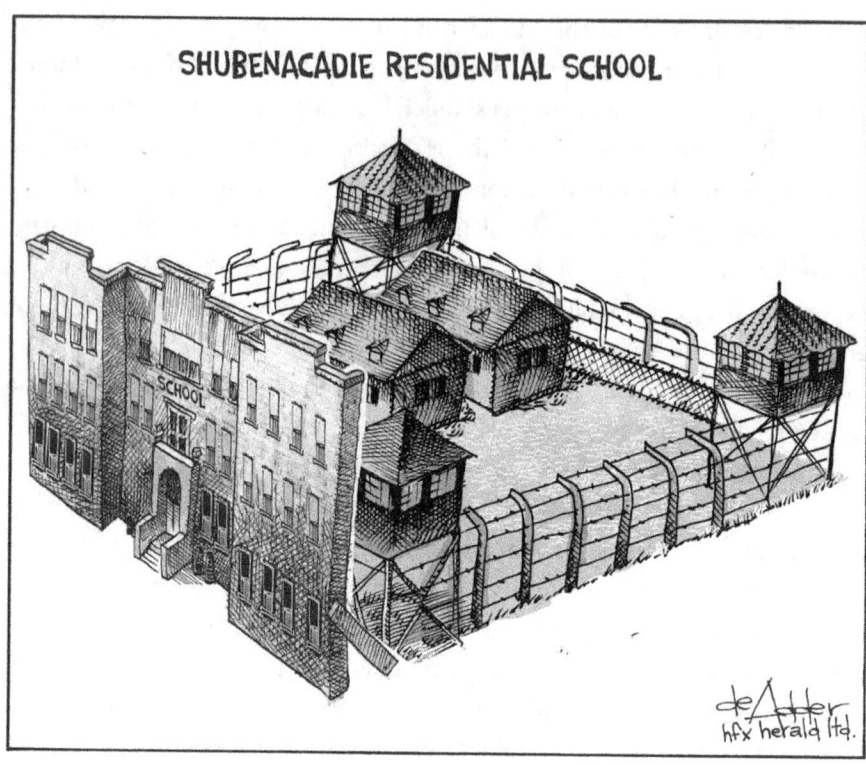

Michael de Adder, "Shubenacadie Residential School." (*Chronicle Herald*, Halifax, NS, July 19, 2013; courtesy Michael de Adder)

morality and ethics point in opposite directions" to characterize the policies of the settler colonial state,[42] and he argues for the necessity of a public inquiry into the schools by drawing on Lawrence Langer's *Holocaust Testimonies: The Ruins of Memory* as "an example of what can be done from people simply being given the opportunity to tell their stories."[43] He also borrows from Jean Améry's insights in *At the Mind's Limits* to expound the psychological burden of Indian residential schools, and he explains the intergenerational damage to Indigenous communities in reference to literature on the children of Holocaust survivors.[44]

Chrisjohn and Young highlight Canada's instrumental role in removing references to cultural genocide from Lemkin's original draft, which, in their view, allowed the state to hide its policies toward Indigenous peoples from possible international scrutiny. In 2000, when the horrific abuses at the schools were becoming publicly known, Chrisjohn and his Mi'kmaw collaborator Sherri Young brought the case against the Canadian government before the Law Commission of Canada, seeking the recognition of the crimes of Indian residential schooling as genocide. The case was dismissed. In Chrisjohn and Young's view, this refusal constituted genocide denial, which served to enable continued perpetration of genocidal policies by consecutive Canadian governments.[45]

For two decades, Chrisjohn and Young's arguments that the treatment of children in residential schools fit the definition of genocide fell on deaf ears, and their writings were only available through small academic presses with limited circulation. In 2013, their cause was rekindled when statements demanding such recognition were made by Shawn Atleo, the national chief of the Assembly of First Nations at the time, and were endorsed by former Prime Minister Paul Martin. In May 2015, Beverley McLachlin, the chief justice of the Supreme Court of Canada, delivered a landmark legal opinion that Canada's policies of assimilation, Indian residential schools in particular, were an attempt to commit "cultural genocide." The statement received wide media coverage and was included in the final report of the Truth and Reconciliation Commission. While the term *cultural genocide*, first introduced by Lemkin, has been gaining traction among Canadian scholars and activists, Chrisjohn objects to describing colonial atrocities as primarily "cultural," on the grounds that such qualification dilutes the magnitude of colonial violence, as well as attenuates the long-term impact of assimilationist policies on Indigenous communities, one of which is an epidemic of suicides.[46]

Intersecting Memories

The dynamics between intersecting memories of the Holocaust and settler colonial genocide have been asymmetrical. While Indigenous scholars and activists frequently invoke the Jewish genocide, and some, such as Paul and Chrisjohn, have extensive knowledge of Jewish history, there is relatively little interest in the plight of the Indigenous people among either Holocaust scholars or members of Jewish communities in Canada. As Daniel Paul has remarked, "It makes me very sad that the Jewish people don't care about us."[47] Yet rectifying this asymmetry and envisioning alliances in which the Jewish memory of the Holocaust and the Indigenous memory of settler colonial genocide can illuminate each other is important for a constructive rethinking of Canada's past to occur.

Joint statements issued by Phil Fontaine and Bernie Farber, the former head of the Canadian Jewish Congress, have been a remarkable expression of solidarity in Canada in recent years. For instance, in a commentary following disclosures about the medical experiments in the Indian residential schools, they wrote: "The time has come for Canada to formally recognize a sixth genocide, the genocide of its own aboriginal communities; a genocide that began at the time of first contact and that was still very active in our own lifetimes; a genocide currently in search of a name but no longer in search of historical facts."[48] In October 2013, in the context of the Canadian Museum for Human Rights (CMHR) debacle (discussed below), Fontaine and Faber met with Special UN Rapporteur for Indigenous People James Anaya and delivered another plea for the official acknowledgment of the "sixth genocide" in Canada, in addition to the five that are currently recognized (the Armenian genocide, the Ukrainian Holodomor, the Holocaust, the massacre in Srebrenica, and the Rwandan genocide).[49] Fontaine and Faber's initiative can be seen as an attempt to forge coalitions between victims of genocidal histories, despite their vastly different historical, cultural, and geographic circumstances.

In a similar vein, the programs for the annual Holocaust Education Week in Canadian cities such as Winnipeg, Toronto, and Halifax have included events featuring conversations between Holocaust survivors living in Canada and survivors of Indian residential schools. An instructive example of such encounters is found in the exchange between Nate Leipciger, who, as a teenager, survived several Nazi concentration camps, and Theodor Fontaine, a member and former chief of the Sagkeeng Ojibway First Nation in Manitoba, a survivor of the Fort Alexander and Assiniboia Residential Schools, which he attended from 1948 to 1960; both survivors are also authors of memoirs, which they wrote relatively late in their lives (2015 and 2010, respectively). Leipciger's testimony is unique among those delivered by male survivors of the Holocaust because, in a frank and direct manner, he describes the sexual assault he suffered at the hands of a kapo in one of the camps, followed by barter sex, which was the price of his survival. Toward the end of his memoir, Leipciger admits how difficult it was for him to finally break the silence about his sexual abuse. What gave him the strength to do so was the example of male survivors of Indian residential schools, such as Phillip Fontaine and Ted Fontaine, who "have come forward and shared their suffering at the hands of people in power over them."[50] In Fontaine's memoir, which details his life's journey to overcome the trauma of abuse, self-blame, and a sense of worthlessness, the horror of childhood experiences is mitigated by a sense of humor and a remarkable spirit of resilience. The pivotal moment for Fontaine was a visit to the Dachau Concentration Camp Memorial Site in 1983. As he reminisces, "I could not imagine the devastation and anguish caused by this atrocity of human history, and my own experience at Indian residential school seemed very minute. Nevertheless, as different as these scenarios are, there was something in the eyes of the people in the photos that was very familiar: I'd seen it in the eyes of residential school survivors."[51] Fontaine and Leipciger's friendship, forged through the recognition of the commonality of trauma that had cast a long shadow over their lives, is testimony to the healing potential of engaging intersecting memories. It also clearly shows that knowledge about the events of one historical atrocity (in this instance, the residential schools) can precipitate invaluable knowledge about another historical event and allow us to uncover past experiences that for various reasons (in this case, social taboos about male sexual shame) would have remained undisclosed.

Another promising example of intersectional memory in Canada is the work of visual artists of mixed Jewish and Indigenous ancestry, such as Kali Spitzer and Steven Loft. In a short film, *2510037901*, which was featured in 2000 as a part of an Ed Video project, *My Life in 5 Minutes*, Steve Loft, who is of mixed Mohawk and Jewish heritage, videotaped his government-issued Indian status card number being tattooed on his forearm. Between footage of the tattooing process, a short text scrolled upward across the screen: "Since the time of his youth, Crazy Horse had known that the world men lived in was only a shadow of the real world. To get into the real world he had to dream, and when he was in the real world everything seemed to float or dance. In this real world his horse danced as if it were wild or crazy, and this is why he called himself Crazy Horse."[52] By summoning the spirit memory of Chief Crazy Horse, a legendary Oglala Lakota warrior and visionary, who laid down his life in the struggle for the rights of his people, Loft beckons the proud legacy of Red Power. Yet he also draws attention to the ongoing stigmatization and pain of First Nations communities by branding himself with

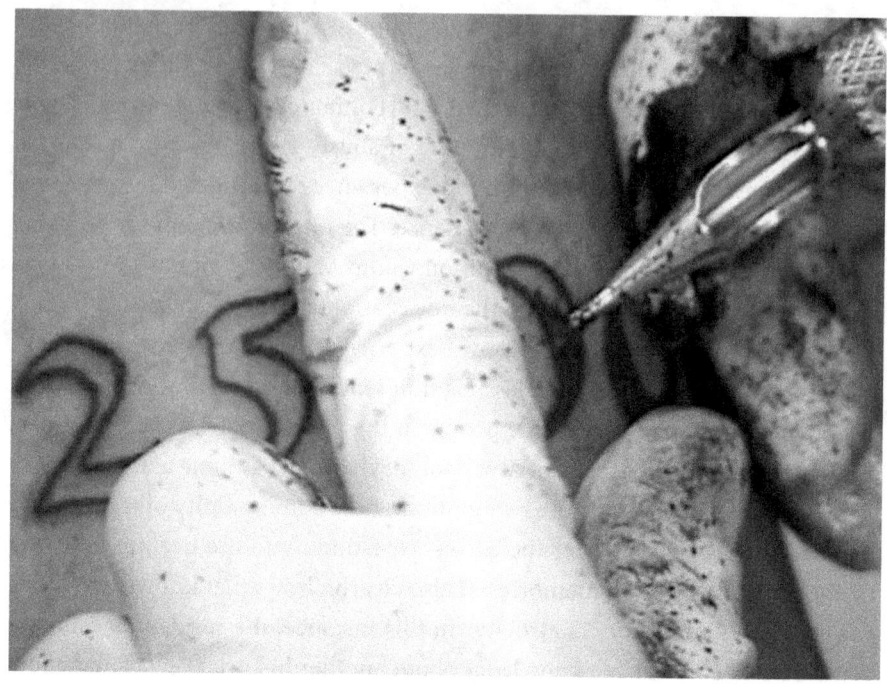

Still from *251003790*. (Courtesy Steven Loft)

his status number in a gesture reminiscent of Auschwitz tattoos.[53] Although this artistic commentary on the complexities of memory politics may appear provocative, it is successful in creating a symbolic space in which acts of solidarity between victims of genocidal events can take place. To quote A. Dirk Moses: "The mutual recognition of common suffering is a powerful moral source for the solidarity needed to prevent future victims of progress."[54]

Holocaust, Genocide, and the Paradoxes of Human Rights in Indigenous Contexts

The relative invisibility of Indigenous claims in the realm of comparative Holocaust studies is reflected in Michael Rothberg's influential book *Multidirectional Memory: Remembering the Holocaust in the Age of Decolonization* (2009), discussed in the introduction to this volume. Although he acknowledges the foundational role of colonial atrocities in the history of the United States, Rothberg makes only passing references to the "legacies of violence . . . that haunt the histories of indigenous peoples."55 Perhaps this omission is inevitable, considering that Rothberg necessarily draws on Western conceptions of history, memory, and trauma. In what way can Holocaust scholars engage with Indigenous systems of knowledge, which are often incommensurate with the conceptual apparatus that gave rise to their understanding of genocidal violence?

In Canada, the inadequacies of Eurocentric epistemic frameworks were exposed during the controversies surrounding the CMHR in Winnipeg, Manitoba, which opened in September 2014, to the accompaniment of protests from a variety of interest groups, most notably representatives of Ukrainian and First Nations communities.56 Manitoba is the province with the largest Indigenous population in the country and the highest incidence of First Nations poverty. The museum is located on Treaty One territory, at the convergence of the Red and Assiniboine Rivers, known as the Forks, which for thousands of years was a meeting place for First Nations and then also Métis peoples. During archaeological digs, cultural artifacts, including sacred objects, were discovered at the site, but since experts did not find evidence of human remains, the architecturally imposing building was erected, thus symbolically entombing ancient Indigenous history and culture.57 The location is also marked by the legacy of environmental racism that has been detrimental to the local Shoal Lake #40 First Nation community: its access to clean drinking water was compromised when, in 1913, the federal government sold a part of the former traditional territory to the city of Winnipeg. The erasure of that history prompted Shoal Lake #40 activists to launch a project called "The Museum of Canadian Human Rights Violations," to coincide with the opening of the CMHR, with the objective of informing tourists about the abysmal living conditions in their community.

The CMHR tells the story of the advancement and triumph of universal human rights, which is symbolically captured in the architecture of the building: it is crowned by the Tower of Hope that protrudes into the sky, while on the inside the Trail of Light—a series of ramps constructed from translucent alabaster—zigzags skyward toward successive galleries. Congruent with the vision of the founder of the museum, Jewish philanthropist Israel Asper, of an all-inclusive Canadian genocide museum, where prominence would be given to the Holocaust as the paradigmatic genocide, the gallery "Examining the Holocaust," which deftly encapsulates the events of the Holocaust and inscribes it into the framework of human rights, is nestled at the heart of the architectural mass. The Holocaust gallery segues into "Breaking the Silence," which features five vignettes dedicated to the genocides officially recognized by Canada (plus one empty window case) and a multimedia display telling the story of sixteen cases of gross human rights violations (including the transatlantic slave trade, the comfort women system, the Cambodian genocide, and the genocide of the Maya in Guatemala). Exhibits pertaining to Canadian Indigenous peoples are interspersed throughout the museum: the most prominent is the large gallery "Indigenous Perspectives," the first one visitors enter after passing through the antechamber "What Are Human Rights?" The Indigenous gallery, flanked by large-scale artworks, is designed to showcase the richness, diversity, and longevity of Indigenous cultures in Canada. Fragments of the history of colonial violence, on the other hand, are spliced into exhibits in other galleries, such as the evocative installation called *REDress*, in the gallery "Canadian Journeys," by Métis artist Jaime Black, which shows five empty red dresses hung against a winter landscape, in a reference to over a thousand missing and murdered Indigenous women. During the 2015–16 season, one of the main temporary exhibits at the CMHR was "Witness Blanket," the monumental collage assembled by master carver Carey Newman from objects once located in Indian residential schools. Nevertheless, the museum's overall design, including the relative centrality of Holocaust remembrance, manifests reluctance to acknowledge the systematic nature of colonial violence and the continuum between past atrocities and social ills suffered by Indigenous communities today.[58] The museum, under federal auspices since 2008, abides by the policy that "the Museum does not have the power to make declarations of genocide."[59] Yet, as Tricia Logan, the former curator for Indigenous content, wonders, "Will the CMHR's treatment of these five recognized genocides further obscure the 'long-lived' quality of settler genocide in the Canadian context?"[60]

The museum's failure to address Indigenous groups' demands for recognition under the definition of genocide, despite its commitment to rectifying historical injustices, reveals the problematic relation between the current conceptualization of genocide and the discourse of human rights. These tensions were noted by Lemkin at the time of the drafting of the Genocide Convention, although the Polish-Jewish lawyer's diatribes against the Universal Declaration of Human Rights, passed one day after the United Nations adopted the Convention, were attributed to his fear that the cause of human rights, championed by Eleanor Roosevelt, would steal the spotlight and hamper his efforts to have the Genocide Convention adopted and ratified by world powers.[61]

The genealogy of "human rights" can be traced to the concept of the "rights of man," which emerged in Europe at the end of the eighteenth century during the time of the French Revolution and was given philosophical justification and moral legitimacy in the writings of thinkers such as Jean-Jacques Rousseau and Immanuel Kant.[62] As scholars of human rights have shown, the philosophical premise of man's universal, natural, and innate rights concealed the fact that the concept was formulated in response to historically contingent sociopolitical circumstances and material conditions. In relation to the history of Indigenous peoples, the assertion of the rights of man coincided with the height of the colonization project in North America. In the context of intensifying colonial genocide, the discourse of inalienable rights did not counteract the expansionist and often lethal creed of Europe's civilizing mission; on the contrary, because of its prominence in new colonial states' founding narratives, it was used to strengthen their territorial and cultural claims, and it ultimately served the goals of European imperialism. In fact, the states that championed the discourse of rights, such as England and France, engaged in particularly aggressive colonialism, which seemed to "depend on withholding these rights from non-white populations."[63]

As Hannah Arendt shows in *The Origins of Totalitarianism*, the rights of man, which emerged in the era of revolutions, were coemergent with the ideas of sovereignty, nationality, and citizenship.[64] In his influential book *The Last Utopia*, Samuel Moyn argues that the contemporary idea of human rights differs radically from the rights of man because it is no longer entangled with these political concepts. Instead, contemporary human rights derive from the intrinsically moral appeal of human suffering, and they are tied to largely conceived humanitarian and transnational agendas that strive to rise above politics. According to Moyn, the decisive shift from the political to moral significance of human rights occurred in the 1970s, following decolonization and the end of imperial world order.[65] This, for Moyn, is unsurprising if we consider that anticolonialism "was a *rights of man* movement, with all the prior fidelity to the state that concept implied in modern history."[66] Yet Moyn's theory of the caesura between the rights of man, as it was inseparable from the interests of the state, and the discourse of human rights does not account for the Indigenous people's struggle for decolonization *within* settler colonial states, a phenomenon that, in the understanding of North American Indigenous scholars and activists, is still unfolding. Reminiscent of Rothberg's terseness on the subject of colonial violence, Moyn's omission indicates that Indigenous groups' version of history and their demands for decolonization do not belong on the timeline from the rights of man to contemporary human rights. Their moral demands for the affirmation of Indigenous rights as human rights remain inseparable from political demands for recognition of their sovereignty as distinct and self-governing nations; moreover, these demands have never been contiguous with the rights of man agenda, in Moyn's understanding of the term. The fact that, in Canada, First Nations were sovereign political entities already prior to contact with Europeans was an impediment in the formation of the settler state and has remained incommensurate with hegemonic national identity.[67]

Historically, the emergence of the rights of man as a precursor to human rights was contemporaneous with the rise of a scientific discourse of race, while the success of colonialization projects was secured by conceptions of racial hierarchies premised on the notion of white supremacy.[68] Hence, colonial settler states' inequitable and for the most part violent relations with Indigenous peoples must be investigated in the context of what philosopher of race Charles Mills calls the "racial contract." Underwriting social contract theory, the racial contract is an unspoken agreement between white people to subordinate and exploit non-whites, on whom they confer an inferior moral, political, and epistemic status.[69] Racial contract theory explains why racist relations of power were formative in the genesis of colonial states and permeated their governing institutions, as well as why they have remained a necessary condition for their continuing economic development and political success. Racism is therefore a sociopolitical system; moreover, it is a system whose mechanisms must remain invisible to its beneficiaries in order to remain in power, requiring the tacit consent of the entire white population.

Sherene Razack, a Canadian scholar of gender and race, has recently called for a more thorough examination of the role of racism "as a weapon in the dispossession of Indigenous people of Canada."[70] Considering the invisibility of white privilege, which secures the continuing legacy of white supremacist thinking in Canada, this is a difficult task to accomplish. It has always been obvious to Indigenous groups, however, that virulent racism propelled the settler colonial genocidal machine and that it continues to infuse, albeit in very different and often covert forms, relations between Indigenous groups and settler populations, even though no politician would dare proclaim it today. For Razack, it is imperative that this historical continuity of racism, which is the basis of Indigenous groups' claims of genocide, not disappear from sight.

Regarding the Holocaust, Mills argues that the prominence of the genocide of the Jews in the discourse of victimization occludes the centrality of the problematic of race and racism in the history of genocidal violence against people of color. Mills views the Holocaust as the climax of murderous Eurocentrism and calls it a "fraternal" genocide between two groups of white people, while assertions of the Holocaust's singularity reflect "an astonishing white amnesia about the actual historical record."[71] Regardless of the glaring limitations of Mills's analysis of the racial dimension of the Nazi extermination of European Jews, his emphasis on the role of racial discourses in genocidal processes is particularly relevant to Indigenous claims to genocide. Yet, if the Holocaust is indeed perceived by people of color as a fratricidal genocide between white people, as Mills—but also Stannard, Churchill, and Chrisjohn—contend, why would comparisons with the Holocaust be used as the main currency in Indigenous claims of genocide? To answer this question, it is important that we give credence to Indigenous uses of the Holocaust rather than, as is often the case, dismiss them as a competition of suffering and rhetorical flourishes in bad taste. A careful examination of these interpellations forces us to reconsider the problematic of race and racism at the intersections of Jewish and Indigenous memories of genocide, with the potential to make visible vestiges of racism, with its settler colonial provenance, which continue to be entrenched in the Canadian social, cultural, and political landscape.

Intersecting Epistemic Spaces

Reflecting on the centrality of racism in the genocidal expropriation of non-white populations, Mills also draws attention to the epistemic dimension of the racial contract. If our knowledge about the world, including knowledge about the past, presupposes a socially constructed consensus about cognitive norms, then the racial contract produces a dissymmetry in the white and non-white knowers' membership in the dominant epistemic community. Western pursuit of epistemic mastery has necessitated the rejection of worldviews that do not conform to the ruling knowledge paradigm, and in relation to Indigenous peoples, it has produced, rather literally, what Tzvetan Todorov described as the "understanding that kills."[72]

Moreover, for its white signatories, the racial contract prescribes an epistemology of ignorance in matters related to race, resulting in a cognitive dysfunction that precludes transparent understanding of the racial social reality that its members themselves have created. In Europe's colonial past, the economy of cognitive ethnocentrism was an enabling condition for the conquest of territories inhabited by non-white people. As Mills demonstrates, it continues to secure and perpetuate white privilege in today's postcolonial settler states, although patterns of racial oppression, that is, the ways in which white people hold on to power, have changed. On that count, Mills's insights coincide with the theses put forth by Vine Deloria Jr., an influential contemporary thinker of mixed Oglala Sioux and European ancestry. Deloria reflects on the incommensurability and power differential between Indigenous and Eurocentric knowledge practices, resulting in racist presuppositions about Indigenous history and culture and the denigration and silencing of Indigenous perspectives. Deloria's project aims to give legitimacy to an alternative account of history, including the history of the planet, "as seen through the eyes and memory of American Indians."[73]

As Indigenous thinkers have shown, cognitive colonialism has served to exclude Indigenous knowledge claims from the realm of intelligibility and, what follows, from the universe of moral obligation.[74] Thus, the covert imposition of colonial epistemic frameworks continues to perpetuate the project of annihilation even in the spaces dedicated to making these voiced "heard," such as the CMHR. In Indian residential schools, these cognitive mechanisms of abjecting Indigenous knowledge were reinforced with coercive "linguicidal" measures, when punishments were meted out to First Nations and Inuit children for speaking their native tongues.[75]

"White" epistemic blindness rests on the fact that a different conceptual framework cannot be recognized within the Eurocentric knowledge paradigm, which structurally depends on this exclusion. This poses a conundrum: if marginalized epistemic spaces have been subjugated by Eurocentric concepts of history, memory, personhood, and trauma, how can they be incorporated into dominant systems of historical knowledge, moral obligation, and frameworks of remembrance, let alone be allowed to transform them? Mills's insight that non-white systems of knowledge have to be verified by the white epistemic apparatus in order to be recognized as valid allows us to understand Indigenous uses of the Holocaust not as egregious examples of victim envy but rather as a case of displacement in the discourse of racial victimization and of epistemic injustice that requires that Indigenous scholars and Indian residential school survivors alike mediate their claim to historical intelligibility through "white cognition."

At the height of the CMHR controversy, in 2012, grassroots movement Idle No More swept through Canada, empowering Indigenous groups and forcing the reluctant hand of the federal government to enter into negotiations regarding treaty rights, land use, Indian status, environmental protections, and living conditions in First Nations and Inuit communities. In 2015, these demands were strengthened by the Truth and Reconciliation Commission's ninety-four calls to action. Coinciding with the growing demand for self-determination, we have witnessed a proliferation of scholarly and literary work by Indigenous authors, often published by prestigious Canadian and international presses, which attests to the resurgence of not only political but also epistemic Indigenous sovereignty. In recounting the plight of their communities in the course of Canadian history, they emphasize resistance, resilience, and affirmation of Indigeneity rather than victimhood. The authors draw on traditions of oral storytelling in order to reclaim Indigenous worldviews based on interconnectedness, embodiment, and ties to the land and to denounce regnant Western concepts as inseparable from the history of violence and colonial appropriation. Anishinaabe poet and thinker Leanne Simpson, for instance, interweaves the stories taught to her by the Elders in order to explain the Nishnaabeg understanding of truth and knowledge that is embodied and relationally located: "For Indigenous Peoples, thought is fully integrated into living being and performance of our traditions," against the Cartesian dualism of mind and body. Simpson concludes: "We need to step out of the [cognitive] box, remove our colonial blinders and at least see the potential for radically different ways of existence."⁷⁶ However, dislodging dominant epistemic structures also requires that members of settler populations, who have benefited from the legacy of white power and privilege, begin to develop epistemic humility and discard *their* cognitive blinders.⁷⁷

An example of the reclamation of Indigenous knowledge with important epistemic implications is *Ta'n Weji-sqalia'tiek: Mi'kmaw Place Names Digital Atlas* (2015), which contains the Mi'kmaw names of over seven hundred places throughout the province of Nova Scotia. The project, which took Mi'kmaw linguist Bernie Francis five years to complete, probes the palimpsests of collective Indigenous memory in this small Atlantic province. It is simple and unassuming in comparison with political protests, yet it radically reconfigures imperial historical narratives. The proclamation of Indigenous names brings into visibility what has been rendered unseen in the geographical and symbolic space of the province and reinserts the Mi'kmaw presence into Canadian topography and national imaginary. I find it both exhilarating and unsettling to walk around my neighborhood in K'jipuktuk with Francis's *Atlas* as a guide, catching glimpses of traditional Mi'maw names as if surging forth from the cracks in the pavement that has sealed that history in the cement of oblivion.

Interestingly, in these recent works, which are sometimes militantly separatist with respect to Western traditions of knowledge and political practice, the Holocaust recedes as a comparative device and a constant term of reference, an indication that these Indigenous scholars and activists no longer wish to position themselves as beneficiaries of Holocaust memory, burdened as it has been with Western conceptual baggage.

To what extent do Eurocentric and therefore discriminatory epistemic measures also operate within our current understanding of the concept of genocide? It is likely that the incommensurability of its official definition with non-Western knowledge systems has undermined the efficacy of Indigenous thinkers and activists' claims to the recognition of historical wrongs as genocide. This is perhaps the full import of Chrisjohn's acerbic remark that the lesson of the Holocaust's "never forget" for First Nations is that "no one will remember what they never knew happened in the first place."⁷⁸ It is difficult to learn about and therefore remember events that do not fit into a socially sanctioned conceptual framework. This is also why Chrisjohn and other Indigenous thinkers and activists have relied on the Holocaust as an emblematic genocide that not only happened in Europe, "between White people," but also whose memory, interpretation, and representation up until now have been ensconced in a hegemonic conceptual grid. As Deloria asks, "Why is such knowledge [about the world] only valid and valuable when white scientists document and articulate it?"[79] If the idea of human rights, which historically originated in colonial Europe, does not capture Indigenous notions of personhood and sovereignty, and the definition of genocide, with its postulate to protect individual members of groups and punish the perpetrators is premised on the belief in inalienable human rights, then perhaps the distinctions and key terms of the very definition merit scrutiny. The debate around "intent" in the UN definition of *genocide*, for instance, has to be reassessed in light of Indigenous critiques of Western notions of personhood and individual agency, that is, of the anthropocentric prescription that we "imagin[e] the world in terms of atomistic [human] agents."[80] Eventually, these may be the lessons to be drawn from the CMHR debacle, which was precipitated by a lack of conceptual clarity around the terms *human rights, genocide,* and *the Holocaust*.

Dominick LaCapra, in his works on the politics of Holocaust memory, has identified an affective modality of writing about traumatic history, to which he refers as "empathic unsettlement in the face of traumatic limit events."[81] Holocaust and genocide scholars' responses to the "uses" of the Holocaust in Indigenous scholarship and activism, therefore, must entail the recognition that empathic unsettlement coincide with the task of "unsettling the settler within," to use the expression coined by Paulette Regan, the former director of research for the Truth and Reconciliation Commission of Canada.[82]

From my perspective as a Holocaust scholar, it appears that the interpellations of the Holocaust in Indigenous contexts also unmask a crisis in received modalities of Holocaust remembrance. In what way could our knowledge about the Holocaust be augmented and transformed if we were to consider it through the prism of settler colonial genocide? What blind spots would be revealed in current understanding of the genesis of the Holocaust, the processes of extermination, and victims' diverse experiences if it were refracted through the lens of non-Eurocentric perspectives and knowledge systems? An exploration of the intersections of Jewish memory of the Holocaust and

Indigenous memories of settler colonial genocide thus shines a spotlight on the urgent need to decolonize Holocaust studies as a discipline, that is, to challenge inherent presumptions and biases that stem from its Eurocentric conceptual frameworks. Perhaps only when, as Holocaust scholars, we acknowledge our complicity in perpetuating an oppressive system of knowledge and actively seek to critique its foundational concepts will we be true to the injunction of "never again!" and only then will we hear its profound reverberations in Chrystos's poem. It is my hope, therefore, that the project of decolonizing Holocaust studies has the potential to introduce an intersectional model of memory based on productive coalitions of Western and non-Western epistemic spaces, rooted in the intersecting memories of the past. And such an earnest attempt to decolonize our disciplines of knowledge and our habits of being must arise from the topographies of specific places and locales in which we live, in which we practice these disciplines and engage in knowledge transmission.

Notes

This chapter was made possible in part by funds granted to the author through a William J. Lowenberg Memorial Fellowship at the Jack, Joseph and Morton Mandel Center for Advanced Holocaust Studies at the United States Holocaust Museum. The statements made and views expressed, however, are solely the responsibility of the author.

1. The term *Indigenous peoples* used in this chapter conforms to the current nomenclature in Canada. Canadian Indigenous people comprise the Inuit (northern communities in Nunavut, Northwest Territories, Nunavik, and Labrador), the Métis (of mixed Indigenous and French ancestry), and over six hundred First Nation communities, altogether constituting an estimated 4.3 percent of Canada's population.

    The Menominee are a small tribe located in today's Wisconsin. After losing their Indigenous status by a federal decree in the 1950s, they successfully fought to regain it and were reestablished as a nation in 1973. Chrystos's family on her mother's side came to the United States from Lithuania and Alsace-Lorraine.
2. Chrystos, "Winter Count," in *Dream On* (Vancouver: Press Gang), 13.
3. Winter counts were pictographic records of important events that had occured during the year, created to aid in the preservation of an Indigenous group's oral

history. Winter counts were kept by the Lakota, Teton Sioux, Blackfeet, Mandan, and Kiowa tribes. See National Museum of the American Indian, *Lone Dog's Winter Count: Keeping History Alive*, teaching poster, http://nmai.si.edu/sites/1/files/pdf/education/poster_lone_dog_final.pdf, accessed November 15, 2017.

4. For the historical context of the violence at Wounded Knee, see Peter Mathiessen, *In the Spirit of Crazy Horse* (New York: Viking, 1980); and Leon Peltier, *Prison Writings: My Life Is My Sun Dance* (New York: St. Martin's Press, 1999).

5. For instance, Russell Thornton's account of the calamitous decline of Indigenous populations in North America is titled *American Indian Holocaust and Survival: A Population History since 1492* (Norman: University of Oklahoma Press, 1987), but the only reference to the Holocaust in this work appears in the title of the book.

6. For an account of the Oka crisis, see Geoffrey York and Loreen Pindera, *People of the Pines: The Warriors and the Legacy of Oka* (Boston: Little Brown, 1991); and *Kanehsatake: 270 Years of Resistance*, directed by Alanis Obomsawin, National Film Board of Canada, 1993.

7. The first National Conference on Indian Residential Schools took place in June 1991 in Vancouver.

8. In the period leading to World War II, the government of Mackenzie King was also notorious for adopting the policy of "none is too many" with respect to Jewish immigration. The phrase has been attributed to Frederick Blair, then head of the Immigration Branch.

9. Pamela Palmater, *Indigenous Nationhood: Empowering Grassroots Citizens* (Halifax: Fernwood, 2015), 2–3.

10. For a comprehensive account of the debate, see Benjamin Madley's "Re-examining the American Genocide Debate: Meaning, Historiography, and New Methods," *American Historical Review* 120, no. 1 (2015): 98–139. For a discussion of "intent" in the definition of the genocide in relation to settler colonial genocide, see Tony Barta, "Relations of Genocide: Land and Lives in the Colonization of Australia," in *Genocide and the Modern Age: Etiology and Case Studies of Mass Death*, ed. Isidor Wallimann and Michael N. Dobkowski (Syracuse, NY: Syracuse University Press, 2000), 237–52; A. Dirk Moses, "Conceptual Blockages and Definitional Dilemmas in the 'Racial Century': Genocides of Indigenous Peoples and the Holocaust," *Patterns of Prejudice*, 36, no. 4 (2002), 7–36; and Andrew Woolford, *This Benevolent Experiment: Indigenous Boarding Schools, Genocide, and Redress in Canada and the United States* (Lincoln: University of Nebraska Press, 2015), 35–40.

11. Steven Katz, for instance, has argued repeatedly that the destruction of Indigenous peoples in America was an "inadvertent" consequence of colonization. See

Katz, *The Holocaust in Historical Contexts*, vol. 1, *The Holocaust and Mass Death before the Modern Age* (New York: Oxford University Press, 1994).

12. In the United States, the best documented case was the settlers' rush for the mineral-rich Black Hills Mountains in South Dakota, on the traditional Lakota territory, which culminated in the Wounded Knee massacre in 1890. The 1973 stand-off at the same location followed the discovery of uranium. According to Peter Mathiessen, already in the 1970s AIM leaders were denouncing these practices as genocidal. Mathiessen, *In the Spirit of the Crazy Horse*, 415.

13. The last Beothuk died in St. John's, Newfoundland, in 1829.

14. Germany's 1904 murderous campaign against the Herero and Nama people was recognized by the United Nations in 1985 as the first genocide of the twentieth century.

15. See Marco Duranti, "The Holocaust, the Legacy of 1789 and the Birth of International Human Rights Law: Revisiting the Foundation Myth," *Journal of Genocide Research* 14, no. 2 (2012): 159–86.

16. Although in *Axis Rule in Occupied Europe* (Washington, DC: Carnegie Endowment for International Peace, 1944) Lemkin enumerates the Jews as one of the targeted national groups, together with Poles, Russians, Czechs, the Roma (referred to as "gypsies"), he also emphasizes that they were "one of the main objects of German genocide policy." He writes that "the treatment of the Jews in the occupied territory is one of the most flagrant violations of the international law," and he provides extensive details regarding that treatment throughout the book, especially in chapter 9, in which he formulates the definition of genocide.

17. See Michael A. McDonnell and A. Dirk Moses, "Raphael Lemkin as Historian of Genocide in the Americas," in *The Origins of Genocide: Raphael Lemkin as a Historian of Mass Violence*, ed. Dominik J. Schaller and Jürgen Zimmerer (London: Routledge, 2009), 57–85.

18. Lemkin based his account of the Tasmanian genocide on James Bonwick's 1870 *Last of the Tasmanians*. The most recent accounts of the genocide, however, dispute Lemkin's (and others) biological understanding of Tasmanians' racial identity and draw attention to the survival of thousands of Aboriginal Tasmanians of mixed heritage. As Tom Lawson argues, the insistence on the totality of destruction "is in some ways a perpetuation of colonizing thinking." Lawson, *The Last Man: A British Genocide in Tasmania* (London: I. B. Tauris, 2014), 10. In contrast, the Beothuk of Newfoundland are considered an extinct Indigenous tribe.

19. See Raphäel Lemkin, *Totally Unofficial: The Autobiography of Raphael Lemkin*, ed. Donna-Lee Frieze (New Haven, CT: Yale University Press, 2013), chaps. 8–10.

20. Lemkin, *Axis Rule in Occupied Europe*, 79.
21. David Stannard, *The Conquest of the New World* (New York: Oxford University Press, 1992), 246.
22. The United States and Canada were signatories of the Convention on the Prevention and Punishment of the Crime of Genocide, which was adopted by the United Nations on December 9, 1948, and came into force in 1951. Canada ratified the convention in 1952, while the United States delayed ratification until 1988.
23. Alice M. Azure, "From Wasouk to Shoah and Back: A Mi'kmaq Honor Song," in *Eating Fire, Tasting Blood: An Anthology of the American Indian Holocaust*, ed. MariJo Moore (New York: Thunder's Mouth Press, 2006), 250.
24. Eric Gansworth, "American Heritage," in Moore, *Eating Fire, Tasting Blood*, 273.
25. See David B. MacDonald, *Identity Politics in the Age of Genocide: The Holocaust and Historical Representation*, Routledge Advances in International Relations and Global Politics (New York: Routledge, 2008), 42.
26. In an interview with the Saskatoon *Star Phoenix*, Ahanakew applauded Hitler's extermination of the Jews in light of what he believed had been the Jewish international conspiracy to dominate the world. Indigenous leaders and organizations immediately distanced themselves from Ahanakew's remarks. See Erin Anderssen, "Native Leader Applauds Hitler" in *Globe and Mail* (Toronto), December 16, 2002, www.theglobeandmail.com/news/national/native-leader-applauds-hitler/article4140793/.
27. This satirical paraphrase of the Canadian anthem could be heard during anti-fracking protests at the Elsipogtog First Nation in New Brunswick in October 2013. Quoted in Palmater, *Indigenous Nationhood*, ix.
28. According to John Reid, Cornwallis was generally unsuccessful in settling Mi'kma'ki, which he renamed Nova Scotia. It is only in the early twentieth century that he began to be celebrated as the "founder" of the city, to bolster the Canadian nationalist narrative and celebrate the success of the East Coast branch of the Canadian National Railway. See John Reid, "Three Lives of Edward Cornwallis," *Journal of the Royal Nova Scotia Historical Society* 16 (2013): 19–45.
29. The Mi'maq and the British signed a succession of Peace and Friendship Treaties (in 1725, 1749, 1752, and in 1760).
30. See John Reid, "Imperial-Aboriginal Friendship in Eighteenth-Century Mi'kma'ki/Wulstukwik," in *The Loyal Atlantic: Remaking the British Atlantic in the Revolutionary Era*, ed. Jerry Bannister and Liam Riordan (Toronto: University of Toronto Press, 2012), 75–102.

31. Chrystos, "Winter Count," 13.
32. Tim Bousquet, "Cornwallis Renaming Is the Right Thing to Do: We Shouldn't Honour the Architects of Genocide," *The Coast*, June 26, 2011, at www.thecoast.ca/RealityBites/archives/2011/06/26/cornwallis-renaming-is-the-right-thing-to-do.
33. John Reid points out the stakes of the Cornwallis controversy are high since they concern the legitimacy of the entire Nova Scotia settlement. Reid, "Three Lives of Edward Cornwallis," 37.
34. Daniel N. Paul, *We Were Not the Savages: Collision between European and Native American Civilizations* (Halifax: Fernwood, 2006), 179.
35. Canada's Truth and Reconciliation Commission, chaired by Honorable Justice Murray Sinclair, a First Nations lawyer and legal scholar from Manitoba, published a comprehensive final report, *Honouring the Truth, Reconciling for the Future: Summary of the Final Report of the Truth and Reconciliation Commission of Canada* (Toronto: James Lorimer, 2015). The report contains ninety-four calls to action, which are recommendations for changes in education, health, governance, and other areas concerning Indigenous peoples. For an analysis of the Indian residential schools' assimilationist policies, see Andrew Woolford, *This Benevolent Experiment: Indigenous Boarding Schools, Genocide, and Redress in Canada and the United States* (Lincoln: University of Nebraska Press, 2015). For the history of the Shubenacadie Indian Residential School in Nova Scotia, see Isabelle Knockwood, *Out of the Depths: The Experiences of Mi'kmaw Children at the Indian Residential School at Schubenacadie Nova Scotia* (Lockport, NS: Roseway, 1992) and Chris Benjamin, *Indian School Road: Legacies of Schubenacadie Residential School* (Halifax: Nimbus, 2014).
36. Paul, *We Were Not the Savages*, 125.
37. Some of the previous measures of redress included the Statement of Reconciliation (1998), which established the Aboriginal Healing Foundation; Alternative Dispute Resolution (2003), which implemented a 1.9 billion compensation package in 2005; and the Settlement Agreement (2006), which provided funding for the Aboriginal Healing Foundation and its successor, the Legacy of Hope Foundation.
38. Sean Glen Coulthard, *Red Skin, White Masks: Rejecting the Colonial Politics of Recognition* (University of Minnesota Press, 2014), 107–10.
39. See "Change Comes Slowly, Mi'kmaq Elder Says," *Chronicle Herald* (Halifax), January 28, 2013, A3.
40. Joseph Auguste Merasty, *The Education of Augie Merasty: A Residential School Memoir* (Regina, SK: University of Regina Press, 2015), 48.

41. Roland Chrisjohn and Sherri Young, *The Circle Game: Shadows and Substance in the Indian Residential School Experience in Canada* (Penticton, BC: Theytus, 1997), 41.
42. Zygmunt Bauman, quoted in Chrisjohn and Young, *Circle Game*, 45–46
43. Lawrence Langer, quoted in Chrisjohn and Young, *Circle Game*, 39.
44. Jean Améry, quoted in Chrisjohn and Young, *Circle Game*, 80; and Aaron Haas, *The Aftermath: Living with the Holocaust*, in Chrisjohn and Young, *Circle Game*, 145–46.
45. Chrisjohn and Young complained that while "Holocaust Deniers are the lunatic fringe in the mainstream society . . . , Genocide Deniers are the legitimate authorities and scholars when Indians are the subjects." Roland Chrisjohn and Sherri Young, "Genocide and Indian Residential Schooling: The Past Is Present," in *Canada and International Humanitarian Law: Peacekeeping and War Crimes in the Modern Era*, ed. Richard D. Wiggers and Ann L. Griffiths (Halifax: Center for Foreign Policy Studies, Dalhousie University, 2002), 331.
46. Chrisjohn and Young, *Circle Game*, 63; and Roland D. Chrisjohn and Shaunessy M. McKay, *Dying to Please You: Indigenous Suicide in Contemporary Canada* (Pentiction, BC: Theytus, 2017). See also David Nercessian, "Rethinking Cultural Genocide under International Law," *Human Rights Dialogue*, April 22, 2005, 507–8.
47. Daniel Paul, private conversation with the author, March 2016.
48. Phil Fontaine and Bernie Farber, *Toronto Star*, July 19, 2013, www.thestar.com/opinion/commentary/2013/07/19/a_canadian_genocide_in_search_of_a_name.html.
49. See Phil Fontaine and Bernie Farber, "What Canada Committed against First Nations Was Genocide. The UN Should Recognize It," *Globe and Mail* (Toronto), October 14, 2013.
50. Nate Leipciger, *The Weight of Freedom* (Toronto: Azrieli Foundation), 260.
51. Theodore Fontaine, *Broken Circle: The Dark Legacy of Indian Residential Schools* (Victoria, BC: Heritage House, 2010), 171.
52. *2510037901*, created by Steven Loft, Vtape, Winnipeg, 2000. The text used in the videorecording is based on John G. Neihardt, *Black Elk Speaks: The Life Story of a Holy Man of the Oglala Sioux* (1932), in which the author documented his conversation with Black Elk, Crazy Horse's cousin.
53. Loft's self-presentation as a person of mixed ancestry is very different from Kali Spitzer's artistic portraiture. Spitzer is Kaska Dena from British Columbia on her father's side and Jewish Romanian from Transylvania on her mother's side. In

contrast to Loft's amalgam of the two sides of his heritage, Spitzer immerses herself fully in her Kaska ancestry to create an "art of resilience" that would help offset the impact of settler colonialism. See Kali Spitzer, "An Exploration of Resilience," *Narrative Witness 2. Indigenous Peoples: Australia–US*, International Writing Program, March 2016, www.iwpcollections.org/nw2-kali-spitzer.

54. Moses, "Conceptual Blockages," 36.
55. Michael Rothberg, *Multidirectional Memory: Remembering the Holocaust in the Age of Decolonization* (Stanford, CA: Stanford Universitiy Press, 2009), 28.
56. Erica Lehrer, "Thinking through the Canadian Museum for Human Rights," *American Quarterly* 67, no. 4 (2015): 1195–1216.
57. Karen Busby et al., "Introduction," in *The Idea of a Human Rights Museum*, ed. Karen Busby, Adam Muller, and Andrew Woolford (Winnipeg: University of Manitoba Press, 2015), 4–5.
58. See A. Dirk Moses, "Does the Holocaust Reveal or Conceal Other Genocides?," in *Hidden Genocides: Power, Knowledge, Memory*, ed. Alexander Laban Hinton, Thomas La Pointe, and Douglas Irvin-Erickson (New Brunswick, NJ: Rutgers University Press, 2014), 21–51.
59. Stuart Murray, former CEO for the museum, in a statement in July 2013, quoted in *Honouring the Truth, Reconciling for the Future*, 250.
60. Tricia Logan, "National Memory and Museums: Remembering Settler Colonial Genocide of Indigenous People in Canada," in *Remembering Genocide*, ed. Nigel Eltringham and Pam MacLean (New York: Routledge, 2014), 114.
61. See Samantha Power, *A Problem from Hell: America and the Age of Genocide* (New York: Basic Books, 2013), chap. 4.
62. See Rowan Cruft, S. Matthew Liao, and Massimo Renzo, eds., *Philosophical Foundations of Human Rights* (Oxford: Oxford University Press, 2015); and Johannes Morsink, *Inherent Human Rights: Philosophical Roots of the Universal Declaration* (Philadelphia: University of Pennsylvania Press, 2009).
63. Stephan-Ludwig Hoffman, "Introduction: Genealogies of Human Rights," in *Human Rights in the Twentieth Century*, ed. Stephan-Ludwig Hoffman (Cambridge: Cambridge University Press, 2011), 7.
64. Hannah Arendt, "The Perplexities of the Rights of Man and Citizen," in chap. 9 of *The Origins of Totalitarianism* (New York: Harcourt, 1976), 290–302.
65. Samuel Moyn, *The Last Utopia: Human Rights in History* (Cambridge, MA: Belknap Press, 2010). Another significant factor was the Cold War détente, culminating in the Helsinki Accords in 1975. See also Samuel Moyn, "The Return of

the Prodigal: The 1970's as the Turning Point in Human Rights History," in *The Breakthrough: Human Rights in the 1970's*, ed. Jan Eckel and Samuel Moyn (Philadelphia: University of Pennsylvania Press, 2014).

66. Moyn, *The Last Utopia*, 85.
67. Mohawk scholar Audra Simpson asks, "How to proceed as a nation if the right to determine the terms of legal belonging, a crucial component of sovereignty, have been dictated by a foreign government?" in *Mohawk Interruptus: Political Life across the Borders of Settler States* (Durham, NC: Duke University Press, 2014), 10.
68. The period of 1850–1950, in which the phenomenon of racialized nation building corresponded to the height of colonial expansion, has been referred to as "the racial century." See Moses, "Conceptual Blockages," 33.
69. Charles Mills, *The Racial Contract* (Ithaca, NY: Cornell University Press, 1997), 11.
70. Sherene Razack, Malinda Smith, and Sunera Thobani, eds., *States of Race: Critical Race Feminism for the 21st Century* (Toronto: Between the Lines, 2010), xvi. See also Sherene H. Razack, *Dying from Improvement: Inquests and Inquiries into Indigenous Deaths in Custody* (Toronto: University of Toronto Press, 2015).
71. Mills, *Racial Contract*, 102.
72. Tzvetan Todorov, *The Conquest of America: The Question of the Other*, trans. Richard Howard (New York: Harper & Row, 1984).
73. Vine Deloria Jr., *Red Earth, White Lies: Native Americans and the Myth of Scientific Fact* (New York: Scribner, 1995), 35.
74. The terms *cognitive ethnocentrism* and *cognitive colonialism* have lately been used in Indigenous pedagogy. See, for instance, Leanne Simpson, *Dancing on Our Turtle's Back: Stories of Nishnaabeg Re-creation, Resurgence, and New Emergence* (Winnipeg: Arp Books, 2011), 44; and Marie Battiste, *Decolonizing Education: Nourishing the Learning Spirit* (Saskatoon, SK: Purich, 2013), 26.
75. "Linguicide" is a term used by Andrea Bear Nicholas, who defines it as "the killing of languages without killing the speakers." In "Linguicide: Submersion Education and the Killing of Languages in Canada," *Briarpatch* March 1, 2011, briarpatchmagazine.com/articles/view/linguicide.
76. Simpson, *Dancing*, 148.
77. Angela Failler and Roger Simon, "Curatorial Challenges: Curatorial Practice and Learning from Difficult Knowledge," in Busby, Muller, and Woolford, *Idea of a Human Rights Museum*, 174.
78. Chrisjohn and Young, "Genocide and Indian Residential Schooling," 14.
79. Deloria, *Red Earth, White Lies*, 59.

80. See Moses, "Conceptual Blockages," 21.
81. LaCapra, *Writing History, Writing Trauma* (Baltimore: Johns Hopkins University Press, 2001), 102.
82. See Paulette Regan, *Unsettling the Settler Within: Indian Residential Schools, Truth Telling, and Reconciliation in Canada* (Vancouver: University of British Columbia Press, 2010).

Conclusion

Shirli Gilbert and Avril Alba

THE STARTING POINT FOR this project was our skepticism about the anti-racist discourse that characterizes much contemporary Holocaust education and memorialization. Over the few years that we have been working on this volume, we have witnessed Trumpism, the Brexit vote, and the alarming resurgence of far-right and neo-Nazi movements across Europe, the United States, and beyond. Such political developments only strengthen our conviction that Holocaust remembrance and education, while often sincerely conceived, is premised on largely untested assumptions. So far, there has been little concrete evidence to suggest that remembering or learning about the Holocaust imparts the kinds of lessons that politicians or educators might hope.

Memorialization initiatives nonetheless continue apace, accompanied by the familiar discourse of anti-racism and tolerance. In October 2017, the winning design was announced for the UK Holocaust Memorial that David Cameron envisioned. This new "national landmark" will be built alongside the Houses of Parliament in London, along with a learning center that will "use the stories and facts of the Holocaust to explore anti-Semitism, extremism, Islamophobia, racism, homophobia and other forms of hatred and prejudice in society today," with the aim of "encouraging respect for others and preventing hatred."[1]

Explaining why "the Holocaust is not—and is not likely to become—a global memory," the historian Peter Novick cautions against the conflation of genuinely collective memory with what he calls "mnemonics": commemorations, memorials, museums, and artifacts intended to spur or support memory work. The latter, he argues, are not necessarily an index to how, and how much, a society actually remembers. Collective memories that do real work in the world, that are "consequential," speak to people's "essential and enduring" identities. While many Holocaust mnemonics dot the American landscape, Novick writes, most Americans do not feel that the Holocaust is *their* memory; rather, it is an "inconsequential" memory that primarily advances the objectives of particular individuals and groups.²

Our reading is perhaps not as cynical as Novick's, even if some memorialization initiatives might reflect the kind of contrivance he suggests. As the contributions to this volume show, memory of the Holocaust has emerged in diverse contexts around the world across more than seven decades. It has informed racist and anti-racist discourse in sometimes transparently political ways, in unexpected ways, and at times because it has been a productive or evasive or provocative medium for engaging with contemporary racism. The rich and sustained history of encounters between the Holocaust and anti-racism nevertheless contrasts markedly with many of the mnemonics produced today, whose messages of tolerance and anti-racism seem to bear less and less relation to the societies from which they emerge.

This volume was intended, first and foremost, to advance a scholarly debate on how Holocaust memory has informed thinking about racism since 1945. Its emphasis on historicization, however, is perhaps of even greater potential importance in the public sphere. A longer historical perspective forces us to look differently, and more critically, at the connections we often unthinkingly make today. It should also hopefully lead us to consider more carefully how Holocaust memory work is rationalized and implemented. In this way, the ever-expanding variety of Holocaust remembrance and educational initiatives might have a better chance of achieving their intended effects.

Notes

1. "Adjaye Associates and Ron Arad Architects Win UK Holocaust Memorial International Design Competition," press release, Gov.UK, October 24, 2017, www.gov.uk/government/news/adjaye-associates-and-ron-arad-architexts-win-uk-holocaust-memorial-international-design-competition.
2. Peter Novick, "The Holocaust Is Not—and Is Not Likely to Become—a Global Memory," in *Marking Evil: Holocaust Memory in the Global Age*, ed. Amos Goldberg and Haim Hazan (New York: Bergahn Books, 2015), 47–55.

Contributors

Avril Alba is a senior lecturer in Holocaust studies and Jewish civilization in the Department of Hebrew, Biblical and Jewish Studies at the University of Sydney. She has published in the areas of Holocaust memory and representation, including *The Holocaust Memorial Museum: Sacred Secular Space* (Palgrave Macmillan, 2015). From 2002 to 2011, Avril was the education director at the Sydney Jewish Museum where she also served as the project director/curator for the permanent exhibition *Culture and Continuity* (2009). She was also project director/consulting curator for the permanent exhibition *The Holocaust* (2017) and co-chief investigator/consulting curator with Associate Professor Jennifer Barrett and Professor A. Dirk Moses for the permanent exhibition *The Holocaust and Human Rights* (2018).

Shirli Gilbert is a professor of modern history and director of the Parkes Institute for the Study of Jewish/ non-Jewish Relations at the University of Southampton. She has published widely on themes relating to Holocaust history and memory and is the author of *Music in the Holocaust* (Oxford University Press, 2005) and, most recently, *From Things Lost: Forgotten Letters and the Legacy of the Holocaust* (Wayne State University Press, 2017). Her current research focuses on Holocaust memory in apartheid and post-apartheid South Africa.

Bashir Bashir is associate professor in the Department of Sociology, Political Science and Communication at the Open University of Israel and a research fellow at the Van Leer Jerusalem Institute. His primary research interests are nationalism and citizenship studies, democratic theory, and the politics of reconciliation. His publications include "Reconciling Historical Injustices: Deliberative Democracy and the Politics of Reconciliation," *Res Publica* (2012); "On Citizenship and Citizenship Education; A Levantine Approach and Reimagining Israel/Palestine," *Citizenship Studies* (2015); (with Amos Goldberg), "'Deliberating the Holocaust and the Nakba: Disruptive Empathy and Binationalism in Israel/Palestine,"

Journal of Genocide Research (2014); "The Strengths and Weaknesses of Integrative Solutions for the Israeli-Palestinian Conflict," *Middle East Journal* (2016); and (coedited with Will Kymlicka), *The Politics of Reconciliation in Multicultural Societies* (Oxford University Press, 2008).

Sarah Phillips Casteel is a professor of English at Carleton University, where she is cross-appointed to the Institute of African Studies and the Institute for Comparative Studies in Literature, Art and Culture and where she cofounded the Centre for Transnational Cultural Analysis. The recipient of a Polanyi prize and a Horst Frenz prize, she is the author of *Second Arrivals: Landscape and Belonging in Contemporary Writing of the Americas* (University of Virginia Press, 2007) and the coeditor (with Winifried Siemerling) of *Canada and Its Americas: Transnational Navigations* (McGill-Queen's University Press, 2010). Her most recent book, *Calypso Jews: Jewishness in the Caribbean Literary Imagination* (Columbia University Press, 2016), won a Canadian Jewish Literary Award.

Steven Cooke is a cultural and historical geographer with interests in heritage, memory, and identity, particularly the history, interpretation, and management of sites associated with war and genocide. Between 2002 and 2011, he worked in the heritage sector at some of Australia Victoria's most significant places, including Melbourne Maritime Museum and the Shrine of Remembrance. He is a senior lecturer in Cultural Heritage and course director for the Cultural Heritage and Museum Studies Program at Deakin University. In 2015, he was appointed as a representative to the International Holocaust Remembrance Alliance by the Australian Government.

Marjorie N. Feld is a professor of history at Babson College in Wellesley, MA, where she teaches courses on American social, gender, and labor history. She is the author of *Lillian Wald: A Biography* (University of North Carolina Press, 2008) and *Nations Divided: American Jews and the Struggle over Apartheid* (Palgrave Macmillan, 2014) Feld is a member of the Academic Councils of Jewish Voice for Peace and Open Hillel. At Babson, she has been the recipient of the LGBTQ+ Pride Award (2017) and the Deans' Award for Teaching Excellence (2018).

Donna-Lee Frieze is a genocide studies scholar with the Contemporary Histories Research Group at Deakin University in Melbourne. She has published widely on twentieth-century genocides in relation to philosophy and cultural studies; is the editor and transcriber of Raphael Lemkin's autobiography, *Totally Unofficial* (Yale University Press, 2013), which has recently been translated into Spanish and Polish; and is coauthor (with Steven Cooke) of *The Interior of Our Memories: A History of Melbourne's Jewish Holocaust Centre* (Hybrid, 2015). She a delegate for the Australian government in the Academic Working Group and the Committee on Holocaust, Genocide and Crimes Against Humanity for the International Holocaust Remembrance Alliance.

Dorota Glowacka is a professor of humanities at the University of King's College in Halifax, NS, where she teaches classes in Holocaust and genocide studies, gender studies, philosophy of race, and critical theory. She has an MA in English from the University of Wrocław, Poland, and a PhD in comparative literature from the State University of New York–Buffalo. She is the author of *Po tamtej stronie: świadectwo, afekt, wyobraźnia* (On the other side: Testimony, affect, imagination) (Institute of Literary Studies, Polish Academy of Science, 2017) and *Disappearing Traces: Holocaust Testimonials, Ethics, and Aesthetics* (University of Washington Press, 2012). She coedited (with Joanna Zylinska) *Imaginary Neighbors: Mediating Polish-Jewish Relations after the Holocaust* (Nebraska UP, 2007) and (with Stephen Boos) *Between Ethics and Aesthetics: Crossing the Boundaries* (SUNY Press, 2002), and she edited a special issue of *Culture Machine* (2006). Glowacka has published numerous book chapters, journal articles, reviews, and encyclopedia entries in Holocaust studies and critical theory. In 2017, Glowacka was William J. Lowenberg Memorial Fellow on America, the Holocaust, and the Jews at the United States Holocaust Memorial Museum.

Amos Goldberg is associate professor at the Hebrew University of Jerusalem, where he teaches Holocaust history. Among his recent publications are *Trauma in First Person: Diary Writing during the Holocaust* (Indiana University Press, 2017) and his coedited volume (with Bashir Bashir) *The Holocaust and the Nakba: A New Grammar of Trauma and History* (Columbia University Press, 2018).

James Jordan is associate professor of Jewish/non-Jewish relations in the Parkes Institute and English Department at the University of Southampton. He is the author of *From Nuremberg to Hollywood: The Holocaust and the Courtroom in American Fictive Film* (Vallentine Mitchell, 2015), and coeditor of several books, including (with Lisa Leff and Joachim Schlör) *Jewish Migration and the Archive* (Taylor & Francis, 2016), (with Tony Kushner and Sarah Pearce) *Jewish Journeys:*

From Philo to Hip Hop (Vallentine Mitchell, 2010), and (with Tom Lawson) *The Memory of the Holocaust in Australia* (Vallentine Mitchell, 2008). He is also coeditor (with Hannah Holtschneider, Tom Lawson and Joanne Pettitt) of *Holocaust Studies: A Journal of Culture and History* (www.tandfonline.com/rhos). He is currently writing a monograph on the BBC and the Holocaust, alongside a broader project on the role and representation of Jews in British television.

Tony Kushner is a professor of Jewish/non-Jewish relations in the Parkes Institute and History Department at the University of Southampton. He is the author of eight monographs, including *Remembering Refugees: Then and Now* (Manchester University Press, 2006) and *Anglo-Jewry since 1066: Place, Locality and Memory* (Manchester University Press, 2009). His most recent book is *The Battle of Britishness: Migrant Journeys, 1685 to the Present* (Manchester University Press, 2012). He is currently working on a study of the construction of ethnicity in the British armed forces and two books relating to Holocaust journeys: *Journeys from the Abyss: The Holocaust and Forced Migration* and (with Aimee Bunting) *Co-Presents to the Holocaust*. He is coeditor (with Tony Kushner, Dan Stone and Barbara Rosenbaum) of the *Journal Patterns of Prejudice* and deputy editor of *Jewish Culture and History*.

Dan J. Puckett is a professor of history at Troy University. He received his PhD at Mississippi State University and is the author of *In the Shadow of Hitler: Alabama's Jews, the Second World War, and the Holocaust* (University of Alabama Press, 2014). His work has been published in *Holocaust and Genocide Studies*, *Alabama Review*, *Alabama Heritage*, and *Southern Jewish History*, among other publications. He is currently working on his second book, *The Jim Crow of All the Ages: Adolf Hitler, World War Two, and Civil Rights in the Heart of Dixie, 1933–1948*. Puckett has been a Starkoff Fellow at the Jacob Rader Marcus Center of the American Jewish Archives and a Chancellor's Fellow at Troy University. He is the chair of the Alabama Holocaust Commission, the immediate past president of the Southern Jewish Historical Society, and a member of the Executive Committee of the Association of Alabama Historians.

Michael Rothberg is the 1939 Society Samuel Goetz Chair in Holocaust Studies and Professor of English and comparative literature at the University of California–Los Angeles. His latest book is *The Implicated Subject: Beyond Victims and Perpetrators* (forthcoming), which will be published in Stanford University

Press's Cultural Memory in the Present series. Previous books include *Multidirectional Memory: Remembering the Holocaust in the Age of Decolonization* (2009), *Traumatic Realism: The Demands of Holocaust Representation* (2000), and (coedited with Neil Levi) *The Holocaust: Theoretical Readings* (2003). With Yasemin Yildiz, he is currently completing *Inheritance Trouble: Migrant Archives of Holocaust Remembrance* for Fordham University Press.

Suzanne D. Rutland, OAM, PhD, is professor emerita in the Department of Hebrew, Biblical and Jewish Studies at the University of Sydney and a renowned Australian Jewish historian. She has published widely on Australian Jewish history, edits the Sydney edition of the *American Jewish Historical Society* journal, and writes on issues relating to the Shoah, Israel, and Jewish education. She is the author of *The Jews in Australia* (Cambridge University Press, 2005); her latest book (with Sam Lipski), *Let My People Go: The Untold Story of Australia and Soviet Jews, 1959–1989* (Hybrid, 2015), was joint winner of the Prime Minister's Literary Award, Australian History. She is a member of the Australian expert delegation for the International Holocaust Remembrance Alliance. In 2008, she received the Medal of the Order of Australia for services to higher Jewish education and interfaith dialogue.

Milton Shain is a professor emeritus of historical studies at the University of Cape Town. He has written, coauthored, and coedited several books on South African Jewish history, South African politics, and the history of antisemitism, including *The Roots of Antisemitism in South Africa* (University Press of Virginia, 1994); *Antisemitism* (Bowerdean Press, 1998); (with coauthor Richard Mendelsohn) *The Jews in South Africa: An Illustrated History* (Jonathan Ball, 2008 and 2014); *A Perfect Storm: Antisemitism in South Africa, 1930–1948* (Jonathan Ball, 2015); and (with coeditors Christopher Browning, Susannah Heschel, and Michael Marrus) *Holocaust Scholarship: Personal Trajectories and Professional Interpretations* (Palgrave Macmillan, 2015).

David Slucki is an assistant professor in the Yaschik/Arnold Jewish Studies Program at the College of Charleston. He received his PhD from Monash University in 2010. His first book, *The International Jewish Labor Bund after 1945: Toward a Global History* (Rutgers, 2012), was the first to look closely at the attempts of Bundists to adapt to the post-Holocaust world. His forthcoming book, *Sing This at My Funeral: A Memoir of Fathers and Sons*, in press with Wayne State

University Press, is a scholarly memoir telling the story of three generations of fathers and sons as they grappled with the Holocaust and its aftermath. Along with Gabriel Finder and Avinoam Patt, he is also coediting a volume on humor after the Holocaust.

Michael E. Staub is a professor of English and American studies at Baruch College, City University of New York. His books include *Torn at the Roots: The Crisis of Jewish Liberalism in Postwar America* (Columbia University Press, 2002), *Madness Is Civilization: When the Diagnosis Was Social, 1948–1980* (University of Chicago Press, 2011), and, most recently, *The Mismeasure of Minds: Debating Race and Intelligence between "Brown" and "The Bell Curve"* (University of North Carolina Press, 2018). He is also the editor of a primary source collection, *The Jewish 1960s: An American Sourcebook* (University Press of New England, 2004). His articles have appeared in *American Quarterly, American Studies, History of Psychology, Representations, MELUS, Shofar, Radical History Review, Minnesota Review,* as well as numerous anthologies.

INDEX

Note: Italic locators reference images in the text.

Aarons, Mark, 285
Abella, Irving, 110
Abeng (Cliff), 252–54, 259, 261
Aboriginal Australians. *See* Indigenous Australians
"Aborigines—Extinction Ballad" (poem; Ravitch), 128–29
Abrahams, Israel, 84–85, 90n66
Abrahams, Sidney, 28–29, 35
Absentees' Property Law (Israel; 1966), 299
Achcar, Gilbert, 296
Acutt, Frank, 81–82
Adler, Jacques, 278, 279, 283
African Americans: armed forces discrimination, 20, 25–26; black nationalism and black power, 173, 208, 212–13, 214–15; employment rights, 53, 55–61, *56*, *60*; history museums, 263; Jewish relations, 173, 181–82, 196–97, 198, 202–9, 212–13, 214, 242, 247–48, 249; racism and Nazism comparisons, Jim Crow era and civil rights, 14, 41–66, 196–209; rights/freedom considered, WWII context, 14, 44, 46, 53, 61, 63; veterans, 66;
voting rights, 46, 50–53, 63, 66; whites' discrimination and stereotyping, 26, 43, 45, 199, 204, 205, 206–7
African diaspora and literature, 248, 256, 260
African governors, 24, 28
African student recruiting, United Kingdom, 24, 27–29
Afrikaner Unity Committee, 80–81
Agamben, Giorgio, 312
Ahenakew, David, 391–92, 413n26
Ajzenbud, Moshe, 339
Alabama. *See* American South
Alabama Democratic Party, 52
Alabama Dry Dock and Shipbuilding Company (ADDSCO), 58, 59
Alba, Avril, 146, 220, 272–89, 332–33, 419–20
Alberta, Canada, 394
Alexander, Jeffrey, 5, 247, 260–61
Aliens Act (South Africa; 1937), 77
Aliens Amendment and Immigration Bill (South Africa; 1939), 78
Allen and Unwin, 276–77
American Indian Movement (AIM), 387, 388, 395, 412n12

427

American Jewish Congress: anti-apartheid activism, 171–72, 176, 182, 187, 193n56; anti-racism messaging and activism, 198–99, 202, 205

American Jewish Historical Society, 196

American South: economics and geography, 44, 58–59; equality vs. segregation policy, 55–57, 58, 59, 64, 66; Jewish politics and activism, 196–97, 204; lynching, 42, 43, 46–50; Nazism vs. racism, 14, 41–66, 196–97; north-south relations, 45, 46–47, 47–48, 55, 57, 59, 65–66; political history, 45, 46–47, 50–53, 61, 65, 68n24; voting rights and registration, 50–53, 63, 68nn24–25; whites' racial attitudes, 45, 47–50, 55, 56–57, 59, 62–64, 65

Améry, Jean, 6, 396

Anaya, James, 398

Anderson, Fay, 97

Anishinaabe peoples, 407–8

Anne Frank House (Amsterdam), 240–42, 259

Anschluss (1938), 107, 222

Anstey, Fred, 103

anticolonialism: activism, 34, 168–69, 174–75, 179, 181–82, 184–85, 187, 260, 261; human rights thinking, 403–4; literature, 224–28, 243, 245, 250, 261; South African history education, 364

anti-communism, 201–2

anti-racism activism. *See also* anti-racism discourse: anti-apartheid, 166–88, 363–64; Jewish activism, 3, 28–29, 117, 118, 136, 140–41, 168–74, 179–88, 196–209, 215, 327–29, 332–33, 335, 338–41, 342; motivations, 117, 168, 196–97, 198–99, 200–201; post-Holocaust projects, 3–4, 196–205, 293, 343–44, 419, 420; and "tolerance," 327–28, 336, 342; universalism and particularism, 118, 172–74, 343

anti-racism discourse. *See also* anti-racism activism; literature and literary connections: containment of Holocaust memory, 7–8, 14–15; Holocaust memory assumptions and, 1–2, 3, 7–8, 294, 372, 419, 420

Anti-Semite and Jew (Sartre), 226–27

antisemitism: activist/movement clashes, 173–74, 391–92, 413n26; Australia, 91–96, 100–106, 107–11, 122, 124, 272, 273, 276–78, 280–83, 288–89; Canada, 411n8; and colonialism, 226–28, 245; vs. and compared with racism, 3, 43, 73, 147–48, 151–53, 196–97, 198–202, 204, 226–28, 333, 335, 336, 341, 367; European history, 72, 299, 357, 358, 361; history education, 357, 358, 359–61, 362, 365; Jewish responses to, 117, 200–201, 234, 327–29, 332–33, 335, 336, 339, 341; media portrayals and communication, 99–100, 101–6, 272, 333; of Nazism, 43, 151, 200–201, 359–61, 362, 366–67, 368–69; "new," 36n9; South Africa, 14, 72–85; stereotypes, 73, 92, 93, 94, 100–106, 110, 211, 314; Ukrainian, 275–76, 277, 278, 281,

282; United Kingdom, 13–14, 17, 20, 26–27, 30–31

apartheid (South Africa), 2, 78, 83–85, 350, 352, 361–62; education system within, 353–55, 356–57, 370, 375n16; Holocaust education, Nazism, and racism, 293–94, 350–72; Jewish attitudes and Holocaust memory, 118, 168–88; personal accounts, 148; South African history education, 351–52, 364–65, 367, 368, 369, 371–72; South African Jewish racial identity, 14, 170, 182–83; term and language, 170, 186, 352

apologies. *See* reconciliation movements

Arab-Israeli conflicts: challenges of asymmetry, 297, 298–301, 309–10, 314–15; military, 174, 209, 215, 299, 307; personal discourse, 307, 309–11; political discourse, 175–76, 178, 179, 183–84, 316–18; State of Israel creation and Palestinian Nakba, 293, 295–319

Arabs and the Holocaust, The (Achcar), 296

Arafat, Yasser, 183–84, 193n60

archaeological excavations, 401

Arendt, Hannah, 6–7, 211, 245, 312–13, 325n57, 403

armed forces discrimination: United Kingdom, 14, 21–24, 25; United States, 20, 25–26

Armenian genocide and refugees, 312, 398

Armstrong, Judith, 281–82

Aronsfeld, C.C., 189n3

Art of the Holocaust (temporary exhibition, JHC), 336–37

art projects and exhibitions, 334, 336–37, 399–400, 402

Aryanism, 43–44, 64, 87n29, 106, 207, 359–60, 366–67

Asian immigration: Australia, 93–94, 340; South Africa, 77, 78; United Kingdom and London's East End, 117, 147, 149–51, 154, 158, 161, 162, 163, 165

Asmal, Kader, 355–56

Asper, Israel, 401–2

assimilation: Canadian attitudes, 388, 389, 394, 397, 404; immigration policy and exclusion, 79, 80, 81, 106; Indigenous Australians, 121, 132–34, 138–39; Jewish, into whiteness and privilege, 117, 122–24, 130, 134–35, 139–40, 141, 154, 165, 173, 209, 213, 226; Jews assumed "unassimilable," Australia, 92, 103, 105, 107, 109–10; Jews assumed "unassimilable," South Africa, 73, 75, 76–78, 79, 81–82; Jews assumed "unassimilable," United Kingdom, 31; melting pot concept, 153, 154, 162; price on peoples, 138–39, 207; rejections, 162–63, 208, 211–13, 231, 232–34

Assmann, Aleida, 247, 260, 261

asymmetry challenges: Arab-Israeli conflicts, 297, 298–301, 309–10, 314–15; Holocaust, and Canadian Indigenous genocide, 397–98, 405, 408–9; race and epistemic communities, 405–6

Atlantic Charter (1941), 66

Atlas (Francis), 408

Atleo, Shawn, 397

Attenborough, David, 161
At the Mind's Limits (Améry), 396
Attwood, Bain, 133
Auron, Yair, 307–8
Auschwitz, 97, 204, 205–6, 208
Australia. *See also* Indigenous Australians; Melbourne, Australia; Sydney, Australia: bicentennial (1988), 338–40; colonialism, 122–23, 127–28, 129–30, 131, 135–36, 138, 329, 338–39, 345, 390, 412n18; genocide, 293, 345, 390, 412n18; Holocaust memorial centers and messaging, 293, 326–46; Holocaust memory and literature, 220, 272–89; immigration and immigration policy, 91–92, 93–96, 99, 100–101, *102*, 103, 104–11, 123–24, 129, 280, 329–30, 337, 340, 341–43, 345, 349n48; Indigenous policy, 93, 94, 95, 117, 121, 132–34, 136–37, 138, 145n42, 146, 339, 343, 345; literary establishment, 276–78, 280, 283–84, 288–89; media, and anti-Jewish racism, 92, 93, 94, 96, 100–106, 110, 220, 272–73, 276–77, 289; population statistics and history, 106–7, 110, 123–24, 124, 127, 131, 136, 140, 338–39; war crimes and trials, 274, 276, 279, 284, 285–89, 292n50; white supremacy, amidst Holocaust memory, 2, 93–96, 100, 105, 106–9, 338–39, 342, 345; WWII, 97–98; Yiddish writers on Indigenous people/culture, 121–41
Australia Day, 145n42
Australian Jewish Almanac, 121, 125, 126, 127, 128, 129, 131, 132, 136

Australian Jewish Herald, 125
Australian Jewish News, 278
Australian Jewish Post, 125
Australian Labor Party, 92, 94, 103, 106, 109–10, 340
Australian literature, 132, 137
Australian Literature Society Gold Medal, 277
Austria, 107, 222, 228–30, 234
authoritarianism. *See also* fascism and fascist societal conditions; Nazism: aspects and actions, 282; avoidance, American history, 201–2; South African politics, 79, 80
authorship and fraud, 272, 273, 277, 280, 283, 290n8
autobiographical writing and memoirs: Caribbean and Jewish identity and writing, 249–50, 251–53, 254–55, 259, 260, 263, 269n63; genre and "permission to write," 254–55, 263; Holocaust, and witnesses, 219–20, 221–37, 251–52, 252–53, 254–55, 270n72; literary fraud, 275; slave narratives, 254–55; survivor narratives, Indian residential schools, 398–99
Axelrad, Albert, 180–81, 192nn48–49
Axis Rule in Occupied Europe (Lemkin), 390–91, 396–97, 412n16
Ayers, Harry M., 44
Azure, Alice M., 391

Bachrach, Hershl, 136
Bantu Education Act (South Africa; 1953), 354–55
Baranowski, Shelley, 6–7

Barbados, 256
Barkan, Elazar, 20
Barromi, Joel, 169
Bart, Lionel, 147, 154, 155–56, 163–64
Bartrop, Paul, 96, 124, 341
Bashir, Bashir, 293, 295–319
Basson, Johannes, 75
Bauer, Yehuda, 298
Bauman, Zygmunt, 395–96
Beasley, Daniel, 66
Beddow, Noel, 58
Belafonte, Harry, 184
Bell, Charles, 65
benchmark, Holocaust as. *See* Holocaust education; Holocaust memory
Bennett, Tony, 331
Bennie, Angela, 280, 292n50
Bentley, David, 275
Beothuk peoples, 390
Berezowsky, Mikolay, 285
Bergen-Belsen, 98
Berlin, Isaiah, 251
Berman, Judith, 343
Bessel, Richard, 322n20
Bethlehem, Louise, 308
Bettelheim, Bruno, 211
Between Camps (Gilroy), 250–51
Bevin, Ernest, 32
Bhabha, Homi K., 264n10
Bikel, Theodore, 182–83, 193n56
binary oppositions, and dangers: Arab/Israeli relations, 297, 316, 318; north/south paradigm, Holocaust memory, 220; racial relations and othering, 106, 228, 233, 316
binationalism, Israel/Palestine, 295, 296, 297–98, 311–19

Birmingham Age-Herald (newspaper), 47, 49–50, 54, 69n38
Birmingham News (newspaper), 55, 63
Birmingham World (newspaper), 49, 51, 52, 54, 56, 60, 61–62
Birth of a Community (Abrahams), 84–85, 90n66
Bischoff, Sam, 99
Bisk, Tsvi, 213–15
Black, Jaime, 402
black Britons and Britons of color: anti-discrimination aims and messages, 21–22, 25, 152; immigration, integration, and discrimination, 17–18, 20–21, 24–25, 26, 27–29, 29–32, 148–49, 151–52, 153–54, 158–59, 162–64, 165; media coverage, 153–54, 156–65; personal accounts, 149–51
black power movement (United States), 208, 212–13, 214–15
Black Skin, White Masks (Fanon), 222–23, 224–26, 229, 233, 236, 245
blacks, United States. *See* African Americans; black power movement (United States)
Blum, Yehuda Z., 177
Blunden, Godfrey, 97, 113n33
Bodenstein, Helgard, 75
Boer culture, 79
Bone, Pamela, 280–81
Bonwick, James, 412n18
Border Protection Bill (Australia; 2001), 349n48
Borensztajn, Heniek, 136
Boswell, E.C., and Boswell Amendment (1946), 52, 68nn24–25

"both sides" justifications, 278–79, 281, 286–87
boycotts. *See* divestment and boycotts
Brady Club (London), 160–61, 162–63, 164
Brandeis University, 180–81
Brattain, Michelle, 3–4
Bremer, Karl, 83
Breton, André, 261
Brighter Sun (Selvon), 256–57
Britain. *See* United Kingdom
Britain's Promise to Remember: The Prime Minister's Holocaust Commission Report, 1, 8n1, 419
British Broadcasting Corporation programs, 148, 151, 154, 155, 161, 163
British Columbia, Canada, 388, 394
British Mandate for Palestine (1923–1948), 32–34
Broder, Henryk M., 292n57
Bromley, Patricia, 352
Brown, Georgia, 117–18, 147, 148, 153–65, 167n24
Browning, Christopher, 72
Brown v. Board of Education of Topeka (United States; 1954), 171–72
Bulletin, The (newspaper), 94, 96, 100, 101, *102*
Burger, Die (newspaper), 75
Burnside, Julian, 342, 343
Burra, Edward, 31–32
Butler, Judith, 317–18
bystanderism: enabling Holocaust, 199, 202–3, 204, 222, 362, 365–66; Jewish awareness and American civil rights activism, 184–85, 199, 202–5; South African consciousness and education, 362, 365–66, 369

Cadogan, Alexander, 25–26
Cahier d'un retour au pays natal (Césaire), 261
Calwell, Arthur, 101, *102*, 107–8, 110
"Calypso Jews," 256–57, *257*
Cameron, David, 1, 419
Cameron, James, 148, 150
Canada: colonial history and genocide, 294, 388–410; First Nations, political status, 388, 389, 394, 404; immigration policy, 411n8; Indigenous history education, 394, 398–99; racism, 388–89, 404–5, 411n8
Canadian Jewish Congress, 398
Canadian Museum for Human Rights, 398, 401–3, 406, 407
"Can Minorities Oppose 'De Facto' Segregation?" (essay; Syrkin), 207–8, 218n27
Capek, Irene, 339
Caribbean: black-Jewish relations, 242, 246, 248; Jewish populations and identities, 243, 248, 249–54, 256–57, *257*, 258–59, 262–63, 267n35, 269n56; literature, and Holocaust memory, 220, 240, 242, 246, 248–63
Carl Peters (film), 221–22, 223, 231–32, 234–36
Casper, Bernard Moses, 182
Casteel, Sarah Phillips, 220, 240–63
Castro, Brian, 276–77
censorship, 283
Césaire, Aimé, 6, 243, 245, 250, 261

Chamberlain, Houston Stewart, 360
Chats with Australian Writers (Kahn), 137–39
Cheyette, Bryan, 6, 7, 18, 19, 34, 226, 237n9, 243
Chicago Defender (newspaper), 67n5
child immigrants, 341–42
children of Holocaust survivors, 251, 396
children of immigrants, 80, 152, 153
child sexual abuse and survivors, 394, 395, 398–99
Chow, Rey, 233–34
Chrisjohn, Roland, 395–97, 405, 408–9, 415n45
Christianity and politics: Australian nationalism, 103; South African nationalism, 79–80, 80, 81, 82–83
Christian National Education (South Africa), 354–55
Christoff, Peter, 272, 278, 283
Chrystos, 386–87, 393, 410n1
Churchill, Ward, 391, 405
Churchill, Winston, 26
Circle Game, The: Shadows and Substance in the Indian Residential School Experience in Canada (Chrisjohn and Young), 395–97
citizenship rights: Germany, 313, 361, 362, 368; Indigenous Australians, 133, 138, 339; South African nationalism, 79–80, 81, 89n51; United States, 52
civic institutions, 330–31, 332–33, 345–46
civil rights. *See* civil rights movement, United States; human rights

civil rights movement, United States, 41–66, 196–209, 215; American opposition, 41, 50–53, 54, 61–66, 205–9, 214; beginnings, 44, 45, 66; "establishment" Jews and, 173–74; Jewish involvement, 171–72, 174, 189n15, 196–209, 213; "Jewish power" amidst, 209–11; "Jewish radicalism" amidst, 211–15; "Jewish survival" amidst, 205–9; marches and demonstrations, 51, 53, 68n28, 172; Red Scare effects, 201–2; voting rights work, 50–53, 66; war effort and equality, 53–54, 55–61, 65–66
claims to justice, 302–3
Clarke, Frank, 94
Cliff, Michelle, 252–54, 255, 256, 259, 261, 262–63
Clifford, James, 246
Cobbs, Hamner, 51, 59, 67n18
"cognitive colonialism," 406–7, 417n74
cognitive dissonance: American South, equality and civil rights, 57, 62–63, 64; concept inception, 92–93; Jews, racial identity and attitudes, 122–23, 141; post-Holocaust antisemitism, Australia, 92–93, 96, 99, 100, 103, 109–10; reaction options, 93
Cohen, Andrew, 28–29, 34–35
Cold War: American political environment, 201–2; human rights, 416n65; issues and activism, 173, 177–78
collective memory: Indigenous Canadians, place names, 408; vs. mnemonics, 419–20
Collins, Lottie, 155

colonialism and imperialism. *See also* anticolonialism; apartheid (South Africa); immigration and immigration policy; postcolonial societies and studies: African independence, 28, 169, 171; antisemitism and, 226–28, 245; Australia, 122–23, 127–28, 129–30, 131, 135–36, 138, 329, 338–39, 345, 390, 412n18; British, and postcolonial Britain, 17–36, 146, 392–93, 403; British Colonial Office, administration, 24, 25–29, 29–32; British Colonial Office, and military recruitment, 21–24; Canada, 388–410; Caribbean identities and literature, 240, 242–43, 252–53, 259, 261–63; "cognitive," 406–7, 417n74; contact zones theory, 122, 135; Dutch, and Holocaust, 240, 259; French, 261, 392, 403; German, and Holocaust, 6–7, 221–23, 229–30, 231–32, 234–36, 239n37, 367, 390, 412n14, 412n16; global timelines, 19, 35, 133, 171, 173, 239n37, 248, 388, 392, 403–4, 417n68; identities of colonized, 224–25, 409–10; Israeli/Zionist, 33, 174–75, 175–76, 184, 186–88, 299–301, 307, 308–9, 314–15; moral atrocity narratives, 244–45, 246–47, 248, 395–96; Native American identities and literature, 386–87; North America, 386–410; racism, 6–7, 18, 19, 20–21, 24–26, 27–29, 122, 138, 168–69, 186, 221–22, 224–27, 234–35, 364, 367, 404–5, 406; South African history education, 364; works about, 122, 221–23, 224–37

"color bar," United Kingdom, 20, 21–22, 24–29, 30, 35
Columbus, Christopher, 248, 262, 388, 392
commemoration of the Holocaust. *See* Holocaust commemoration
Commentary (periodical), 200, 205–6, 209
Commonwealth Immigrants Act (United Kingdom; 1968), 148
Commonwealth Restrictive Immigration Law (Australia; 1901), 93
communism: Communist Party, 34; press, 202–3; and Red Scare, 201–2; South African history education, 358, 362; Ukrainian propaganda and beliefs, 276, 278, 282
community-based museums, 309, 328–29, 331–46
concentration camps. *See* Holocaust conditions
Confino, Alon, 4, 322n20
confiscation of property, 299
Congress of Racial Equality, 208
Conrad, Sebastian, 247
Conservative Judaism, 203–4
contact zones theory, colonialism, 122, 135
Convention on the Prevention and Punishment of the Crime of Genocide (1948), 389, 390, 402–3, 413n22
Cooke, Steven, 293, 327–46
Cooper, William, 345
Corney, Hyam, 162–63
Cornwallis, Edward, 393–94, 413n28, 414n33
Cosic, Miriam, 282
"cosmopolitan" memory cultures, 5, 260

Coulthard, Glenn Sean, 395
Cowan, Paul, 197
Craps, Stef, 7, 246, 265n18, 266n25
Crazy Horse, 399
Crisis (NAACP publication), 53–54
critical thinking skill development, 362–63, 369, 370–71
Crooke, Elizabeth, 331
Crossfire (film), 99–100
Crownshaw, Rick, 246
Cuba, 256, 258–59
cultural genocide: Australia, 138–39; Canada, 390–91, 393, 394, 396–97, 398
cultural memory studies: field history and breadth, 243–47; Holocaust memory within, 246–47, 248–49, 259–61, 266n25, 294; multidirectional, 245–46, 251–52, 265n18, 400; and postcolonial studies/global Holocaust memory, 244–45, 248–49, 259–61, 294, 320n13, 400–401, 405; transnational, 243–44, 245–46
"cultural situation" of colonized, 224
Cummings, Ivor, 24–25, 26, 27–30, 31
Curaçao, 240, 256, 259

Dabney, Virginius, 44
Dabydeen, David, 262, 270n76
Dafner, Alex, 344
Daily Telegraph (British newspaper), 158, 162
Daily Telegraph (Sydney newspaper), 97
Daily Worker (newspaper), 69n42
Dallaire, Roméo A., 343–44
Dark, Eleanor, 137
Darville, Helen. *See* Demidenko/Darville, Helen

Darwish, Mahmoud, 323n24, 325n53
Davis, Frank Marshall, 61
Dawidowicz, Lucy, 208
Day-Lewis, Sean, 158, 162
Days of Awe (Obejas), 258–59
decolonization: German, 239n37; global timelines, 19, 35, 133, 171, 173, 239n37, 248, 388, 392, 403–4, 417n68; Holocaust memory amidst, 5–6, 238n19, 242–44, 253–54, 294, 400–401; Holocaust studies, 294, 409–10; human rights thinking, 403–4; postwar discourse and politics, 2, 245, 251–52, 400–401
de Gobineau, Arthur, 360
deliberation, public, 296–97, 298, 301, 307, 315–16
Deloria, Vine, Jr., 406, 409
Demidenko/Darville, Helen, 220, 272–89, 290n8
Demidenko Debate, The (Reimer), 283–84
Democratic Party (United States), 52, 60, 68n28
democratic values: vs. "American fascism," 46, 52, 53, 59–61, 60, 62; American responses to Nazism, 42–43, 44, 61, 198–99; American responses to racism, 61, 63–64, 198–99; American, WWII involvement and hypocrisy, 44, 46, 48–49, 52–55, 57–58, 59–61, 60, 63, 64–65; democracy for whites only, 57, 63–64, 136; Germany, 358, 359; South Africa, and history education, 351, 355–56, 359, 362–63, 365, 369, 371; voting rights struggles, 50–53, 63

demonstrations and protests: American civil rights, 51, 53, 68n28, 172, 196, 202–3; anti-apartheid, 170, 182, 190n27; British anti-immigration, 158–59, 165; British fascist and anti-fascist, 159–60; Indigenous Australians, 145n42; inherent power, 203; labor, 53, 68n28, 172; Palestinian, 301, 308

deportation policy, 30

Dershowitz, Alan, 287

desegregation. *See also* civil rights movement, United States; segregation: American Jewish rejection, 207–8, 214; U.S. military, 65

de Toth, André, 99

Devine, Frank, 283

Diab, Saleh, 308, *309*

diary genre. *See* autobiographical writing and memoirs

Diary of Anne Frank, The (film), 252–53

Diary of a Young Girl, The (Frank), 240–42, 252, 253, 254, 255, 259, 263, 379n43

Diasporas of the Mind (Cheyette), 18

dictation tests, immigration policy, 93–94, 95

Dimbleby, Richard, 160

Diner, Hasia, 169

Dinkins, David, 184

Dinnerstein, Leo, 110

"disciplinary thinking," 243

Discourse on Colonialism (Césaire), 245

discrimination. *See* "color bar," United Kingdom; racism; segregation

disease transmission, 96, 127, 389, 393

"disidentification," 231, 232–34, 236–37

displaced persons: Australian immigration journeys, 337–38; Australian immigration policy, 92, 95, 108–9; immigration, United Kingdom, 155; labor policy, Australia, 108–9; labor policy, United Kingdom, 30; post-Holocaust Jews, 312

"disruptive politics," 298, 311–12, 315

divestment and boycotts: anti-apartheid, 176, 180–81, 182–83, 190n27, 193n56; boycott law, Israel, 187; Israel, 118, 186–87, 188

Dixiecrats, 45, 65

Dixon, Frank, 41, 46, 56–58, 64–65, 69nn39–42

Doane, Mary Ann, 225

documentary materials: Holocaust archives, 328, 332, 337, 340; television series, 117–18, 147, 148, 149, 153, 155–65, 250, 255, 267n35

Dominican Republic, 256, 269n56

Dominion Party (South Africa), 81–82

Donges, Ebenhaezer, 75

Dowrick, Stephanie, 276–77

Draft for a Republic (Malan), 81

drama and theater, 307

Dream On (Chrystos), 386–87, 393

Duff Cooper, Alfred, 33

Duker, Abraham G., 206–7, 208

Dunera (ship), 107, 341

du Plessis, Otto, 80

Durr, Robert, 53, 61, 68n27

Dutch colonialism, 240, 259

East End (documentary), 153

East End, London, 117–18, 147, 148, 153–65

East End Story (Levy), 153–54
Eastern European Jews: Australian immigration policy, 94, 100, 101–2, 103, 105–6, 107–8, 124; South African immigration policy, 73–74
East Jerusalem, 308
Ebony (periodical), 204
economic and labor rights. *See* labor law and rights
economic scapegoating, 152
editorial cartoons: Alabama, *49*, *56*, *60*; Australia, 101, *102*, 103
education. *See* education laws; Holocaust education; state education oversight; textbooks
education laws, 354–55, 394
Edugyan, Esi, 256
Eichmann, Adolf, and trial, 150–51, 215
Eichmann in Jerusalem (Arendt), 211
election law, 52
Elliot, John, 152
empathy. *See also* Holocaust memory: cross-cultural, and otherness in literature, 243, 249–50, 252–53, 257, 263, 303–4; "disruptive," Israel/Palestine binationalism, 295, 311, 315; empathetic engagement and Holocaust studies, 294; "empathic unsettlement," 293, 297, 303–19, 409; Holocaust learning, and assumptions, 1, 7–8, 293–94; refugees, and political considerations, 313–14
Empire Windrush (ship), 29–30
employment law and rights. *See* labor law and rights
environmental racism, 401

epistemology and epistemic spaces, 405–10
equality values. *See also* civil rights movement, United States: American southern attitudes and system, 45, 46, 47, 57, 59, 61–62, 65–66; anti-racism work and goals, 3–4, 196–216, 293, 342; societal messaging, 19, 22, 25–26, 45, 200
Erll, Astrid, 246
Etheridge, Mark, 44, 55, 69n37, 69n39
ethnic cleansing, 1, 322n20, 325n59, 338
étoile noire, L' (Maillet), 253, 254–55, 256
eugenics: Canada, 394, 398; education, 364, 368; Nazism, 368
Eurocentrism: colonialism effects, 403, 406; "genocide" thought and centering, 390, 391, 400–401, 405, 408–9, 409–10; history education, 354, 356; Holocaust studies, 294, 409–10; knowledge paradigms, 405–7, 408–10
Europa (television program), 152
Europe. *See also* colonialism and imperialism; Eurocentrism; specific nations: history, and Holocaust, 72, 152–53, 222, 235–36, 298, 299; Holocaust, and memorial cultures, 4–5, 244–45, 246, 260, 266n25, 270n71; Palestine/Israel influence, 295, 312–15; shared television programming, 152
European Tribe (Phillips), 249, 250
Evatt, Herbert Vere, 96–97
evil: apartheid as, 181; Holocaust as global symbol, 5, 187–88, 247, 298; ordinary people allowing, 187–88, 202–3, 204, 365–66

exil selon Julia, L' (Pineau), 263
Exodus (Uris), 250, 267n33
Exodus 1947 (ship), 32–33

"face" of the other, 303
Fair Employment Practices Committee (FEPC), 53, 55–61, *56*, *60*, 68n28
false equivalence justifications, 278–79, 281, 286–87
Fanon, Franz, 6, 219–20, 222–30, 233–34, 236, 243, 245, 250
Farber, Bernie, 398
fascism and fascist societal conditions. *See also* Nazism: American racism and, 46, 52–53, 59–62, 200, 201–2; logic and thought, 61, 282, 305, 324n41; South Africa, 79; South African history education, 356–57, 358, 359, 364, 365–66, 369, 370, 371; United Kingdom, 118, 159–60
Federal Bureau of Investigation (FBI), 387
federal contracting practices. *See* Fair Employment Practices Committee (FEPC)
Federation of Polish Jews, 327
Feldman, Marty, 148
Feld, Marjorie N., 118, 168–88
feminist theory, 234
Feniger, Saba, 335–36
Festinger, Leon, 93
fiction: Caribbean literature, 243, 249, 251–55, 256–57, 258–59, 261–62, 262–63; literary hoaxes and controversies, 220, 272–89; nature and qualities, 219, 280; on Palestinian catastrophe, 297, 301–6, 323n26

50 Years in Stepney (Henriques), 154
films: Holocaust, 98–100, 252–53, 387; immigration, 151–52, 154–55; Jewish/Indigenous Canadian intersectional memory, 399–400; Nazi cinema, 220, 221–22, 228–37; racialization processes, 224–25
Fineberg, Warren, 344
Fink, Leo, 327, 346n1
Fink, Mina, 327–28, 346n1
First Nations (Canada). *See* Indigenous Canadians
Flanagan, Bud, 154
Flint, John, 19, 20, 22
Fontaine, Phil, 388, 398–99
Fontaine, Theodor, 398–99
forgetting. *See also* silence: cultural memory cultures, 244, 253, 405; cultural tendencies and erasure, 138, 273–74, 279, 282, 288–89, 386–87, 388–89, 408–9; Holocaust memory and knowledge, 215–16, 340, 408
Forman, James, 210
Fort Alexander Residential School (Manitoba), 388, 398–99
Four Freedoms, 14, 44, 53, 61
Fowlkes, William A., 62
France, colonialism, 261, 392, 403
Francis, Bernie, 408
Frank, Anne, *241*, 252, 253, 254, 255, 259, 263
Frantzman, Seth J., 322n20
Fraser, Malcolm, 339
Fredrickson, George M., 3
Free Enterprise (Cliff), 259
free will, 282, 365–66
Freud, Sigmund, 311

438 • Index

Friedländer, Saul, 324n41
Frieze, Donna-Lee, 293, 327–46
Frith, Nicola, 244
From Holocaust to New Life (temporary exhibition, JHC), 338–41

Gadsden Call-Post (newspaper), 52, 67n5
"Gadsden twelve," 58
Galchinsky, Michael, 174–75
Gansworth, Eric, 391
Gaon, Boaz, 307
Gascoyne-Cecil, Robert Arthur James (Viscount Cranborne), 26
Gate of the Sun (Khoury), 297, 301–6, 310, 323n26
Gaza, 187, 194n69, 299–300
Geason, Susan, 282
genocide. *See also* Holocaust: Australia, 138, 293, 345, 390, 412n18; causes, and prevention, 7–8, 12n19, 343–44, 366, 369, 371, 389; cultural, 138–39, 390–91, 393, 394, 396–97, 398; defining, and issues of intent, 389–91, 396–97, 402–3, 408, 409, 411n10, 412n16; Eurocentrism, 390, 391, 400–401, 405, 408–9, 409–10; global, 1–2, 398, 402, 405; museums, 401–2; North America, 386–410, 415n45; South African history education, 351–52, 357, 360, 362, 364, 365–69; statutes, 389, 390–91, 402–3, 413n22
Gentleman's Agreement (film), 99
Georgia, 47
Germany. *See also* Holocaust; World War II: Berlin Olympics (1936), 42; colonialism, and effects, 6–7,
221–23, 229–30, 231–32, 234–36, 239n37, 367, 390, 412n14, 412n16; Holocaust, and bystanders, 187–88, 202–3, 204, 222, 362; Holocaust, and memorial culture, 4, 270n71; Jewish and non-Jewish emigration, Australia, 93, 105–6, 110–11, 124; Jewish emigration, South Africa, 74–75, 78; Nazism's changes to, 43, 47, 359–60, 369; WWII, 356–59, 365–67
ghettos: colonial control, 34; documentary archives and exhibitions, 328, 332, 340; Holocaust, and "ghetto neurosis," 177, 208, 214; United States (Jewish takes), 204, 214
Gilbert, Shirli, 293–94, 350–72, 419–20
Gilman, Sander, 228, 258
Gilroy, Paul, 18, 250–51
Glowacka, Dorota, 294, 386–410
Goebbels, Joseph, 358, 359, 361
Goering, Hermann, 358, 359
Goldberg, Abram, 332
Goldberg, Amos, 5, 247, 266n25, 293, 295–319
Goldhar, Pinchas, 125, 131–32, 135, 142n14
Goldstein, Eric, 139–40
Goldstone, Richard, 194n69
Goulbourne, Harry, 17–18
Grant, Cy, 24, 25
Graves, John Temple, 41, 44, 45, 46, 54–55, 63, 65
Green, Cooper, 60
Grosse, Pascal, 239n37
Grüber, Heinrich, 151
Gruber, Ruth, 33
Gullett, Henry "Jo," 103, 109–10

Gypsy Reflections: Remembering the Romani Victims of the Holocaust through Art (temporary exhibition, JHC), 341

Haake, Claudia, 322n20
Haebich, Anna, 133
Hale, Sabine, 235
Half-Blood Blues (Edugyan), 256
Halifax, Nova Scotia, 392, 393–94, 413n28
Hall, Grover C., 44–45
Hammerstein, David, 179–80
Hammond, Samuel B., 104–5
Hand That Signed the Paper, The (Demidenko/Darville), 272–89
Harlot's Progress, A (Dabydeen), 262, 270n76
Harper, Stephen, 395
Harriet's Daughter (Philip), 253
Harris, Cyril, 85
Harrisson, Tom, 153, 167n23
Hart, Mitchell, 141, 143n21
Harvard University, 176
Hashomer Hatzair, 168, 169, 188n1
Hasluck, Paul, 133
Hawke, Bob, and administration, 276, 287
Haynes, George Edmund, 61
Healy, Chris, 131
Hearne, John, 257, 262–63
Hebrew Immigrant Aid Society, 91
Henderson, D.E., 69n40
Henderson, Gerard, 278, 283
Henriques, Rose, 154
Hentoff, Nat, 204
Herbert, Xavier, 137
Herero peoples, 390, 412n14

Hertzog, J.B.M., 73, 75, 77, 168
Hertz, Richard, 204
Herzl, Theodor, 185
Heseltine, Harry, 277–78
Hess, Rudolf, 359
Hever, Hannan, 303
Heyes, Tasman, 95
"hierarchy of suffering": avoiding, 18, 238n19; Indigenous Canadians and Holocaust memory, 388, 391, 393–94, 397–98
High Court of Australia, 143n19
Hijuelos, Oscar, 256
Himmelfarb, Milton, 205
Himmler, Heinrich, 359
Hirschbein, Peretz, 126–28, 129–30, 143n15
Hirsch, Marianne, 246
historicization, Holocaust-racism intersections, 2–3, 4, 7–8, 420
historiography: Holocaust memory, 4–7, 332; postcolonial memory, 253–54, 260–61; sources, 4, 12n19, 332
history education: goals and aims, 362–63, 369, 370–71; South Africa, 293–94, 350–72; storytellers' racial perspectives and power, 406–7, 408, 409
Hitler, Adolf. *See also* Nazism: American racism and Nazism, 41, 42, 46, 53–56, 63, 199; British policy compared, 32, 152; German Jewish population policies, 312–13, 366–67, 368; South African history education, 356, 357–59, 360, 366–67, 368
Hodgson, Kate, 244
Hofmeyr, Jan, 74, 82

Hollingsworth, David, 93, 112n27
Holman, W.A., 103
Holmes, Colin, 26
Holocaust. *See also* Holocaust commemoration; Holocaust conditions; Holocaust education; Holocaust memory: American Jewish politics, and race, 196–216; within European history, 72, 152–53, 298, 299, 389, 390; Jewish survival struggle and themes, 205–9, 300–301; journalism and media coverage, 61–62, 96–97, 98–100, 109, 113n35, 151; moral atrocity narratives, 244–45, 246–47, 248; Nakba considered with, 293, 295–319; racialization process and "othering," 204, 222, 223; resistance movements, 334, 365–66; "silence" following, 197–98, 202–3; South African history education, 351–52, 357, 359–61, 362, 364–69; South African reactions, 82, 83, 183

Holocaust, The (television program), 98, 267

Holocaust and Memory in the Global Age, The (Levy and Sznaider), 5, 242–43, 270n71

Holocaust and the Nakba, The (study), 293

Holocaust commemoration. *See also* Holocaust education; Holocaust memory: assumed effects, 1; Caribbean, 248, 259; in centers and exhibitions, and going beyond, 203, 308–10, *310*, 329, 332–33, 335, 340, 345–46; globalization and events, 5, 248, 260, 261, 352; personal and media accounts, 157, 160; United Kingdom, 1, 157, 160; United States, 203, 215–16, 270n66

Holocaust commissions and reports (national), 1, 8n1, 419

Holocaust conditions: American racism compared, 41–42, 46, *60*, 61–62, 64, 65–66, 196–97, 198–99, 201, 204, 207–8; artistic portrayals, 336–37; Australian literary portrayals, 274–75, 277–82, 283, 286–87; Caribbean literary reactions, 251–52, 254–55; evidence and witnessing, 328, 332, 333, 335, 336–37, 340; Jewish struggle and psychology, 206–7, 208, 211, 214; Native American abuses and genocide, comparisons, 395–97, *396*, 398–400, *400*; personal accounts, 160, 187–88, 202–3, 332, 333, 334, 336–37, 396; racism and antisemitism following, 92–93, 96, 103, 141, 288; South African history education, 351, 362, 365, 368

Holocaust education: assumed and actual effects, 1, 7–8, 294, 372, 419, 420; Australian media, 98–99; Australian memorial centers, 293, 327–28, 329, 333, 335, 345; Canada, 398–99; exhibitions, 308–10, *310*, 333; global trends, 1, 352, 369, 371, 372, 385n120, 419; Holocaust studies field, 294, 352, 373n13, 375n16; Jewish initiatives, 375n16; "lesson making" ethics, 198–99; "lesson making" shortfalls, 293, 352, 372; South Africa and textbooks, 293–94, 350–72

Holocaust literature. *See under* literature and literary connections

Holocaust memorial centers and museums: Jewish education initiatives, 203, 375n16; local and community focus, 309, 328–29, 331–46; professional museums, 178, 309, 328, 330–31, 332, 333, 387, 401–2, 419; temporary exhibitions, 293, 308–10, 327, 329–32, 334–44

Holocaust memory. *See also* Holocaust commemoration; Holocaust education; Holocaust memorial centers and museums; victimization and victimhood: American cultural and media trends, 198, 387, 391; anti-apartheid stances and, 168–88; antiracist stances considered, 196–209, 215; globalization/global nature debate, 5, 151–53, 242–43, 243–44, 245, 246–47, 248, 256, 259–61, 266n25, 270n66, 320n13, 419–20; inability to penetrate racism, 14–15, 19–20, 92–93, 122–23, 205–9, 293–94, 372; inspiring activism, 187–88, 196–205, 209, 215, 293; intersectional memory and understanding, 399–400, 409–10; literary hoaxes, 220, 272–89; literature and literary connections, 4, 7, 219–20, 238n19, 240–63, 272, 386–87, 391; memorial centers, 178, 203, 240–42, 261, 270n66, 293, 327–46, 387; memory studies and memorial cultures, 4–7, 238n19, 242–47, 259–61; mnemonics, 419–20; nature of, and fallibility, 4, 215–16; North American colonial genocide and, 386–410; and potential of history repeating, 152–53, 159, 160, 165, 279, 369; and race relations, Australia, 146; and race relations, United Kingdom, 147, 150–52, 158–59; and race relations, United States, 196–215; self-defense and -determination tenets, 210, 212, 213; South Africa, 168–70, 350–51

Holocaust, Rebirth, and the Nakba, The (Auron), 307–8

Holocaust studies: considering decolonization of, 294, 409–10; education field, 373n13, 375n16; global consciousness and trends, 352; postcolonial studies and, 245, 246–49

Holocaust survivors, 298–99; Australian immigration and treatment, 91–93, 105–6, 107–10, 124, 337–38, 340; Australian literary criticism by, 278, 279; Australian portrayals and presentations, 293; children of, 251, 396; on Israeli policies, 187–88, 300; memorial center participation and exhibitions, 327, 328–30, 332–34, 335–39, 340–41, 344, 345–46; memorial service participation, 160; Palestine immigration and Zionism, 33; racial identities, 122, 134–35, 204, 220, 235, 251, 340; terminology and language, 308; war criminal protests, 285, 287–88; writers and works, 121–22, 134–35, 219–20, 221–37, 251

Holocaust Testimonies: The Ruins of Memory (Langer), 396

Holocaust victims. *See* Holocaust; Holocaust conditions; victimization and victimhood
Holodomor (Ukraine), 275–76, 278, 283, 398
Honouring the Truth, Reconciling for the Future: Summary of the Final Report of the Truth and Reconciliation Commission of Canada (2015), 407, 414n35
Hook, Sidney, 201
House for Mr. Biswas, A (Naipaul), 257
housing. *See also* property law and land rights: American discrimination, 200, 204; British discrimination, 20
Howard, John, and administration, 274, 289n4, 339, 340, 342, 343, 349n48
human behavior: genocides, 151, 152–53; racializing and racism, 106, 148, 316
Human Genome Project, 367
human rights. *See also* civil rights movement, United States; universalism vs. particularism: and anti-Israel/anti-Jewish accusations, 175–76, 186–87, 194n69; Holocaust as comparison/benchmark, 1, 186, 196–97, 198, 351, 352, 368; Holocaust education as human rights education, 352, 363–64, 368–69, 372; Indigenous Australians, 121, 132–33, 136, 138, 140–41; museums and exhibitions, 330–31, 334, 398, 401–3, 406, 407; philosophy and theory, 403–4, 409; South African apartheid and activism, 169, 172–73, 174–81, 363–64; statutes, 133, 364, 365, 368, 402–3

Hunte, Joseph, 152
Huppert, Paul, 339
Husseini, Mohammed Amin al-, 321n19
Huyssen, Andreas, 243–44, 256, 270n66

Iberian expulsion of Jews, 242, 248, 258–59, 262, 263, 392
identification markers, 23, 204, 230. *See also* "disidentification"
imaginative literature, 243
immigrants and immigrant families. *See also* immigration and immigration policy; refugees: children of/1st-generation British, 152, 153, 156–57, 164; community museums, 331–32; fiction portrayals, 280; film portrayals, 151–52, 154–55; identities, 149–51, 156–57, 163, 341–42; personal accounts, 149–51, 156–57, 163, 164, 184–85, 337, 341–42, 343
immigration and immigration policy, 19. *See also* immigrants and immigrant families; Australia, 91–92, 93–96, 99, 100–101, *102*, 103, 104–11, 123–24, 129, 280, 329–30, 337, 340, 341–43, 345, 349n48; Canada, 411n8; government assistance, 109; group classification, 73, 76, 77, 81, 87n29, 91–92, 95, 96, 104–6, 107, 109; Jewish immigration into Palestine, 32–34; language tests, 93–94, 95; legislation, 30, 74, 75, 76–77, 78, 82, 93, 95, 100, 106–9, 148–49, 349n48; morality issues, 342; national reports, 30–31; quotas, 73–74, 107, 108; South Africa, 14, 72, 73–74, 75, 76–80, 81–83, 84;

immigration and immigration policy (*continued*)
surveys, 104–6; transportation modes, 108; United Kingdom, 14, 17–18, 20–21, 26, 29–32, 117–18, 147–65; United States, 73–74

Imperial Eyes (Pratt), 122

imperialism. *See* colonialism and imperialism

Indian Act (Canada; 1876), 394

Indian immigrants and populations, United Kingdom, 147, 149–51, 154, 158, 161

Indian residential schools (Canada), 388, 389, 394–97, *396*, 398–99, 402, 406, 414n35

Indigenous Australians: activists, 345; assimilation, 121, 132–34, 138–39; Australian racial policy, 93, 94, 95, 117, 121, 132–34, 136–37, 138, 145n42, 146, 339, 343, 345; culture, 129, 137–39; genocide, 138, 293, 345, 390, 412n18; human rights, 121, 132–33, 136, 138, 140–41; populations, 127, 131, 140, 142n11; racist media coverage, 100, 131; reconciliation language and policy, 140–41, 146; stereotypes and "othering," 117, 121, 122–23, 126, 132, 135, 137, 138, 140; Tasmanians, 412n18; Yiddish writers' encounters, 117, 121–41, 142n14

Indigenous Canadians, 410n1; colonialism and genocide, 294, 386, 388–410; Jewish genocide and asymmetry considered, 397–98, 405; political status/sovereignty, 388, 389, 394, 404, 407–8, 409, 417n67; populations, 401, 410n1; residential schools, 388, 389, 394–97, 398–99, 402, 406, 414n35

individual responsibility, 282, 365–66, 369

Informed Heart (Bettelheim), 211

"intent" issues, genocide, 338, 389–90, 409, 411n10

International Holocaust Remembrance Day, 5, 309, 352

International Jewish Labor Bund, 136

International Refugee Organization, 108–9

International Task Force on Holocaust Education, Remembrance and Research, 261

intersectional memory and understanding, 399–400, 409–10

intertextual literary works, 222, 249, 254–55

Israel. *See also* Arab-Israeli conflicts; Zionism: American Jewish attitudes and social justice, 118, 170, 173, 174–81, 187–88, 209; BDS movement, 118, 186–87, 188; black African relations, 177, 178–79; colonialism and occupation, 33, 174–75, 175–76, 184, 186–88, 299–301, 307, 308–9, 314–15; Holocaust, and memorial culture, 4; literature, 306–7; military conflicts, 174, 209, 215; modern state, politics, and policies, 33, 169, 170, 173, 174–75, 176–79, 180, 183–84, 186–88, 263, 299–301, 308, 315; Palestine relations, 170, 175, 176, 179, 183–84,

186–87, 293, 295–96, 298, 299–301, 307–10, 314–19; South Africa policy and apartheid, 85, 169, 170, 175–81, 191n35; state creation, 34, 295
Israel Apartheid Week, 186–87
Israel Horizons/Labor Israel (newspaper), 168, 169
Itzkovitz, Daniel, 247

Jackson, Emory O., 51, 52, 54–55, 67n5
Jamaica, 252–53, 256
Jansen, Jonathan, 354, 355
Jaworsky, George, 278–79
Jenkins, Jay, 60
Jensen, Harold I., 101, 103
Jewish Chronicle, The (London), 162–63
Jewish Committee of the Communist Party (UK), 34
Jewish Defense League (JDL), 209–11, 212
Jewish East End, London, 147–65
Jewish Holocaust Centre (Melbourne Australia), 293, 327–46
Jewish Labor Bund, 136
Jewish Liberation Journal, 212, 213–14
Jewish Life (periodical), 200–201
Jewish organizations, 91, 160–61, 171, 181, 182, 184–85
Jewish Post, The, 121
Jewish power and radicalism, 209–15
Jewish Press (Brooklyn-based newspaper), 209–10
Jews. *See also* American Jewish Congress; antisemitism; immigration and immigration policy: American Jewish politics, and race, 196–216; American Jews and South African apartheid, 169–88; Australian Jewish identity, 123–24, 130, 134–35, 137, 139–40, 141; Caribbean Jewish identity, 243, 248, 249–54, 256–57, 258–59, 260, 262–63; European Jewish identity, 314; German population policies, 312–13, 360, 361, 362; identities of, following Holocaust, 6, 14, 85, 122–23, 139–40, 197, 206, 207, 208, 209, 210–11, 213–14; perceptions of, following Holocaust, 3, 18, 83, 84–85, 91–92, 96–97, 98, 100, 211, 312; postcolonial Britain, and race, 17–18, 20, 30–31; "race" and race issues, 3, 8n3, 14, 72–85, 91–92, 96, 105, 106, 109, 122–23, 129, 135, 139–40, 143n21; refugee populations, 169, 312–13; Sephardim, 258–59, 262, 263; South Africa, race and assimilation, 14, 72–85; world Jewry, activism solidarity and fractures, 170, 171, 172–73, 174, 176, 183–84, 186
Jews for Racial and Economic Justice, 184–85, 194n66, 194nn63–64
Jim Crow laws: racism considered, vs. Nazism, 14, 41–66, 196, 201; white southerners' values, 44–45, 46–47, 50–53, 54, 55, 56–57, 61, 62–63
Johnson-Reed Act (United States; 1924), 74
Jordan, James, 117–18, 146–65
Joseph, Jo, 154, 157
journalism. *See also* editorial cartoons: African American publications and press, 42, 48–49, 51–52, 54, 56, 58,

journalism (*continued*)
59–61, *60*, 61–62, 65, 67n5; African independence movements, 28; American Jewish press, 198, 199, 200–201, 202–3, 205, 209–10, 278; American white southern press, 44–45, 47, 49–50, 50, 54, 55, 63–64; Australian literary criticism and investigations, 275, 277, 278–79, 280–84; Australian war criminals, 285; Australian "yellow press" and antisemitism, 92, 93, 94, 96, 100–103, *102*, 110; Australian Yiddish writers and press, 121–22, 125; British media reviews, 158, 161–62; drama criticism, 307; Holocaust coverage, 61–62, 96–98; Israel, 168, 169, 171; on Israel/South Africa ties, 178, 179–80; South Africa, 75, 76, 82

Jud Süss (film), 221

Jukes, Geoffrey, 277

justice claims, 302–3

Kadimah, 327, 346n1

Kahane, Meir, 209–10

Kahn, Leora, 343

Kahn, Yitzhak, 137–39

Kanafani, Ghassan, 307

Kant, Immanuel, 403

Katz, Shlomo, 205

Katz, Steven, 411n11

Keating, Paul, and administration, 285–86

Keith, J.L., 24, 26, 27

Khoury, Elias, 297, 301–6, 310, 317, 323n26, 323n28

Kincaid, Jamaica, 257

Kingdom on Shylock, The (pamphlet), 103

King, Mackenzie, and administration, 389, 411n8

King, Martin Luther, Jr., 202, 204

Kisch, Egon, 95

Kitson, Jill, 276, 277–78, 280

Kleinbaum, Sharon, 176, 190n27

Klemperer, Victor, 238n25

Klot, Lillian. *See* Brown, Georgia

Klüger, Ruth, 219–20, 221–37

Knockwood, Doug, 395

knowledge paradigms, 405–10

Kontinentn un okeanen (Ravitch), 128–29

Kramer, Leonie, 277–78

Kugelmass, Jack, 125–26

Ku Klux Klan, 44–45, 64, 200

Kushner, Tony, 13–14, 17–36

Kwiet, Konrad, 288

Labor Israel/Israel Horizons (newspaper), 168, 169, 171

labor law and rights: American federal policy and FEPC, 53, 55–61, *56*, *60*, 68n28; American labor discrimination, 200; Australian nationalist thought, 94, 101, 103, 106; displaced persons, Australia, 108–9; displaced persons, United Kingdom, 30; South African nationalist thought, 80, 82

Labor Party (Australia), 92, 94, 103, 106, 109–10, 340

Labuschagne, Frans, 75

LaCapra, Dominick, 293, 297, 303–6, 315–16, 318, 409

Lamidey, Noel, 91–92
land and property law: Canada, 388, 389–90, 392–93; Palestine, 299, 308; United States/territories, 412n12
Land of the Living (Hearne), 257
Landsberg, Alison, 246
Langer, Lawrence, 396
Langfield, Michele, 341
Lang, Jack, 103, 109–10
language rights, Native Americans, 394, 406, 417n75
language tests, 93–94, 95
language use and terminology: apartheid, 170, 186, 352; genocide, 389, 390, 396–97; Holocaust, 62, 187, 294, 308, 351, 357, 387; immigrants, 82, 93–94, 95, 124, 142n8, 339; Nakba, 308, 319n1; "Nazis," 186, 195n69; race and racism, 3, 294, 333, 351, 364, 370; terrorism, 187
Last Chance, The (film), 99
Last of the Tasmanians (Bonwick), 412n18
Last Utopia, The (Moyn), 403–4
Law Commission of Canada, 396–97
Lawson, Tom, 146, 412n18
League of Colored Peoples, 21
LeFlore, John L., 51, 67n5, 67n21
legal briefs and opinions: Canadian Indigenous peoples policy, 397; United States segregation, 171–72
legislation and regulation: anti-lynching, 46–47, 50; anti-poll tax, 51; boycotts, 187; education, 354–55, 394; employment rights, 53, 55–57, 68n28; genocide statutes, 389, 390–91, 402–3, 413n22; human rights statutes, 133, 364, 365, 368, 402–3; immigration, 30, 74, 75, 76–77, 78, 82, 93, 95, 100, 106–9, 148–49, 349n48; national racial policies, 83–84, 86n7, 93–94, 95, 100, 106, 117–18, 133, 143n19, 148–49, 152, 361–62, 394; political participation, 75–76; property confiscation, 299, 308; race relations, 117–18, 148–49; war crimes, 285
Leipciger, Nate, 398–99
Lekakis, George, 341
Lemkin, Raphaël, 390–91, 396–97, 402–3, 412n16, 412n18
Lerner, Max, 198–99
Lerner, Michael, 194n69
Levinas, Emmanuel, 303
Lévi-Strauss, Claude, 256, 261
Levy, A.B., 153–54
Levy, Daniel, 5, 242, 270n71
Leyburn, James, 134
LGBTQ issues, 176
liberalism: American liberalism, 169, 174, 179–80, 198, 199–200; English liberalism, 150–51, 159; Jewish left, 179–81, 187, 199–200, 201–2, 209; South African Jewish liberalism, 168–69; white southern liberalism and civil rights, 44, 45, 50, 53–55, 63
Liberal Party (Australia), 92, 103, 106, 109–10
Lichtheim, Richard, 113n35
Liebler, Isi, 283
"linguicide," 394, 406, 417n75
Lippmann, Walter, 339–40
literary archives, Holocaust materials, 328, 332

literary awards, 276–78, 280, 286, 288–89
literary hoaxes, 220, 272–89
literature and literary connections. *See also* drama and theater; fiction; poets and poetry; textbooks: global kinship, Anne Frank's *Diary*, 240–42, 252–53, 254, 255, 259, 263; Holocaust and colonialism, 219–20, 221–37, 386–87, 391; Holocaust memory, 4, 7, 219–20, 238n19, 240–63, 272, 386–87, 391; on Palestinian catastrophe, 297, 301–6, 323n26; travel writing, 122, 125–27, 128, 129, 130, 132, 142n14
Locke, John, 403
Łódź Ghetto, 332
Loft, Steve, 399–400, 415n53
Logan, Tricia, 402
London, England, 31–32, 117–18, 147, 148, 153–65
Long, B. K., 73
Louw, Eric, 78, 81, 82
lynching: language, Holocaust descriptions, 62; legislation struggles, 46–47, 50; press coverage, 47–50; United States, 42, 43, 46–50
Lyotard, Jean-François, 324n41

Mabo v. Queensland (Australia; 1992), 143n19
MacArthur, Douglas, 98
Madison, Arthur, 51
Mahameed, Khaled Kasab, 309–10
Maier, Charles S., 244–45, 246
Maillet, Michèle, 253, 254–55, 256
Malan, Daniel François, 14, 74, 75, 76–78, 81, 82, 83–85, 90n66, 168–69

Malinek, Malvina, 339
Mandatory Palestine (1923–1948), 32–34
Mandela, Nelson, 85, 183–84, 185, 193nn58–59
Mandel, Naomi, 266n28
Man from the Sun, A (Elliot), 151–52
Manicheanism, 225
Manitoba, Canada, 388, 398, 401
Mankowitz, Wolf, 147, 159
Manne, Robert, 273, 277, 278, 283, 288–89
Mantel, Hilary, 267n29
Maoris, 127–28
Marks, Eva, 335
Marks, Peter, 307
Markus, Andrew, 329
Martinique, 256, 261
Martin, Paul, 397
Marx, Christoph, 79
Masalha, Nur, 322n20
Mathiessen, Peter, 412n12
McCorvey, Gessner, 52
McDonald, Roger, 276, 277
McGill, Ralph, 44
McGuiness, Padraic P., 283
McLachlin, Beverley, 307
McLeod, Cynthia, 251
media. *See* editorial cartoons; films; journalism; newsreels, WWII; propaganda; television programs and series; textbooks
Meeting Point (television series), 151
Meir, Golda, 169, 170
Melbourne, Australia: Jewish Holocaust Centre, 293, 327–46; Jewish immigration, 110, 124, 125, 332, 340, 341–43; populations and culture,

107, 124–25, 127, 140, 142n11, 327, 334, 339–40
melting pot concept, 153, 154, 162. *See also* assimilation
memoirs. *See* autobiographical writing and memoirs
memorialization of the Holocaust. *See* Holocaust commemoration; Holocaust memorial centers and museums; Holocaust memory
memory. *See* collective memory; cultural memory studies; forgetting; Holocaust memory; mnemonics
Memory of the Holocaust in Australia, The (Lawson and Jordan), 146
Mendes, Philip, 136, 140
Menominee peoples, 386–87, 410n1
Merasty, Augie, 395
Messinger, Ruth, 176, 184
"metaphysics of comprehension," 296
Métis peoples, 401
"metropolitan" memories, 244, 261
Mexico, 388
Mikardo, Ian, 152
Mi'kmaq peoples and Mi'kma'ki, 391, 392–94, 395, 408, 413n28
Miles Franklin Award, 277–78, 280, 287
militarism, 210–11
Mills, Charles, 404, 405–6, 407
Milton, George Fort, 44
mineral resources and rights, 412n12
Ministry of Information (United Kingdom), 22
miscegenation fears: American south, 45; Nazi Germany, 361, 362; South Africa, 73, 75, 76, 77, 79; U.S. troops abroad, 20, 25, 31, 35

Mitchell, Adrian, 277–78
mnemonics, 246, 419
Mobile, Alabama, 58–59, 67n21
Mohawk peoples, 388
Montgomery Advertiser (newspaper), 44–45
Montgomery Voter League, 51
Moody, Harold, 21–22
Mooney, W.H., 69n38
Moraes, Dom, 149–51
Morely, Grace McCann, 330
Morrison, Herbert, 20
Moses, A. Dirk, 400
Moses and Monotheism (Freud), 311
Mosley, Oswald, 159–60
movies. *See* films
Moyn, Samuel, 403–4
Mr. Potter (Kincaid), 257
Muchnicki, Mietek, 336
Mufti, Aamir R., 11n16
multiculturalism. *See also* race relations: activism and civic values, 339; Australia, and cultural status quo, 220, 272–74, 279, 287, 288–89; Australia, and Jewish civic engagement, 329, 338–39, 340, 341–42; Canadian considerations, 389; literature, 257–58; London, United Kingdom, 153, 154, 161–63; South Africa, 85
"multidirectional memory": literary illustrations, 251–52, 254–55; theory, 245–46, 265n18, 400
Multidirectional Memory (Rothberg), 5–6, 18, 238n19, 245, 400–401
Mulvey, Laura, 234
Muñoz, José, 231, 232–33, 234
Munz, Hirsch, 130–31, 132, 135

museums. *See* Holocaust memorial centers and museums
Muslim immigrants, United Kingdom, 165
Mussolini, Benito, 358
"My Negro Problem—and Ours" (essay; Podhoretz), 205–6, 209

Naipaul, V.S., 257
Nakba, 319n1, 321n18; anniversaries, 323n24; considered alongside Holocaust, 293, 295–319; "ethics of catastrophe," 296; as ethnic cleansing, 322n20; literary portrayals, 297, 301–6, 310; present-day, 299
Nakba survivors, 308–11, *309*
Nama peoples, 390, 412n14
Nassy, Josef, 261, 270n72
National Association for the Advancement of Colored People (NAACP), 42, 46, 51, 53–54, 67n5
nationalism. *See also* Zionism: Australia, 94, 96, 100, 101, 103; black, United States, 173, 212–13, 214–15; Canada, 413n28; South Africa, 14, 75, 77–78, 79–81, 168–69, 351, 352, 355, 361–62, 365
National Jewish Community Relations Advisory Council, 181
national liberation and independence movements, 19, 173; African nations, 28, 178–79, 185; Holocaust memory influence, 170; Palestine, 34, 301–2; South Africa, 85, 350, 355
National Museum of African American and Culture, 263

National Party (South Africa), 73, 75–78, 81, 82, 83–84, 168–69
national racial policy. *See* legislation and regulation; racialized political systems
national songs, 392, 413n27
Native American history. *See also* Indigenous Canadians: activism, 387–88, 391, 392, 393–94, 395–97, 397–99, 401, 407, 412n12; land rights, 388, 389–90, 392–93, 412n12; literary portrayals, 386–87; North American colonialism and genocide, 386–410, 415n45; residential schools, 388, 389, 394–97, *396*, 398–99, 402, 406, 414n35; writing of, 406–7, 408, 409, 410n3, 415n45
nativism, South Africa, 73, 75, 76, 77, 82
natural rights philosophy, 403–4, 409
Nature of Blood, The (Phillips), 243, 249, 255, 261, 266n29
Nazism. *See also* Holocaust; Holocaust conditions: American racism and inequality compared, 14, 41–66, 196–209; American responses, 42–43, 44, 61, 63–64, 172, 187–88, 198; British responses, 150–51, 152–53; cinema, 220, 221–22, 228–37; German colonialism and, 6–7, 221–22, 239n37, 367; modern language use, 186, 194n69; racial discourse and responses, 3, 4, 7–8, 22, 198–99, 351; racialization processes, 204, 222, 223, 229–30, 233, 361, 362, 365; South Africa and apartheid, 170, 172, 173, 175, 178, 180, 294, 350–52, 354, 356–72;

South African education, 293–94, 351, 354, 356–61, 362, 363, 364–71; specific racism, 3, 13, 22, 31, 43, 62, 64, 72, 151, 222, 312, 351, 359–60, 364, 366–68, 371

Neate, Charles, 81–82

Neimark, Marilyn Kleinberg, 184, 194n66

Netanyahu, Benjamin, 177–78, 188, 194n69

Netherlands Antilles, 240, 254, 259

Nettleford, Rex, 251

Neumann, Alfred, 99

Neumann, Charlotte, 340

Nevel, Donna, 184, 194n66

"new Cockneys," London, 117–18, 147, 148, 153, 155–65

New Era (South African newspaper), 82, 89n58

Newfoundland, Canada, 390

"New Jewish Agenda," 176, 181–82, 184–85, 187

New Left Jews, 212–13

Newman, Carey, 402

newspapers. *See* journalism; specific newspapers

newsreels, WWII, 96, 98

New World Order, A (Phillips), 269n63

New York City, 184, 194n66, 210

New Zealand, 127–28

Nigeria, 24–25, 27–28, 35

Nigger-Hunting in England? (Hunte), 152

Ni'lin, West Bank, 308–10

Nixon, E.D., Sr., 51

None Shall Escape (film), 98–99

Nordicism, 62, 73, 77, 87n29

North American colonialism and genocide, 386–410

Norton, John, 101, 103

Nova Scotia, Canada, 392–94, 395, 408, 413n28, 414n33

Novick, Peter, 5, 247, 321n19, 419–20

Nuremberg Laws (Germany; 1935), 361, 362, 365, 368

Nuremberg Trials (Germany; 1945–1946), 364

Nuwe Orde (South Africa), 79–80

Obejas, Achy, 258–59

Occupied Palestinian Territories, 299–300, 317; Holocaust exhibitions, 308–10; literary portrayals, 307

Oeser, Oscar A., 104–5

Ofarim, Esther, 161–62

Of Black America (television documentary), 162

Ofer, Dalia, 4

Ohm Krüger (film), 221

Oka crisis (Canada; 1990), 388

Olympic Games (1936), 42

One Australia policy, 339, 342, 343

"One Black Englishman" (television documentary episode), 149–51

One Pair of Eyes (television documentary series), 148, 149–51, 153, 155–65

Ontario, Canada, 388

"On 'The Nature of Blood' and the Ghost of Anne Frank" (essay; Phillips), 240

"On the Social Construction of Moral Universals" (essay; Alexander), 5, 260–61

Origins of Totalitarianism, The (Arendt), 6, 403
Ossewa Brandwag (South Africa), 79, 81
Othello (Shakespeare), 249
Our East End (radio program), 154
Oyneg Shabes archive, 328
Oystralyer lebn (newspaper), 125

Pacific campaign, WWII, 98
Pakistani immigrants and populations, United Kingdom, 117, 147, 150, 154, 158, 161, 162, 163
Palestine: BDS movement, 118, 186–87, 188; Israel relations, 170, 175, 176, 179, 183–84, 186–87, 293, 295–96, 298, 299–301, 307–10, 314–19; Mandate (1923-1948), and immigration, 32–34; Nakba, 293, 295–319, 321n18, 322n20; occupation and statelessness, 299–301, 307, 308–9, 317
Palestinian Liberation Organization, 183–84
Pappé, Ilan, 322n20
Pardoe, John, 152–53
particularism. *See* universalism vs. particularism
"Passover on Caves" (poem; Yeshurun), 306–7
Patterson, Frederick, 66
Paul, Daniel N., 392, 393–94, 397
peace activism, 65, 336, 337–38. *See also* anti-racism activism
Peberdy, Sally, 76
Perlzweig, Maurice, 171–73
permanent vs. temporary collections, museums, 330–31, 333, 334–36
"permission to write," 254–55
Petegorsky, David, 171–73
Peters, Carl, 221–22, 231–32, 234–35
Pfeffer, Leo, 199
Philip, M. NourbeSe, 249–50, 251–52, 253, 267n33
Phillips, Caryl, 240–42, *241*, 243, 249–51, 255, 259, 261; literary criticism, 266n29, 267n30; nonfiction, 269n63
Phillips, Mike, 25
Phillips, Trevor, 25
photograph collections: Holocaust perpetrators, 333, 336; Holocaust victims and exhibits, 308–10, *309*, 333–34, 336–37, 343–44
Pilger, John, 281
Pineau, Gisèle, 263
Pinkard, Otis, 66
Pirow, Oswald, 79
Pittsburgh Courier (newspaper), 53
place names, resources, 408
Podhoretz, Norman, 205–6, 209, 214
poets and poetry: American, 386–87, 393; Caribbean, 251, 261, 268n37; English, 149, 150; Israeli, 306–7; Palestinian, 325n53; Yiddish, 128–29
Polakow-Suransky, Sasha, 191nn34–35, 192n51
Poland, 97
police: Nazi enforcement, 229, 230, 365, 369; United Kingdom, 152; United States, 204
Polier, Justine Wise, 209
Polier, Shad, 209
poll taxes, 50–51
Polyukhovich, Ivan, 285, 286

Portugal, Jewish expulsions, 258–59, 262
Posel, Deborah, 352, 361
postcolonial societies and studies: Canada, 389; considering Holocaust literature, 219–20, 222–37, 242–63; field and funding, 18, 264n7; memory studies, 5–6, 242–47, 251–52, 253–54, 259–60, 266n22, 294; postcolonial shift, 19, 35, 133, 171, 173, 239n37, 403–4; racialization theories, 224–25, 228, 229–30, 233–34; United Kingdom, 17–36, 146
poverty: Indigenous Australians, 132, 135–36; Indigenous Canadians, 401
Powell, Enoch, 117–18, 148–49, 150, 152, 154, 158, 159, 165
Pratt, Mary Louise, 122, 135
Pratt, Richard H., 394
press coverage. *See* journalism
Price, Charles, 109
primary elections, 52
Primitive Passions (Chow), 233–34
Prinz, Joachim, 172–73, 202–3
progressive Jewish activism, 176, 181–82, 184–85, 187, 199, 203–4
propaganda. *See also* editorial cartoons: Nazi, 207, 358, 361, 369; Nazi cinema, personal accounts, 221, 230–36; racial policies, WWII era, 22, 207; Zionism and British Mandate, 32–34
property law and land rights: Canada, 388, 389–90, 392–93; Palestine, 299, 308; United States/territories, 412n12
"prophetic Judaism," 199, 207

"prosthetic memory," 245, 246
pseudoethnography, 126
public deliberation, 296–97, 298, 301, 307, 315–16
publishers, 276–77
Puckett, Dan J., 14, 41–66
Purified National Party (South Africa), 75
Purser, Philip, 161–62

Quota Act (South Africa; 1930), 73–74, 82

Rabbinical Assembly, 203–4
rabbis: activism and affiliation, American civil rights, 196–97, 199, 202–4; activism and affiliation, anti-apartheid and colonialism, 176, 180–82, 190n27, 192nn48–49; prophetic Judaism, 199
race. *See also* anti-racism discourse; race relations; "race thinking"; racism: British immigration and, 26, 29–32; group classifications, 73, 76, 77, 81, 95, 96, 106, 109, 129, 134, 404; Jewish views on, 122–23, 128, 134–35, 137, 143n21, 177; Jews and, 3, 8n3, 14, 72–85, 91–92, 96, 105, 106, 109, 135, 139–40, 143n21; Palestine immigration and, 32–34; as social construct, 3, 404; South African race thinking, 72, 73, 76, 77, 168, 170, 294, 352, 361–62, 364, 372
race relations. *See also* multiculturalism: Australia, 125, 130–32, 134–35, 137–38, 146–47, 273, 282–83, 288, 342; Caribbean, 258–59, 260, 262,

race relations (*continued*)
267n29; legislation, 117–18, 148–49; South Africa, 78, 84, 352, 369; United Kingdom, 117–18, 146, 147, 148–65; United States, 41, 43–44, 45, 53–54, 58, 64–66, 181–82, 199, 202–9, 212–13, 215, 242, 247–48

Race Relations Act (United Kingdom; 1965), 117–18

"race thinking," 17, 19–20, 31, 72

racial contract theory, 404, 405–6

racial differentiation: group classification, immigration, 73, 76, 77, 81, 95, 96, 104–6, 107, 109; Jewish, 73, 76, 81, 91–92, 96, 227, 228–30; "near-white" races, 23; skin color and shades, 18, 73, 76

racial equality. *See* equality values

racialization processes: Nazi, 204, 222, 223, 229–30, 233, 313, 361, 362, 365; personal, described, 219–20, 222, 223, 224–25, 226–27, 228–30, 233; postcolonial theory, 224–25, 228, 229–30, 233–34

racialized political systems: American South/Jim Crow, 41–42, 44–45, 46–47, 50–53, 62–64, 201, 204; Australia, 2, 93–96, 100, 105, 106, 145n42, 146, 339, 342, 343; history education and textbooks, 359–60, 368; Nazi Germany, 43, 47, 62, 64, 200, 230, 359–61, 362, 365, 367–68, 371; personal accounts, 148, 187–88, 202; South Africa/apartheid, 2, 13, 14, 20, 75–76, 78, 81, 82, 83–85, 118, 168–88, 350, 352, 354–55, 356, 359, 361–62, 368

racism. *See also* anti-racism activism; anti-racism discourse; antisemitism; racialized political systems; segregation: antisemitism compared, 3, 43, 73, 147–48, 151–53, 196–97, 198–202, 204, 226–28, 333, 335, 336, 341, 367; Australia, 92, 93–96, 100–106, 110, 117, 122, 132, 137–38, 146, 279, 282–83, 340, 342, 345; Canada, 388–89, 404–5; colonial, 6–7, 18, 19, 20–21, 24–26, 27–29, 122, 138, 168–69, 186, 221–22, 224–27, 234–35, 364, 367, 404–5, 406; contexts and meanings, 3, 404; contra to American war effort, 55–66; environmental, 401; Holocaust memory's inability to address, 14–15, 19–20, 92–93, 122–23, 205–9, 293–94, 372; Jews and: Australia, 117; Jews and: United States, 118, 196–216; modern society and global relations, 419, 420; postwar forms and evolution, 4, 13–14, 19–29, 30–32, 35, 117–18, 147–48, 148–49, 152, 154, 158–59, 200, 204, 406; postwar responses, 13–15, 20, 22, 152; scholarship, postwar cultures, 5–6, 17–18; scientific, 13, 20, 23–24, 25, 94, 95, 199, 222, 359–60, 361, 366–67, 368; societal and political messaging and denial, 19–20, 22, 23–24, 25–26, 30–31, 41–42, 43, 62–66, 154; South Africa, 72–73, 80–81, 168–69, 351–52, 354, 356, 359, 361, 364–65, 371–72; theories of behavior, 148, 151, 367; United Kingdom, 13–14, 20–34, 117–18,

147–48, 158, 162, 165; United States, 41–66, 196–216, 406; Zionism and apartheid, 178–79, 186
radical Zionism, 211–15, 300
Radical Zionist Alliance, 212
Radio Times (periodical), 147, 148
Ralling, Christopher, 163
Randolph, A. Philip, 53, 68n28
Rankin, John E., *60*
Ravitch, Melech, 126, 128–30, 131, 132, 135, 141, 143n23
Razack, Sherene, 404–5
reconciliation movements: Australia, 140–41, 146; Canada, 394–95, 397, 407, 409, 414n35, 414n37; Jewish reparations, 210, 212; South Africa, 350, 351, 355, 364
recruitment: academic, 24, 27–29; labor, and discrimination, 30; military, and discrimination, 21–24, 25
Redner, Harry, 333–34
Red Power movement, 387, 399–400
Reed, Merl, 59
Reform Judaism, 181–82
refugees: and Australian immigration, 91, 94, 95, 103, 106–8, 124, 142n9, 329–30, 341–43, 349n48; and Caribbean immigration, 256–57, 258–59, 261, 269n56; detention conditions, 343; Holocaust outcomes, 297–98, 301–2, 311–13, 314, 315; International Refugee Organization, 108–9; Israel policy, 169; literary portrayals, 307; Nakba outcomes, 297–98, 299, 301–3, 307, 308–11, 313, 314–15; political status, 312–14, 315; and South African immigration, 75

Regan, Paulette, 409
Reid, John, 413n28, 414n33
Reimer, Andrew, 278, 283–84
. . . reitet für Deutschland (film), 221
reparations, 210, 212
Republican Party (United States), 52
Rescuers, The (temporary exhibition, JHC), 334, 343–44
Return to Haifa (Gaon), 307
Return to Haifa (Kanafani), 307
Rex, Zvi, 288
Reynolds, David, 20, 26
Reynolds, Henry, 143n19
Richards, Arthur, 24, 28
Ringelblum, Emanuel, 328
Rising Tide, The: An Exposition of Australian Socialism (Jensen), 101, 103
"Rivers of Blood" speech, E. Powell, 1968, 117–18, 148–49, 152
Robinson, Robert, 58
Rogers, Andrew, 328–29
Romain, Gemma, 267n35
Romani people, 341
Romaniw, Stefan, 279
Roosevelt, Eleanor, 403
Roosevelt, Franklin D., 53, 57, 60, 64–65, 68n28, 107
Rosenberg, M. Jay, 213, 214
Rosie, George, 148
Rossington, Michael, 264n7, 264n10
Rothberg, Michael: Holocaust memory theory and work, 5–6, 7, 18–19, 219–20, 244, 245–46, 251, 260, 265n18, 266n22, 266n25, 400–401; postcolonial countermemory, 266n22; postcolonial theory and racialization, 219–20, 221–37

Rothfield, Robin, 343
Rothschild, Jacob M., 203
Rousseau, Jean-Jacques, 403
Rowe, Jennifer, 276
Royal Air Force, 22, 23, 24, 25
Royal Commission on Population (UK), 30–31
Royal Navy, 23, 33
Rubenstein, Richard, 203–4
Ruchames, Louis, 196–97
Rudd, Kevin, 146
Rupprecht, Anita, 253, 266n22
Russell, Susan Garnett, 352
Rutland, Suzanne D., 14, 91–111
Rwandan genocide, 398

Said, Edward, 311, 317, 325n53
Sancton, Thomas, 65
Sanctuary: Nazi Refugees in Australia (Aarons), 285
Sandell, Richard, 330–31
Saperstein, David, 182
Saphir, Jacob, 142n14
Sarna, Jonathan, 174
Sartre, Jean-Paul, 226–27
Sassoon, Vidal, 147
Sauer, Paul, 78, 83–84
scapegoating mechanisms, 152, 282, 306, 316
Schach, Leonard, 379n43
Schappes, Morris, 179, 184
Scholl, Sophie, 366
Schumann, Christian, 75
Schwarzchild, Henry, 184–85, 194n64
Schwarz, Jan, 142n8
"scientific" racism: Australia, 94, 95, 138; Nazism, 20, 222, 359–60, 361, 366–67, 368; US and UK, 23–24, 25, 199; world history, 13, 364, 367–68
Scott, Duncan Campbell, 394
sculpture, 328–29
Searle, Anthony, 164–65
Segal, Lynne, 276–77
Segev, Tom, 4
segregation. *See also* desegregation: educational systems, 171–72, 354–55; Holocaust conditions, 62, 64, 230; Jewish communities, London's East End, 162, 164; racial, American education and housing, 171–72, 200, 204; racial, American labor, 59, 70n44, 172; racial, American military, 20, 25, 66; racial, Australia, 132, 133, 145n42; racial, South Africa, 75–76, 78, 83–85, 86n7, 168–88, 352, 354–55, 361–62; racial, United States, 44–45, 50–53, 55, 56–58, 59, 64, 66, 196, 204, 207–8, 214
self-defense, 209–11, 300
self-hatred, 174, 206, 207, 208, 209, 213
Selpin, Hubert, 221–22, 231–32
Selvon, Sam, 256
"separate but equal" policies, 171–72, 361
separation walls, 308–9
Sephardim, 258–59, 262, 263
sexual abuse and survivors, 394, 395, 398–99
Shaiak, Gedaliah, 121–22, 132, 133–35, 137, 141
Shain, Milton, 14, 72–85
Shakespeare, William, 249
Sheikh Jarrah, East Jerusalem, 308

Shelter from the Storm: Jewish Refugees to Australia 1933–1945 (temporary exhibition, JHC), 341–43

Shohat, Ella, 225

Shores, Arthur D., 52

Shubenacadie Residential School (Nova Scotia), 395, *396*, 414n35

Siegman, Henry, 187–88

silence. *See also* forgetting: Australian colonialism and genocide, 293, 329; enabling American racism, 203, 204, 406; enabling Holocaust, 202–3, 204; post-Holocaust, 197–98, 215, 250, 293

Simple Habana Melody (Hijuelos), 256

Simpson, Audra, 417n67

Simpson, Leanne, 407–8

Simpson, Moira G., 331

Sinclair, Murray, 414n35

Sinden, Donald, 35

Six Day War (1967), 174, 209, 215

slave narratives, 254–55

slavery and slave trade: British history, 32–33; Caribbean, and literary responses, 242, 247, 248, 250–51, 252, 254–55, 256, 257, 258, 262, 263; Holocaust memory and, 242, 270n71; media portrayals, 234–35, 263; 21st century responses, 263; United States, and literary responses, 266n28

Slucki, David, 117, 121–41

Smith's Weekly (Sydney newspaper), 96, 101

Smith v. Allwright (United States; 1944), 52

Smuts, Jan, 83

Snow White and the Seven Dwarves (film), 221, 228–30, 234

Snyder, Timothy, 320n10

social contract theory, 404–3

social Darwinism, 94, 95, 364

Sokolowicz, Aron, 340

Sokolowicz, Cyla, 333

Solarz, Stephen, 193n56

Solomon, Alisa, 184

Soreson, Rosemary, 275

South Africa: Holocaust education and apartheid, 293–94, 350–72; immigration policy, 14, 72, 73–74, 75, 76–80, 81–83, 84; Jews, politics, and apartheid, 168, 170, 171, 172–88; Jews, race, and assimilation, 14, 72–85; racialized political system, 2, 13, 14, 20, 75–76, 81, 82, 83–85, 118, 180, 350, 352, 354–55, 356, 359, 361–62, 368; state education policy, 353–56, 363–65, 369, 375n16; voting rights, 76

South African Party, 73, 74

southern United States. *See* American South

sovereignty, Indigenous notions, 389, 404, 407–8, 409

Spain: Iberian expulsion of Jews, 242, 248, 258–59, 262, 263, 392; War of the Spanish Succession, 392

Special Investigations Unit (Australia), 285, 292n48

Spitzer, Kali, 399, 415n53

Spivak, G.C., 264n10

sponsorship, immigration, 107–8

Srebrenica massacre (1995), 398

Stalinism, 199, 244–45, 275–76, 283

Stam, Robert, 225
Stannard, David A., 391, 405
Stanner, W.E.H., 329
Star (Johannesburg newspaper), 73
state constitutions, United States, 52
state education oversight: Canada, and Indigenous peoples, 388, 389, 393–97, *396*, 398–99; South Africa, 353–56, 363–65, 369, 375n16
state-run museums, 332
states' rights: political parties, 45, 65; values and issues, 46–47, 55, 56–58, 59
States' Rights Democratic Party (Dixiecrats), 45, 65
Staub, Michael E., 118–19, 174, 189n9, 196–216
Steinberg, Gerald M., 186–87
Still Alive (Klüger), 221, 228–36
Stockholm International Forum on the Holocaust (2000), 5, 352
"Stop Frame" (short story; Philip), 251–52
Stratton, Jon, 96, 106
Strijdom, J.G., 76, 77
Student Nonviolent Coordinating Committee (SNCC), 208, 210
Students for a Democratic Society (SDS), 208
Stuttgart (ship), 75
suffrage. *See* voting rights
suicide, 397
Sullivan, K.J., 52, 67n5
Sundquist, Eric J., 267n30
Supreme Court (Canada), 397
Supreme Court (United States), 52, 171–72

Suriname, 259
surveys, immigration, 104–6
survivors. *See* Holocaust survivors; Nakba survivors; sexual abuse and survivors
Survivors amongst Us Work for Peace (temporary exhibition, JHC), 336, 337–38, 342
Svonkin, Stuart, 173, 189n15
Swallow, Norman, 163
Sydney, Australia: Indigenous Australians, 127; Jewish immigration, 106–7, 124, 125, 142n9; WWII, 98
Sydney Jewish News, 97, 113n35
synagogues, 164
Syrkin, Marie, 207–8, 218n27
Sznaider, Natan, 5, 242, 270n71

Talmon, Jacob, 72
Tampa affair (Australia; 2001), 343, 349n48
Ta'n Weji-sqalia'tiek: Mi'kmaw Place Names Digital Atlas (Francis), 408
Tarzan movies, 224, 225, 226
Tasmania, 390, 412n18
tattoos, 399–400, *400*
Tatz, Colin, 125, 140
Tavan, Gwenda, 93–94, 108
teachers, South Africa, 353–54, 355, 376n21
television programs and series: Holocaust content and trends, 98, 198, 263, 267n35; *One Pair of Eyes*/"Who Are the Cockneys Now?", 117–18, 147, 148, 153, 155–65; *The World At War*, 250, 255, 267n35

temporary exhibitions: Holocaust centers, 293, 327, 329–32, 334–44; Holocaust exhibitions in Palestine, 308–10
terra nullius, 143n19
terrorism: language, Arab-Israeli relations, 183–84, 187, 193n60; white supremacists, United States, 47, 200
Texas: lynching, 48, 49, 67n16; voting rights, 52
textbooks: biased content, 357–58; publishing and selection, 353–54, 355, 370; South African education, Nazism and racism, 293–94, 350–72
Than, Joseph, 99
Thomas, Neil, 277
Thornton, Russell, 411n5
Todorov, Tzvetan, 406
tolerance, teaching and concept, 327–28, 336, 342
totalitarianism. *See* fascism and fascist societal conditions
trade, Israel-South Africa, 178–79, 180–81
Transcultural Memory (Crownshaw), 246
transnational circulation of memory, 245–46
travel writing, 122, 125–27, 128, 129, 130, 132, 142n14
Treaty of Utrecht (1713), 392
treaty rights, Indigenous Canadians, 388, 389, 393
Trinindad and Tobago, 240, 256–57, 257, 269n56
Tristes tropiques (Lévi-Strauss), 256
Troper, Harold, 110

Trudeau, Pierre, 388
Truman, Harry S., 65
Truth (Australian newspaper), 96, 101, 103
Truth and Reconciliation Commission (Canada), 394–95, 397, 407, 409, 414n35
Truth and Reconciliation Commission (South Africa), 364
Tuskegee Institute: leaders, and civil rights movement, 66; lynching reports, 48
2510037901 (film), 399–400, *400*

Uganda, 35
Ukraine and Ukrainians, 274–76, 277–79, 280–82, 283, 284, 285–86, 287
"Uncle Jake, Come Home!" (essay, Bisk), 213–15
Union of American Hebrew Congregations, 181
United Australia Party, 106
United Kingdom: British colonialism and empire, 19, 20, 22, 33–34, 34–35, 136, 390, 392–93, 403; British Colonial Office, administration, 24, 25–29, 29–32, 34; British Colonial Office, and military recruitment, 21–24, 25; British Mandate for Palestine (1923–1948), 32–34; Holocaust Commission, reports, and memorials, 1, 8n1, 419; Holocaust memory, and modern immigration and race relations, 146–65; immigration policy, 14, 17–18, 20–21, 26, 29–32, 117–18, 148–49; immigration

United Kingdom (*continued*)
populations and geography, 147–65;
museum collections and care, World
War II, 330; postcolonial Britain,
and race issues, 17–36, 146–65;
postwar racism and antisemitism,
13–14, 17, 20–34, 117–18, 147–48,
158, 162, 165

United Nations: genocide and genocide
statutes, 389, 390–91, 402–3, 409,
412n14, 413n22; Human Rights
Council, 194n69; human rights
statues, 133, 365, 402–3; International Holocaust Remembrance Day,
5, 309, 352; International Year of
Peace, 337; Israel, and South African
apartheid, 169, 171, 176–78; peacekeeping missions, 343; Rapporteur
for Indigenous People, 398; UNESCO projects, 3–4

United Party (South Africa), 75, 77, 79

United Sates Holocaust Memorial
Museum (Washington, DC), 332

United States. *See also* American South;
civil rights movement, United
States: African American voting
rights, 46, 50–53, 63, 66, 68n24;
American Jews, apartheid, and the
Holocaust, 118, 168–88; armed
forces discrimination, 20, 25–26;
colonialism and genocide, 386–88,
400–401; Holocaust, and memorial
culture, 4, 198, 199–200, 202; Holocaust memory globalization/Americanization, 247, 260–61, 270n66;
race relations, 41, 43–44, 45, 53–54,
58, 64–66, 181–82, 199, 202–9,
212–13, 215, 242, 247–48

United States Constitution, 50, 52

United States Holocaust Memorial
Museum, 270n66, 270n72, 387

Universal Declaration of Human Rights
(1948), 133, 365, 402–3

universalism vs. particularism: Holocaust memory and writing, 256,
263; Holocaust memory cultures,
5, 260–61, 266n25; Jewish social
attitudes and activism, 118, 172–78,
188, 343

university recruiting, United Kingdom,
24, 27–29

Uris, Leon, 250, 267n33

Vajda, Frank, 339
"Valaida" (short story; Wideman), 256
van der Merwe, Nico, 77
van der Post, Laurens, 148
Vanishing Street, The (film), 154–55, 164
Van Leer Jerusalem Institute, 325n51
van Rensburg, Hans, 79
Vas, Robert, 154–55, 164
victimization and victimhood: ArabJewish collective identity, 295, 296,
297–98, 301–3, 311–12; global
genocides, 398, 405; "hierarchy of
suffering" and zero-sum logic, 5–6,
18, 236, 238n19, 388, 391, 397–98;
Holocaust memory and articulation,
5–6, 175, 177–78, 210–11, 212, 219,
238n19, 245, 248, 249; Holocaust
victims, groups and inclusion, 341,
343–44, 365, 367, 412n16; Jewish,

and human rights, 175; Jewish, and nationalism, 6, 175–76, 212; Jewish power responses, 209–11, 212, 299, 329; literary portrayals, 249; narrative, Jewish history, 118; racial influence, cognition and recognition, 407; victim-blaming, 288
visual culture, 223, 224, 225, 228, 230, 236
Vogel Literary Award, 276–77, 280, 286
Vogt, Paul, 97, 113n35
Volkan, Vamik, 306
volkekunde, 87n32
Vorster, John, 178–79, 180, 191n35
voter registration, 51, 52, 53, 66
voting rights: African Americans, 46, 50–53, 63, 66, 68n24; Australians, 94; class issues, 50; court cases, 52, 68n24; South Africans, 76

Wagner, Heinrich, 285
Walcott, Derek, 251, 262–63, 267n37
War Crimes Amendment Act (Australia; 1988), 285
war crimes and trials: Australia, 274, 276, 279, 284, 285–89, 292n50; criminal investigations, 285, 292n48; Eichmann, documentation and memory, 150–51, 215; literary portrayals, 286–87, 292n50
War Criminals Welcome: Australia, A Sanctuary for Fugitive War Criminals since 1945 (Aarons), 285
War of the Spanish Succession (1701–1714), 393
Warsaw Ghetto and uprising, 328, 334, 365

Weekly Review (newspaper), 48, 58, 61
Weiss, Peter, 176, 184
weiter leben (Klüger), 221, 228–36
Werder, Felix, 339
West African Pilot (newspaper), 28, 34
West Bank, 299–300, 307, 308–10
We Were Not the Savages: Collision between European and Native American Civilizations (Paul), 392
"White Australia" policy, 2, 93–96, 100, 105, 106, 145n42, 146
"white cognition," 406–8
Whitehead, Anne, 264n7, 264n10
white privilege, 404–5, 406, 408
white supremacy systems, 62, 404; Canada, 404–5; Nazism, 43–44, 62, 63, 64, 366–68; South Africa, 78, 79–81, 83–85, 170, 352, 354–55, 356; United States, 14, 42–45, 46–48, 51, 52, 54–55, 56–57, 61–64, 200; world history, 367–68, 404, 406–7
White, T.E., 107
"Who Are the Cockneys Now?" (television documentary episode), 117–18, 147, 148, 153, 155–65
Wideman, John Edgar, 256
Wiener, Bono, 332, 340, 344
Winter, Jay, 4
"Winter Count" (poem; Chrystos), 386–87, 393, 410n3
"Woman Who Plays the Trumpet" (short story; Cliff), 256
World at War, The (television documentary series), 250, 255
World Jewish Congress, 171, 172

World War I: ending, and WWII precursors, 239n37, 365; refugee populations following, 313

World War II. *See also* Holocaust: American labor, 53, 55–61; American messaging and values, 14, 43, 46, 53, 61, 172; American war effort and racial inequality, 44, 46, 48–49, 52–66, 60; Australian war effort and reporting, 97–98; British messaging and values, 21–22; British museum exhibitions, 330; British personal accounts, 164; Caribbean literature, 251–52; Caribbean personal accounts, 251; films, 98–100, 252–53; German precursors, 239n37, 357, 365; journalism and reporting, 61–62, 96–98; Middle East outcomes, 295, 312–15; South Africa, 79; South African history education, 356–58, 364–69; Ukraine, 274–75, 278–79, 281–82, 284

Wright, Eileen, 341

Wright, Susanne, 341

Yad Vashem Foundation, 375n16

Yad Vashem memorial and museum, 178, 180, 309, 332, 333

Yeshurun, Avot, 306–7

Yiddish cultural centers, 124–25, 339

Yiddishe Nayes, Di (newspaper), 125

Yiddish writers and writing, 117, 130, 139, 142n8; encountering Indigenous Australia, 121–41; journalism, 121, 125; Yiddish language, 124, 139, 142n8

Younge, Gary, 267n35

Young, Sherri, 395–97, 415n45

Yunqian, Chen, 332

zachor, 332–33, 335, 342, 387

zero-sum game logic, victimization, 5–6, 18, 236, 238n19

Zertal, Idith, 4, 301

Zierler, Wendy, 267n30

Zimmerer, Jürgen, 6–7

Zionism: American Jewish concerns, 173, 175, 179, 211; apartheid and racism and, 178–79, 186, 188; armed forces, 299; Australian portrayals, 276, 287; British Mandate-era immigration, 32–34; organizations, 168, 209; Palestinian experiences and opinions, 300–301, 307–8, 314–15; postcolonial Jewish victimhood, 6; radical Zionist movement, 211–15, 300

Zochrot, 308

Zuckerman, Moshe, 301

Zuckoff, Aviva Cantor, 212

www.ingramcontent.com/pod-product-compliance
Lightning Source LLC
Chambersburg PA
CBHW071354300426
44114CB00016B/2064